second edition

PROGRAMMING LANGUAGES

Design and Implementation

Terrence W. Pratt

Department of Applied Mathematics and Computer Science
University of Virginia

PRENTICE-HALL, Inc., Englewood Cliffs, New Jersey 07632

Library of Congress Cataloging in Publication Data

Pratt, Terrence W.
  Programming languages.

  Bibliography: p. 583
  Includes index.
  1. Programming languages (Electronic computers)
I. Title.
QA76.7.P7   1984   001.64'24   83-4567
ISBN 0-13-730580-X

Editorial/production supervision by Linda Mihatov
Interior design by Anne Bonanno and Linda Mihatov
Cover design by Anne Bonanno
Manufacturing buyer: Gordon Osbourne

©1984, 1975 by PRENTICE-HALL, INC.,
Englewood Cliffs, New Jersey 07632

Printed in the United States of America

10 9 8 7 6 5 4 3 2 1

ISBN 0-13-730580-X

Prentice-Hall International, Inc., *London*
Prentice-Hall of Australia Pty. Limited, *Sydney*
Editora Prentice-Hall do Brasil, Ltda., *Rio de Janeiro*
Prentice-Hall Canada Inc., *Toronto*
Prentice-Hall of India Private Limited, *New Delhi*
Prentice-Hall of Japan, Inc., *Tokyo*
Prentice-Hall of Southeast Asia Pte. Ltd., *Singapore*
Whitehall Books Limited, *Wellington, New Zealand*

For Kirsten, Randy, and Laurie

Contents

PART 1
CONCEPTS

CHAPTER 1
The Study
of Programming
Languages   *3*

CHAPTER **5**

Subprograms
and Programmer-Defined
Data Types   *124*

CHAPTER **6**

Sequence
Control   *149*

CHAPTER 7

Data
Control   *215*

CHAPTER 8

Storage
Management   *280*

CHAPTER 9

Syntax
and
Translation   *303*

PART 2
LANGUAGES

CHAPTER 19

APL

REFERENCES

INDEX

Preface

Computer programming language design and the interplay between language design and implementation are the two central concerns of this book. The design and implementation of programming languages, during the almost thirty-year span from the first version of FORTRAN in the mid-1950s to the design of Ada[1] in the early 1980s, have been more art than science. The underlying principles have always been vague at best, and the accumulation of accepted design alternatives has been far slower than one might expect considering the hundreds of programming languages that have come into existence during the period. The central goal of this book is to bring together the various facets of language design and implementation within a single conceptual framework. The most difficult problem has been to find a framework with both the breadth to encompass the concepts in a wide variety of languages and the depth to allow the relationships among variants of the same concept in different languages to be clearly seen. The result of this endeavor is found in Part I of this book, in which many of the central concepts in programming languages are identified and discussed, along with their implementations on conventional computers. In Part II, eight of the most widely used programming languages are described individually in terms of the concepts developed in Part I. The book is intended as a text for an undergraduate or beginning graduate survey

[1] Ada is a registered trademark of the U.S. Dept. of Defense.

course on programming languages and as a useful reference to concepts, terminology, and languages for practicing programmers.

Part I is organized in the following manner: Chapter 1 develops some of the motivation for the study of programming languages and provides a brief history. Chapter 2 outlines the basic approaches to language implementation. Chapters 3 through 8 form the core of the book, developing the key concepts in the areas of data objects, data types, abstraction mechanisms, control structures, and storage management. *Syntax*, which often makes up a major part of discussions about programming languages, plays a lesser role here. Chapters 3 through 8 are concerned primarily with *semantic structures* and *run-time representations* in languages. Syntax enters only occasionally as a topic of interest, although many examples of various syntactic structures are found in these chapters. Chapter 9 considers directly the topic of syntax and its effect on language structure and translator design. Chapters 10 and 11 round out the conceptual underpinnings through brief discussions of language environments and theoretical models.

Topic selection has been a major problem throughout Part I. What are the central concepts in programming languages? Those selected here have seemed most central, but inevitably some topics have been slighted, and some have been omitted altogether. Doubtless few readers will find the selection entirely to their liking. In an area where there is so little agreement on general principles this cannot be helped. Nevertheless perhaps the overall breadth and balance of the treatment may serve to outweigh somewhat its deficiencies in particular topic areas.

The choice of languages to include in Part II has also been difficult. Two major criteria have guided the selection: widespread use and diversity of concept. On the one hand, inclusion of the most widely used languages has seemed a necessity if the book is to have value as a text and reference. On this basis I have been guided toward the older, more well-established languages: FORTRAN, COBOL, PL/I and Pascal. On the other hand, variety of language design concept is also to be desired if the languages are to exemplify as many of the concepts of Part I as possible. On this basis I have included the list processing language LISP, the string processing language SNOBOL4, and the array processing language APL. Ada is included for its variety of concept, because it promises to be in widespread use within a few years, and because in major aspects it represents the distillation of many language design concepts developed through experience with dozens of other language designs, beginning with ALGOL 60.

Many other languages besides these eight were considered for inclusion, but ultimately restrictions of space and time narrowed the choice. The particular choice of languages should not be too significant, for the intent in Part I is to build a framework for the analysis of languages that may be applied by the reader to any language. Part II only illustrates how this analysis might be done in eight specific cases.

As a Text

This book is intended as an upper-division undergraduate text for a one-semester course in programming languages (such as the course CS 8 in the ACM Curriculum '78). It is suitable as a beginning graduate text with some supplementary material from the literature. Since it presumes only an elementary background—knowledge of at least one high-level language and a basic knowledge of machine organization and assembly language programming—it could also be used as a lower-division undergraduate text by suitable choice of topics.

A survey course on programming languages is difficult to teach because of the multiplicity of language and implementation concepts that might be treated. There are dozens of languages in fairly wide use, each with its own set of concepts and implementation techniques. How is one to survey this diversity without the result being simply a hodgepodge of unrelated detail? The answer provided by this book is found in the conceptual framework of Part I. The study of a language is organized around the central areas of data objects and data types, abstraction mechanisms, sequence control and data control, storage management, syntax, and operating and programming environments. Part II provides example analyses of eight of the most widely used programming languages, using the concepts developed in Part I. Each chapter provides references for further reading and problems involving, for the most part, application of the concepts to new situations.

There are two different approaches that might be used in a course organized around this material. The simplest approach is to take Part I more or less sequentially, with the instructor providing examples from particular languages to illustrate the material more fully as appropriate. I have found this approach successful with more mature students in a beginning graduate course. At this level the text was supplemented with readings in the literature, and class discussion concentrated on the more complex concepts in the text. The course involved only a few programming problems; the primary emphasis lay with design questions.

The alternative approach, which I have used at the advanced undergraduate level with students having only two or three previous computer science courses, is to work back from the languages to the concepts. The instructor chooses two to four of the languages in Part II, including one that the entering students have already used. The text is supplemented by the usual manuals for these languages, and the students write elementary programs in each language as the course progresses. The appropriate chapters in Part II, beginning with the chapter on the known language, are taken up after an initial quick pass through Part I. As the concepts in each of the chosen languages are developed and contrasted, the relevant sections of Part I are brought in to provide the necessary depth to support the discussion. By staying close to particular languages, which the student is at the same time applying in practical programming exercises, proper motivation is provided for the study of the general concepts of Part I. The choice of exactly which languages to study in depth is dependent on three factors: the background of the students entering, the languages available on the computer at hand, and the interests of the instructor. For the greatest breadth of concept, at least one of the first five languages in Part II (FORTRAN, COBOL, PL/I, Pascal, Ada) and one of the last three (LISP, SNOBOL4, APL) make an effective combination. It has been my experience that for the undergraduate student a detailed study of a language loses its interest and effectiveness unless coupled with the opportunity to write and run programs in the language at the same time. The organization of the text should allow considerable flexibility in the choice of languages to meet local situations. At the end of the course, if time permits, a particularly useful larger project is to have the student learn and analyze a locally available language that is not described in Part II.

Changes from the First Edition

Our understandings about programming languages have changed in major ways between 1973, when the first edition was being written, and today. As a result, this edition represents almost a complete rewriting of the original text. The central core of the book, Chapters 3 through 8, has been extensively modified. The major changes begin with a new emphasis on the data-object/data-type distinction, and the view of a data type as a set of data objects and the operations on those objects. A more integrated treatment of data types and type checking is used in Chapters 3 and 4 (in contrast to the separate treatment of data and operations in the first edition).

Chapter 5, which is entirely new, brings together a number of concepts treated briefly or not at all in the first edition. The importance of abstraction as a central concept in the construction of programs is emphasized, and the concepts of procedural and data abstraction are introduced. Subprograms are treated for the first time here in their role as abstraction mechanisms. The issues of sequence and data control related to subprograms are taken up in the subsequent chapters.

The discussion of sequence control at the statement level and at the subprogram level (Chapter 6) has been extensively modified and extended. An extended discussion of concurrency is now included, based on the Ada rather than the PL/I approach to tasks and concurrent programming.

Data control structures (scope rules and parameter transmission) are central issues in programming languages. Chapter 7 now deals with these issues in what I hope is a more satisfactory fashion. The distinction between static and dynamic scope is clearly drawn, aliasing is treated, and the entire discussion is reorganized to reflect a better understanding of the issues on my part. In the section on parameter transmission, *call by name* transmission and transmission of label parameters (important topics in ALGOL 60), have been deemphasized.

Other additions include a section on programming environments to complement that on operating environments in Chapter 10 and a brief history of the field in Chapter 1. Deletions have come in two major areas: variable-size data structures (stacks, queues, linked lists) and heap storage management. Several reviewers of the first edition noted that these topics ordinarily are treated in other courses and thus these sections are usually skipped.

Theoretical models (Chapter 11) is a new topic, treated far too superficially. It includes the discussion of universal languages and Turing machines from the first edition, but touches on several additional areas where theory has influenced practice in obvious ways (e.g., compiler construction, program verification, formal semantic definition). It would be more satisfying in many ways to use formal theoretical models throughout the book in a much stronger way, but this is not yet possible. There is no single theoretical framework that encompasses the breadth and depth of topics that need to be treated, and introduction of several different formal structures to treat different topics would obscure rather than clarify. Chapter 11 is intended to provide only motivation for further study of theoretical models and some pointers to the literature.

Finally, the most obvious change: Pascal and Ada have replaced ALGOL 60 in Part II, and Pascal and Ada are the primary sources of examples now in Part I. This change reflects the obvious shift of concerns in language design and implementation during the 1970s.

A Note on Terminology

Many technical terms related to programming languages and language implementations lack a generally accepted definition. Often the same term has been used by different writers to name different concepts, e.g., the term *interpreter*, or alternatively, the same concept has been denoted by a variety of different terms, e.g., the data structure termed a *stack* here, which is also known as a *pushdown list* and *LIFO* (*last-in-first-out*) *list*. I have tried to choose the terminology that seems most generally accepted, e.g., *stack*. In cases where there seems to be little agreement on a standard definition, however, a precise definition is adopted for the purposes of this book (see, for example, the definition of *interpreter* in Chapter 2), maintaining what seems to be the major denotation of the term insofar as possible. The reader should exercise due caution, however, in the case of terms that are already familiar from other contexts.

A more difficult problem concerns concepts for which there is no generally accepted terminology. In these few cases an appropriate terminology has been introduced in the text. The two most prominent examples are the term *data control structure* (Chapter 7) for those aspects of a language concerned with the visibility and accessibility of data at different points in a program, and the distinction between the operations of *referencing* (Chapter 7) and *selection* (or *accessing*, Chapter 4) on data objects. In choosing these terms, I have tried to avoid conflict with other occasional uses of the same terms, but perhaps without complete success. Again the reader is cautioned.

Terrence W. Pratt
Charlottesville, Virginia

Acknowledgments

This book is based largely on experience teaching programming language concepts at the University of Virginia, and before that at the University of Texas at Austin. A number of people have contributed through their thoughtful reviews of the manuscript or of individual chapters: John Knight, Paul Reynolds, John Gannon, Mary Dee Fosberg, Bob Collins, and Stefan Feyock for the second edition, and Jeffrey Ullman, Ralph Griswold, Saul Rosen, and Dan Friedman for the first. Felix Saltor and Jaume Argila provided an extended review of the first edition, which was extremely helpful. Numerous other users of the first edition also contributed suggestions over the years.

My wife, Barbara Kraft, handled the entry of most of the revised text on our word processor and aided in many other ways in the preparation of the manuscript. The University of Virginia provided financial support, and the Institute for Computer Applications in Science and Engineering (ICASE) at the NASA Langley Research Center provided a congenial working environment for much of the writing. Ruthie Pratt, Ann Patterson, and the University of Texas at Austin contributed to the preparation of the manuscript of the first edition. To these people and institutions, my thanks.

PART 1

CONCEPTS

CHAPTER 1

The Study
of Programming
Languages

Any notation for the description of algorithms and data structures may be termed a programming language, although we usually also require that a programming language be implemented on a computer. The sense in which it may be "implemented" is considered in the next chapter. In the remainder of Part I the design and implementation of the various components of a language are considered in detail. Part II illustrates the application of the concepts in the design of eight major programming languages: FORTRAN, COBOL, PL/I, Pascal, Ada, LISP, SNOBOL4, and APL. Before approaching the general study of programming languages, however, it is worth considering the possible value of such a study to a computer programmer.

1-1   WHY STUDY PROGRAMMING LANGUAGES?

Hundreds of different programming languages have been designed and implemented. Even in 1969, Sammet [1969] listed 120 that had been fairly widely used, and many others have been developed since that time. Most programmers, however, never venture to use more than a few languages, and many confine their programming entirely to one or two. In fact practicing programmers often work at computer installations where use of a particular language such as PL/I, COBOL, or FORTRAN is required. What is to be gained, then, by study of a variety of different languages that one is unlikely ever to use?

In fact there are excellent reasons for such a study, provided that you go beneath the superficial consideration of the "features" of languages and delve into the underlying design concepts and their effect on language implementation. Five primary reasons come immediately to mind:

1. *To improve your understanding of the language you are using.* Many languages provide features which when used properly are of benefit to the programmer but when used improperly may waste large amounts of computer time or lead the programmer into time-consuming logical errors. Even a programmer who has used a language for years may understand some features poorly or not at all. A typical example is *recursion*, a handy programming feature available in many languages. When properly used it may allow the direct implementation of elegant and efficient algorithms, but in other cases it may cause an astronomical increase in execution time for a simple algorithm. Moreover, the cost of recursion varies depending on the language implementation. The programmer who knows nothing of the design questions and implementation difficulties which recursion implies is likely to shy away from this somewhat mysterious construct. However, a basic knowledge of its principles and implementation techniques allows the programmer to understand the relative cost of recursion in a particular language and from this understanding to determine whether its use is warranted in a particular programming situation. Alternatively, if you are using a language such as FORTRAN or COBOL in which recursion is not allowed, an understanding of the design and implementation difficulties of recursion may clarify what otherwise appears as a rather arbitrary language restriction.

2. *To increase your vocabulary of useful programming constructs.* It has often been noted that language serves both as an aid to thinking and a constraint. Properly, a person uses a language to express what he is thinking, but language serves also to structure how one thinks, to the extent that it is difficult to think in ways which allow no direct expression in words. Familiarity with a single programming language tends to have a similar constraining effect. In searching for data and program structures suitable to the solution of a problem, one tends to think only of structures that are immediately expressible in the languages with which one is familiar. By studying the constructs provided by a wide range of languages, and the manner in which these constructs are implemented, a programmer increases his programming "vocabulary." The understanding of implementation techniques is particularly important, because in order to use a construct while programming in a language that does not provide it directly, the programmer must provide his own implementation of the new construct in terms of the primitive elements actually provided by the language. For example, the subprogram control structure known as *coroutines* is useful in

many programs, but few languages provide a coroutine feature directly. A FORTRAN programmer, however, may readily simulate a coroutine structure in a set of FORTRAN programs if he is familiar with the coroutine concept and its implementation, and in so doing may be able to provide just the right control structure for a large program.

3. *To allow a better choice of programming language.* Of course, when the situation arises, a knowledge of a variety of languages may allow choice of just the right language for a particular project, thereby reducing enormously the coding effort required. For example, FORTRAN or COBOL programmers are often faced with the need to write a program to do some minor string processing, e.g., reformatting some improperly formatted input data. Such a program may be used only once of a few times. Coded in FORTRAN or COBOL the program might be tedious and time-consuming to write, but written in the string-processing language SNOBOL4 it might require only a few minutes and a dozen lines to code. The programmer with a knowledge of SNOBOL4 enjoys a decided advantage.

4. *To make it easier to learn a new language.* A linguist, through a deep understanding of the underlying structure of natural languages, often can learn a new foreign language more quickly and easily than the struggling novice who understands little of the structure even of his native tongue. Similarly, a thorough knowledge of a variety of programming language constructs and implementation techniques allows the programmer to learn a new programming language more easily when the need arises.

5. *To make it easier to design a new language.* Few programmers ever think of themselves as language designers, yet any program has a *user interface* that in fact is a form of programming language. The user interface consists of the commands and data formats that are provided for the user to communicate with the program. The designer of the user interface for a large program such as a text editor, an operating system, or a graphics package must be concerned with many of the same issues that are present in the design of a general-purpose programming language. This aspect of program design is often simplified if the programmer is familiar with a variety of constructs and implementation methods from ordinary programming languages.

From this discussion it should be apparent that there is much more to the study of programming languages than simply a cursory look at their features. In fact, many similarities in features are deceiving—the same feature in two different languages may be implemented in two very different ways, and thus the two versions may differ greatly in the cost of use. For example, almost every language provides an addition operation as a primitive, but the cost of performing an addition in, e.g., FORTRAN and SNOBOL4 may vary by an order of magnitude. The study of programming languages must necessarily include the study of implementation techniques, particularly techniques for the run-time representation of different constructs.

The emphasis on implementation structures in this book is somewhat in conflict with a much more prevalent view that language descriptions should be *implementation-independent*; i.e., the programmer should be unaware of the underlying run-time structures used in the language implementation. The latter view is characteristic of most language manuals and texts in which a language is described as a collection of features—data types, operations, statement types, etc.—which the programmer may combine into programs according to certain specified rules. Implementation-independent descriptions are of value to the beginner or the occasional user of a programming language, but a serious programmer who intends to make more than casual use of a language needs the depth provided by an understanding of the language implementation.

In Parts I and II of this book numerous language constructs are discussed, accompanied in almost every case by a design for the implementation of the construct on a conventional computer. Where the implementation techniques are fairly standard, only a single technique may be mentioned. In more complex cases more than one technique may be suggested, and often the problems suggest further alternatives. However, no attempt has been made to be comprehensive in covering possible implementation methods. The same language or construct, if implemented on the reader's local computer, may differ radically in cost or detail of structure when different implementation techniques have been used or when the underlying computer hardware differs from the simple conventional structure assumed here.

1-2   A BRIEF HISTORY

Programming language designs and implementation methods have evolved rapidly since the earliest high-level languages appeared in the 1950s. Of the eight major languages described in Part II, FORTRAN, LISP, and COBOL were designed originally during the 1950s; PL/I, SNOBOL4, and APL came into use in the 1960s; and Pascal and Ada represent more recent designs from the 1970s. The older languages have undergone periodic revisions to reflect changing influences from other areas of computing; the newer languages reflect a composite of experience gained in the design and use of these and the hundreds of other older languages. Some of the major influences on the evolution of language designs are listed below.

1. *Computer hardware and operating systems.* Computers have evolved from the small, slow, and costly vacuum-tube machines of the 1950s to the supercomputers and microcomputers of today. At the same time, layers of microprogram and operating system software have been inserted between the programming language and the underlying computer hardware. These factors have influenced both the structure and the cost of using the features of high-level languages.

2. *Applications.* Computer use has spread rapidly from the original concentration on critical military, scientific, business, and industrial applications in the 1950s, where the cost could be justified, to the computer games, personal computers, and applications in almost every area of human activity seen today. The requirements of these new application areas affect the designs of new languages and the revisions and extensions of older ones.

3. *Programming methods.* Language designs have evolved to reflect our changing understanding of good methods for writing large and complex programs and to reflect the changing environment in which programming is done.

4. *Implementation methods.* The development of better implementation methods has affected the choice of features to include in new designs.

5. *Theoretical studies.* Research into the conceptual foundations for language design and implementation, using formal mathematical methods, has deepened our understanding of the strengths and weaknesses of language features and has thus influenced the inclusion of these features in new language designs.

6. *Standardization.* The need for "standard" languages that can be implemented easily on a variety of computer systems and that allow programs to be transported from one computer to another has provided a strong conservative influence on the evolution of language designs.

To illustrate, Table 1-1 briefly lists some of the languages and influences that were important during each five-year period from 1950 to 1980. Many of these topics are taken up again in later chapters. Of course, missing from this table are the hundreds of languages and influences that have played a lesser but still important part in this history.

1-3   WHAT MAKES A GOOD LANGUAGE?

The design of high-level languages has yet to be perfected. Each language in Part II has many shortcomings, but each might be considered "successful" in comparison with the many hundreds of other languages that have been

TABLE 1-1 Some Major Influences and Programming Languages

	Influences	*Languages*

1950–55:	Primitive computers
	Assembly and machine language programming
	Foundation concepts:
	  Subprograms
	  Data structures
	Possibility of high-level languages
		Assembly languages
		Experimental high-level
		  languages; none in use
		  today

1956–60:	Small, slow, and expensive computers Magnetic-tape mass storage systems Compilers Software interpreters Code optimization Dynamic storage management Linked data structures and list processing BNF grammars	FORTRAN ALGOL 58 and ALGOL 60 COBOL LISP
1961–65:	Large, expensive computers Magnetic-disk mass storage systems Operating systems Multiprogramming Syntax-directed compilers "General-purpose" as a language design goal	FORTRAN IV COBOL 61 Extended ALGOL 60 Revised SNOBOL APL (as a notation; not implemented)

1966–70:	Instruction-set compatible computers of varying
	  size, speed, and cost
	Large, expensive mass storage systems
	Time-sharing, interactive operating systems
	Microprogramming
	Optimizing compilers
	Translator-writing systems
	First "standard" languages
	Flexibility and generality as language design
	  goals
		PL/I
		FORTRAN 66 (standard)
		COBOL 65 (standard)
		ALGOL 68
		SNOBOL4
		SIMULA 67
		BASIC
		APL\360

1971–75:	Microcomputers Small, inexpensive mass storage systems Proofs of program correctness Structured programming Software engineering Reaction against large, complex languages Simplicity as a language design goal	Pascal COBOL 74 (standard) PL/I (standard)

1976–80:	Powerful, inexpensive computers
	Large, inexpensive mass storage systems
	Distributed computer systems
	Embedded computer systems
	Concurrent and real-time programming using
	  high-level languages
	Interactive programming environments
	Data abstraction
	Software components
	Formal semantic definitions
	Reliability and ease of maintenance as language
	  design goals
		Ada
		FORTRAN 77 (standard)

designed, implemented, used for a period of time, and then allowed to fall into disuse.

In part the reasons for the success or failure of a language tend to be external to the language itself. For example, part of the reason the success of COBOL in the United States may be laid to governmental regulations for its use in certain areas of programming directed by government agencies. Likewise, part of the reason for the success of FORTRAN and PL/I may be attributed to the strong support of various computer manufacturers who have expended large amounts of money and manpower in providing sophisticated implementations and extensive documentation for these languages. The success of SNOBOL4 may be due in part to an excellent early text describing the language (Griswold et al. [1971]). Pascal and LISP have benefited from their use as objects of theoretical study by students of language design as well as from actual practical use.

The task of implementing a language on a given computer is almost always a major one. Preparation, testing, documentation, and maintenance of an implementation for any language of substantial complexity require years of labor. Reimplementation of a language on a new computer may tax the resources of any computing center, and thus languages often fall into disuse as computer installations move to new machines.

In spite of the major importance of some of these external influences, it is the programmer who ultimately, if sometimes indirectly, determines which languages live and die. Many reasons might be suggested to explain why programmers prefer one language over another. Let us consider some of these.

1. *Clarity, simplicity, and unity of language concept.* A programming language provides both a conceptual framework for thinking about algorithms and a means of expressing those algorithms for machine execution. The language should be an aid to the programmer long before he reaches the actual coding stage in programming. It should provide him with a clear, simple, and unified set of concepts that he can use as primitives in developing algorithms. To this end it is desirable to have a minimum number of different concepts, with the rules for their combination being as simple and regular as possible. It is this semantic clarity, this clarity of concept, that seems the most significant determiner of the value of a language.

2. *Clarity of program syntax.* The syntax of a language greatly affects the ease with which a program may be written, tested, and later understood and modified. The *readability* of programs in a language is a central issue here. A syntax that is particularly terse or cryptic often makes a program easy to write (for the experienced programmer) but difficult to read when the program must be modified later. APL programs are often so cryptic that their own designers cannot easily decipher them a few months after they are

completed. Many languages contain syntactic constructs that encourage misreading by making two almost identical statements actually mean radically different things. For example, the presence of a single blank character in a SNOBOL4 statement may entirely alter its meaning. A language should have the property that constructs which *mean* different things look different; i.e., semantic differences should be mirrored in the language syntax.

More important to the programmer than a syntax which is simply not misleading or error-prone is a syntax which when properly used allows the program structure to reflect the underlying logical structure of the algorithm. In the approach to good program design known as *structured programming*, programs are designed hierarchically from the top down (main program to lowest-level subprograms) using only a restricted set of control structures at each level—simple statement sequences, iterations, and certain kinds of conditional branching. When properly done, the resulting algorithm structures are easy to understand, debug, and modify. Ideally it should be possible to translate such a program design directly into appropriate program statements which reflect the structure of the algorithm. Often, however, the language syntax does not allow such a direct encoding. For example, FORTRAN relies heavily on statement labels and GOTO statements as control structures and provides few alternatives. As a result the form of a FORTRAN program cannot ordinarily be made to reflect very clearly the control structure of the underlying algorithm, and much of the effort expended in developing a properly structured algorithm is likely to be lost in the translation into FORTRAN code. This is part of the basis for the controversy over the use of GOTO statements in programming (see Sec. 6-3). One of the major arguments favoring Pascal over FORTRAN in the teaching of introductory programming, in spite of the much wider practical use of FORTRAN, is that Pascal gives more encouragement to elegant program design.

3. *Naturalness for the application.* The language should provide appropriate data structures, operations, control structures, and a natural syntax for the problem to be solved. One of the major reasons for the proliferation of languages is just this need for naturalness. A language particularly suited to a certain class of applications may greatly simplify the creation of individual programs in that area. COBOL, for business applications involving file handling, and SNOBOL4, for string processing, are two languages in Part II with an obvious slant toward particular (although very large) classes of applications.

4. *Support for abstraction.* Even with the most natural programming language for an application, there is always a substantial gap remaining between the abstract data structures and operations that characterize the

solution to a problem and the particular primitive data structures and operations built into a language. For example, Pascal may be an appropriate language for constructing a program to do class scheduling for a university, but the abstract data structures of "student," "class section," "instructor," "lecture room," and the abstract operations of "assign a student to a class section," "schedule a class section in a lecture room," etc., that are natural to the application are not provided directly by Pascal. A substantial part of the programmer's task is to design the appropriate abstractions for the problem solution and then to implement these abstractions using the more primitive features provided by the actual programming language. The programming language may substantially aid or hinder the expression of these abstractions. Ideally the language should allow data structures, data types, and operations to be defined and maintained as self-contained abstractions, so the programmer may use them in other parts of the program knowing only their abstract properties, without concern for the details of their implementation. Almost all languages provide subprogram mechanisms for defining abstract operations, but most are notably weak in their support for other types of abstraction.

5. *Ease of program verification.* The reliability of programs written in a language is always a central concern. There are many techniques for verifying that a program correctly performs its required function. A program may be *proved correct* by a formal verification method (see Chapter 11), it may be informally proved correct by *desk checking* (reading and visually checking the program text), it may be *tested* by executing it with test input data and checking the output results against the specifications, etc. For large programs some combination of all these methods is often used. A language that makes program verification difficult may be far more troublesome to use than one that supports and simplifies verification, even though the former may provide many more features that superficially appear to make programming easier. Simplicity of semantic and syntactic structure are two primary aspects that tend to simplify program verification.

6. *Programming environment.* The technical structure of a programming language is only one aspect affecting its utility. The presence of an appropriate *programming environment* may make a technically weak language easier to work with than a stronger language that has little external support. A long list of factors might be included as part of the programming environment. The availability of a reliable, efficient, and well-documented implementation of the language must head the list. Special editors and testing packages tailored to the language may greatly speed the creation and testing of programs. Facilities for maintaining and modifying multiple versions of a program may make working with large programs much simpler.

7. *Portability of programs.* An important criterion for many programming projects is that of the *transportability* of the resulting programs from the computer on which they are developed to other computer systems. A language which is widely available and whose definition is independent of the features of a particular machine forms a useful base for the production of transportable programs. FORTRAN and COBOL are two languages whose success in part has been based on a concern for program portability.

8. *Cost of use.* The tricky criterion of cost has been left for last. Cost is certainly a major element in the evaluation of any programming language, but a variety of different measures of cost might be used:

a. Cost of program execution. In the earlier years of computing, questions of cost were concerned almost exclusively with program execution. Research on the design of optimizing compilers, efficient register allocation, and the design of efficient run-time support mechanisms was important. Cost of program execution, although always of some importance in language design, is of primary importance for large production programs which will be executed many times.

b. Cost of program translation. When a language like FORTRAN or PL/I is used in teaching, the question of efficient translation (compilation) rather than efficient execution may be paramount. Typically, student programs are compiled many times while being debugged but are executed only a few times. In such a case it is important to have a fast and efficient compiler rather than a compiler that produces optimized executable code.

c. Cost of program creation, testing, and use. Yet a third aspect of cost in a programming language is exemplified by the language APL. For a certain class of problems a solution may be designed, coded, tested, modified, and used in APL with a minimum waste of the programmer's time and energy. APL is cost effective in that the overall time and effort expended in solving a problem on the computer is minimized. Concern with this sort of overall cost in use of a language has become as important in many cases as the more traditional concern with efficient program execution and compilation.

d. Cost of program maintenance. Many studies have shown that the largest cost involved in any program that is used over a period of years is not the cost of initial design, coding, and testing of the program, but the cost of maintenance of the program while it is in production use. Maintenance includes the repair of errors discovered after the program is put into use, changes in the program required as the underlying hardware or operating system is updated, and extensions and enhancements to the program that are needed to meet new needs. A language that makes it easy for a program to be repeatedly modified, repaired, and extended by different programmers over a period of many years may be, in the long run, much less expensive to use than any other.

1-4 REFERENCES AND SUGGESTIONS FOR FURTHER READING

Numerous texts discuss particular programming languages at an intro- ductory level. More general texts that consider language structure, design, and implementation issues are relatively few. Ghezzi and Jazayeri [1982], Tennent [1981], Ledgard and Marcotty [1981], Organick et al. [1978], Barron [1977], and Nicholls [1975] provide alternative views of many of the same issues treated here. The *Ada Rationale* (Ichbiah et al. [1979]) provides a deeper insight into current thought on many advanced language design issues. A useful collection of papers on language design is provided by Wasserman [1980]. The series edited by Yeh [1977-78] provides a somewhat more theoretically oriented collection.

The history of programming languages is treated extensively by Sammet [1969 and 1972]. Wexelblat [1981] and Metropolis [1980] have edited collections of papers from the original designers of many major languages that are also of interest.

The literature on *structured programming* is particularly relevant as background for the study of language design because of the general emphasis in this work on the relation between languages and the ease of program construction and verification. An excellent starting point is the book by Dahl, Dijkstra, and Hoare [1972]. The ACM Turing Award Lectures by Dijkstra [1972b] and Hoare [1981] are also important. The December 1974 issue of *Computing Surveys* contains a classic set of articles on the subject.

1-5 PROBLEMS

1. For a language that is heavily used on your local computer system, evaluate the reasons for its success according to the list of criteria given in Sec. 1-3. Should the list be extended?

2. Standardization of language definitions helps to make programs portable among implementations on *different* computers. When the standard definition of a language is revised (usually every five to ten years), a major influence on the revision is the requirement to make programs written in the earlier version portable to implementations of the revised version on the *same* computer system. Thus there is pressure during the revision to make the new version include the earlier version, so that programs are portable without modification. For the first and second standard definitions of FORTRAN or COBOL, compare the features and list several poor ones whose appearance in the second standard is attri- butable primarily to the desire to maintain compatibility with the first.

CHAPTER 2

Programming
Language
Processors

A *computer* is an integrated set of algorithms and data structures capable of storing and executing programs. A computer may be constructed as an actual physical device using wires, integrated circuits, circuit boards, and the like, in which case it is termed an *actual computer* or *hardware computer*, or it may be constructed via software by programs running on some other computer, in which case it is a *software-simulated computer*. A programming language is implemented by construction of a *translator* which translates programs in the language into *machine language programs* that can be directly executed by some computer. The computer that executes the translated programs may occasionally be a hardware computer, but ordinarily it is a *virtual computer* composed partially of hardware and partially of software. An understanding of these concepts provides the necessary foundation for understanding the more specialized topics in the following chapters.

2-1 THE STRUCTURE AND OPERATION OF A COMPUTER

For our purposes it is convenient to divide the discussion of a computer's structure into six major aspects, which correspond closely to the major aspects of a programming language:

1. *Data.* A computer must provide various kinds of elementary data items and data structures to be manipulated.

2. *Primitive operations.* A computer must provide a set of primitive operations useful for manipulating the data.

3. *Sequence control.* A computer must provide mechanisms for controlling the sequence in which the primitive operations are to be executed.

4. *Data control.* A computer must provide mechanisms for controlling the data supplied to each execution of an operation.

5. *Storage management.* A computer must provide mechanisms to control the allocation of storage for programs and data.

6. *Operating environment.* A computer must provide mechanisms for communication with an external environment containing programs and data to be processed.

These six topics form the subject matter for the main chapters in this part of the book. They also form the basis for the analysis and comparison of the languages described in Part II. However, before looking at these topics in the rather complex context of high-level programming languages, it is instructive to view them within the simple context of an actual hardware computer.

Hardware computer organizations vary widely, but Fig. 2-1 illustrates a fairly typical conventional organization. A *main memory* contains programs and data to be processed. Processing is performed by an *interpreter* which takes each machine language instruction in turn, decodes it, and calls the designated *primitive operation* with the designated operands as input. The primitives manipulate the data in main memory and in high-speed registers and also may transmit programs or data between memory and the *external operating environment*. Let us consider the six major parts of the computer in more detail.

Data. The schematic of Fig. 2-1 shows three major data storage components: main memory, high-speed registers, and external files. Each of these has an assumed internal organization. Main memory is usually organized as a linear sequence of bits subdivided into fixed-length words or bytes. The high-speed registers consist of word or address-length bit sequences and may have special subfields which are directly accessible. External files are usually subdivided into records, each of which is a sequence of bits or bytes.

An actual computer also has certain built-in data types which can be manipulated directly by hardware primitive operations. A common set might include integers, single-precision reals (floating-point numbers), fixed-length character strings, and fixed-length bit strings (where the

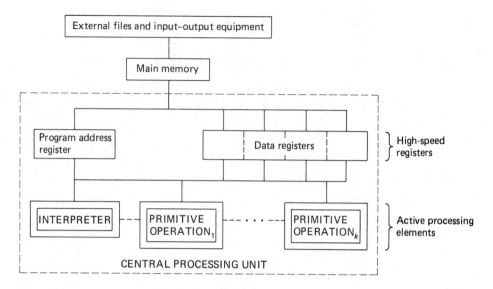

Fig. 2-1 Schematic of the organization of a conventional computer

length is equal to the number of bits or characters that fit into a single word of storage).

Besides these obvious hardware data elements we must also consider programs as a form of data. As with the other built-in data types there must be a built-in representation for programs, termed the *machine language representation* of the computer. Typically a machine language program would be structured as a sequence of memory locations, each containing one or more instructions. Each instruction in turn is composed of an operation code and a set of operand designators.

Operations. A hardware computer must contain a set of built-in primitive operations, usually paired one-to-one with the operation codes that may appear in machine language instructions. A typical set would include primitives for arithmetic on each built-in number data type (e.g., real and integer addition, subtraction, multiplication, and division), primitives for testing various properties of data items (e.g., test for zero, positive, and negative numbers), primitives for accessing and modifying various parts of a data item (e.g., retrieve or store a character in a word and retrieve or store an operand address in an instruction), primitives for controlling input-output devices, and primitives for sequence control (e.g., unconditional and return jumps).

Sequence control. The next instruction to be executed at any point during execution of a machine language program is usually determined by the contents of a special *program address register*, which always contains the memory address of the next instruction. Certain primitive operations are allowed to modify the program address register in order to transfer control to another part of the program, but it is the *interpreter* that actually uses the program address register and guides the sequence of operations.

The interpreter is so central to the operation of a computer that its operation deserves more detailed study. Typically the interpreter executes the simple cyclic algorithm shown in Fig. 2-2. During each cycle the interpreter gets the address of the next instruction from the program address register (and increments the register value by 1), fetches the designated instruction from memory, decodes the instruction into an operation code and a set of operand designators, fetches the designated

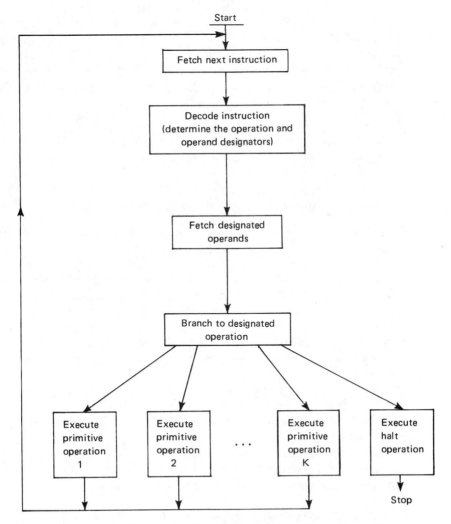

Fig. 2-2 Basic procedure for program interpretation and execution

operands (if necessary), and calls the designated operation with the designated operands as arguments. The primitive operation may modify data in
memory or registers, access input-output devices, or change the execution
sequence by modifying the contents of the program address register. After
execution of the primitive the interpreter simply repeats the above cycle.

Data control. Besides an operation code, each machine language
instruction must specify the operands that the designated operation is to
use. Typically an operand might be in main memory or in a working
register. An actual computer must incorporate a means of designating
operands and a mechanism for retrieving operands from a given operand
designator. Likewise the result of a primitive operation must be stored in
some designated location. We term these facilities the *data control* of the
computer. The conventional scheme is to simply associate integer *addresses*
with memory locations and provide operations for retrieving the contents of
a location given its address (or alternatively for storing a new value in a
location whose address is given). Similarly, registers are also often designated by simple integer addresses.

Storage management. Hardware storage management mechanisms
are often nonexistent. In the simplest design no storage management
facilities are built into the hardware; programs and data reside in one fixed
place in memory throughout program execution. In more sophisticated
computer designs it is now common to include facilities for *paging* or
dynamic program relocation directly in the hardware.

Operating environment. The operating environment of an actual
computer ordinarily consists of a set of peripheral storage and input-output
devices. These devices represent the "outside world" to the computer, and
any communication with the computer must be by way of the operating
environment. Often there are hardware distinctions between various classes
of devices in the environment, based on differences in use or in speed of
access, e.g., high-speed storage (magnetic drums, extended core), medium-
speed storage (magnetic disks), low-speed storage (tapes), and input-output
devices (readers, printers, user terminals, operator console).

An understanding of the *static organization* of a computer in terms of
data, operations, control structures, and the like provides only part of the
picture. Full understanding requires that we also see clearly the *dynamic
operation* of the computer during program execution: What are the contents
of the various storage components at the start of execution, what operations
are executed in what sequence, how are the various data components
modified as execution proceeds, and what is the final result of program
execution?

A convenient means of viewing the dynamic behavior of a computer is
through the concept of *computer state*. Consider the process of program

execution by the computer to proceed through a series of states, each defined by the contents of memory, registers, and external storage at some point during execution. The initial contents of these storage areas define the *initial state* of the computer. Each step in program execution transforms the existing state into a new state through modification of the contents of one or more of these storage areas. This transformation of state is termed a *state transition*. When program execution is complete, the *final state* is defined by the final contents of these storage areas. Program execution may be seen in terms of the sequence of state transitions made by the computer. We understand the dynamic operation of the computer if we can predict the sequence of state transitions which execution of any given program will cause.

2-2 HARDWARE AND FIRMWARE COMPUTERS

Earlier we defined a computer as an integrated set of algorithms and data structures capable of storing and executing programs. The programs executed by a computer are, of course, written in the machine language of the computer. Ordinarily we think of computers as operating on a rather low-level machine language, with simple instruction formats and operations such as "add two numbers" and "load a register with the contents of a memory location." However, machine languages are not restricted to be low-level. Choose any programming language—FORTRAN, PL/I, APL, etc.—and specify precisely a set of data structures and algorithms which define the rules for execution of any program written in the language. In so doing you are necessarily defining a computer, a computer whose "machine language" is the programming language you chose. Each program defines an initial state for the computer, and the rules for program execution define the sequence of state transitions that the computer will make during program execution. The result of execution of the program is determined by the final state of the computer when program execution is complete (if ever).

Given a precise definition of a computer, it is always possible to *realize the computer in hardware*—that is, to construct a hardware device whose machine language is precisely that of the defined computer. This is true even if the machine language is FORTRAN, APL, or some other high-level language. In suggesting this possibility we are appealing to an important basic principle behind computer design: *Any precisely defined algorithm or data structure may be realized in hardware*. Because a computer is simply a collection of algorithms and data structures, we may assume that its hardware realization is a possibility, regardless of the complexity of the computer or its associated machine language.

Actual hardware computers usually have a rather low-level machine language only because of practical considerations—a computer with FORTRAN or APL as its machine language is likely to be considerably more complex (and hence more costly) and considerably less flexible in a variety of computing tasks than a computer with a low-level machine language. A hardware computer with a low-level general-purpose instruction set and a simple, unstructured main memory and register set may be programmed to "look like" any of a broad range of computers relatively efficiently, as we shall see in the following sections. Computers with high-level machine languages have occasionally been constructed, but other techniques for implementation of high-level languages are usually preferable to hardware realization.

A common alternative to the strict hardware realization of a computer is the *firmware computer*, simulated by a *microprogram* running on a special *microprogrammable hardware computer*. The machine language of this computer consists of an extremely low-level set of *microinstructions*, which usually specify simple transfers of data between main memory and high-speed registers, between the registers themselves, and from registers through processors such as adders and multipliers to other registers. A special microprogram is coded, using this simple instruction set, that defines the interpretation cycle and the various primitive operations of the desired computer. The microprogram *simulates* the operation of the desired computer on the microprogrammable *host* computer. Ordinarily the microprogram itself resides in a special read-only memory in the host computer and is executed at high speed by the host computer hardware. This microprogram simulation of a computer is essentially the same, in concept, as the software simulation technique discussed in the next section, except that the host computer in this case is especially designed for microprogramming and provides execution speeds for the simulated computer comparable to those obtained by direct hardware realization. Microprogram simulation of a computer is sometimes termed *emulation*.

The implementation through microprogram simulation of firmware computers with high-level machine languages is likely to become an increasingly attractive alternative for programming language implementation. Microprogrammed implementations of a number of languages have already been proposed or constructed, including implementations of APL and Pascal.

2-3   TRANSLATORS AND SOFTWARE-SIMULATED COMPUTERS

In theory it may be possible to construct a hardware or firmware computer to execute directly programs written in any particular programming language, and thus to construct a LISP, APL, or PL/I computer, but it is not ordinarily economical to construct such a machine. Practical considerations tend to favor actual computers with rather low-level machine languages, on the basis of speed, flexibility, and cost. Programming, of course, is most often done in a high-level language far removed from the hardware machine language itself. The question that actually faces the language implementor, then, is how to get programs in the high-level language executed on the actual computer at hand, regardless of its machine language.

There are two basic solutions to this implementation question:

1. *Translation (compilation).* A translator could be designed to translate programs in the high-level language into equivalent programs in the machine language of the actual computer. Translated programs could then be executed directly by the interpreter and primitive operations built into the hardware. The general term *translator* denotes any language processor that accepts programs in some *source language* (which may be high- or low-level) as input and produces functionally equivalent programs in another *object language* (which may also be high- or low-level) as output. Several specialized types of translator have particular names:

a. A *compiler* is a translator whose source language is a high-level language and whose object language is close to the machine language of an actual computer, either being an assembly language or some variety of machine language.

b. An *assembler* is a translator whose object language is also some variety of machine language for an actual computer but whose source language, an *assembly language*, represents for the most part a simple transliteration of the object machine code. Most instructions in the source language are translated one-for-one into object language instructions.

c. A *loader* is a translator whose object language is actual machine code and whose source language is almost identical, usually consisting of machine language programs in *relocatable* form together with tables of data specifying points where the relocatable code must be modified to become truly executable.

d. A *link editor* is a translator whose source language is the same as that of a loader: programs in relocatable form. The link editor takes collections of such programs that have been compiled separately, usually including subprograms stored in program libraries of various sorts, and links them together into a single unit of actual machine code ready for execution by an actual computer.

e. A *preprocessor* is a translator whose source language is an extended form of some high-level language such as FORTRAN or Pascal and whose object language is the standard form of the same language. The object program produced by a preprocessor is then ready to be translated and executed by the usual processors for the standard language.

Translation of a high-level source language into executable machine language programs often involves more than one translation step. For example, it is not uncommon to have FORTRAN programs first compiled into assembly language, then assembled to produce relocatable machine code, and finally link-edited and loaded to produce executable machine code. Moreover, the compilation step itself may involve a number of passes which progressively translate the program into various intermediate forms before producing the final object program.

2. *Software simulation* (*software interpretation*). Rather than translating the high-level language programs into equivalent machine language programs, we might instead *simulate*, through programs running on another host computer, *a computer whose machine language is the high-level language*. To do this we construct a set of programs in the machine language of the host computer that represent the algorithms (and data structures) necessary for the execution of programs in the high-level language. In other words, we construct with software running on the host computer the high-level language computer which we might otherwise have constructed in hardware. This is termed a *software simulation* (or *software interpretation*) of the high-level language computer on the host computer. The simulated computer accepts as input data a program in the high-level language. The main simulator program performs an interpretation algorithm similar to that of Fig. 2-2, decoding and executing (with the aid of other programs representing the primitive operations of the language) each statement of the input program in the appropriate sequence and producing (with the aid of other programs representing the output operations of the high-level language) the specified output from the program.

Note the difference between software simulation and translation. Both translator and simulator accept programs in the high-level language as input. However, the translator simply produces an equivalent program in its object language, which must then be executed by an interpreter for the object language. The simulator executes the input program directly. If we were to follow the processing of the input program by both translator and simulator, we would observe the translator processing the program statements in their physical input sequence and the simulator following the logical flow of control through the program. The translator would ordinarily process each program statement exactly once, while the simulator might process some statements repeatedly (if they were part of a loop) and might ignore others completely (if control never reached them).

Pure translation and pure simulation form two extremes. In practice pure translation is seldom used except in cases where the input language is in fact quite similar to the machine language, as in the case of assembly languages. Pure simulation is also relatively rare except in the case of operating system control languages or interactive languages. More commonly a language is implemented on a computer by a combination of translation and simulation, as shown in Fig. 2-3. A program is first translated from its original form into a form which is more easily execut-

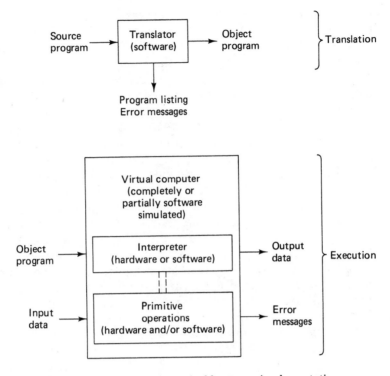

Fig. 2-3   Structure of a typical language implementation

able, and then this executable form of the program is decoded and executed by simulation. In Part II of this book we shall have occasion to study a number of different combinations of translation and simulation in language implementations.

Translation and simulation provide different advantages in a programming language implementation. Some aspects of program structure are best translated into simpler forms before execution; other aspects are best left in their original form and processed only as needed during execution. We can see the basic advantages of translation by considering statements in the original source language program that are executed repeatedly, e.g., statements within program loops or statements in subprograms that are called more than once. Execution of such a statement typically requires a fairly complicated decoding process to determine the operations to be executed and their operands. Often most or all of this process is identical each time the statement is executed. Thus if the statement is executed 1000 times, the identical decoding must be performed 1000 times. If instead the statement is translated into a form which is very simple to decode, for example, as a sequence of machine language instructions, then the complex decoding process need be executed only once by the translator, and only a simple decoding of the translated statement is needed during each of the 1000 repetitions during execution. The total savings in processing time may be substantial.

The disadvantage of translation is connected with storage. Typically a single source language statement may expand during translation into hundreds of machine language instructions. Although execution of these machine language instructions is more efficient, they may take up a great deal more storage than the original statement. For example, execution of a single PRINT statement might require hundreds or even thousands of machine language instructions, because of the need to format the output, check the status of the output device, manipulate buffers, etc. Moreover, *each* PRINT statement requires a similar expansion.

Simulation provides almost an inverted set of advantages. By leaving statements in their original form until they need to be executed, no space is wasted storing multiple copies of long code sequences; the basic code need be stored only once in the simulation routine. However, the total cost of decoding must be paid each time the statement is to be executed. As a general rule translation is used when a source language construct has some rather direct representation in the object language, for then the code expansion is likely not too severe and the advantage of efficient execution outweighs the loss in storage. In other cases simulation is likely the rule.

The key question overall in a language implementation tends to be whether the base representation of the program during execution is that of the machine language of the actual computer being used. This provides the basis for the common division of languages (more precisely, language implementations) into those which are *compiled* and those which are *interpreted*:

1. *Compiled languages.* FORTRAN, Pascal, Ada, PL/I and COBOL are commonly thought of as languages that are compiled. This means that programs in these languages are usually translated into the machine language of the actual computer being used before execution begins, with simulation being confined to a set of *run-time support routines* which simulate primitive operations in the source language that have no close analogue in the machine language. The advantage of utilizing a machine language representation for programs during execution is that the hardware interpreter may be utilized to decode and initiate execution of primitive operations. By using the hardware interpreter, very fast program execution is often realized. It is important to understand, however, that extensive software simulation may be used in implementing parts of the language processor other than the interpreter; for example, data control structures and storage management, as well as many primitive operations, may be software-simulated in a compiled language. Typically, the translator for a

compiled language is relatively large and complex, and the emphasis in translation is on the production of a translated program that executes as efficiently as possible.

2. *Interpreted languages*. LISP, SNOBOL4, and APL are languages often implemented by use of a software interpreter. In such a language implementation, the translator does not produce machine code for the computer being used. Instead the translator produces some intermediate form of the program that is more easily executable than the original program form yet that is different from machine code. The interpretation procedure for execution of this translated program form must be represented by software because the hardware interpreter cannot be used directly. Use of a software interpreter ordinarily results in relatively slow program execution. In addition, languages which are software-interpreted also tend to require extensive software simulation of primitive operations, storage management, and other language features. Translators for interpreted languages tend to be rather simple, with most of the complexity of the implementation coming in the simulation software.

2-4   SYNTAX, SEMANTICS, AND VIRTUAL COMPUTERS

At the beginning of this chapter a computer was defined to be an integrated set of algorithms and data structures capable of storing and executing programs. In the preceding sections we have considered a variety of ways in which a given computer might actually be constructed:

1. Through a *hardware realization*, representing the data structures and algorithms directly with physical devices.

2. Through a *firmware realization*, representing the data structures and algorithms by microprogramming a suitable hardware computer.

3. Through *software simulation*, representing the data structures and algorithms by programs and data structures in some other programming language.

4. Through some *combination* of these techniques, representing various parts of the computer directly in hardware, in microprograms, or by software simulation as appropriate.

A hardware computer is termed an *actual computer*. A computer that is partially or wholly simulated by software or microprograms is termed a *virtual computer*. When a programming language is implemented, the run-time data structures and algorithms used in program execution define a computer. Because this computer is almost always at least partially software-simulated, we speak of this as the *virtual computer defined by the language implementation*. The machine language of this virtual computer is the executable program form produced by the translator for the language, which may take the form of actual machine code if the language is compiled, or, alternatively, may have some arbitrary structure if the language is interpreted. The data structures of this virtual computer are the run-time data structures that are used during program execution. The primitive operations are those operations that are actually executable at run time. Sequence control, data control, and storage management structures are those used at run time, regardless of representation by software, hardware, or microprogram.

Syntax and Semantics

The *syntax* of a programming language is the form in which programs are written. To give the rules of syntax for a programming language means to tell how statements, declarations, and other language constructs are written. The *semantics* of a programming language is the meaning given to the various syntactic constructs. For example, to give the syntax used in Pascal to declare a ten-element vector, V, of real numbers you would show how such a Pascal declaration would be written:

$$V:\textbf{array}[1..10] \textbf{ of } real;$$

To understand the meaning of such a Pascal declaration, you need to know the semantics in Pascal for such array declarations—that is, you need to know that such a declaration placed at the beginning of a subprogram means to create on each entry to that subprogram, and destroy on exit, a vector that has storage for ten real numbers and that can be referenced by the name V during execution of the subprogram.

In programming language manuals and other language descriptions, it is customary to organize the language description around the various syntactic constructs in the language. Typically the syntax is given for a language construct such as a particular type of statement or declaration, and then the semantics for that construct is also given, describing the intended meaning.

In this text, a different style of description is used, organized around the structure associated with a virtual computer. This style describes the semantics of a programming language in terms of the data structures and operations used in the virtual computer for that programming language. Sometimes these data structures and operations are tied directly to particular constructs in the syntax of the language, but often the tie is much less direct. For example, the Pascal virtual computer may use a vector V during execution of a program, where V has a structure that is directly given by the declaration above. However, the Pascal virtual computer may have other data structures, such as a central stack of subprogram "activation records," that are not seen directly in the syntax of programs at all.

These "hidden" virtual computer structures are as important to an understanding of the language as are the "visible" structures that correspond directly to something that the programmer has written in the program. For this reason, the discussion of language elements here is organized around structures seen in virtual computers, rather than in terms of syntactic elements. A particular virtual computer element may have no syntactic representation in a program, may be directly represented by a single syntactic element, or may be represented by several separate syntactic elements that are brought together by the language translator to produce one virtual computer element.

Virtual Computers and Language Implementations

If programming languages were originally defined in terms of their virtual computers, so that each language was associated with a single commonly understood virtual computer, then description of the semantics of each language in terms of its virtual computer would be straightforward. Unfortunately, because languages are usually defined by giving a semantics for each syntactic construct individually, language definitions specify only implicitly an underlying virtual computer. Each time the language is implemented on a different computer, the implementor tends to see a slightly different (and sometimes very different) virtual computer in the language definition. Thus two different implementations of the same language may utilize a different set of data structures and operations in the implementation, particularly for data structures and operations that are "hidden" in the program syntax. Each implementor has wide latitude in determining the virtual computer structures that are the basis for his particular implementation.

When a programming language is being implemented on a particular computer, the implementor first determines the virtual computer that represents his understanding of the semantics of the language, and then he chooses a particular way of constructing that virtual computer out of the hardware and software elements provided by the underlying computer. For example, if the virtual computer contains both an integer-addition operation and a square-root operation, the implementor may choose to represent the integer-addition operation using an integer-addition operation provided directly by the underlying hardware, while the square-root operation may be represented by a software simulation, as a subprogram for computing square roots. If the virtual computer contains a simple integer variable X, then the implementor may choose to represent X directly by a storage location in memory containing the value of X, or he may choose to represent X by a storage location that contains a "type tag" designating "integer" together with a pointer to another storage location that contains the value of X. The organization and structure of an implementation of a language are determined by the many detailed decisions of this sort made by the implementor, taking into account the various hardware and software facilities available in the underlying computer and the costs of their use.

The implementor must also determine precisely what is to be done during translation of a program and what during execution. Often, a particular way of representing a virtual computer data structure or operation during program execution can be used only if certain kinds of actions are taken during program translation to set up the run-time structure. If the implementor chooses to simplify the translator by omitting these actions, then different run-time representations may be necessary.

Thus, three factors lead to differences among implementations of the same language:

1. Differences in each implementor's conception of the virtual computer that is implicit in the language definition,

2. Differences in the facilities provided by the host computer on which the language is to be implemented, and

3. Differences in the choices made by each implementor as to how to simulate the virtual computer elements using the facilities provided by the underlying computer and how to construct the translator so as to support these choices of virtual computer representation.

2-5   HIERARCHIES OF COMPUTERS

The virtual computer that a programmer uses when he programs in some high-level language is in fact formed from a *hierarchy of virtual computers*. At the bottom there must, of course, lie an actual hardware computer. However, the ordinary programmer seldom has any direct dealing with this computer. Instead this hardware computer is successively transformed by layers of software (or microprograms) into a virtual computer which may be radically different. The second level of virtual computer (or the third if a microprogram forms the second level) is usually defined by the complex collection of routines known as the *operating system*.

Typically the operating system provides simulations for a number of new operations and data structures that are not directly provided by the hardware, e.g., external file structures and file management primitives. The operating system also deletes certain hardware primitives from the operating-system-defined virtual computer so that they are not accessible to the operating system user, e.g., hardware primitives for input-output, error monitoring, multiprogramming, and multiprocessing. The operating-system-defined virtual computer is usually that which is available to the implementor of a high-level language. The language implementor provides a new layer of software that runs on the operating-system-defined computer and simulates the operation of the virtual computer for the high-level language. He also provides a translator for translating user programs into the machine language of the language-defined virtual computer.

The hierarchy in fact does not end with the high-level language implementation. The programs that a programmer runs add yet another level to the hierarchy. What is the machine language of this programmer-defined, software-simulated virtual computer? The machine language is

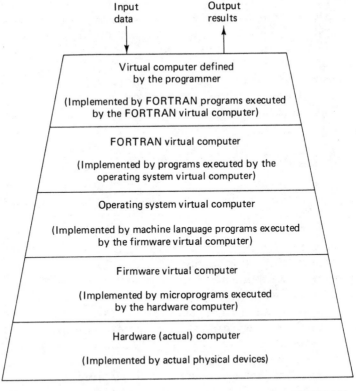

Fig. 2-4 Layers of virtual computer used by a FORTRAN programmer

composed of the *input data* for these programs. Once the programmer has his programs running, he "writes a program" to operate the virtual computer defined by these programs by choosing an appropriate set of input data. If this view seems far-fetched it is because for many programs the input data formats are so simple as to constitute only a most trivial programming language. However, it is apparent that every programmer constructing the lower levels in our hierarchy must have held exactly that view, because at each level the programs and data structures constructed in fact represented a simulation of a virtual computer that programmers at the next level programmed. Figure 2-4 illustrates such a hierarchy of virtual computer layers as they might appear to a FORTRAN programmer.

Implicit in the above discussion is a central concept that deserves explicit mention: *the equivalence of programs and data*. We are accustomed to considering certain kinds of objects in programming as "program" and others as "data." This is often a useful intuitive distinction, but, as the above discussion makes clear, it is a distinction that is more apparent than real. That which is program in one context is likely to become data in another. For example you may write a Pascal program, but to the Pascal compiler that program is input data to be processed. The output data produced by the compiler is, to you, a program in machine language. You may request execution of this program, but a closer look at the manner of program execution might convince you that in fact the program is just data to the interpreter used by the executing computer. In the same vein we may always consider the input to any program equivalently as data to be processed or as a program to be executed.

2-6   BINDING AND BINDING TIME

The preceding sections have described the *translator/virtual computer* structure common to all programming language implementations. We have stressed the importance of understanding the gross structure of a language implementation if one is to use the language properly in programming. In this section the same question is viewed in a somewhat different light. We may encompass much of the discussion in terms of the central concepts of *binding* and *binding time*.

Binding is not a concept that allows a single precise definition, nor is binding time. There are many different varieties of bindings in programming languages, as well as a variety of binding times. Without attempting to be too precise, we may speak of the *binding* of a program element to a particular characteristic or property as simply the choice of the property from a set of possible properties. The time during program formulation or processing when this choice is made is termed the *binding time* of that property for that element. In addition we wish to include within the concepts of binding and binding time the properties of program elements that are fixed either by the definition of the language or by its implementation.

Classes of Binding Times

While there is no simple categorization of the various types of bindings, a few main binding times may be distinguished if we recall our basic assumption that the processing of a program, regardless of the language, always involves a translation step followed by execution of the translated program:

1. *Execution time* (*run time*). Many bindings are performed during program execution. These include bindings of variables to their values, as well as (in many languages) the binding of variables to particular storage locations. Two important subcategories may be distinguished:

a. *On entry to a subprogram or block.* In most languages important classes of bindings are restricted to occur only at the time of entry to a subprogram or block during execution. For example, in Pascal the binding of formal to actual parameters and the binding of formal parameters to particular storage locations may occur only on entry to a subprogram.

b. *At arbitrary points during execution.* Other important classes of bindings may occur at any point during execution of a program. The most important example here is the basic binding of variables to values through assignment.

2. *Translation time* (*compile time*). In all languages, but especially those that are compiled, important classes of bindings are performed during translation. Two different classes of translation time bindings may be distinguished:

a. *Bindings chosen by the programmer.* In writing a program, the programmer consciously makes many decisions regarding choices of variable names, types for variables, program statement structures, etc. that represent bindings during translation. The language translator makes use of these bindings in determining the final form of the object program.

b. *Bindings chosen by the translator.* Other bindings are chosen by the language translator without direct programmer specification. For example, in FORTRAN, bindings of variables to particular storage locations are performed at *load time*, the last stage of translation when translated programs are linked and loaded into memory in their final executable form. In all languages, the binding of the source program to a particular object program representation is made by the translator.

3. *Language implementation time*. Some aspects of a language definition may be the same for all programs that are run using a particular implementation of a language, but they may vary between implementations. For example, often the details associated with the representations of numbers and of arithmetic operations are determined by the way that arithmetic is done in the underlying hardware computer. A program written in the language that uses a feature whose definition has been fixed at implementation time will not necessarily run on another implementation of the same language; even more troublesome, it may run and give different results.

4. *Language definition time*. Most of the structure of a programming language is fixed at the time the language is defined, in the sense of specification of the alternatives available to a programmer when writing a program. For example, the possible alternative statement forms, data structure types, program structures, etc. are all often fixed at language definition time.

To illustrate the variety of bindings and binding times, consider the simple assignment statement

$$X := X + 10$$

Suppose that this statement appeared within some program written in a language L. We might inquire into the bindings and binding times of at least the following elements of this statement:

1. *Set of possible types for variable X*. The variable X in the statement usually has a data type associated with it, such as *real*, *integer*, or *Boolean*. The set of allowable types for X is often fixed at language definition time; e.g., only types *real*, *integer*, *Boolean*, *set*, and *character* might be allowed. Alternatively, the language may allow each program to define new types, as in Pascal and Ada, so that the set of possible types for X is fixed at translation time.

2. *Type of variable X*. The particular data type associated with variable X is often fixed at translation time, through an explicit declaration in the program such as the Pascal:

$$X : real;$$

In other languages, such as APL and LISP, the data type of X may be bound only at execution time through assignment of a value of a particular type to X. In these languages, X may refer to an array at one point and to an integer at a later point in the same program.

3. *Set of possible values for variable X*. If X has data type *real*, then its value at any point during execution is one of a set of bit sequences representing real numbers. The precise set of possible values for X is

determined by the real numbers that can be represented and manipulated in the virtual computer defining the language, which ordinarily is the set of real numbers that can be represented conveniently in the underlying hardware computer. Thus the set of possible values for X is determined at language implementation time; different implementations of the language may allow different ranges of possible values for X.

4. *Value of the variable X*. At any point during program execution, a particular value is bound to variable X. Ordinarily this value is determined at execution time through assignment of a value to X. The assignment X:= X + 10 changes the binding of X, replacing its old value by a new one that is ten more than the old one.

5. *Representation of the constant 10*. The integer ten has both a representation as a constant in programs, using the string 10, and a representation at execution time, commonly as a sequence of bits. The choice of decimal representation in the program (i.e., using 10 for ten) is usually made at *language definition time*, while the choice of a particular sequence of bits to represent ten at execution time is usually made at *language implementation time*.

6. *Properties of the operator +*. Let us consider the binding times of the various properties of the operator + in the statement. The choice of the symbol + to represent the addition operation is made at *language definition time*. However, it is common to allow the same symbol + to represent *real addition*, *integer addition*, *complex addition*, etc., depending on the context. In a compiled language it is common to make the determination of which operation is represented by + at *compile time*. The mechanism for specifying the binding desired is usually the typing mechanism for variables: If X is type integer, then the + in X + 10 represents integer addition; if X is type real, then the + represents real addition; etc.

Another property of the operation represented by + is its value for any given pair of operands. Thus, in our example, if X has the value 12, then what is the value of X + 10? Or if X has the value 2^{49}, then what is the value of X + 10? In other words, when is the meaning of addition defined? The meaning is usually fixed at language implementation time and is drawn from the definition of addition used in the underlying hardware computer.

In summary, for a language like Pascal the symbol + is bound to a set of *addition operations* at language definition time, each addition operation in the set is defined at language implementation time, each particular use of the symbol + in a program is bound to a particular addition operation at translation time, and the particular value of each particular addition operation for its operands is determined only at execution time. This set of bindings represents one choice of possible bindings and binding times typical of a variety of programming languages. Note, however, that many other bindings and binding times are also possible. In SNOBOL4, all these bindings could be made at execution time.

Importance of Binding Times

In the analysis and comparison of programming languages in the following chapters many distinctions are based on differences in binding times. We shall be continuously in the process of asking the question: Is this done at translation time or at execution time? Many of the most important and subtle differences among languages involve differences in binding times. For example, almost every language allows numbers as data and allows arithmetic operations on these numbers. Yet not all languages are equally suited for programming problems involving a great deal of arithmetic. For example, while both SNOBOL4 and FORTRAN allow one to set up and manipulate arrays of numbers, solving a problem requiring large arrays and large amounts of arithmetic in SNOBOL4 would probably be most inappropriate if it could also be done in FORTRAN. If we were to try to trace the reason for this by comparing the features of SNOBOL4 and FORTRAN, we ultimately would ascribe the superiority of FORTRAN in this case to the fact that in SNOBOL4 most of the bindings required in the program will be set up at execution time while in FORTRAN most will be set up at translation time. Thus a SNOBOL4 version of the program would spend most of its execution time creating and destroying bindings, while in the FORTRAN version most of the same bindings would be set up once during translation, leaving only a few to be handled during execution. As a result the FORTRAN version would execute much more efficiently. On the other hand, we might turn around and ask a related question: Why is FORTRAN so inflexible in its handling of arrays, numbers, and arithmetic, as compared to SNOBOL4? Again the answer turns on binding times. Because most bindings in FORTRAN are performed at translation time, before the input data are known, it is difficult in FORTRAN to write programs that can adapt to a variety of different data-dependent situations at execution time. For example, the size of arrays and the type of variables must be fixed at translation time in FORTRAN. In SNOBOL4 bindings may be delayed during execution until the input data have been examined and the appropriate bindings for the particular input data determined.

A language like FORTRAN in which most bindings are made during translation, early in the processing of a program, is said to have *early binding*; a language with *late binding*, such as SNOBOL4, delays most bindings until execution time.

The advantages and disadvantages of early binding versus late binding revolve around this conflict between efficiency and flexibility. In languages where execution efficiency is a prime consideration, such as FORTRAN, Pascal, and COBOL, it is common to design the language so that as many bindings as possible may be performed during translation. Where flexibility is the prime determiner, as in SNOBOL4 and LISP, most bindings are delayed until execution time so that they may be made data-dependent. In a language designed for both efficient execution and flexibility, such as Ada or PL/I, multiple options are often available that allow choices of binding times.

Binding Times and Language Implementations

Language definitions are usually permissive in specifying binding times. A language is designed so that a particular binding *may* be performed at, e.g., translation time, but the actual time at which the binding is performed is in fact defined only by the implementation of the language. For example, Pascal is designed to permit the type of variables to be determined at compile time, but a particular Pascal implementation might instead do type checking at execution time. Thus while the definition of Pascal permits compile-time type checking, it does not require it. In general a language design specifies the earliest time during program processing at which a particular binding is possible, but any implementation of the language may in fact delay the binding to a later time. However, usually most implementations of the same language will perform most bindings at the same time. If the language is designed to permit compile-time bindings, then to delay these bindings until execution time will probably lead to less efficient execution at no gain in flexibility. It ordinarily is expedient to perform the bindings at the earliest possible moment.

One additional caution is needed, however. Often seemingly minor changes in a language may lead to major changes in binding times. For example, in FORTRAN the change to allow recursion and computed array dimensions, two rather simple changes in the language, would modify many of the binding times of important FORTRAN features. Because binding times are implementation-dependent, we place emphasis on knowing the language implementation. In Part II a number of languages are analyzed. In each case a "typical" implementation of the language is assumed and the binding times of the various language elements in the context of this implementation are discussed. When approaching your own local implementation of the same language, it is important to ask about the binding times in that implementation. Are they the usual ones, or have local modifications to the language caused the usual binding times to be modified?

2-7   REFERENCES AND SUGGESTIONS FOR FURTHER READING

Software simulation, translation, virtual computers, and binding times are central topics in the chapters that follow. Tanenbaum [1976] provides an excellent overview of computer organization at the hardware, firmware, and operating system levels. His discussion of microprogramming is particularly recommended. Husson [1970] also discusses microprogramming in some depth. Siewiorek, Bell, and Newell [1982] provide a collection of articles describing different computer organizations. The texts by Kuck [1978] and Baer [1980] are also recommended.

The general class of computers described in Sec. 2-1 are usually termed *von Neumann computers*, because the basic organizational principles may be traced to the early work of John von Neumann. Alternative computer organizations based on radically different principles have not been discussed here. The Turing Award Lecture of Backus [1978] critiques the von Neumann computer organization and offers an alternative. Many other alternatives have been suggested; Myers [1981] provides an excellent discussion and survey of organizations directed toward support of high-level languages. The April 1982 issue of *SIGPLAN Notices* also contains a useful collection of articles on this subject.

Compilers and translation are discussed further in Chapter 9. Assemblers, loaders, and link editors are treated by Barron [1972] and Presser and White [1972].

2-8   PROBLEMS

1. Analyze the implementation of a programming language with which you are familiar. What is the executable form of a program (i.e., what is the output of the translator)? What sorts of translations are made in translating the various statements and expressions into executable form? What software simulation is necessary during program execution? Is the interpreter software-simulated? Which of the primitive operations require software simulation?

2. Analyze the structure of your local actual (hardware) computer. Determine the data types, primitive operations, sequence and data control structures, storage management facilities, and operating environment which are built into the hardware.

3. If your local computer has an operating system, determine the structure of the virtual computer defined by the operating system. How does this virtual computer differ from the actual hardware computer? Are there features of the hardware which are restricted by the operating system, e.g., hardware instructions which are not allowed in user programs in the operating-system-defined virtual computer? What new features are provided directly in the operating system virtual computer which could be simulated only by complex software on the basic hardware computer, e.g., input-output?

4. The use of an operating system to provide the programmer with a virtual computer different from the basic hardware computer has three advantages. It allows the user to work with a simpler computer than is provided directly by the hardware—for example, by providing simpler and more powerful input-output

facilities. It also protects the computer system from the user, in that each user may be effectively "sealed off" in his own virtual computer, so that any errors he makes will hurt only his virtual computer and not bring down the whole system and its other users as well. It also allows the operating system to allocate the resources of the system more appropriately to different users. Analyze your local operating system and the virtual computer it provides the programmer. How well does it achieve these goals?

5. The BASIC programming language is often implemented using a complete software simulation of the BASIC virtual computer. If the programs that simulate the BASIC virtual computer were written in FORTRAN (as they might well be), then another layer would be added to the layers of virtual computer in Fig. 2-4. Draw the new layer. If you know both BASIC and FORTRAN, explain the parts of the BASIC virtual computer that the FORTRAN programs might simulate. Where does the *translator* that translates BASIC programs into their executable form fit into this diagram?

6. Write a statement in a language with which you are familiar. For each syntactic component of the statement (variable names, operation symbols, etc.), list the various bindings that are necessary to completely determine the semantics of the statement when it is executed. For each binding, identify the binding time used in the language.

7. Do Problem 6, but use a *declaration* instead of a statement. Declarations are usually said to be *elaborated* instead of executed, so list the bindings (and their binding times) necessary for a complete elaboration of the declaration.

CHAPTER 3

Elementary Data Types

Any program, regardless of the language used, may be viewed as specifying a set of operations that are to be applied to certain data in a certain sequence. Basic differences among languages exist in the types of data allowed, in the types of operations available, and in the mechanisms provided for controlling the sequence in which the operations are applied to the data. These three areas—data, operations, and control—form the basis for the next five chapters and also provide the framework for much of the discussion and comparison of languages in Part II. This chapter and the next consider the *primitive* data types and operations that are usually built into languages. Chapter 5 considers language mechanisms that allow the *programmer* to define new operations and data types. The topic of control is taken up in Chapters 6 and 7.

3-1 DATA OBJECTS, VARIABLES, AND CONSTANTS

The data storage areas of an actual computer, such as the memory, registers, and external storage, usually have a relatively simple structure as bit sequences grouped into bytes or words. However, the data storage areas of the virtual computer for a programming language tend to have a much more complex organization, with various arrays, stacks, numbers, character strings, and other pieces of data existing at different points during execution of a program. It is convenient to use the term *data object* to refer to a run-time grouping of one or more pieces of data in a virtual computer. During execution of a program, many different data objects of different types exist. Moreover, in contrast to the relatively static organization of the underlying storage areas of an actual computer, these data objects and their interrelationships change dynamically as execution of the program progresses.

Some of the data objects that exist during program execution will be *programmer-defined*; that is, they will be variables, constants, arrays, files, etc. that the programmer explicitly creates and manipulates through declarations and statements in his program. Other data objects will be *system-defined*; that is, they will be data objects that the virtual computer set up for "housekeeping" during program execution and that are not directly accessible to the programmer, such as run-time storage stacks, subprogram activation records, file buffers, and free-space lists. System-defined data objects are ordinarily generated automatically as needed during program execution without explicit specification by the programmer. To understand the virtual computer defined by a language, it is important to understand the run-time data objects that exist during program execution. Programmer-defined data objects are the subject of this and the next two chapters. System-defined data objects are a primary concern of Chapters 6, 7, and 8.

A data object represents a *container for data values*—a place where data values may be stored and later retrieved. A data object is characterized by a set of *attributes*, the most important of which is its *data type*. The attributes determine the number and type of values that the data object may contain and also determine the logical organization of those values.

A *data value* might be a single number, character, or possibly a pointer to another data object. A data value is ordinarily represented by a particular pattern of bits in the storage of a computer. Many copies of the same value may exist; that is, the same pattern of bits may appear in many places in storage. Two values are the same if the patterns of bits representing them in storage are identical. It is easy to confuse data objects and data values, and in many languages the distinction is not clearly made. Both data objects and data values are abstract concepts useful in understanding languages. The distinction is perhaps most easily seen by noting the difference in implementation: a data object is usually represented by a block of storage in the computer memory. A data value is represented by a pattern of bits. To say that a data object A contains the value B means that the block of storage representing A is set to contain the particular bit pattern representing B, as shown in Fig. 3-1.

If we observe the course of execution of a program, some data objects exist at the beginning of execution and others are created dynamically during execution. Some data objects are destroyed during execution; others

A :
```
┌─────────────────┐
│                 │
└─────────────────┘
```

(a) A data object named A, represented by one word in a
computer memory.

10001

(b) A data value, the number 17, represented in
binary as a bit pattern.

A : | 00000010001 |

(c) The data object A containing (bound to) the data
value 17.

Fig. 3-1 A simple variable data object with value 17

persist until the program terminates. Thus each object has a *lifetime* during execution of a program, and during its lifetime it may be used to store data values.

A data object is *elementary* if it contains only a single data value that is always manipulated as a unit. It is a *data structure* if it is an aggregate of other data objects. This chapter considers elementary data objects; data structures are considered in the next chapter.

A data object may also participate in various *bindings* during its lifetime. While the attributes of a data object are invariant during its lifetime, the bindings may change dynamically. The most important bindings are:

1. The binding of a data object to one or more *values*. This binding may usually be modified by an assignment operation.

2. The binding of a data object to one or more *names* by which it may be referenced during program execution. These bindings are usually set up by declarations and modified by subprogram calls and returns, as discussed in Chapter 7.

3. The binding of a data object to one or more data objects of which it is a *component*. Such a binding is often represented by a pointer value, and it may be modified by a change in the pointer, as discussed in Chapter 4.

4. The binding of a data object to a *storage location* in memory where the data object is represented. This binding ordinarily is not directly modifiable by the programmer but is set up and may be changed by the storage management routines of the virtual computer, as discussed in Chapter 8.

EXAMPLE 3-1. Pascal Simple Variables. In Pascal a subprogram may include the declaration:

$$\textbf{var } N : \text{integer;}$$

which declares a simple variable N of type *integer*. Subsequently in the subprogram, the assignment:

$$N := 27$$

may be used to assign the value 27 to N. In the terms used above, we would describe the situation somewhat more completely as follows:

1. The declaration specifies an elementary data object of type *integer*, its sole attribute. This data object is to be created on entry to the subprogram and destroyed on exit; thus its lifetime is the duration of execution of the subprogram.

2. During its lifetime, the data object is to be bound to the name "N" through which it may be referenced, as happens in the assignment statement above. Other names may be bound to the data object if it is passed as an argument to another subprogram.

3. No value is bound to the data object initially, but the assignment statement binds the value 27 to it temporarily until some later assignment to N changes the binding.

4. Hidden from the programmer are other bindings done by the virtual computer: the data object N is made a component of an *activation record* data object that contains all the local data for the subprogram, and this activation record and all the data objects it contains are allocated storage in a *run-time stack* (another hidden data object) at the time that execution of the subprogram begins. When the subprogram terminates, this storage is freed for reuse, and the binding of data object to storage location is destroyed.

Variables and Constants

A data object that is defined and named by the programmer explicitly in a program is usually termed a *variable*. A *simple variable* is an elementary data object with a name. We usually think of the value (or values) of a variable as being modifiable by assignment operations; i.e., the binding of data object to value may change during its lifetime.

A *constant* is a data object with a name which is bound to a value (or values) permanently during its lifetime. A *literal* (or *literal constant*) is a constant whose name is just the written representation of its value (e.g., "21" is the written decimal representation of the literal constant data object with value 21). A *programmer-defined constant* is a constant whose name is chosen by the programmer in a definition of the data object.

The concept of *data object* is more general than that of *variable* or *constant* because data objects need not have names and need not be created explicitly by the programmer. All the terms used above in relation to data objects may also be specialized to variables, however, since a variable is just a special form of data object. Thus we may use the terms "value of a variable," "location of a variable," "name of a variable," "type of a variable," etc. The same is true for constants—e.g., "value of a constant," "location of a constant."

EXAMPLE 3-2. Pascal Variables, Constants, and Literals. In Pascal a subprogram may include the definition:

$$\textbf{const } MAX = 30;$$

Then with the declaration:

$$\textbf{var } N : integer;$$

we may write the assignments:

$$N := 27;$$
$$N := N + MAX$$

N is a simple variable; MAX, 27, and 30 are constants. N, MAX, "27," and "30" are names for data objects of type *integer*. The constant definition specifies that the data object named MAX is to be bound permanently (for the duration of execution of the subprogram) to the value 30. The constant MAX is a *programmer-defined constant* because the programmer explicitly defines his own name for the value 30. The name "27," on the other hand, is a *literal* that names a data object containing the value 27. Such literals are defined as part of the language definition itself. The important but confusing distinction here is between the *value* 27, which is an integer represented as a sequence of bits in storage during program execution, and the *name* "27," which is a sequence of two characters "2" and "7" that represents the same number in decimal form as it is written in a program.

Note that in this example, the constant 30 has two names, the programmer-defined name "MAX" and the literal name "30," both of which may be used to refer to a data object containing the value 30 in the program.

3-2   DATA TYPES

A *data type* is a class of data objects together with a set of operations for creating and manipulating them. Although a program deals with particular *data objects* such as an array A, the integer variable X, or the file F, a programming language necessarily deals more commonly with *data types* such as the class of arrays, integers, or files and the operations provided for manipulating arrays, integers, or files.

Every language has a set of *primitive* data types that are built into the language. In addition a language may provide facilities to allow the programmer to define new data types. One of the major differences between older languages such as FORTRAN and COBOL and newer languages such as Pascal and Ada lies in the area of programmer-defined data types, a subject taken up in Chapter 5.

A data type in a language may be studied at two different levels: in terms of its *specification* (or *logical organization*) and in terms of its *implementation*. In addition the *syntactic representation* of the data type in the language is important.

The basic elements of a *specification* of a data type are:

1. The *attributes* that distinguish data objects of that type,

2. The *values* that data objects of that type may have, and

3. The *operations* that define the possible manipulations of data objects of that type.

For example, in considering the specification of an array data type, the attributes might include the number of dimensions, the subscript range for each dimension, and the data type of the components; the values would be the sets of numbers that form valid values for array components; and the operations would include subscripting to select individual array components and possibly other operations to create arrays, to change their shape, to access attributes such as upper and lower bounds of subscripts, and to perform arithmetic on pairs of arrays.

The basic elements of the *implementation* of a data type are:

1. The *storage representation* that is used to represent the data objects of the data type in the storage of the computer during program execution, and

2. The manner in which the operations defined for the data type are represented in terms of particular *algorithms* or *procedures* that manipulate the chosen storage representation for the data objects.

Both the storage representation and the algorithms are necessarily defined in terms of more primitive data objects and operations.

The specification of a data type corresponds roughly to the specification of that part of the virtual computer which is defined by the data type, as described in Chapter 2. The implementation of a data type defines the *simulation* of those parts of the virtual computer in terms of the more primitive constructs provided by the underlying layer of virtual computer, which may be directly the hardware computer or a hardware/software combination defined by an operating system or microcode.

The last concern connected with a data type lies in its *syntactic representation*. Both specification and implementation are largely independent of the particular syntactic forms used in the language itself. Attributes of data objects are often represented syntactically by *declarations* or *type definitions*. Values may be represented as literals or defined constants. Operations may be invoked by using special symbols such as "+", built-in procedures or functions such as SIN or READ, or implicitly through combinations of other language elements. The particular syntactic representation makes little difference, but the information present in the program syntax provides information to the language translator that may be vital in determining the binding time of various attributes and thus in allowing the translator to set up efficient storage representations or to perform checking for type errors.

The sections that follow consider in more detail the areas of data type specification, implementation, and syntactic representation and type checking. Particular syntactic representations vary so widely among languages that no comprehensive survey is attempted here, but examples from various languages in Part II are used to illustrate the concepts.

3-3   SPECIFICATION OF ELEMENTARY DATA TYPES

An *elementary* data object contains a single data value. A class of such data objects over which various operations are defined is termed an *elementary data type*. Although each programming language tends to have a somewhat different set of elementary data types, the types *integer, real, character, Boolean,* and *enumeration* treated in this chapter are often included, although the exact specification may differ significantly between two languages. For example, although most languages include an integer data type, it is treated quite differently in FORTRAN and SNOBOL4; in APL it is omitted altogether.

Attributes

The most basic attribute of any data object is its data type. For a particular data type, an additional set of attributes may be needed to completely characterize a particular data object. In the specification of the attributes associated with a data type, we need to specify the attribute's name and possible values. For example, a real-number data type may have the attribute PRECISION with two possible values, SINGLE or DOUBLE.

The attributes of a data object are invariant during its lifetime. They are of primary importance in determining the storage representation of the data object, as described in the next section. Some of the attributes may be stored in a *descriptor*, as part of the data object during program execution; others may be used only to determine the storage representation of the data object and may not appear explicitly during execution at all. Note that the *value of an attribute* of a data object is different from the *value that the data object contains*. The value contained may change during the data object's lifetime and is always represented explicitly during program execution.

Values

The type of a data object determines the set of possible values that it may contain. At any point during its lifetime, an elementary data object contains a single value from this set. For example, the *integer* data type determines a set of integer values that may serve as the values for data objects of this type. This set of values is usually the same as the set of integer values that may be represented conveniently in storage in the underlying hardware computer, although it need not be.

The set of values defined by an elementary data type is usually an *ordered set*; that is, the set has a least value and a greatest value, and for any pair of distinct values, one is greater than the other. For example, for an integer data type, there is usually a greatest integer, corresponding to the greatest integer that can be conveniently represented in memory, and similarly a least integer, with the integers between arranged in their usual numerical ordering.

Operations

The set of operations defined for a data type determine how data objects of that type can be manipulated. The operations considered in this chapter and the next are the *primitive operations* of each data type, which means the operations that are specified as part of the language definition. *Programmer-defined operations*, in the form of subprograms, are considered in subsequent chapters.

An operation in a programming language is logically a *mathematical function*: for a given input *argument* (or arguments) it has a well-defined and uniquely determined *result* (or results). Each operation has a *domain*, the set of possible input arguments on which it is defined, and a *range*, the set of possible results that it may produce. The *action* of the operation defines the results produced for any given set of arguments. An *algorithm* that specifies how to compute the results for any given set of arguments is a common method for specifying the action of an operation, but other specifications are possible. For example, to specify the action of a multiplication operation, you might give a "multiplication table" that simply lists the results of multiplying any two pairs of numbers, rather than an algorithm for multiplying any two numbers.

To specify the domain of an operation, the number, order and data type of the arguments are given. Similarly, to specify the range, the number, order, and data type of the results are given. It is convenient to use the usual mathematical notation for this specification:

operation name : argument-type $\times$ argument-type $\times$ ... →

result-type $\times$ result-type $\times$ ...

EXAMPLE 3-3

(a) Integer addition is an operation that takes two integer data objects as arguments and produces an integer data object as its result (a data object usually containing the sum of the values of its two arguments). Thus its specification is:

$$+: \text{integer} \times \text{integer} \rightarrow \text{integer}$$

(b) The operator "=" that tests for equality of the values of two integer data objects and produces a data object containing a Boolean (true or false) result is specified:

$$=: \text{integer} \times \text{integer} \rightarrow \text{Boolean}$$

(c) A square-root operation, SQRT, on real number data objects is specified:

$$\text{SQRT}: \text{real} \rightarrow \text{real}$$

An operation that has two arguments and produces a single result is termed a *binary* (or *dyadic*) operation. If it has one argument and one result it is a *unary* (or *monadic*) operation. Most of the primitive operations in programming languages are binary or unary operations.

A precise specification of the action of an operation ordinarily requires more information than just the data type of the arguments. In particular, the storage representation of the argument types usually determines how arguments of those types may be manipulated. For example, an algorithm for multiplication of two numbers, where the numbers are represented in binary notation, is different from a multiplication algorithm for decimal numbers. Thus in the specification of an operation, an informal description of the action is usually given. A precise specification of the action then is part of the implementation of the operation, after the storage representations for the arguments have been determined.

In studying a programming language definition, it is often difficult to determine a precise specification of an operation as a mathematical function. The determination of the domain and range of a given operation may be difficult, and even more so the algorithm on which its action is based. There are four main factors that combine to obscure the definition of many programming language operations:

1. *Operations that are undefined for certain inputs.* An operation that apparently is defined over some domain may in fact contain error stops or other internal structures that cause it to be undefined for certain inputs in the domain. The exact domain on which an operation is undefined may be extremely difficult to specify, as, for example, the sets of numbers that cause underflow or overflow in arithmetic operations.

2. *Implicit arguments.* An operation in a program ordinarily is invoked with a set of explicit arguments. However, the operation may access other implicit arguments through the use of global variables or other nonlocal identifier references. Complete determination of all the data that may affect the result of an operation is often obscured by such implicit arguments.

3. *Side effects (implicit results).* An operation may return an explicit result, as in the sum returned as the result of an addition, but it may also modify the values stored in other data objects, both programmer- and system-defined. Such implicit results are termed *side effects.* The most common type of side effect is that produced by the assignment operation. The main result of this operation is the modification of a value stored in a data object; the explicit result of the assignment operation may be taken to be the same as the value stored (as in APL) or may simply be ignored (as in FORTRAN or Pascal). A second type of side effect occurs in a subprogram that modifies its input arguments. Side effects are a basic part of many operations, particularly those that modify data structures. Their presence makes exact specification of the range of an operation difficult.

4. *Self-modification (history sensitivity).* One of the most problematic aspects of programming language operations is the potential for self-modification. An operation may modify its own internal structure, either local data that is retained between executions or its own code. The results produced by the operation for a particular set of arguments then depend not only on those arguments but on the entire history of preceding calls during

the computation, and the arguments given at each call. The operation is said to be *history-sensitive* in its actions. A common example is the *random number generator* found as an operation in many languages. Typically this operation takes a constant argument (unless it is being reinitialized) and yet returns a different result each time it is executed. Of course, the operation not only returns its result but also modifies an internal *seed number* that affects its result on the next execution. Self-modification through changes in local data retained between calls is common; self-modification through change in the code of an operation is less common but possible in languages such as LISP and SNOBOL4.

3-4   IMPLEMENTATION OF ELEMENTARY DATA TYPES

The implementation of an elementary data type consists of a *storage representation* for data objects and values of that type, and a set of *algorithms* or *procedures* that define the operations of the type in terms of manipulations of the storage representation.

Storage Representation

For elementary data types the storage representation for data values ordinarily uses storage representations provided by the underlying hardware computer. For example, the storage representation for integer or real values is almost always taken as the integer or floating-point binary representation for numbers used in the underlying hardware. For character values, the hardware or operating system character codes are used. The reason for this choice is simple: if the hardware storage representations are used, then the basic operations on data of that type may be implemented using the hardware provided operations. If the hardware storage representations are not used, then the operations must be software-simulated, and the same operations will execute much less efficiently.

The *attributes* of elementary data objects are treated in two main ways in different languages:

1. The attributes of a data object may be used by the compiler for the language to determine, at compile time, the run-time storage representation for the data object. The attributes themselves are not stored in the run-time storage representation. The run-time storage representation is usually a representation provided directly by the hardware. This is the usual method in languages such as FORTRAN and Pascal, where efficiency of storage use and execution speed are primary goals.

2. The attributes of a data object may be stored in a *descriptor* as part of the data object at run time. This is the usual method in languages such as LISP and SNOBOL4, where flexibility rather than efficiency is the primary goal. Since most hardware does not provide storage representations for descriptors directly, descriptors and operations on data objects with descriptors must be software-simulated. Examples of both these approaches are given in the sections that follow.

The storage representation of a data object is ordinarily independent of its location in memory. Thus each data object of a given type (and with the same attributes) has the same representation regardless of its particular position in the computer memory. The storage representation is usually described in terms of the size of the block of memory required (the number of memory words, bytes, or bits needed) and the layout of the attributes and data values within this block. Usually the address of the first word or byte of such a block of memory is taken to represent the location of the data object. Note that a data object might be represented by a single bit, a single byte or word, or by a sequence of several bytes or words.

Implementation of Operations

Each operation defined for data objects of a given type may be implemented in one of three main ways:

1. *As a hardware operation directly, if the storage representation for the data objects is precisely that provided by the hardware.* For example, if integers are stored using the hardware representation for integers, then addition, subtraction, and other arithmetic operations on integers may be implemented using the integer arithmetic operations built into the hardware.

2. *As a procedure or function subprogram that implements the operation in software.* For example, a square-root operation is usually not provided directly as a hardware operation, even if numbers are represented using the hardware number representation, and thus it might be implemented as a square-root subprogram that calculates the square root of its argument. If data objects are not represented using a hardware-defined representation, then all operations must be software-simulated, usually in the form of subprograms provided in a subprogram library.

3. *As an in-line code sequence that implements the operation as a short sequence of hardware operations.* An *in-line code sequence* is also a software implementation of the operation, but instead of using a very short subprogram, the operations in the subprogram are copied into the program at

the point where the subprogram would otherwise have been invoked. For example, the absolute-value function on numbers, defined by:

$$ABS(X) = \textbf{if } X < 0 \textbf{ then } -X \textbf{ else } X$$

is usually implemented as an in-line code sequence:

    a. Fetch value of X from memory.
    b. If $X \geqslant 0$, skip the next instruction.
    c. Set $X = -X$.
    d. Store X in memory.

where each line is implemented by a single hardware operation.

3-5   DECLARATIONS

In writing a program, the programmer determines the number and type of data objects that are needed. He also determines the lifetime of each data object—during what part of program execution it is needed—as well as the operations to be applied to it. The syntax of a programming language determines how these things are stated by the programmer in his program.

A *declaration* is a program statement that serves to communicate to the language translator information about the number and type of data objects needed during program execution. By its placement in the program, e.g., at the beginning of a particular subprogram, a declaration may also serve to indicate the desired lifetimes of the data objects. For example, the Pascal declaration:

A,B: real;

at the start of a subprogram F indicates that two data objects of type real are needed during execution of subprogram F. The declaration also specifies the binding of the data objects to the names A and B during their lifetimes.

The Pascal declaration above is an *explicit* declaration. Many languages also provide *implicit* or *default* declarations, which are declarations that hold when no explicit declaration is given. For example, in a FORTRAN subprogram, a simple variable INDEX may be used without explicit declaration, and by default it is assumed by the FORTRAN compiler to be an integer variable because its name begins with one of the letters I-N. Alternatively the FORTRAN program could explicitly declare INDEX to be a real variable by the declaration:

REAL INDEX

The general term *declaration* is used here to refer to any means of making information available to the language translator, whether explicit or implicit. It is not particularly important whether declarations in a programming language are explicit or implicit (except that implicit declarations appear to be somewhat more error-prone in programming), but it is important what *information* is provided by declarations to the translator. The declared information about data objects determines many details of the storage representations used and the manner in which type checking and storage management are performed.

A declaration usually specifies the data type and attributes of a data object. It may also specify the value of the data object if it is a constant, or the initial value of the data object, if not. Other bindings for the data object may also be specified in the declaration: a name for the data object or the placement of the data object as a component of a larger data object. Sometimes implementation details such as binding to a particular storage location or to a particular specialized storage representation are also specified. For example, the COBOL designation of an integer variable as COMPUTATIONAL usually indicates that a binary rather than a character-string storage representation for the value of that data object is needed (to allow more efficient arithmetic operations to be used).

Declarations of Operations

Declarations may also be used to specify information about operations to the language translator. The information required during translation is primarily the number, order, and data types of the arguments and results of each operation. No explicit declaration of argument types and result types for primitive operations that are built into a language is ordinarily required. Such operations may be invoked as needed in writing a program, and the argument and result types are determined implicitly by the language translator. However, argument and result types for programmer-defined operations (subprograms) must usually be made known to the language translator before the subprogram may be called. Usually this is done through an explicit declaration giving the subprogram name and listing the number of arguments and results and their data types. In Pascal, the head of a subprogram definition provides this information—for example:

$$\textbf{function } SUB(X: \text{integer; } Y: \text{real): real;}$$

which declares SUB to have the specification:

$$SUB: \text{integer} \times \text{real} \rightarrow \text{real}$$

Purposes for Declarations

Declarations serve several important purposes:

1. *Choice of storage representations.* If a declaration provides information to the language translator about the data type and attributes of a

data object, then the translator can often determine the best storage representation for that data object, with a consequent reduction in overall storage requirement and execution time for the program being translated. This use of declarations is seen repeatedly in the subsequent sections.

2. *Storage management.* Information provided by declarations about the lifetimes of data objects often makes it possible to use more efficient storage management procedures during program execution. In Pascal, for example, data objects declared at the beginning of a subprogram all have the same lifetime (equal to the duration of execution of the subprogram) and thus may be allocated storage as a single block on entry to the subprogram, with the entire block being freed on exit. Other Pascal data objects are created dynamically by use of a special operation NEW. Since the lifetimes of these data objects are not declared, they must be allocated storage individually in a separate storage area at greater expense.

3. *Generic operations.* Most languages use special symbols such as "+" to designate any one of several different operations depending on the data types of the arguments provided. Thus, for example, "A+B" in Pascal means "perform integer addition" if A and B are of integer type, "perform real addition" if A and B are of real type, and "perform the set union operation" if A and B are of set type. Such an operation symbol is said to be *overloaded* because it does not designate one specific operation but rather denotes a *generic* "add" operation that may have several different *type-specific* forms for arguments of different types. In most languages, the basic operation symbols such as "+", "*", and "/" are overloaded—i.e., they denote generic operations—but other operation names must uniquely identify a particular operation. However, Ada allows the programmer to define overloaded subprogram names and to add additional meanings to existing operation symbols such as "+".

Declarations usually allow the language translator to determine at compile time the particular operation designated by an overloaded operation symbol. In Pascal, for example, the compiler determines from the declarations of variables A and B which of the three possible operations (integer addition, real addition, or set union) is designated by "A+B". No run-time checking is required to determine which operation to perform. In SNOBOL4, on the other hand, because there are no declarations of types for variables, the determination of which "+" operation to perform must be made each time a "+" operation is encountered during program execution.

4. *Type checking.* The most important purpose for declarations, from the programmer's viewpoint, is that they allow *static* rather than *dynamic* *type checking* to be done. Because of the importance of type-checking issues in language design and implementation, this discussion is taken up in a separate section.

3-6   TYPE CHECKING AND TYPE CONVERSION

Data storage representations that are built into the computer hardware usually include no type information, and the primitive operations on the data do no type checking. For example, a particular word in the computer memory during execution of a program may contain the bit sequence:

$$11100101100 \ldots 0011$$

This bit sequence might represent an integer, a real number, a sequence of characters, or an instruction; there is no way to tell which. The hardware primitive operation for integer addition cannot check whether its two arguments represent integers; they are simply bit sequences, and the hardware operation must assume that they represent integers. A common programming error in assembly or machine languages is to invoke an operation such as integer addition on arguments of the wrong type. Such errors are particularly difficult to find because the operation does not fail in some obvious way. The operation "works," but the results produced are completely meaningless. However, since the result is just another bit string with no type information attached, subsequent operations may continue to compute with the "garbage" result to produce more "garbage," until the entire computation fails. Thus at the hardware level, conventional computers are particularly unreliable in detecting data type errors.

Type checking means checking that each operation executed by a program receives the proper number of arguments of the proper data type. For example, before executing the assignment statement:

$$X := A + B * C$$

it must be determined for the three operations, addition, multiplication, and assignment, that each receives two arguments of the proper data type. If "+" is defined only for integer or real-number arguments, and A names a character data object, then there is an argument *type error*. Type checking may be done at run time (*dynamic type checking*) or at compile time (*static type checking*).   A major advantage of using a high-level language in programming is that the language implementation can provide type checking for all (or almost all) operations, and thus the programmer is protected against this particularly insidious form of programming error.

Dynamic type checking is run-time type checking usually performed immediately before the execution of a particular operation. Dynamic type checking is usually implemented by storing a type tag in each data object that indicates the data type of the object. For example, an integer data object would contain both the integer value and an "integer" type tag. Each operation is then implemented to begin with a type-checking sequence in which the type tag of each argument is checked. The operation is performed only if the argument types are correct; otherwise an error is signaled. Each operation must also attach the appropriate type tags to its results so that subsequent operations can check them.

Some programming languages such as SNOBOL4, LISP, and APL are designed so that dynamic type checking is required. In these languages, no declarations for variables are given and no default declaration of type is assumed (in contrast to the default typing structures of FORTRAN and PL/I). The data types of variables such as A and B in the expression "A + B" may change during the course of program execution. In such circumstances, the types of A and B must be checked dynamically each time the addition is performed at run time. In languages without declarations, the variables are sometimes said to be *typeless*, since they have no fixed type.

The major advantage of dynamic type checking lies in the flexibility that it allows in the language design: no declarations are required, and the type of the data object associated with a variable name may change as needed during program execution. The programmer is freed from most concerns about data types. However, dynamic type checking has several major disadvantages:

1. For the programmer, the major disadvantage is the difficulty of debugging a program to completely remove all argument type errors. Because dynamic type checking checks data types at the time of execution of an operation, operations on program execution paths that are not executed are never checked. During program testing not all possible execution paths can be tested, in general. Any untested execution paths may still contain argument type errors, and these errors may only appear at a much later time during use of the program when some unsuspecting user provides input data that takes the program down an untested path.

2. Dynamic type checking requires that type information be kept for each data object during program execution. The extra storage required can be substantial.

3. Dynamic type checking must ordinarily be implemented in software, since the underlying hardware seldom provides support. Since the checking must be done before each execution of each operation, the speed of execution of the program is likely to be greatly slowed.

Because of these disadvantages, many languages attempt to eliminate or minimize dynamic type checking by moving the type checking into the language translator so that it is done at compile time.

Static type checking is performed during translation of a program. In order to allow static type checking, a great deal of information is required about the types of data objects that the program manipulates during its execution. This information is usually provided in part by declarations that the programmer provides and in part by other language structures. The information required is:

1. *For each operation, the number, order, and data types of its arguments and results.* For primitive operations, this information is part of the basic language definition, but for subprograms the programmer must specify it explicitly.

2. *For each variable name, the type of data object named.* The type of the data object associated with a variable name must be invariant during program execution as well, so that in checking an expression such as "A+B" it can be assumed that the type of data object named by A is the same on each execution of the expression, even if the expression is executed repeatedly with different bindings of A to particular data objects (e.g., in the case that A is a formal parameter of a subprogram).

3. *For each constant, the type of the constant data object.* The syntactic form of a literal usually indicates its type; e.g., "2" is an integer, "2.3" is a real number. Each defined constant must be matched with its definition to determine its type.

Static type checking is usually implemented as follows. During the initial phases of translation of a program, the compiler (or other translator) collects information from declarations in the program into various tables, primarily a "symbol table" (see Chapter 9) that contains type information about variables and subprograms. The compiler also has other internal tables that contain type information about language-defined primitive operations, constants, etc. After all the type information is collected, each operation invoked by the program is checked to determine whether the type of each argument is valid. Note that if the operation is a generic one, as discussed above, then any of several argument types may be valid. If the argument types are valid, then the result types are determined and the compiler saves this information for checking later operations. Note that at the same time, the generic operation name may be replaced by the name of the particular *type-specific operation* that uses arguments of the designated types.

Because static type checking includes all operations that appear in any program statement, all possible execution paths are checked, and further testing for type errors is not needed. Thus type tags on data objects at run time are not required, and no dynamic type checking is needed; the result is a substantial gain in efficiency of storage use and execution speed.

In the design of a programming language where static type checking is desired, concern for static type checking tends to affect many aspects of the language: declarations, data-control structures, and provisions for separate compilation of subprograms, to name a few. In most languages, static type checking is not possible for some language constructs in certain cases. These "flaws" in the type-checking structure may be treated in two ways:

1. *By dynamic type checking.* Often the storage cost of this option is high because type tags for data objects must be stored at run time, even though the type tags are checked only rarely.

2. *By leaving the operations unchecked.* Unchecked operations can cause serious and subtle program errors, as noted above, but are sometimes accepted where the cost of dynamic checking is considered too great.

Because type-checking issues permeate many aspects of language design, we shall return to these questions in later chapters.

Type Conversion and Coercion

If, during type checking, a mismatch occurs between the actual type of an argument and the expected type for that operation, then two options arise:

1. The type mismatch may be flagged as an error, and an appropriate error action taken, or

2. A *coercion* (or *implicit type conversion*) may be applied to change the type of the actual argument to the correct type.

A *type conversion* is an operation with the specification:

$$\text{conversion-op: type1} \rightarrow \text{type2}$$

—that is, the conversion takes a data object of one type and produces the "corresponding" data object of a different type. Most languages provide type conversions in two ways:

1. As a set of *built-in functions* that the programmer may explicitly invoke to effect the conversion. For examle, Pascal provides the function ROUND that converts a real-number data object to an integer data object with a value equal to the rounded value of the real.

2. As *coercions* invoked automatically in certain cases of type mismatch. For example, in Pascal, if the arguments for an arithmetic operation such as "+" are of mixed real and integer types, the integer data object is implicitly converted to type real before the addition is performed.

With dynamic type checking, coercions are made at the point that the type mismatch is detected during execution. For static type checking, extra code is inserted in the compiled program to invoke the conversion operation at the appropriate point during execution.

A type-conversion operation may require extensive change in the run-time storage representation of the data object. For example, in COBOL numbers often are stored in character-string form. To perform addition of such numbers on most machines, the character-string storage representation must be converted to a hardware-supported binary-number representation, with the result being converted back to character-string form before it is stored. The type-conversion operations here may take hundreds of times longer than the actual addition itself.

Coercions are an important design issue in most languages. Two opposed philosophies exist regarding the extent to which the language should provide coercions between data types. In Pascal and Ada, almost no coercions are provided; any type mismatch, with few exceptions, is considered an error. In PL/I and COBOL, coercions are the rule; a type mismatch causes the compiler to search for an appropriate conversion operation to insert into the compiled code to provide the appropriate change of type. Only if no conversion is possible is the mismatch flagged as an error.

Type mismatch is a common minor programming error and type conversion is a common need, particularly in languages such as PL/I and COBOL that have a large number of data types. There are also subtle questions as to the meaning of the notion "type mismatch" (see Sec. 5-3). Coercions often free the programmer from concern with what otherwise would be tedious detail—the invocation of numerous-type conversion operations explicitly in a program. However, coercions may also mask serious programming errors that might otherwise be brought to the programmer's attention during compilation. PL/I, in particular, is somewhat famous for the propensity of its compilers to take a minor programming error, such as a misspelled variable name, and through a sometimes surprising coercion, hide the error so that it becomes a subtle program bug that is difficult to detect.

3-7   ASSIGNMENT AND INITIALIZATION

Let us now begin to look at the specification and implementation of some common elementary data types—in particular, numbers, enumerations, Booleans, and characters. Most of the operations defined for these types are straightforward; the operation takes one or two argument data objects of the type, performs a relatively simple arithmetic, relational, or other operation, and produces a result data object, which may be of the same or different type. The operation of assignment defined for these types is somewhat more subtle and deserves special mention.

Assignment

Assignment is a central operation defined for every elementary data type. The syntax for an explicit assignment varies widely, e.g.:

A := B	(Pascal and Ada)
A = B	(FORTRAN, PL/I, and SNOBOL4)
MOVE B TO A	(COBOL)
A ← B	(APL)
(SETQ A B)	(LISP)

Input operations also involve assignment. Parameter transmission (Sec. 7-8) is often defined as assignment of the argument value to the formal parameter. Various forms of implicit assignment are found as well; e.g., in SNOBOL4, each reference to the variable INPUT causes a new value to be assigned to it, and in Pascal, a call of the WRITE procedure causes assignment to the "buffer variable" of a file (see Chapter 15).

Assignment is the basic operation for changing the binding of a value to a data object. This change, however, is a *side effect* of the operation. In some languages, such as APL and LISP, assignment also returns directly a result, which is a data object containing a copy of the value assigned. These factors become clear when we try to write a specification for assignment. In Pascal the specification for assignment of integers would be:

$$\text{assignment (:=): integer}_1 \times \text{integer}_2 \rightarrow \text{void}$$

with the action: Set the value contained in data object $integer_1$ to be a copy of the value contained in data object $integer_2$ and return no explicit result. (The change to $integer_1$ is an implicit result or side effect.) In APL, the specification is:

$$\text{assignment}(\leftarrow): \text{type}_1 \times \text{type}_2 \rightarrow \text{type}_3$$

with the action: Set the value contained in data object $type_1$ to be a copy of the value contained in data object $type_2$ and also create a new data object $type_3$, containing a copy of the value of $type_2$; return $type_3$ as a result.

Since the Pascal assignment operation returns no explicit result, we are required to use it only at the statement level, in an explicit assignment statement, e.g.:

$$X := B + 2*C;$$
$$Y := A + X;$$

while in APL, an assignment operation may be used within an expression:

$$Y \leftarrow A + (X \leftarrow B + 2*C)$$

In the APL assignment, the value of B + 2*C is both assigned to X and returned as a value to become the second operand in A + ... The value returned as the result of the assignment to Y is ignored, since the expression contains no further operations.

A final difference between languages in the semantics of assignment is seen in the following. Consider the Pascal assignment "A := B". In Pascal, as in many other languages, this means "Assign a copy of the value of variable B to variable A," as noted above. Now consider the SNOBOL4 assignment "A = B". In SNOBOL4 this means "Make the variable name A refer to the same data object as variable name B." The SNOBOL4 meaning for assignment appears to contradict the specification above, until you understand that A and B in SNOBOL4 always refer to a *pointer* to a data object, rather than directly to the data object itself. Thus the assignment "A = B" means "Assign a copy of the pointer stored in variable B to variable A," as shown in Fig. 3-2. Note that with the Pascal meaning of assignment, the type of variable A cannot change because of the assignment; only the value of A changes. With the SNOBOL4 semantics, the type of data object referenced by A may change owing to the assignment; for example, before the assignment, A may refer to an array; after, to an integer.

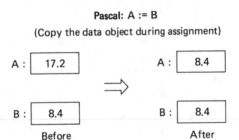

Pascal: A := B

(Copy the data object during assignment)

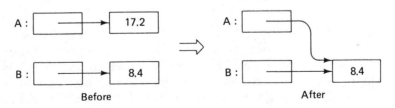

SNOBOL4: A = B

(Copy the pointer to the data object during assignment)

Fig. 3-2 Two views of assignment

Initialization

An *uninitialized variable*, or more generally, an *uninitialized data object*, is a data object that has been created but not yet assigned a value. Creation of a data object ordinarily involves only allocation of a block of storage. Without any further action, the block of storage retains whatever bit pattern it happened to contain when the allocation was made. An explicit assignment is ordinarily required to bind a data object to a valid value. In some languages (e.g., Pascal) initialization must be done explicitly with assignment statements. In other languages (e.g., APL) initial values for each data object must be specified when the object is created; the assignment of initial values is handled implicitly without use of the assignment operation by the programmer.

Uninitialized variables are a serious source of programming error, for professional programmers as well as for beginners. The random bit pattern contained in the value storage area of an uninitialized data object ordinarily cannot be distinguished from a valid value, since the valid value also appears as a bit pattern. Thus a program often may compute with the "value" of an uninitialized variable, and appear to operate correctly, when in fact it contains a serious error. Because of the effect of uninitialized variables on program reliability, immediate initialization of variable values upon creation is often considered good programming practice, and newer languages such as Ada provide facilities to do this more easily. For example, in Ada, each variable declaration may also include an initial value for the variable, using the same syntax used for ordinary assignment. For example:

$$\text{A: } \mathbf{array}(1..3) \textbf{ of } \text{FLOAT} := (17.2, 20.4, 23.6);$$

creates an array A and assigns each element an initial value explicitly in the declaration. Since ordinarily the array A is created dynamically during program execution, the implementation of initial-value assignment requires the generation of code by the compiler that, when executed, explicitly assigns the specified initial values to the data object.

3-8   NUMERIC DATA TYPES

Some form of numeric data is found in almost every programming language, but the details of specification and implementation of such types vary widely. Integer and real number types are the most common because they are often directly supported in the computer hardware. The various classes of numeric data are relatively familiar, and while the details of their treatment vary from language to language (and from implementation to implementation), the variations seldom make major differences in the languages. The properties of numeric data representations and arithmetic on computers differ substantially from the numbers and arithmetic operations discussed in ordinary mathematics. The fascinating subject of computer arithmetic has been treated in other books, however, and is not central to an understanding of the larger structure of programming languages, so only a brief treatment is given here.

Integers

Specification. A data object of type integer usually has no other attributes besides its type. The set of integer values defined for the type forms an ordered subset, within some finite bounds, of the infinite set of integers studied in mathematics. The maximum integer value is sometimes represented as a defined constant; e.g., in Pascal it is the constant MAXINT. The range of values is then ordinarily defined to be from −MAXINT to MAXINT. The value of MAXINT is chosen by the implementor to reflect the maximum integer value conveniently representable on the underlying hardware.

Operations on integer data objects typically include the main groups:

1. *Arithmetic operations.* Binary arithmetic operations have the specification:

$$bin\text{-}op: \text{integer} \times \text{integer} \rightarrow \text{integer}$$

where *bin-op* may be *addition* (+), *subtraction* (−), *multiplication* (∗), *division* (/ or div), *remainder* (mod), or a similar operation. Unary arithmetic operations have the specification:

$$unary\text{-}op: \text{integer} \rightarrow \text{integer}$$

where, for example, *unary-op* may be *negation* (−) or *identity* (+). Commonly other arithmetic operations are included as well, often as library function subprograms.

2. *Relational operations.* The relational operations each have the specification:

$$rel\text{-}op: \text{integer} \times \text{integer} \rightarrow \text{Boolean}$$

where *rel-op* may be *equal, not equal, less-than, greater-than, less-than-or-equal,* and *greater-than-or-equal*. The relational operation compares the values of its two argument data values, and returns a Boolean (true or false value) data object as its result.

3. *Assignment.* Assignment between integer data objects is specified:

$$assignment: \text{integer}_1 \times \text{integer}_2 \rightarrow \text{void}$$

or

$$assignment: \text{integer}_1 \times \text{integer}_2 \rightarrow \text{integer}_3$$

as discussed in the preceding section.

Implementation. The language-defined integer data type is most often directly implemented using a hardware-defined integer storage representation and set of hardware arithmetic and relational primitive operations on integers. Usually this representation uses a complete memory word (or sequence of bytes) to store an integer.

Figure 3-3 shows three possible storage representations for integers. The first has no run-time descriptor; only the value is stored. This representation is possible where the language provides declarations and static type checking for integer data objects as in Pascal and FORTRAN. The second and third show two possible representations that include a run-time type descriptor. The second form stores the descriptor in a separate memory location, with a pointer to the "full-word" integer value. This representation is often used in LISP. Its disadvantage is that it potentially may double the storage required for a single integer data object; its advantage is that the value is stored using the built-in hardware representation, so that hardware arithmetic operations may be used. The third form stores the descriptor and value in a single memory location, by shortening the size of the integer sufficiently to provide space for the descriptor. Here storage is conserved, but the hardware arithmetic operations cannot be used

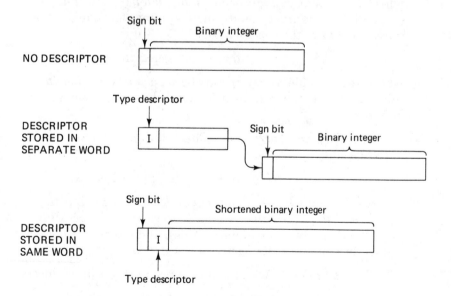

Fig. 3-3   Three storage representations for integers

without first clearing the descriptor from the integer data object, performing the arithmetic, and then reinserting the descriptor. Thus, because a sequence of hardware instructions must be executed to perform a single arithmetic operation, arithmetic is done inefficiently.

Subranges

Specification. A subrange of an integer data type is a sequence of integer values within some restricted range—e.g., the integers in the range 1 to 10 or in the range −5 to 50. A declaration of the form:

A: 1..10 (Pascal)   or   A: INTEGER **range** 1..10 (Ada)

is often used. A subrange type allows the same set of operations to be used as for the ordinary integer type; thus a subrange may be termed a *subtype* of the *base type* integer.

Implementation. Subrange types have two important implementation effects:

1. *Smaller storage requirements.* Since a smaller range of values is possible, a subrange value can usually be stored in fewer bits than a general integer value. For example, an integer in the subrange 1..10 requires only 4 bits of storage for its representation, whereas a full integer value might require 16, 32, or more on typical machines. However, because arithmetic operations on shortened integers must usually be partially software-simulated (and thus be much slower), subrange values are often represented as full integers to allow efficient arithmetic operations.

2. *Better type checking.* Declaration of a variable as being of a subrange type allows more precise type checking to be performed on the values assigned to that variable. For example, if variable MONTH is:

MONTH: 1..12

then the assignment:

MONTH := 0

is illegal and can be detected at compile time, whereas if MONTH is declared to be of integer type, then the assignment is valid and the error must be found by the programmer during testing. Many subrange type checks cannot be performed at compile time, however, if the check involves a computed value. For example, in:

MONTH := MONTH + 1

run-time checking is required to determine if the new value assigned to MONTH is still within the bounds declared. In this case, the bounds must be available at run time to allow the checking.

Floating-Point Real Numbers

Specification. A floating-point real-number data type is often specified with only the single data type attribute REAL, as in FORTRAN and Pascal. As with type integer, the values form an ordered sequence from some hardware-determined minimum negative value to a maximum value, but the values are not distributed evenly across this range. Alternatively, the precision required for floating-point numbers, in terms of the number of digits used in the decimal representation, may be specified by the programmer, as in Ada and PL/I.

The same set of arithmetic, relational, and assignment operations described for integers are usually also provided for reals. In addition most languages provide other operations as built-in functions, such as:

SIN: real → real	(sine function)
COS: real → real	(cosine function)
SQRT: real → real	(square-root function)
MAX: real × real → real	(maximum-value function)

Implementation. Storage representations for floating-point real types are ordinarily based on an underlying hardware representation in which a storage location is divided into a mantissa and an exponent, as shown in Fig. 3-4. A double-precision form of floating-point number is also sometimes available, in which an additional memory word is used to store an extended mantissa. Both single and double precision (if available) are generally supported by hardware arithmetic operations for addition, subtraction, multiplication, and division. Exponentiation is usually software-simulated. Where both single- and double-precision real numbers are supported, the precision declaration for the number of digits in the value of a particular real data object object is used to determine whether single- or double-precision storage representation must be used. Alternatively the programmer may simply declare a real variable to be DOUBLE or LONG REAL to specify use of double precision as the storage representation.

Other Numeric Data Types

Fixed-point real numbers. A fixed-point number is represented as a digit sequence of fixed length, with the decimal point positioned at a given point between two digits. In COBOL and PL/I, the declaration is given as a PICTURE clause, e.g.,

$$\text{X PICTURE 999V99.}$$

which declares X as a fixed-point variable with three digits before the decimal and two digits after. A fixed-point type may be directly supported by the hardware or may be simulated using a hardware floating-point type. The storage representation may be in binary or directly in character form.

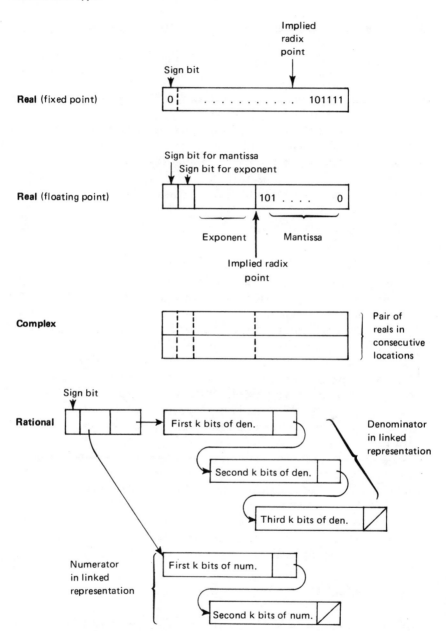

Fig. 3-4 Some storage representations for numbers (without descriptors)

Complex numbers. A complex number consists of a pair of real numbers, representing the number's real and imaginary parts. A complex-number data type may be easily provided by representing each data object as a block of two storage locations containing a pair of real values.

Rational numbers. A rational number is the quotient of two integers. The usual reason for including a rational-number data type in a language is to avoid the problems of roundoff and truncation encountered in floating- and fixed-point representations of reals. As a result, it is desirable to represent rationals as pairs of integers of unbounded length. Such long integers are often represented using a linked representation. Figure 3-4 illustrates some of these number representations.

3-9   ENUMERATIONS

In programming it is common to have a variable that can take on only one of a small number of values. For example, a variable STUDENT_CLASS might have only four possible values representing "freshman," "sopho-more," "junior," and "senior"; similarly a variable EMPLOYEE_SEX might have only two values representing "male" and "female." In older languages such as FORTRAN or COBOL such a variable is ordinarily given the data type *integer* and the values are represented as distinct, arbitrarily chosen integers. For example, "freshman" = 1, "sophomore" = 2, etc., or "male" = 0, "female" = 1. The program then manipulates the values as integers, and the programmer must remember the correspondence between the integer values and their "meaning" in the application. The programmer is also responsible for ensuring that no operations are applied to the integer variables that make no sense in terms of the intended "meaning"—e.g., assigning 2 to variable EMPLOYEE_SEX or multiplying STUDENT_CLASS by 3.

Many recent languages such as Pascal and Ada include an *enumeration* data type that allows the programmer to define and manipulate such variables more directly.

Specification

An enumeration is an ordered list of distinct values. The programmer defines both the literal names to be used for the values and their ordering, using a declaration such as:

            STUDENT_CLASS: (FRESH,SOPH,JUNIOR,SENIOR);
            EMPLOYEE_SEX: (MALE,FEMALE);

Because ordinarily many variables of the same enumeration type are used in a program, it is common to define the enumeration in a separate "type definition" and give it a "type name" that can then be used to specify the type of several variables. Thus in Pascal, the type definition:

type CLASS = (FRESH,SOPH,JUNIOR,SENIOR);

is given, followed by declarations for variables such as:

STUDENT_CLASS: CLASS;
TRANSFER_STUDENT_CLASS: CLASS;

Note that the type definition introduces the type name CLASS, which may be used wherever a primitive type name such as INTEGER might be used, and it also introduces the "literals" FRESH, SOPH, JUNIOR, and SENIOR, which may be used wherever a language-defined literal such as "27" might be used. Thus we can write:

if STUDENT_CLASS = JUNIOR **then** . . .

instead of the less understandable:

if STUDENT_CLASS = 3 **then** . . .

that would be required if integer variables were used.

The basic operations on enumeration types are the relational operations (equal, less-than, greater-than, etc.), assignment, and the operations *successor* and *predecessor*, which give the next and previous value, respectively, in the sequence of literals defining the enumeration (and are undefined for the last and first values, respectively). Note that the full set of relational operations is defined for enumeration types because the set of values is given an ordering in the type definition.

Implementation

The storage representation for a data object of an enumeration type is straightforward: each value in the enumeration sequence is represented at run time by one of the integers $0, 1, 2, \ldots$. However, because only a small set of values are involved and the values are never negative, the usual integer representation is often shortened to omit the sign bit and use only enough bits for the range of values required, as with a subrange value. For example, the type CLASS defined above has only four possible values, represented at run time as $0 =$ FRESH, $1 =$ SOPH, $2 =$ JUNIOR, and $3 =$ SENIOR. Since only two bits are required to represent these four possible values in memory, a variable of type CLASS need be allocated only two bits of storage.

Given this storage representation for enumeration types, implementation of the basic operations on enumerations is also straightforward, because the hardware provided operations on integers may be used. For example, relational operations such as "=", "<", and ">" may be implemented using the corresponding hardware primitives that compare integers. The successor and predecessor operations involve simply adding or subtracting one from the integer representing the value and checking to see that the result is within the proper range.

3-10 BOOLEANS

A *Boolean* or *logical* data type is common in most languages.

Specification

The Boolean data type consists of data objects having one of the two values *true* or *false*. In Pascal and Ada, the Boolean data type is considered simply a language-defined enumeration:

$$\textbf{type } BOOLEAN = (FALSE, TRUE);$$

which both defines the names "TRUE" and "FALSE" for the values of the type and defines the ordering FALSE < TRUE.

The most common operations on Boolean types include assignment as well as:

and: Boolean × Boolean → Boolean   (conjunction)
or: Boolean × Boolean → Boolean   (inclusive disjunction)
not: Boolean → Boolean   (negation or complement)

Other Boolean operations such as equivalence, exclusive or, implication, nand (not-and), and nor (not-or) are sometimes included. *Short-circuit forms* of the operations *and* and *or* are discussed in Sec. 6-1.

Implementation

The storage representation for a Boolean data object is simply a single bit of storage, provided no descriptor designating the data type is needed. Because single bits may not be separately addressable in memory, often this storage representation is extended to be a single addressable unit such as a byte or word. Then the values true and false might be represented in two ways within this storage unit:

1. A particular bit is used for the value (often the sign bit of the number representation), with 0 = false, 1 = true in that bit, and the rest of the byte or word ignored, or

2. A zero value in the entire storage unit represents false, and any other nonzero value represents true.

Because a large amount of storage may be wasted with either of these representations, provision is often made in a language for access to all the bits of a storage unit individually. The BIT STRING data type of PL/I and the *packed array of Boolean* and *set* data types of Pascal are examples.

3-11 CHARACTERS

Most data are input and output in character form. Conversion during input and output to other data types is usually provided, but processing of some data directly in character form is also important. Sequences of characters (character strings) are often processed as a unit. Provision for character-string data may be provided either directly through a *character-string* data type (as in SNOBOL4 and PL/I) or through a *character* data type, with a character string considered as a linear array of characters (as in APL, Pascal, and Ada). Character strings are considered in Sec. 4-7.

Specification

A character data type provides data objects that have a single character as their value. The set of possible character values is usually taken to be a language-defined enumeration corresponding to one of the standard character sets supported by the underlying hardware and operating system, such as the ASCII character set. The ordering of the characters in this character set is called the *collating sequence* for the character set. The collating sequence is important because it determines the alphabetical ordering given to character strings by the relational operations. Since the ordering includes all characters in the set, character strings that include spaces, digits, and special characters may be "alphabetized" as well.

Operations on character data include only the relational operations, assignment, and sometimes operations to test whether a character value is in one of the special classes "letter," "digit," or "special character."

Implementation

Character data values are almost always directly supported by the underlying hardware and operating system because of their use in input-output. Ordinarily a language implementation uses the same storage representation for characters. Occasionally, however, the language definition prescribes use of a particular character set (such as the ASCII set) that is not supported by the underlying hardware. Although the same characters may be represented in both character sets, their storage representation, and thus their collating sequences, may differ; in other cases, some special characters in one set may not exist in the other. Since characters arrive from the input-output system in the hardware-supported representation, the language implementation may have to provide appropriate conversions to the alternative character-set representation or provide special implementation of the relational operations that take account of differences in the collating sequences. If the language-defined character representation is the same as that supported by the hardware, then the relational operations also are usually represented directly in the hardware or may be simulated by short in-line code sequences.

3-12 REFERENCES AND SUGGESTIONS FOR FURTHER READING

Most general texts on programming languages discuss the issues of types and type checking (see the references at the end of Chapter 1). The *Ada Rationale* (Ichbiah et al. [1979]) is particularly relevant; it also includes a discussion of the design problems associated with fixed-point and floating-point real-number types. Knuth [1981] discusses the issues surrounding number representations and computer arithmetic in depth. Fateman [1982] looks at the language implications of the proposed IEEE standard for floating-point arithmetic.

3-13 PROBLEMS

1. For an elementary data type in a language with which you are familiar, do the following:

   (a) Describe the set of values that data objects of that type may contain.
   (b) Determine the storage representation for values of that type (used in your local implementation of the language).
   (c) Define the syntactic representation used for constants of that type.
   (d) Determine the set of operations defined for data objects of that type, and for each operation give its specification and its syntactic representation in the language.
   (e) For each operation, determine whether it is implemented through software simulation or directly as a single hardware instruction.
   (f) Describe any attributes that a data object of that type may have other than its data type.
   (g) Determine if any of the operation symbols or names used to represent operations of the type are overloaded. For each overloaded operation name,

determine when (compile time or run time) the specific meaning of each use of the overloaded name in a statement is determined.

(h) Determine whether static or dynamic type checking is used to determine the validity of each use of each operation of the type.

2. For an elementary data type in a language with which you are familiar, do the following:

  (a) Explain the difference between the type itself, variables of that type, and constants of that type.
  (b) Show a situation during execution where a data object of that type exists that is neither a variable nor a constant.
  (c) Explain the difference between data objects of that type and the values that those data objects may contain.
  (d) Give the ordering of the values for the type (if any).
  (e) Explain the difference between the syntactic representation and the storage representation for literals of that type.
  (f) For an operation of the type, distinguish between the syntactic representation of the operation, the specification of the operation, and the implementation of the operation.

3. For a language with which you are familiar, find an example of a primitive operation

  (a) That has an implicit argument.
  (b) That has a side effect.
  (c) That is undefined for some data objects in its specified domain.
  (d) That is self-modifying.

4. Give a formula for determining the maximum number of bits required for storage of any value in the integer subrange $M..N$, where M and N are any two integers such that $M < N$.

5. For a language with which you are familiar which uses static type checking, give two examples of constructs that cannot be checked statically. For each construct, determine by running a test program whether the language implementation provides dynamic type checking or leaves the construct unchecked during execution.

6. Give two examples of system-defined data objects in a language with which you are familiar.

7. Give an example of an operation in a programming language:

  (a) That is implemented directly in hardware.
  (b) That is implemented as a subprogram.
  (c) That is implemented as an in-line code sequence.

8. Give two examples of coercions in a language with which you are familiar.

9. The potential for overloading of enumeration literal names is a problem in languages that provide enumeration types. In defining an enumeration type in a large program, the programmer may inadvertantly use one of the same literal

names that is used in another enumeration; e.g., the literal JUNIOR might be used in the definition of enumeration CLASS and in the definition of another enumeration OFFICER GRADE. A later reference to the literal JUNIOR is then ambiguous. Propose a means by which a language might allow the programmer to resolve the ambiguity without prohibiting overloaded enumeration literals altogether.

10. Figure 3-3 illustrates two number representations for integers with a run-time type descriptor. One uses extra space to gain speed in arithmetic; the other sacrifices speed for a more compact storage structure. Design two similar representations for your local computer, assuming the run-time descriptor requires at most 6 bits. Write the programs necessary for addition, subtraction, multiplication, and division of numbers in these forms. Compare the relative advantages and disadvantages of the two representations.

11. (a) Describe the elementary data types that are built into the hardware of your local computer. Determine whether any hardware data types carry descriptors.

   (b) Design a complete set of descriptors for the hardware data types. Each descriptor should include enough information so that from the descriptor alone the location, length, and format of the data item it describes can be determined.

   (c) Design a *storage structure* for the descriptors whose logical organization was set up in part (b). Since you do not wish to get into the problem of descriptors for descriptors, design the storage structure so that descriptors are *self-describing*; i.e., given the location of the first bit (on a binary computer) of any descriptor, it should be possible to determine the length and format of the descriptor without additional information.

CHAPTER 4

Structured
Data
Types

A data structure is a data object that contains other data objects as its elements or components. In the preceding chapter the concepts of data object and data type are considered in the simple setting of elementary data types. In this chapter the same issues are taken up again in the more complex setting of data structures. The important data types of arrays, records, strings, stacks, lists, pointers, sets, and files are considered.

4-1 STRUCTURED DATA OBJECTS AND DATA TYPES

A data object that is constructed as an aggregate of other data objects is termed a structured data object or *data structure*. The data objects that it contains are its *components*. A component may be elementary or it may be another data structure; e.g., a component of an array may be a number or it may be a record, character string, or another array.

Many of the issues and concepts surrounding data structures in programming languages are the same as for elementary data objects and have been treated in the preceding chapter. As with elementary data objects, some are programmer-defined and others are system-defined during program execution. The bindings of data structures to values, to names, and to locations are important and somewhat more complex in this setting.

Data structure types involve the same issues of type specification, type implementation, and declarations and type checking that are found for elementary data types, but again the issues are more complex. Two aspects in particular are important. First, the specification and implementation of structural information becomes a central problem: how to indicate the component data objects of a data structure and their relationships in such a way that selection of a component from the structure is straightforward. Second, many operations on data structures bring up storage management issues that are not present for elementary data objects.

4-2   SPECIFICATION OF DATA STRUCTURE TYPES

Specification of the attributes of a data structure type is more complex than for an elementary type. The major attributes include:

1. *Number of components.* A data structure may be of *fixed size* if the number of components is invariant during its lifetime, or of *variable size* if the number of components changes dynamically. Variable-size data structure types usually define operations that insert and delete components from structures. *Arrays* and *records* are common examples of fixed-size data structure types; *character strings, stacks, lists, sets,* and *files* are examples of variable-size types. Variable-size data objects are also sometimes provided through a *pointer* data type that allows fixed-size data objects to be linked together explicitly by the programmer.

2. *Type of each component.* A data structure is *homogeneous* if all its components are of the same type. It is *heterogeneous* if its components are of different types. Arrays, character strings, sets, and files are usually homogeneous; records and lists are usually heterogeneous.

3. *Names to be used for selecting components.* Almost invariably a data structure type includes a *selection* operation that allows individual components of the data structure to be retrieved for processing. To specify which component is desired, a name is provided to the selection operation. For an array, the name may be an integer subscript or sequence of subscripts; for a record, the name is usually an arbitrary identifier. Some data structure types such as stacks and files allow access to only a particular component (the top or current component) at any time, but operations are provided to change the component that is currently accessible.

4. *Maximum number of components.* For a variable-size data structure such as a character string or stack, a maximum size for the structure in terms of number of components may be specified.

5. *Organization of the components.* The most common organization is a simple linear sequence of components. Vectors (one-dimensional arrays),

records, character strings, stacks, lists, and files are data structures with this organization. Array, record, and list types, however, also usually are extended to "multidimensional" forms: multidimensional arrays, records whose components are records, and lists whose components are lists. These extended forms may be treated as separate types or simply as the basic sequential type in which the components are themselves data structures of similar type. For example, a two-dimensional array (matrix) may be considered as a separate type, or as a "vector of vectors"—a vector in which the components (the rows or columns) are themselves vectors. Records also may include "variants": alternative sets of components of which only one is included in each data object of that type.

Operations on Data Structures

Specification of the domain and range of operations on data structure types may be given in much the same manner as for elementary types. Some new classes of operations are of particular importance:

1. *Component selection operations.* Processing of data structures often proceeds by retrieving each component of the structure for processing using various primitive and programmer-defined operations. A *selection operation* is an operation that accesses a component of a data structure and makes it available for processing by other operations. Two types of selection may be distinguished: *random selection*, in which an arbitrary component of the data structure is accessed, and *sequential selection*, in which components are selected one after the other in sequence for processing. For example, in processing a vector, the operation of subscripting is used to select a component at random, e.g., V[4], and subscripting combined with a FOR or DO loop is used to select a sequence of components, e.g.,

$$\textbf{for } I := 1 \textbf{ to } 10 \textbf{ do} \ldots V[I] \ldots ;$$

2. *Whole-data-structure operations.* Operations may take entire data structures as arguments and produce new data structures as results. Most languages provide a limited set of such whole-data-structure operations— e.g., addition of two arrays, assignment of one record to another, or a union operation on sets. Languages such as APL and SNOBOL4 provide rich sets of whole-data-structure operations, however, so that the programmer need seldom select individual components of data structures for processing.

3. *Insertion/deletion of components.* Operations that change the number of components in a data structure have a major impact on storage representations and storage management for data structures, as discussed in the next section.

4. *Creation/destruction of data structures.* Operations that create and destroy data structures also have a major impact on storage management for data structures.

Selection (or *accessing*) of a component or data value in a data object should be distinguished from the related operation of *referencing*, discussed in Chapter 7. Ordinarily a data object is given a name, e.g., the vector named V above. When we write V[4] in a program to select the fourth component of V, we actually invoke a two-step sequence, composed of a *referencing operation* followed by a *selection operation*. The referencing operation determines the current referent of the name V, returning as its result a pointer to the location of the entire vector data object designated by the name V. The selection operation takes the pointer to the vector, together with the subscript 4 of the designated component of the vector, and returns a pointer to the location of that particular component within the vector. Only the selection operation is of concern in this chapter. Discussion of the referencing operation (which may be far more complex and costly than the selection operation) must await a detailed consideration of the problems of names, scope rules, and referencing environments in Chapter 7.

4-3   IMPLEMENTATION OF DATA STRUCTURE TYPES

Implementation considerations for data structure types include the same issues as for elementary types. In addition, two new issues develop that strongly affect the choice of storage representations: selection of components from a data structure should be efficient, and an efficient overall storage management structure for the language implementation should be possible.

Storage Representations

The storage representation for a data structure includes (1) storage for the components of the structure and (2) an optional *decriptor* that stores some or all of the attributes of the structure. The two basic storage representations are shown in Fig. 4-1:

1. *Sequential representation*, in which the data structure is stored in a single contiguous block of storage that includes both descriptor and components.

2. *Linked representation*, in which the data structure is stored in several blocks of storage at different places in memory, with the blocks

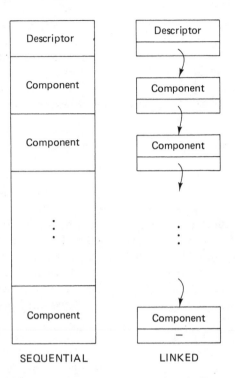

Fig. 4-1 Storage representations for linear
data structures

linked together through pointers. A *pointer* from a block A to a block B is
represented by storing the address of the first location of block B in a
location reserved for the purpose in block A. Such a pointer between two
storage blocks is called a *link*.

Sequential representations are used for fixed-size data structures and
sometimes for homogeneous variable-size structures such as character
strings or stacks. Linked representations are commonly used for variable-
size structures such as lists. Several different varieties of sequential and
linked representations are seen in subsequent sections.

Unfortunately, conventional computer memories provide little aid in
developing storage representations for data structures. Memories in general
are structured simply as a long sequence of bits, broken at fixed intervals
into addressable words or bytes. Hardware operations for accessing components of data structures are also usually lacking, beyond the provision of
simple index registers, base registers, and indexing operations that allow
efficient access to vectors stored sequentially in memory. Most hardware
lacks provisions for data structure descriptors, for manipulation of linked

representations, for storage management for data structures, and for easy manipulation of external files. Thus data structures and operations that work with data structures must usually be software-simulated in a programming language implementation, in contrast to the case with elementary data types and operations, where direct hardware-supported storage representations and operations are common.

Implementation of Operations on Data Structures

Component selection is of primary importance in the implementation of most data structures. Often both efficient random-selection and efficient sequential-selection operations are important. For example, for a vector, A, selection of a component A[I] chosen at random must be efficient, and also it is desirable to be able to step through the array sequentially, selecting A[1], A[2], . . . more efficiently than simply as a sequence of random selections. These two basic types of component selection are implemented differently for sequential and linked storage representations:

1. *Sequential representation.* Random selection of a component often involves a *base-address-plus-offset* calculation using an *accessing formula*. The relative location of the selected component within the sequential block is called its *offset*. The starting location of the entire block is the *base address*. The accessing formula, given the name or subscript of the desired component (e.g., the integer subscripts of an array component), specifies how to compute the offset of the component. The offset is then added to the base address to get the actual location in memory of the selected component, as shown in Fig. 4-2.

For a homogeneous structure such as an array that is stored sequentially, selection of a sequence of components from the structure is possible by the steps:

a. To select the first component of the sequence, use the base-address-plus-offset calculation described above.

b. To advance to each subsequent component in the sequence, add the size of the current component to the location of the current component to get the location of the next component. For a homogeneous structure, the size of each component is the same, and thus each component in the sequence is found by adding a constant value to the location of the preceding component.

2. *Linked representation.* Random selection of a component from a linked structure involves following a chain of pointers from the first block of storage in the structure to the desired component. For this selection algorithm, the position of the link pointer within each component block

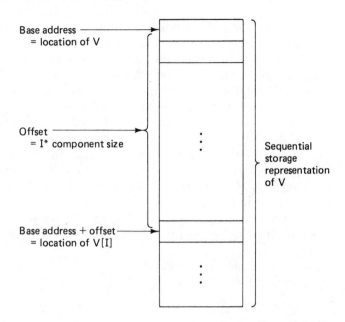

Fig. 4-2 Component selection using base-address-plus-offset calculation

must be known. Selection of a sequence of components proceeds by selecting the first component as above, and then following the link pointer from the current component to the next component for each subsequent selection.

Data structure representations are sometimes extended to include special system-defined substructures that allow efficient component selection. For example, random selection of components of an ordinary sequential file is difficult unless an index is added to the storage representation, as described in Sec. 4-11. Hash-coded tables for set storage are another example seen below.

Storage Management and Data Structures

The lifetime of any data object begins when the binding of the object to a particular storage location is made—that is, when a block (or blocks) of storage is allocated and the storage representation for the data object is initialized. The lifetime ends when this binding of object to storage block is dissolved. For a data structure of variable size, individual components of the structure have their own lifetimes, determined by the time at which they are created and inserted into the structure and by the time at which they are deleted from the structure.

At the time that a data object is created, i.e., at the start of its lifetime, an *access path* to the data object must also be created so that the data object can be accessed by operations in the program. Creation of an access path is accomplished either through association of the data object with an identifier, its *name*, in some referencing environment (see Chapter 7) or through storage of a pointer to the structure in some other existing, already accessible structure. In the latter case the data object becomes a component of the older structure.

During the lifetime of a data object, additional access paths to it may be created, e.g., by passing it as an argument to a subprogram or by creating new pointers to it. Access paths may also be destroyed in various ways, e.g., by assigning a new value to a pointer variable or by return from a subprogram, with the consequent loss of its referencing environment. Thus at any point during the lifetime of a data object, several access paths to it may exist.

Two central problems in storage management arise because of the interplay between the lifetime of a data object and the access paths to it that exist:

1. *Garbage.* When all access paths to a data object are destroyed but the data object continues to exist, the data object is said to be *garbage*. The data object can no longer be accessed from other parts of the program, so it is of no further use, but the binding of data object to storage location has not been broken, so the storage is not available for reuse.

2. *Dangling references.* A *dangling reference* is an access path that continues to exist after the lifetime of the associated data object. An access path ordinarily leads to the location of a data object, i.e., to the beginning of the block of storage for the object. At the end of the lifetime of the object, this block of storage is recovered for reallocation at some later point to another data object. However, the recovery of the storage block does not necessarily destroy the existing access paths to the block, and thus they may continue to exist as dangling references.

Dangling references are a particularly serious problem for storage management, as they may compromise the integrity of the entire run-time structure during program execution. For example, an assignment to a nonexistent data object by the use of a dangling reference can modify storage that has already been allocated to another data object of entirely different type (thus violating the security of the type-checking structure) or it can modify housekeeping data (such as a link to a free space list) that has been stored there temporarily by the storage management system (thus destroying the integrity of the storage management system itself).

Garbage is a less serious, but still troublesome problem. A data object that has become garbage ties up storage that might otherwise be reallocated for another purpose. Since storage is often in short supply during execution of a program, a buildup of garbage can force the program to terminate prematurely because of lack of available free storage.

Storage management structures for dealing with garbage and dangling references are treated in Chapter 8. However, any operation that affects the lifetime of a data object or the access paths to it can potentially impact the overall storage management structure of a language implementation. Thus, in most languages, operations that create and destroy data structures and that insert and delete components of data structures are designed with a careful eye toward their effect on storage management. Often the result is a tight set of restrictions on such operations.

4-4   DECLARATIONS AND TYPE CHECKING FOR DATA STRUCTURES

The basic concepts and concerns surrounding declarations and type checking for data structures are similar to those discussed in Chapter 3 for elementary data objects. Declarations for data structures are ordinarily more complex because there are more attributes to be specified. For example, the Pascal declaration at the beginning of a subprogram P:

$$A: \textbf{array } [1..10, -5..5] \textbf{ of } real;$$

specifies the following attributes of array A:

1. Data type (array).

2. Number of dimensions (2).

3. Subscripts naming the rows (the integers 1, 2, . . . , 10).

4. Subscripts naming the columns (the integers −5, −4, . . . , 5).

5. Number of components (10 rows × 11 columns = 110 components).

6. Data type of each component (real).

Declaration of these attributes allows a sequential storage representation for A and the appropriate accessing formula for selecting any component A[I,J] of A to be determined at compile time, as described in the next section, in spite of the fact that A is not created until entry to subprogram P at run time. Without the declaration, the attributes of A would have to be determined dynamically at run time, with the result that the storage representation and component accessing would be much less efficient.

The point at which a declaration appears in a program often determines the lifetime of the declared data object as well. For example, a Pascal declaration may appear only at the beginning of a main program or subprogram, and the lifetime of the data object becomes the same as the duration of execution of the program or subprogram. Such bounds on data object lifetimes are important in determining the run-time storage management structure, as discussed in the preceding section.

Type checking is somewhat more complex for data structures, because component selection operations must be taken into account. There are two main problems:

1. *Existence of a selected component.* The arguments to a selection operation may be of the right types, but the component designated may not exist in the data structure. For example, a subscripting operation that selects a component from an array may receive a subscript that is "out of bounds" for the particular array; i.e., the subscript is outside the specified subscript range. If a data structure is of variable size, it may be empty (have no components). The failure of a selection operation to find the selected component in the structure is not a type-checking problem in itself, provided that the selection operation fails "gracefully" by noting the error and raising an exception, e.g., a "subscript range error." However, the result of a selection operation is almost always used immediately as an argument by some other operation. If the selection operation produces an incorrect result, e.g., by computing the location of an array component using an out-of-bounds subscript value, then the effect is similar to a type-checking error: the operation receiving the result is given an invalid argument (the location of a block of storage that may contain data of the wrong type, executable code, etc.). Component selection operations that use an accessing formula to compute the offset of the selected component within a sequential storage block are particularly prone to this sort of error; run-time checking is often required to determine whether the selected component exists before the formula is used to determine its precise location.

2. *Type of a selected component.* A selection sequence may define a complex path through a data structure to the desired component. For example, the Pascal:

$$A[2,3].\mathrm{link}\uparrow.\mathrm{item}$$

selects the contents of the component named "item" in the record reached via the pointer contained in the component named "link" of the record that is the component in row 2 and column 3 of array A. To perform static type checking, it must be possible to determine at compile time the type of the component selected by any valid composite selector of this sort. As noted above, it cannot in general be assumed that the selected component exists when needed at run time. Instead, static type checking guarantees only that if the component does exist, then it is of the right type.

4-5   VECTORS AND ARRAYS

Vectors and arrays are the most common type of data structure in programming languages. A *vector* is a data structure composed of a fixed number of components of the same type organized as a simple linear sequence. A component of a vector is selected by giving its *subscript*, an integer (or enumeration value) indicating the position of the component in the sequence. A vector is also termed a *one-dimensional array* or *linear array*. A *two-dimensional array*, or *matrix*, has its components organized into a rectangular grid of rows and columns. Both a row subscript and a column subscript are needed to select a component of a matrix. Multidimensional arrays of three or more dimensions are defined in a similar manner.

Vectors

Specification and syntax.   The attributes of a vector are:

1. *Number of components*, usually indicated implicitly by giving the subscript range.

2. *Data type of each component* (a single data type suffices, since the components are of the same type).

3. *Subscript to be used to select each component*, usually given as a range of integers, with the first integer designating the first component, the second designating the second component, etc.

A typical declaration for a vector is the Pascal:

V: array [1..10] of real;

which defines a vector of ten components, each a real number, where the components are selected by the subscripts 1, 2, . . . , 10.

The subscript range need not begin at one; for example in

W: array [−5..10] of real;

W is a vector of 16 components. The subscript range need not be a subrange of integers; it may be any enumeration (or a subsequence of an enumeration). For example:

type CLASS = (FRESH,SOPH,JUNIOR,SENIOR);
var X: array [CLASS] of . . .

Operations on vectors.   The operation that selects a component from a vector is called *subscripting* and is usually written as the vector name followed by the subscript of the component to be selected, e.g., V[2] or

X[SOPH]. However, the subscript may generally be a computed value, in which case an expression may be given that computes the subscript, e.g., V[I+2]. Usually the same syntax is used to specify subscripting that returns the location of the selected component and subscripting that returns the value of the selected component. For example, in the assignment:

$$V[2] := V[2] + 1$$

the first V[2] designates the location of the second component of V, while the second V[2] designates the value of that data object. For our purposes here it is convenient to consider a subscripting operation as returning the *location* of a data object as its result, rather than a value. Accessing the value, given the location, is then a simple operation that may follow if the value rather than the location is required.

Other operations on vectors include operations to create and destroy vectors, assignment to components of a vector, and operations that perform various arithmetic operations on pairs of vectors of the same size, such as addition of two vectors (add corresponding components). Since vectors are of fixed size, insertion and deletion of components is not allowed; only the value of a component may be modified. Most languages provide only a limited set of such operations, but APL contains a large set that allows vectors to be decomposed and new vectors to be constructed in quite general ways.

Implementation. The homogeneity and fixed size of a vector make storage and accessing of individual components straightforward and efficient. Homogeneity implies that the size and structure of each component is the same, and fixed size implies that the number and position of each component is invariant throughout the lifetime of the vector. A sequential storage representation is appropriate, as shown in Fig. 4-3. The components are stored in sequence in a block of memory. A descriptor may also be included to store some or all of the attributes of the vector. The upper and lower bounds of the subscript range are commonly stored in the descriptor if range checking for computed subscript values is required (see below). The other attributes often are not stored in the descriptor at run time; they are needed only during translation for type checking and for setting up the storage representation.

The subscripting operation is efficient if this storage representation is used. The location of component I of the vector may be computed using the *accessing formula*:

$$\text{locn } A[I] = \alpha + D + (I - LB) \times E$$

where I is the subscript of the desired element, α is the *base address* of the block of storage (the memory address of the first word or byte in the block), D is the *size of the descriptor*, LB is the *lower bound* of the subscript range

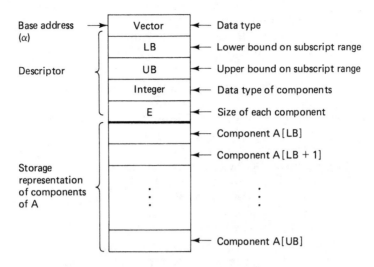

Fig. 4-3 Storage representation for a vector A with full descriptor

(subscript of the first component of the vector), and E is the *size of each component data object* (number of words or bytes required for storage). If the subscript is a value from some enumeration other than an integer, then the values used for I and LB are chosen appropriately.

Observe that in the accessing formula, the computation of the offset, $D + (I - LB) \times E$, uses three values, D, LB, and E, that can often be determined during translation from the information in the declaration of the vector. If the values of D, LB, and E are known, then the translator can compute $K = D - LB \times E$, and the accessing formula would be $\alpha + K + I \times E$. If the value of subscript I is also known to the translator, e.g., $A[2]$, then $I \times E$ may be computed during translation, so that the accessing formula reduces to $\alpha + K'$, where $K' = D + (I - LB) \times E$ is computed during translation.

The above formula assumes that the value of I is known to be a valid subscript for A. To check for a subscript range error, the test $LB \le I \le UB$ must precede use of the accessing formula, and the values of both LB and UB must be present in the run-time descriptor. In general, the exact variation of the accessing calculation (and range checking) that is most efficient depends on the particular hardware configuration and hardware operations available.

Packed- and unpacked-storage representations. The accessing formula given above presumes that the size, E, of each component is an integral number of addressable storage units (words or bytes). For example, if the basic unit of addressable storage in the computer is a word, then each component is presumed to fill one word, two words, etc. as appropriate for the declared component type. If the component type is *Boolean* or *character*, only a small part of a word may be required to store one component, and thus several components might be packed into a single word. A *packed-storage representation* is one in which components of a vector (or other structure) are packed into storage sequentially without regard for placing each component at the beginning of an addressable word (or byte) of storage. A packed-storage representation may allow substantial savings in the amount of storage required for a vector. Unfortunately, access to a component of a packed structure is usually much more expensive, because the simple accessing formula above cannot be used. Instead, a more complex series of calculations is required to access the memory word that contains the component, and then clear away the other components in the word, shift the component to one end of the word, etc. If a component may cross over a word boundary, then access is even more difficult.

Because of the cost of access of a packed vector, vectors are often stored in *unpacked* form; each component is stored beginning at the boundary of an addressable unit of storage, and between each pair of components there is unused storage that represents *padding*. Accessing is then possible using the above formula, but at a cost in lost storage. Distinctions between packed- and unpacked-storage representations for vectors and other data structures are often seen in programming languages (e.g., Pascal, COBOL); they allow the programmer some control over the tradeoff between storage cost and access cost in these two representations.

Whole-vector operations.   Operations that work on entire vectors as a unit are readily implemented using the sequential storage representation for vectors. Assignment of one vector to another with the same attributes is implemented by simply copying the contents of the storage block representing the first into the storage block representing the second. Arithmetic operations on vectors, or specialized operations such as inner product, are implemented as loops that process the elements of the vectors in sequence.

A major implementation problem with such whole-vector operations concerns the storage required for the result. The result of adding two vectors of 100 components each is itself a vector of 100 components. Storage must be allocated temporarily to store this result, unless it is immediately assigned to an existing vector. If a program involves many whole-vector operations, a substantial amount of storage for temporary results may be required, and the management of this temporary storage may increase the complexity and cost of program execution.

Multidimensional Arrays

A vector is an array of one dimension; a matrix composed of rows and columns of components is a two-dimensional array; a three-dimensional array is composed of planes of rows and columns; similarly arrays of any number of dimensions may be constructed from arrays of fewer dimensions. The storage representation and accessing formula for vectors generalize readily to multidimensional arrays.

Specification and syntax. A multidimensional array differs from a vector in its attributes only in that a subscript range for each dimension is required, as in the Pascal declaration:

$$\text{B: } \textbf{array } [1..10, -5..5] \textbf{ of } \text{real};$$

Selection of a component requires that one subscript be given for each dimension, e.g., B[2,4].

Implementation. A matrix is conveniently implemented by considering it as a vector of vectors; a three-dimensional array is a vector whose elements are vectors of vectors, etc. Note that all the subvectors must have the same number of elements of the same type.

Whether a matrix is viewed as a "column of rows" or a "row of columns" is important in some contexts (most often, where a matrix is to be passed as an argument to a subprogram written in another language). Most common is the column-of-rows structure in which the matrix is considered as a vector in which each element is a subvector representing one row of the original matrix. This representation is known as *row-major order*. In general an array of any number of dimensions is organized in row-major order when the array is first divided into a vector of subvectors for each element in the range of the first subscript, then each of these subvectors is subdivided into subsubvectors for each element in the range of the second subscript, etc. *Column-major order* is the representation in which the matrix is treated as a single row of columns.

The storage representation for a multidimensional array follows directly from that for a vector. For a matrix, we store the data objects in the first row (assuming row-major order), followed by the data objects in the second row, etc. The result is a single sequential block of memory containing all the components of the array in sequence. The descriptor for the array is the same as that for a vector, except that an upper and a lower bound for the subscript range of each dimension are needed. Figure 4-4 illustrates this storage representation for a matrix.

The subscripting operation, using an accessing formula to compute the offset of a component from the base address of the array, is similar to that for vectors. For a vector, the accessing formula might be understood as: To find the Ith component, start from the base address, α, and skip down past the descriptor and the components that precede the Ith one. There are $I - LB$ such components, and each is of size E, so $(I - LB) \times E$ computes the number of storage locations to skip.

For a two-dimensional array, we use the same idea: To find the location of $A[I, J]$, first determine the number of rows to skip over, $(I - LB_1)$,

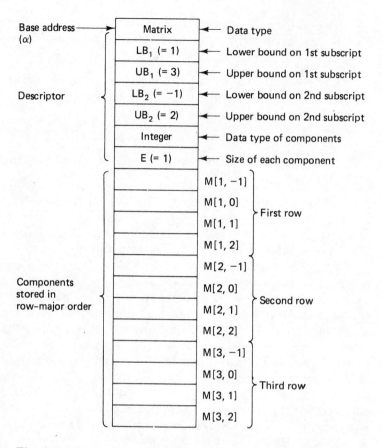

Fig. 4-4 Matrix storage structure with full descriptor, declared as
M: **array** [1..3,–1..2] **of** integer

multiply by the length of a row to get the location of the start of the Ith row, and then find the location of the Jth component in that row, as for a vector. Thus, if A is a matrix with M rows and N columns and A is stored in row-major order, the location of element $A[I, J]$ is given by

$$\text{locn } A[I, J] = \alpha + D + (I - LB_1) \times S + (J - LB_2) \times E$$

where

α = base address
D = length of the descriptor
S = length of a row = $(UB_2 - LB_2 + 1) \times E$
LB_1 = lower bound on first subscript
LB_2, UB_2 = lower and upper bounds, respectively, on the second subscript

Collecting constant terms, this simplifies to

$$\text{locn } A[I, J] = \alpha + K + I \times S + J \times E$$

with $K = D - LB_1 \times S - LB_2 \times E$. Note that K, S, α, and E are fixed when the array is created and thus need be computed only once and stored. The worst-case computation necessary on each access then becomes

$$\text{locn } A[I, J] = \alpha' + I \times S + J \times E$$

where $\alpha' = \alpha + K$. The generalization of these formulas to higher dimensions is straightforward.

4-6   RECORDS

A data structure composed of a fixed number of components of different types is usually termed a *record*.

Specification and Syntax

Both records and vectors are forms of fixed-length linear data structures, but records differ in two ways:

1. The components of records may be *heterogeneous*—i.e., of mixed data types—rather than homogeneous.

2. The components of records are named with *symbolic names* (identifiers) rather than with integer subscripts.

The Pascal syntax for a record declaration is fairly typical:

```
EMPLOYEE: record
          ID: integer;
          AGE: integer;
          SALARY: real;
          DEPT: char
       end
```

The declaration defines a record of four components of types integer, integer, real, and character, respectively. The components have the "subscripts" ID, AGE, SALARY, and DEPT. To select a component of the record, one writes in Pascal:

EMPLOYEE.ID   or   EMPLOYEE.SALARY, etc.

The attributes of a record are seen in the above declaration:

1. The number of components.
2. The data type of each component.
3. The subscript used to name each component.

The components of a record are often called *fields*, and the component names then are the *field names*. Records are also sometimes called "structures" (e.g., in PL/I).

Component selection is the basic operation on a record, as in the selection EMPLOYEE.SALARY. This operation corresponds to the subscripting operation for arrays, but with one crucial difference: the "subscript" here is always a *literal component name*; it is never a computed value. For example, the selection above of the third component of the record EMPLOYEE corresponds to the selection VECT[3] of the third component of a vector, but there is no selection for records that corresponds to VECT[I], where the value of I is computed.

Operations on entire records are usually few. Most commonly assignment of records of identical structure is provided, e.g.,

$$\text{EMPLOYEE} := \text{INPUTREC}$$

where INPUTREC has the same attributes as EMPLOYEE. The correspondence of component names between records is also made the basis for assignment in COBOL and PL/I, e.g., in the COBOL:

$$\text{MOVE CORRESPONDING EMPLOYEE TO OUTPUTREC}$$

which assigns each component of EMPLOYEE to the corresponding component of OUTPUTREC, where corresponding components must have the same name and data type but need not appear in the same order in each record.

Implementation

The storage representation for a record consists of a single sequential block of memory in which the components are stored in sequence, as shown in Fig. 4-5. Individual components may need descriptors to indicate their data type or other attributes, but ordinarily no run-time descriptor for the record itself is required.

Component selection is easily implemented because subscripts (field names) are known during translation rather than being computed during execution. The declaration for the record also allows the size of each component and its position within the storage block to be determined during translation. As a result, the *offset* of any component may be computed

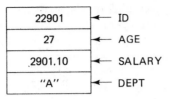

Fig. 4-5 Storage representation for record EMPLOYEE

during translation. The basic accessing formula used to compute the location of the Ith component is:

$$\text{location R}.\,I = \alpha + \sum_{j=1}^{I-1} (\text{size of R}.\,j)$$

where α is the base address of the storage block representing R and R. j is the jth component. The summation is necessary because of the possibly differing sizes of each component. However, the summation may always be computed during translation to give the offset, K_I, for the Ith component, so that during execution only the base address for the storage block need be added:

$$\text{location R}.\,I = \alpha + K_I$$

The operation of assignment of an entire record to another of identical structure may be implemented as a simple copy of the contents of the storge block representing the first record into the storage block representing the second record. The more complex MOVE CORRESPONDING operation may be implemented as a sequence of assignments of individual components of one record to another.

Records and Arrays with Structured Components

In languages that provide both arrays and records as basic data structure types, provision is usually made for components of the two types to be intermixed with components of elementary types (and usually of other structured types such as character strings). For example, a vector in which each component is a record is often useful, as in the Pascal:

EMPLOYEE_LIST: **array** [1..500] **of record**

               ID: integer;

               AGE: integer;

               SALARY: real;

               DEPT: char

           end

which declares a vector of 500 components, each of which is a record. A component of such a composite data structure is selected by using a sequence of selection operations to select first a component of the vector and then a component of the record, as in EMPLOYEE_LIST[3].SALARY.

A record may also have components that are arrays or other records, leading to records that have a hierarchical structure consisting of a top level of components, some of which may be arrays or records. The components of these second-level components may also be arrays or records. In COBOL and PL/I this hierarchical organization is indicated syntactically by assigning *level numbers* to specify each new level of components. The PL/I declaration is typical:

```
1 EMPLOYEE,
   2 NAME,
      3 LAST CHARACTER(10),
      3 FIRST CHARACTER(15),
      3 MIDDLE CHARACTER(1),
   2 AGE FIXED(2),
   2 ADDRESS,
      3 STREET,
         4 NUMBER FIXED(5),
         4 ST-NAME CHARACTER(20),
      3 CITY CHARACTER(15),
      3 STATE CHARACTER(10),
      3 ZIP FIXED(5);
```

Note that the declaration syntax resembles that of an outline, with major headings, subheads, etc. The data structure resulting from this declaration is composed of a single record EMPLOYEE, whose components are those numbered "2", and whose names are NAME, AGE, and ADDRESS. AGE is an elementary component (an integer), but NAME and ADDRESS are each records, and their components are numbered "3". The component STREET of record ADDRESS is itself a record, and its components are numbered "4". Note that the numbers 1, 2, 3, and 4 are not subscripts but are only *level numbers* used to indicate to which record a given component belongs. Selection of a component uses the component names only, not the level numbers, as in EMPLOYEE.ADDRESS.STREET.NUMBER.

Implementation. Although complex data structures may be constructed out of hierarchies of arrays and records, the implementation of such structures is straightforward. The storage representations developed for simple vectors and records extend without change to vectors and records whose components are themselves vectors or records. We considered vectors of vectors of vectors, etc. in Sec. 4-5. A vector of records has the same storage representation as a vector of integers or any other elementary type, except that the storage block representing a component in the larger block representing the vector is the storage block for a record, as described above.

Thus a vector of records is stored much as the vector of vectors in Fig. 4-4, but with each row replaced by the storage representation of a record. Similarly a record whose components are records (or vectors) retains the same sequential storage representation, but with each component represented by a subblock that may be itself the representation of an entire record. Figure 4-6 shows the storage representation for the PL/I data

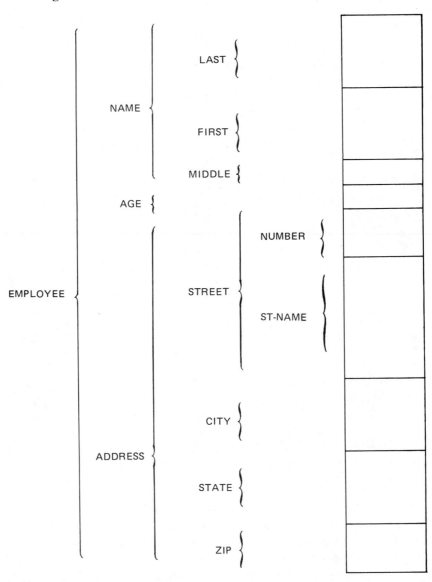

Fig. 4-6 Storage representation for a multilevel PL/I record (without descriptor)

structure declared above. Selection of components requires only a sequence of selections starting from the base address of the complete structure and computing an offset to find the location of the first-level component, followed by computation of an offset from this base address to find the second-level component, etc.

Variant Records

Often it is useful to have a single record that has several *variants*. Such a record ordinarily has one or more components that are common to all variants, and then each variant has, in addition, several other components with names and data types that are unique to that variant. For example, a record containing employee payroll information may have two variants, one for salaried employees paid by the month, and one for employees paid by the hour. The Pascal declaration:

```
type PAY_TYPE = (SALARIED,HOURLY);
var  EMPLOYEE: record
                   ID: integer;
                   DEPT: char;
                   AGE: integer;
                   case PAY_CLASS: PAY_TYPE of
                       SALARIED: (MONTHLY_RATE: real;
                                   START_DATE: integer);
                       HOURLY: (RATE_PER_HOUR: real;
                                 REG_HOURS: integer;
                                 OVERTIME_HOURS: integer)
             end
```

defines such a variant record. The record always has components ID, DEPT, AGE, and PAY_CLASS. When the value of PAY_CLASS = "SALARIED," then the record also has the components MONTHLY_RATE and START_DATE, while if the value of PAY_CLASS = "HOURLY," then it has components RATE_PER_HOUR, REG_HOURS, and OVERTIME_HOURS. The component PAY_CLASS is called the *tag* (Pascal) or *discriminant* (Ada) because it serves as a tag to indicate which variant of the record exists at a given point during program execution.

In using a variant record such as EMPLOYEE, values associated with a particular employee might be stored in the record for processing and subsequently replaced repeatedly as the data for each employee is processed. Suppose the first employee is salaried. Then values might be assigned to the common components ID, DEPT, and AGE. The tag component PAY_CLASS is assigned the value "SALARIED," and then components MONTHLY_RATE and START_DATE are assigned appropriate values. When data for the next employee are to be processed, the common components again are assigned values as before. However, if this employee is paid by the hour, then the tag PAY_CLASS is assigned "HOURLY" and the components RATE_PER_HOUR, REG_HOURS, and OVERTIME_HOURS are then assigned appropriate values. As this example shows, an assignment of a new value to the tag component indicates a change to a new variant of the record. Components of the old variant "disappear"; components of the new variant "appear."

The selection operation for components of a variant record is just the same as that for an ordinary record. For example, EMPLOYEE. MONTHLY_RATE and EMPLOYEE.REG_HOURS select components from the variants defined above. For ordinary records, each component exists throughout the lifetime of the record, but for a component in a variant, the component may exist at one point during execution (when the tag component has a particular value), may later cease to exist (when the value of the tag changes to indicate a different variant), and later may reappear (if the tag changes back to its original value). Thus the selection EMPLOYEE.REG_HOURS may attempt to select a component during execution that does not exist at that time. This problem of selection of a nonexistent component of a variant record is similar to the subscript range error discussed in the preceding section, and the possible solutions are similar:

1. *Dynamic checking.* The tag component may be checked at run time before the component is accessed to insure that the tag value indicates that the component exists. If the tag has the proper value, then the component is accessed; if not, then it is a run-time error, and some special exception processing is invoked, much as is done when checking for subscript range errors.

2. *No checking.* The language design may allow variant record definitions without an explicit tag component that may be checked at run time, so that selection of a component of a variant record is presumed to be valid whenever executed. Because of the implementation of variant records, described below, such a selection is always possible, but if the component does not exist, values in the current variant that does exist may be inadvertently retrieved or overwritten. COBOL, PL/I, and Pascal provide forms of variant records without designated tag fields, and implementations of these forms cannot provide checking.

Record types with variants are also commonly known as *union types*, because each variant may be considered as a separate class of record data object, and then the overall record type appears as the union of these sets of data objects. If there is no designated tag field, then it is a *free-union* type; if there is, then it is a *discriminated-union* type. The term "discriminated" refers to the fact that it is possible (by checking the tag field) to discriminate the variant class to which each data object of the overall type belongs.

Implementation of Variant Records

The storage representation for a variant record is straightforward. During translation, the amount of storage required for the components of each variant is determined, and storage is allocated in the record for the *largest* possible variant, as shown in Fig. 4-7. With this storage block, each variant describes a different layout for the block in terms of number and types of components. Since the block is large enough for the largest variant, there is space in the block for any one of the variants at a given time during program execution, but smaller variants may not use some of the allocated storage. The effect of the variant record declaration is to give multiple layouts for the same block of storage. The layouts are determined during translation and are used to compute offsets for component selection; during execution no special descriptor is needed for a variant record, because the tag component is considered just another component of the record.

Selection of a component of a variant is identical to selection of a component of an ordinary record, provided no checking is to be done. During translation, the offset of the selected component within the storage block is computed, and during execution, the offset is added to the base address of the block to determine the location of the component. If the component does not exist, this accessing calculation gives the location where the component *would be stored* if it did exist, but the location instead will contain a value (or part of a value or several values) representing a component of the current variant. An assignment to a component that does not exist, if unchecked,

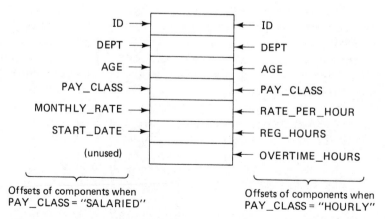

Fig. 4-7   Storage representation for variant form of EMPLOYEE_REC

changes the contents of the location accessed. If that location is currently being used as part of a component in the current variant, then unpredictable changes are made in the value of that component (with possibly disastrous results).

If dynamic checking is provided for selection of components of variants, then at run time the base-address-plus-offset calculation to locate the component is the same, but first the value of the tag field must be checked to insure that the tag indicates that the proper variant currently exists.

Records in Languages Without Declarations

Language such as SNOBOL4 and LISP provide linear data structures of fixed size in which the components may be of mixed type. However, no declaration of the type of each component is given. Instead the structure is created with a fixed number of components, and the type of each component is allowed to vary dynamically during execution, using assignment to assign a data object of possibly different type to each component. These data structures are termed *arrays* in both languages, and components are selected using integer subscripts, as for arrays. However, because they are heterogeneous rather than homogeneous, they are actually more closely akin to records than arrays.

For example, in SNOBOL4, the statement:

$$A = ARRAY(10)$$

is used to create an array A of 10 components. The assignments:

$$A\langle 1 \rangle = \text{``XYZ''}$$
$$A\langle 2 \rangle = 27$$

assign data objects of different types to components of A. A later assignment, e.g., $A\langle 2 \rangle$ = "UVW", may change the type of data object assigned to a component of A.

Implementation.   Such a data structure is ordinarily implemented as a vector in which each component contains a *pointer* to the data object stored there (and possibly a type descriptor for the data object), rather than the data object itself. This storage representation allows the ordinary accessing formula for vectors to be used for subscripting and also allows the assignment operation to readily change the type of data object stored in a component, simply by changing the pointer value and type descriptor. Figure 4-8 shows a storage representation of this sort.

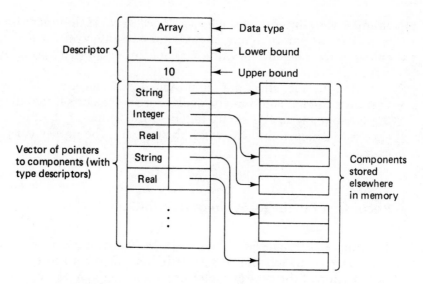

Fig. 4-8 Storage representation for a SNOBOL4 array

4-7 CHARACTER STRINGS

A *character string* is a data object composed of a sequence of characters. A character-string data type is important in most languages, owing in part to the use of character representations of data for input and output.

Specification and Syntax

At least three different treatments of character-string data types may be identified:

   1. *Fixed declared length.* A character-string data object may have a fixed length that is declared in the program. The value assigned to the data object is always a character string of this length. Assignment of a new string value to the data object results in a length adjustment of the new string through truncation of excess characters or addition of blank characters to produce a string of the correct length. This is the basic technique used in COBOL, where a PICTURE declaration is used to specify the number of characters, as in:

LAST_NAME   PICTURE X(20)

which declares a character-string variable LAST_NAME containing a string of 20 characters. In Pascal, a character-string data type is not provided; instead a character data type (Sec. 3-11) is used as the base type for a vector, giving a character string represented as a *vector of characters*, as in:

LAST_NAME: packed array [1..20] of char;

The effect is to make each character string of fixed declared length.

2. *Variable length to a declared bound.* A character-string data object may have a *maximum* length that is declared in the program as above, but the actual value stored in the data object may be a string of shorter length, possibly even the "empty string" of no characters. During execution, the length of the string value of the data object may vary, but it is truncated if it exceeds the bound. This technique is used in PL/I.

3. *Unbounded length.* A character-string data object may have a string value of any length, and the length may vary dynamically during execution with no bound (beyond available memory). This is the basic technique used in SNOBOL4.

The first two methods of handling character-string data allow storage allocation for each string data object to be determined at translation time; if strings have unbounded length, then dynamic storage allocation at run time is required. The different methods also make different sorts of operations on strings appropriate.

A wide variety of operations on character string data are provided in the languages described in Part II. Some of the more important are briefly described here:

1. *Concatenation.* Concatenation is the operation of joining two character strings to make one long string. For example, if "//" is the symbol for the concatenation operation, then "BLOCK"//"HEAD" gives "BLOCKHEAD".

2. *Relational operations on strings.* The usual relational operations—equal, less-than, greater-than, etc.—may be extended to strings. The basic character set always has an ordering, as described in Sec. 3-11. Extending this ordering to character strings gives the usual *lexicographic* (alphabetic) ordering, in which string A is considered to be less than string B (i.e., comes before it in the ordering) if either the first character of A is less than the first character of B, or the first characters are equal and the second character of A is less than the second character of B, etc., with the shorter of strings A and B extended with blank characters (spaces) to the length of the longer.

3. *Substring selection using character-position subscripts.* Manipulation of character-string data often involves working with a contiguous substring of the overall string. For example, a string may often contain a

leading sequence of blank characters or be composed of words separated by blanks and punctuation marks. To facilitate manipulation of substrings of a string, many languages provide an operation for selecting a substring by giving the positions of its first and last characters (or first character position and length of the substring), as in the FORTRAN "NEXT = STR(6:10)", which assigns the five characters in positions 6 through 10 of string STR to string variable NEXT.

The meaning of the substring selection operation is particularly troublesome to define because it must be allowed to appear on both sides of an assignment, so that a new value may be assigned to the selected substring. Consider the FORTRAN:

$$STR(1:5) = STR(I:I+4)$$

which might be used to move a five-character substring beginning in position I to the first five-character positions of the string. If the substrings referenced on the left and right of the assignment happen to overlap, the meaning of this statement must be carefully defined (see Problem 14).

4. *Input-output formatting.* Operations for manipulating character strings are often provided primarily to aid in formatting data for output or for breaking up formatted input data into smaller data items. The formatted input-output features of FORTRAN and PL/I are examples of extensive sets of operations provided for this purpose.

5. *Substring selection using pattern matching.* Often the position of a desired substring within a larger string is not known, but its relation to other substrings is known. For example, we might want to select the first nonblank character of a string, or a sequence of digits followed by a decimal point, or the word following the word "THE". A *pattern-matching operation* takes as one argument a pattern data structure, where the pattern specifies the form of the substring desired (e.g., its length, or that it is composed of a sequence of decimal digits) and possibly other substrings that should adjoin it (e.g., a following decimal point or a preceding sequence of blank characters). The second argument to the pattern-matching operation is a character string that is to be scanned to find a substring that matches that specified by the pattern. Thus the result of the pattern-matching operation is selection of a substring, which may then be assigned a new value or otherwise manipulated in the usual ways. SNOBOL4 provides a powerful pattern-matching operation and set of language features for constructing patterns to be used in this form of substring selection.

Implementation

Each of the three methods for handling character strings utilizes a different storage representation, as shown in Fig. 4-9. Storage representations for characters are discussed in Sec. 3-11. For a string of fixed declared length,

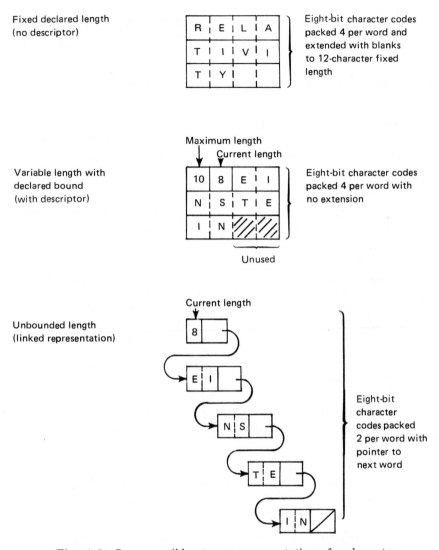

Fig. 4-9 Some possible storage representations for character strings

the representation is essentially that used for a packed vector of characters, as described in Sec. 4-5. For the variable-length string to a declared bound, the storage representation utilizes a descriptor containing both the declared maximum length and the current length of the string stored in the data object. For strings of unbounded length, a linked storage representation may be used, with a descriptor containing the current length of the string.

Hardware support for the simple fixed-length representation is usually available, but other representations for strings must usually be software-simulated. Operations on strings such as concatenation, substring selection, and pattern matching are ordinarily entirely software-simulated.

4-8   VARIABLE-SIZE DATA STRUCTURES

A *variable-size* data structure is one in which the number of components may change dynamically during program execution. Some of the major types of variable-size data structures are:

Lists and list structures.   A *list* is a linear data structure with a variable number of components of possibly differing types. If the components of a list may themselves be lists, the list is usually called a *list structure.* Components may be inserted into a list and deleted from it. Components may also be selected from a list, but since the position of a component in a list may change due to the insertion and deletion of neighboring components, selection operations do not ordinarily use subscripts to designate components. Instead, selection is based on relative position of a component within the list, e.g., first, second, third, next, or last component. Linked storage representations for lists and list structures are commonly used to accommodate the varying number of components.

Stacks and queues.   Two restricted forms of lists are important. A *stack* is a list in which component selection, insertion, and deletion are restricted to one end. A *queue* is a list in which component selection and deletion are restricted to one end and insertion is restricted to the other end. Both sequential and linked storage representations for stacks and queues are common.

Trees.   A list in which the components may be lists as well as elementary data objects is termed a *tree*, provided that each list is only a component of at most one other list.

Directed graphs.   A data structure in which the components may be linked together using arbitrary linkage patterns (rather than just linear sequences of components) is termed a *directed graph.*

Property lists.   A *record* with a varying number of components is usually termed a *property list* if the number of components may vary without restriction. (The variant record structure described in Sec. 4-6 allows variation only within a predefined set of alternatives.) In a property list, both the component names (field names) and their values must be stored. Each field name is termed a *property name*, the corresponding value of the field is the *property value.* A common representation for a property list is as an ordinary linked list, with the property names and their values alternating in a single long sequence, as illustrated in Fig. 4-10. To select a

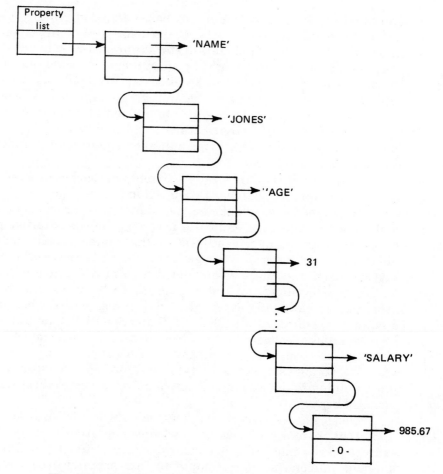

Fig. 4-10   Linked storage representation for a property list with the properties NAME, AGE, and SALARY

particular property value, e.g., the value for the AGE property, the list is searched, looking only at the property names, until the desired property is found. The next list component is then the value for that property. When a new property is inserted in the property list, two components are inserted— the property name and its value. Property lists are found under a variety of names in programming languages; in LISP they are called property lists, but in SNOBOL4 they are *tables* (and a mixed sequential and linked representation is used for their storage, see Problem 18). The terms *attribute-value list* and *description list* are also used.

Variable-size data objects are natural to use when the amount of data in a problem is not known in advance. For example, the data may be entering from an input device or may be generated internally by a program in an unpredictable manner. Use of fixed-size arrays and records may be impossible unless large amounts of storage are reserved in advance for the maximum size data that might be encountered. Variable-size data structures instead allow storage to be allocated gradually as needed during program execution. However, the storage management associated with variable-size data objects presents a fundamental problem for a language implementation, and thus the treatment of these data types in any language is tied closely to the basic storage management structures underlying the language implementation.

There are two fundamentally different approaches to these data types in programming languages. In some languages, such as LISP, a list structure, property list, stack, or queue data type is provided directly—it is built into the language—and the language implementation provides a hidden storage management system that automatically manages the allocation and recovery of storage for these structures. In other languages, such as Pascal and Ada, a *pointer* data type is provided, along with facilities for the dynamic allocation of storage explicitly by the programmer, and the programmer builds his own linked structures, as described in the next section. Some languages, such as PL/I and SNOBOL4, provide versions of both facilities. Because the use of pointers and programmer-constructed data objects is most common, and also because of the large variety of variable-size data structures (and storage representations) used in different programming languages, no comprehensive survey of these data types is included here.

Stacks, queues, trees, and other types of variable-size data objects are important in many phases of the implementation of a language. For example, a run-time stack is a central system-defined data object in most language implementations (Chapter 6), trees are often used to represent the symbol table in a compiler (Chapter 9), and queues are often used in the scheduling and synchronization of concurrent subprograms (Chapter 6). These system-defined data structures are discussed as appropriate in subsequent chapters.

4-9   POINTERS AND PROGRAMMER-CONSTRUCTED DATA OBJECTS

Commonly, rather than build a variety of types of variable-size, linked data objects into a programming language, facilities are provided to allow the programmer to construct his own, using pointers to link together the component data objects as desired. Several language features are needed to make this possible.

1. An elementary data type *pointer* (also called a *reference* or *access* type). A pointer data object contains the location of another data object, or it may contain the null pointer, *nil*. Pointers are ordinary data objects that may be simple variables or components of arrays and records.

2. A *creation operation* for data objects of fixed size, such as arrays, records, and elementary types. The creation operation both allocates a block of storage for the new data object and returns a pointer to its location, which may then be stored as the value of a pointer data object. The creation operation differs in two ways from the ordinary creation of data objects caused by declarations: (a) the data objects created need have no names, since they are accessed through pointers, and (b) data objects may be created in this way at any point during execution of a program, not just on entry to a subprogram.

3. A *selection operation* for pointer values that allows a pointer to be followed to the data object to which it points.

Specification

A pointer data type defines a class of data objects whose values are the locations of other data objects. A single data object of pointer type might be treated in two ways:

1. *Pointers may reference data objects only of a single type.* The pointers (locations) that are allowed as a value of the pointer data object may be restricted to point only to data objects of the same type. This is the approach used in Pascal and Ada, where type declarations and static type checking are used. To declare a pointer variable in Pascal, for example, that may point to any data object of type VECT:

P: ↑VECT;

The "↑" designates the type of P as type pointer. The type VECT designates the type of data object to which a pointer value for P may point. A separate type definition (see Chapter 5) must be given to define the structure of data objects of type VECT, e.g.:

type VECT = **array** [1..20] **of** real;

2. *Pointers may reference data objects of any type.* An alternative is to allow a pointer data object to point to data objects of varying type at different times during program execution. This is the approach used in languages like SNOBOL4, where data objects carry type descriptors during execution and dynamic type checking is performed.

The creation operation both allocates storage for (and thus creates) a fixed-size data object and also creates a pointer to the new data object that may be stored in a pointer data object. In Pascal and Ada, this operation is named NEW. Consider a subprogram containing a declaration of pointer variable P (as defined above). On entry to the subprogram, only space for the data object P is allocated (storage for a single pointer value). Later during execution of the subprogram, an array of type VECT may be created by executing the statement:

$$\textbf{new}(P)$$

Since P has been declared to point to objects only of the type VECT, this statement has the meaning "Create a 20-component vector of real numbers (i.e., allocate storage for it and initialize the descriptor as required) and assign a pointer to its location to P."

The selection operation allows a pointer value to be followed to reach the data object designated. Since pointers are ordinary data objects, the pointer data object itself may also be selected using only the ordinary mechanisms for selection. In Pascal, for example, the selection operation that follows a pointer to its designated object is written "↑". To select a component of the vector pointed to by P, you write "P↑[5]" or "P↑[20]", as in

$$\textbf{if } P <> \text{NIL } \textbf{then } \text{SUM} := P\uparrow[1] + P\uparrow[2]$$

Note that the first reference to P selects P's pointer value to compare against the null pointer value NIL. The reference P↑ selects P's pointer value and then follows the pointer to the designated vector.

Implementation

A pointer data object is represented as a storage location containing the address of another storage location. The address is the base address of the block of storage representing the data object pointed to by the pointer. Two major storage representations are used for pointer values:

1. *Absolute addresses.* A pointer value may be represented as the actual memory address of the storage block for the data object.

2. *Relative addresses.* A pointer value may be represented as an *offset* from the *base address* of some larger *heap* storage block within which the data object is allocated.

If absolute addresses are used for pointer values, then data objects created by the creation operation, NEW, may be allocated storage anywhere in memory. Usually this allocation takes place within a general *heap* storage area. Selection using absolute addresses is efficient, because the pointer value itself provides direct access to the data object using the hardware memory-accessing operation. The disadvantage of absolute addresses is that storage management is more difficult, because no data object may be moved within memory if there exists a pointer to it stored elsewhere, unless the pointer value itself is changed to reflect the new position of the data object. Recovery of storage for data objects that have become garbage is also difficult, because each such data object is recovered individually and its storage block must be integrated back into the overall pool of available storage. These issues are treated in Chapter 8.

The use of relative addresses as pointers requires the initial allocation of a block of storage, called an *area* in PL/I, within which subsequent allocation of data objects by NEW takes place. There may be one area for each type of data object to be allocated, or a single area for all data objects. Each area is managed as a *heap* storage area. Assuming one area for each type of data object, then NEW may allocate storage in fixed-size blocks within the area, which makes storage management particularly simple (see Chapter 8). Selection using this form of pointer value is more costly than for an absolute address, because the offset must be added to the base address of the area to obtain an absolute address before the data object may be accessed. However, the advantage of relative pointers lies in the opportunity to move the area block as a whole at any time without invalidating any of the pointers. For example, the area might be written out to a file and later read back in to a different place in primary memory. Since the offset of each pointer value is unchanged, access to a data object in the new area may use the same offset with the new base address of the area. An additional advantage is that the entire area may be treated as a data object which is created on entry to a subprogram, used by NEW within that subprogram (and any subprograms it calls), and then deleted on exit. No storage recovery of individual data objects within the area is necessary; they may be allowed to become garbage because the entire area is recovered as a whole when the subprogram is exited.

Static type checking is possible for references using pointer values if each pointer data object is restricted to point to other data objects of a single type, as described above. Without this restriction, it cannot be determined during translation what type of data object a pointer will designate at run time, so dynamic type checking is necessary, or else, in some languages, selections using pointer values are simply left unchecked. Run-time checking for a *nil* pointer value is also required before selection.

The major implementation problem associated with pointers and programmer-constructed data objects that use pointer linkages is the storage allocation associated with the creation operation. Because this operation may be used to create data objects of different sizes at arbitrary times during program execution, it requires an underlying storage management system capable of managing a general *heap* storage area. For Pascal, the other parts of the language require only a stack-based storage management system, so the addition of pointers and the NEW operation to the language requires a substantial extension of the overall run-time storage management structure. Pointer data objects introduce the potential for generating garbage if all pointers to a created data object are lost. Dangling references are also possible if data objects can be destroyed and the storage recovered for reuse. These issues are treated again in Chapter 8.

4-10   SETS

Logically a set may be viewed as in mathematics: a *set* is a data object containing an *unordered* collection of *distinct* values. In contrast, a list is an ordered collection of values, some of which may be repeated. The basic operations on sets are:

1. *Membership test.* Is data value X a member of set S?

2. *Insertion and deletion of single values.* Insert data value X in set S, provided it is not already a member of S. Delete data value X from S if a member.

3. *Union, intersection, and difference of sets.* Given two sets, S_1 and S_2, create set S_3 that contains all members of both S_1 and S_2 with duplicates deleted (*union* operation), create S_3 to contain only values that are members of both S_1 and S_2 (*intersection operation*), or create S_3 to contain only values that are in S_1 but not in S_2 (*difference operation*).

Note that accessing of components of a set by subscript or relative position plays no part in set processing.

Implementation

In programming languages the term *set* is sometimes applied to a data structure representing an *ordered* set. An ordered set is actually a list with duplicate values removed; it requires no special consideration. The unordered set, however, admits two specialized storage representations that merit attention.

Bit-string representation of sets.   The bit-string storage representation is appropriate where the size of the underlying universe of values (the values that may appear in set data objects) is known to be small. Suppose that there are N elements in the universe. Order these elements arbitrarily as e_1, e_2, ..., e_N. A set of elements chosen from this universe may then be represented by a bit string of length N, where the ith bit in the string is a 1 if e_i is in the set and 0 if not. The bit string represents the *characteristic function* of the set. With this representation, insertion of an element into a set consists of setting the appropriate bit to 1, deletion consists of setting the appropriate bit to 0, and membership is determined simply by interrogating the appropriate bit. The union, intersection, and difference operations on whole sets may be represented by the Boolean operations on bit strings that are usually provided by the hardware: the Boolean OR of two bit strings represents union, AND represents intersection, and the AND of the first string and the complement of the second represents the difference operation.

The hardware support for bit-string operations, if provided, makes manipulation of the bit-string representation of sets efficient. However, the hardware operations usually apply only to bit strings up to a certain fixed length (e.g., the word length of the central memory). For strings longer than this maximum, software simulation must be used to break up the string into smaller units that can be processed by the hardware. Thus languages such as Pascal that ordinarily use this set representation allow each implementation to restrict the size of sets to some small maximum number of elements. The maximum is chosen to be equal to the length of one or a few words or bytes, depending on the ease of processing on the underlying hardware.

Hash-coded representation of sets. A common alternative representation for a set is based on the technique of *hash coding* or *scatter storage*. This method may be used when the underlying universe of possible values is large (e.g., when the set contains numbers or character strings). It allows the membership test, insertion, and (with some methods) deletion of values to be performed efficiently. However, union, intersection, and difference operations must be implemented as a sequence of membership tests, insertions, and deletions of individual elements, so they are inefficient. To be effective, hash-coding methods also require a substantial allocation of storage. Most commonly, a language does not provide this representation for a set *data type* available to the user, but the language implementation uses this representation for some of the system-defined data required during translation or execution. For example, most LISP implementations use this storage representation for the set called the *object list* (Chapter 17), which consists of the names of all the atomic data objects in use by a LISP program during its execution. Most SNOBOL4 implementations maintain a hash-coded representation of a set containing all the string data objects created during execution of a SNOBOL4 program (Chapter 18).

In the hash-coded storage representation, a block of storage (sometimes termed the *hash table*) is reserved for the set. Rather than storing elements of the set in sequential locations within this block, however, the elements are scattered randomly through the block. The trick is to store each new element in such a way that its presence or absence can later be immediately determined without a search of the block.

Consider how this may be done. Suppose that we wish to add a new element x, represented by bit string B_x, to the set S, represented by the block of storage M_S. First we must determine if x is already a member of S, and if not, add it to the set. We determine a position for B_x within the block M_S by the application of a *hashing function* to the bit string B_x. The hashing function "hashes" (chops up into little pieces and mixes together) the bit string B_x and then extracts a *hash address* I_x from the result. This hash address is used as an index pointing to a position in the block M_S. We look at that position in the block, and if x is already in the set, then it must be stored at that position. If not, then we store the bit string B_x at the location designated by I_x. Any later attempt to find whether x is a member of S will be answered by hashing the new bit string B_x representing x, obtaining I_x, accessing the block M_S at that position, and finding the previously stored string B_x. No search of the table is ever needed.

Exactly how the hashing function works is not critical as long as it is relatively fast and generates hash addresses that are fairly randomly distributed. An example will illustrate the idea more directly. Suppose that we allocate a block of 1024 words (a block length equal to a power of 2 for a binary computer is most convenient) for the block M_S and suppose that the data items to be stored are character strings represented by double-word bit strings. We may represent a set of up to 512 distinct elements within this block. Suppose that the starting address of the block in memory is α. An appropriate hash address for such a table would be a string I_x of nine bits, since then the formula

$$\alpha + 2 \times I_x$$

would always generate an address within the block. We might compute I_x from a given two-word-long bit string B_x by the following algorithm: Assume that B_x is stored in words a and b; then

1. Multiply a and b, giving c (two-word product).
2. Add together the two words of c, giving d.
3. Square d, giving e.
4. Extract the center nine bits of e, giving I_x.

Different hashing functions are appropriate depending on the properties of the bit-string representations of the data to be stored.

Even the best hashing function cannot in general guarantee that different data items will generate different hash addresses when hashed. While it is desirable that the hashing function spread the generated hash addresses throughout the block as much as possible, almost inevitably two data items may be hashed to the same hash address, leading to a *collision*. A collision occurs when we have a data item to be added to the set, go to the block at the designated hash address, and find the block entry at that point filled with a data item *different from the one to be stored* (but which just happened to hash to the same hash address). Many techniques for handling collisions are known; for example:

1. *Rehashing.* We might modify the original bit string B_x (e.g., by multiplication by a constant), and then rehash the result, generating a new hash address. If another collision occurs, we rehash again until either B_x is found or an empty block location is encountered.

2. *Sequential scan.* From the original point of the collision in the block we might begin a sequential (end-around) search until either B_x is found or an empty block location is encountered.

3. *Bucketing.* In place of direct storage in the block we might substitute pointers to linked *bucket lists* of the elements having the same hash addresses. After hashing B_x and retrieving the pointer to the appropriate bucket list, we search the list for B_x, and if not found, add it to the end of the list.

4-11   FILES AND INPUT-OUTPUT

A *file* is a data structure with two special properties:

1. It ordinarily is represented primarily on a secondary storage device such as a disk or tape and thus may be much larger than most data structures of other types.

2. Its lifetime may encompass a greater span of time than that of the program creating it.

Sequential files are the most common type of file, but many languages also provide *direct-access files* and *indexed sequential files.* Two general uses for files are seen: for input and output of data to an external operating environment (see Chapter 10) and as temporary *scratch storage* for data when not enough high-speed memory is available. The components of a file are often termed *records,* but this use of the term is avoided here because of the conflict with the record data structure discussed in Sec. 4-6.

Sequential Files

A *sequential file* is a data structure composed of a linear sequence of components of the same type. It is of varying length, with no fixed maximum bound (beyond available storage). Language structures for declaring sequential files vary widely. The Pascal approach is straight-forward. In Pascal a file is declared by giving its name and the type of component it contains. For example:

MASTER_LIST: **file of** EMPLOYEE_REC;

defines a file named MASTER_LIST whose components are of type EMPLOYEE_REC. The component type may be an elementary type or a data structure type of fixed size such as an array or record. Variable-size data structures ordinarily cannot be components of files (thus, no files of files or files of stacks). In addition, data structures that are in linked representation or that include pointer values are often not allowed as components of files, because the pointer values usually become meaningless after the lifetime of the program creating the file. When the data are later read from the file, the storage locations referenced by the pointer values may be in use for another purpose.

For input-output, data are usually represented in character form. Each component of such a file is then a single character, and the file is known, in Pascal, as a *textfile*. Most languages provide a special set of input-output operations for textfiles, in addition to the ordinary file operations. A textfile also commonly divides character sequences into groups called *lines*. We consider ordinary sequential files first and then note some special characteristics of textfiles.

A distinctive characteristic of a sequential file is the manner in which its components may be accessed. Typically the file may be accessed in one of two modes, *read* mode or *write* mode. In either mode there is a *file-position pointer* that designates a position either before the first file component, between two components, or after the last component. In write mode, the file-position pointer is always positioned after the last component, and the only operation possible is to assign (WRITE) a new component to that position, thus extending the file by one component. In read mode, the file-position pointer may be positioned anywhere in the file, and the only access provided is access (READ) to the component at (immediately following) the position designated. No assignment of new components or component values is provided. In either mode, a READ or WRITE operation advances the file position pointer to the position immediately following the component accessed or assigned. If the file-position pointer is positioned after the last component, the file is said to be positioned at *end-of-file* (or at the *end-of-file mark*).

The major operations on sequential files are:

1. *Open*. Ordinarily, before a file may be used, it must be opened. The OPEN operation is given the name of a file and the access mode (read or write). If the mode is *read*, then the file is presumed to already exist. The OPEN operation ordinarily requests information from the operating system

about the location and properties of the file, allocates the required internal storage for buffers and other information (see the implementation discussion below), and sets the file-position pointer to the first component of the file. If the mode is *write*, then a request is made to the operating system to create a new empty file, or if a file already exists with the given name, to delete all the existing components of the file, so that it is empty. The file position pointer is set to the start of the empty file.

Ordinarily an explicit OPEN statement is provided. In Pascal the procedure *reset* opens a file in read mode, and procedure *rewrite* opens a file in write mode. Sometimes a language provides for an implicit OPEN operation on a file at the time of the first attempt to read or write the file.

2. *Read.* A READ operation transfers the contents of the current file component (designated by the file-position pointer) to a designated variable in the program. The transfer is usually defined as having the same semantics as an assignment from the file component to the program variable. This variable may be an ordinary programmer defined variable or it may be a special *buffer variable* defined implicitly for each file. For example, in Pascal, the declaration of a file F in a program creates implicitly also a program variable named F↑, called the *buffer variable* for F. The READ operation (called *get* in Pascal) assigns the next file component to F↑. The programmer may then reference F↑ as an ordinary program variable in the usual way.

3. *Write.* A WRITE operation creates a new component at the current position in the file (always at the end) and transfers the contents of a designated program variable to the new component. Again this transfer is usually defined as a form of assignment. The program variable may be created explicitly by the programmer, or it may be a buffer variable, as for READ.

4. *End-of-file test.* In write mode, the current file position is always at the end of the file. In read mode, however, a READ operation fails if the file position pointer designates the end of the file. Since the file is of variable length, an explicit test for the end-of-file position is needed so that the program may take special action. Pascal provides a function:

$$\textbf{eof: } \textit{file} \rightarrow \textit{Boolean}$$

that returns true if the file is positioned at its end, and false otherwise. In COBOL, Ada, and FORTRAN, an explicit designation of action to take for an end-of-file condition is specified as part of a READ operation, for example the COBOL:

$$\text{READ } \textit{file-name} \text{ AT END } \textit{statement}$$

specifies a statement to be executed if the READ operation fails owing to an end-of-file condition.

5. *Close.* When processing of a file is complete, it must be closed. Ordinarily this operation involves notification to the operating system that the file can be detached from the program (and potentially made available to other programs), and possibly also deallocation of internal storage used for the file (such as buffers and buffer variables). Often files are closed implicitly when the program terminates, without explicit action by the programmer. However, to change the mode of access to a file from write to read, or vice versa, the file must often be explicitly closed and then reopened in the new mode.

Implementation.   In most computer systems, the underlying operating system has the primary responsibility for the implementation of files, since files are created and manipulated by various programming language processors and utilities. A particular programming language implementation provides only the necessary local data structures needed for the interface with the operating system. File operations are primarily implemented by calls on primitives provided by the operating system.

From the language viewpoint, the primary implementation problem comes from the need to provide storage for system data and buffers required by the operating system primitives. Typically when a program opens a file during its execution, storage for a *file information table* and a *buffer* must be provided. The operating system OPEN primitive stores information about the location and characteristics of the file in the file information table. The buffer is used as a sequential representation of a queue. Assume the file is opened in *write* mode. When a WRITE operation transfers a component to be appended to the end of the file, the data is sent to an operating system WRITE primitive. The WRITE primitive stores the data in the next available position in the buffer, in memory. No actual transfer of data to the file takes place until enough WRITE operations have been performed to allow a complete block of components to have accumulated in the buffer. At this time, the block of components is transferred from the buffer to the external storage device (e.g., disk or tape). The next sequence of WRITE operations executed by the program again fills the buffer, until a complete block may be transferred to external storage. When a file is read, the inverse process occurs: data are transferred from the file into the buffer in blocks of components. Each READ operation executed by the program transfers a single component from the buffer to the program variable. The buffer is refilled as needed. Often the filing and emptying of the buffer may take place simultaneously with execution of other parts of the program, using separate input-output processors available in the computer system. The cost, for the program, of a READ or WRITE operation is then reduced to the cost of copying a component from program variable into the buffer or vice versa, which is fast and inexpensive compared to the speed and cost of the actual transfer of a block to the file. This organization is shown in Fig. 4-11.

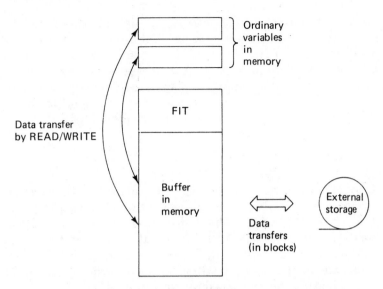

Fig. 4-11 File representation using a buffer and file information table (FIT)

The file information table is used to maintain the pointers to the top and bottom of the queue of components in the buffer, and to maintain the location of the current block on the external storage device as well. The file position pointer corresponds in the implementation to the current point at which components are being inserted into (for *write* mode) or moved from (for *read* mode) the buffer.

Textfiles

A *textfile* (the term comes from Pascal) is a file of characters. Textfiles are the primary form of file for input-output to the user in most languages, since textfiles may be printed and may be created directly from keyboard input. Files with components of other types ordinarily are only written by programs and read by programs. Textfiles are a form of ordinary sequential file and may be manipulated in the same ways. However, special operations are often provided for textfiles that allow numeric data (and sometimes other types of data) to be automatically converted to internal storage representations during input without storage in character form. Similar operations on output allow conversion of numbers and other data from internal representations to character form. Along with these conversions, provision is ordinarily made for formatting the data on output into lines of the appropriate length that include headings, spaces, and converted data items as desired for printed output. This *output formatting* is an important part of the implementation of output operations for textfiles; similar formatting operations may be used for input, or the input operations may be *free-format*, allowing numbers to appear anywhere on a line separated by spaces. The free-format READ operation scans the line (*or* lines) as necessary to find the numbers needed to satisfy the read request. The details of textfiles and formatted and free-format input-output vary widely between languages, so no detailed survey is attempted here.

Interactive Input-output

Consider a textfile that represents an interactive terminal at which a programmer is sitting. During execution of the program, a WRITE operation on this file is interpreted as a command to display the characters on the terminal screen. A READ operation is a command that requests input of data from the keyboard, usually beginning with display of a "prompt" character on the screen. In this setting, several aspects of the ordinary view of sequential files described above are modified:

1. The file must be in *both* read mode and write mode at the same time, since ordinarily READ and WRITE operations alternate—first some data are displayed, then some input data are requested, and so on.

2. Buffering of data on input and output is restricted. Seldom can more than one line of data be collected in an input buffer before it is processed. Data collected in an output buffer must be displayed before a read request is made to the terminal.

3. The file-position pointer and end-of-file test have relatively little significance. An interactive file has no position, in the sense described above, and it has no end, since the programmer may continue to enter data indefinitely. A special control character may be used by the programmer to signal the end of a portion of his input from the terminal, but the usual notions of end-of-file test and end-of-file processing are often inappropriate.

Because of these substantial differences between interactive files and ordinary sequential files, many language designs have experienced difficulty accommodating interactive files within an input-output structure designed for ordinary sequential files.

Direct-Access Files

In a sequential file, the components must be accessed in sequence in the order in which they appear on the file. While limited operations to advance or backspace the file-position pointer are usually available, access to any component at random is usually not possible. A *direct-access file* is organized so that any single component may be accessed at random, just as in an array or record. The subscript used to select a component is called its *key*, and may be an integer or other identifier. If an integer, the key looks much like an ordinary subscript used to designate a component of the file. However, because a direct access file is stored on a secondary storage device rather than in central memory, the implementation of the file and the selection operation is quite different from that for an array.

A direct-access file is organized as an unordered set of components, with a key value associated with each component. Initially the file is empty. A WRITE operation is given a component to copy to the file, and the key value to be associated with that component. The WRITE operation creates a new component on the external storage device and copies the designated value into it. The key value is ordinarily associated with the location of the component (on the external storage device) by storing the pair (key, location) in an index. An *index* is a vector of such pairs. Each WRITE operation that writes a component with a new key value adds another pair to the index, but if a WRITE operation is given the key of an existing component, that component is *overwritten* with the new value. Thus writing on a direct-access file is similar to assignment to a component of a vector, where the key value is the subscript.

A READ operation is given the key of the desired component in the file. The index is searched to find the pair with that key, and then the component is read from the designated location in secondary storage.

Implementation. The details of implementation of direct-access files are primarily hidden in the operating system. The language implementation must provide space for a file information table, but the index for the file must be permanently a part of the file, and thus ordinarily it is not a concern of the language implementation (in contrast to buffers for sequential files, which exist only for the lifetime of the program accessing the file).

Indexed Sequential Files

An indexed sequential file is similar to a direct-access file, with the additional facility to access components in sequence, beginning from a component selected at random. For example, if component with key value 27 is selected (read), then the subsequent READ operation may choose the "next" component in sequence, rather than giving a key value. This file organization provides a compromise between the pure sequential and pure direct-access organizations.

An indexed sequential file requires an index of key values, just as for a direct-access file, but the entries in the index must be *ordered* by key values. When a READ or WRITE operation selects a component with a particular key value, then that pair in the index becomes the *current component* of the file; that is, the file-position pointer is positioned at that component. To advance to the next file component in sequence, the next entry in the index is accessed, and that entry becomes the current component. Thus sequential access to components is possible without a major change from the direct-access organization.

Implementation. As with other file organizations, the implementation details are the primary responsibility of the operating system. Blocking and buffering of sequences of components are often provided, in a manner similar to that used for sequential files, so that sequential access to components is more efficient than a simple sequence of random selections of components.

4-12 REFERENCES AND SUGGESTIONS FOR FURTHER READING

The two volumes by Knuth [1973a, b] contain a wealth of material on data structures and their manipulation. Standish [1980], Aho et al [1983], Pfaltz [1977], Wirth [1976], and Horowitz and Sahni [1976] are representative of the selection of general texts available on data structures. Two papers by Hoare [1968, 1972] are important in their emphasis on the relation between language design and data structure handling. A study of individual languages that emphasize treatment of particular kinds of data structures is also useful: APL for arrays, SNOBOL4 for strings, LISP for lists and property lists, Pascal and Ada for records, pointers, and programmer-constructed data objects. Nicholls [1975] provides a language-oriented view of files and an extensive bibliography.

4-13 PROBLEMS

1. Pick a language and a data structure type in that language. List the *attributes* of data objects of that type. List the *operations* provided for data objects of that type. Determine the storage representation for data objects of that type in your local implementation of the language. Is there a run-time descriptor? What attributes are stored in the descriptor? Do any operations require the allocation or freeing of storage when this storage representation is used?

2. Pick a language and a data structure type in that language. Determine the selection operations provided for selecting individual components or substructures of data objects of that type. For each selection operation (or class of operations) determine (a) whether the existence of the selected component can be determined statically (at compile time), and (b) whether the data type of the selected component can be determined statically. If either existence or data type

cannot be determined statically, determine whether you, the programmer, or the language implementation is responsible for checking at run time whether a selected component exists and is of the correct type before it is used in a computation.

3. Write an algorithm for finding the location of the component V[N] of a vector V if V is stored in linked representation, as in Fig. 4-1. Assume the address of the descriptor is α, its link field is at offset j, and each component is stored in a separate block with the link stored at offset k in that block.

4. Suppose the declaration of a vector V is given using an enumeration type as the subscript range, e.g.,

   CLASS_TYPE = (FRESH, SOPH, JUNIOR, SENIOR, GRADUATE);
   V: **array** [CLASS_TYPE] **of** real;

   (a) Show the storage representation (including descriptor) that would be appropriate for V and give the accessing formula for computing the location of a component V[i].
   (b) How would the storage representation and accessing formula change if V were declared as

   V: **array** [JUNIOR..GRADUATE] **of** real;

5. Give the accessing formula for computing the location of component A[I,J] of a matrix A declared as

   A: **array** [LB$_1$..UB$_1$, LB$_2$..UB$_2$]

   where A is stored in *column-major order.*

6. Extend the matrix storage representation and accessing formula of Sec. 4-5 to arrays of an arbitrary number of dimensions. Assume row-major order of components.

7. Many computations using matrices involve sequential processing of all the elements of a single row or column. The loop in which the processing is done likely involves references to A[I,J] with the subscript I or J increased by one each time through the loop. In such cases it is inefficient to compute locn A[I,J] independently on each loop; instead (assuming subscript I is the one which is varying) locn A[I,J] may be computed more simply from locn A[I-1,J]. Give the formula for computing locn A[I,J] in terms of locn A[I-1,J]. Extend this formula to arrays of arbitrary dimension where an arbitrary subscript is the one being incremented.

8. In the language SIMSCRIPT a multidimensional homogeneous array is represented as a vector of pointers that point to other vectors of pointers, etc., to as many levels as the array has dimensions. A 3×4 matrix of numbers, for example, is represented by a vector of three pointers, each of which points to another vector of four numbers. Give an algorithm for accessing A[I,J] when such a representation is used. Compare the relative efficiency of accessing and storage use between this representation and the usual sequential representation. Consider both the case of matrices and arrays of higher dimension.

9. A *cross section* of a homogeneous multidimensional array is a subarray obtained by fixing one or more subscripts and letting the other subscripts vary through their ranges. For example, if A is a matrix, then any row or column of A is a cross section. In PL/I an array cross section is designated by a subscripted variable with ∗ in one or more subscript positions. Thus A[3,∗] designates the third row of A, A[∗,4] designates the fourth column of A, and A[∗,∗] is the entire array. Assume that arrays are stored in row-major order sequentially in the usual way. It is desirable that a descriptor for cross sections of arrays be used that allows the same accessing formula to be used for cross sections that is used for ordinary arrays.

(a) Design a run-time descriptor for linear array cross sections (e.g., rows or columns of matrices) that has this property. The descriptor should contain the elements α, LB, and E needed to compute the location of the Ith element of the cross section according to the usual vector accessing formula $\alpha + (I - LB) \times E$.

(b) Design a run-time descriptor for two-dimensional cross sections (e.g., planes of three-dimensional arrays) that has this property.

10. Because most hardware provides no direct support, subscript range checking on each access to an array component during a computation can be costly in both execution time and storage for the extra code involved. For a language with which you are familiar, determine the relative cost, in both execution time and storage, of access to a component of a matrix, A[I,J]. Preferably, obtain a listing of the object code produced by the compiler for a simple program that includes some array accessing, and determine the instructions generated and their timings for the checked and unchecked cases.

11. Suppose you modified Pascal records (without variants) to allow field names to be integers, and modified the selection of fields to allow integer field names to be computed, so that, e.g., R.(I + 2) could be used to select a component.

(a) Explain why the storage representation of Sec. 4-6 would no longer be adequate.

(b) Modify the storage representation so that it would work, and give the accessing formula (or algorithm) to be used with the new representation to select a component R.K, where K is a computed value.

12. Repeat Problem 11, but allow records *with variants*.

13. For a language that allows variant records without tag fields (free-union types) such as Pascal, write a procedure

procedure GIGO(I: integer; **var** R: real;)

that uses a record with two variants whose only purpose is to compromise the type-checking system. GIGO takes an argument I of type *integer* and returns the same bit pattern as a result R of type *real*, without actually converting the value of I to a real number.

14. Consider a substring selection operation, ⟨*string variable*⟩(⟨*first char. posn.*⟩: ⟨*last char. posn.*⟩), such as described in Sec. 4-7. Give two different possible

definitions for the meaning of this selection operation when used as both the source and object in an assignment such as

$$STR(I{:}J) := STR(K{:}L)$$

where the selected substrings may overlap.

15. *Concatenation* is a central operation on character strings.

   (a) Assuming the representation of Fig. 4-9 for character strings of variable length with a declared bound, design a concatenation operation CAT1. CAT1 is called with three parameters A, B, and C. A and B are pointers to the two storage blocks containing the strings to be concatenated, and C is the receiving block, which initially contains some other character string. The string composed of the characters of string B concatenated to the characters of string A is to be stored in block C (with the appropriate descriptor, of course). Blocks A and B are to be unchanged by the operation.
   (b) Strings without a declared bound may also be stored sequentially using the same storage representation, with the maximum length deleted from the descriptor. Design an appropriate storage structure assuming that characters may be packed four per word. Then design the concatenation operation CAT2. CAT2 has two parameters, A and B, representing the strings to be concatenated, and returns a pointer to a new block of storage containing the concatenated strings. Assume that CAT2 calls a function ALLOCATE(N) that returns a pointer to a newly allocated block of N words of storage.
   (c) Design CAT3, a routine that concatenates strings represented as linked lists in the manner of Fig. 4-9.

16. In studying the preliminary design of language BL you note that BL includes a stack data structure and three operations:

   1. NEW-TOP(S,E), which adds the element E to the top of stack S,
   2. POP-TOP(S), which deletes the top element of stack S, and
   3. GET-TOP(S), which returns a pointer to the location in stack S of the current top element.

   What is wrong with the design of these three operations? How could they be redefined to correct the problem?

17. A property list might be represented as a set rather than a list because elements are accessed randomly by subscript rather than sequentially. Design a storage representation for property lists using the technique of Sec. 4-10.

18. In SNOBOL4 a property list, or *table* in SNOBOL4 terminology, is created by a statement such as

$$X = TABLE(50{,}20)$$

Tables are stored using a mixed sequential and linked representation. An initial block big enough for 50 subscript-value pairs is set up by the statement above, and a pointer to the block is assigned as the value of X. Subscript-value pairs are entered into the table by an assignment such as

$$X[AGE] = 52$$

which enters the pair (AGE,52) into the table if the subscript AGE is not already present. If AGE is found, then its value is changed to 52. When 50 pairs have been entered into the initially allocated block, a new block big enough for 20 pairs (the second parameter in the call to the TABLE function) is allocated and linked to the first block. New pairs are now put in the new block until it is full, at which time another block for 20 pairs is allocated. Deletion of a pair is not allowed. Design a detailed storage structure appropriate for such tables, including run-time descriptor, and then give an algorithm for execution of the assignment given above on an arbitrary table.

19. For a language that provides a *pointer* type for programmer-constructed data objects and operations such as NEW and DISPOSE that allocate and free storage for data objects, write a program segment that generates *garbage* (in the storage management sense). Write a program segment that generates a *dangling reference*. If one or the other program segment cannot be written, explain why.

20. In hash-coding methods for set storage, both the rehashing and sequential-scan techniques for handling collisions encounter difficulties if deletions from the set are allowed. Explain the difficulties encountered.

21. In many SNOBOL4 implementations the set of character strings that exist at any point during program execution is kept in a *central strings table*. This table is organized as a hash table in which each entry is a pointer to a linked bucket list. A *double-hashing* scheme is used to test for membership of a given string X in the set. X is hashed twice to produce both a hash address, which is used to index the central table to obtain a pointer to the appropriate bucket, and a *bucket order number*. Each entry on a bucket list is composed of a bucket order number and a pointer to a string. Entries on a given bucket list are ordered by bucket order number. To determine if X is stored in the bucket designated by its hash address, the bucket is searched, matching X's bucket order number against those in the bucket list until either a match is found or a bucket order number greater than that of X is found. In the latter case X is immediately inserted in the list, and otherwise a character-by-character match of X with any other strings in the list with the same bucket order number is required. Program this double-hashing scheme, assuming that strings are stored in sequential blocks with a length descriptor. The function coded would accept a pointer to a string as input, look up the string in the table, enter it if it were not found, and return the address of the old entry if found and the address of the new entry if not.

22. File input and end-of-file tests are usually done in advance of the need for the data or for the result of the test because input is done through a buffer in blocks, as shown in Fig. 4-11. An alternative, *lazy input*, is more appropriate with interactive input-output: neither input of data nor an end-of-file test is ever performed until required by the program being executed. Design a READ operation and an END-OF-FILE test for lazy input from an interactive file. The user should be able to input several values at once when input is requested, so a buffer may still be needed.

23. Some computers have been constructed with hardware data descriptors and hardware-supported type checking. Survey the use of hardware data descriptors (two good starting points are the book by Myers [1981] and the paper by Feustal [1973]). Of the different data structure types described in this chapter, how many have been implemented directly in hardware or with extensive hardware support?

CHAPTER 5

Subprograms
and Programmer-defined
Data Types

In the construction of large programs, the programmer is almost inevitably concerned with the design and implementation of new data types, although the term is seldom used explicitly. For example, in constructing a program to generate registration assignments and class rolls for a university, one of the early steps in the design might be to define a type of data object that represents a single "section" of a course. Certain information would be stored in such a data object: the instructor's name, room assignment, maximum enrollment, and so on. These might be considered the attributes of the data type "section" because they would not be expected to change over the lifetime of such a data object. A section would also contain a list of the students enrolled, which might be considered the components of the data object. A particular data object of this type would represent a particular class section, with values assigned for each attribute and for the current student list. A set of operations would then be defined to provide the basic manipulations of such "section" data objects: create a new section, assign a student to a section, destroy a section, and so on. All of this design activity might properly be considered as designing the *specification* of the *abstract data type* "section"—i.e., designing the attributes and operations required.

Implementation of the "section" data type comes at a later step in constructing the program. A particular representation for section data objects must be chosen, using the data types provided by the language (or perhaps using other abstract data types such as a type "student," a type "instructor," etc.). Thus the instructor's name might be implemented as a character string of 10 characters or less, or as an integer (the identification number of the instructor), while the student roll list might be represented as a linear array of integers (student identification numbers). Once this representation for "section" data objects is defined, the operations on sections may be implemented as subprograms whose arguments represent such data objects.

Programmers who are designing and coding other parts of the larger program now may use the "section" data type. That is, they may use the defined representation and subprograms to create and manipulate "sections" using the specification given for the subprograms, without much concern with exactly how sections are implemented. For these programmers the effect is similar to the addition of a new data type to the language. The base language provides a primitive type *integer* and operations on integers that effectively make it unnecessary for the programmer to concern himself with the details of the underlying representation of integers as bit sequences. Now there exist a higher-level type *section* and a set of operations on sections that make it unnecessary for the programmer to be concerned with the details of the implementation of sections as arrays, records, character strings, and the like.

Because this construction of new data types is a pervasive part of the programming process, the facilities a language provides to support these activities are important. Earlier languages, such as FORTRAN and COBOL, provide support primarily through subprogram definition facilities that allow new operations to be defined. As the concept of data type has evolved, new language designs have provided better facilities for specifying and implementing entire abstract data types.

5-1   EVOLUTION OF THE DATA TYPE CONCEPT

The evolution of the concept of *data type* was a major development in programming languages in the 1970s. In older languages such as FORTRAN and COBOL we see the beginnings of the concept. Where hardware computers ordinarily include no provision for defining and enforcing data type restrictions (e.g., real arithmetic on bit strings representing character or integer data is usually allowed), these higher-level languages provide a set of basic data types, such as *real*, *integer*, and *character string*. Type checking is provided to insure that operations such as arithmetic are not applied to data of the wrong type. The early notion of data type centers around the idea that a data type defines a *set of values* that a variable might take on. Data types in these older languages are always associated directly with individual variables, so that each declaration names a variable and defines its type. If a program uses several arrays, each containing 20 real numbers, each array is declared separately and the entire array description is repeated for each.

The next step in evolution of the type concept is seen in Pascal. Separate *type definitions* may be made that define the structure of a set of data objects and the possible value bindings. To get a particular data object of the defined type, a declaration requires only the variable name and the name of the type to be given, rather than a complete redefinition of the type. Here, a data type defines a *set of data objects* and their possible value bindings.

The final step in this evolution lies in understanding that a data type includes not just a *set of data objects*, but also a *set of operations* that manipulate those data objects. For primitive types such as *real* and *integer*, a language provides not only the facility to declare variables of that type, but also a set of operations on reals and integers that represent the *only way* that reals and integers can be manipulated by the programmer. Thus the storage representation of reals and integers is effectively *encapsulated*; that is, it is hidden from the programmer. The programmer may use real and integer data objects without knowing exactly how they are represented in storage. All the programmer sees is the name of the type and the list of operations available for manipulating data objects of that type. For the programmer, these types are true data abstractions, but abstractions provided directly by the language.

In this deeper understanding of the primitive data types provided in older languages we see the basis for language facilities to allow a programmer to define data types such as the type *section* described above. The language needs to allow the definition of the type to include: (1) a name for the type, (2) the storage representation for data objects of the type, and (3) a set of operations (subprograms) for manipulating data objects of the type that represent the *only* operations that can directly manipulate the storage representation of data objects of the type. The entire definition should be encapsulated in such a way that the user of the type needs to know only the type name and the list of available operations. This evolution leads to the concept of *abstract data type*, as embodied, for example, in the Ada *package* facility. Since both subprograms and type definitions play a role in programmer-defined data types, and both are found separately in older languages, we take up these topics individually first. The complete concept of abstract data type is treated in the final section of this chapter.

5-2 ABSTRACTION, ENCAPSULATION, AND INFORMATION HIDING

To understand the design of language facilities for programmer-defined operations and data types, it is important to understand the problems that these facilities are designed to solve. The central problem is that of *abstraction*. A large program, or even one of moderate size, when all its details are considered at once, easily exceeds the intellectual grasp of a single person. To construct a large program, a form of "divide and conquer" must be used: the program is divided into a set of pieces, often called *modules*, each of which may be viewed from the other modules as a simple abstraction. The data type "section" described above is exactly such an abstraction—the specification of the data type is all that must be understood to make use of it; the implementation details are hidden and can be ignored. Thus the programmer designing the overall strategy for assigning students to sections in the program can forget about exactly how sections are implemented and remember only that students can be assigned to sections, sections have instructors and room numbers, and so on.

Abstraction is so pervasive in programming activities that it often goes without notice. The layering of software and hardware described in Chapter 2 is another example of abstraction. A flow chart is an abstraction of the statement-level control structure of a program. Methods for designing programs, given various names such as *stepwise refinement, structured programming, modular programming*, and *top-down programming*, are concerned with the design of abstractions.

A programming language provides support for abstraction in two ways. First, by providing a virtual computer that is simpler to use and more powerful than the actual underlying hardware computer, the language directly supplies a useful set of abstractions that we think of as the "features" of the language. Second, the language provides facilities that aid the programmer in constructing his own abstractions, the abstractions that together form the virtual computer defined by a particular program. Subprograms, subprogram libraries, type definitions, and packages are some of the facilities provided by different languages to support programmer-defined abstractions.

Information hiding is the term used for one of the central principles in the design of programmer-defined abstractions such as subprograms and new data types: each such program component should hide as much information as possible from the users of the component. Thus the language-provided square-root function is a successful abstract operation because it hides the details of the number representation and the square-root computation algorithm from the user. Similarly a programmer-defined data type such as the "section" type described above is a successful abstraction if it may be used without knowledge of the representation of "sections" or of the algorithms used by the operations on "sections."

When information is *encapsulated* in an abstraction it means that the user of the abstraction:

a. *Does not need to know* the hidden information in order to use the abstraction and

b. *Is not permitted* to directly use or manipulate the hidden information even if he wishes.

For example, the integer data type in a programming language such as FORTRAN or Pascal not only hides the details of the integer number representation, but also effectively encapsulates the representation so that the programmer cannot manipulate individual bits of the representation of an integer (except by use of flaws in the encapsulation mechanism of the language to get "illegal" access to the bits). It is much more difficult for the user of FORTRAN or Pascal to encapsulate the representation of the new data type "section" described above. Although a set of subprograms can be constructed that allow sections to be created and manipulated as abstractions in those languages (thus giving information hiding), it is impossible to encapsulate the data representation used for sections so that the user of the abstraction cannot write another subprogram that will manipulate sections in improper ways. For example, if the student roll list is represented as a linear array of integers, a subprogram could be written that would add 3 to each integer in the array. Such an operation is meaningless in terms of the abstraction, where the integers represent student identification numbers, but it is perfectly valid in terms of the particular data representations used.

Encapsulation is particularly important in its effect on the ease of modification of a program. If the "section" data type were encapsulated, then we could modify the representation of sections at any time by simply modifying the subprograms that manipulate sections so that they work with the new representation instead of the old. However, if not encapsulated, then subprograms may exist in other parts of the program that presume a particular representation for sections. Any change in the representation will invalidate those other subprograms. Often it is difficult to determine which subprograms are dependent on a particular representation for data objects if there is no encapsulation, and thus changes in a data representation give rise to subtle errors in other parts of the program that seemingly should not be affected by the change.

Subprograms form a basic encapsulation mechanism that is present in almost every language. Mechanisms that allow encapsulation of entire data type definitions are more recent and, of the languages presented here, appear only in Ada. Note that information hiding is primarily a question of *program design*; information hiding is possible in any program that is properly designed, regardless of the programming language used. Encapsulation, however, is primarily a question of *language design*; an abstraction is effectively encapsulated only when the language prohibits access to the information hidden within the abstraction.

5-3 SUBPROGRAMS

A subprogram is an abstract operation defined by the programmer. Subprograms form the basic building block out of which most programs are constructed, and facilities for their definition and invocation are found in almost every language. Two views of subprograms are important here. At the *program design* level, we may ask about the sense in which a subprogram represents an abstract operation that the programmer defines, as opposed to the primitive operations that are built into the language. At the *language design* level, the concern is with the design and implementation of the general facilities for subprogram definition and invocation. Although the views overlap, it is helpful to take them up separately.

Subprograms as Abstract Operations

A subprogram definition has two parts, a *specification* and an *implementation*, just as does a primitive operation. However, for a subprogram both parts are provided by the programmer when the subprogram is defined.

Specification of a subprogram. Since a subprogram represents an abstract operation, we should be able to understand its specification without understanding how it is implemented. The specification for a subprogram is the same as that for a primitive operation. It includes:

1. The *name* of the subprogram.

2. The number of *arguments*, their order, and the data type of each.

3. The number of *results*, their order, and the data type of each.

4. The *action* performed by the subprogram—i.e., a description of the function it computes.

A subprogram represents a mathematical function that maps each particular set of arguments into a particular set of results. If a subprogram returns a single result data object explicitly, it is usually termed a *function subprogram* (or simply, *function*), and a typical syntax for its specification is the Pascal:

function FN(X: real; Y: integer): real

which specifies a function:

FN: real × integer → real

Note that the specification also includes the names X and Y by which the arguments may be referenced within the subprogram; these *formal parameters* and the general topic of transmission of parameters to a subprogram are taken up in Chapter 7.

If a subprogram returns more than one result, or if it modifies its arguments rather than returning results explicitly, then it is usually termed a *procedure* or *subroutine*, and a typical syntax for its specification is the Pascal:

procedure SUB(X: real; Y: integer; **var** Z: real; **var** U: Boolean);

In this specification, a formal parameter name preceded by **var** may indicate a result or an argument that may be modified. The syntax in Ada for this specification clarifies these distinctions:

procedure SUB(X: **in** REAL; Y: **in** INTEGER;
Z: **in out** REAL; U: **out** BOOLEAN)

This procedure heading declares a subprogram with the specification:

SUB: $real_1 \times integer \times real_2 \rightarrow real_2 \times Boolean$

The tags **in**, **out**, and **in out** distinguish the three cases as follows: **in** designates an argument that is not modified by the subprogram, **in out** designates an argument that may be modified, and **out** designates a result. These ideas are treated more extensively in Chapter 7.

Although a subprogram represents a mathematical function, the same problems arise as for primitive operations in attempting to describe precisely the function computed:

1. A subprogram may have *implicit arguments*, in the form of nonlocal variables that it references (see Chapter 7).

2. A subprogram may have *implicit results* (*side effects*), returned through changes in nonlocal variables or through changes in its in_out arguments.

3. A subprogram may not be defined for some possible arguments, so that it does not complete execution in the ordinary way if given those arguments, but instead transfers control to some external exception handler (Chapter 6) or terminates execution of the entire program abruptly.

4. A subprogram may be *history-sensitive* (self-modifying), so that its results depend on the arguments given over the entire past history of its calls and not just on the arguments given in a single call. History sensitivity may be due to the subprogram's retaining local data between invocations or, less often, through modification of its own code.

Implementation of a subprogram. A *primitive operation* is implemented using the data structures and operations provided by the layer of virtual computer underneath the programming language. A *subprogram* represents an operation of the layer constructed by the programmer, and thus a subprogram is implemented using the data structures and operations provided by the programming language itself. The implementation is defined by the subprogram *body*, which consists of *local data declarations* defining the data structures used by the subprogram and *statements* defining the actions to be taken when the subprogram is executed. The declarations and statements are usually encapsulated, so that neither the local data nor the statements are accessible separately to the user of the subprogram; the user may only invoke the subprogram with a particular set of arguments and receive the computed results. The Pascal syntax for the body of a subprogram is typical:

```
function FN(X: real; Y: integer): real;   —specification
    var M: array [1..10] of real;         —declarations of local
        N: integer;                          data objects
    begin
        .                                  —sequence of statements
        .                                     defining the actions
        .                                     of the subprogram
    end;
```

Ordinarily the body may also include definitions of other subprograms that represent programmer-defined operations used only within the larger subprogram. These "local" subprograms are also encapsulated so that they cannot be invoked from outside the larger subprogram.

Type checking is an important issue for subprograms. Each invocation of a subprogram requires arguments of the proper types, as given in the subprogram specification. The types of the results returned by a subprogram must also be known. The type-checking issues are similar to those for primitive operations. Type checking may be performed statically, during translation, if declarations are given for the argument and result types of each subprogram. Alternatively, type checking may be dynamic, during program execution. Coercion of arguments to convert them to the proper types may also be provided automatically by the language implementation. These problems and implementation methods are straightforward generalizations of the concepts presented in Chapter 3 for primitive operations. The major difference comes from the need for the programmer to explicitly declare information about argument and result types that is implicit for primitive operations. Once this information is provided, however, the type-checking problems are treated similarly.

Language Structures for Subprogram Definition and Invocation

The design of facilities for subprogram definition and invocation is a central problem, perhaps even *the* central problem, in the design of most languages. Much of the overall implementation structure is determined by the subprogram structure in the language. Because of the importance and complexity of the topics surrounding subprograms, this and the following several chapters treat different aspects of subprogram design. Some general concepts are taken up here. In the next chapter we consider various sequence-control structures that might be used to control how subprograms are invoked for execution. In Chapter 7 we consider methods for giving subprograms access to data on which to operate. Chapter 8 considers how the various design decisions about subprogram structure affect the overall storage management structure for the language implementation. Finally, some topics concerning translation of subprograms are treated in Chapter 9.

Subprogram definitions and subprogram activations. A programmer writes a subprogram *definition* in a program. During execution of the program, if the subprogram is called, an *activation* of the subprogram is created. When execution of the subprogram is complete, the activation is destroyed. If another call is made, a new activation is created. Thus from a single subprogram definition, many activations may be created during program execution. The definition serves as a *template* for creating activations during execution.

The distinction between definitions and activations of subprograms is important. Note that a definition is what is present in the program as written, and thus it is the definition that is available during translation. Subprogram activations exist only during program execution. During execution, the definition exists only in the form of a template from which activations may be created.

The distinction between definition and activation for subprograms is quite similar to the distinction between a type definition and a data object of that type, as taken up in the next section. The type definition is used as a template to determine the size and structure of the data objects of that type. However, the data objects themselves usually are created during execution, either when a subprogram is entered or on execution of a creation operation such as NEW. The use of NEW to create new data objects as needed during program execution corresponds to the use of CALL to create new subprogram activations as needed. In fact, a subprogram activation *is* a type of data object. It is represented as a block of storage that contains certain component data items relevant to the subprogram activation. Storage must be allocated when it is created, and storage is freed when it is destroyed. An activation has a *lifetime*, the time during execution between the CALL that creates it and the RETURN that destroys it. However, there are concepts surrounding subprogram activations that have no direct analog for other data objects—e.g., the concept of *executing* an activation and the concept of referencing and modifying other data objects during this execution. Because of these differences, and because intuitively a strong distinction is made in most languages between subprograms and other data objects, the term *data object* is not used here to refer to a subprogram activation.

Implementation of subprogram definition and invocation. Consider again a subprogram definition, as it might appear in Pascal:

```
function FN(X: real; Y: integer): real;
    const MAX = 20;
    var M: array [1..MAX] of real;
        N: integer;
begin
    .
    .
    .
    N := MAX;
    X := 2 * X + M[5];
    .
    .
    .
end;
```

This definition defines the components needed for an activation of the subprogram at run time:

1. Storage for *parameters*, the data objects X and Y.

2. Storage for the *function result*, a data object of type *real*.

3. Storage for *local variables*, the array M and variable N.

4. Storage for *literals* and *defined constants*, the constants 20, 2, and 5.

5. Storage for the *executable code* generated from the statements in the subprogram body.

The definition of the subprogram allows these storage areas to be organized and the executable code determined during translation. The result from translation is the template used to construct each particular activation at the time the subprogram is called during execution. Figure 5-1 shows the subprogram definition as translated into a run-time template.

To construct a particular activation of the subprogram from its template, the entire template might be copied into a new area of memory. However, rather than making a complete copy, it is far better to split the template into two parts:

1. A static part, called the *code segment*, consisting of items 4 (constants) and 5 (executable code) above. This part is invariant during execution of the subprogram, and thus a single copy may be shared by all activations.

2. A dynamic part, called an *activation record*, consisting of items 1 (parameters), 2 (function result), and 3 (local data) above, plus various other items of implementation-defined "housekeeping" data such as temporary storage areas, return points, and linkages for referencing nonlocal variables (discussed in Chapters 6-8). This part has the same structure for each

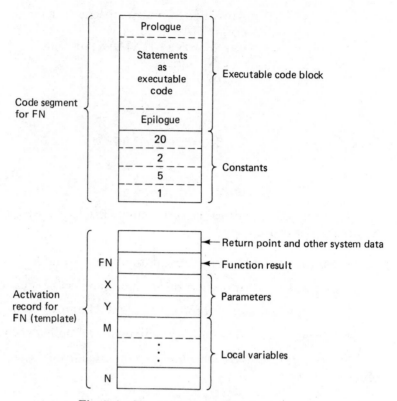

Fig. 5-1 Structure of a subprogram activation

activation, but it contains different data values. Thus each activation necessarily has its own copy of the activation record part.

The resulting structure during execution is shown in Fig. 5-2. For each subprogram, a single code segment exists in storage throughout program execution. Activation records are dynamically created and destroyed during execution each time the subprogram is called and each time it terminates an activation with a return. This dynamic creation and destruction of activation records has a major impact on the overall storage management structure of the language implementation, as discussed in Chapters 6 and 8.

The size and structure of the activation record required for a subprogram can ordinarily be determined during translation; that is, the compiler (or translator) can determine how large the activation record needs to be, and the position of each component within it. Access to the components may then be made using the base-address-plus-offset calculation, as described in Sec. 4-6 for ordinary record data objects. For this reason, an activation record is in fact ordinarily represented in storage just as any other record data object. To create a new activation record requires

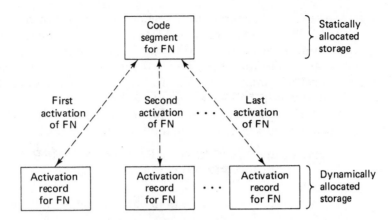

Fig. 5-2 Shared code segment, separate activation records on different calls of a subprogram

only that the *size* of the record storage block be known, rather than its detailed internal structure (since the offsets into the block are already computed during translation, and only the base address is needed to complete the accessing calculation during execution). Thus, rather than storing a complete activation record template at run time, usually only the size of the activation record must be stored for use by the CALL operation in creating an activation record. Storage management on subprogram call and return involves only allocation of a block of the appropriate size when a subprogram is called, and freeing of the block on return.

When a subprogram is called, a number of hidden actions take place that are concerned with the setting up of the activation record, the transmission of parameters, the creation of linkages for nonlocal referencing, and similar "housekeeping" activities. These actions must take place before the actual code for the statements in the body of the subprogram is executed. Commonly the translator inserts a block of code to perform these actions, called the *prologue*, at the start of the executable code block for the subprogram. On termination of a subprogram a similar set of housekeeping actions are required to return results and free the storage for the activation record. An *epilogue* is a set of instructions inserted by the translator at the end of the executable code block to perform these actions. Thus prologue and epilogue instructions for a subprogram usually handle much of the detail involved with subprogram call and return operations. Further details are found in each of the next three chapters.

Generic Subprograms

The specification of a subprogram ordinarily lists the number, order, and data types of the arguments. A *generic subprogram* is one with a single name but several different definitions, distinguished by different numbers, orders, or types of arguments. A generic subprogram name is said to be *overloaded*. The general concepts of a generic operation and an overloaded operation name are treated in Chapter 3 in relation to primitive operations. Subprograms may also be generic in the same manner. For example, in writing a set of subprograms for a university class registration program, two routines might be needed, one to enter a "section" in a table of class sections, and another to enter a "student" in a class roll for a "section." Both subprograms might be defined using the name ENTER:

```
procedure ENTER(STUDENT: in INTEGER; SECT:
       in out SECTION) is
   begin
           —statements to enter student in a section
              roll list
   end;
procedure ENTER(S: in SECTION; TAB:
       in out CLASSLIST) is
   begin
           —statements to enter a section in a classlist
   end;
```

The name ENTER is overloaded and has become the name of a generic ENTER subprogram. When a call to ENTER is made:

ENTER(A,B);

the translator must resolve the ambiguity by comparing the types of the arguments A and B with the specified types for the first and second parameters of each definition of a subprogram named ENTER. In this case if A is of type *integer*, then the call is a call on the first definition of the ENTER subprogram, and if A is of type *section*, then it is a call on the second. Since this resolution is made during translation, in a language such as Ada or PL/I, there is no effect on the run-time organization of the language. Once the overloading is resolved, translation of the subprogram call proceeds as for any other subprogram call. Generic subprograms thus introduce no major change in the language implementation beyond some extra complexity in the early phases of translation.

Subprogram Definitions as Data Objects

In most compiled languages, such as FORTRAN and Pascal, subprogram definitions are processed into their run-time form by the compiler. During execution the static part of the subprogram definition is both inaccessible and invisible to the programmer. However, in languages such as LISP and SNOBOL4 (which are usually implemented by software interpreters), it is common to provide some facilities that allow subprogram *definitions* to be treated as run-time data objects in themselves.

Translation is an operation that takes a subprogram definition in the form of a character string and produces the run-time data object representing the definition. *Execution* is an operation that takes a definition in run-time form, creates an activation from it, and executes the activation. The execution operation is invoked by the usual CALL primitive, but the translation operation is often considered a separate *meta-operation* that takes place for all subprograms before the execution of the overall program begins. In both LISP and SNOBOL4, however, translation is also an operation that may be invoked at *run time* on a character-string data object to produce the executable form of a subprogram body. Both languages also provide an operation DEFINE that takes a subprogram body and specification and produces a complete callable subprogram definition.

Thus in both languages it is possible to begin program execution without having a particular subprogram in existence. During execution, the subprogram body may be read in or created as a character-string data object and then translated into executable form. The DEFINE operation may then be used to provide a name and define parameters for the body so that a complete definition results. Subsequently the subprogram may be called as needed. Later the definition of the subprogram may be modified (in LISP by directly manipulating the executable form of the subprogram body; in SNOBOL4 by manipulating the character-string representation and retranslating to get a new body for the subprogram). Subprogram definitions thus become true data objects in these languages.

5-4   TYPE DEFINITIONS

For the programmer to be able to define a complete new abstract data type, some mechanism is required for definition of a class of data objects. In newer languages such as Pascal and Ada this mechanism is termed a *type definition* (but note that a type definition does not define a complete abstract data type, because it does not include definition of the *operations* on data of that type).

In a type definition, a *type name* is given, together with a declaration that describes the structure of a class of data objects. The type name then becomes the name for that class of data objects, and when a particular data object of that structure is needed, we need give only the type name, rather than repeating the complete description of the data structure. In Pascal, for example, if several vectors, A, B, and C are needed, each of which has the same structure, then the program may contain the type definition:

type REALVECT = **array** [1..10] **of** real;

followed by the declarations:

$$\textbf{var } A: REALVECT;$$
$$\vdots$$
$$B,C: REALVECT;$$
$$\vdots$$

so that the definition of the structure of a data object of type REALVECT is given only once rather than being repeated three times for each of A, B, and C.

Besides simplifying program structure, type definitions have other advantages for the programmer. Should the structure of a REALVECT need to be modified, the use of a type definition allows the modification to be made only to the single type definition, rather than to many separate instances of declarations of individual variables. Also, if a data object is transmitted as an argument to a subprogram, the subprogram definition must usually include a description of the argument. Here again, rather than repeating the entire structure description, we need use only the type name.

A type definition is used as a *template* to construct data objects during program execution. A data object of the type may be created on entry to a subprogram (if a declaration for a variable of that type is included among the local data declarations for the subprogram) or it may be created dynamically through use of a creation operation such as the NEW operation discussed in Sec. 4-9, with subsequent access through pointer variables. In its role as a template a type definition is quite similar to a subprogram definition, as described in the preceding section.

Type definitions allow the separation of the definition of the *structure* of a data object from the definition of the points during execution at which data objects of that structure are to be *created*. However, note also that we have, potentially, a new form of *encapsulation* and *information hiding*. A subprogram may declare a variable to be of a particular type by simply using the type name. The type definition effectively hides the internal structure of data objects of that type. If a subprogram only creates objects of the type, using the type name, but never accesses the internal components of the data objects, then the subprogram becomes independent of the particular structure declared in the type definition. The type definition may be modified without changing the subprogram. If the language design enforces the restriction, so that only a few designated subprograms can access the internal components of the data objects, then the type definition has effectively encapsulated the structure of data objects of the type. In the next section we consider how this encapsulation allows construction of a complete programmer-defined abstract data type.

Implementation

As we saw in the preceding chapters, the information contained in the declaration of a variable is used primarily during translation, to determine the storage representation for the data object, and for storage management and type-checking purposes. Declarations themselves are not present at run time; they are used only to set up the appropriate run-time data objects. A type definition, similarly, is used only during translation. The language translator enters the information from a type definition into a table during translation and, whenever the type name is referenced in a subsequent declaration, uses the tabled information to produce the appropriate executable code for setting up and manipulating the desired data objects during execution. The type definition allows some aspects of translation, such as determining storage representations, to be done only once for a single type definition rather than many times for different declarations. However, inclusion of type definitions in a language does not ordinarily change the run-time organization of the language implementation.

Equivalence of Defined Types

Type checking, whether static or dynamic, involves a comparison between the data type of the actual argument given to an operation and the data type of the argument that is expected by the operation. If the types are the same, then the argument is accepted and the operation proceeds; if different, then either it is considered an error or a coercion is used to convert the type of the argument to match that expected.

What does it mean to say that two types are "the same"? This is a subtle question that we have ignored when dealing with primitive data types such as integers or arrays (although the question is present with primitive types). Type definitions allow the question to be raised directly in a form that must be answered if a language is to have a clear definition.

Consider the following type definitions and declarations:

```
type VECT1: array [1..10] of real;
     VECT2: array [1..10] of real;
var X,Z: VECT1;
    Y: VECT2;
procedure SUB(A: VECT1);
    :
    :
end;        —of procedure SUB
```

    begin   —main program

             .
             .
             .

             X: = Y;
             SUB(Y);

             .
             .
             .

    end.   —of main program

The question is whether variables X and Y and Y and A have the same type, so that the assignment X := Y and the procedure invocation SUB(Y) are considered correct, or whether they have different types, so that the use of Y as an argument in either case is invalid.

There are two general solutions to this problem: name equivalence and structural equivalence.

Name equivalence. Two data types are considered equivalent only if they have the same name. Thus types VECT1 and VECT2 above are different types, even though the defined data objects have the same structure. An assignment X := Z is valid, but X := Y is not. Name equivalence of types is the method used in Ada and for subprogram parameters in Pascal (although not for other cases in Pascal).

Name equivalence has the disadvantages:

1. Every type must have a name; there can be no *anonymous types*, such as in the direct declaration:

    var W: **array** [1..10] **of** real;

Variable *W* is of a distinct type, but the type has no name. Thus *W* cannot be used as an argument to an operation that requires an argument of a particular named type.

2. A single type definition must serve all or large parts of a program, since the type of a data object transmitted as an argument through a chain of subprograms cannot be defined again in each subprogram; the single "global" type definition must be used.

Structural equivalence. Two data types are considered equivalent if they define data objects that have the same *internal structure*. Usually "the same internal structure" means that the same storage representation may be used for both classes of data objects. For example, VECT1 and VECT2 are equivalent types under this definition because each data object of type VECT1 and each data object of type VECT2 have exactly the same number of components of equivalent types. The storage representation for data objects of either type is the same, so that the same accessing formulas can be used to select components, and in general the run-time implementation of the data types is identical.

Structural equivalence does not have the disadvantages of name equivalence, but it has its own set of problems:

1. Several subtle questions arise as to when two types are structurally equivalent. For example, for records, must the component names be identical, or does it suffice to have the same number of components and type of components in the same order; if record component names must be identical, then must the components be in the same order; must array subscript ranges be identical, or is it sufficient to have the same number of components; must the literals in two enumeration types be the same and in the same order?

2. Two variables may inadvertently be structurally equivalent, even though the programmer declares them as separate types, as in the simple example:

type METERS = integer;
LITERS = integer;
var LEN: METERS;
VOL: LITERS;

Variables LEN and VOL have structurally equivalent types, and thus an error such as computing LEN + VOL would not be detected by static type checking. Where several programmers are working on a program, inadvertent type equivalence may destroy much of what is gained from static type checking, since many type errors may go undetected.

3. Determining whether two complex type definitions are structurally equivalent, if done frequently, may be a costly part of translation.

The issues involved in the choice of a definition of type equivalence are important in the design of newer languages, such as Ada and Pascal, where type definitions play a central role. In older languages, such as FORTRAN, COBOL, and PL/I, there are no type definitions, and thus some form of structural equivalence of types is used. The Pascal design raises the issues but does not consistently use either method. The Ada design consistently uses name equivalence, but the issue is still considered a research question (see the references and problems at the end of this chapter).

Type Definitions with Parameters

Where many similar type definitions must be made, it is often useful to have a way to make a single "parameterized" type definition that can be used repeatedly with different substitutions for the parameters, without rewriting it each time. For example, suppose we wish to define a type SECTION as a record, as in the Ada definition:

type SECTION **is**
    record
        ROOM: INTEGER;
        INSTRUCTOR: INTEGER;
        CLASS_SIZE: INTEGER **range** 0..100;
        CLASS_ROLL: **array** (1..100) **of** STUDENT_ID;
    end record;

Note the problem: this definition of SECTION defines a section of maximum size 100; to get sections of any other maximum size requires another type definition.

A parameterized type definition for SECTION allows the type definition to have a MAX_SIZE parameter that determines the maximum class size:

type SECTION(MAX_SIZE: **integer**) **is**
    record
        ROOM: INTEGER;
        INSTRUCTOR: INTEGER;
        CLASS_SIZE: INTEGER **range** 0..MAX_SIZE;
        CLASS_ROLL: **array** (1..MAX_SIZE) **of** STUDENT_ID;
    end record;

With this type definition, the maximum class size may be declared as part of the declaration of each individual variable:

        X: SECTION(100)   —gives maximum size 100
        Y: SECTION(25)   —gives maximum size 25

Type definitions with parameters are used as templates during compilation, just as any other type definition, except that when the compiler translates a declaration of a variable with a parameter list following the type name (as SECTION(100) above), the compiler first fills in the parameter value in the type definition to get a complete type definition without parameters, then processes it just as it would any other type definition. Parameters in type definitions have an effect on the run-time organization of the language implementation in only a few cases, e.g., where a subprogram must accept any data object of the parameterized type as an argument (and thus must be prepared for an argument of possibly different size on each call).

5-5   ABSTRACT DATA TYPES

An *abstract data type* is a new data type defined by the programmer that includes:

1. Definition of a set of *data objects*, ordinarily using one or more type definitions,

2. Definition of a set of *abstract operations* on those data objects, using one or more subprogram definitions to define each abstract operation, and

3. *Encapsulation* of the whole in such a way that the user of the new type cannot manipulate data objects of the type except by use of the operations defined.

Data abstraction—that is, the design of abstract data objects and operations on those objects—is a fundamental part of programming, as discussed at the beginning of this chapter. In a programming language that provides little direct support for data abstraction beyond the ordinary subprogram mechanism, the programmer may still design and use his own abstract data types, but the concept is not present in the language itself. Instead the programmer must use "coding conventions" to organize his program so that the effect of an abstract data type is achieved. Without language support for the definition of abstract data types, however, encapsulation of a new type is not possible. Thus if the coding conventions are violated, whether intentionally or not, the language implementation cannot detect the violation. Such programmer-created abstract data types often appear as special subprogram libraries in languages such as FORTRAN, PL/I, and APL, e.g., a library of subprograms to manipulate "sparse" arrays.

Type definitions, such as are provided by Pascal, make it simpler to declare new variables of the type, since only the type name is needed in the declaration. However, the internal structure of data objects of the type is not encapsulated. Any subprogram that can declare a variable to be of the new type is also allowed to access any component of the representation of the type. Thus any such subprogram may bypass the defined operations on the data objects and instead directly access and manipulate the components of the data objects. The intent of encapsulation of an abstract data type definition is to make such access impossible, so that the only subprograms that know how data objects of the type are represented are the operations defined as part of the type itself.

Of the languages described in Part II, only Ada provides language support for encapsulation of such abstract type definitions. In Ada such an abstract type definition is one form of a *package*. A package defining an abstract data type SECTION_TYPE might take the form shown in Fig. 5-3. The declaration *private* for type SECTION indicates that the internal structure of section data objects is not to be accessible from subprograms using the package. Only subprograms within the package definition have access to the components of sections. Thus, for example, procedures ASSIGN_STUDENT and CREATE_SECTION may access the array

```
package SECTION_TYPE is
    type STUDENT_ID is INTEGER;
    type SECTION(MAX_SIZE: INTEGER) is private;
    procedure ASSIGN_STUDENT(SECT: in out SECTION;
                             STUD: in STUDENT_ID);
    procedure CREATE_SECTION(SECT: in out SECTION;
                             INSTR: in INTEGER;
                             ROOM: in INTEGER);
private
    type SECTION(MAX_SIZE: INTEGER) is
        record
            ROOM: INTEGER;
            INSTRUCTOR: INTEGER;
            CLASS_SIZE: INTEGER range 0 . . MAX_SIZE := 0;
            CLASS_ROLL: array (1 . . MAX_SIZE) of STUDENT_ID;
        end record;
end;

package body SECTION_TYPE is
    procedure ASSIGN_STUDENT( . . . ) is
        —statements to insert student on class_roll
    end;
    procedure CREATE_SECTION( . . . ) is
        —statements to initialize components of SECTION record
    end;
end;
```

Fig. 5-3   Abstract data type SECTION defined as an Ada package

CLASS_ROLL that is one component of a SECTION, but any other procedure (outside the package) cannot access this component, even though the other procedure may declare a variable to be of type SECTION (and specify a maximum class size as a parameter).

Implementation. Abstract data types defined as Ada packages involve few new implementation ideas. In the preceding sections we considered the implementation of type definitions and subprogram definitions. A package provides encapsulation for a set of type definitions and subprograms. Thus its primary new effect is to restrict the visibility of the names declared in the package, so that users of the abstract type cannot gain access to the internal elements of the definition. Issues concerned with the visibility of names are treated in Chapter 7.

Generic Abstract Data Types

The primitive data types built into a language often allow the programmer to declare the basic type of a new class of data objects, and then specify several attributes of the data objects as well. For example, Pascal provides the basic data type *array* on which several primitive operations such as subscripting are defined. However, the type definition:

$$\text{type VECT} = \textbf{array } [1..10] \textbf{ of } real;$$

specifies additional attributes of the class of data objects of type VECT: each has ten components of type real, accessible through the subscripts $1, 2, \ldots,$ 10. Additional subprograms may be written to manipulate VECT data objects, but the operations provided by the base type *array* are still available as well. A similar structure is desirable for the definition of abstract data types. For example, to define a new abstract type *stack* with operations of *push* and *pop* to insert and delete elements in the stack, the stack might be defined as an Ada package as in Fig. 5-4. Note the problem that arises: The type of element in a stack data object is part of the type definition for *stack*, so this definition is for a *stack of integers* data type. A *stack of reals* or a *stack of sections* type requires a separate package definition, even though the representation of the stack and of the PUSH and POP operations may be defined identically.

A *generic abstract type definition* allows such an attribute of the type to be specified separately, so that one base type definition may be given, with the attributes as parameters, and then several specialized types derived from the same base type may be created. The structure is similar to that of a type definition with parameters, as described in the preceding section, except that here the parameters may affect the definition of the operations in the abstract type definition as well as the type definitions themselves, and the parameters may be type names as well as values. The Ada package of Fig. 5-5 shows such a generic type definition for a *generic stack* type in which both the type of element stored in the stack and the maximum size of the stack are defined as parameters.

Instantiation of a generic abstract type definition. A generic package definition represents a *template* that can be used to create particular

```
package INT_STACK_TYPE is
    type STACK(SIZE: POSITIVE) is private;
    procedure PUSH(I: in INTEGER; S: in out STACK);
    procedure POP(I: out INTEGER; S: in out STACK);
private
    type STACK(SIZE: POSITIVE) is
        record
            STK_STORAGE: array (1 . . SIZE) of INTEGER;
            TOP: INTEGER range 0 . . SIZE := 0;
        end record;
end INT_STACK_TYPE;
package body INT_STACK_TYPE is
    procedure PUSH(I: in INTEGER; S: in out STACK) is
        begin
            —body of PUSH procedure
        end;
    procedure POP(I: out INTEGER; S: in out STACK) is
        begin
            —body of POP procedure
        end;
end INT_STACK_TYPE;
```

Fig. 5-4   "Stack of integers" data type defined as an Ada package

```
generic
    type ELEM is private;
packageSTACK_TYPE is
    type STACK(SIZE: POSITIVE) is private;
    procedure PUSH(I: in ELEM; S: in out STACK);
    procedure POP(I: out ELEM; S: in out STACK);
private
    type STACK(SIZE: POSITIVE) is
      record
          STK_STORAGE: array (1 . . SIZE) of ELEM;
          TOP: INTEGER range 0 . . SIZE : = 0;
      end record;
end STACK_TYPE;
package body STACK_TYPE is
    procedure PUSH(I: in ELEM; S: in out STACK) is
      begin
              —body of PUSH, as before
      end;
    procedure POP(I: out ELEM; S: in out STACK) is
      begin
              —body of POP, as before
      end;
end STACK_TYPE;
```

Fig. 5-5   Generic abstract type "stack" defined as an Ada package

abstract data types. The process of creating the particular type definition from the generic definition for a given set of parameters is called *instantiation*. For example, given the Ada generic stack type definition in Fig. 5-5, it may be instantiated to produce a definition of the INT_STACK type equivalent to that in Fig. 5-4 by the declaration:

> **package** INT_STACK_TYPE **is**
> **new** STACK_TYPE(ELEM => INTEGER);

A stack data type containing "sections" may be defined by the instantiation:

> **package** SECT_STACK_TYPE **is**
> **new** STACK_TYPE(ELEM => SECTION);

Subsequently integer stacks of different sizes may be delcared:

> STK1: INT_STACK_TYPE.STACK(100);
> NEW_STK: INT_STACK_TYPE.STACK(20);

and similarly, section stacks may be declared

> SS_STACK: SECT_STACK_TYPE.STACK(10);

Note that the generic type STACK_TYPE may be instantiated many times for many different values of the parameters, and each instantiation produces another definition for the type name STACK within the package. Thus when STACK is referenced in a declaration, it may be ambiguous. Ada requires that the package name precede the type name in the declaration in order to resolve the ambiguity, e.g., INT_STACK_TYPE.STACK or SECT_STACK_TYPE.STACK.

Implementation. A generic abstract data type, in principle, usually has a straightforward implementation. The parameters to the generic package must be given in the program when the package definition is instantiated. The compiler uses the generic package definition as a template, inserts the specified values for the parameters, and then compiles the definition just as though it were an ordinary package definition without parameters. During program execution, only data objects and subprograms appear; the package definition serves primarily as a device to restrict the visibility of these data objects and subprograms. The package itself does not appear as a part of the run-time structure.

If a generic type definition is instantiated many times (as might happen, for example, if the generic package were provided in a library), then this straightforward implementation may be too inefficient, because the instantiation produces a copy of the entire package, including all the subprograms defined in the package, which must then be completely recompiled. A better implementation would avoid the generation of a new copy of each subprogram and would also avoid the complete recompilation of the entire package. The best methods for doing this are still a subject for research.

5-6 REFERENCES AND SUGGESTIONS FOR FURTHER READING

Three important papers raising the problems of abstraction and information hiding as central concerns in programming are those by Dijkstra [1972a], Hoare [1972], and Parnas [1972]. Welsh, Sneeringer, and Hoare [1977] develop the notions of type equivalence in a critique of the Pascal design.

The definition and implementation of various forms of abstract data types are the subject of many papers. Several experimental languages have included such facilities, e.g., CLU (Liskov et al. [1977]), EUCLID (Lampson et al. [1977]), and ALPHARD (Shaw et al. [1977]). There is much more to both the design and implementation of such data abstraction facilities than we have mentioned here. The *Ada Rationale* (Ichbiah et al. [1979]) is useful as an introduction to these issues. Wasserman [1980] and Yeh [1978, Vol. IV] have collected selections of papers that treat many of these issues.

5-7 PROBLEMS

1. For a language with which you are familiar, consider how effective its encapsulation of each primitive data type is by trying to determine how many properties of the storage representations of data objects of that type can be determined by writing test programs. For example:

(a) *Arrays*. Can you determine whether arrays are stored in row-major or column-major order? Can you determine if there is a run-time descriptor, and its contents and format?

(b) *Records*. Can you determine the order in which components of the record are stored, and whether components are packed or aligned on storage-unit boundaries?

2. In a language of your choice, attempt to define an abstract data type *stack of integers* and the operations of PUSH and POP that insert and delete elements in a stack. Suppose you are part of a programming group that will use stacks of integers in many places in constructing a large program. Explain how your abstract data type may be most effectively set up in the language (using a combination of language-provided protections and "coding conventions" that the group must follow when working with stacks) so that the storage representation of stacks is hidden and is manipulated only by your PUSH and POP operations.

3. For a program you have written recently, give a complete specification of the arguments and results of each subprogram. Be sure to include implicit arguments and results in the specifications. Are any of the subprograms history-sensitive? What makes them so? Are any of them undefined for some arguments in the domain you specified? Explain. List at least one piece of information that is *hidden* by each subprogram.

4. A subprogram that is compiled into a separate code segment and activation record is sometimes said to be *reentrant*, because it can be entered (called) during execution a second time before the first activation has terminated. Thus there may be many simultaneous activations, each sharing the same code segment, as shown in Fig. 5-2. For a language of your choice, determine if subprograms are reentrant. What language feature (or features) allows you to begin a second activation before the first has terminated?

5. For a language of your choice, determine whether *name equivalence* or *structural equivalence* of data types is used. Consider each data type individually (because the rules tend to vary among types) and explain precisely when two variables of that type are considered to have the "same type" and when a variable (actual parameter) and a formal parameter in a subprogram call are considered to have the "same type." Are the rules different for primitive types and programmer-defined types (if allowed)?

6. For data objects of type *record*, give three different possible rules for determining when two records have the same type, using *structural equivalence* as the basic approach. Give two possible rules for determining when two *vectors* have the same type, using structural equivalence.

CHAPTER 6

Sequence
Control

Control structures in a programming language provide the basic framework within which operations and data are combined into programs and sets of programs. To this point we have been concerned with data and operations in isolation; now we must consider their organization into complete executable programs. This involves two aspects: the control of the order of execution of the operations, both primitive and user-defined, which we term *sequence control* and discuss in this chapter, and the control of the transmission of data among sets of operations, which we term *data control* and discuss in the next chapter. This division is convenient, as both subjects are rather complex, but it also serves to differentiate sharply two aspects of programming languages which are often confused.

6-1   IMPLICIT AND EXPLICIT SEQUENCE CONTROL

Many different sequence-control structures are in use in various programming languages. They may be conveniently categorized in three groups:

1. Structures used in *expressions* (and thus within statements, since expressions form the basic building blocks for statements), such as precedence rules and parentheses,

2. Structures used between *statements* or groups of statements, such as conditional and iteration statements, and

3. Structures used between *subprograms*, such as subprogram calls and coroutines.

This division is necessarily somewhat imprecise. For example, some languages, such as LISP and APL, have no statements, only expressions, yet versions of the usual statement sequence-control mechanisms are used.

Sequence-control structures may be either implicit or explicit. *Implicit* (or default) sequence-control structures are those defined by the language to be in effect unless modified by the programmer through some explicit structure. For example, most languages define the physical sequence of statements in a program as controlling the sequence in which statements are executed, unless modified by an explicit sequence-control statement. Within expressions there is also commonly a language-defined hierarchy of operations that controls the order of execution of the operations in the expression when parentheses are absent. *Explicit* sequence-control structures are those that the programmer may optionally use to modify the implicit sequence of operations defined by the language, as, for example, by using parentheses within expressions, or **goto** statements and statement labels.

6-2   SEQUENCE CONTROL WITHIN EXPRESSIONS

Consider the formula for computing one root of the quadratic equation

$$\text{root} = \frac{-B + \sqrt{B^2 - 4AC}}{2A}$$

This apparently simple formula actually involves at least fifteen separate operations (assuming a square-root primitive and counting the various data references). Coded in a typical assembly or machine language it would require at least fifteen instructions, and probably far more. Moreover, the programmer would have to provide storage for and keep track of each of the five or ten intermediate results generated. He would also have to worry about optimization: Can the two references to the value of B (and also A) be combined; in what order should the operations be performed to minimize temporary storage and make best use of the hardware, and so on? In a high-level language such as FORTRAN, however, the formula can be coded as a single expression almost directly:

$$\text{ROOT} = (-B+\text{SQRT}(B**2-4*A*C)) \, / \, (2*A)$$

The notation is compact and natural, and the language processor rather than the programmer concerns itself with temporary storage and optimization. It seems fair to say that the availability of expressions in high-level languages is one of their major advantages over machine and assembly languages.

Expressions are a powerful and natural device for representing sequences of operations, yet they raise new problems. While it may be tedious to write out long sequences of instructions in machine language, at least the programmer has a clear understanding of exactly the order in which the instructions will be executed. But what of the expression? Take the FORTRAN expression for the quadratic formula. Is the expression correct? How do we know, for example, that the expression indicates the subtraction should take place *after* the multiplication of 4 * A * C rather than before? The sequence-control mechanisms that operate to determine the order of operations within this expression are in fact rather complex and subtle.

Tree-Structure Representation of Expressions

In discussing operations and their arguments and results in the preceding chapters, the syntax used for invoking operations and for designating their arguments has been treated only briefly. Within expressions, which may contain many operations, the syntactic issues come out more clearly. In considering operations within expressions, the arguments of an operation are termed its *operands*.

The basic sequence-control mechanism in expressions is *functional composition*: A main operation and its operands are specified; the operands may be either constants or the results of data references or other operations, whose operands in turn may be constants or the results of data references or still other operations, to any depth. Functional composition gives an expression the characteristic structure of a tree, where the root node of the tree represents the main operation, nodes between the root and the leaves represent intermediate-level operations, and the leaves represent data references (or constants). For example, the expression for the quadratic formula may be represented (using M to represent the unary minus operation) by the tree of Fig. 6-1.

The tree representation clarifies the control structure of the expression. Clearly the results of data references or operations at lower levels in the tree serve as operands for operations at higher levels in the tree, and thus these data references and operations must be evaluated (executed) first. Yet the tree representation leaves part of the order of evaluation undefined. For example, in the tree in Fig. 6-1 it is not clear whether −B should be evaluated before or after B**2, nor is it clear whether the two data references to the identifier B may be combined into a single reference. Unfortunately, in the

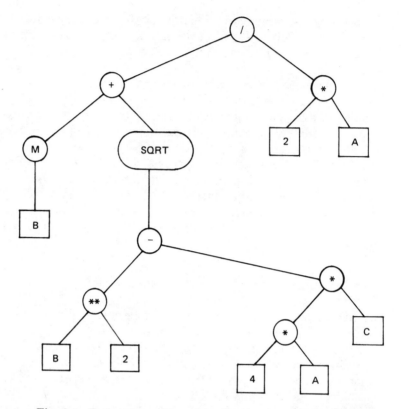

Fig. 6-1 Tree representation of quadratic formula in FORTRAN

presence of operations with side effects it may make a difference, as we shall see below. It is common in a language definition to define the order of evaluation of expressions only at the level of the tree representation and to allow the language implementer to decide on the detailed order of evaluation (such as whether −B or B**2 comes first). Before looking at the problems that arise in determining the exact order of evaluation, however, it is appropriate to look at the various syntactic representations for expressions which are in use.

Syntax for Expressions

If we take expressions as characteristically represented by trees, then in order to use expressions within programs some linearization of trees is required; i.e., one must have a notation for writing trees as linear sequences of symbols. Let us look at the most common notations:

Prefix notation (ordinary, Polish, and Cambridge Polish). In *prefix* notation one writes the operation symbol first, followed by the operands in order from left to right. If an operand is itself an operation with operands, then the same rules apply. In *ordinary prefix* notation one simply encloses the sequence of operands in parentheses, separating operands by commas. The tree of Fig. 6-2 then becomes

$$*(+(A,B),-(C,A))$$

A variant of this notation used in LISP is sometimes termed *Cambridge Polish*. In Cambridge Polish notation the left parenthesis following an operator symbol is moved to immediately precede it, and the commas separating operands are deleted. An expression then looks like a nested set of lists, where each list begins with an operator symbol followed by the lists representing the operands. In Cambridge Polish the tree of Fig. 6-2 becomes

$$(* (+ A\ B)(- C\ A))$$

A second variant, called *Polish* (or parenthesis-free) notation, allows the parentheses to be dropped altogether. If we assume that the number of operands for each operator is known and fixed, then the parentheses are unnecessary. For example, the tree of Fig. 6-2 represented in Polish notation becomes

$$* + A\ B - C\ A$$

Because the Polish mathematician Lukasiewiez invented the parenthesis-free notation, the term "Polish" has been applied to this notation and its derivatives.

Consider now the quadratic formula (Fig. 6-1) represented in prefix notation (using ↑ for exponentiation and M for minus):

$/(+(M(B),SQRT(-(\uparrow(B,2),*(*(4,A),C)))),*(2,A))$	(ordinary prefix)
$(/ (+ (M\ B)(SQRT(- (\uparrow B\ 2)(* (* 4\ A)C))))(* 2\ A))$	(Cambridge Polish)
$/ + M\ B\ SQRT - \uparrow B\ 2 * * 4\ A\ C * 2\ A$	(Polish)

The most obvious fact about these prefix expressions is that they are

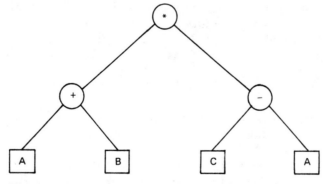

Fig. 6-2 Tree form of the simple expression $(A + B)*(C - A)$

difficult to decipher. In fact, we cannot decipher the Polish form of the expression at all without knowing for each symbol the number of operands it requires (treating data references as operators with no operands). The ordinary prefix and Cambridge Polish forms require large numbers of parentheses, and, of course, the notation is simply unfamiliar to those accustomed to the more common infix notation.

Prefix notation is not without value, however. In fact, ordinary prefix notation is the standard mathematical notation for most operations other than binary arithmetic and logical operations; e.g., $f(x, y, z)$ is written in prefix notation. More important, prefix notation may be used to represent operations with any number of operands, and thus it is completely general—only one syntactic rule need be learned in order to write any expression. For example, in LISP, where programs are expressions, one need master only the Cambridge Polish notation for writing expressions and one has learned most of the syntactic rules of the language. Prefix notation is also relatively easy to decode mechanically, and for this reason translation of prefix expressions into simple code sequences is easily accomplished. Occasionally a prefix representation is used directly during execution as the executable form of an expression (e.g., in SNOBOL4).

Postfix (suffix or reverse Polish) notation. Postfix notation is similar to prefix notation except that the operation symbol *follows* the list of operands. For example, the expression in Fig. 6-2 is represented as

$$((A,B)+,(C,A)-)* \qquad \text{or} \qquad A\ B + C\ A - *$$

Postfix is not a common syntactic representation for expressions in programming languages, but it does have importance as the basis for a particularly valuable execution-time representation for expressions (see below).

Infix notation. Infix notation is suitable only for binary (dyadic) operations, i.e., operations taking two operands. In infix notation the operator symbol is written between the two operands. Because infix notation for the basic arithmetic, relational, and logical operations is so commonly used in ordinary mathematics, the notation for these operations has been widely adopted in programming languages and in some cases extended to other operations as well. In infix form the tree of Fig. 6-2 is represented

$$(A + B) * (C - A)$$

Although infix notation is common, its use in a programming language leads to a number of unique problems:

1. Because infix notation is suitable only for binary operators, a language cannot use only infix notation but must necessarily combine infix

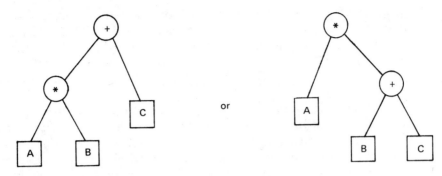

Fig. 6-3

and prefix (or postfix) notations. The mixture makes translation correspondingly more complex.

2. When more than one infix operator appears in an expression, the notation is inherently ambiguous unless parentheses are used. For example, the infix expression

$$A * B + C$$

might represent either of the trees of Fig. 6-3. Parentheses may be used to explicitly indicate the grouping of operators and operands, as in $(A * B) + C$ or $A * (B + C)$, but in complex expressions the resulting deep nests of parentheses become confusing. For this reason languages commonly introduce implicit control rules that make most uses of parentheses unnecessary. The two common types of implicit rules are:

a. *Hierarchy of operations* (*precedence rules*). The operators that may occur in expressions are placed in a hierarchy or precedence order. The Ada hierarchy is typical (see Table 6-1). In an expression involving operators from more than one level in the hierarchy the implicit rule is that operators with higher precedence are to be executed first. Thus in $A * B + C$, $*$ is above $+$ in the hierarchy and will be executed first.

b. *Associativity*. In an expression involving operations at the same level in the hierarchy an additional implicit rule for associativity is needed

TABLE 6-1   Ada Hierarchy of Operations

Highest precedence level	**	(exponentiation)
	* /	(multiplication, division)
	+ − *not*	(unary operations)
	+ −	(addition, subtraction)
	= < ⩽ > ⩾	(relational operations)
Lowest precedence level	*and or xor*	(Boolean operations)

to completely define the order of operations. For example, in $A - B - C$, is the first or second subtraction to be performed first? Left-to-right associativity is the most common implicit rule, so that $A - B - C$ is treated as $(A - B) - C$. However, in APL associativity is from right to left: $A - B - C$ is treated as $A - (B - C) = A - B + C$.

Each of the notations for expressions that we have mentioned has its own particular difficulties. Infix notation with the implicit precedence and associativity rules and explicit use of parentheses (when required) gives a rather natural representation for most arithmetic, relational, and logical expressions. However, the need for the complex implicit rules and the necessary use of prefix (or other) notation for nonbinary operations makes the translation of such expressions complex. Infix notation without the implicit rules (i.e., with full parenthesization) is cumbersome because of the large number of parentheses required. However, both Cambridge Polish and ordinary mathematical prefix notation share this problem with parentheses. The Polish notation avoids use of parentheses altogether, but one must know in advance the number of operands required for each operator, a condition that is often difficult to satisfy when programmer-defined operations are involved. In addition the lack of any structuring cues makes reading complex Polish expressions difficult. All the prefix and postfix notations share the advantage of applying to operations with differing numbers of operands.

The major and minor differences in notation among languages make the situation even more difficult. In APL, for example, infix notation is used for both primitive and programmer-defined operations, but without a hierarchy of operations, and with right-to-left rather than left-to-right associativity. LISP uses only Cambridge Polish. Many languages adopt infix notation for the basic arithmetic, logical, and relational operations; Polish prefix notation for built-in unary operators like negation and logical not; and ordinary mathematical prefix notation for everything else, including both programmer-defined operations and some built-in functions such as *sine* and *cosine*. SNOBOL4 represents relational operations in ordinary prefix notation but adds a considerable number of new unary and binary operators in Polish prefix and infix notation, respectively. It is apparent that no general agreement exists on the best notation for expressions in programming languages.

Translation of Expressions into Tree Representations

Translating an expression from its syntactic representation in a program text into its executable form is most easily conceptualized as a two-stage process. First the expression is translated into its tree representation, and then the tree is translated into a sequence of executable instructions. The first stage ordinarily is concerned only with establishing the basic tree control structure of the expression, utilizing the implicit rules of precedence and associativity when the expression involves infix notation. In the second stage the detailed decisions concerning order of evaluation are made, including optimization of the evaluation process. Both stages of expression translation have received extended study, because both are of central importance in the construction of compilers for high-level languages. A brief discussion is found in Chapter 9.

Execution-Time Representations of Expressions

Various run-time representations of expressions are used in language implementations. Because of the difficulty of decoding expressions in their original form in the program text, especially where infix notation is used, it is commonplace to translate into an executable form that may be easily decoded during execution. The following are the most important alternatives in use:

1. *Machine code sequences*. The most common technique is to simply translate expressions into actual machine code. The ordering of the instructions reflects the sequence-control structure of the original expression. On conventional computers such machine code sequences must make use of explicit temporary storage locations to hold intermediate results. Machine code representation, of course, allows use of the hardware interpreter, providing very fast execution.

2. *Tree structures*. Expressions may be executed directly in their natural tree-structure representation, using a software interpreter. Execution may then be accomplished by a simple tree traversal. This is the basic technique used in (software-interpreted) LISP, where entire programs are represented as tree structures during execution.

3. *Prefix or postfix form*. Expressions in prefix or postfix form may be executed by relatively simple interpretation algorithms that scan the expression from left to right. Postfix representation is particularly useful here, as the order of symbols in the postfix expression corresponds closely to the order in which the various operations must be executed. In some actual computers based on a stack organization, the actual machine code is essentially represented in postfix form. Prefix representation is the executable form of programs in SNOBOL4 in many implementations. Execution is by a left-to-right scan, with each operation calling the interpreter recursively to evaluate its operands.

Evaluation of Tree Representations of Expressions

Although translation from expressions in programs into tree representations occasionally causes difficulty, the basic translation procedure is straightforward. The second stage, in which the tree is translated into an executable sequence of primitive operations, involves most of the subtle questions of order of evaluation. It is not our concern here to study algorithms for the generation of executable code from the tree representation but rather to consider the problems of order of evaluation which arise in determining exactly the code to generate.

   Problem 1. Uniform evaluation rules.   In evaluating an expression, or in generating code for its evaluation, one would expect the following uniform evaluation rule to apply regardless of the operations involved or of the complexity of the expression: For each operation node in the expression tree, first evaluate (or generate code to evaluate) each of its operands, and then apply the operation (or generate code to apply the operation) to the evaluated operands. The exact order in which these evaluations occur should not matter, so that the order of evaluation of operands or of independent operations may be chosen to optimize use of temporary storage or other machine features. Under this evaluation rule, for the expression of Fig. 6-2 either of the following orders of evaluation would be acceptable:

   Order 1:

   1. Fetch the value of A, obtaining a.

   2. Fetch the value of B, obtaining b.

   3. Add a and b, obtaining d.

   4. Fetch the value of C, obtaining c.

   5. Subtract a from c, obtaining e.

   6. Multiply d and e, obtaining f, the value of the expression.

   Order 2:

   1. Fetch the value of C, obtaining c.

   2. Fetch the value of B, obtaining b.

   3. Fetch the value of A, obtaining a.

   4. Subtract a from c, obtaining e.

   5. Add a and b, obtaining d.

   6. Multiply d and e, obtaining f.

This is all quite natural, and one would like to adopt the uniform evaluation rule mentioned. Unfortunately it is not always correct to evaluate the

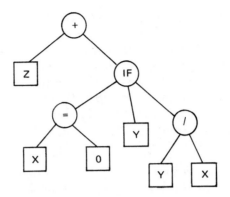

Fig. 6-4 An expression containing a conditional

operands before applying the operation. The best example is the case of expressions containing conditionals, for example, in ALGOL: Z + (if $X = 0$ then Y else Y/X). One would like to treat such a conditional simply as an operation with a "funny syntax" and three operands, as in Fig. 6-4. In fact in LISP this is exactly what is done, utilizing the Cambridge Polish notation for conditionals as well as for all other operations. But now the problem with the uniform evaluation rule appears. If we evaluate the operands of the conditional operator IF in Fig. 6-4, we produce the effect of doing exactly what the conditional is set up to avoid, namely dividing Y by X even if X is zero. Clearly, in this case we do not wish all the operands evaluated before the operation is applied. Instead we need to pass the operands (or at least the last two operands) to the operation IF *unevaluated* and let the operation determine the order of evaluation.

The problem with conditionals suggests that perhaps an alternative uniform evaluation rule would be better: *Never* evaluate operands before applying the operation; instead always pass the operands unevaluated and let the operation decide if evaluation is needed. In fact, it may be shown that this evaluation rule works in all cases and thus theoretically would serve. However, implementation turns out to be impractical in most cases, for how is one to simulate the passing of unevaluated operands to operations? While it can be done, it requires substantial software simulation to accomplish. Moreover, as the need for unevaluated operands commonly arises only in a few cases, it is difficult to justify the expense of simulation.

The two uniform evaluation rules suggested above correspond to two common techniques for passing parameters to subprograms, transmission *by value* and *by name*, respectively. The details of these concepts and their simulation are discussed in greater depth when parameter transmission is taken up in the next chapter. For our purposes here it suffices to point out that no simple uniform evaluation rule for expressions (or for generating code for expressions) is satisfactory. In language implementations one commonly finds a mixture of the two techniques. In LISP, for example, functions (operations) are split into two categories depending on whether the function receives evaluated or unevaluated operands. In SNOBOL4 programmer-defined operations (subprograms) always receive evaluated operands while language-defined primitive operations receive unevaluated operands. ALGOL primitive operations receive evaluated operands, with conditionals being simulated by in-line code sequences, but programmer-defined subprograms may receive both evaluated and unevaluated operands.

Problem 2. Side effects. The use of operations that have side effects (or that are self-modifying) in expressions is the basis of a long-standing controversy in programming language design. Consider the expression

$$A * FUN(X) + A$$

Before the multiplication can be performed, the value of A must be fetched and FUN(X) must be evaluated. The addition requires the value of A and the result of the multiplication. It is clearly desirable to fetch the value of A only once and simply use it in two places in the computation. Moreover, it should make no difference whether FUN(X) is evaluated before or after the value of A is fetched. However, if FUN has the side effect of changing the value of A, then the exact order of evaluation is critical. For example, if A has the value 1 on beginning evaluation of the expression and FUN(X) evaluates to 3 and, as a side effect, increases the value of A by 1, then different orders of evaluation might produce any of the results 4, 5, 7, or 8.

Two positions on the use of side effects in expressions have emerged. One position is that side effects should be outlawed in expressions, either by disallowing functions with side effects altogether or simply by making undefined the value of any expression in which side effects might affect the value (e.g., the value of the expression above). Another view is that side effects should be allowed and that the language definition should make it clear exactly what the order of evaluation of an expression is to be so that the programmer can make proper use of side effects in his code. The difficulty with this latter position is that it makes many kinds of optimization impossible. In many language definitions the question is simply ignored altogether, with the unfortunate result that different implementations provide conflicting interpretations.

Ordinarily, statements are allowed to have side effects. For example, the assignment operation necessarily produces a side effect—a change in the value of a variable or data structure element. And clearly we expect the side effects produced by one statement to affect the inputs of the next statement in sequence. The problem is whether this sort of interdependence through side effects should be allowed below the statement level, in expressions. If disallowed, we need to specify the order of evaluation in expressions only to the tree representation level; expression evaluation, for the programmer, is without "tricks"; and optimization of expression evaluation sequences by the translator is possible. However, if optimization is not a prime concern, it is often valuable to allow side effects and specify the order of evaluation completely. In this case we lose much of the reason for distinguishing between statements and expressions in a language. In a number of languages, notably LISP and APL, the distinction between expressions and statements has in fact almost or entirely disappeared. For the programmer this represents a valuable simplification. Thus there is no dominant position on side effects in expressions—either approach has its adherents.

Problem 3. Error conditions. A special kind of side effect is involved in the case of operations that may fail and generate an error condition. Unlike ordinary side effects, which usually are restricted to programmer-defined functions, error conditions may arise in many primitive operations (overflow or underflow on arithmetic operations, divide by zero, etc.). It is undesirable to outlaw side effects of this sort, yet the meaning, and even the occurrence of such error conditions, may be affected by differences in the order of evaluation of expression components. In such situations the programmer may need precise control of the order of evaluation, yet the demand for optimization may preclude this (see Problem 5 at the end of the chapter). The solution to these difficulties tends to be essentially ad hoc and varies from language to language and implementation to implementation.

Problem 4. Short-circuit Boolean expressions. In programming it is often natural to use the Boolean operations *and* and *or* to combine relational expressions such as:

$$\textbf{if } (A = 0) \textit{ or } (B/A > C) \textbf{ then } \ldots$$

or

$$\textbf{while } (I \leqslant UB) \textit{ and } (V[I] > 0) \textbf{ do } \ldots$$

In both these expressions, evaluation of the second operand of the Boolean operation may lead to an error condition (division by zero, subscript range error); the first operand is included to insure that the error does not occur. The intent is that if the left expression evaluates to *true* in the first example and *false* in the second, then the second expression is never evaluated at all. Logically, this intent makes sense, because clearly the value of expression (α or β) is *true* if α by itself is *true*, and likewise (α and β) is *false* if α alone is *false*. Unfortunately the uniform evaluation problem mentioned above is also present here: ordinarily both operands are evaluated before the Boolean operation is evaluated. Many programming errors arise from the expectation that the value of the left operand of a Boolean operation may "short-circuit" the rest of the evaluation if the value of the overall expression may be decided from the value of the left operand alone. A solution to this problem in Ada is to include two special Boolean operations, *and then* and *or else*, that explicitly provide short-circuit evaluation, in addition to the ordinary Boolean operations *and* and *or*, which do not. For example, in Ada:

$$\textbf{if } (A = 0) \textit{ or else } (B/A > C) \textbf{ then } \ldots$$

cannot fail because of division by zero, since if $A = 0$ evaluation of the entire expression is terminated and the value is taken to be *true*.

6-3   SEQUENCE CONTROL BETWEEN STATEMENTS

In this section we shall take up the basic mechanisms in use for controlling the sequence in which the individual statements are executed within a program, leaving for the following sections the larger sequence-control structures concerned with programs and subprograms.

Basic Statements

At its center, a program is composed of *basic statements* that apply operations to data objects. Examples of such basic statements are assignment statements, subprogram calls, and input and output statements. Within a basic statement, sequences of operations may be invoked by using expressions, as discussed in the preceding section, but for our present purposes each basic statement may be considered as a unit that represents a single step in the computation.

Forms of Statement-Level Sequence Control

Three main forms of statement-level sequence control are usually distinguished:

1. *Composition.* Statements may be placed in a textual sequence, so that they are executed in order whenever the larger program structure containing the sequence is executed.

2. *Alternation.* Two sequences of statements may form alternatives, so that one or the other sequence is executed, but not both, whenever the larger program structure containing both sequences is executed.

3. *Iteration.* A sequence of statements may be executed repeatedly, zero or more times (zero meaning execution may be omitted altogether), whenever the larger program structure containing the sequence is executed.

In constructing programs, we are engaged in putting together the basic statements that perform the computation into the appropriate sequences by repeatedly using composition, alternation, and iteration to get the effect desired. Within each of these general control-form categories, we often use variations appropriate for particular purposes. For example, instead of an alternation consisting of only two alternatives, we often need one consisting of several alternatives. The programming language usually provides various sequence-control structures intended to allow these control forms to be easily expressed.

Sequence Control Using Statement Labels and GOTO Statements

A primitive mechanism for sequence control is found in the facility in most languages to label statements and then transfer control explicitly to a labeled statement from another point in the program. The transfer of control is most often indicated by use of a **goto** statement, although other notations are also used. For convenience, we shall adopt the term **goto** *statement* to refer to any notation for the explicit transfer of control to a labeled statement from elsewhere in a program.

Two forms of **goto** statement are:

1. *Unconditional* **goto**. Within a sequence of statements, an unconditional **goto**, such as

goto NEXT

transfers control to the statement labeled NEXT. The statement following the **goto** is not executed as part of the sequence.

2. *Conditional* **goto**. Within a sequence of statements, a conditional **goto**, such as:

if $A = 0$ then goto NEXT

transfers control to the statement labeled NEXT only if the specified condition holds. Using these two forms of **goto**, we can easily express the basic control forms, as shown in Fig. 6-5.

The **goto** statement has the advantage that it is easy to use, completely general-purpose (since all control forms may be expressed with it), and efficient to execute, since, at least in its simple form, it reflects the basic underlying structure of conventional computers, in which each instruction word or byte has an address, and the hardware has a built-in *jump* instruction that transfers control to a designated address. Because of this hardware influence, **goto** statements represent a natural control structure

(a) Composition	(b) Alternation	(c) Iteration

S_0
    goto L1
 L2: S_2
    goto L3
 L1: S_1
    goto L2
 L3: S_3
	S_0
	 if A=0 **then goto** L1
	 S_1
	    goto L2
	 L1: S_2
	 L2: S_3
		S_0
		 L1: **if** A=0 **then goto** L2
		 S_1
		    goto L1
		 L2: S_2

Execution sequence: $S_0 S_1 S_2 S_3$	Execution sequence: $S_0 S_1 S_3$ or $S_0 S_2 S_3$	Execution sequence: $S_0 S_2$ or $S_0 S_1 S_2$ or $S_0 S_1 S_1 S_2$ or $S_0 S_1 S_1 S_1 S_2$ etc.

(Each S_i is a sequence of statements)

Fig. 6-5 Basic control forms expressed using only GOTO statements

to a programmer moving to a high-level language from an assembly language. Most older languages include both the basic **goto** statement and various augmented forms based on the use of labels as data. In newer languages such as Pascal and Ada, however, sequence control based on **goto** statements is much less important, although the construct is still included, as discussed below.

It is convenient to identify three basic approaches to the use of statement labels and **goto** statements:

1. *Labels as local syntactic tags in programs during translation.* The simplest approach is to restrict the use of labels and **goto** statements to situations that may be directly translated into the hardware *instruction word address/jump instruction* construct. Such restricted use allows simple and efficient implementation of the label/**goto** structure. To set up such an implementation it must be possible for the translator to equate each label with an execution-time address so that **goto** statements may be translated into equivalent jump instructions. This is the approach used in Ada.

2. *Labels as restricted data items at run time but without run-time computation of labels.* A more complex approach is to allow statement labels to be represented at run time as a restricted type of data. The most important restriction is to avoid constructs that allow statement labels to be read in or computed at run time, because such constructs would necessarily require that a table of statement labels and pointers to corresponding code positions be maintained during program execution. Within this restriction the language may still allow label variables and arrays, references to nonlocal labels, and label parameters to subprograms. ALGOL is typical of languages allowing use of labels at this intermediate level.

3. *Labels as unrestricted data items during execution.* The most general approach is to accept statement labels as simply another data type during execution by allowing labels to be read in or computed as needed, as, for example, in

$$\vdots$$

READ X

Y := 2

GO TO X+Y

$$\vdots$$

To allow this generality it must be possible to determine during execution for each label the corresponding position in the executable form of the program. Thus a run-time table of labels and code positions is required. SNOBOL4 and APL are typical of languages taking this approach.

Structured Programming and the GOTO Controversy

Although every language in Part II allows the use of labels and **goto** statements in programs, considerable controversy surrounds their continued inclusion in new languages. In some new languages, **goto**'s and statements are completely eliminated. Some of the *advantages* of **goto**'s are mentioned above: (1) direct hardware support for efficient execution if labels are simply local syntactic tags on statements, (2) simple and easy to use in *small* programs, (3) familiar to programmers trained in assembly language or older languages, and (4) completely general-purpose as a building block for representing (simulating) any of the other control forms discussed below.

What are the *disadvantages* of statement labels and **goto**'s? There are three central ones:

1. *Lack of hierarchical program structure.* A program of more than a few statements is difficult to understand unless statements are organized into groups hierarchically, with each group representing one conceptual unit of the underlying computation. The hierarchical structure means that a few groups, organized into one of the basic control forms mentioned above, make up the top level of the program. Each of these groups is itself organized as a few subgroups using one of the control forms, and so on. In the design of a program, this sort of hierarchical organization is essential to allow the programmer to comprehend how all the parts of the program fit together. (Psychologists set the limit to the number of such "chunks" that a person

can comprehend and remember at a time at less than ten.) When a program design that is organized hierarchically in this way is written as a program containing only basic statements and **goto**'s, the hierarchical structure is largely obscured. The original programmer may still see the structure, but finding it becomes difficult for anyone else. We say that the program has a very "flat" structure; all statements appear to be on one level rather than being organized hierarchically.

2. *Order of statements in the program text need not correspond to the order of execution.* Using **goto**'s, it is easy to write programs in which control jumps between different sequences of statements in irregular patterns. Then the order in which statements appear in the program has little connection with the order in which the statements are executed, as in Fig. 6-5(a). To understand a program, we must understand the order of execution of the statements, and it is much simpler to understand a program in which the statements appear in approximately the sequence in which they are executed. A program written with **goto**'s and that has been modified several times often loses so much of the connection between textual sequence and execution sequence that it is said to have *spaghetti logic,* because tracing a possible execution sequence through the program text is somewhat akin to following a single strand of spaghetti through a bowl full.

3. *Groups of statements may serve multiple purposes.* A program is more easily understood if each group of statements serves a single purpose within the overall program structure, i.e., computes a clearly defined separate part of the entire computation. Often two separate groups of statements may contain several statements that are identical in both. Using **goto**'s, we can combine two such groups of statements so that the identical statements are written only once, and control is transferred to this common set during execution of each group. The resulting program is shorter and initially may be as easy to understand as the original, but the multipurpose nature of statements tends to make the program difficult to modify. When one statement of a multipurpose group is changed to correct or modify the group for one purpose (i.e., one execution path), the use of the same group in other execution sequences may be subtly damaged.

The term *structured programming* is often used for a style of programming that emphasizes (1) hierarchical design of program structures using only the simple control forms of composition, alternation, and iteration described above, (2) representation of the hierarchical design directly in the program text, preferably using the "structured" control statements described below, (3) program text in which the textual sequence of statements corresponds to the execution sequence, and (4) use of single-purpose groups of statements, even if statements must be copied. When a program is written by following these tenets of structured programming it usually is much easier to understand, debug, verify to be correct, and later modify and reverify.

Structured programming can be done in a language using only **goto** statements for sequence control, if careful attention is paid to adopting coding conventions that limit the ways in which groups of statements may be connected with **goto**'s to only the basic forms mentioned above. However, the disadvantage of **goto**'s is that they may be too easily used instead to construct programs with multipurpose statement groups, connected by "spaghetti logic," that lack any coherent hierarchical organization. During modification of an existing program, **goto** statements are particularly likely to be used to construct "patches" that destroy what originally might have been a properly structured program.

It is because **goto** statements are so easily misused that new language designs have tended to deemphasize or eliminate them altogether, replacing them with the alternative control statements discussed below. There is little question that **goto** statements are seldom needed if the language provides a rich set of alternative control structures. However, there remain situations in most languages in which use of a **goto** statement may be the most appropriate way to represent a particular sequence-control requirement. Several of these situations are discussed below.

Sequence Control Using "Structured" Control Statements

Most languages provide a set of control statements for expressing the basic control forms of composition, alternation, and iteration without the use of **goto** statements. We shall look at some of the most common, but variations in both syntax and semantics are found in most languages.

One important aspect of the statements discussed below is that each is a *one-in, one-out* control statement, meaning that in each statement there is only one entry point to the statement and one exit point from it. If one of these statements is placed in sequence with some other statements, then the sequence of execution will necessarily proceed from the preceding statement into the one-in, one-out statement, through the statement, and out to the following statement (provided the statement cannot include an internal **goto** statement that sends control elsewhere). In reading a program constructed only from one-in, one-out control statements, without **goto**'s, the flow of program execution must match the sequence of statements in the program text. Each one-in, one-out control statement may include internal branching and looping, but control may leave the statement only through its single exit point. Because one-in, one-out control statements force the sequence of execution to match the sequence of program text, their use enforces one of the tenets of structured programming noted above.

Compound Statements

A *compound statement* is a sequence of statements that may be treated as a single statement in the construction of larger statements. Often a compound statement is written:

> **begin**
>   ⋮   —sequence of statements (one or more)
> **end**

Within the compound statement, statements are written in the sequence in which they are to be executed. Thus the compound statement is the basic structure for representing the *composition* of statements. Because a compound statement is itself a statement, groups of statements representing single conceptual units of computation may be kept together as a unit by the **begin** . . . **end** bracketing, and hierarchies of such groups may be constructed.

    Implementation. A compound statement is implemented in a conventional computer by placing the blocks of executable code representing each constituent statement in sequence in memory. The order in which they appear in memory determines the order in which they are executed.

Conditional Statements

A *conditional statement* is one that expresses alternation of two or more statements, or optional execution of a single statement, where by *statement* we mean either a single basic statement, a compound statement, or another control statement. The choice of alternative is controlled by a test on some condition, usually written as an expression involving relational and Boolean operations. The most common forms of conditional statement are:

    If statements. The optional execution of a statement is expressed as a *single-branch* **if**:

> **if** ⟨*condition*⟩ **then** ⟨*statement*⟩ **endif**

A choice between two alternatives uses a *two-branch* **if**:

> **if** ⟨*condition*⟩ **then** ⟨*statement₁*⟩ **else** ⟨*statement₂*⟩ **endif**

A choice among many alternatives may be expressed by nesting additional **if** statements within the alternative statements of a single **if**, or by a *multibranch* **if**:

$$\textbf{if} \ \langle condition_1 \rangle \ \textbf{then} \ \langle statement_1 \rangle$$
$$\textbf{elsif} \ \langle condition_2 \rangle \ \textbf{then} \ \langle statement_2 \rangle$$
$$\vdots$$
$$\textbf{elsif} \ \langle condition_n \rangle \ \textbf{then} \ \langle statement_n \rangle$$
$$\textbf{else} \ \langle statement_{n+1} \rangle \ \textbf{endif}$$

Case statements. The conditions in a multibranch **if** often take the form of repeated testing of the value of a variable, such as:

```
if TAG = 0 then
              —statement S₀
elsif TAG = 1 then
              —statement S₁
elsif TAG = 2 then
              —statement S₂
else
              —statement S₃
endif
```

This common structure is expressed more concisely as a **case** *statement*:

```
case TAG of
       0: begin
              —statement S₀
          end;
       1: begin
              —statement S₁
          end;
       2: begin
              —statement S₂
          end;
  others: begin
              —statement S₃
          end
endcase
```

In general, the variable TAG may be replaced by any expression that evaluates to a single value, and then the actions for each of the possible values are represented by a compound statement preceded by the value for the expression that would cause that compound statement to be executed. Enumeration types and integer subranges are particularly useful in setting up the possible values that the expression in a **case** statement may return. For example, if variable TAG above is defined as having the subrange $0..5$ as its type, then during execution of the **case** statement, values for TAG of 0,

1, or 2 will cause S_0, S_1, or S_2, respectively, to be executed, and values 3, 4, or 5 will cause S_3 to be executed.

Implementation of conditional statements. **If** statements are readily implemented using the usual hardware-supported branch and jump instructions (the hardware form of conditional and unconditional **goto**). The result is similar to that shown in Fig. 6-5(b). **Case** statements are commonly implemented using a jump table to avoid repeated testing of the value of the same variable. A *jump table* is a vector, stored sequentially in memory, each of whose components is an unconditional jump instruction. The expression

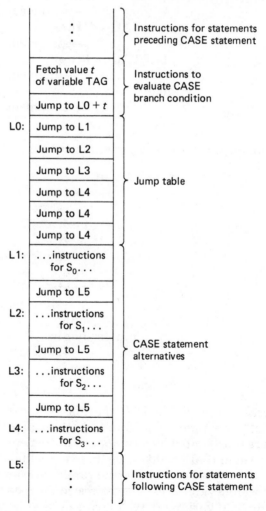

Fig. 6-6 Jump-table implementation of a CASE statement.

forming the condition of the **case** statement is evaluated, and the result is transformed into a small integer representing the offset into the jump table from its base address. The jump instruction at that offset, when executed, leads to the start of the code block representing the code to be executed if that alternative is chosen. The resulting implementation structure for the **case** statement above is shown in Fig. 6-6.

Guarded commands. Another important form of conditional statement, the *guarded command*, allows a number of alternative statements to be specified, with each preceded by the condition (its *guard*) that allows it to be executed. When the guarded command statement is executed, all the guards are evaluated, and if more than one of the guard conditions are true, then one of the corresponding alternative statements is chosen and executed, but the choice is made nondeterministically. Guarded commands are important primarily when considering concurrent execution of subprograms; they are treated in more depth in Sec. 6-9.

Iteration Statements

The basic structure of an iteration statement consists of a *body* and a *head*. The body is ordinarily composed of a single statement, which may be compound; the head consists of an expression designating the number of times the body is to be executed. Although the bodies of iteration statements are fairly unrestricted, many variants of head structure may be seen. Let us look at some typical ones.

Simple repetition. The simplest type of iteration statement head specifies that the body is to be executed some fixed number of times. The COBOL PERFORM statement is typical.

PERFORM *body* 12 TIMES.   or   PERFORM *body* K TIMES.

In this simple form the body is simply executed 12 times, or the current value of K times. This seems straightforward, yet already a subtle question arises in the second form of the statement. The problem concerns the point of evaluation of the variable K. Is K evaluated only once before the first execution of the body, or is K evaluated before *each* execution of the body? The result will be the same unless the value of K is changed within the body. If this happens, the result can be very confusing; e.g., the iteration might never terminate if the value of K were to be increased each time through the body. For this simple iteration statement it is reasonable to assume that K is evaluated once only before execution begins. A second question of concern: What if the initial value of K is negative or *zero*? Should we simply skip execution of the body, execute it once, or treat it as an error condition and halt execution of the program altogether?

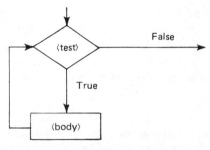

Fig. 6-7

Although these questions may seem like hairsplitting for this simple iteration statement, the same questions arise in each form of the statement, and thus it is important to look at them in their simplest form here. In each case it is important to ask: (1) when is the termination test made? and (2) when are the variables used in the statement head evaluated?

Repetition while condition holds. A somewhat more complex iteration may be constructed using a *repeat while* head. A typical form is

$$\textbf{while } \langle test \rangle \textbf{ do } \langle body \rangle$$

The meaning of this construct may be represented by the flow chart of Fig. 6-7. In this form of iteration statement the test expression is reevaluated each time after the body has been executed. Note also that here it is to be expected that execution of the body will change some of the values of variables appearing in the test expression; otherwise the iteration, once begun, would never terminate.

Repetition while incrementing a counter. The third alternative form of iteration statement of interest—and in many languages the most important—is the statement whose head specifies a variable which serves as a counter or index during the iteration. An initial value, final value, and increment are specified in the head, and the body is executed repeatedly using first the initial value as the value of the index variable, then the initial value plus the increment, then the initial value plus twice the increment, and so on, until the final value is reached. In FORTRAN this is the only form of iteration statement available. The ALGOL **for** statement illustrates the typical structure

$$\textbf{for } I := 1 \textbf{ step } 2 \textbf{ until } 30 \textbf{ do } \langle body \rangle$$

The meaning of this statement is defined by the flow chart of Fig. 6-8. In its general form both the initial value, final value, and increment may be given by arbitrary expressions, as in

$$\textbf{for } K := N{-}1 \textbf{ step } 2{\times}(W{-}1) \textbf{ until } M{\times}N \textbf{ do } \langle body \rangle$$

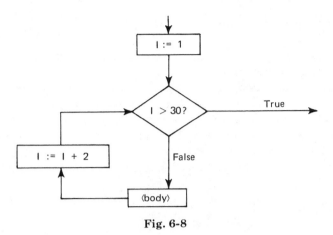

Fig. 6-8

Again the question arises as to when the termination test is made and when and how often the various expressions are evaluated. Here the question is of central importance additionally for the language implementor because such iteration statements are prime candidates for optimization, and the answers may affect greatly the sorts of optimizations which can be performed.

Indefinite repetition. Where the conditions for loop exit are complex and not easily expressible in the usual loop head, a loop with no explicit termination test in the head is often used, e.g., as in the Ada:

loop

⋮

exit when ⟨*condition*⟩;

⋮

end loop;

or in Pascal, using a **while** loop with a condition that is always true:

while true **do begin . . . end**

Implementation of loop statements. Implementation of loop-control statements using the hardware branch/jump instruction is straightforward. The run-time organization is similar to that shown in Fig. 6-5(c) for **while** loops. To implement a **for** loop, the expressions in the loop head defining the final value and increment must be evaluated on initial entry to the loop and saved in special temporary storage areas where they may be retrieved at the beginning of each iteration for use in testing and incrementing the controlled variable.

Problems in Structured Sequence Control

A **goto** statement is often viewed as a last resort when the structured control statements described above prove inadequate for the expression of a difficult sequence-control structure. Although in theory it is always possible to express any sequence-control structure using only the structured statement forms, in practice a difficult form may not have any natural expression directly using only those statements. Several such problem areas are known, and often special control constructs are provided for these cases that make use of a **goto** statement unnecessary. The most common are:

1. *Multiple exit loops.* Often several conditions may require termination of a loop. The search loop is a common example: a vector of K elements is to be searched for the first element that meets some condition. The loop terminates if either the end of the vector is reached or an appropriate element is found. Iteration through the elements of a vector is naturally expressed using a **for** loop:

```
for I := 1 to K do
    if VECT[I] = 0 then goto α (α is outside the loop)
endfor
```

In a language such as Pascal, however, either a **goto** statement must be used to escape from the middle of the loop as above, or the **for** loop must be replaced by a **while** loop, which obscures the information contained in the **for** loop head about the existence and range of the index variable *I*.

The **exit** statement in Ada provides an alternative construct for expressing such loop exits without use of a **goto** statement:

```
for I in 1..K loop
    exit when VECT(I) = 0;
end loop;
```

The **exit** statement is a restricted form of **goto** statement that may transfer control only to the statement immediately following the loop.

2. *Loop and a half.* Often the most natural place to test whether to exit a loop comes not at the beginning or end of the loop but in the middle, after some processing has been done, as in

```
loop
    read(X)
    if X = 0 then goto α (outside the loop)
    process(X)
end loop;
```

This form is sometimes called the "loop and a half," because the entire loop body is executed as many times as needed, and then only the first half (down to the exit test) is executed on the last iteration. A **while** loop with the test at the beginning of each iteration (or a **repeat-until** loop with the test at the end) cannot directly express this structure. Again the **exit** statement of Ada provides an alternative, a restricted **goto** that allows exit only to the end of the loop.

3. *Exceptional conditions.* **Goto** statements are often used in Pascal, FORTRAN, and other languages to represent control transfers caused by exceptional conditions that require special handling outside the normal course of execution. These exceptions may represent error conditions of various kinds, such as unexpected end-of-file conditions, subscript range errors, or bad data to be processed. The statements that handle the processing of these exceptional conditions are often grouped at a special place in the program, such as at the end of the subprogram in which the exception might be detected, or possibly in another subprogram used only to handle exceptions. Transfer from the point where the exceptional condition is detected to the exception handler (group of statements) often is best represented using a **goto** statement. However, this use of **goto** statements may be avoided in languages such as Ada and PL/I that provide special language mechanisms for defining exception handlers and for specifying the control transfer needed when an exception is detected. The Ada **raise** statement is typical of this restricted form of **goto**:

raise BAD_CHAR_VALUE

This statement transfers control to the exception-handling statements that are associated with the exception name BAD_CHAR_VALUE. Exceptions and exception handlers are discussed further in Sec. 6-6.

6-4 SUBPROGRAM SEQUENCE CONTROL: SIMPLE CALL-RETURN

In this and the following sections our concern is with mechanisms for controlling the sequence in which sets of programs and subprograms are executed. The simple subprogram CALL and RETURN statement structure is common to almost all programming languages, but more sophisticated control structures involving recursion, coroutines, exceptions, tasks, and scheduling of subprogram calls are also important.

Simple Subprogram Call-Return Structure

We are accustomed in programming to mentally structuring our sets of programs and subprograms into hierarchies. A program is composed of a single main program, which during execution may call various subprograms, which in turn may each call other subsubprograms, and so forth to any depth. Each subprogram at some point is expected to terminate its execution and return control to the program that called it. During execution of a subprogram, execution of the calling program is temporarily halted. When execution of the subprogram is completed, execution of the calling program resumes at the point immediately following the call of the subprogram. This control structure is often explained by the *copy rule*: The effect of the subprogram CALL statement is the same as would be obtained if the CALL statement were replaced by a copy of the body of the subprogram (with suitable substitutions for parameters and conflicting identifiers) before execution. Viewed in this way, subprogram calls may be considered as control structures that simply make it unnecessary to copy large numbers of identical or nearly identical statements that occur in more than one place in a program. However, if a particular subprogram turned out to be very short (e.g., only one or two statements), then we could actually apply the copy rule explicitly and replace the subprogram call by *in-line* code during translation. In fact, this sort of replacement of subprogram calls by in-line code is often done in compilers for languages such as FORTRAN when simple standard function subprograms are involved (a typical example is computation of the absolute value of a number).

Before looking at the implementation of the simple call-return structure used for the copy-rule view of subprograms, let us look briefly at some of the implicit assumptions present in this view that may be relaxed to get more general subprogram control structures:

1. *Subprograms cannot be recursive.* A subprogram is *directly recursive* if it contains a call on itself (e.g., if subprogram B contains the statement CALL B); it is *indirectly recursive* if it calls another subprogram that calls the original subprogram or that initiates a further chain of subprogram calls that eventually leads back to a call of the original subprogram. In the case of simple nonrecursive subprogram calls we may apply the copy rule during translation to replace subprogram calls by copies of the subprogram body and completely eliminate the need for the separate subprogram (in principle, not in practice). But if the subprogram is directly recursive, then this is not possible even in principle, because the substitution of subprogram call for subprogram body is obviously unending: Each substitution that deletes a CALL statement introduces a new call on the same subprogram, for which another substitution is necessary, and so on. Indirect recursion may allow some subprograms to be deleted but must lead eventually to making others directly recursive. But many algorithms are recursive and lead naturally to recursive subprogram structures.

2. *Explicit CALL statements are required.* For the copy rule to apply, each point of call of a subprogram must be explicitly indicated in the

program to be translated. But for a subprogram used as an *exception handler*, no explicit call may be present.

3. *Subprograms must execute completely at each call.* Implicit in the copy rule is the assumption that each subprogram is executed from its beginning to its logical end each time it is called. If called a second time, the subprogram begins execution anew and again executes to its logical end before returning control. But a subprogram used as a *coroutine* continues execution from the point of its last termination each time it is called.

4. *Immediate transfer of control at point of call.* An explicit CALL statement in a program indicates that control is to transfer directly to the subprogram at that point, and thus copying the body into the calling program has the same effect. But for a *scheduled subprogram* call, execution of the subprogram may be deferred until some later time.

5. *Single execution sequence.* At any point during execution of a program-subprogram hierarchy exactly one program has control. Execution proceeds in a single sequence from calling program to called subprogram and back to calling program. If we halt execution at some point, we may always identify one program that is in execution (i.e., that has control), a set of others whose execution has been temporarily suspended (the calling program, its calling program, etc.), and the remainder, which either have never been called or have completely executed. But subprograms used as *tasks* may execute concurrently, so that several are in execution at once.

Of the major languages discussed in Part II, only FORTRAN and COBOL are based directly on the copy-rule view of subprograms. Each of the others allows more flexible structures. In the sections that follow we shall consider the various subprogram control structures that result from the relaxation of each of the above five assumptions in turn.

Note that the emphasis here is on sequence-control structure, i.e., on the mechanisms for transfer of control between programs and subprograms. Closely tied to each of these sequence-control structures is the question of data control: parameter transmission, global and local variables, and so on. These topics are taken up separately in the next chapter so that we can keep our focus here on the sequence-control mechanisms themselves. For example, even simple subprogram calls ordinarily arise in two forms, the *function call*, for subprograms that return values directly, and the *procedure* or *subroutine call*, for subprograms that operate only through side effects on shared data. These distinctions are based on methods of data control, however, and thus are taken up in the next chapter. For our purposes in this chapter the two types of subprograms are identical in the sequence-control structures they require, and thus we do not distinguish the two cases.

Implementation

To understand the implementation of the simple call-return control structure, it is important to build a more complete model of what it means to say
that a program is "being executed." For expressions and statement
sequences we think of each as represented by a block of executable code at
run time. Execution of the expression or statement sequence means simply
execution of the code, using a hardware or software interpreter, as discussed
in Chapter 2. For subprograms, a deeper understanding is needed. Recall
from the preceding chapter:

1. There is a distinction between a subprogram *definition* and a
subprogram *activation*. The definition is what we see in the written
program, which is translated into a template. An activation is created each
time a subprogram is called, using the template created from the definition.

2. An activation is implemented as two parts, a *code segment* containing the executable code and constants, and an *activation record* containing
local data, parameters, and various other data items.

3. The code segment is *invariant* during execution. It is created by the
translator and stored statically in memory. During execution it is used but
never modified. Every activation of the subprogram uses the same code
segment.

4. The activation record is *created* anew each time the subprogram is
called, and it is *destroyed* when the subprogram returns. While the
subprogram is executing, the contents of the activation record are con-
stantly changing as assignments are made to local variables and other data
objects.

To avoid confusion, we cannot simply talk of "execution of a particular
statement *S* in the subprogram," but rather we must talk of "execution of *S*
during activation *R* of the subprogram." Thus to keep track of the point at
which a program is "being executed," we need two pieces of data, which we
consider as stored in two system-defined pointer variables:

1. *Current-instruction pointer (CIP)*. Statements and expressions in a
subprogram are represented by instructions of some sort in the executable
code produced by the translator and stored in the code segment. We consider
that at any point during execution there is some instruction in some code
segment that is currently being (or just about to be) executed by the
hardware or software interpreter. This instruction is termed the *current
instruction*, and a pointer to it is maintained in the variable called the
current-instruction pointer or CIP. The interpreter acts by fetching the

instruction designated by the CIP, updating the CIP to point to the next instruction in sequence, and then executing the instruction (which may itself change the CIP again to effect a jump to some other instruction).

2. *Current-environment pointer (CEP)*. Since all activations of the same subprogram use the same code segment, it is not enough simply to know the current instruction being executed; a pointer to the activation record being used is also needed. For example, when the instruction in the code references a variable X, that variable ordinarily is represented in the activation record. Each activation record for that subprogram has a different data object named X. The activation record represents the "referencing environment" of the subprogram, as discussed in Chapter 7, so a pointer to an activation record is commonly known as an *environment pointer*. The point to the current activation record (current referencing environment) is maintained during execution in the variable we term the *current-environment pointer* or CEP. The activation record designated by the CEP is used to resolve the reference to X.

With the CIP and CEP pointers it now becomes easy to understand how a program is executed. An activation record for the main program is created (since there is only one such activation, this activation record is often created during translation along with the code segment). The CEP is assigned a pointer to it. The CIP is assigned a pointer to the first instruction in the code segment for the main program. The interpreter goes to work, fetching and executing instructions as designated by the CIP.

When a subprogram CALL instruction is reached, an activation record for the subprogram is created and a pointer to it is assigned to the CEP. The CIP is assigned a pointer to the first instruction of the code segment for the subprogram. The interpreter continues from that point, executing instructions in the subprogram. If the subprogram calls another subprogram, new assignments are made to set the CIP and CEP for the activation of that subprogram.

In order to be able to return correctly from a subprogram call, the values of the CIP and CEP must be saved somewhere by the subprogram CALL instruction before the new values are assigned. When a RETURN instruction is reached that terminates an activation of a subprogram, the old values of the CIP and CEP that were saved when the subprogram was called must be retrieved and reinstated. This reinstatement of the old values is all that is necessary to return control to the correct activation of the calling subprogram at the correct place so that execution of that subprogram may continue.

Where should the CALL instruction save the values of the CIP and CEP before assigning the new values? A convenient place is to store them in the activation record of the subprogram being called. An additional system-defined data object, the *return point*, is included in the activation record. The return point contains space for two pointer values, the pair (instruction pointer, environment pointer) or *(ip,ep)*. After the CALL instruction creates the activation record, it stores the old values, *(ip,ep)*, of the CIP and CEP in the return point and assigns the new *(ip,ep)* to the CIP and CEP, thus effecting the transfer of control to the called subprogram. The RETURN instruction fetches the old *(ip,ep)* from the return point and reinstates them as the values of the CIP and CEP, thus effecting the return of control to the calling subprogram.

Now if we were to watch the overall pattern of execution of a program, we would see the interpreter plodding along, executing the instruction designated by the CIP on each cycle and using the CEP to resolve data references (a subject taken up in detail in the next chapter). The CALL and RETURN instructions swap *(ip,ep)* values in and out of the CIP and CEP to effect transfers of control back and forth to subprograms. If execution were halted at some point, it would be simple to determine which subprogram was currently being executed (look at the CIP and CEP), which subprogram had called it (look at the return point of the subprogram being executed), which subprogram had called that subprogram (look at its return point), and so on. Figure 6-9 shows this organization for a main program and two subprograms, each called at two places.

This model for the implementation of subprogram call and return is general enough to serve as a basis for several of the varieties of subprogram control structure considered below. Returning to look at the implementation of only the simple call-return structure described above, we might note one important property of the copy-rule view of subprograms: *at most one activation of any subprogram is in use at any point during program execution*. A subprogram P may be called many different times during execution, but each activation is complete and terminated before the next activation begins.

From this property, a simpler model of subprogram implementation may be derived, provided we are willing to pay a penalty in storage in order to increase execution speed. The simpler implementation is to allocate storage for the single activation record of each subprogram statically, as an extension of the code segment, rather than creating the activation record at the time of call of the subprogram. In this simpler model (which is used in many implementations of FORTRAN and COBOL) execution of the overall program begins with a code segment and activation record for each subprogram and the main program already present in memory. Execution proceeds without any dynamic allocation of storage when a subprogram is called. Instead, the same activation record is used repeatedly, simply being reinitialized each time the subprogram is called again. Since only one activation is in use at any point, this reuse of the same activation record on

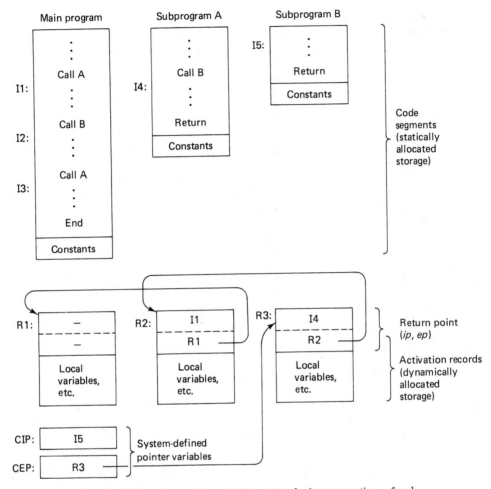

Fig. 6-9 Snapshot of execution state during execution of subprogram B, showing subprogram return points

each call cannot destroy any information needed from an earlier call, since all earlier calls have already terminated.

By allocating a code segment and an activation record as a single block of storage, some other simplifications are also gained. The CEP pointer is no longer needed, since the current activation record is always just an extension of the code segment that the CIP designates. A reference in the instructions to a variable X always may be resolved by going to the attached activation record rather than to the CEP. With the CEP omitted, only a single *ip* pointer, the CIP, need be saved and restored on subprogram call and return.

With the more general implementation of call and return, the under-lying hardware often provides little support. However, with this simplified implementation, the hardware often provides a *return-jump instruction* that allows a subprogram call to be implemented in a single hardware instruc-tion. Assuming the executable code for a subprogram is represented in machine language instructions, then the hardware interpreter is used to execute the program. The CIP of our model is represented directly by the *program address register* of the hardware (as discussed in Chapter 2). The return-jump instruction stores the contents of this program address register in a memory location or register (often the memory location immediately before the location to which control is transferred) and assigns a designated location as the new value of the program address register (thus effecting a jump to the instruction at that location). The effect is exactly what is desired: the old value of the CIP is saved and the location of the first instruction of

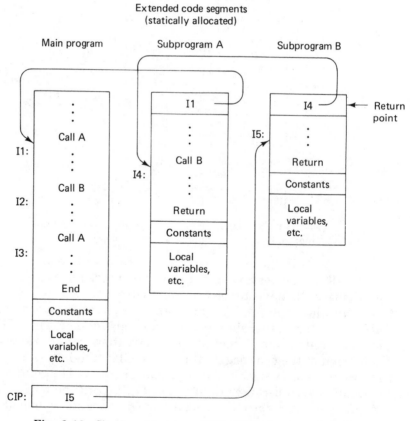

Fig. 6-10 Simple subprogram CALL-RETURN structure during execution of subprogram B

the subprogram code is assigned as the new value. The return from a subprogram is also usually implementable as a single instruction: the saved value is reassigned to the program address register (a jump instruction does this). The result is a simple implementation of subprogram call and return, at a cost in storage due to the static allocation of activation records for all subprograms. An example of this structure is shown in Fig. 6-10.

6-5   RECURSIVE SUBPROGRAMS

Recursion, in the form of recursive subprogram calls, is one of the most important sequence-control structures in programming. Many algorithms are most naturally represented using recursion, particularly algorithms that manipulate list structures and trees. In LISP, where list structures are the primary data structure available, recursion is the primary control mechanism for repeating sequences of statements, replacing the iteration of most other languages.

Specification

Suppose we relax restriction 1 mentioned above and allow recursive subprogram calls. That is, a subprogram A may call any other subprogram, including A itself, a subprogram B that calls A, and so on. Syntactically, in writing the program, probably nothing changes, since a recursive subprogram call looks the same as any other subprogram call. In concept, also, there is no difficulty, provided that the distinction between a subprogram definition and activation is clear. The only difference between a recursive call and an ordinary call is that the recursive call creates a second activation of the subprogram *during the lifetime of the first activation*. If the second activation leads to another recursive call, then three activations may exist simultaneously, and so on. In general, if the execution of the program results in a chain of a first call of subprogram A followed by k recursive calls that occur before any return is made, then $k + 1$ activations of A will exist at the point just before return from the kth recursive call. The only new element introduced by recursion is the multiple activations of the same subprogram that all exist simultaneously at some point during execution.

Implementation

Because of the possibility of multiple activations, the simplified implementation model for subprograms that is described in the preceding section cannot be used, but the general model with both the CIP and CEP is quite adequate. At the time of each subprogram call, a new activation record is created, which is subsequently destroyed upon return.

When an activation record is created, a block of storage must be allocated for it. This storage must remain allocated throughout the lifetime of the activation. When the activation ends, through execution of a RETURN instruction, the storage is freed for reuse. Potentially this storage management, the allocation and freeing of storage for activation records, might be difficult to implement, except for one important property of the lifetimes of subprogram activations: *lifetimes cannot overlap in time*; for any two activations A and B, either the lifetime of A *completely includes* that of B, the lifetime of B *completely includes* that of A, or the lifetimes are entirely *separate* in time, with one activation complete before the other begins. Because of this property, if subprogram A calls subprogram B, the activation of B must terminate before that of A. If B calls C, C must terminate before B, and so on. In terms of storage management, this means that storage is allocated for A's activation record, then for B's activation record, and then for C's activation record. When C terminates, its storage is freed, then B's when it terminates, and then A's. B cannot terminate before C, nor A before either B or C.

Storage management in such circumstances is straightforward, because a simple *central stack* may be used. The allocation and freeing of activation records obeys the rules for a stack: the last item created on the stack must be the first item deleted. The implementation of subprogram call and return proceeds as follows. At the start of program execution, a large block of storage is reserved for the central stack. The activation record for the main program is allocated at one end of the block. This becomes the bottom of the stack.

When a subprogram A is called, storage for its activation record is allocated adjacent to that of the main program's activation record. If A calls B, B's activation record is allocated adjacent to A's. If B calls C, C's activation record is adjacent to B's, and so on. When C terminates and returns control to B, any storage allocated beyond C's in the central stack must already have been freed. C's storage is freed, and then B's when B returns, and so on. The central-stack implementation for a series of subprogram calls and returns is shown in Fig. 6-11.

Each activation record contains a return point, as explained above, to store the values of the (*ip*,*ep*) pair used by CALL and RETURN. If you observe only the *ep* values stored in the return points in Fig. 6-11, you note that they form a linked list that links together the activation records on the central stack in the order of their creation. From the CEP pointer itself, the "top" activation record in the central stack is reached. From the *ep* value in its return point, the second activation record in the stack may be reached; from the *ep* value in that activation record the third activation record in the stack may be reached. At the end of this chain, the last link leads to the activation record for the main program. This chain of links is called the *dynamic chain* because it chains together subprogram activations in the order of their dynamic creation during program execution. (In Chapter 7 a related *static chain* is discussed that links activation records together for referencing purposes.)

Conventional computer hardware sometimes provides some hardware support for this central-stack organization, but it is generally somewhat more costly to implement than the simple call-return structure without recursion. There is no difficulty in mixing subprograms implemented in the simple way with those using a central stack, provided the compiler knows which is which when compiling CALL and RETURN instructions. Only subprograms that are actually called recursively need the central-stack implementation. Thus in some languages, such as PL/I, subprograms called recursively must be tagged RECURSIVE as part of the subprogram definition. The compiler then uses the simple implementation for other subprograms.

6-6   EXCEPTIONS AND EXCEPTION HANDLERS

During execution of a program, events or conditions often occur that might be considered "exceptional." Rather than continue with normal program execution, a subprogram needs to be called to perform some special processing. For example:

   1. *Error conditions.* Call a subprogram to process an error such as an arithmetic operation overflow or reference to an array element with a subscript out of bounds.

   2. *Conditions that arise unpredictably during normal program execution.* Call a subprogram to handle special output headings at the end of a printer page or to process an end-of-file indicator on an input file.

   3. *Tracing and monitoring during program testing.* Call a subprogram to print trace output during program testing when a subprogram is entered or exited or when the value of a variable changes.

   While it may often be possible to insert an explicit test in the program to test for the exceptional condition and call the subprogram, such extra statements can quickly obscure the program's basic structure. It is simpler to relax the requirement that subprograms must be invoked by *explicit* calls and to provide a way that a subprogram may be invoked when a particular condition or event occurs. Such a condition or event is usually termed an *exception.* The subprogram that performs the special processing is termed an *exception handler.* The action of noticing the exception, interrupting program execution, and transferring control to the exception handler is called *raising the exception.*

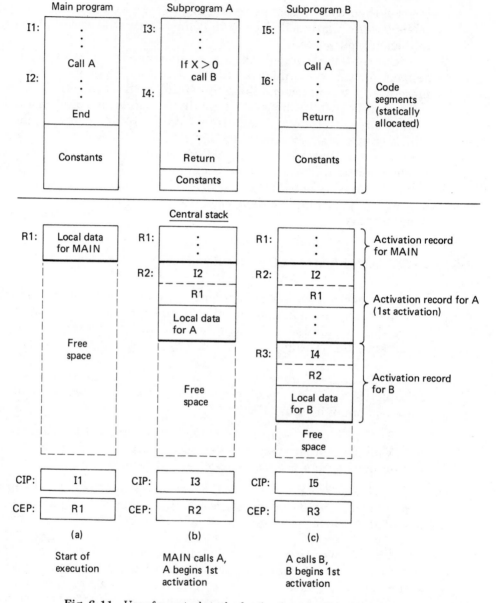

Fig. 6-11   Use of a central stack of activation records to implement recursive subprogram calls

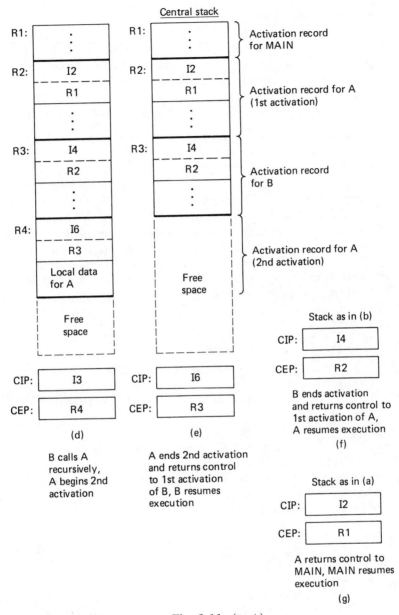

Fig. 6-11 (cont.)

Exception Handlers

Because an exception handler is invoked without an explicit call, it ordinarily does not require a name or parameters. The definition of an exception handler typically contains only

1. A set of declarations of local variables (if any), and

2. A sequence of executable statements.

To provide the connection between exceptions and their handlers, each class of exceptions is given a name. Some exceptions are ordinarily predefined in the language, e.g., OVERFLOW, UNDERFLOW, SUBSCRIPT_RANGE_ERROR, END_OF_FILE. Others may be programmer-defined, e.g., the program may include a declaration "STACK_EMPTY: *exception*" or "BAD_DATA_VALUE: *exception*". Each exception handler is then paired with the name (or names) of the exception(s) that it is to handle. Usually all the exception handlers are grouped at the beginning or end of the larger program or subprogram where the exception might occur. The Ada structure is typical:

```
procedure SUB
    BAD_DATA_VALUE: exception;
            —other declarations for SUB
begin
            —statements for normal processing in SUB
exception
    when BAD_DATA_VALUE =>
            —handler for bad data values
    when NUMERIC_ERROR =>
            —handler for predefined exception NUMERIC_ERROR
    when others =>
            —handler for all other exceptions
end;
```

Raising an Exception

An exception may be raised by a language-defined primitive operation; e.g., an addition or multiplication operation might raise the exception OVERFLOW. Alternatively, an exception may be raised explicitly by the programmer using a statement provided for that purpose, such as the Ada:

```
raise BAD_DATA_VALUE;
```

which might be executed in a subprogram after determining that a particular variable or input file contained an improper value.

In a subprogram, if an explicit **raise** statement is used and the subprogram itself contains a handler for the exception raised, as for example when the statement

if X = 0 **then raise** BAD_DATA_VALUE **end if;**

appears within the body of the procedure SUB above, then the **raise** statement has the effect of a **goto** from the point of the **raise** statement to the associated handler. One of the major uses for **goto** statements in languages without explicit exception-handling features is to provide transfers to exception-handling code, as discussed in Sec. 6-3.

Propagating an Exception

Often, in constructing a program, the place at which an exception occurs is not the best place to handle it. For example, one subprogram may have the function of reading data values from a file and passing them to a nest of subprograms to be processed. Suppose that several different types of bad data values may be found on the file and each subprogram tests for a different class of such errors, but the response in all cases is the same: print an error message and advance the file past the bad data. In this case, the handler might properly be a part of the subprogram that reads the file, and each subprogram might properly raise the exception BAD_DATA_VALUE. When an exception is handled in a subprogram other than the subprogram in which it is raised, the exception is said to be *propagated* from the point at which it is raised to the point at which it is handled.

The rule for determining which handler handles a particular exception is usually defined in terms of the *dynamic chain* of subprogram activations leading to the subprogram that raises the exception. When an exception P is raised in subprogram C, then P is handled by a handler defined in C if there is one. If there is none, then C terminates. If subprogram B called C, then the exception is propagated to B, and raised again at the point in B where B called C. If B provides no handler for P, then B is terminated, the exception propagates to B's caller, and so on. If no subprogram or the main program provides a handler, then the entire program is terminated and a standard language-defined handler is invoked.

One important effect of this rule for propagating exceptions is that it allows a subprogram to remain as a programmer-defined *abstract operation*, even in processing exceptions. A primitive operation may suddenly interrupt its normal processing and raise an exception. Similarly, through execution of a RAISE statement, a subprogram may suddenly interrupt its normal processing and raise an exception. To the caller, the effect of a subprogram's raising an exception is just the same as the effect of a primitive operation's raising an exception, if the subprogram does not itself handle the exception. If the exception is handled within the subprogram, then the subprogram returns in the normal way, and the caller is never aware that an exception has been raised.

After an Exception is Handled

After a handler completes the processing of an exception, and the handler is ready to terminate, there is a sticky question as to where control is to be transferred, because there was no explicit call of the handler. Should control return to the point where the exception was raised (which may be several levels of subprogram distant)? Should control return to the statement in the subprogram containing the handler where the exception was raised after being propagated? Should the subprogram containing the handler itself be terminated, but terminated normally, so it appears to its caller as if nothing had happened? The latter solution is that adopted in Ada; PL/I provides several options; and other languages have chosen other alternatives.

Implementation

Exceptions may be raised directly by hardware interrupts or traps, such as arithmetic overflow, or they may be raised in support software in the operating system, such as end-of-file condition. Often, however, checking for exceptions is done by special code inserted by the language translator into the executable code. For example, to detect the exception SUBSCRIPT_RANGE_ERROR caused by an array subscript that was too large or too small, the translator inserts an explicit sequence of instructions at each reference to an array, such as A[I,J], to check that the values of I and J are within the declared bounds. Thus, unless the hardware or operating system provides the exception checking, checking for an exception requires some software simulation. Often the cost of this software checking, in both code storage and execution time, is large. For example, it may take longer to perform the subscript bounds check on A[I,J] than it does to access the element of the array. Because of this extra cost, most languages provide a means to turn off checking for exceptions in parts of the program where the programmer determines it is safe to do so.

Once the exception is raised, transfer of control to a handler in the same program is usually implemented by a direct jump to the start of the handler code. Propagation of exceptions down the dynamic chain of subprogram calls can make use of the dynamic chain formed by the return points of the subprogram activation records in the central stack, as discussed in the preceding section. In proceeding down the dynamic chain, each subprogram activation must be terminated, using a special form of RETURN instruction to both return control to the caller and raise the exception in the caller again.

The sequence of returns continues down the dynamic chain until a subprogram is reached that has a handler for the exception raised.

Once the appropriate handler is found, it is invoked as in an ordinary subprogram call. When the handler terminates, however, it may also terminate the subprogram that contains it (e.g., in Ada), thus leading to two normal subprogram returns, one immediately after the other. Once the dynamic chain has been unwound in this way to a final normal return to a subprogram, that subprogram continues its execution in the usual manner.

6-7   COROUTINES

Suppose that we drop restriction 3 in Sec. 6-4 and admit subprograms that do not execute completely before returning control to their calling program. Such subprograms are termed *coroutines*. When a coroutine receives control from another subprogram, it ordinarily executes only partially. The execution of the coroutine is suspended when it returns control, and at a later point the calling program may "resume" execution of the coroutine from the point at which execution was suspended.

Note the symmetry that has now been introduced into the *calling program/called program* structure. If A calls subprogram B as a coroutine, then B executes for a while and returns control to A, just as any ordinary subprogram would do. When A again passes control to B, now by a *resume* call, B again executes for a while and returns control to A, just as an ordinary subprogram. Thus to A, B appears as an ordinary subprogram. But now the situation is very similar viewed from subprogram B. B, in the middle of execution, gives control to A. A executes for a while and returns control to B. B continues execution for a while and returns control to A. A executes for a while and returns control to B. From subprogram B, A appears very much like an ordinary subprogram. The name *coroutine* derives from this symmetry. Rather than a calling program and a called program, the two programs appear more as equals—two subprograms swapping control back and forth as each executes, with no one of them clearly controlling the other. Figure 6-12 illustrates the control transfer between two coroutines.

From two coroutines it is natural to extend this sequence control structure to a set of coroutines. The coroutine A in execution may transfer control to another coroutine B with a statement of the form

resume B

Let us take the simplest case in which coroutines may be activated only by **resume** statements (interpreting a **resume** call of a coroutine which has not yet been activated or which has completed its execution to indicate an

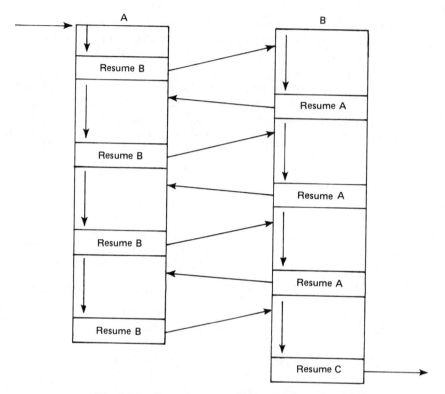

Fig 6-12   Control transfer between two coroutines

ordinary subprogram call). The **resume** statement acts much like an
ordinary subprogram call except that the entry point to the subprogram is
variable. Note, however, that there is now no analogue of the **return**
statement, with its special property that the subprogram to which control is
to be returned is not specified. Instead the **resume** statement always
specifies explicitly which of the other coroutines is to receive control.

Coroutines are not currently a common control structure in programming languages outside of discrete simulation languages (see Sec. 6-8).
However, they provide a control structure in many algorithms that is more
natural than the ordinary subprogram hierarchy. Moreover, the simple
coroutine structure may be readily simulated in many languages using the
goto statement and a *resume point* variable specifying the label of the
statement at which execution is to resume (see Problem 13).

Implementation

The **resume** instruction that transfers control between coroutines specifies
the resumption of some particular activation of the coroutine. If there are
multiple recursive activations of a coroutine B, then the statement **resume**

B has no clear meaning. For this reason, it is simplest to think of coroutines in a context where only at most one activation of a given coroutine exists at a time. This restriction allows us to use an implementation for coroutines similar to that used for the simple call-return structure in Sec. 6-4. A single activation record is allocated storage statically at the beginning of execution, as an extension of the code segment for the coroutine. A single location, now called the *resume point*, is reserved in the activation record to save the old *ip* value of the CIP when a **resume** instruction transfers control to another coroutine. However, unlike the return point in a simple subprogram, this resume-point location in a coroutine B is used to store the *ip* value *for B itself*. Execution of a **resume** B instruction in coroutine A then involves two steps:

1. The current value of the CIP is saved in the resume-point location of the activation record for A.

2. The *ip* value in the resume point location of B is fetched from B's activation record and assigned to the CIP, to effect the transfer of control to the proper instruction in B.

Since there is no explicit return instruction, B does not need to know that A gave it control. Figure 6-13 illustrates this implementation structure for coroutines.

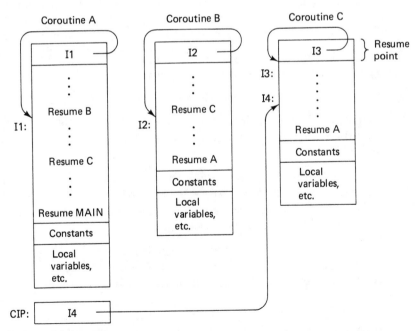

Fig. 6-13 Snapshot of execution state during execution of coroutine C

Control structures in which subprograms may be invoked either as coroutines or ordinary subprograms and in which coroutines may be recursive (i.e., may have multiple simultaneous activations) require more complex implementations. Problem 14 explores some of these structures.

6-8   SCHEDULED SUBPROGRAMS

The concept of subprogram scheduling results from relaxation of the assumption that execution of a subprogram should always be initiated immediately upon its call. One may think of an ordinary subprogram call statement as specifying that the called subprogram is to be scheduled for execution immediately, without completing execution of the calling program. Completion of execution of the calling program is rescheduled to occur immediately on termination of the subprogram. The exception-handling control structure may be viewed also as a means of subprogram scheduling. The exception handler is scheduled to be executed when a particular exception is raised.

Generalizing further, other subprogram scheduling techniques come to mind:

1. Schedule subprograms to be executed before or after other subprograms, as, for example: CALL B AFTER A, which would schedule execution of subprogram B after execution of subprogram A is completed.

2. Schedule subprograms to be executed when an arbitrary Boolean expression becomes true, as, for example:

$$\text{CALL B WHEN } X = 5 \wedge Z > 0$$

Such scheduling provides a sort of generalized exception-handling feature—B is called whenever the values of Z and X are changed to satisfy the given conditions.

3. Schedule subprograms on the basis of a simulated *time scale*, as, for example: CALL B AT TIME = 25 or CALL B AT TIME = CURRENT-TIME + 10. Such scheduling allows a general interleaving of subprogram calls scheduled from different sources.

4. Schedule subprograms according to a priority designation, as, for example, CALL B WITH PRIORITY 7, which would activate B when no other subprogram with higher priority has been scheduled.

Generalized subprogram scheduling is a feature of programming languages designed for discrete system simulation, such as GPSS, SIMSCRIPT, and SIMULA, although the concepts have wide applicability.

Each of the above scheduling techniques appears in at least one of the simulation languages mentioned. The most important technique in system simulation is the third in the list: scheduling based on a simulated time scale. We shall emphasize this technique in our discussion.

When we speak of subprogram scheduling we mean scheduling of subprogram *activations*, because this scheduling is a run-time activity in which the same subprogram may be scheduled to be activated at many different points during execution. In generalized subprogram scheduling the programmer no longer writes a main program. Instead the main program is a system-defined *scheduler program* that typically maintains a list of currently scheduled subprogram activations, ordered in the sequence in which they are to be executed. Statements are provided in the language through which subprogram activations may be inserted into this list during execution. The scheduler operates by calling each subprogram on the list in the indicated sequence. When execution of one subprogram terminates, execution of the next subprogram on the list is initiated. Usually provision is also made for ordinary subprogram calls, sometimes simply by allowing a subprogram to suspend its own execution and schedule immediate execution of another subprogram.

In simulation languages the most common approach to subprogram scheduling is based on a type of generalized coroutine. Execution of a single subprogram activation proceeds in a series of *active* and *passive* phases. During active phase the subprogram has control and is being executed; in a passive phase the subprogram has transferred control elsewhere and is awaiting a resume call. However, rather than each coroutine directly transferring control to another coroutine when it switches from active to passive, control is returned to the scheduler, which then transfers control to the next subprogram on its list of scheduled activations. This transfer of control may take the form of a resume call if the subprogram is already partially executed, or an entirely new activation of the subprogram may be initiated.

The coroutine scheduling concept is particularly direct using a simulated time scale. Assume that each active phase of execution of a subprogram may be scheduled to occur at any point on an integer time scale beginning at time $T = 0$. T is a simple integer variable that always contains the value of the current time on the simulated scale. Execution of an active phase of a subprogram always occurs instantaneously on this simulated time scale; i.e., the value of T does not change during execution of an active phase of a subprogram. When a subprogram completes an active phase and returns control to the scheduler, the scheduler updates the value of T to that at which the next subprogram on the list of scheduled subprograms is to be activated and transfers control to that subprogram. The newly activated routine partially executes and returns control to the scheduler, which again updates T and activates the next routine on the list.

6-9   TASKS AND CONCURRENT EXECUTION

The final and most important restriction from Sec. 6-4 is the restriction to a single execution sequence in executing a program. More generally, several subprograms might be executing *simultaneously*. Where there is a single execution sequence, the program is termed a *sequential program* because execution of its subprograms proceeds in a predefined sequence. In the more general case, the program is termed a *concurrent* or *parallel* program. Each subprogram that can execute concurrently with other subprograms is called a *task*.

Computer systems capable of executing several programs concurrently are now quite common. A *multiprocessor* system has several central processing units (CPU's) sharing a common memory. A *distributed* or *parallel* computer system has several computers (possibly hundreds), each with its own memory and CPU, connected with communication links into a network in which each can communicate with the others. In such systems, many tasks may execute concurrently.

Even on a single computer, it is often useful to design a program so that it is composed of many separate tasks that run concurrently on the *virtual* computer, even though on the actual computer only one can be executing at once. The illusion of concurrent execution on a single processor is obtained by interleaving execution of the separate tasks, so that each executes a portion of its code, then is swapped out to be replaced by another task that executes a portion of its code, and so on. Operating systems that support *multiprogramming* and *time sharing* provide this sort of concurrent execution for separate user programs. Our concern here, however, is with concurrent execution of tasks *within a single program*. Facilities to support concurrent tasks are still rather rare in high-level programming languages. Some versions of PL/I provide tasks and concurrency, but the standard PL/I language described in Chapter 14 does not. Of the languages described in Part II, only Ada provides tasks and concurrent execution.

The basic idea behind tasks is quite simple. Consider a subprogram A being executed in the normal fashion. If A calls subprogram B, then ordinarily execution of A is suspended while B is executed. However, if B is initiated as a *task*, then execution of A continues while B is being executed. The original execution sequence has now split into two parallel execution sequences. Continuing, either A or B or both may initiate further tasks, allowing any number of parallel execution sequences to coexist.

In general, each task is considered a *dependent* of the task that initiated it. When a task is ready to terminate, it must wait until all its dependents have terminated before it may terminate. Thus the splitting into multiple execution sequences is reversed as tasks terminate, coalescing into fewer and fewer sequences until finally only a single sequence remains. For many applications involving tasks, however, termination of the top-level group of tasks is presumed to occur only in case of a major error that shuts down the entire system. In normal circumstances, each of these top-level tasks controls a major part of the system (often now a distributed computer system) and, once initiated, is expected to run "forever."

Defining, Initiating, and Terminating Tasks

The definition of a task in a program differs little from the definition of an ordinary subprogram, except at places defining how the task synchronizes and communicates with other tasks. Most of the body of a task definition contains ordinary declarations and statements concerned with the processing performed by the task while working independently of other tasks. In Ada, which is our primary example here, a task definition takes the form:

```
task NAME is
           — special declarations allowing
             synchronization and communication
             with other tasks
    end;
task body NAME is
           — usual local declarations as
             found in any subprogram
    begin
           —sequence of statements
    end;
```

Methods for synchronizing and communicating with other tasks are discussed below.

Initiating execution of a task may take the form of an ordinary subprogram call. For example, in many implementations of PL/I, a task B is initiated by executing the statement:

CALL B (*parameters*) TASK;

In Ada the method is somewhat different. The definition of a task, as given above, is included among the declarations of some larger program structure such as the main program. When that larger program structure is entered, all the tasks declared within it are automatically initiated. Thus no explicit **call** statement is needed; the tasks begin execution concurrently as soon as the larger program structure is entered.

Multiple simultaneous activations of the *same* task are often required in applications. For example, consider a computer system that controls a set of user terminals. The primary task might be the program that monitors the status of all the terminals. When a user logs on at a terminal, this task,

MONITOR, initiates a new task, TERMINAL, to control the interactions with the user at that particular terminal. When the user logs off, the TERMINAL task terminates. The MONITOR task, of course, runs continuously except in the case of a catastrophic system failure. When several users are logged on simultaneously at different terminals, several activations of the task TERMINAL are required, one for each user.

If a task is initiated using an ordinary subprogram call, as in PL/I, then repeatedly executing a CALL suffices to create multiple activations. In Ada, a slightly different method is used. The Ada task definition described above may be used to create only a single task activation, owing to the implicit initiation of tasks in Ada. Thus the task MONITOR would probably be defined as above. For the task TERMINAL, multiple activations are required, and they must be created and initiated by MONITOR as needed. In Ada, TERMINAL is defined as a *task type*:

> **task type** TERMINAL **is**
> —rest of definition in the same form as above
> **end;**

Definition of TERMINAL as a task type allows an activation of the task to be treated as a type of data object, in the same way that an ordinary type definition is used to define a class of data objects, as described in Sec. 5-3. Creation and initiation of a new task activation is then done in the same manner that a new data object is created using a type definition as a template. To create several activations and give them the names A, B, and C, the Ada programmer writes the declarations as ordinary variable declarations:

> A: TERMINAL;
> B, C: TERMINAL;

These declarations appear at the beginning of a larger program structure, and on entry to this larger program the three activations of TERMINAL are created and initiated. Alternatively, a pointer variable may be defined whose value is a pointer to a *task activation*, as in:

type TASK_PTR **is access** TERMINAL;   —defines pointer type
        NEW_TERM: TASK_PTR := **new** TERMINAL
                                —declares pointer variable

Pointer variable NEW_TERM points to an activation of a task of type TERMINAL that is created and initiated at the time NEW_TERM itself is created.

Once a task is initiated, the statements in its body are executed in sequence, just as for an ordinary subprogram. When a task terminates, it does not return control; its separate parallel execution sequence simply ends. However, a task cannot terminate until its dependents have terminated, and when it does terminate, any task of which it is a dependent must be notified so that that task may also terminate. A task terminates when it completes execution of the statements in its body; a task that never terminates is written to contain an infinite loop that cycles continuously (until an error occurs).

Synchronization of Tasks

During the concurrent execution of several tasks, each task proceeds *asynchronously* with the others; that is, each task executes at its own speed, independently of the others. Thus, when task A has executed ten statements, task B, which was initiated at the same time, may have executed only six statements or no statements, or it may have already run to completion and terminated.

In order for two tasks running asynchronously to coordinate their activities, the language must provide a means of *synchronization*, so that one task can tell the other when it completes execution of a particular section of its code. For example, one task may be controlling an input device and the second task processing each batch of data as it is input from the device. The first task reads in a batch of data, signals the second that a batch has arrived, and then begins preparation for input of the next batch of data. The second task waits for the signal from the first task, then processes the data, then signals the first that it has completed the processing, and then waits again for the signal that another batch has arrived. The signals sent between the tasks allow the tasks to synchronize their activities so that the second does not start processing data before the first has finished reading it in, and so that the first does not overwrite data that the second is still processing.

Tasks that are synchronizing their activities in this way are somewhat like coroutines—the signals serve to tell each task when to wait and when to proceed, somewhat like the use of resume calls between coroutines to signal a coroutine to proceed. However, with coroutines, there is only a single execution sequence, while here there may be several.

Many language features have been proposed to allow synchronization of tasks. Synchronization to allow safe access to shared data, as in the example above, is a common requirement. This special form of synchronization is treated more fully in the next chapter, after we consider shared data in sequential programs. First we consider only synchronization based on simple signaling, regardless of its connection to data sharing.

Interrupts. Synchronization of concurrent tasks through the use of interrupts is a common mechanism found in computer hardware. If task A wishes to signal to task B that a particular event has occurred (e.g., completion of a particular segment of code), then task A executes an instruction that causes execution of task B to be interrupted immediately. Control is transferred to a subprogram or code segment whose sole purpose is to handle the interrupt by performing whatever special actions are required. When this interrupt handler completes its execution, task B continues its execution from the point where the interrupt occurred. This method of signaling is similar to the exception-handling mechanisms described in Sec. 6-6 and is often used for that purpose. For example, in a hardware computer, a task that handles an input-output device may synchronize with the central processor through the use of interrupts. In high-level languages, however, interrupts have several disadvantages as a synchronization mechanism: (1) the code for interrupt handling is separate from the main body of the task, leading to a confusing program structure; (2) a task that wishes to wait for an interrupt must usually enter a *busy waiting loop*, a loop that does nothing but cycle endlessly until the interrupt happens; (3) the task must be written so that an interrupt at any time can be correctly handled, which usually requires that data shared between the task body and the interrupt routine be protected in special ways. Because of these (and several other) problems with interrupts, high-level languages usually provide other mechanisms for synchronization.

Semaphores. A *semaphore* is a data object used for synchronization between tasks. A semaphore consists of two parts: (1) an integer counter, whose value is always positive or zero, that is used to count the number of signals sent but not yet received, and (2) a queue of tasks that are waiting for signals to be sent. In a *binary semaphore*, the counter may only have the values zero and one. In a *general semaphore*, the counter may take on any positive integer value.

Two primitive operations are defined for a semaphore data object P:

SIGNAL(P). When executed by a task A, this operation tests the value of the counter in P; if zero, then the first task in the task queue is removed from the queue and its execution is resumed; if not zero or if the queue is empty, then the counter is incremented by one (indicating a signal has been sent but not yet received). In either case, execution of task A continues after the SIGNAL operation is complete.

WAIT(P). When executed by a task B, this operation tests the value of the counter in P; if nonzero, then the counter value is decremented by one (indicating that B has received a signal) and task B continues execution; if zero, then task B is inserted at the end of the task queue for P and execution of B is suspended (indicating that B is waiting for a signal to be sent).

As an example of the use of semaphores and the WAIT and SIGNAL operations, consider again the two tasks that cooperate to (1) input a batch of data (task A) and (2) process a batch of data (task B). To synchronize their activities, two binary semaphores might be used. Semaphore P is used by task A to signal that input of a batch of data is complete. Semaphore Q is used by task B to signal that processing of a batch of data is complete. Figure 6-14 shows the structure of tasks A and B, using WAIT and SIGNAL operations.

Semaphores have some disadvantages for use in high-level-language programming of tasks: (1) a task can wait for only one semaphore at a time, but often it is desirable to allow a task to wait for any of several signals, (2) if a task fails to SIGNAL at the appropriate point (e.g., because of a coding error), the entire system of tasks may *deadlock*—that is the tasks may each be waiting in a semaphore queue for some other task to signal, so that no task remains executing, and (3) programs involving several tasks and semaphores become increasingly difficult to understand, debug, and verify. In essence, the semaphore is a relatively low-level synchronization construct that is adequate primarily in simple situations.

Guarded commands. The problem of a task's waiting for a signal from any of several other tasks is a common synchronization problem, regardless of the use of semaphores or some other mechanism for synchronization. The *guarded command* mentioned in Sec. 6-3 is a statement-level control

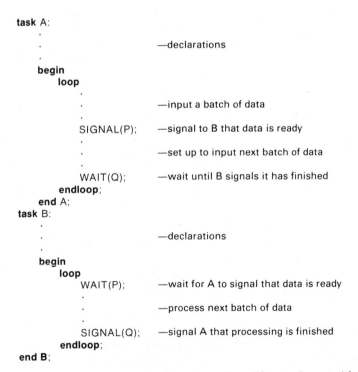

```
task A:
        .                       —declarations
        .
        .
    begin
        loop
            .                   —input a batch of data
            .
            SIGNAL(P);          —signal to B that data is ready
            .                   —set up to input next batch of data
            .
            WAIT(Q);            —wait until B signals it has finished
        endloop;
    end A;
task B:
    .                           —declarations
    .
    .
    begin
        loop
            WAIT(P);            —wait for A to signal that data is ready
            .                   —process next batch of data
            .
            SIGNAL(Q);          —signal A that processing is finished
        endloop;
    end B;
```

Fig. 6-14 Two tasks synchronizing through semaphores with WAIT and SIGNAL operations

structure that provides a solution to this problem. A guarded command has a form somewhat similar to a **case** statement. It is a form of conditional statement with multiple alternative statements, and each time it is executed, exactly one of the alternative statements is executed. In Ada it is termed a **select** statement and has the general form (Ada makes some further restrictions not mentioned here):

> **select**
> > **when** ⟨ *condition* ⟩ => ⟨ *statement* ⟩
> **or   when** ⟨ *condition* ⟩ => ⟨ *statement* ⟩
> > $\vdots$
>
> **or   when** ⟨ *condition* ⟩ => ⟨ *statement* ⟩
> **else**   ⟨ *statement* ⟩   —*optional else clause*
> **end select;**

Each of the conditions is termed a *guard*, and each statement is a *command*, hence "guarded command." The meaning of the guarded-command statement is that first each guard is evaluated to determine which commands are available for execution. Then *one* of the available commands is chosen and executed. If no guard returns true (indicating that the corresponding command is available for execution), then the statement following **else** is executed. If only one guard evaluates to true each time, then the guarded command becomes equivalent to an ordinary conditional statement. For example, the guarded command:

> **select**
> > **when** X = 0 => *statement*$_1$
> **or   when** X < 0 => *statement*$_2$
> **else**   *statement*$_3$
> **end select;**

is equivalent to:

> **if** X = 0 **then**
> > *statement*$_1$
> **elsif** X < 0 **then**
> > *statement*$_2$
> **else** *statement*$_3$
> **end if;**

However, if two or more guards may be true when the guarded command is executed, then the guarded command has no equivalent in an ordinary conditional statement, because the statement to execute is chosen *arbitrarily* from among those available. While guarded commands may be used as part of a variety of task-synchronization mechanisms, their use in the Ada rendezvous mechanism illustrates the concept well.

Rendezvous. When two tasks synchronize their actions for a brief period, that synchronization is termed a *rendezvous* in Ada. The rendezvous works as follows. Suppose that one task A is used to input data, as in the example above, and the second task B processes the data. However, assume B *copies* the data into a local data area before processing it, so that A may input a new batch without waiting. Now a rendezvous is necessary to allow A to signal to B that a new batch of data is ready. Task A must then wait while B copies the new data into its local area, and then both tasks may continue concurrently until A has input a new batch of data and B has processed the last batch, at which point another rendezvous takes place.

A rendezvous point in B is called an *entry*, which in this example might be named NEW_DATA_READY. When task B is ready to begin processing a new batch of data, it must execute an **accept** *statement*:

>**accept** NEW_DATA_READY **do**
>>—statements to copy new data from A into
>>>local data area of B
>
>**end;**

When task A has completed the input of a new batch of data, it must execute the *entry call*:

>NEW_DATA_READY;

When task B reaches the **accept** statement, it waits until task A (or some other task) executes an entry call for the entry NEW_DATA_READY named in the **accept** statement. Similarly, when task A reaches the entry call NEW_DATA_READY, it waits until B reaches the **accept** statement. When both are at that point, the rendezvous takes place: A continues to wait while B executes all the statements contained within the **do** . . . **end** of the **accept** statement. Then the rendezvous is complete, and both A and B continue their separate executions.

To see how guarded commands might be used to allow B to wait for any of several rendezvous, suppose B is extended so that it can process data from any of three input devices, each controlled by separate tasks, A1, A2, and A3. Each of the three input tasks runs concurrently with B and each other. When an input task has a batch of data ready to be processed, it executes the corresponding entry call, READY1 (in task A1), READY2 (in task A2), or READY3 (in task A3). When one of these entry calls is issued, task B may be waiting already, or B may still be processing a previous batch of data. If B were waiting already, then without a guarded-command structure, B could not wait for any of READY1, READY2, and READY3, but instead would have to wait for only one of these. To wait for any one of the three, B executes the guarded command:

```
    select
        accept READY1 do
                —copy data from A1 into local area of B
            end;
    or  accept READY2 do
                —copy data from A2 into local area of B
            end;
    or  accept READY3 do
                —copy data from A3 into local area of B
            end;
    end select;
```

When B reaches this statement, it waits until A1, A2, or A3 signals the appropriate entry call. The entry call is accepted (if more than one are signaled at the same time, only one is accepted) and the rendezvous takes place as before. Note that the explicit guards "**when** ⟨*condition*⟩ =>" and the **else** clause have been omitted here, since all three **accept** statements are to be available for execution when the **select** statement is reached. In some cases, however, an explicit guard might be included. For example, each input device might have an associated "status" indicating whether it was operating properly. The rendezvous might be made conditional on the status of each device:

```
    select
        when DEVICE1_STATUS = ON => accept READY1 do ... end;
    or  when DEVICE2_STATUS = ON => accept READY2 do ... end;
    or  when DEVICE3_STATUS = CONNECTED => accept READY3
            do ... end;
    else ...  —no device is ready; do something else
    end select;
```

Tasks and Real-Time Processing

A program that must interact with input-output devices or other tasks within some fixed time constraints is said to be operating in *real time*. For example, a program that is used to monitor the pressures within a nuclear reactor may be required to receive and process pressure information from an external pressure sensor attached to the reactor every 100 milliseconds. A program that controls the rocket engines on a spacecraft may be required to produce start and stop commands as needed within intervals of $\frac{1}{4}$ second. When tasks are executing concurrently, their interactions are often subject to timing constraints if the overall computer system is being used for real-time processing. Thus, for example, a task A that wishes to rendezvous with another task B may not be able to delay more than a fixed length of time before proceeding, even without starting the rendezvous. In real-time computer systems, failure of part of the hardware or of an external input-output device often leads to a task's being abruptly terminated. If other tasks wait on such a failed task, the entire system of tasks may deadlock and cause a crash of the system.

The special demands of real-time processing require the programming language to include some explicit notion of time that can be used in the control and synchronization of tasks. Unlike the simulated time scale discussed in Sec. 6-8 in regard to scheduled subprograms, a *real-time clock* is required here. In Ada there is a language defined package CALENDAR (an abstract data type) that includes a type TIME and a function CLOCK. The implementation of this package is intended to make use of a hardware-provided time clock whose current value is accessible through the function CLOCK. In waiting for a rendezvous with another task, a task may "watch the clock" by specifying a delay of a certain duration. If the rendezvous is not started within the specified duration according to the clock, then the process continues without the rendezvous. In the example above with task A that inputs data and task B that processes the data, A might be taking data from a sensor such as an airspeed indicator on an aircraft. Suppose task A must sample the sensor every $\frac{1}{2}$ second, but task B may not always be able to process the data every $\frac{1}{2}$ second. Task A may then wish to wait for a rendezvous with B for at most $\frac{1}{2}$ second, and if no rendezvous occurs, then simply continue so as to sample the sensor again, overwrite the old data with the new batch, and again try for a rendezvous with B. Instead of the simple entry call

NEW_DATA_READY;

in A, this timing constraint would be indicated by using the *timed entry call*:

```
select
    NEW_DATA_READY;
or
    delay 0.5;   —wait at most .5 seconds for a rendezvous
end select;
```

Note that the syntax is that for a guarded command. No explicit guards are given, so either alternative is available for execution. The timing for the delay alternative begins as soon as the rendezvous is attempted (usually when the task executing the entry call enters a queue of tasks waiting for that particular entry name). Either the rendezvous defined by the entry call is made, or the delay is completed. Ada also provides several other methods for taking account of real-time constraints in the interactions of tasks (see Chapter 16).

Implementation of Tasks

Implementation of tasks is a subject too complex for the space available here. The implementation methods differ greatly, depending on the particular language structures involved, the synchronization methods used, the underlying operating system (if any), and the computer hardware—whether a single processor or a distributed system. Thus (unhappily) we cannot attempt to treat these intriguing issues here.

6-10   DATA STRUCTURES AND SEQUENCE CONTROL

While most of the sequence-control mechanisms discussed in this chapter are *general-purpose* in the sense that they occur in most programming languages regardless of the data structures or operations used in the language, it is not appropriate to leave the subject without considering the close relationship between sequence-control mechanisms and the data structures and operations in a language. While a variety of sequence-control mechanisms may contribute to the *generality* of a language, a most important component of the *naturalness* of a programming language comes from the choice of the appropriate sequence-control mechanisms for the data structures and operations available. For example, FORTRAN and Pascal would be crippled without the iteration statement, yet APL gets along quite well without it. Similarly LISP without recursive subprogram calls is unthinkable, yet FORTRAN allows no recursion, and in PL/I, although permitted, recursion is of fairly minor impact. Why? The answer has to do with the appropriateness of iteration for element-by-element array processing and of recursion for list structure processing.

The grouping of data items together into structures has many advantages in programming, but clearly a major one is the ability to process the elements of such a structure in sequence, applying the same operations to each element in turn. Array processing is a typical case. In a language like FORTRAN, where the array is the basic data structure, one of the most common program structures is a loop that involves a sequential scan of all or part of an array, taking each element in turn and applying the same sequence of tests and operations to it. We use a simple integer variable as a pointer into the array, an index, which takes on successively the subscripts of the appropriate array elements as values. The DO statement of FORTRAN or the **for** statement of Pascal reflects this natural structure, allowing such loops and index variables to be set up, initialized, incremented, and tested easily. Because sequential processing of arrays, element by element, is such a common process in these languages, these iteration statements are heavily used, and their omission would greatly weaken these languages.

In APL the basic data structures are also arrays, yet APL has no iteration statement, and in fact such a statement would be relatively unimportant even were it included. The reason is that sequential element-by-element array processing in APL is uncommon. Most of the operators work directly on entire arrays as operands. While these operations may internally process the array sequentially, to the programmer this is hidden. Instead APL programs ordinarily involve relatively little statement-level control structure. Thus the iteration statement does not provide the natural sequence-control mechanism for processing arrays in APL.

In LISP the basic data structures are list structures. Again sequential processing of these structures is an important aspect of many LISP programs. But iteration using index variables with integer values is not the natural sequence control mechanism. The elements of LISP list structures cannot be referenced by integer subscripts, and the structures are quite irregular in shape. In LISP it is *recursion* that provides the natural sequence-control mechanism. One processes a list structure recursively by first applying the tests and operations to each element of the main list, and whenever an element of this list is itself a sublist, then one simply invokes the process recursively to process this sublist. Basically one uses the recursive subprogram structure to "keep track" of a position in the list structure.

As data structures increase in complexity from the simple arrays of FORTRAN or the list structures of LISP to more complex structures involving elements interconnected in irregular fashion, the "natural" sequence-control mechanisms become more obscure. Consideration of mechanisms appropriate to processing such general data structures clarifies the nature of the relation between data and sequence control.

Readers. One of the simplest approaches is that of the data structure *reader*, a term introduced by Weizenbaum [1963] in his *symmetric list processing* language SLIP. A simple reader may be viewed as just a pointer to an element of a data structure. One processes a data structure using a reader by first initializing the reader to point to the desired *first* element of the structure. The reader is then "advanced" through the structure, pointing in sequence to various elements of the structure. At each point one may access (read off) the element pointed to by the reader for processing. For a simple linear array an integer variable serves as a most appropriate reader, and incrementing or decrementing the value of this variable is a perfectly adequate way of advancing the reader. An iteration statement which allows such an *array reader* to be set up together with a specification for how to initialize it and advance it through the structure then becomes a powerful and natural array-processing mechanism.

For a list structure (tree) a simple stack-structured reader is appropriate. The list structure reader either advances down the main list or "descends" into a sublist, saving its place in the main list on the reader stack. Within a sublist other descents into sublists may be necessary, using further stack locations. Then, as the reader "ascends" through the structure, the information stored on the stack is used to unwind the processing, assuring return to the proper point on each list after sublist processing is complete. In fact, Weizenbaum's original use of readers in SLIP was in the processing of list structures using stack-structured readers. Note that sequential processing of list structures using recursion in LISP is essentially a use of the central system stack (used to store subprogram return points and activation records) to simulate a stack-structured reader for list structures. Because this may be easily done in LISP, recursion becomes the natural processing technique for list structures.

Generators. A second approach to the sequential processing of data structures is found in the concept of *generator*, introduced in the list-processing language IPL-V (Newell [1964]). A generator is a subprogram A which accepts as input (1) a data structure and (2) another subprogram B to be applied to the various elements of the data structure in sequence. The generator subprogram processes the data structure in some arbitrary manner, producing a sequence of elements from the structure. As each element is produced, the subprogram B is called with the generated element as its input. When B returns, it signals either *continue* or *halt* to the generator subprogram. The generator then proceeds to generate the next element of the structure for processing by B, or it halts and returns control to the original program.

The generator concept appears in LISP in the form of *functionals*, of which **mapcar** is typical. **Mapcar**(L,F) generates each element of the input list L in sequence and applies the function F to it. These generator functions in LISP provide an alternative to the use of recursion to set up *readers* for list structures.

Iterators. In some recent languages with mechanisms for programmer-defined abstract data types, such as CLU (Liskov [1977]), another means of processing data structures is provided, called an *iterator*. An iterator is defined as one of the operations available on a data structure of a programmer-defined abstract type. When an iterator is first invoked on a data structure of the type, it returns the "first" component of the structure. On each subsequent call it returns the "next" component of the structure. When the "last" component of the structure is reached, the iterator returns an indication that it is finished. In this setting, it is the programmer building the abstract data type who determines the meaning of "first," "next," and "last." Since the representation of the abstract type is encapsulated, the user of the iterator does not necessarily know exactly how the data structure is represented or how the iterator works. The iterator is used within an extended form of **for** loop, where calls to the iterator replace the usual index variable and initial and final values. For example, if GEN_NEXT_ ITEM is the name of an iterator that produces components (of type ITEM) in sequence from a data structure L of type ITEM_LIST, then a program using the iterator might include a loop:

> **for** I: ITEM in GEN_NEXT_ITEM(L) **loop**
> —statements to process item I
> **end loop;**

The **for** loop is translated into an initial call to the iterator to get the first item in L, followed by execution of the loop body, followed by another call to the iterator to get the second item in L, followed by execution of the loop body, and so on, until the iterator signals that the last element has been returned, at which point the loop terminates. An iterator is similar to a generator, but the loop body forms the "subprogram" that is applied to each component generated from the data structure.

6-11 REFERENCES AND SUGGESTIONS FOR FURTHER READING

There is an extensive literature on the design of sequence control structures in programming languages. Wasserman [1980] and Yourdon [1979] provide collections containing some of the more important papers, including Edsger Dijkstra's famous letter that precipitated the controversy over the use of **goto** statements. Most general texts on programming languages also treat these topics at length, e.g., Ledgard and Marcotty [1981].

Techniques for efficient translation and evaluation of expressions are a central topic in compiler design (see the references at the end of Chapter 9). The problem of side effects in expression evaluation stirred considerable controversy in the design of ALGOL 60; see Knuth's discussion [1967].

Statement-level control structures are a central concern in papers by Knuth [1974] and many others. Leavenworth [1972] provides a collection of relevant articles; see also the general references above.

Recursion is the subject of monographs by Burge [1975] and Barron [1968], and, of course, it is a common programming structure in many languages, especially LISP (Chapter 17). General coroutine structures are treated at length by Marlin [1980] and Dahl and Hoare [1972]. The issues surrounding the design of exception-handling features are treated by Goodenough [1975]; see also Wasserman's collection [1980] and the *Ada Rationale* (Ichbiah et al. [1979]). Subprogram scheduling in discrete simulation languages is a central topic in the survey by Dahl [1968].

Control structures for tasks and concurrent processing have been a central topic in the literature. The issues are more complex and less well understood than for sequential programs. Most texts on operating system design treat task scheduling, synchronization, and communication at length, e.g., Holt et al. [1978], Brinch Hansen [1977]. Guarded commands are introduced by Dijkstra [1975] and used extensively in an important monograph (Dijkstra [1976]). Surveys and examples of various techniques are given by Brinch Hansen [1973] and Presser [1975]. The *Ada Rationale* (Ichbiah et al. [1979]) provides an excellent overview of these considerations in the Ada design. Practical experience with the use of monitors in the MESA language is described by Lampson and Redell [1980]. Iterators and generators in the context of definition of abstract data types are an important issue in CLU (Liskov [1977]) and ALPHARD (Shaw et al. [1977]).

Two more specialized control structures that are not considered here are *decision tables*, treated by Metzner and Barnes [1977], and *backtracking*, see Prenner et al. [1972]. A general technique for the implementation of subprogram control structures, including coroutines and backtracking, is the subject of Bobrow and Wegbreit [1973].

6-12   PROBLEMS

1. *Translation of infix expressions to postfix.* One common compilation technique for expressions is to translate infix expressions first into a postfix (reverse Polish) form. The reverse Polish is then translated directly into machine code or optimized and then translated into machine code. The translation into reverse Polish is based on use of a stack and a table of precedences. Consider a simple expression composed only of identifiers and binary infix operators, such as A * B + C / D − E. Assuming the usual hierarchy of infix operations (e.g., as given in Table 6-1), the translation algorithm is based on a simple left-to-right scan of the infix expression using two processing rules:

   1. Identifiers are moved directly into the output reverse Polish string as they are encountered.
   2. Operators are stacked on an intermediate stack, with a number indicating their precedence level in the hierarchy. Before an operator is stacked, all operators on the top of the stack with higher precedence are first deleted from the stack one by one and moved into the output reverse Polish string.

   For the expression above the output reverse Polish string is

$$A \ B * C \ D \ / + E \ -$$

   (a) Give a flow chart for this translation algorithm in the simple case of expressions containing only identifiers and the binary arithmetic infix operators +, −, *, /, and ↑.
   (b) Expand the algorithm of part (a) to include expressions with parentheses. Note that the parentheses do not appear in the output string, although, of course, they control the order in which the output string is generated.

(c) Expand the algorithm of part (a) to include the unary operator − (negation) in Polish prefix notation. What is an appropriate precedence for unary −?

(d) Expand the algorithm of part (a) to include function calls in ordinary mathematical notation, e.g., SIN(X) or MAX(A,B,C). What precedence is appropriate for such function calls?

2. Give the tree representation of the following expressions:

(a) $- (A - B \ast\ast C) \ast D \, / \, E \ast\ast F + G$

(b) $A \ast B > C - D \ast\ast - E \, / \, F$

(c) $A \, / \, B \, / \, C = D \ast\ast E \textbf{ and } F + G > H \ast J$

(d) $\textbf{not } A - B > C \textbf{ and } (D < E \textbf{ or } F) \textbf{ or not } G \textbf{ and } H = J$

Case 1. (Ada) Assume the Ada hierarchy of operations from Table 6-1, with left-to-right associativity.

Case 2. (APL) Assume that all operations have equal precedence, that associativity is from *right-to-left*, and that parentheses indicate grouping in the usual way.

3. Give the representation of the expressions in Problem 2 in Cambridge Polish and Polish prefix representations. Assume the hierarchy of operations of Table 6-1 and left-to-right associativity. In the Polish form, subscript each operator symbol with an integer specifying the number of operands of the operator. For example, $((-A) \ast B) - C$ becomes $-_2 \ast_2 -_1 ABC$.

4. In the discussion of side effects in expression evaluation the expression A*FUN(X)+A was considered. Under the assumption that A has the value 1 on beginning evaluation of the expression and FUN(X) evaluates to 3 and increases the value of A by 1, then the expression may evaluate to any of the values 4, 5, 7, or 8, depending on the order of evaluation. List evaluation sequences which produce each of these values.

5. *Evaluation of expressions involving logical or.* Consider the expression

$$(A) \lor (B)$$

where A and B are arbitrary logical or relational expressions. If subexpression A evaluates to *true*, then it is desirable for efficiency to avoid evaluation of B, as the result of the entire expression must be true in any case. As B may itself be a complex expression the savings may be substantial. The following is a useful optimization rule: Evaluate the shorter or "simpler" of A and B; if the value is *true*, skip evaluation of the other expression. Explain the potential complications to the programmer caused by such optimization in a language like FORTRAN or Pascal. Note that this is a form of *short-circuit* Boolean expression, but one in which the *compiler* determines the evaluation order.

6. Give a simple algorithm for left-to-right evaluation of arithmetic expressions in postfix form when only simple variables, constants, and binary arithmetic operations are involved. The evaluation rule should use a stack for temporary storage of intermediate results.

7. Give an algorithm for evaluation of arithmetic expressions represented in tree form, assuming that only simple variables, constants, and binary arithmetic operations are involved. Base the algorithm on a reader which initially points to the root of the tree and which "walks" through the tree, pointing to the various nodes in sequence. The algorithm should use a stack for temporary storage of intermediate results.

8. Consider the following ALGOL program segment:

(initialization)   SUM := 0; J := 1; N := 20;
(iteration head)   **for** I :=1 **step J until** N **do**
(iteration body)   **begin** SUM := SUM + A[I]; J := J + I; N := N − J **end;**

Which elements of the array A will be summed under each of the following evaluation strategies for evaluation of the variables J and N in the iteration head?

(a) Evaluate both J and N once on initial entry to the iteration statement.
(b) Evaluate J once on initial entry; evaluate N once on entry and again after each execution of the body.
(c) Evaluate N once on initial entry; evaluate J once on entry and again after each execution of the body.
(d) Evaluate both J and N on entry and reevaluate after each execution of the body.

9. In languages such as BASIC and APL that provide few statement-level "structured" control forms, *coding conventions* are often adopted governing the use of **goto** statements that provide for their use only in fixed patterns, corresponding to the various structured control forms described in Sec. 6-3. For example, an **if** . . . **then** . . . **else** . . . **endif** form may be represented as in Fig. 6-5. Design a set of coding conventions for one of the above languages that would provide the basic structured control forms through disciplined use of **goto** statements.

10. One of the major theoretical results supporting the replacement of **goto** statements by "structured" statement forms is due to Böhm and Jacopini [1966]. Their results prove that any flow graph with a single entry point and single exit point that might be programmed using **goto** statements may also be programmed using only sequences of statements, **if-then-else** alternation, and **while** loops. Draw a one-in, one-out flow graph with several loops and branches. Program it using only **goto**'s and using only the structured forms mentioned above. Evaluate the results on the basis of the ease of writing and reading the programs.

11. In the simple (nonrecursive) call-return implementation for subprograms described in Sec. 6-4, which is often used in FORTRAN, usually no checking is done for the occurrence of a recursive call during execution. Instead, the recursive call is allowed, but later the program falls into an infinite loop.

(a) Explain the reason for this behavior in terms of the implementation model for nonrecursive subprograms.
(b) Revise the implementation model so that a run-time check is possible to determine if a call is recursive, before the call is executed.

12. After an exception handler has completed processing an exception, a return of control to the point of the exception to resume execution is not always appropriate. In general, the exception may have occurred when some operation was only partially executed, and it may be undesirable (or impossible) to attempt to resume execution of the partially complete operation. Discuss the point(s) where it might be natural to resume execution in case of each of the following types of exceptions that might be raised by the language primitive operations:

   (a) Overflow on an integer multiplication.
   (b) Second subscript out of range in a reference to an element of a three-dimensional array.
   (c) End-of-page condition after output of the second line of a four-line block of printing.
   (d) Nonnumeric character encountered during conversion of a character string to internal binary integer representation.
   (e) End-of-file encountered on an input file during a READ statement.

13. An argument favoring retention of statement labels and **goto** statements is that other control structures may often be simulated using these primitive features. Simulation of simple coroutines in FORTRAN is an example. Design a simulation for coroutines in FORTRAN using the CALL statement, the ASSIGN statement (e.g., ASSIGN 20 TO L;—where 20 is a statement number), and the *assigned* **goto** GO TO L, (list of statement numbers). The simulation should operate so that the CALL statement actually acts like a RESUME statement for subprograms in which the coroutine simulation is being used.

14. *Recursive coroutines*. Consider a language in which subprogram execution may be initiated with an ordinary CALL or may be resumed with a coroutine RESUME. For example, if A and B are subprograms and A calls B, then control transfers to B as in an ordinary subprogram call. B may then return control to A either through a RETURN in the usual way or through a coroutine RESUME A command. In addition, B may initiate another activation of A through a recursive call of A using the statement CALL A. If A is called recursively, then A may later call B recursively, setting up another activation of B, or A may return control to B through a RETURN or a RESUME B command. Of course, there may be many subprograms, and each may contain CALLs or RESUMEs on any of the others.

   (a) Define precisely a reasonable interpretation for the statements RESUME and RETURN in this context of recursive coroutines, assuming that CALL always initiates a new activation of the called subprogram as with ordinary recursive subprograms. Note that each subprogram may have been activated recursively a number of times and that the subprogram being executed may have been initially called from one subprogram and then later resumed from another. Thus it is not immediately obvious where control is to be transferred when a RETURN or RESUME is encountered.
   (b) Design a simulation for this control structure on a conventional computer. Specify the storage requirements for return and/or resume points and the

manner in which this information is used during execution of the CALL, RESUME, and RETURN statements.

15. An alternative view of a data structure generator is as a coroutine generator. A coroutine generator is a coroutine which on initial activation is given a data structure as input parameter and returns the first element of the sequence of elements. On each subsequent resume call it generates the next element of the sequence and returns it. Design such a generator for:

 (a) Generating the main diagonal on a FORTRAN, ALGOL, or PL/I matrix.
 (b) Generating the integer-valued leaf nodes on a LISP tree.
 (c) Generating the nodes breadth-first on a LISP tree—for example, the nodes in numbered order from the following tree:

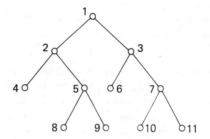

16. A **for** loop, e.g., **for** I := 1 **to** N **do** . . . **end loop**, can be used to create a *reader* I for a vector V. I takes on the possible subscript values for V, and thus allows access to each component of V in sequence. A second nested **for** loop might create a second reader, J, for V that points to a different component of the vector. However, I and J cannot be advanced independently of each other, e.g., I cannot be advanced to its next value until J has completed an entire cycle through its range. Suppose you want to advance I and J independently, so that either may be advanced at the end of a cycle through the loop. Explain how you would set up two independent readers for a vector in a language like Pascal or FORTRAN.

17. Extend the program of Fig. 6-14 to include a third task A2, similar to task A, which also inputs batches of data for B to process. Assume both A and A2 use the same shared data area to pass a batch of data to B and that both A and A2 may want to simultaneously write in the area. Write A, A2, and B so that they synchronize their activities correctly using WAIT and SIGNAL and semaphores.

CHAPTER 7

Data
Control

The data-control features of a programming language are those parts concerned with the accessibility of data at different points during program execution. The sequence-control mechanisms of the preceding chapter provide the means to coordinate the sequence in which operations are invoked during program execution, for both primitive operations and programmer-defined operations (subprograms). Once an operation is reached during execution, it must be provided with the data on which it is to operate. The data-control features of a language determine how data may be provided to each operation, and how a result of one operation may be saved and retrieved for later use as an operand by a subsequent operation.

When writing a program, one ordinarily is well aware of the operations that the program must execute and their sequence, but seldom is the same true of the operands for those operations. For example, a Pascal program contains

$$X := Y + 2 * Z$$

Simple inspection indicates three operations in sequence: a multiplication, an addition, and an assignment. But what of the operands for these operations? One operand of the multiplication is clearly the number 2, but the other operands are marked only by the identifiers Y, Z, and X, and these obviously are not the operands but only designate the operands in some manner. Y might designate a real number, an integer, or the name of a parameterless subprogram to be executed to compute the operand. Or perhaps the programmer has erred and Y designates a Boolean value or a string or serves as a statement label. Y may designate a value computed nearby, perhaps in the preceding statement, but equally as likely it may designate a value computed at some point much earlier in the computation, separated by many levels of subprogram call from the assignment where it is used. To make matters worse, Y may be used as a name in different ways in different sections of the program. Which use of Y is current here?

In a nutshell, the central problem of data control is the problem of what Y means in each execution of such an assignment statement. Because Y may be a local or nonlocal variable, the problem involves what are known as "scope rules" for declarations; because Y may be a formal parameter, the problem involves techniques for parameter transmission; and because Y may name a parameterless subprogram, the problem involves mechanisms for returning results from subprograms. Each of these topics is taken up in turn in the following sections.

7-1 NAMES AND REFERENCING ENVIRONMENTS

There are basically only two ways that a data object can be made available as an operand for an operation:

1. *Direct transmission.* A data object computed at one point as the result of an operation may be directly transmitted to another operation as an operand, as, for example, the result of the multiplication $2 * Z$ is transmitted directly to the addition operation as an operand in the Pascal statement $X := Y + 2 * Z$. In this case, the data object is allocated storage temporarily during its lifetime and may never be given a name.

2. *Referencing through a named data object.* A data object may be given a name when it is created, and the name may then be used to designate it as an operand of an operation. Alternatively, the data object may be made a component of another data object that has a name, so that the name of the larger data object may be used together with a selection operation to designate the data object as an operand.

Direct transmission is used for data control within expressions, but most data control outside of expressions involves the use of names and the referencing of names. The problem of the meaning of names forms the central concern in data control.

Program Elements That May Be Named

What kinds of names are seen in programs? Each language differs, but some general categories seen in many languages are:

1. Variable names.

2. Formal parameter names.

3. Subprogram names.

4. Names for defined types.

5. Names for defined constants.

6. Statement labels (names for statements).

7. Exception names.

8. Names for primitive operations, e.g., +, *, SQRT.

9. Names for literal constants, e.g., 17, 3.25.

Categories 1-3, names for variables, formal parameters, and subprograms, form the center of our concern here. Of the remaining categories, most references to names in these groups are resolved during translation rather than during program execution, as discussed below. Some special cases exist, e.g., exceptions may be propagated at run time up the dynamic chain of calling programs in Ada, **goto** statements may reference statement labels in other subprograms in Pascal, and primitive operation symbols may be redefined in SNOBOL4, but these special cases are relatively rare and add few new concepts. Once the basic ideas underlying data control for variables, formal parameters, and subprogram names are understood, the extension to these new cases is relatively straightforward.

A name in any of the above categories may be termed a *simple name*. A *composite name* is a name for a component of a data structure, written as a simple name designating the entire data structure, followed by a sequence of one or more selection operations that select the particular component of the named structure. For example, if A is the name of an array, then A is a simple name, and A[3] is a composite name. Composite names may be quite complex, e.g., A[3].CLASS[2].ROOM. Selection operations and the accessing of components of data structures given the structure itself are discussed in Chapter 4. In this chapter, only the meaning of simple names remains to be discussed. In most languages, simple names are represented by identifiers such as X, Z2, and SUB1, and thus the terms *identifier* and *simple name* are used interchangeably here.

Associations and Referencing Environments

Data control is concerned in large part with the binding of identifiers (simple names) to particular data objects and subprograms. Such a binding is termed an *association* here, and may be represented as a pair consisting of the identifier and its associated data object or subprogram.

If we observe the course of execution of a program in most languages, we see the following:

1. At the beginning of execution of the main program, identifier associations exist that bind each variable name declared in the main program to a particular data object and that bind each subprogram name invoked in the main program to a particular subprogram definition.

2. As the main program executes, it invokes *referencing operations* to determine the particular data object or subprogram associated with an identifier. For example, to execute the assignment:

$$A := B + FN(C)$$

four referencing operations are required to retrieve the data objects associated with the names A, B, and C and the subprogram associated with the name FN.

3. When the main program calls a subprogram, a new set of associations is created for the subprogram. Each of the variable names and formal parameter names declared in the subprogram is associated with a particular data object. New associations for subprogram names may also be created.

4. As the subprogram executes, it invokes referencing operations to determine the particular data object or subprogram associated with each identifier. Some of the references may be to associations created on entry to the subprogram, while others may be to associations created back in the main program.

5. If the subprogram invokes another subprogram, another set of associations will be created and used in referencing, and so on.

6. When the subprogram returns control to the main program, its associations are destroyed (or become inactive).

7. When control returns to the main program, execution continues as before, using the associations originally set up at the start of execution.

In this pattern of creation, use, and destruction of associations, we see the main concepts of data control:

1. *Referencing environments.* Each program or subprogram has a set of identifier associations available for use in referencing during its execution. This set of identifier associations is termed the *referencing environment* of the subprogram (or program). The referencing environment of a subprogram is ordinarily invariant during its execution. It is set up when the subprogram activation is created, and it remains unchanged during the lifetime of the activation. The values contained in the various data objects

may change, but the associations of names with data objects and sub-programs do not. The referencing environment of a subprogram may have several components:

    a. Local referencing environment (or simply *local environment*). The set of associations created on entry to a subprogram that represent formal parameters, local variables, and subprograms defined only within that subprogram form the *local referencing environment* of that activation of the subprogram. The meaning of a reference to a name in the local environment may be determined without going outside the subprogram activation.

    b. Nonlocal referencing environment. The set of associations for identifiers that may be used within a subprogram but that are not created on entry to it is termed the *nonlocal referencing environment* of the subprogram.

    c. Global referencing environment. If the associations created at the start of execution of the main program are available to be used in a subprogram, then these associations form the *global referencing environment* of that subprogram. The global environment is part of the nonlocal environment.

    d. Predefined referencing environment. Some identifiers have a pre-defined association, defined directly in the language definition. Any program or subprogram may use these associations without explicitly creating them.

    2. *Visibility.* An association for an identifier is said to be *visible* within a subprogram if it is part of the referencing environment for that sub-program. An association that exists but is not part of the referencing environment of the subprogram currently in execution is said to be *hidden* from that subprogram. Often an association is hidden when a subprogram is entered that redefines an identifier already in use elsewhere in the program.

    3. *Dynamic scope.* Each association has a *dynamic scope*, which is that part of program execution during which it exists as part of a referencing environment. Thus the dynamic scope of an association consists of the set of subprogram activations within which it is visible.

    4. *Referencing operations.* A *referencing operation* is an operation with the specification:

ref-op: identifier $\times$ referencing environment $\rightarrow$ data object or subprogram

where *ref-op*, given an identifier and a referencing environment, finds the appropriate association for that identifier in the environment and returns the associated data object or subprogram definition.

    5. *Local, nonlocal, and global references.* A reference to an identifier is a *local reference* if the referencing operation finds the association in the

local environment; it is a *nonlocal* or *global* reference if the association is found in the *nonlocal* or *global* environment, respectively. (The terms *nonlocal* and *global* are often used interchangeably to indicate any reference that is not local.)

EXAMPLE 7-1. Figure 7-1 shows a simple Pascal subprogram with the referencing environment for each subprogram marked. Note that identifiers A, D, and C are each declared in two places. Identifier A is a formal parameter name in SUB1 and is also declared as a variable in the main program. Identifier C is a formal parameter in SUB2 and also a variable name in the main program, and D is a local variable name in both SUB1 and SUB2. However, in each referencing environment, only one association for each of these names is visible. Thus, in SUB2, the local association for C is visible, and the global association for C in the main program is hidden. In the statement C := C + B in SUB2 both a local reference to C and a global reference to B in the main program appear.

The predefined referencing environment is not shown. In Pascal it consists of constants such as MAXINT (the maximum integer value) and subprograms such as *read*, *write*, and *sqrt*. Any of these predefined identifiers may be given a new association through an explicit program declaration, and thus the predefined association may become hidden for part of the program.

```
program MAIN(OUTPUT);
var A,B,C: real;
procedure SUB1(A: real);
    var D: real;
    procedure SUB2(C: real);
        var D: real;
        begin
            —statements
            C := C + B;
            —statements
        end;
    begin
        —statements
        SUB2(B);
        —statements
    end;
begin
    —statements
    SUB1(A);
    —statements
end.
```

Referencing environment for SUB2:
local: C,D
nonlocal: A, SUB2 in SUB1
           B, SUB1, OUTPUT in MAIN
global: B, SUB1, OUTPUT in MAIN

Referencing environment for SUB1:
local: A, D, SUB2
nonlocal, global: B, C, SUB1, OUTPUT in MAIN

Referencing environment for MAIN:
local: A, B, C, SUB1, OUTPUT

Fig. 7-1   Referencing environments in a Pascal program

Aliases for Data Objects

During its lifetime a data object may have more than one name; that is, there may be several associations in different referencing environments, each providing a different name for the data object. For example, when a data object is transmitted "by reference" (see Sec. 7-8) to a subprogram as a parameter, it may be referenced through a formal parameter name in the subprogram, and it also retains its original name in the calling program. Alternatively, a data object may become a component of several data objects through pointer linkages and thus have several composite names through which it may be accessed. Multiple names for the same data object are possible in various ways in almost every programming language.

When a data object is visible through more than one name (simple or composite) *in a single referencing environment*, each of the names is termed an *alias* for the data object. Where a data object has multiple names, but a unique one in each referencing environment in which it appears, no problems arise. However, the ability to refer to the same data object using different names within the same referencing environment raises serious problems for both the user and implementor of a language. Figure 7-2 shows

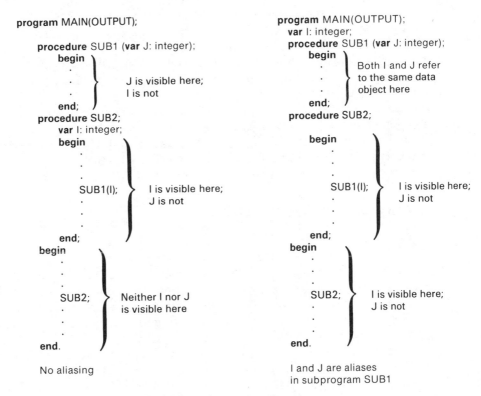

Fig. 7-2   Aliasing in a Pascal program

two Pascal programs in which an integer variable has two names I and J at different points during program execution. In the first program, no aliasing occurs, because at no point during execution can both names I and J be used in the same subprogram. In the second program, within subprogram SUB1, I and J are aliases for the same data object because I is passed "by reference" to SUB1, where it becomes associated with the name J, and at the same time I also is visible in SUB1 as a nonlocal name.

Aliasing is troublesome for the programmer because it makes understanding a program difficult. For example, if within a program you see the statement sequence:

$$X := A + B;$$
$$Y := C + D;$$

the assignments to X and Y apparently are independent and could take place in either order, or if the variable X were not referenced later, the first assignment might be deleted altogether. However, suppose X and C are aliases for the same data object. Then the statements are in fact interdependent, and no reordering or deletion is possible without introducing a subtle error in the program. The possibility of aliasing makes it difficult to verify that a program is correct, because no two variable names may be assumed to refer necessarily to different data objects. Often a separate analysis is needed to determine whether aliasing is present.

The problems caused by aliasing for the implementor are similar. As a part of the optimization of program code during translation, it is often desirable to reorder the steps in a computation or to delete unnecessary steps. Where aliasing is possible, this cannot be done without additional analysis to insure that two apparently independent computational steps are not dependent due to aliasing, as above. Because of the problems caused by aliasing, new language designs sometimes attempt to restrict or eliminate altogether features that allow aliases to be constructed.

7-2   STATIC AND DYNAMIC SCOPE

The *dynamic scope* of an association for an identifier, as defined in the preceding section, is that set of subprogram activations in which the association is visible during execution. The dynamic scope of an association always includes the subprogram activation in which that association is created as part of the local environment. It may also be visible as a nonlocal association in other subprogram activations.

A *dynamic scope rule* defines the dynamic scope of each association in terms of the dynamic course of program execution. For example, a typical dynamic scope rule states that the scope of an association created during an activation of subprogram P includes not only that activation but also any activation of a subprogram called by P, or called by a subprogram called by P, and so on, unless that later subprogram activation defines a new local association for the identifier that hides the original association. With this rule, the dynamic scope of an association is tied to the *dynamic chain* of subprogram activations described in Sec. 6-5.

When we look at the written form of a program, the *program text*, we notice that the association between references to identifiers and particular declarations or definitions of the meaning of those identifiers is also a problem. For example, in Fig. 7-1, the references to B and C in the statement C := C + B in SUB2 need to be tied to particular declarations of C and B as variables or formal parameters—but which declarations? Each declaration or other definition of an identifier within the program text has a certain scope, called its *static scope*.

For simplicity, the term *declaration* is used here to refer to a declaration, subprogram definition, type definition, constant definition, or other means of defining a meaning for a particular identifier within a program text. A declaration creates an association in the program text between an identifier and some information about the data object or subprogram that will be named by that identifier during program execution. The *static scope* of a declaration is that part of the program text where a use of the identifier is a reference to that particular declaration of the identifier. A *static scope rule* is a rule for determining the static scope of a declaration. In Pascal, for example, a static scope rule is used to specify that a reference to a variable X in a subprogram P refers to the declaration of X at the beginning of P, or if not declared there, then to the declaration of X at the beginning of the subprogram Q whose declaration contains the declaration of P, and so on.

Static scope rules relate references with declarations of names in the program text; dynamic scope rules relate references with associations for names during program execution. What should be the relation between the two? Clearly the scope rules must be *consistent*. For example, if the static scope rules for Pascal relate the reference to variable B in the statement C := C + B in Fig. 7-1 to the declaration of B in the main program, then the dynamic scope rules must also relate the reference to B at run time to the data object named B in the main program. There may be several declarations for B in the program text, and several data objects named B in various subprogram activations during execution. Thus maintaining the consistency between static and dynamic scope rules is not entirely straightforward. Several different approaches are considered below.

The Importance of Static Scope

Suppose a language makes no use of static scope rules. Consider a statement such as X :=X + MAX that occurs in a subprogram. Without static scope rules, nothing about the names X and MAX can be determined during translation of the program. During execution of the program, when the statement is reached, a referencing operation must first find the relevant associations for X and MAX, and then the type and other attributes of X and MAX must be determined. Does there exist an association for each identifier? Is MAX a subprogram name, variable name, statement label, type name, or formal parameter name? If X is a variable name, is it of a type that can be added to MAX? None of these questions can be answered until the attempt to reference names X and MAX is made during execution. Moreover, each time the statement is executed, the entire process must be repeated, because the associations for X and MAX may change between two executions of the statement. Of the languages in Part II, LISP, SNOBOL4, and APL make almost no use of static scope rules, and thus each reference to a name in these languages requires a rather complex and costly interpretation process to be invoked that first finds the relevant association for the name (if any) and then determines the type and attributes of the associated data object or subprogram.

Static scope rules allow much of this process to be performed once during program translation rather than repeatedly during execution for most references to names in a program. For example, if the assignment statement $X := X + MAX$ appears in Pascal, and MAX is defined by a constant declaration "**const** MAX = 30" somewhere in the program, then the static scope rules of Pascal allow the reference to MAX to be related to this (or some other) declaration of MAX during translation. The Pascal compiler can then determine that MAX always has the value 30 when this statement is executed and may translate the statement into executable code that simply adds 30 to X, with no referencing operation for the name MAX at all. Similarly, if the Pascal static scope rules allow the reference to X to be related to the declaration "X: real" somewhere in the program text, then the Pascal compiler may perform static type checking; that is, it may determine that when the statement is executed, (1) an assocation relating X to a data object will exist, (2) that data object will be a real number, and (3) its value will be of the right type to serve as an argument for the addition operation. The compiler cannot tell from the declaration the *location* of the data object that X references (since the location is determined dynamically during execution and may be different on different executions of the statement), nor can the compiler determine the *value* of X (since it also is determined dynamically during execution). However, the static type checking makes program execution both much faster and also more reliable (since type errors are detected for all program paths during translation).

Static scope rules allow many different sorts of connections to be established between references to names and their declarations during translation. Two have been mentioned above: relating a variable name to a declaration for the variable and relating a constant name to a declaration for a constant. Other connections include relating type names to type declarations, relating formal parameters to formal parameter specifications, relating subprogram calls to subprogram declarations, and relating statement labels referenced in **goto** statements to labels on particular statements. In each of these cases, a different set of simplifications may be made during translation that make execution of the program more efficient.

Static scope rules are also important for the programmer in reading a program, because they make it possible to relate a name referenced in the program to a declaration for the name without tracing the course of program execution. For example, the static scope rules of Pascal allow a reference to X in a statement to be related to a declaration for X elsewhere in the program without any consideration for the sequence of subprogram calls that lead from the main program to the actual execution of the statement. The static scope rules thus make the program easier to understand. Static scope rules play an important part in the design and implementation of most programming languages, e.g., FORTRAN, COBOL, PL/I, Pascal, and Ada.

7-3   BLOCK STRUCTURE

The concept of *block structure* as found in *block-structured languages* such as Pascal, PL/I, and Ada deserves special mention. Block-structured languages have a characteristic program structure and associated set of static scope rules. The concepts were originated in the language ALGOL 60, one of the most important early languages, and because of their elegance and effect on implemention efficiency, they have been adopted in other languages.

In a block-structured language, each program or subprogram is organized as a set of nested blocks. The chief characteristic of a *block* is that it introduces a new local referencing environment. A block begins with a set of declarations for names (variable declarations, type definitions, constant definitions, etc.), followed by a set of statements in which those names may be referenced. For simplicity, we shall consider a block as equivalent to a subprogram declaration, although the exact definition of a block varies from language to language. The declarations in a block define its local referencing environment. This local environment is invariant during the execution of the statements that form its body.

The nesting of blocks is accomplished by allowing the definition of one block to entirely contain the definitions of other blocks. At the outermost level, a program consists of a single block, defining the main program. Within this block are other blocks defining subprograms callable from the main program; within these blocks may be other blocks defining subprograms callable from within the first-level subprograms, and so on. Figure 7-3 illustrates the typical layout of a block-structured program. In languages

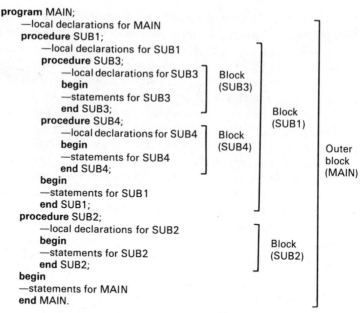

Fig. 7-3 Static block structure of a program

such as PL/I and Ada the outermost level may consist of several independent nests of blocks (each of which may be compiled separately), but it is sufficient here to consider only a single nest.

The *static scope rules* associated with a block-structured program are as follows:

1. The declarations at the head of each block define the local referencing environment for the block. Any reference to an identifier within the body of the block (not including any nested subblocks) is considered a reference to the local declaration for the identifier, if one exists.

2. If an identifier is referenced within the body of the block and no local declaration exists, then the reference is considered a reference to a declaration within the block that immediately encloses the first block. If no declaration exists there, then it refers to a declaration in the block that immediately encloses that block, and so on. If the outermost block is reached before a declaration is found, then the reference is to the declaration within that outermost block. Finally, if no declaration is found there, the declaration in the predefined language environment is used, if any, or the reference is taken to be an error. The predefined environment thus acts like a block enclosing the outermost block (or blocks) of the program.

3. If a block contains another block definition, then any local declarations within the inner block or any blocks it contains are completely hidden

from the outer block and cannot be referenced from it. Thus inner blocks encapsulate declarations so that they are invisible from outer blocks.

4. A block may be named (usually when it represents a named subprogram). The block name becomes part of the local referencing environment of the *containing block*. For example, if a Pascal main program contains a subprogram definition that begins

procedure P(A: real);

then the procedure name P is a local name in the main program, while the formal parameter name A is part of P's local environment. Within the main program, P may be referenced, but A may not.

Note that, using these static scope rules, a declaration for the same identifier may occur in many different blocks, but a declaration in an outer block is always hidden within an inner block if the inner block gives a new declaration for the same identifier.

These static scope rules for block-structured programs allow every reference to a name within any block to be associated with a unique declaration for the name during program translation (if the reference is not an error), with little explicit action by the programmer other than to provide the proper *local* declarations in each block and the proper nesting of blocks. The compiler for the language may provide static type checking and other simplifications of the run-time structure based on use of the static scope rules. For these reasons, block structure has been adopted as a program structure in many major languages.

7-4 LOCAL DATA AND LOCAL REFERENCING ENVIRONMENTS

With the concepts of the preceding sections, we may now begin to look at the various data-control structures used in programming languages. Local referencing environments, which form the simplest structure, are treated in this section. The sections that follow consider nonlocal environments, and parameters and parameter transmission.

The *local environment* of a subprogram Q consists of the various identifiers declared in the head of subprogram Q (but not "Q" itself). Variable names, formal parameter names, and subprogram names are the concern here. Other types of names present no new problems. The subprogram names of interest are the names of subprograms that are defined locally within Q (i.e., subprograms whose definitions are nested within Q).

For local environments, static and dynamic scope rules are easily made consistent. The static scope rule specifies that a reference to an identifier X in the body of subprogram Q is related to the local declaration for X in the head of subprogram Q (assuming one exists). The dynamic scope rule specifies that a reference to X during execution of Q refers to the association for X in the current activation of Q (note that in general there may be several activations of Q, but only one will be currently in execution). To implement the static scope rule, the compiler simply maintains a table of the local declarations for identifiers that appear in the head of Q, and while compiling the body of Q, it refers to this table first whenever the declaration of an identifier is required.

Implementation of the dynamic scope rule may be done in two ways, and each gives a different semantics to local references. Consider subprograms P, Q, and R, with a local variable X declared in Q:

```
procedure R;
    .
    .
end;
procedure Q;
var X: integer := 30;          —initial value of X is 30
begin
    write(X);                  —print value of X
    R;                         —call subprogram R
    X := X + 1;                —increment value of X
    write(X)                   —print value of X again
end;
procedure P;
    .
    .
    Q;                         —call subprogram Q
    .
    .
end;
```

Subprogram P calls Q, which in turn calls R, which later returns control to Q, which completes its execution and returns control to P. Let us follow variable X during this execution sequence. The steps are:

1. When P is in execution, X is not visible in P, since X is local to Q.

2. When P calls Q, X becomes visible as the name of an integer data object with initial value 30. As P executes, the first statement references X and prints its current value, 30.

3. When Q calls R, the association for X becomes hidden, but it is retained while R executes.

4. When R returns control to Q, the association for X becomes visible again. X still names the same data object, and that data object still has the value 30.

5. Q resumes its execution, X is referenced and incremented, and then its new value, 31, is printed.

6. When Q returns control to P, the association for X again becomes hidden, but two different meanings might be provided for what else happens:

   a. *Retention.* The association for X might be *retained* until Q is called again, just as it was while Q called R. If the association is retained, then when Q is called the second time, X is still associated with the same data object, which still has its old value, 31. Thus the first statement executed will reference X and print the value 31. If the entire cycle repeats and Q is called a third time, X will have the value 32, and so on.

   b. *Deletion.* Alternatively, the association for X might be *deleted*; that is, the association binding X to the data object might be broken, and the data object destroyed and its storage reallocated for some other use. When Q is called a second time, a new data object is created and assigned the initial value 30, and the association with X is recreated as well. The first statement in Q then prints the value 30 every time Q is executed.

Retention and deletion are two different approaches to the semantics of local environments. Pascal, Ada, LISP, APL, and SNOBOL4 use the deletion approach: local variables do not retain their old values between successive calls of a subprogram. COBOL and many versions of FORTRAN use the retention approach: variables do retain their old values between calls. PL/I and ALGOL provide both options; each individual variable may be treated differently.

Implementation

In discussing the implementation of referencing environments, it is convenient to represent the local environment of a subprogram as a *local environment table* consisting of pairs, each containing an identifier and the associated data object, as shown in Fig. 7-4. Since the details of the storage representations for the data objects are not important here (and are discussed in Chapters 3 and 4), we consider each data object as represented only by a block of storage, with the identifier naming it associated with the first location of the block (the base address of the block). Drawing a local environment table this way does not imply that the actual identifiers, e.g., "X" are stored during program execution; often only the data objects are

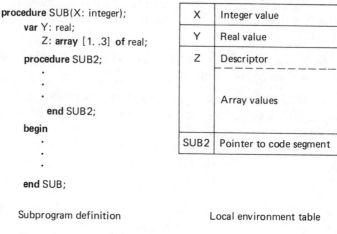

```
procedure SUB(X: integer);
    var Y: real;
        Z: array [1..3] of real;
    procedure SUB2;
        .
        .
        .
        end SUB2;
    begin
        .
        .
        .
    end SUB;
```

X	Integer value
Y	Real value
Z	Descriptor
	Array values
SUB2	Pointer to code segment

Subprogram definition   Local environment table

Fig. 7-4 A Pascal subprogram and its local environment table

stored and the identifiers are translated into offsets from a base address, as discussed below. Using local environment tables, implementation of the retention and deletion approaches to local environments is straightforward.

Retention. If the local environment of a subprogram Q is to be retained between calls, then a single local environment table containing the retained variables is allocated as part of the *code segment* of Q, as shown in Fig. 7-5. Since the code segment is allocated storage statically and remains in existence throughout execution, any variables in the local environment part of the code segment are also retained. If a variable has an initial value, such as the value 30 for X above, then the initial value may be stored in the data object when the storage is allocated (just as the value for a constant in the code segment would be stored). Assuming each retained local variable is declared at the start of the definition of Q, the compiler can determine the size of each variable in the local environment table and compute the offset of the start of the data object from the start (the base address) of the code segment. When a statement within the code references a variable X during execution, the offset of X is added to the base address of the code segment to find the location of the data object associated with X. The identifier "X" is not needed during execution and need not be stored at all.

With this implementation of retention for the local environment, no special action is needed to retain the values of the data objects; the values stored at the end of one call of Q will still be there when the next call begins. Also no special action is needed to change from one local environment to another as one subprogram calls another. Since the code and local data for each subprogram are part of the same code segment, a transfer of control to

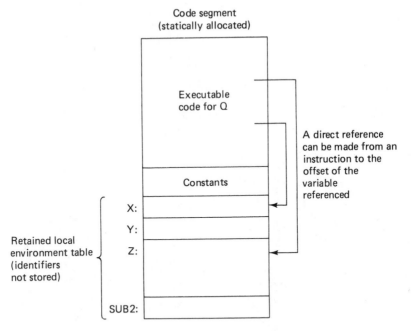

Fig. 7-5 Allocation and referencing of retained local variables

the code for another subprogram automatically results in a transfer to the local environment for that subprogram as well.

Deletion. If the local environment of Q is to be deleted between calls and recreated anew on each entry, then the local environment table containing the deleted variables is allocated storage as part of the *activation record* for Q. Assuming the activation record is created on a central stack on entry to Q, and deleted from the stack on exit, as discussed in Sec. 6-4, deletion of the local environment follows automatically. Assuming each deleted local variable is declared at the start of the definition of Q, the compiler again can determine the number of variables and the size of each in the local environment table and may compute the offset of the start of each data object from the start of the activation record (the base address). Recall that the CEP pointer (current-environment pointer) is maintained during execution so that it points to the base address of the activation record in the stack for the subprogram that is currently executing at any point. If Q is executing and references variable X, then the location of the data object associated with X is found by adding the offset for X to the contents of the CEP. Again the identifier "X" need not be stored in the activation record at all; only the data objects are needed. Figure 7-6 shows this implementation.

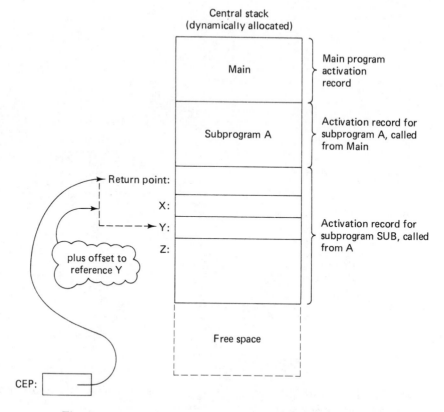

Central stack
(dynamically allocated)

Main program
activation
record

Main

Activation record for
subprogram A, called
from Main

Subprogram A

Return point:

X:

Y:

Z:

Activation record for
subprogram SUB, called
from A

plus offset to
reference Y

Free space

CEP:

Fig. 7-6 Allocation and referencing of deleted local variables

Both the retention and deletion approaches are easy to implement in our general model of subprogram implementation as given in Chapter 6. Several additional points deserve notice:

1. In the implementation of the *simple* call-return structure (without recursion) described in Sec. 6-4, retention and deletion lead to essentially the same implementation, as there is never more than one activation record, allocated statically anyway. However, if initial values are provided for variables, two different meanings for initialization result (see Problem 2).

2. *Individual variables* may readily be given either treatment, with those whose values are to be retained allocated storage in the code segment, and those whose values are to be deleted allocated storage in the activation record. This is the approach used in PL/I, where a variable declared STATIC is retained and a variable declared AUTOMATIC is deleted.

3. A *subprogram name*, which is associated with a declaration for the subprogram in the local environment, may always be treated as retained. The association of name and definition may be represented as a pointer data object in the code segment, where the pointer points to the code segment representing the subprogram.

4. A *formal-parameter* name represents a data object that is reinitialized with a new value on each call of the subprogram, as described in Sec. 7-8 below. This reinitialization precludes retaining an old value for a formal parameter between calls. Thus formal parameters are appropriately treated as deleted associations.

5. If *recursive* subprogram calls are allowed, then multiple activations of a subprogram Q may exist as separate activation records in the central stack at the same time. If a variable X is treated as deleted, then each activation record will contain a separate data object named X, and as each activation executes, it will reference its own local copy of X. Ordinarily separate copies of X in each activation are what is desired, and thus for languages with recursion (or other subprogram control structures that generate multiple simultaneous activations of a subprogram) the deletion of local environments is ordinarily used. However, retention of some local variables is often of value. In ALGOL 60, for example, a local variable declared as *own* is treated as a retained variable, even though the subprogram containing the declaration may be recursive. If multiple activations of a subprogram Q reference the retained variable X, then there is only one data object X that is used by every activation of Q, and its value persists from one activation to another.

Advantages and disadvantages. Both retention and deletion are used in a substantial number of important languages. Each technique has advantages not shared by the other. Consider the situation from the programmer's viewpoint. The retention approach allows the programmer to write subprograms which are *history sensitive* (in the sense of Chapter 3), in that their results on each call are partially determined by their inputs and partially by the local data values computed during previous activations. The deletion approach does not allow any local data to be carried over from one call to the next, so a variable that must be retained between calls must be declared as nonlocal to the subprogram. For recursive subprograms, however, deletion is the more natural strategy. Deletion also provides a savings in storage space in that local environment tables exist only for those subprograms which are in execution or suspended execution. Local environment tables for all subprograms exist throughout execution using retention. Other advantages and disadvantages will become apparent as we try to generalize these approaches in the following sections.

7-5   SHARED DATA: EXPLICIT COMMON
ENVIRONMENTS

A data object that is strictly local is used by operations only within a single
local referencing environment—that is, within a single subprogram. Many
data objects, however, must be *shared* among several subprograms, so that
operations in each of the subprograms may use the data. A data object may
be transmitted as an explicit parameter between subprograms, as discussed
in Sec. 7-8, but there are numerous occasions in which use of explicit
parameters is cumbersome. For example, consider a set of subprograms that
all make use of a common table of data. Each subprogram needs access to
the table, yet transmitting the table as an explicit parameter each time it is
needed is tedious. Every language in Part II provides mechanisms for
subprograms to share data objects without use of parameters. Such data
sharing is usually based on sharing of identifier associations. If subprograms P, Q, and R all need access to the same variable X, then it is
appropriate to simply allow the identifier X to have the same association in
each subprogram. The association for X is then no longer part of the local
environment for more than one of the subprograms; it has become a
common part of the *nonlocal* environment of the others. Sharing of data
objects through nonlocal environments is an important alternative to the
use of direct sharing through parameter transmission.

Three basic approaches to nonlocal environments are in use in
programming languages. In this section we consider the use of *explicit
common environments*; in the following two we consider *implicit* nonlocal
environments based on *dynamic scope* and *static scope*, respectively.

A *common environment* set up explicitly for the sharing of data
objects is the most straightforward method. A set of data objects that are to
be shared among a set of subprograms is allocated storage in a separate
named block. Each subprogram contains a declaration that explicitly
names the shared block. The data objects within the block are then visible
within the subprogram and may be referenced by name in the usual way.
Such a shared block is known by various names: *COMMON block* in
FORTRAN and *compool* in several languages; in Ada it is a form of a
package; and in PL/I single variables tagged EXTERNAL are shared in
this way. The term *common environment* is appropriate in our setting here.

Specification

A common environment is identical to a local environment for a subprogram, except that it is not a part of any single subprogram. It may
contain definitions of variables, constants, and types, but no subprograms
or formal parameters. The definition in Ada uses a **package** specification.

For example:

```
package SHARED_TABLES is
      TAB_SIZE: constant INTEGER := 100;
      type TABLE is array (1 . . TAB_SIZE) of real;
      TABLE1,TABLE2: TABLE;
      CURR_ENTRY:INTEGER range 1 . . TAB_SIZE;
end SHARED_TABLES
```

The package specification defines a type, a constant, two tables, and an integer variable which together represent a group of data objects (and type definitions) that are needed by several subprograms. The package definition is given outside of any subprograms that use the variables.

If a subprogram P requires access to the common environment defined by this package, then an explicit **with** statement is included among the declarations of P:

with SHARED_TABLES;

Within the body of P, any name in the package may now be used directly, as though it were part of the local environment for P, using the syntax ⟨*package name*⟩.⟨*variable name*⟩. Thus we can write, in P:

SHARED_TABLES.TABLE1(SHARED_TABLES.CURR_ENTRY) :=
      SHARED_TABLES.TABLE2(SHARED_TABLES.CURR_ENTRY) + 1;

without any further declaration of any of these names. The package name must be used as a prefix on each name because a subprogram may use many packages, some of which may declare the same name. (If there are no such conflicts, the package name prefix may be avoided by a **use** statement in Ada, e.g., **with** SHARED TABLES; **use** SHARED_TABLES). In general, any number of other subprograms may use the same common environment by including the statement "**with** SHARED_TABLES", and any number of common environments may be used by a single subprogram.

Implementation

In FORTRAN and PL/I, each subprogram using the common environment must also include declarations for each shared variable, so that the compiler knows the relevant declarations even though the common environment is also declared elsewhere. In Ada, the compiler is expected to retrieve the declaration for the common environment from a library or another part of the program text when a **with** statement is encountered during compilation of a subprogram.

The declarations for the common environment are added to the compiler symbol table as an additional set of local names that may be referenced in the subprogram. Each reference to a name in the subprogram body is then looked up in the table in the usual way for purposes of static type checking and generation of executable code.

At run time, a common environment is represented as a block of storage containing the data objects declared in the definition. Since the data objects are potentially of mixed type and their declarations are known during compilation, the block may be treated as though it were a *record*. The name of the block represents the name of the record, and the individual variables in the block represent the components of the record. References to individual variables within the block are then translated into the usual base-address-plus-offset calculation for record component references.

The block of storage representing a common environment must continue to exist in memory for as long as any of the subprograms that use it are still potentially callable, because each activation of any of these subprograms may access the block. Thus the block is ordinarily allocated storage statically, so that it is set up at the beginning of execution of the program and is retained throughout execution. There may be many such common blocks in memory, interspersed with the blocks representing code segments for subprograms and other statically allocated blocks of run-time storage.

A subprogram that references a data object in a common block must know the base address of the block. A simple implementation is to allocate a location in the code segment for the subprogram to contain a pointer to the block (i.e., to contain the base address of the block). These pointer linkages between a subprogram and the common blocks that it uses are similar to the linkages between a subprogram and the code segments for the subprograms that it calls. One of the primary tasks of the link editor that assembles a collection of subprograms and common blocks in memory prior to the start of execution is the storing of the actual linkage pointers in each code segment as required for execution. Figure 7-7 illustrates this structure. During execution, a reference to a data object in a common environment is handled by taking the base address of the appropriate common block from the code segment for the subprogram making the reference, and adding the precomputed offset to get the actual memory location of the shared data object.

Import/Export of Shared Variables

A related form of explicit sharing of data objects is that of providing a means for a data object in the *local* environment of a subprogram to be made visible to other subprograms. Thus instead of a group of variables in a common environment separate from any subprogram, each variable has an

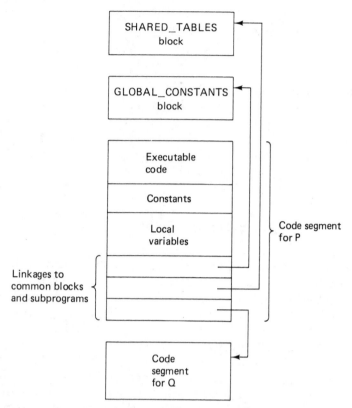

P uses SHARED_TABLES and GLOBAL_CONSTANTS and calls subprogram Q

Fig. 7-7 Linkages from a subprogram to common blocks and other subprograms

"owner," the subprogram that declares it. To make a local variable visible outside the subprogram, an explicit *export definition* must be given, such as the **defines** declaration in:

    procedure P(. . .);
        defines X, Y, Z;   —X, Y, and Z become available for
                                 "export"
        X, Y, Z: real;   —usual declarations for X, Y, and Z
        U, V: integer;   —other local variables
        begin . . . end;   —statements

Another subprogram that needs access to an exported variable uses an explicit *import definition* to import the variable, e.g., by including a **uses** declaration naming both the subprogram and the exported variable:

procedure Q(. . .);
    uses P.X, P.Z;   —imports X and Z from P
    Y: integer;   —other declarations
    begin . . . **end**   —statements may include references to X and Z

The effect is similar to use of a variable in a common environment. Storage for an exported local variable must be retained between activations of the subprogram defining it, so it ordinarily would be allocated storage in the code segment for the subprogram, as for ordinary retained local variables. Referencing of such a variable from another subprogram that imports it then uses the base address of the code segment for the exporting subprogram, and adds the appropriate offset.

7-6   SHARED DATA: DYNAMIC SCOPE

An alternative to the use of explicit common environments for shared data is the creation of an *implicit nonlocal environment* for each subprogram when it is entered. The implicit nonlocal environment for a subprogram P consists of a set of local environments of other subprogram activations that are made accessible to P during its execution. When a variable X is referenced in P and X has no local association, then the implicit nonlocal environment is used to determine the association for X. What should be the implicit nonlocal environment for P? In block-structured languages, the static scope rules determine the implicit nonlocal environment for each subprogram; this fairly complex approach is considered in the next section. A simpler, but less widely used, alternative is considered here, use of the local environments for subprograms in the current dynamic chain.

Consider a language in which local environments are deleted upon subprogram exit and in which subprogram definitions are not nested within one another. Each is defined separately from the others. In this case, found in APL, LISP, and SNOBOL4, there is no static program structure on which to base scope rules for references to *nonlocal* identifiers. For example, if a subprogram P contains a reference to X, and X is not defined locally within P, then which definition for X in some other subprogram is to be used? The natural answer is found by considering the *dynamic chain* of subprogram activations that leads to the activation of P. Consider the course of program execution: assume the main program calls a subprogram A, which calls B, which calls P. If P references X and no association for X exists in P, then it is natural to turn to the subprogram B that called P and ask if B has an association for X. If B does, then that association for X is used; otherwise, we go to the subprogram A that called B, and check if A has an association for X. We have used the *most recently created association* for X in the dynamic chain of subprogram calls leading to P. This meaning for a nonlocal reference is termed the *most-recent-association rule*; it is a referencing rule based on dynamic scope.

With an implicit nonlocal environment determined by the most-recent-association rule, no static scope rules are used; that is, no attempt is made during program translation to determine the definition associated with a reference to an identifier that is not defined locally in the subprogram. During program execution, when a data object X is created as part of the activation of subprogram P, the *dynamic scope* of the association for X becomes all the activations of subprograms called by P or by those subprograms, and so on. X is visible within this dynamic scope (except where it is hidden by a later subprogram that has its own local association for X). Viewed from the other direction, the *implicit nonlocal environment* of a subprogram activation P consists of the entire dynamic chain of subprogram activations leading to it.

The most troublesome aspect of this nonlocal environment is that it may *change* between activations of P. Thus on one activation of P, when a nonlocal reference to X is made, the most recent association in the calling chain may have X as the name of an array. On a second activation of P, invoked through a different sequence of prior subprogram calls, the dynamic chain may change so that the most recent association for X is as the name of a character string. On a third activation of P, there may be no association for X in the calling chain at all, so that the reference to X is an error. This variability in the association for X means that *dynamic type checking* is required; thus the method is only used in languages such as LISP, APL, and SNOBOL4 where dynamic type checking is used for other reasons.

Implementation. Implementation of the most-recent-association rule for nonlocal references is straightforward, given the central-stack implementation for storing subprogram activation records. The local environment for each subprogram is made part of its activation record. On entry to the subprogram the activation record is created; on return, the activation record is deleted.

Suppose that a subprogram P calls subprogram Q, which calls R. When R is executing, the central stack might look as shown in Fig. 7-8. To resolve a nonlocal reference to X, the stack is searched, beginning with the local environment for R and working back through the associations in the stack until the most recent association for X is found. As the figure shows, some of the associations in the stack will be hidden by later associations for the same identifier.

This implementation of the most-recent-association rule is costly. The search required at each nonlocal reference takes time and reintroduces the necessity of storing some representation of the *identifiers themselves* in the local association tables, because the position of the association for X may

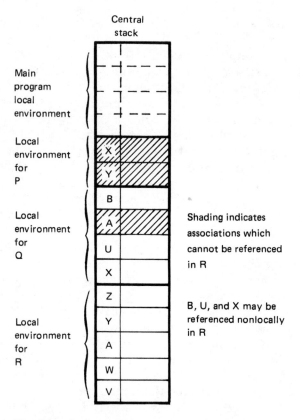

Fig. 7-8 Active referencing environment during execution of R

differ in each local table. Thus no base address plus offset computation is possible in nonlocal referencing.

How may searching for nonlocal references be avoided? A tradeoff is possible between the cost of nonlocal referencing and the cost of subprogram entry and exit, which may be advantageous if nonlocal referencing is assumed to be much more frequent than subprogram entry and exit, i.e., if the nonlocal environment is likely to be used more frequently than it is modified.

The alternative implementation uses a central table common to all subprograms, the *central referencing environment table*. The central table is set up to contain at all times during program execution *all the currently active identifier associations*, regardless of whether they are local or nonlocal. If we assume, also for simplicity, that the set of identifiers referenced in any of the subprograms may be determined during translation, then the central table is initialized to contain one entry for each identifier, regardless of the number of different subprograms in which that identifier appears. Each entry in the table also contains an *activation flag* which indicates whether or not that particular identifier has an active association, as well as space for a pointer to the object of the association.

All referencing in subprograms is direct to this central table using the base-address-plus-offset scheme described previously. Since the current association for identifier X is always located at the same place in the central table, regardless of the subprogram in which the reference occurs, and regardless of whether the reference is local or nonlocal, this simple referencing computation is adequate. Each reference requires only that the activation flag in the entry by checked to insure that the association in the table is currently active. By use of the central table we have obtained our objective of relatively efficient nonlocal referencing without search.

Subprogram entry and exit is more costly, because each change in referencing environment requires modification of the central table. When subprogram P calls Q, the central table must be modified to reflect the new local environment for Q. Thus each entry corresponding to a local identifier for Q must be modified to incorporate the new local association for Q. At the same time if the old table entry for an identifier was active, the entry must be saved so that it may be reactivated when Q exits to P. Because the entries that require modification are likely to be scattered throughout the central table, this modification must be done piecemeal, entry by entry. On exit from Q, the associations deactivated and saved on entry to Q must be restored and reactivated. Again an execution-time stack is required, as in the earlier simulations, but it is used here as a *hidden stack* to store the deactivated associations. As each local identifier association is updated on entry to Q, the old association is stacked in a block on the hidden stack. On return from Q the top block of associations on the stack is restored into the appropriate positions in the central table. This central table simulation is shown in Fig. 7-9. An additional advantage accrues when using the central table if the language does not allow new references to be generated during execution. In this case, as was the case earlier in regard to local tables, the identifiers themselves may be dropped from the table, for they will never be used, having been replaced by the base-address-plus-offset computation. (In a sense the identifier is simply represented by its table offset during execution.)

The central environment table has many variants. The SNOBOL4 implementation described in Chapter 18 is based on this approach. Other variants are taken up in the problems at the end of this chapter.

7-7   SHARED DATA: STATIC SCOPE AND BLOCK STRUCTURE

In languages such as Pascal, PL/I, Ada, and ALGOL that utilize a block-structured form for programs, the handling of nonlocal references to shared

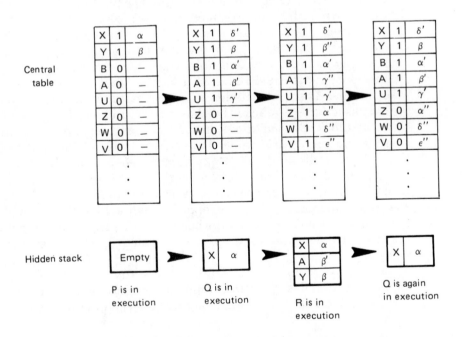

Fig. 7-9 The central environment table implementation of nonlocal referencing

data is more complex. If you look again at the static scope rules for block-structured programs given in Sec. 7-3, you will note that they associate each reference to an identifier within a subprogram to a definition for that identifier in the program text, even if the identifier is not local to the subprogram. Thus the nonlocal referencing environment of each subprogram during execution is already determined by the static scope rules used during translation. The implementation problem is to retain consistency between the static and dynamic scope rules, so that a nonlocal reference during program execution is correctly related to the data object corresponding to the definition for that identifier in the program text.

Figure 7-10 shows an example of the static scope rules for a block-structured Pascal program. Subprogram R is called from subprogram Q which is called from P. Both P, Q, and the main program define a variable X. Within R, X is referenced nonlocally. The static scope rules define the reference to X as a reference to the X declared in the main program, not as a reference to either of the definitions for X within P or Q. The meaning of the nonlocal reference to X is independent of the particular dynamic chain of calls that leads to the activation of R, in contrast to the most-recent-association rule of the preceding section, which relates X to the X either in P or in Q depending on which subprogram called R.

The static scope rules are straightforward to implement in the compiler. As each subprogram definition is processed during compilation, a local table of declarations is created and attached to a chain of such local tables that represent the local environments of the main program and other subprograms within which this subprogram is nested. Thus, in compiling R the compiler adds the local table of declarations for R to the chain containing only the main program definition. During compilation, this chain is searched to find a declaration for a reference to X, starting with the local declarations for R, and proceeding back down the chain to the declarations in the main program. When compilation of R is complete, the compiler deletes the local table for R from the chain. Note the similarity with the searching for a meaning for X done with the most-recent-association rule described in Sec. 7-6; however, this search for a declaration for X is done during *compilation*, not during execution. The chains of local tables of declarations represent the static nesting of subprogram definitions in the program text rather than the dynamic subprogram calling chain during execution.

During program execution in a block-structured language, a central stack is used for subprogram activation records. The local environment for each subprogram is stored in its activation record. The difficulty in maintaining consistency between the static and dynamic scope rules becomes apparent in Fig. 7-11, which shows the contents of the central stack during execution of subprogram R of Fig. 7-10. When R is executing and the nonlocal reference to X is encountered, the referencing operation must find

```
program MAIN;
    var X,Y: integer;
    procedure R;
        var Y: real;
        begin
            .
            .
            X := X + 1; —nonlocal reference to X
            .
            .
            .
        end;
    procedure Q;
        var X: real;
        begin
            .
            .
            R; —call procedure R
            .
            .
            .
        end;
    procedure P;
        var X: Boolean;
        begin
            .
            .
            Q; —call procedure Q
            .
            .
            .
        end;
    begin
        .
        .
        .
        P; —call procedure P
        .
        .
        .
    end.
```

Fig. 7-10   A Pascal procedure with nonlocal references

the association for X in the main program, rather than that in subprogram Q which called R. Unfortunately, a simple search down the stack leads to the association for X in Q. The problem is that the sequence of local tables in the stack represents the *dynamic nesting* of subprogram *activations*, the nesting based on the execution-time calling chain. But it is the *static nesting* of subprogram *definitions* which now determines the nonlocal environ-

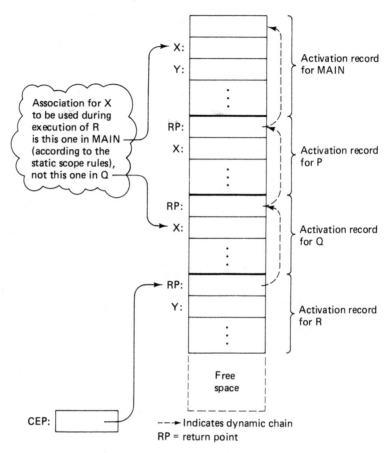

Fig. 7-11 Incorrect central stack during execution of R (Fig. 7-10)

ment, and the stack as currently structured contains no information about static nesting.

To complete the implementation it is necessary to represent the static block structure during execution in such a way that it may be used to control nonlocal referencing. Observe that in many respects the rule for nonlocal referencing in this case is similar to that for nonlocal referencing using the most recent association rule: To find the association to satisfy a reference to X we search a chain of local environment tables until an association for X is found. However, the chain of local environment tables to search is not composed of *all* the local tables currently in the stack but only of those *which represent blocks or subprograms whose definition statically encloses the current subprogram definition in the original program text*. The search then is still down some of the tables in the stack, but only those tables that are actually part of the referencing environment.

    Static chain implementation.   These observations lead to the most direct implementation of the correct referencing environment: the *static chain* technique. Suppose that we modify the local environment tables in the stack

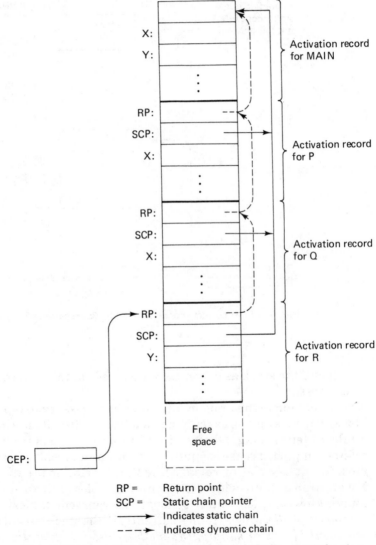

RP =	Return point
SCP =	Static chain pointer
———▶	Indicates static chain
– – –▶	Indicates dynamic chain

Fig. 7-12 Central stack during execution of R (Fig. 7-10) showing static chain pointers

slightly so that each table begins with a special entry, called the *static chain pointer*. This static chain pointer always contains the base address of another local table further down the stack. The table pointed to is the table representing the local environment of the statically enclosing block or subprogram in the original program. (Of course, since each local environment table is just a part of an activation record, we may use the base address of the activation record, rather than just the base address of the local environment part.)

The static chain pointers form the basis for a simple referencing scheme. To satisfy a reference to X we follow the CEP pointer to the current local environment on top of the stack. If no association for X is found in the local environment, then we follow the static chain pointer in that local table down the stack to a second table. If X is not in that table, the search continues down the static chain pointers until a local table is found with an association for X. The first one found is the correct association. Figure 7-12 illustrates the static chain for the Pascal program of Fig. 7-10.

If a nonlocal reference involves a *search* of a sequence of local environment tables, then we have returned to one of the problems which caused difficulty before. However, the search here may be eliminated without difficulty. To see how, we need a few preliminary observations.

First note that, for any subprogram R, when R is in execution (and its local environment table is therefore on top of the stack), the length of the static chain leading from R's local table down the stack (and ultimately to the table for the main program) is *constant*. This length is constant regardless of the current size of the stack and regardless of the point of call of R. Of course, the reason is simply that the length of the static chain is equal to the depth of static nesting of subprogram R's definition back in the original program at compile time, and this depth of nesting is fixed throughout execution. For example, if R is defined within a block which is directly contained within the outermost block of the program, then the static chain for R during execution always has length 3: R's local table, the local table for the directly containing block, and the local table for the outermost block (the main program). In Figs. 7-10 and 7-12, for example, the static chain for R always has length 2.

Second, note that in this chain of constant length a nonlocal reference will always be satisfied at exactly the same point in the chain. For example, in Fig. 7-12 the nonlocal reference to X in R will always be satisfied in the second table in the chain. Again this fact is a simple reflection of the static program structure. The number of levels of static nesting that one must go out from the definition of R to find the declaration for X is fixed at compile time.

Third, note that the position in the chain at which a nonlocal reference will be satisfied may be determined at compile time. For example, we may determine at compile time that a reference to X in R will be found in the second table down the static chain during execution. In addition, we know at compile time the relative position of X in that local table. Thus, for example, at *compile time* we can conclude that the association for X will be the second entry in the second table down the static chain during execution.

The basis for a fairly efficient referencing operation is now apparent. Instead of explicitly searching down the static chain for an identifier, we need only skip down the chain a fixed number of tables, and then use the base-address-plus-offset computation to pick out the appropriate entry in the table. In fact, under the usual assumption that new references cannot be generated during execution, we no longer need the identifiers represented explicitly at all, because no search is used. Instead it is natural to represent an identifier in the form of a pair (chain position, offset), during execution. For example, if X, referenced in R, is to be found as the third entry in the first table down the chain, then in the compiled code for R, X may be represented by the pair (1,3). This representation provides a rather simple referencing algorithm.

The static chain technique allows straightforward entry and exit of subprograms. When a subprogram is called, its activation record is created on top of the stack. At this time the appropriate static chain pointer must be installed in it, pointing to an activation record further down the stack. On exit it is necessary only to delete the activation record from the stack in the usual way; no special action is needed for the static chain pointer.

How can we determine the appropriate static chain pointer to install on entry to a subprogram? Suppose that subprogram R is called from subprogram Q and that R is defined in the original program text nested directly within MAIN, as in Fig. 7-11. When R is entered during execution, the appropriate static chain pointer is back to the activation record for MAIN. At the point of call, the activation record for Q is on top of the stack, and that for R is to be stacked on top of Q's. How is it determined that the proper static chain pointer is the one to MAIN? Observe that the identifier "R", the subprogram name, is itself referenced nonlocally in Q in the call statement invoking R. If "R" is determined (at compile time) to be defined at one level of nesting out from the call statement in Q, then at run time the static chain pointer for R should point to the activation record one step back down Q's static chain. Thus at the point of call in Q, the static chain pointer for R can be determined to point to the activation record for MAIN, because MAIN's activation record is one step back down Q's static chain. The situation is exactly as though R were defined as a local variable in MAIN that was referenced nonlocally in Q, except that after following the static chain from Q to the appropriate activation record, no offset is added. Instead the activation record found is made the object of R's static chain pointer after R's activation record is created. Figure 7-13 illustrates this structure for the program of Fig. 7-10.

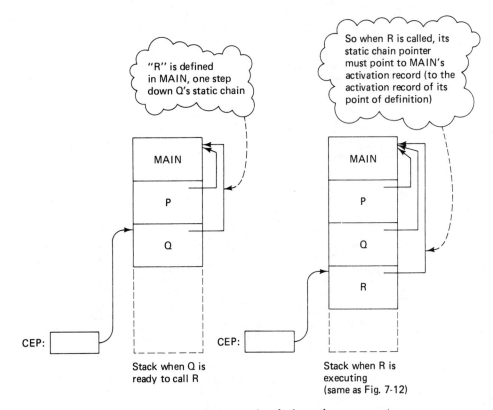

Fig. 7-13 Static chain creation during subprogram entry

The display implementation.   The necessity of following the static chain for each nonlocal reference is a drawback of the above technique. We may avoid this referencing cost by using an alternative implementation, but only at a cost on subprogram entry and exit. In this implementation the current static chain is copied into a separate vector, termed the *display*, on entry to each subprogram. The display is separate from the central stack and is often represented in a set of high-speed registers. At any given point during execution the display contains the same sequence of pointers that occur in the static chain of the subprogram currently being executed. Figure 7-14 illustrates the display for the example of Fig. 7-10.

Referencing using a display is particularly simple. Let us adopt a slightly modified representation for identifiers during execution. Again pairs of integers are to be used, but let the 3 in a pair like (3,2) represent the number of steps back from the *end* of the chain to the appropriate activation record (rather than down from the start of the chain as before). The second

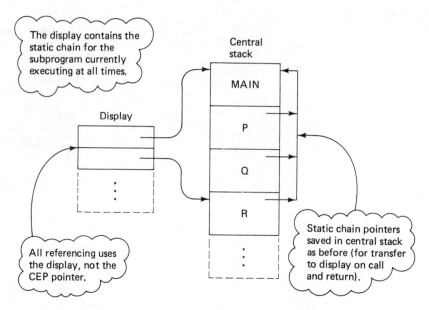

Fig. 7-14 Central stack and display during execution of R
(Fig. 7-10), using the display implementation

integer in the pair still represents the offset in the activation record. Now, given a nonlocal reference such as (3,2), the appropriate association is found in two steps:

    1. Consider the first entry (3) as a subscript into the display. Thus *display* [3] contains a pointer to the base address of the appropriate activation record.

    2. Compute the location of the desired entry as base address plus offset, where the offset is the second entry in the pair.

Ordinarily these two steps combine into one using indirect addressing through the display entry. If the display is represented in high-speed registers during execution, then only one memory access per identifier reference is required.

    Although referencing is simplified using a display, subprogram entry and exit are more difficult because the display must be modified on each entry and exit to reflect the *currently active* static chain. The simplest procedure is to maintain the static chain pointers in the central stack, as described above, and reload the display with the appropriate static chain pointers on each entry and exit, using instructions inserted by the compiler into the prologue and epilogue of each subprogram code segment.

7-8   SHARED DATA: PARAMETERS AND PARAMETER TRANSMISSION

Explicitly transmitted parameters and results are the second major method for sharing data objects among subprograms. In contrast to the use of nonlocal referencing environments, where sharing is achieved by making certain nonlocal names visible to a subprogram, data objects transmitted as parameters and results are transmitted without a name attached. In the receiving subprogram a data object is given a new *local name* through which it may be referenced. The sharing of data through parameters is most useful when a subprogram is to be given different data to process each time it is called. Sharing through a nonlocal environment is more appropriate where the same data objects are used on each call. For example, if subprogram P is used on each call to enter a new data item into a table shared with other subprograms, then typically the table would be shared through references to a nonlocal environment and the data item itself would be transmitted as an explicit parameter on each call of P.

Actual and Formal Parameters

Several terms related to parameter transmission need to be carefully distinguished. We shall consider first the sharing of *data* through parameters, and then later the use of parameters to transmit *subprograms* and *statement labels*. In the preceding chapters, the term *argument* is used for a data object (or a value) that is sent to a subprogram or primitive operation as one of its operands, i.e., as a piece of data to use in processing. The term *result* refers to a piece of data (data object or value) that is returned from an operation at the end of its execution. The arguments of a subprogram may be obtained both through parameters and through nonlocal references (and less commonly, through external files). Similarly the results of a subprogram may be returned through parameters, through assignments to nonlocal variables (or files), or through explicit function values. Thus the terms *argument* and *result* apply to data sent to and returned from the subprogram through a variety of language mechanisms. In narrowing our focus to parameters and parameter transmission, the term *actual parameter* and *formal parameter* become central.

A *formal parameter* is a particular kind of local data object within a subprogram. The subprogram definition ordinarily lists the names and declarations for formal parameters as part of the specification part (heading). A formal parameter name is a simple identifier, and the declaration ordinarily gives the type and other attributes, as for an ordinary local variable declaration. For example, the Pascal procedure heading:

procedure SUB(X:integer; Y:Boolean);

defines two formal parameters named X and Y and declares the type of each. The declaration of a formal parameter, in general, does not mean the same thing as a declaration for a variable, although the differences are not great. Various meanings used in different languages are discussed below.

An *actual parameter* is a data object that is shared with the subprogram by being explicitly transmitted from the caller. An actual parameter may be a local data object belonging to the caller, it may be a formal parameter of the caller, it may be a nonlocal data object visible to the caller, or it may be a result returned by a function invoked by the caller and immediately transmitted to the called subprogram. An actual parameter is represented at the point of call of the subprogram by an expression, termed an *actual-parameter expression*, that ordinarily has the same form as any other expression in the language (e.g., such as an expression that might appear in an assignment statement). For example, in Pascal, the subprogram SUB specified above might be called with any of the following types of actual parameter expressions:

Procedure Call in P	Actual Parameter in P
SUB(I,B)	I,B: local variables of P
SUB(27,true)	27,true: constants
SUB(P1,P2)	P1,P2: formal parameters of P
SUB(G1,G2)	G1,G2: global or nonlocal variables in P
SUB(A[I],D.B1)	Components of arrays and records
SUB(I+3,FN(Q))	Results of primitive or defined functions

The syntax for procedure calls in Pascal is typical of many languages. The subprogram call is written in prefix form, as discussed in Sec. 6-2, with the subprogram name first, followed by a list of actual parameter expressions in parentheses (other notations are used, however, e.g., infix notation in APL, Cambridge Polish in LISP). For simplicity, we adopt the conventional Pascal prefix representation and speak of *actual-parameter lists* and *formal-parameter lists* to indicate the sequence of actual and formal parameters designated in a subprogram call and subprogram definition, respectively.

When a subprogram is called with an actual-parameter expression of any of the forms above, the expression is *evaluated* at the time of the call, before the subprogram is entered. The data objects that result from the evaluation of the actual-parameter expressions then become the actual parameters transmitted to the subprogram. The special case in which the actual-parameter expressions are *not* evaluated at the time of call, but are passed *unevaluated* to the subprogram, is treated separately below.

Establishing the Correspondence

When a subprogram is called with a list of actual parameters, a correspondence must be established between the actual parameters and the formal parameters listed in the subprogram definition. Two methods are:

1. *Positional correspondence.* The correspondence is established by pairing actual and formal parameters based on their respective positions in the actual- and formal-parameter lists; the first actual and first formal parameters are paired, then the second in each list, and so on.

2. *Correspondence by explicit name.* In Ada and some other languages, the formal parameter to be paired with each actual parameter may be named explicitly in the calling statement. For example, in Ada, one could call SUB with the statement:

$$SUB(Y => B, X => 27);$$

which pairs actual parameter B with formal parameter Y and actual parameter 27 with formal parameter X during the call of SUB.

Most languages use positional correspondence exclusively, so examples here use this method. Ordinarily, the number of actual and formal parameters must correspond, so that the pairing is unique; however, some languages relax this restriction and provide special conventions for interpreting missing or extra actual parameters. For simplicity here, all parameters are assumed to be paired.

Methods for Transmitting Parameters

When an actual-parameter expression is evaluated, just before the transfer of control to the subprogram that has been called, the result is a data object that is to serve as the actual parameter. That data object, however, is located at some storage location in memory. To *transmit* that data object as a parameter means ordinarily that a *pointer* to the location of the data object is made available to the subprogram. *The data object itself does not change position in memory.* At the beginning of execution of the subprogram, the pointers to actual parameters are used to initialize local storage locations for the formal parameters. This initialization takes one of two forms: (1) the pointer to the actual parameter is copied into the formal-parameter location, or (2) the entire actual-parameter data object is copied into the formal parameter location. Thus parameter transmission takes place in two stages:

1. In the calling subprogram, each actual-parameter expression is evaluated to give a pointer to the actual-parameter data object. A list of these

pointers is stored in a common storage area that is also accessible to the subprogram being called (often in a set of registers). Control is then transferred to the subprogram, as described in the preceding chapter; that is, the activation record for the subprogram is created (if necessary), the return point is established, and so on.

2. In the called subprogram, as it begins execution, the list of pointers to actual parameters is accessed and the formal parameters are appropriately initialized before the statements in the subprogram body are executed.

During execution of the subprogram, references to formal parameter names are treated as ordinary local variable references (except that there may be a hidden pointer selection, see below). On termination of the subprogram, results may be returned to the calling program through the actual-parameter data objects as well. The details of the semantics of parameter transmission differ among languages, but several methods are widely used. The most general methods allow a single parameter to be used both to send arguments to a subprogram and to return results (**in out** parameters). More restricted forms provide only for arguments to be sent (**in** parameters) or only for results to be returned (**out** parameters). A result may also be returned as an explicit function value, which acts somewhat like an additional **out** parameter. Most languages provide more than one alternative, with the programmer specifying the option as part of the declaration of each formal parameter in the subprogram definition.

IN OUT Parameters

Transmission by reference (location).   If a parameter is *transmitted by reference*, the formal parameter is a local data object of type *pointer*. The pointer to the actual parameter is copied into this formal-parameter location at the time of call. Each reference to the formal parameter in the called subprogram then invokes an implicit pointer-selection operation that follows the pointer to the actual parameter. Thus the actual-parameter data object is made directly accessible to the subprogram through the formal-parameter pointer. The subprogram may obtain values from the actual parameter or assign new values to it. When the subprogram terminates, the formal-parameter pointer is deleted, but any changes made to the value of the actual parameter remain.

Transmission by value-result.   If a parameter is *transmitted by value-result*, the formal parameter is a local variable (data object) of the same data type as the actual parameter. The value (contents) of the actual-parameter data object is copied into the formal-parameter data object at the time of call, so that the effect is the same as if an explicit assignment of actual parameter to formal parameter were executed. During execution of the subprogram, each reference to the formal-parameter name is treated as an ordinary reference to a local variable. When the subprogram terminates, the final contents of the formal-parameter data object is copied into the actual-parameter data object, just as though an explicit assignment of formal parameter to actual parameter were executed. Thus the actual parameter retains its original value until termination of the subprogram, when its new value is assigned as a result from the subprogram.

Both transmission by reference and by value-result are widely used. Many languages are defined so that the implementor may choose which method to use for **in out** parameters. For the programmer, the particular method used makes no difference in the final result, provided the called subprogram terminates normally (see Problem 8) and provided the called subprogram cannot also access the actual parameter through an alias (see below).

IN-only Parameters

Transmission by value. If a parameter is *transmitted by value*, the formal and actual parameters are treated exactly as for transmission by value-result, except that the final value of the formal parameter is not assigned back to the actual parameter. Thus the formal parameter is initialized with a local copy of the value of the actual parameter on entry to the subprogram. The actual parameter cannot be modified by the subprogram. Any changes made in the formal-parameter values during execution of the subprogram are lost when the subprogram terminates.

Transmission by constant value. If a parameter is *transmitted by constant value*, then no change in the value of the formal parameter is allowed during program execution, that is, no assignment of a new value or other modification of the value of the parameter is allowed, and the formal parameter may not be transmitted to another subprogram except as a constant-value parameter. The formal parameter thus acts as a *local constant* during execution of the subprogram. Because no change in its value is possible, two implementations are possible. The formal parameter may be treated exactly as a parameter transmitted by value, so that it is a local data object whose initial value is a copy of the actual-parameter value. Alternatively, it may be treated as a parameter transmitted by reference, so that the formal parameter contains a pointer to the actual-parameter data object.

Both transmission by value and transmission by constant value have the effect of protecting the calling program from changes in the actual parameter. Thus from the viewpoint of the calling program, the actual parameter is only an input argument for the subprogram. Its value cannot be modified by the subprogram, either inadvertently or in order to transmit results back.

OUT-only Parameters: Transmission by Result

A parameter *transmitted by result* is used only to transmit a result back from a subprogram. The initial value of the actual-parameter data object makes no difference and cannot be used by the subprogram. The formal parameter is a local variable (data object) with no initial value (or with the usual initialization provided for local variables). When the subprogram terminates, the final value of the formal parameter is assigned as the new value of the actual parameter, just as in transmission by value-result.

Explicit Function Values

In most languages, a single result may be returned as an explicit *function value* rather than as a parameter. The subprogram must be declared to be a function subprogram, and the type of the result returned must be declared as part of the subprogram specification, as in the Pascal declaration:

function FN(A: integer): real;

which specifies FN to be a function subprogram returning a result of type *real*. Within the function subprogram, the result to be returned as the function value may be specified in one of two ways. One method, used in PL/I, is to designate the function value to be returned by an explicit result expression given as part of the RETURN statement that terminates execution of the subprogram, e.g., RETURN(2∗X) to designate that the value 2∗X is to be returned as the function value. An alternative method, used in Pascal, is to designate the value to be returned by an assignment of the value to the *function name* within the subprogram, e.g., FN := 2∗X. In this latter method, the subprogram may contain several assignments to the function name. The function value returned is the last value assigned to the function name before the subprogram terminates. With either method, the function value may best be considered as an extra implicit OUT parameter from the subprogram.

Implementation of Parameter Transmission

Because each activation of a subprogram receives a different set of parameters, storage for the formal parameters of a subprogram is ordinarily allocated as part of the activation record of the subprogram, rather than in the code segment. Each formal parameter is a local data object in the subprogram. If a formal parameter P is specified in the subprogram heading as being of a particular type T (that is, the actual parameter transmitted is of type T), then the formal parameter is implemented in one of two ways, depending on the method of parameter transmission being used (as discussed above). Either P is treated as a local data object of type T (whose initial value may be a copy of the actual parameter value) or P is treated as a local data object of type *pointer to T* (whose initial value is a pointer to the actual-parameter data object). The former method is used for parameters transmitted by value-result, by value, and by result; the latter is used for parameters transmitted by reference. Either method may be used to implement parameters transmitted by constant-value. An explicit function value may be treated with the former method. If the language does not provide a type specification for formal parameters (as in LISP, APL, and SNOBOL4), then the formal parameter is implemented as a local pointer variable, but the pointer may point to a data object of arbitrary type.

The various actions associated with parameter transmission are split into two groups, those associated with the *point of call* of the subprogram in each calling subprogram and those associated with the *entry and exit* in the subprogram itself. At the point of call, in each calling subprogram, each actual-parameter expression is evaluated, and the list of pointers to actual-parameter data objects (or, sometimes, just copies of their values) is set up. Note that it is important that this evaluation take place at the point of call, in the referencing environment of the calling subprogram. When the actual parameters have been determined, control is transferred to the called subprogram. Ordinarily this involves a change in the CIP and CEP pointers, as discussed in Chapter 6, to transfer control to the start of the executable code for the subprogram, and also to change the referencing environment to that appropriate for the called subprogram.

After the transfer of control to the subprogram, the *prologue* for the subprogram completes the actions associated with parameter transmission, by either copying the entire contents of the actual parameter into the formal parameter, or by copying the pointer to the actual parameter into the formal parameter. Before the subprogram terminates, the *epilogue* for the subprogram must copy result values into the actual parameters transmitted by result or value-result. Function values must also be copied into registers or into temporary storage provided by the calling program. The subprogram then terminates and its activation record is lost, so all results ordinarily must be copied out of the activation record before termination.

The compiler has two main tasks in the implementation of parameter transmission. First it must generate the correct executable code for transmission of parameters, for return of results, and for each reference to a formal-parameter name. Because most languages provide more than one parameter-transmission method, the executable code required in each case is often slightly different. This code generation is also difficult because it often involves coordinated actions taken at each point of call, in the subprogram prologue, and in its epilogue. The second major task of the compiler is to perform the necessary static type checking to insure that the type of each actual-parameter data object matches that declared for the corresponding formal parameter. For this checking, the compiler must know the specification of the subprogram being called (number, order, and type of parameters) but need not know the internal structure of the subprogram body. This specification must be available at each point of call of the subprogram. In many languages, particularly where subprograms may be compiled separately from each other, if a subprogram Q is called from a subprogram P, then a separate specification for Q must be provided when compiling P, even though Q is defined elsewhere, in order to allow the compiler to perform the necessary static type checking and to generate the appropriate code for parameter transmission at each point of call (see the discussion in Sec. 10-4).

Parameter-Transmission Examples

The combination of parameter-transmission method with the different types of actual parameters leads to a variety of effects. Some examples are of use in explaining the subtleties. For these examples, transmission *by reference* and *by value* are the two methods used. The differences that result from using other methods are taken up in some of the problems. Pascal is used as the base for these examples. In our version of Pascal a formal-parameter name that is preceded by **var** in the subprogram heading is transmitted by reference, while one without the **var** is transmitted by value.

Simple variables and constants.   Figure 7-15 shows a Pascal subprogram Q with two formal parameters, I, transmitted by value, and J, transmitted by reference. Suppose we write a subprogram P that calls Q with two integer variables, A and B, as actual parameters:

```
procedure P;
    var A,B: integer;
        begin
        A := 2;
        B := 3;
        Q(A,B);
        write(A,B)
    end;
```

If P is executed, the results printed by the two *write* statements are: 12 13   2 13. Let us follow each parameter in turn.

When P calls Q, the actual-parameter expressions "A" and "B" are

```
procedure Q(I: integer; var J: integer);
    begin
        I := I + 10;
        J := J + 10;
        write(I,J)
    end Q ;
```

Fig. 7-15 Pascal procedure with value and reference parameters

evaluated; that is, a referencing operation is invoked to determine the current association of the names A and B. Each name represents an integer variable data object, so the actual parameters transmitted are these data objects (actually pointers to these data objects). Since A is being transmitted by value, formal parameter I is represented as a local integer variable within Q, and when subprogram Q begins execution, the value of A at the time of the call is assigned as the initial value of I. Subsequently A and I have no further connection (the pointer to A is not used again). Thus when I is assigned the new value 12, A is not changed. After the call to Q is complete, A still has the value 2. Parameter B, on the other hand, is transmitted by reference. This means that J is a local variable in Q of type *pointer to integer*.

When Q begins execution, the pointer to data object B is stored as the value of J. When 10 is added to the value of J, J itself does not change. Instead each reference to J (which leads to the location containing the pointer value) is followed implicitly by a pointer value selection operation, so that the reference to J actually gives access to the location of the data object B. As a result the assignment to J, although it looks identical to the assignment to I, actually means something quite different—the value of actual parameter B is changed to 13. When the values of the formal parameters I and J are printed in Q, the results are 12 and 13, but after return to P, when the values of the corresponding actual parameters A and B are printed, only B has changed value. The value 12 assigned to I in Q is lost when Q terminates, since local variables in Q are deleted at termination. The value of J, of course, is also lost, but this is the pointer, not the value 13.

Data structures. Suppose we write a different version of Q in which the formal parameters are vectors:

```
type VECT = array [1 . . 3] of integer;
procedure Q(K: VECT; var L: VECT);
    var N: integer;
    begin
        K[2] := K[2] + 10;
        L[2] := L[2] + 10;
        for N := 1 to 3 do write(K[N]);
        for N := 1 to 3 do write(L[N])
    end;
```

We might write procedure P as follows:

```
procedure P;
    var C,D: VECT;
        M: integer;
    begin
        C[1] := 6;
        C[2] := 7;
        C[3] := 8;
        D[1] := 6;
        D[2] := 7;
        D[3] := 8;
        Q(C,D);
        for M := 1 to 3 do write(C[M]);
        for M := 1 to 3 do write(D[M]);
    end;
```

When P is executed, the values printed are:

$$6 \quad 17 \quad 8 \qquad 6 \quad 17 \quad 8 \qquad 6 \quad 7 \quad 8 \qquad 6 \quad 17 \quad 8$$

To follow the transmission of C and D as parameters, we first note that the evaluation of the actual parameter expressions "C" and "D" in P leads to pointers to the blocks of storage for the vectors C and D within P's activation record (just as for A and B above). These pointers are transmitted to Q. Since vector C is transmitted by value, the corresponding formal parameter K is a local array in Q having the same shape as C (three components plus a descriptor). The three values in vector C are copied into the corresponding positions of K, and thereafter C and K have no further contact, so on return to P, vector C is unmodified by the assignment to K in Q. The vector D transmitted by reference, however, is modified by the assignment to formal-parameter vector L, because L is not a vector, but only a pointer to a vector. When Q begins execution, L is initialized to point to vector D, and each subsequent reference to L in Q leads via this pointer to D. Thus the assignment to L[2] modifies D[2]. The printed values reflect these distinctions. Figure 7-16 shows the run-time stack at the end of execution of Q.

In general, a data structure such as an array or record that is transmitted by value is copied into a local data structure (the formal parameter) in the called subprogram. The subprogram works on this local copy and has no access to the original. A data structure transmitted by reference is not copied, and the called subprogram works directly on the actual-parameter data structure (using the formal-parameter pointer for access).

Components of data structures. Suppose that we go back to the procedure Q in Fig. 7-15, but instead of simple variables or constants, we

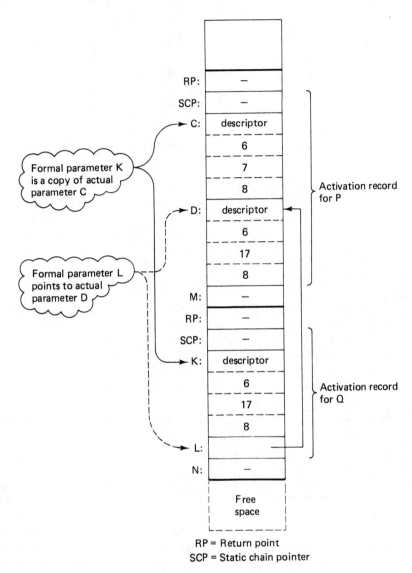

RP = Return point
SCP = Static chain pointer

Fig. 7-16 Run-time stack just before Q terminates (vectors as parameters)

pass components of data structures as parameters to Q—for example, by writing P as:

```
procedure P;
    var C: VECT;
        M: integer;
    begin
        C[1] := 6;
        C[2] := 7;
        C[3] := 8;
        Q(C[1],C[2]);
        for M := 1 to 3 do write(C[M]);
    end;
```

When P is executed, the values printed are:

$$16 \quad 17 \quad \quad 6 \quad 17 \quad 8$$

Transmission of C[1] by value follows the same pattern as before. The expression "C[1]" is evaluated by referencing "C" and then selecting its first component. The result is a pointer to the location of that component (rather than to the entire vector). Formal parameter I is initialized to the value of the data object designated by the transmitted pointer, as before, so the rest of the actions are the same. Similarly, "C[2]" is evaluated and a pointer to the component transmitted. Assignments within Q then directly change the component of C via the pointer stored in formal parameter J.

Nothing is too surprising here, provided the components of C are represented in storage *exactly as are simple variable data objects of the same type*, because within Q, the code that is executed to manipulate I and J is the same, regardless of whether the call of Q is "Q(A,B)" or "Q(C[1],C[2])". If the components of C were represented in storage differently from simple variables A and B (for example, if they were "packed" in some way), then a special conversion would have to be made before Q was called to convert the actual parameters to the proper representation (whatever is expected by Q), store the converted parameters in temporary storage, and pass pointers to the temporary storage to Q. For transmission by value, this conversion might be acceptable, but for transmission by reference, the resulting pointer is no longer a pointer to the original data object, so assignments to the formal parameter no longer modify the actual parameter directly. For this reason, transmission of components of packed arrays and records is often prohibited (e.g., in Pascal).

Array components with computed subscripts. Suppose subprogram R has two integer parameters transmitted by reference:

procedure R(**var** I,J: integer);
   begin
      I := I + 1;
      J := J + 1;
      write(I,J)
   end R;

Suppose P is as above, with vector C, but R is called instead of Q, using the statements:

M := 2;
R(M,C[M]);
for M := 1 **to** 3 **do** write(C[M]);

What values are printed when P is executed now? Note that M has the value 2 initially, but because it is a reference parameter, its value is changed to 3 in R before C[M] is incremented via the pointer in J. Does the statement "J := J + 1" then add one to C[2] or C[3]? Clearly it must be C[2] that is incremented, not C[3], because the actual-parameter expression "C[M]" is evaluated *at the time of call of R* to get a pointer to a component of C. At the time of call of R, M has the value 2, so it is a pointer to C[2] that is transmitted to R. R knows nothing of the existence of C[3], since within R the pointer to C[2] appears the same as a pointer to any other integer data object. Thus the values printed are "3 8   6 8 8". (A different effect appears if parameters are transmitted *by name*, see below.)

Pointers. Suppose an actual parameter is a simple variable of type *pointer* or is a data structure such as an array or record that contains pointers as components. For example, suppose X in P is declared as:

type VECTPTR = ↑VECT;
X: VECTPTR;

and suppose that the corresponding formal parameter in Q is declared likewise:

H: VECTPTR;

Regardless of whether H is declared as transmitted by value or by reference, the effect of transmitting X as the actual parameter is to allow Q to directly access the vector to which X points. If transmission is by value, then Q has its own copy of the pointer that X contains, so both X and H point to the same vector. If transmission is by reference, then H contains a pointer to X which contains a pointer to the vector. As a general rule, whenever the actual-parameter data object contains a pointer or pointer components, the data objects designated by these pointers will be directly accessible from the subprogram, regardless of the method of parameter transmission. Note that if a linked list (or other linked data structure) is transmitted *by value* as a parameter to a subprogram, this usually means that only the pointer to the first element is copied during transmission; the entire linked structure is not copied into the subprogram.

Results of expressions. Suppose we return a final time to the procedure Q of Fig. 7-15, and write procedure P as follows:

procedure P;
    var A,B: integer;
    begin
        A := 2;
        B := 3;
        Q(A+B, A*B);
        write(A,B);
    end;

When P is exececuted, the values printed are "15 16 2 3". Here the actual parameters are not named data objects but the unnamed data objects that result from evaluation of the actual-parameter expressions "A+B" and "A*B". To transmit the result of such an expression as a parameter means to first evaluate the expression at the point of call, then store the resulting value in a *temporary storage location* in P, and then transmit a pointer to that location to the procedure Q as the parameter. Execution of Q continues as before. Transmission by value or by reference is acceptable, except that transmission by reference leads to the formal parameter containing a pointer to the temporary storage location in P. Since this location has no name by which it can be referenced in P, any assignment made to it by Q does not change a value that P can later reference. Thus Q cannot transmit a result back to P through the reference parameter. Pascal prohibits an expression as an actual parameter where the transmission is by reference, because assignments to the formal parameter have no effect observable in the calling program (and thus a parameter transmitted by value should be used).

Aliases and Parameters

The possibility of aliases (multiple names for the same data object in a single referencing environment) arises in connection with parameter transmission in most languages. As explained in Sec. 7-1, aliases are a problem in understanding and verifying the correctness of programs and in program optimization. An alias may be created during parameter transmission in one of two ways:

    1. *Formal parameter and nonlocal variable.* A data object transmitted as an actual parameter by reference may be directly accessible in the

subprogram through a nonlocal name. The formal-parameter name and the nonlocal name then become aliases, because each refers to the same data object. Figure 7-2 shows an example of this type of aliasing.

2. *Two formal parameters*. The same data object may be transmitted as an actual parameter by reference in two positions in the same actual-parameter list. The two formal-parameter names then become aliases, because the data object may be referenced through either name. For example, the procedure R above, defined with the specification:

procedure R(**var** I,J: integer);

could be called by P using:

R(M,M)

During execution of R, both I and J contain pointers to the same data object M in P; thus I and J are aliases.

Subprograms as Parameters

In many languages, a subprogram may be transmitted as an actual parameter to another subprogram. The actual-parameter expression in this case consists of the *name* of the subprogram. The corresponding formal parameter is then specified as of *subprogram* type. In Pascal, for example, a subprogram Q may be defined with a formal parameter R of type procedure or function:

procedure Q(X:integer; **function** R(Y,Z: integer): integer);

and Q may then be called with a function subprogram as its second parameter, e.g., the call:

Q(27,FN)

which invokes Q and passes function subprogram FN as a parameter. Within Q, the subprogram passed as the parameter may be invoked by using the formal-parameter name, R, e.g.,

Z := R(I,X)

invokes the actual-parameter subprogram (FN in the call above) with the actual parameters I and X; thus R(I,X) is equivalent to FN(I,X) in this case. On a different call, if the actual parameter is function subprogram FN2, then R(I,X) invokes FN2(I,X).

Two major problems are associated with subprogram parameters:

1. *Static type checking*. When a subprogram parameter is called using the formal-parameter name, e.g., R(I,X) above, it is important that static type checking be possible to insure that the call includes the proper number

and type of actual parameters for the subprogram being called. Since the actual name of the subprogram being called is not known at the point of call (in the example above, it is FN on one call and FN2 on another), the compiler cannot ordinarily determine whether the actual parameters I and X in the call R(I,X) match those expected by FN or FN2 without additional information. What the compiler needs is a full specification for formal parameter R that includes not only the type *procedure* or *function*, but also the number, order, and type of each parameter (and result) of that procedure or function, e.g., as given above in the specification for Q. Then within the subprogram Q, each call of R may be checked statically for the correctness of its parameter list. In addition, at each call of Q the actual parameter that corresponds to R may be checked as to whether its specification matches that given for R. Thus FN and FN2 must both have the same number, order, and type of parameters as specified for R.

2. Nonlocal references (free variables). Suppose that a subprogram such as FN or FN2 contains a reference to a nonlocal variable. For example, suppose FN references Z and FN2 references Z2, and neither subprogram contains a local definition for the variable referenced. Such a nonlocal reference is often termed, in mathematics, a *free variable*, because it has no local binding within the subprogram definition. Ordinarily when a subprogram is called, a nonlocal referencing environment is set up, and this nonlocal environment is used during execution of the subprogram to provide a meaning for each reference to a nonlocal variable (as described in the preceding sections). However, suppose that a subprogram FN that contains a nonlocal reference is passed as a parameter from a calling subprogram P to a called subprogram Q. What should be the nonlocal environment used when FN is invoked within Q [by using the corresponding formal parameter R, e.g., R(I,X) to invoke FN(I,X)]? The simplest answer is to say that the nonlocal environment should be the same as that used if the call R(I,X) were simply replaced by the call FN(I,X) in subprogram Q, but that turns out to be the wrong answer in most cases. Figure 7-17 illustrates the difficulty. Function FN contains nonlocal references to both "X" and "I". According to the Pascal static scope rules, "X" references the X declared in the main program and "I" references the I declared in procedure P. However, P passes FN as a parameter to Q, and it is Q that actually calls FN via the formal-parameter name "R". Q has local definitions for both "I" and "X", and FN cannot be allowed to incorrectly retrieve these local variables when it is called.

This problem of free variables in functions passed as parameters is not unique to languages like Pascal that use static scope rules and block structure. It also occurs in LISP and other languages that use the most-recent-association rule for nonlocal referencing. The general solution is to invoke the following rule about the meaning of free variables in functional

```
program MAIN;
    var X: integer;
    procedure Q(var I: integer; function R(J: integer):integer);
        var X: integer;
        begin
            X := 4;
            write("IN Q, BEFORE CALL OF R, I = ",I," X = ",X);
            I := R(I);
            write("IN Q, AFTER CALL OF R, I = ",I," X = ",X);
        end Q;
    procedure P;
        var I: integer;
        function FN(K: integer):integer;
            begin
                X := X + K;                          }   "I" and "X" are free
                FN := I + K;                         }   variables here
                write("IN FN, I = ",I,               }
                        "K = ",K," X = ",X);         }
            end FN ;
        begin
            I := 2;
            Q(X,FN);
            write("IN P, I = ",I," X = ",X);
        end P ;
    begin
        X := 7;
        P;
        write("IN MAIN, X = ",X);
    end MAIN .
```

Fig. 7-17 A subprogram with free variables transmitted as a parameter in Pascal

parameters: a nonlocal reference (reference to a free variable) should mean the same thing during the execution of the subprogram passed as a parameter as it would *if the subprogram were invoked at the point where it appears as an actual parameter in the parameter list.* For example, in Fig. 7-17 the subprogram FN appears as an actual parameter in the parameter list of the call to Q within P. Thus the nonlocal references to "X" and "I" in FN, regardless of where FN is actually called later (in this case within Q), are to mean just what they would mean if FN were called where Q is called within P.

To correctly implement this rule for the meaning of nonlocal references within subprograms passed as parameters, it must be possible to recreate the correct nonlocal environment at the point of call of the subprogram parameter, so that it executes using the correct nonlocal environment. In the static chain implementation of nonlocal referencing, as discussed in Sec. 7-7, this is fairly straightforward. All that is necessary is to determine the correct static chain pointer for the subprogram parameter, and pass that along as part of the information transmitted with a subprogram parameter. The subprogram parameter then becomes a pair of pointers (CP,SCP), where CP is a pointer to the code segment for the subprogram and SCP is the static chain pointer to be used when the subprogram is invoked. This pair may be passed through many levels of subprogram until it becomes time to invoke the subprogram. At that point the activation record is created, the transmitted SCP is installed, and execution of the subprogram code segment proceeds as for any other call.

Figure 7-18 illustrates the main steps in execution of the Pascal program of Fig. 7-17. In order to illustrate the interplay between static and

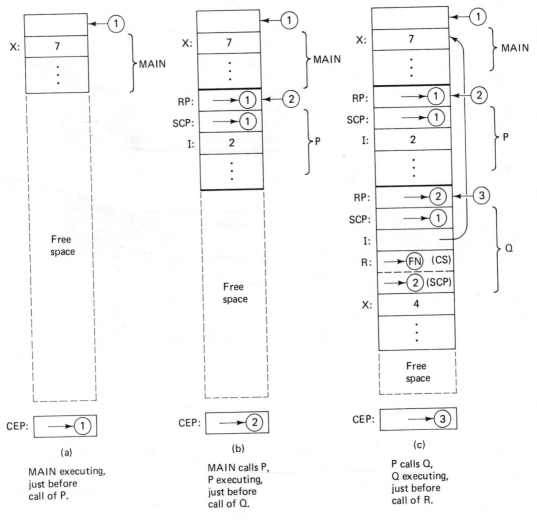

Fig. 7-18   Snapshots of the central stack during execution of the Pascal program of Fig. 7-17

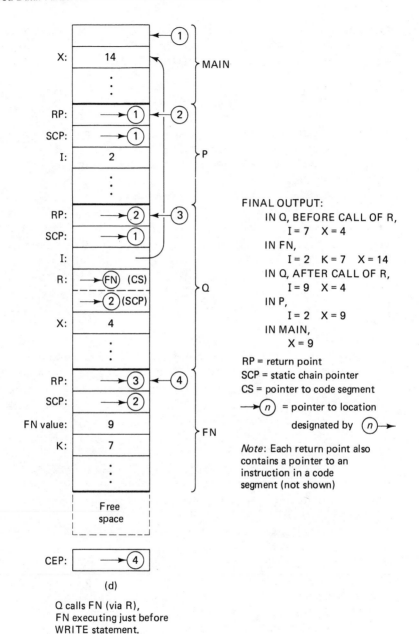

  IN Q, BEFORE CALL OF R,
    I = 7   X = 4
  IN FN,
    I = 2   K = 7   X = 14
  IN Q, AFTER CALL OF R,
    I = 9   X = 4
  IN P,
    I = 2   X = 9
  IN MAIN,
    X = 9

RP = return point
SCP = static chain pointer
CS = pointer to code segment

$\longrightarrow$(n) = pointer to location
        designated by (n)$\longrightarrow$

Note: Each return point also
contains a pointer to an
instruction in a code
segment (not shown)

(d)

Q calls FN (via R),
FN executing just before
WRITE statement.

Fig. 7-18 (cont.)

dynamic chains, as well as subprogram parameters and nonlocal referencing, the example shows the values of variables and the return points and static chain pointers during the main steps in execution of the program.

Unevaluated Parameters: Transmission by Name

The basic concept in parameter transmission by name is that of leaving actual parameters *unevaluated until the point of use* in the called subprogram. The parameters are transmitted unevaluated, and the called subprogram determines when, if ever, they are actually evaluated. Recall from our earlier discussion of uniform evaluation rules that this possibility was useful in treating operations such as the *if-then-else* conditional as ordinary operations. In primitive operations the technique is occasionally useful; in programmer-defined subprograms its utility is more problematic because of the cost of implementation. Parameter transmission by name plays a major role in ALGOL and is of considerable theoretical importance. It has not been widely used outside of ALGOL, being replaced in later languages by more appropriate mechanisms based on subprograms as actual parameters.

The basic transmission-by-name rule may be stated in terms of substitution: The actual parameter is to be substituted everywhere for the formal parameter in the body of the called program before execution of the subprogram begins. While this seems straightforward, consider the problem of even the simple CALL SUB(X). If the formal parameter in SUB is Y, then X is to be substituted for Y throughout SUB before SUB is executed. But this is not enough, because when we come to a reference to X during execution of SUB, the association for X referenced is that *back in the calling program*. not the association in SUB (if any). When X is substituted for Y, we must also indicate a different referencing environment for use in referencing X. This is precisely the problem which arises with subprogram parameters in general, a topic which is discussed above.

Not surprisingly, the basic technique for implementing transmission by name is to treat actual parameters as simple parameterless subprograms (traditionally called *thunks*). This technique allows a uniform handling of the problems of referencing environments for both *by-name* parameters and subprogram parameters. Whenever a formal parameter corresponding to a by-name actual parameter is referenced in a subprogram, the thunk compiled for that parameter is executed, resulting in the evaluation of the actual parameter in the proper referencing environment and the return of the resulting value (or location) as the value of the thunk.

For the programmer, transmission of a parameter by name is identical in effect to transmission by reference for most types of actual-parameter expressions. The major observable difference comes in the case where the actual parameter is an expression containing several variables, and one of these is also transmitted separately as a parameter to the subprogram. For example, consider the case discussed above under "Components of data structures." The procedure R is defined as:

procedure R(**var** I,J: integer);
    begin
        I := I + 1;
        J := J + 1;
        write(I,J);
    end;

and R is called from P with:

M := 2;
R(M,C[M]);

Note that the actual-parameter expression C[M] includes a reference to variable M, and M is also transmitted separately as a parameter to R. With transmission by reference, execution of R caused one to be added to C[2] rather than C[3], because the subscript M was evaluated at the time of call of R (when its value was 2) rather than when J was referenced in R. With transmission by name, however, one is added to C[3], because the actual-parameter expression is reevaluated each time the corresponding formal parameter is referenced within R. Thus each reference to J within R causes the expression "C[M]" to be reevaluated (using the referencing environment of the calling program). Since M has the value 3 when J is referenced in R, the reference to J is a reference to C[3] within R. If later in R, "I := 1" were executed, then any later reference to J would be a reference to C[1], and so on. As you can see, parameter transmission by name is not only somewhat difficult and costly to implement but also leads to potentially confusing programs.

Statement Labels as Parameters

Many languages allow a statement label to be passed as a parameter to a subprogram and then used as the object of a **goto** statement within the subprogram. Besides the usual difficulties associated with the use of **goto** statements, as described in Chapter 6, this mechanism introduces two new difficulties:

1. *Which activation should be used?* A statement label refers to a particular instruction in the code segment of a subprogram during execution. However, a **goto** cannot simply transfer control to that instruction by changing the CIP in the usual way, because the code segment may be shared by several activations of the subprogram. The statement label, when passed

as a parameter, must designate an instruction *in a particular activation* of the subprogram. Thus the label becomes a pair (instruction pointer, activation record pointer) that is transmitted as the parameter.

2. *How is the* **goto** *to a label parameter implemented?*   When a **goto** is executed that designates a formal parameter of type label as its object, it does not suffice to simply transfer control to the designated instruction in the designated activation in most cases. Instead the dynamic chain of subprogram calls must ordinarily be unwound until the designated subprogram activation is reached. That is, the current subprogram executing the **goto** statement must be terminated, then the subprogram that called it, then that subprogram's caller, and so on, until the subprogram activation designated in the **goto** is reached. That activation then begins executing at the instruction designated by the **goto** rather than at the instruction designated by the original return point. Depending on the details of the language definition and implementation, especially regarding the final values of value-result and result parameters in such aborted calling chains, this process may be fairly complex to implement correctly.

7-9   TASKS AND SHARED DATA

Each different treatment of subprogram control structures, e.g., coroutines, exception handlers, tasks, and scheduled subprograms, as discussed in Chapter 6, leads to somewhat different structures for shared data. In most cases these structures are straightforward variations on the concepts presented in the preceding sections, but tasks present special problems due to the concurrent execution involved. The problem is that of *mutual exclusion* from shared data. If task A and task B each have access to a single data object X, then A and B must synchronize their access to X, so that task A is not in the process of assigning a new value to X while task B is simultaneously referencing that value or assigning a different value. For example, if variable X has the value 1 and task A executes the statement:

$$\textbf{if } X > 0 \textbf{ then } X := X + 1;$$

and B executes the statement:

$$\textbf{if } X > 0 \textbf{ then } X := X - 2;$$

then X may end up with the value 0 (if A goes first), the value -1 (if B goes first), or possibly the value 2 (if A and B happen to interleave their actions by attempting to execute both statements concurrently). To insure that two tasks do not simultaneously attempt to access and update a shared data object, one task must be able to gain *exclusive access* to the data object while it manipulates it. There are several different approaches to solution of the problem of mutual exclusion when tasks work on shared data.

Critical Regions

A *critical region* is a sequence of program statements within a task where the task is operating on some data object shared with other tasks. If a critical region in task A is manipulating data object X, then mutual exclusion requires that no other task be simultaneously executing a critical region that also manipulates X. During execution of task A, when it is about to begin execution of the critical region, A must wait until any other task has completed a critical region that manipulates X. As task A begins its critical region, all other tasks must be locked out, so that they cannot enter their critical regions (for variable X) until A has completed its critical region. Critical regions may be implemented in tasks by associating a semaphore with each shared data object (or group of objects). The shared data objects ordinarily are made part of an explicit common environment (or several common environments) that is accessible to each task.

Monitors

Another approach to mutual exclusion is through the use of a monitor. A *monitor* is a shared data object together with the set of operations that may manipulate it. Thus a monitor is similar to a data object defined by an abstract data type, as described in Sec. 5-4. A task may manipulate the shared data object only by using the defined operations, so that the data object is encapsulated, as is usual for data objects defined by abstract data types. To enforce mutual exclusion, it is only necessary to require that *at most one* of the operations defined for the data object may be executing at any given time.

The requirement for mutual exclusion and encapsulation in a monitor make it natural to represent the monitor itself as a task. The shared data object is made a local data object within the task, and the operations are defined as local subprograms within the task. For example, suppose the shared data object is a table, BIG_TABLE, and two operations, ENTER_NEW_ITEM and FIND_ITEM are defined. Mutual exclusion is necessary so that one task will not be entering a new item at the same time that another task is attempting to find an item at the same position in the table. In Ada, the monitor might be represented as a task TABLE_MANAGER, with two entries, ENTER_NEW_ITEM and FIND_ITEM, defined as shown in Fig. 7-19. Within TABLE_MANAGER, BIG_TABLE is a local variable. A **select** statement with two **accept** alternatives is used to allow the monitor

```
task TABLE_MANAGER is
    entry  ENTER_NEW_ITEM(. . .);
    entry FIND_ITEM (. . .);
end;
task body TABLE_MANAGER is
    BIG_TABLE: array (. . .) of . . . ;
    procedure ENTER(. . .) is
        —statements to enter item in BIG_TABLE
    end ENTER;
    function FIND(. . .) returns . . . is
        —statements to find item in BIG_TABLE
    end FIND;
begin
        —statements to initialize BIG_TABLE
    loop       —loop forever to process entry requests
        select
            accept ENTER_NEW_ITEM( . . . ) do
            —call ENTER to enter received item in BIG_TABLE
            end;
        or   accept FIND_ITEM( . . . ) do
            —call FIND to look up received item in BIG_TABLE
            end;
        end select;
    end loop;
end TABLE_MANAGER;
```

Fig. 7-19   A monitor represented as an Ada task

to respond to requests from other tasks to perform one or the other of the operations ENTER_NEW_ITEM or FIND_ITEM in such a way that only one such operation is ever in execution at once. Two tasks may simultaneously request items to be entered or looked up in the table. For example, task A may execute the entry call statement:

ENTER_NEW_ITEM(. . .);

and task B may execute concurrently the entry call:

FIND_ITEM(. . .);

The first entry call received by TABLE_MANAGER is processed (i.e., the rendezvous takes place as described in Sec. 6-9). If the second entry statement is executed before the first is processed by TABLE_MANAGER, the second task must wait. Thus BIG_TABLE is protected from simultaneous access by two tasks.

Message Passing

Another solution to the problem of shared data between tasks is to prohibit shared data *objects* and provide only the sharing of data *values* through passing the values as parameters. When a data value is transmitted between two tasks, it is usually termed a *message*. Using message passing as the basis for data sharing insures mutual exclusion without any special mechanism, since each data object is owned by exactly one task, and no other task may access the data object directly. The owner task A may send a copy of the values stored in the data object to task B for processing. B then has its own local copy of the data object. When B has finished processing its local copy, B sends a copy of the new values to A, and A then changes the actual data object. Task A, of course, may continue to change the actual data object while B changes its local copy.

Message passing is the natural extension of parameter-passing concepts, as discussed in Sec. 7-8, to communication between concurrent tasks. Message passing is seen in Ada in Fig. 7-19, where the entry calls and accept statements for ENTER_NEW_ITEM and FIND_ITEM each are followed by a list of parameters, indicating values to be passed (as messages) between other tasks and the monitor task.

Implementation of message passing is more complex than it might seem. Several tasks may simultaneously attempt to send messages to a single receiving task. If some of these messages are not to be lost, the implementation must include a mechanism to store the messages in a queue (usually called a *buffer*) until the receiver can process them. Alternatively, the sending task itself (rather than just its message) can be made to wait in a queue until the receiver is ready to receive the message. The latter method is used in Ada, where a sending task must rendezvous with the receiving task (and thus synchronize with it) before the message may be transmitted.

7-10   REFERENCES AND SUGGESTIONS
FOR FURTHER READING

Most of the books and papers referenced in Chapter 6 that deal with subprogram-level control structures also deal with the associated problems of referencing environments, shared data, and parameters. Wasserman [1980] has collected some papers of interest. Jones and Muchnick [1978] and the volume edited by Tou and Wegner [1971] provide additional material. The *contour model* of referencing environments is introduced by Johnston in the latter volume and provides the basis for the text by Organick et al. [1978]. These topics are also a central issue in the construction of compilers (see Chapter 9). Ada and Euclid (Lampson, et al. [1977]) are two languages in which the issues of visibility, aliasing, and shared data have been central concerns.

7-11   PROBLEMS

1. When local referencing environments are deleted between subprogram activations, using a central stack as in Pascal, it sometimes appears as if values are *retained*. For example, in most Pascal implementations, if procedure SUB has a local variable X and SUB assigns the value 5 to X on the first call, then on a second call, if X is (inadvertently) referenced before it is assigned a new value, sometimes X still has its old value 5. However, in the same program a third call on SUB may find X *not* retaining its old value from the second call. Explain this apparent anomaly: In what circumstances could an activation of SUB that references an uninitialized variable X find that X still had the value assigned on a previous call? In what circumstances would X not have its previously assigned value?

2. Suppose a language allows initial values to be specified for local variables—for example, the Ada declaration

$$X: INTEGER := 50$$

which initializes X to 50. Explain the two meanings that such an initialization might have in the cases (1) local variables are *retained* between calls and (2) local variables are *deleted* between calls.

3. Pascal (and many other languages) allow *pointer* type variables to be used together with a NEW operation to construct data objects. Pascal also uses the deletion approach to local referencing environments. The combination has a high potential for the generation of *garbage* (inaccessible storage) during program execution. Explain the difficulty.

4. For a program you have written recently in a language that uses *static scope rules*, take each subprogram and list the names in (1) its local referencing environment, (2) its nonlocal referencing environment, (3) its global referencing environment, and (4) its predefined referencing environment. Then invert the problem: For a name declared in each of these referencing environments, (1) list the subprogram definitions in its static scope and (2) the subprogram activations in its dynamic scope.

5. Repeat Problem 4, but with a language that uses *dynamic scope rules*. [Delete part (1) of the inverted problem.]

6. In languages such as Pascal that use static scope rules and that allow recursive subprogram calls, it is sometimes difficult to relate a nonlocal reference in one subprogram to a particular variable in another subprogram if there are several recursive activations of that second subprogram in existence. For example, suppose A, B, C, and D are the subprograms of program MAIN, and A is called by MAIN. Suppose A calls B, B calls A recursively, A calls C, and then C calls D.

expression, the expression may be evaluated for many different values of the variables. A simple example of the technique is in the general-purpose summation routine SUM, defined in ALGOL as follows:

> **real procedure** SUM (EXPR,INDEX,LB,UB); **value** LB,UB;
> **real** EXPR; **integer** INDEX,LB,UB;
> **begin real** TEMP; TEMP := 0
> **for** INDEX := LB **step** 1 **until** UB **do** TEMP := TEMP + EXPR;
> SUM := TEMP
> **end** proc SUM;

In this program EXPR and INDEX are transmitted by name, and LB and UB by value. The call of SUM

$$SUM(A[I],I,1,25)$$

will return the sum of the first 25 elements of vector A. The call

$$SUM(A[I] \times B[I],I,1,25)$$

will return the sum of the products of the first 25 corresponding elements of vectors A and B (assuming that A and B have been appropriately declared). The call

$$SUM(C[K,2],K,-100,100)$$

will return the sum of the second column of matrix C from C[-100,2] to C[100,2].
(a) What call to SUM would give the sum of the elements on the main diagonal of a matrix D, declared as **real array** D[1:50,1:50]?
(b) What call to SUM would give the sum of the squares of the first 100 odd numbers?
(c) Use Jensen's device to write a general-purpose MAX routine that will return the maximum value from a set of values obtained by evaluating an arbitrary expression EXPR containing an index INDEX which varies over a range from LB to UB in steps of STEP size (an integer).
(d) Show how the effect of Jensen's device may be obtained by using subprograms as parameters in a language without parameter transmission by name.

17. Explain why it is *impossible* in a language with only parameters transmitted by value or name, such as ALGOL, to write a subprogram SWAP of two parameters which simply swaps the values of its two parameters (which must be simple or subscripted variables). For example, SWAP called by SWAP(X,Y) should return with X having the original value of Y and Y the original value of X. Assume that SWAP works only for arguments of type integer.

CHAPTER 8

Storage
Management

Storage is often a scarce resource in a computing system. Storage management is one of the central concerns of the programmer, language implementor, and language designer. In this chapter the various problems and techniques in storage management are considered.

Programming language design is strongly influenced by storage management considerations. Typically languages contain many features or restrictions which may be explained only by a desire on the part of the designers to allow one or another storage management technique to be used. Take, for example, the restriction in FORTRAN to nonrecursive subprogram calls. Recursive calls could be allowed in FORTRAN without change in the syntax, but their implementation would require a run-time stack of return points, a structure necessitating dynamic storage management during execution. Without recursive calls FORTRAN may be implemented with only static storage management. Pascal is carefully designed to allow stack-based storage management, LISP to allow garbage collection, and so on.

Storage management is one of the first concerns of the language implementor as well. While each language design ordinarily permits the use of certain storage management techniques, the details of the mechanisms, and their representation in hardware and software, are the task of the implementor. For example, while the LISP design may point to a free-space list and garbage collection as the appropriate basis for storage management, there are a number of different garbage-collection techniques known. The implementor must choose or design one appropriate to the available hardware and software.

The programmer is also deeply concerned with storage management, but his position is somewhat anomalous. While it is of major importance to the programmer to design programs that use storage efficiently, he is likely to have little direct control over storage management. His program affects storage management only indirectly through the use or lack of use of different language features. His position is made more difficult by the tendency of both language designers and language implementors to treat storage management as a *machine-dependent* topic which should not be directly discussed in language manuals. Thus it is often difficult for a programmer to discover what storage management techniques are actually used.

8-1 MAJOR RUN-TIME ELEMENTS REQUIRING STORAGE

The programmer tends to view storage management largely in terms of storage of his data structures and translated programs. However, run-time storage management encompasses many other areas besides these. Some, such as return points for subprograms, have been touched on in preceding chapters; others have not yet been mentioned explicitly. Let us look at the major program and data elements requiring storage during program execution.

Code segments for translated user programs. A major block of storage in any system must be allocated to store the code segments representing the translated form of user programs, regardless of whether programs are hardware- or software-interpreted. In the former case programs will be blocks of executable machine code; in the latter case, in some intermediate form.

System run-time programs. Another substantial block of storage during execution must be allocated to system programs that support the execution of the user programs. These may range from simple *library routines*, such as sine, cosine, or square-root functions, to software interpreters or translators present during execution. Also included here are the routines that control run-time storage management. These system programs would ordinarily be blocks of hardware-executable machine code, regardless of the executable form of user programs.

User-defined data structures and constants. Space for user data must be allocated. This includes mainly data structures declared in or created by user programs, although constants used in programs must also be stored.

Subprogram return points. Internally generated sequence-control information, such as subprogram return points, coroutine resume points, or event notices for scheduled subprograms, must be allocated storage. As noted in Chapter 6, storage of these data may require only single locations, a central stack, or other run-time storage structure.

Referencing environments. Storage of referencing environments (identifier associations) during execution may require substantial space, as, for example, the LISP A-list (Chapter 17).

Temporaries in expression evaluation. Expression evaluation requires use of system-defined temporary storage for the intermediate results of evaluation. For example, in evaluation of the expression $X \times Y + U \times V$, the result of the first multiplication must be stored in a temporary while the second multiplication is performed. When expressions may involve recursive function calls, a potentially unlimited number of temporaries may be required to store partial results at each level of recursion.

Temporaries in parameter transmission. When a subprogram is called, a list of actual parameters must be evaluated and the resulting values stored in temporary storage until evaluation of the entire list is complete. Where evaluation of one parameter may require evaluation of recursive function calls a potentially unlimited amount of storage may be required, as in expression evaluation.

Input-output buffers. Ordinarily input and output operations work through buffers which serve as temporary storage areas where data are stored between the time of the actual physical transfer of the data to or from external storage and the program-initiated input and output operations. Often hundreds of memory locations must be reserved for these buffers during execution.

Miscellaneous system data. In almost every language implementation, storage is required for various system data: tables, status information for input-output, and various miscellaneous pieces of state information (e.g., reference counts or garbage-collection bits).

From the foregoing list it is clear that storage management concerns storage for much more than simply user programs and data. More important, much of the information requiring storage is hidden from the language user.

Besides the data and program elements requiring storage, it is instructive also to consider the various operations that may require storage to be allocated or freed. The major operations are:

1. *Subprogram call and return operations.* The allocation of storage for a subprogram activation record, the local referencing environment, and other data on call of a subprogram is often the major operation requiring

storage allocation. The execution of a subprogram return operation usually requires freeing of the storage allocated during the call.

2. *Data structure creation and destruction operations.* If the language provides operations that allow new data structures to be created at arbitrary points during program execution (rather than only on subprogram entry), then these operations ordinarily require storage allocation that is separate from that allocated on subprogram entry. The Pascal NEW operation and the PL/I ALLOCATE operation are examples of such creation operations. The language may also provide an explicit destruction operation, such as the Pascal DISPOSE and the PL/I FREE operations, which may require that storage be freed.

3. *Component insertion and deletion operations.* If the language provides operations that insert and delete components of data structures, storage allocation and freeing may be required to implement these operations, e.g., the SNOBOL4 concatenation operation that inserts characters in a string, and the LISP **cons** operation that inserts a component into a list.

While these operations require explicit storage management, many other operations require some hidden storage management to take place. Much of this storage management activity involves the allocation and freeing of temporary storage for housekeeping purposes (e.g., during expression evaluation and parameter transmission).

8-2 PROGRAMMER- AND SYSTEM-CONTROLLED STORAGE MANAGEMENT

To what extent should the programmer be allowed to directly control storage management? On the one hand, PL/I allows some direct control by the programmer through statements such as ALLOCATE and FREE, which allocate and free storage for programmer-defined data structures. On the other hand, many high-level languages allow the programmer no direct control; storage management is affected only implicitly through the use of various language features.

The difficulty with programmer control of storage management is twofold: It may place a large and often undesirable burden on the programmer, and it may also interfere with the necessary system-controlled storage management. No high-level language can allow the programmer to shoulder the entire storage management burden. For example, the programmer can hardly be expected to concern himself with storage for temporaries, subprogram return points, or other system data. At best he might control storage management for his data (and perhaps programs). Yet even simple allocation and freeing of storage for data structures, as in

PL/I, is likely to permit generation of garbage and dangling references. Thus programmer-controlled storage management is "dangerous" to the programmer because it may lead to subtle errors or loss of access to available storage. Programmer-controlled storage management also may interfere with system-controlled storage management, in that special storage areas and storage management routines may be required for programmer-controlled storage, allowing less efficient use of storage overall.

The advantage of allowing programmer control of storage management lies in the fact that it is often extremely difficult for the system to determine when storage may be most effectively allocated and freed. The programmer, on the other hand, often knows quite precisely when a particular data structure is needed or when it is no longer needed and may be freed.

8-3   STORAGE MANAGEMENT PHASES

It is convenient to identify three basic aspects of storage management:

1. *Initial allocation.* At the start of execution each piece of storage may be either already allocated for some use or free. If free initially, it is available to be allocated dynamically as execution proceeds. Any storage management system requires some technique for keeping track of free storage as well as mechanisms for allocation of free storage as the need arises during execution.

2. *Recovery.* Storage which has been allocated and used for a while and which subsequently becomes available must be recovered by the storage manager for reuse. Recovery may be very simple, as in the repositioning of a stack pointer, or very complex, as in garbage collection.

3. *Compaction and reuse.* Storage recovered may be immediately ready for reuse, or compaction may be necessary to construct large blocks of free storage from small pieces. Reuse of storage ordinarily involves the same mechanisms as initial allocation.

Many different storage management techniques are known and in use in language implementations. It is impossible to survey them all, but a relative handful suffice to represent the basic approaches. Most techniques are variants of one of these basic methods.

8-4   STATIC STORAGE MANAGEMENT

The simplest form of allocation is *static allocation*—that is, allocation during translation which remains fixed throughout execution. Ordinarily storage for the code segments of user and system programs is allocated statically, as is storage for I/O buffers and various miscellaneous system data. Static allocation requires no run-time storage management software, and, of course, there is no concern for recovery and reuse.

In the usual FORTRAN implementation all storage is allocated statically. Each subprogram is compiled separately, with the compiler setting up the code segment (including an activation record) containing the compiled program, its data areas, temporaries, return-point location, and miscellaneous items of system data. The loader allocates space in memory for these compiled blocks at load time, as well as space for system run-time routines. During program execution no storage management takes place.

Static storage allocation is efficient, because no time or space is expended for storage management during execution. However, it is incompatible with recursive subprogram calls, with data structures whose size is dependent on computed or input data, and with many other desirable language features. In the remaining sections of this chapter we shall discuss various techniques for *dynamic* (run-time) *storage management*. However, the reader should not lose sight of the importance of static allocation—for many programs static allocation is quite satisfactory. Two of the most widely used programming languages, FORTRAN and COBOL, are designed for static storage allocation.

8-5   STACK-BASED STORAGE MANAGEMENT

The simplest run-time storage management technique is the stack-based technique. Free storage at the start of execution is set up as a sequential block in memory. As storage is allocated, it is taken from sequential locations in this stack beginning at one end. Storage must be freed in the reverse order of allocation, so that a block of storage being freed is always at the top of the stack. This organization makes trivial the problems of storage recovery, compaction, and reuse.

A single *stack pointer* is basically all that is needed to control storage management. The stack pointer always points to the next available word of free storage in the stack block, representing the current top of the stack. All storage in use lies in the stack below the location pointed to by the stack pointer. All free storage lies above the pointer. When a block of k locations is to be allocated, the pointer is simply moved to point k locations farther up the stack area. When a block of k locations is freed, the pointer is moved back k locations. There are no problems of compaction; compaction is automatic.

It is the strictly nested last-in, first-out structure of subprogram calls and returns in most languages that makes stack storage management an appealing technique. Many of the program and data elements requiring storage are tied to subprogram activations.

Grouping those elements associated with a subprogram activation which require stack allocation into a single *activation record* as discussed in Sec. 5-2 is a common technique. When a subprogram is called, a new activation record is created on the top of the stack. Termination causes its deletion from the stack.

Most Pascal implementations are built around a single central stack of activation records for subprograms together with a statically allocated area containing system programs and subprogram code segments. The structure of a typical activation record for a Pascal subprogram is shown in Fig. 8-1. The activation record contains all the variable items of information associated with a given subprogram activation. Figure 8-2 shows a typical memory organization during Pascal execution (the heap storage area is used for storage allocated by NEW and freed by DISPOSE).

The use of a stack in a LISP implementation is somewhat different. Here also subprogram (function) calls are strictly nested and a stack may be used for activation records. Each activation record contains a return point and temporaries for expression evaluation and parameter transmission. Local referencing environments might also be allocated in the same stack, except that the programmer is allowed to directly manipulate these associations. Therefore they are ordinarily stored in a separate stack, represented as a linked list, called the *A-list*. The stack containing return points and temporaries may then be hidden from the programmer and allocated sequentially. LISP implementation requires also a *heap* storage area, which is managed through a free space list and garbage collection, with a special area and storage manager for *full-word* data items such as numbers. A typical LISP memory organization is illustrated in Fig. 8-3.

The use of a stack of subprogram activation records (or partial activation records as in LISP) is characteristic of implementation of every language in Part II except FORTRAN and COBOL. Stack-based storage management is the most widely used technique for run-time storage management.

The division of storage into an area allocated statically, an area allocated as a stack, and an area allocated as a heap that is seen in Pascal and LISP is characteristic of a number of languages. Ada, SNOBOL4, and PL/I also use this tripartite division of memory into areas managed in different ways.

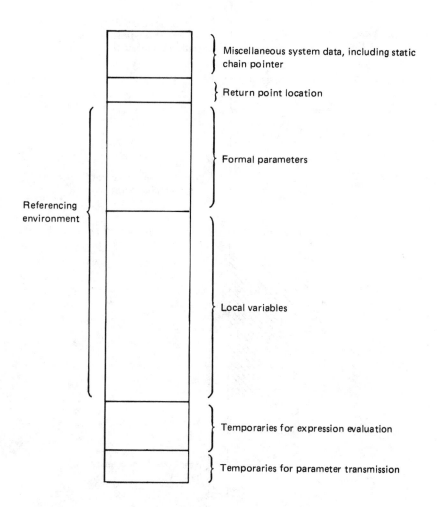

Fig. 8-1   Structure of a Pascal subprogram activation record

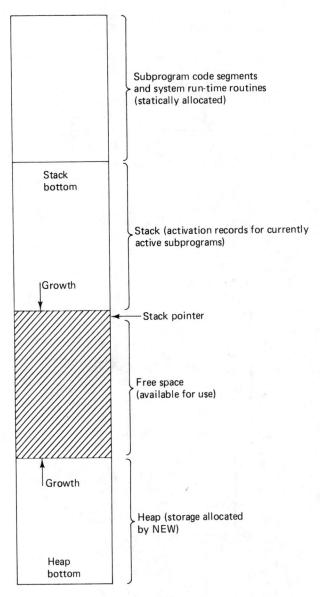

Fig. 8-2 Typical Pascal memory organization during execution

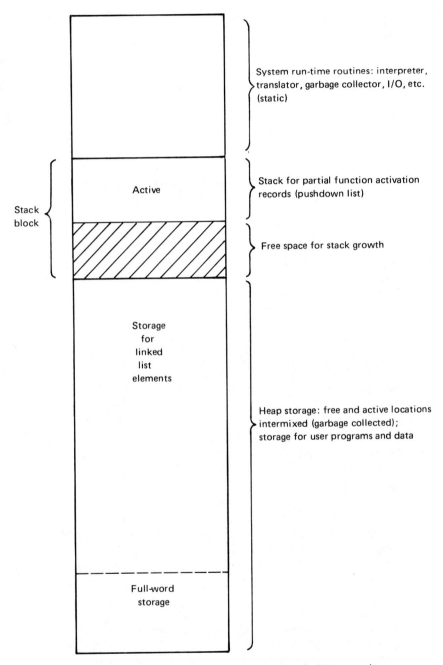

Fig. 8-3 Typical LISP memory organization during execution

8-6   HEAP STORAGE MANAGEMENT: FIXED-SIZE ELEMENTS

The third basic type of storage management, besides static and stack-based management, is termed *heap storage management*. A *heap* is a block of storage within which pieces are allocated and freed in some relatively unstructured manner. Here the problems of storage allocation, recovery, compaction, and reuse may be severe. There is no single heap storage management technique, but rather a collection of techniques for handling various aspects of heap storage management. We shall survey the basic techniques here, without attempting to be comprehensive.

The need for heap storage and storage management arises when a language requires storage to be allocated and freed at arbitrary points during program execution, as when a language allows creation, destruction, or extension of programmer data structures at arbitrary program points. For example, in SNOBOL4 two strings may be concatenated to create a new string at any arbitrary point during execution. Storage must be allocated for the new string at the time it is created. In LISP a new element may be added to an existing list structure at any point, again requiring storage to be allocated. In both SNOBOL4 and LISP, storage may also be freed at unpredictable points during execution.

It is convenient to divide heap storage management techniques into two categories, depending on whether the elements allocated are always of the same fixed size or of variable size. Where fixed-size elements are used, management techniques may be considerably simplified. Compaction, in particular, is not a problem. We shall consider the fixed-size case in this section, leaving the variable-size case until the following section.

Assume that the fixed-size elements which are allocated from the heap and later recovered occupy N words of memory each. Typically N might be 1 or 2. Assuming the heap occupies a contiguous block of memory, we conceptually divide the heap block into a sequence of K elements, each N words long, where $K \times N$ = length of the heap block. This division of the heap into K fixed-size elements forms the basis for our heap storage management. Whenever an element is needed, one of these is allocated from the heap. Whenever an element is freed, it must be one of these original heap elements.

Initially the K elements are linked together to form a *free-space list*. To allocate an element, the first element on the free-space list is removed from the list and a pointer to it is returned to the operation requesting the storage. When an element is freed, it is simply linked back in at the head of the free-space list. Figure 8-4 illustrates such an initial free-space list, as well as the list after allocation and freeing of a number of elements.

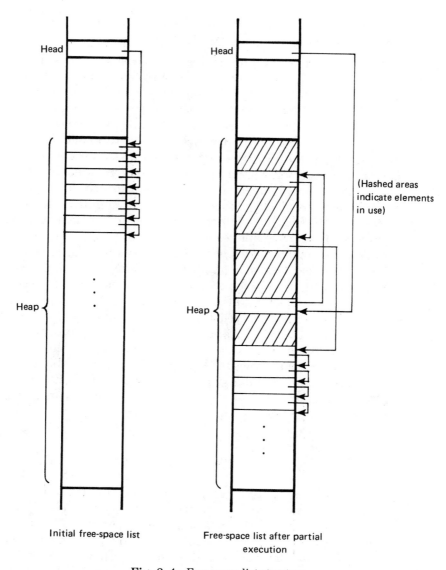

Initial free-space list

Free-space list after partial
execution

Fig. 8-4 Free-space list structure

Recovery: Explicit Return, Reference Counts, and Garbage Collection

Return of newly freed storage to the free-space list is simple, provided such storage may be identified and recovered. But identification and recovery may be quite difficult. The problem lies in determining which elements in the heap are available for reuse and therefore may be returned to the free-space list. Three solutions are in fairly wide use.

Explicit return by programmer or system. The simplest recovery technique is that of *explicit return*. When an element which has been in use becomes available for reuse, it must be explicitly identified as "free" and returned to the free-space list. Where the space has been used for a programmer-defined data structure, the programmer is provided with a FREE or ERASE command which is used to explicitly designate data structures to be returned. Where elements are used for system purposes, such as storage of referencing environments, return points, or temporaries, or where all storage management is system-controlled, each system routine is responsible for returning space as it becomes available for reuse, through explicit call of a FREE routine with the appropriate element as a parameter.

Explicit return would seem the natural recovery technique for heap storage, but unfortunately it is not always feasible. The reasons lie with two old problems: *garbage* and *dangling references*. We first discussed these problems in Chapter 4 in connection with destruction of data structures. If a structure is destroyed (and the storage freed) before all access paths to the structure have been destroyed, the remaining access paths become dangling references. On the other hand, if the last access path to a structure is destroyed without the structure itself being destroyed and the storage recovered, then the structure becomes garbage. In the context of heap storage management a dangling reference is a pointer to an element that has been returned to the free-space list (or a pointer to an element that has been returned and later reallocated for another purpose). A garbage element is one that is available for reuse but not on the free-space list and which thus is inaccessible.

Both garbage and dangling references are potentially troublesome for a storage management system. If garbage accumulates, available storage is gradually reduced until the program may be unable to continue for lack of known free space. Dangling references may cause chaos. If a program attempts to modify through a dangling reference a structure that has already been destroyed, the contents of an element on the free-space list may be modified inadvertently. If this modification overwrites the pointer linking the element to the next free-space-list element, the entire remainder of the free-space list may become garbage. Even worse, a later attempt by the storage allocator to use the pointer in the overwritten element leads to completely unpredictable results; e.g., a piece of an executable program may be allocated as "free space" and later modified. Similar sorts of problems arise if the element pointed to by the dangling reference has already been reallocated to another use before a reference is made.

Recovery of heap storage by explicit return often leads to the potential to create garbage and dangling references. For example, consider the PL/I statements:

ALLOCATE ELEM SET(P)

P = Q

(allocates an element from free space and sets variable P to contain a pointer to it) (destroys the only pointer to the element, leaving it as garbage)

or

ALLOCATE ELEM SET(P)
Q = P
FREE P − > ELEM

(copies the pointer in P into Q) (destroys the element pointed to by P, freeing the storage for reuse; the pointer in Q is not destroyed, however, leaving a dangling reference)

It is easy in such cases for the programmer inadvertently to create garbage or dangling references, with the resulting sometimes dire consequences.

It may be equally difficult for the run-time system to avoid creating garbage or dangling references. In LISP, for example, linked lists are a basic data structure. One of the primitive LISP operations is CDR, which, given a pointer to one element on a linked list, returns a pointer to the next element in the list (see Fig. 8-5). The element originally pointed to *may* have been freed by the CDR operation, provided the original pointer given CDR was the only pointer to the element. If CDR does not return the element to the free-space list at this point, it becomes garbage. However, if CDR does return

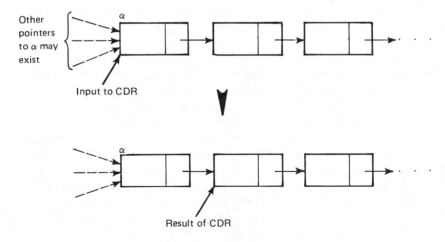

Fig. 8-5 The LISP CDR operation

the element to free space and other pointers to it exist, then they become dangling references. If there is no direct way to determine whether such pointers exist, then the CDR primitive must potentially generate garbage or dangling references.

Owing to these problems with explicit return, alternative approaches are desirable. One alternative, called *garbage collection*, is to allow garbage to be created but no dangling references. Later if the free-space list becomes exhausted, a *garbage-collector* mechanism is invoked to identify and recover the garbage. A second alternative, that of *reference counts*, requires explicit return but provides a way of checking the number of pointers to a given element so that no dangling references are created.

Reference counts.   The use of reference counts is the simpler of the two techniques, so we shall take it up first. The basic concept is this: Within each element in the heap allow some extra space for a *reference counter*. The reference counter of an element contains at all times an integer, the *reference count*, indicating the number of pointers to that element which exist. When an element is initially allocated from the free-space list, its reference count is set to 1. Each time a new pointer to the element is created, its reference count is increased by 1. Each time a pointer is destroyed, the reference count is decreased by 1. When the reference count of an element reaches zero, the element is free and may be returned to the free-space list.

Reference counts allow both garbage and dangling references to be avoided in most situations. Consider the LISP CDR operation again (Fig. 8-5). If each list element contains a reference count, then it is simple for the CDR operation to avoid the previous difficulties. CDR must subtract 1 from the reference count of the element originally pointed to by its input. If the result leaves a reference count of zero, then the element may be returned to the free-space list, and if nonzero, then the element is still pointed to by other pointers and cannot be considered free (see Fig. 8-6).

Where the programmer is allowed an explicit FREE or ERASE statement, reference counts also provide protection. The result of a FREE statement is only to decrement the reference count of the structure by 1. Only if the count then is zero is the structure actually returned to the free-space list. A nonzero reference count indicates that the structure is still accessible and that the FREE command should be ignored.

The most important difficulty associated with reference counts is the *cost of maintaining* them. Reference-count testing, incrementing, and decrementing must go on continuously throughout execution, often causing a substantial decrease in execution efficiency. Consider, for example, the simple assignment P := Q, where P and Q are both pointer variables. Without reference counts it suffices to simply copy the pointer in Q into P. With reference counts we must do the following:

1. Access the element pointed to by P and decrement its reference count

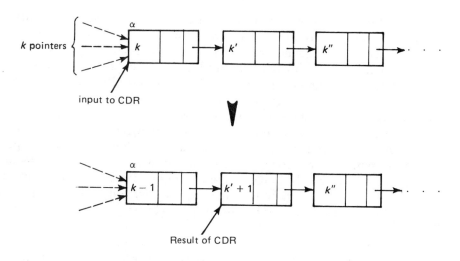

If $k - 1 = 0$, element α may be freed safely

Fig. 8-6 The LISP CDR operation with reference counts

by 1. Test the resulting count, and if zero, return the element to the free-space list.

2. Copy the pointer in Q into P.

3. Access the element pointed to by Q and increment its reference count by 1.

The total cost of the assignment operation has been increased substantially. Any similar operation which may create or destroy pointers must modify reference counts also. In addition, there is the cost of the extra storage for the reference counts. If extra space exists in heap elements already, this storage may be no problem. More commonly an extra location would be necessary in each element to contain the reference count. Where elements are only one or two locations in length to begin with, storage of reference counts may substantially reduce the storage available for data.

Garbage collection. Returning to the basic problems of garbage and dangling references, we may readily agree that dangling references are potentially far more damaging than garbage. Garbage accumulation causes a drain on the amount of usable storage, but dangling references may lead to complete chaos because of random modification of storage in use. Of course, the two problems are related: Dangling references result when storage is freed "too soon," and garbage when storage is not freed until "too late." Where it is infeasible or too costly to avoid both problems simultaneously through a mechanism such as reference counts, garbage generation is clearly to be preferred in order to avoid dangling references. It is better not to recover storage at all than to recover it too soon.

The basic philosophy behind garbage collection is simply to allow garbage to be generated in order to avoid dangling references. When the free-space list is entirely exhausted and more storage is needed, the computation is suspended temporarily and an extraordinary procedure instituted, a *garbage collection*, which identifies garbage elements in the heap and returns them to the free-space list. The original computation is then resumed, and garbage again accumulates until the free-space list is exhausted, at which time another garbage collection is initiated, and so on.

Because garbage collection is done only rarely (when the free-space list is exhausted), it is allowable for the procedure to be fairly costly. Two stages are involved:

1. *Marking active elements*. In the first stage each element in the heap which is active, i.e., which is part of an accessible data structure, must be marked. Each element must contain a *garbage-collection bit* set initially to "on." The marking algorithm sets the garbage-collection bit of each active element "off."

2. *Collecting garbage elements*. Once the marking algorithm has marked active elements, all those remaining whose garbage-collection bit is "on" are garbage and may be returned to the free-space list. A simple sequential scan of the heap is sufficient. The garbage-collection bit of each element is checked as it is encountered in the scan. If "off," the element is passed over; if "on," the element is linked into the free-space list. All garbage-collection bits are reset to "on" during the scan (to prepare for a later garbage collection).

The marking part of garbage collection is the most difficult. Since the free-space list is exhausted when garbage collection is initiated, each element in the heap is either active (i.e., still in use) or garbage. Unfortunately, inspection of an element cannot indicate its status, because there is nothing intrinsic to a garbage element to indicate that it is garbage. Moreover, the presence of a pointer to an element from another heap element does not necessarily indicate that the element pointed to is active; it may be that both elements are garbage. Thus a simple scan of the heap which looks for pointers and marks the elements pointed to as active does not suffice.

When is a heap element active? Clearly, an element is active if there is a pointer to it from *outside the heap* or in another *active* heap element. If it is possible to identify all such outside pointers and mark the appropriate heap elements, then an iterative marking process may be initiated which searches these active elements for pointers to other unmarked elements. These new elements are then marked and searched for other pointers, and so on. A fairly disciplined use of pointers is necessary, because three critical assumptions underlie this marking process:

1. Any active element must be reachable by a chain of pointers beginning outside the heap.

2. It must be possible to identify every pointer outside the heap which points to an element inside the heap.

3. It must be possible to identify within any active heap element the fields which contain pointers to other heap elements.

If any of these assumptions are unsatisfied, then the marking process will fail to mark some active elements. The result will be recovery of active elements and thus the generation of dangling references.

The manner in which these assumptions are satisfied in a typical LISP implementation is instructive. First each heap element is formatted identically, usually with two pointer fields and a set of extra bits for system data (including a garbage-collection bit). Since each heap element contains exactly two pointers, and these pointers are always in the same positions within the element, assumption 3 is satisfied. Second, there is only a small set of *system data structures* which may contain pointers into the heap (the A-list, the OB-list, the pushdown list, etc.). Marking starting from these system data structures is guaranteed to allow identification of all external pointers into the heap, as required by assumption 2. Finally, it is impossible to reach a heap element other than through a chain of pointers beginning outside the heap. For example, a pointer to a heap element cannot be computed by addition of a constant to another pointer. Thus, assumption 1 is satisfied.

Satisfying the assumptions necessary for garbage collection may be difficult. Consider assumption 3. It requires that every heap element have the same format, that the position of pointers within an element be tagged, that a format designator be stored in each element, or that the marking algorithm "know" where the pointers are in any element it reaches, using some external rules about the structure of data and pointer chains. Such special requirements for garbage collection place an extra burden on the designer of a language implementation in addition to those imposed directly by the language design.

8-7 HEAP STORAGE MANAGEMENT: VARIABLE-SIZE ELEMENTS

Heap storage management where variable-size elements are allocated and recovered is more difficult than with fixed-size elements, although many of the same concepts apply. Variable-size elements arise in many situations.

For example, if space is being used for programmer-defined data structures stored sequentially, such as arrays, then variable-size blocks of space will be required, or activation records for tasks might be allocated in a heap in sequential blocks of varying sizes.

The major difficulties with variable-size elements concern reuse of recovered space. Even if we recover two five-word blocks of space in the heap, it may be impossible to satisfy a later request for a six-word block. This problem did not arise in the simpler case of fixed-size blocks; recovered space could always be immediately reused.

Initial Allocation and Reuse

With fixed-size elements it was appropriate to immediately split the heap into a set of elements and then base initial allocation on a free-space list containing these elements. Such a technique is not acceptable with variable-size elements. Instead we wish to maintain free space in blocks of as large a size as possible. Initially then we consider the heap as simply one large block of free storage. A *heap pointer* is appropriate for initial allocation. When a block of N words is requested, the heap pointer is advanced by N and the original heap pointer value returned as a pointer to the newly allocated element. As storage is freed behind the advancing heap pointer, it may be collected into a free-space list.

Eventually the heap pointer reaches the end of the heap block. Some of the free space back in the heap must now be reused. Two possibilities for reuse present themselves, because of the variable size of the elements.

1. Use the free-space list directly for allocation, searching the list for an appropriate size block and returning any leftover space to the free list after the allocation.

2. Compact the free space by moving all the active elements to one end of the heap, leaving the free space as a single block at the end and resetting the heap pointer to the beginning of this block.

Let us look at these two possibilities in turn.

Reuse Directly from a Free-Space List

The simplest approach, when a request for an N-word element is received, is to scan the free-space list for a block of N or more words. A block of N words can be allocated directly. A block of more than N words must be split into two blocks, an N-word block, which is immediately allocated, and the remainder block, which is returned to the free-space list. The basic idea is

straightforward. A number of particular techniques for managing allocation directly from such a free-space list are known:

  1. *First-fit method*. When an N-word block is needed, the free-space list
is scanned for the *first* block of N or more words, which is then split into an
N-word block, and the remainder, which is returned to the free-space list.

  2. *Best-fit method*. When an N-word block is needed, the free-space list
is scanned for the block with the *minimum* number of words greater than or
equal to N. This block is allocated as a unit, if it has exactly N words, or is
split and the remainder returned to the free-space list.

Recovery with Variable-Size Blocks

Before considering the memory compaction problem, let us look at
techniques for recovery where variable-size blocks are involved. Relatively
little is different here from the case of fixed-size blocks. Explicit return of
freed space to a free-space list is the simplest technique, but the problems of
garbage and dangling references are again present. Reference counts may
be used in the ordinary manner.
  Garbage collection is also a feasible technique. Some additional
problems arise with variable-size blocks, however. Garbage collection
proceeds as before, with a marking phase followed by a collecting phase.
Marking must be based on the same pointer-chain-following techniques.
The difficulty now is in collecting. Before, we collected by a simple
sequential scan of memory, testing each element's garbage-collection bit. If
the bit was "on," the element was returned to the free-space list; if "off," it
was still active and was passed over. We should like to use the same scheme
with variable-size elements, but now there is a problem in determining the
boundaries between elements. Where does one element end and the next
begin? Without this information the garbage cannot be collected.
  The simplest solution is to maintain along with the garbage-collection
bit in the first word of each block, active or not, an integer *length indicator*
specifying the length of the block. With the explicit length indicators
present, a sequential scan of memory is again possible, looking only at the
first word of each block. During this scan, adjacent free blocks may also be
compacted into single blocks before being returned to the free-space list,
thus eliminating the partial-compaction problem discussed below.
  Garbage collection may also be effectively combined with full compaction to eliminate the need for a free-space list altogether. Only a simple heap
pointer is needed in this case.

Compaction and the Memory Fragmentation Problem

The problem that any heap storage management system using variable-size elements faces is that of memory *fragmentation*. One begins with a single large block of free space. As computation proceeds, this block is progressively fragmented into smaller pieces through allocation, recovery, and reuse. If only the simple first-fit or best-fit allocation technique is used, it is apparent that free-space blocks continue to split into ever smaller pieces. Ultimately one reaches a point where a storage allocator cannot honor a request for a block of N words because no sufficiently large block exists, even though the free-space list contains in total far more than N words. Without some compaction of free blocks into larger blocks, execution will be halted by a lack of free storage faster than necessary.

Depending on whether active blocks within the heap may be shifted in position, one of two approaches to compaction is possible:

1. *Partial compaction.* If active blocks *cannot* be shifted (or if it is too expensive to do so), then only adjacent free blocks on the free-space list may be compacted.

2. *Full compaction.* If active blocks *can* be shifted, then all active blocks may be shifted to one end of the heap, leaving all free space at the other in a contiguous block. Full compaction requires that when an active block is shifted, all pointers to that block be modified to point to the new location.

8-8   REFERENCES AND SUGGESTIONS FOR FURTHER READING

Most texts on compiler construction treat stack and static storage allocation strategies (see the references for Chapter 9). Bobrow and Wegbreit [1973] consider a more general stack management technique, the *spaghetti stack*, that can be used with a variety of control structures.

Techniques for heap storage management have been widely studied. The programmer often needs to implement his own heap storage management for linked data structures when the language does not provide it directly. As a result, the study of heap storage management has become a standard part of the general study of data structures. For example, see Knuth [1973], Standish [1980], Aho et al. [1983], and Pfaltz [1977]. Cohen [1981] gives a compact survey of garbage-collection methods.

Operating systems also provide storage management facilities that often overlap the facilities provided by programming languages. *Virtual memory systems* are now commonly provided by many operating systems to provide storage allocation in fixed-size *pages* or variable-size *segments*. These facilities may support but usually do not supplant heap storage management provided by the language implementation. Discussion of storage management by the operating system is a topic in most texts on operating systems.

8-9   PROBLEMS

1. Analyze the storage management techniques used in a language implementation available to you. Consider the various elements requiring storage mentioned in Sec. 8-1. Are there other major run-time structures requiring storage besides those mentioned in Sec. 8-1.

2. Analyze the primitive operations used in a language with which you are familiar. Which operations require storage to be allocated or freed? Is the size of the storage block always the same, or are blocks of variable size required? Is storage allocated and freed only on subprogram entry and exit or at unpredictable points during execution? What does the overall pattern of storage allocation and freeing suggest about the storage management structures used in the language implementation? Can you prove that a heap of fixed-size or variable-size blocks is required? Can you prove that only a central stack is sufficient?

3. As Fig. 8-2 illustrates, most Pascal implementations use a single large block of storage for both the central stack and the heap. The stack and heap grow toward each other from opposite ends of the storage block during execution, allocating storage from the block of free space between. Suppose the stack and heap meet, because the free space is entirely used up. Explain the options available to the implementor if (a) the next request is for a new block for the stack or (b) the next request is for a new block for the heap.

4. One of the striking features of garbage collection as a method of storage recovery is that its cost is *inversely proportional* to the amount of storage recovered; i.e., the less storage recovered, the more it costs to perform a garbage collection.
   (a) Explain why this is so.
   (b) When a program is just about to run out of storage altogether, it often performs a series of lengthy and costly garbage collections (that recover very little storage) before it terminates altogether. Give a method for avoiding repeated useless garbage collections of this sort.

5. In the SLIP list-processing extension to FORTRAN each list has a special header (containing a reference count). When a list is freed, instead of returning all the list elements to the head of the free-space list, only the list header is returned, and it is placed at the *end* of the free-space list (using a special pointer to the end of the free-space list). Thus the cost of returning a list to free space is minimal. The list elements are returned to the free-space list only when the header of the list reaches the top of the free-space list. What is the advantage of this technique for shifting

the cost of freeing the list elements from the time of *recovery* of the list to the time of *reuse* of the storage?

6. *Full-word* data items such as numbers present special problems in garbage collection. Ordinarily the data themselves take up the entire heap element, with no extra bit available for garbage-collection marking. It is usual in such cases to separate all such full-word elements into a special section of the heap and store all the garbage-collection bits for these full-word elements in a special packed array (a *bit vector*) outside the heap. Assuming that the full-word data items are numbers (and thus contain no pointers to other heap elements), design a garbage-collection algorithm which allows the possibility of pointers to full-word items in the heap. The algorithm should include marking and collecting. Maintain a separate free-space list for the full-word portion of the heap.

7. Give an algorithm for the *collection* of marked blocks during garbage collection in a heap with variable-size elements. Assume that the first word of each block contains a garbage-collection bit and a length indicator. Compact all adjacent blocks during the collection.

8. *APL array storage.* Design a storage management system for a heap B of variable-size blocks under the following assumptions:

   1. B is used only to store arrays of real numbers (one word per number). Arrays always have at least two elements.
   2. Each array block is accessible only through a single external pointer stored in the array descriptor. All array descriptors are stored in a block A separate from the heap B.
   3. Requests for blocks to be allocated from the heap occur at random (and frequently) during execution.
   4. Blocks are explicitly returned to "free" status when arrays are destroyed. This also occurs randomly and frequently during execution.
   5. Permanent loss of storage through memory fragmentation cannot be tolerated. (Note that a one-word free block can never be reused.)

   Your design should specify:

   (a) The *initial organization* of the heap block B, together with any special external structures needed for storage management (e.g., free-space list heads).
   (b) The *storage allocation* mechanism, given a request for a block of N words from B.
   (c) The *storage recovery* mechanism, given a call on the storage manager with the address of a block of M words to be freed.
   (d) The *compaction* mechanism, if any, including a specification of how it works and when it is invoked.

CHAPTER 9

Syntax
and
Translation

In earlier chapters, syntax has played a relatively minor role. Instead the discussion has concentrated largely on semantic structures, with only an occasional comment on the syntactic elements used to represent the semantics. In this chapter we shall take up syntactic structure directly. There are three main aspects of this discussion: the syntactic elements themselves, the structure of the translators which process the syntax, and the formal specification of syntax.

One of the chief reasons syntax has not been more central in the discussion to this point is that many of the most important semantic elements of programs are not represented in the syntax of the program directly but appear only implicitly. For example, we have noted the use of implicit declarations, implicit data structures, implicit operations, implicit sequence control, and implicit referencing environments. If we look only at the syntax of a program, we miss much that is of central importance.

A second reason for slighting the study of program syntax is that so much here is arbitrary. Variations among languages in syntactic structures are far greater than variations in underlying semantic structures; even a brief look at the example programs for the languages in Part II shows this clearly. These variations in syntax are largely a matter of the personal taste of the language designers and deserve no extended consideration. In fact there are few generally agreed-upon rules for syntactic structure in programming languages—each language designer tends to choose structures that seem natural and appropriate to him. This lack of uniformity may be seen even in the simplest case of a syntax for referencing elements of linear arrays: The first element of linear array A may be designated A(1), A[1], A⟨1⟩, (CAR A), FIRST OF A, or A.FIRST, depending on the language and whether the array is homogeneous, heterogeneous, or variable-length, considering only the languages of Part II. In the larger syntactic structures—expressions, statements, declarations, and subprograms— there is even less uniformity (if that is possible).

When you undertake to master a new programming language, you are likely to be confronted with an entirely new syntax masking an underlying semantics not greatly different from that of other languages with which you are familiar. This choice of a new syntax may not be entirely perverse— often the new syntactic structures are more elegant, more readable, less error-prone, or have other advantages over the familiar ones. The important thing is to move as quickly as possible to the underlying semantics of a new language. The semantic structures are likely both to be more familiar and to explain some of the reasons for syntactic peculiarities.

9-1   GENERAL SYNTACTIC CRITERIA

The primary purpose of syntax is to provide a notation for communication of information between the programmer and the programming language processor. It is in this context that syntax has entered the discussions of the preceding chapters—we were concerned with the information communicated by the syntax rather than the details of syntactic structure. The choice of particular syntactic structures, however, is constrained only slightly by the necessity to communicate particular items of information. For example, the fact that a particular variable has a value of type *real number* may be represented in any of a dozen different ways in a program—through an explicit declaration as in Pascal, through an implicit *naming convention* as in FORTRAN, and so on. The details of syntax are chosen largely on the basis of secondary criteria, such as readability, which are unrelated to the primary goal of communicating information to the language processor. There are many such secondary criteria, but they may be roughly categorized under the general goals of making programs easy to read, easy to write, easy to translate, and unambiguous. We shall consider some of the ways that language syntactic structures may be designed to satisfy these often conflicting goals.

Readability

A program is readable if the underlying structure of the algorithm and data represented by the program is apparent from an inspection of the program text. A readable program is often said to be *self-documenting*—it is understandable without any separate documentation (although this goal is seldom achievable in practice). Readability is enhanced by such language features as natural statement formats, structured statements, liberal use of keywords and noise words, provision for embedded comments, unrestricted length identifiers, mnemonic operator symbols, free-field formats, and complete data declarations. Readability, of course, cannot be guaranteed by the design of a language, because even the best design may be circumvented by poor programming. On the other hand, syntactic design can force even the best-intentioned programmer to write unreadable programs (as is often the case in APL). Of the languages in Part II the COBOL design emphasizes readability most heavily, often at the expense of ease of writing and ease of translation.

Readability is enhanced by a program syntax in which syntactic differences reflect underlying semantic differences so that program constructs which do similar things look similar, and program constructs which do radically different things look different. For example, the difference between a conditional branch, an iteration, and a **goto** control structure is made clear in most languages by the use of different statement types with different syntactic structures. In general the greater the variety of syntactic constructs used, the more easily the program structure may be made to reflect different underlying semantic structures. Languages which provide only a few different syntactic constructs in general lead to less readable programs. In APL, for example, only one statement format is provided. The differences among an assignment statement, a subprogram call, a simple **goto**, a subprogram return, a multiway conditional branch, and various other common program structures are reflected syntactically only by differences in one or a few operator symbols within a complex expression. It often requires a detailed analysis of a program to determine even its gross control structure. Moreover, a simple syntax error, such as a single incorrect character in a statement, may radically alter the meaning of a statement without rendering it syntactically incorrect. A similar problem arises in SNOBOL4, which also provides only one basic statement syntax. The presence of a single extra blank character within a SNOBOL4 statement may change the statement from a simple subprogram call to a pattern-matching statement, leading to a cascade of run-time errors in other parts of the program which can be traced back to the offending syntax error only with great difficulty. In LISP, errors in matching parentheses cause similar problems. During the program testing stage, we may well ask that a readable program not look correct when it is grossly incorrect.

Writeability

The syntactic features which make a program easy to write are often in conflict with those features which make it easy to read. Writeability is enhanced by use of concise and regular syntactic structures, while for readability a variety of more "verbose" constructs are helpful. Implicit syntactic conventions that allow declarations and operations to be left unspecified make programs shorter and easier to write but harder to read. Other features advance both goals; for example, the use of structured statements, simple natural statement formats, mnemonic operation symbols, and unrestricted identifiers usually make program writing easier by allowing the natural structure of the problem algorithms and data to be directly represented in the program.

A syntax is *redundant* if it communicates the same item of information in more than one way. Some redundancy is useful in programming language syntax because it makes a program easier to read and also allows more error checking to be done during translation. The disadvantage is that redundancy makes programs more verbose and thus harder to write. Most of the default rules for the meaning of language constructs are intended to reduce redundancy by eliminating explicit statement of meanings that can be inferred from the context. For example, rather than require explicit declaration of the type of every simple variable, FORTRAN uses a naming convention that implicitly declares variables whose names begin with one of the letters I-N to be type integer and all other variables to be type real. Now the mere occurrence of a new variable name in a program suffices to "declare" it. The redundancy of a separate declaration is avoided. Unfortunately the added convenience is offset by a more serious negative effect: a misspelling of a variable name cannot be detected by the FORTRAN compiler. If the program uses a variable INDEX that at some point is referenced inadvertently as INDX, the compiler assumes INDX to be a new integer variable (of course, with no initial value), and a subtle error is introduced into the program. If an explicit declaration is required for each variable, as in Pascal, then the compiler flags the misspelled variable name as an error. Because of this effect of masking errors in programs, languages that lack all redundancy are often difficult to use.

Ease of Translation

Yet a third conflicting goal is that of making programs easy to translate into executable form. Readability and writeability are criteria directed to the needs of the human programmer. Ease of translation relates to the needs of the translator that processes the written program. The key to easy translation is regularity of structure. The LISP syntax provides an example of a program structure which is neither particularly readable nor particularly writeable but which is extremely simple to translate. The entire syntactic structure of any LISP program may be described in a few simple rules, because of the regularity of the syntax. Programs become harder to translate as the number of special syntactic constructs increases. For example, COBOL translation is made extremely difficult by the large number of statement and declaration forms allowed, even though the semantics of the language is not particularly complicated.

Lack of Ambiguity

Ambiguity is a central problem in every language design. A language definition ideally provides a unique meaning for every syntactic construct that a programmer may write. An ambiguous construction allows two or more different interpretations. The problems of ambiguity usually arise not in the structure of individual program elements but in the interplay between different structures. For example, Pascal and ALGOL allow two different forms of conditional statement:

$$\textbf{if} \langle \textit{Boolean expression} \rangle \textbf{ then } \langle \textit{statement}_1 \rangle \textbf{ else } \langle \textit{statement}_2 \rangle$$

and

$$\textbf{if} \langle \textit{Boolean expression} \rangle \textbf{ then } \langle \textit{statement}_1 \rangle$$

The interpretation to be given to each statement form is clearly defined. However, when the two forms are combined by allowing $\langle \textit{statement}_1 \rangle$ to be another conditional statement, then the structure

$$\textbf{if} \langle \textit{Boolean expression}_1 \rangle \textbf{ then if} \langle \textit{Boolean expression}_2 \rangle \textbf{ then}$$
$$\langle \textit{statement}_1 \rangle \textbf{ else } \langle \textit{statement}_2 \rangle$$

is found. This statement form is ambiguous, because it is not clear which of the two flow charts of Fig. 9-1 is intended. FORTRAN syntax provides another example. A reference to A(I,J) might be either a reference to an element of the two-dimensional array A or a call of the function subprogram A, because the syntax in FORTRAN for function calls and array references is the same. Similar ambiguities arise in almost every programming language.

The ambiguities in FORTRAN and ALGOL mentioned above have in fact been resolved in both languages. In the ALGOL conditional statement the ambiguity has been resolved by changing the syntax of the language to introduce a required **begin** . . . **end** delimiter pair around the embedded conditional statement. Thus the natural but ambiguous combination of two conditional statements has been replaced by the two less natural but unambiguous constructions

$$\textbf{if} \langle \textit{Boolean expression}_1 \rangle \textbf{ then begin if} \langle \textit{Boolean expression}_2 \rangle \textbf{ then}$$
$$\langle \textit{statement}_1 \rangle \textbf{ end else } \langle \textit{statement}_2 \rangle$$

and

$$\textbf{if} \langle \textit{Boolean expression}_1 \rangle \textbf{ then begin if} \langle \textit{Boolean expression}_2 \rangle \textbf{ then}$$
$$\langle \textit{statement}_1 \rangle \textbf{ else } \langle \textit{statement}_2 \rangle \textbf{ end}$$

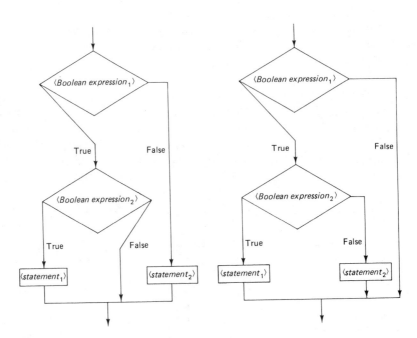

Fig. 9-1   Two interpretations of the ALGOL conditional

A simpler solution is found in Ada: each **if** statement must end with the delimiter **end if**. In Pascal and PL/I another technique is used to resolve the ambiguity: An arbitrary interpretation is chosen for the ambiguous construction, in this case the final **else** is paired with the nearest **then** so that the combined statement has the same meaning as the second of the above ALGOL constructions. The ambiguity of FORTRAN function and array references is resolved by a similar rule: The construct A(I,J) is assumed to be a function call if no declaration for an array A is given. Since each array must be declared prior to its use in a program, the translator may readily check whether there is in fact an array A to which the reference applies. If none is found, then the translator assumes that the construct is a call on an external function A. This assumption cannot be checked until load time when all the external functions (including library functions) are linked into the final executable program. If the loader finds no function A, then a loader error message is produced. In Pascal a different technique is used to distinguish function calls from array references: A syntactic distinction is made—square brackets are used to enclose subscript lists in array references (e.g., A[I,J]) and parentheses are used to enclose parameter lists of function calls (e.g., A(I,J)).

Ambiguities are usually resolved by one of the two techniques: either some syntactic modification is made to distinguish ambiguous constructions or some fixed interpretation is chosen, which may be dependent on the context, and the ambiguous syntactic construction is left intact (as in the Pascal conditionals and the FORTRAN parentheses). Either technique raises difficulties. Modifying the syntax is often only possible by introducing unnatural syntactic constructs. For example, to many beginning ALGOL programmers the need for the **begin** ... **end** delimiters in a nested ALGOL conditional is not natural, and the construct leads to many errors. Yet the alternative of providing an implicit interpretation for the ambiguous construct may lead to even more subtle errors. A beginning FORTRAN programmer, for example, is likely to be mystified at a loader error message SUBPROGRAM A NOT FOUND when all he had done was to omit inadvertently a declaration for array A.

9-2   SYNTACTIC ELEMENTS OF A LANGUAGE

The general syntactic style of a language is set by the choice of the various basic syntactic elements. We shall consider briefly the most prominent of these.

Character Set

The choice of character set is one of the first to be made in designing a language syntax. There are several widely used character sets, such as the ASCII set, each containing a different set of special characters in addition to the basic letters and digits. Usually one of these standard sets is chosen, although occasionally a special nonstandard character set may be used, as, for example, in APL (see Chapter 19). The choice of character set is important in determining the type of input and output equipment which can be used in implementing the language. For example, the basic FORTRAN character set is available on most input and output equipment. The APL character set, on the other hand, cannot be used directly on most I/O devices.

The choice of character set is also important in determining the number of available special characters which may be used in programs and data as delimiters, operator symbols, and the like. This choice can be an important factor in making the language syntax natural and unambiguous. For example, the use of the semicolon to separate statements and declarations in Pascal provides a natural punctuation similar to that of English and also provides a unique statement terminator. Using the FORTRAN character set without the semicolon, no suitable terminator is available. In particular, neither commas nor periods may be used because of the ambiguities which arise because of other uses of these characters.

Identifiers

The basic syntax for identifiers—a string of letters and digits beginning with a letter—is widely accepted. Variations among languages are mainly in the optional inclusion of special characters such as . or - to improve readability and in length restrictions. Length restrictions, such as the FORTRAN restriction to six characters, force the use of identifers with little mnemonic value in many cases and thus restrict program readability significantly.

Operator Symbols

Most languages use the special characters + and − to represent the two basic arithmetic operations, but beyond that there is almost no uniformity. Primitive operations may be represented entirely by special characters, as is done in APL. Alternatively identifiers may be used for all primitives, as in the LISP PLUS, TIMES, and so on. Most languages adopt some combination, utilizing special characters for some operators, identifiers for others, and often also some character strings which fit in neither of these categories (for example, the FORTRAN .EQ. and **).

Key Words and Reserved Words

A *key word* is an identifier used as a fixed part of the syntax of a statement—for example, IF, THEN, and ELSE in PL/I conditional statements or DO beginning a FORTRAN iteration statement. A key word is a *reserved word* if it may not also be used as a programmer-chosen identifier. Key words serve a variety of purposes in programming languages. Commonly statements begin with a key word designating the statement type: READ, IF, GOTO, and so on. Others may be used within statements as delimiters—for example, the THEN and ELSE of the PL/I conditional.

Syntactic analysis during translation is made easier by using reserved words. FORTRAN syntactic analysis, for example, is made difficult by the fact that a statement beginning with DO or IF may not actually be an iteration or conditional statement. Because DO and IF are not reserved words, a programmer may legitimately choose these as variable names. COBOL uses reserved words heavily, but there are so many identifiers reserved that it is difficult to remember them all, and as a result one often inadvertently chooses a reserved identifier as a variable name. The primary difficulty with reserved words, however, comes when the language needs to be extended to include new statements using new reserved words, e.g., as when COBOL is periodically revised to prepare an updated standard. Addition of a new reserved word to the language means that every old program that uses that identifier as a variable name (or other name) is no longer syntactically correct, even though it has not been modified. A compiler that implements the extended language will thus reject many old programs and force them to be modified.

Comments and Noise Words

Inclusion of comments in a program is an important part of its documentation. A language may allow comments in several ways: (1) As separate comment lines in the program, as in FORTRAN, (2) delimited by special markers, such as the Pascal { and }, with no concern for line boundaries, or (3) beginning anywhere on a line but terminated by the end of the line, as in Ada. The third alternative includes the first, and also allows a short comment to be included after the statement or declaration on a line. The second alternative suffers from the disadvantage that a missing terminating delimiter on a comment will turn the following statements (up to the end of the next comment) into "comments," so that even though they appear to be correct when reading the program, they are not in fact translated and executed.

Noise words are optional words which may be inserted in statements to improve readability. COBOL provides many such options. For example, in the COBOL **goto** statement, written GO TO ⟨*label*⟩, the keyword GO is required, but TO is an optional noise word which carries no information and is used only to improve readability.

Blanks (Spaces)

Rules on the use of blanks vary widely between languages. In FORTRAN, for example, blanks are not significant anywhere except in literal character-string data. Other languages use blanks as separators, so that they play an important syntactic role. In SNOBOL4 one of the primitive operations (concatenation) is represented by a blank, and the blank is also used as a separator between elements of a statement (leading to much confusion).

Delimiters and Brackets

A *delimiter* is a syntactic element used simply to mark the beginning or end of some syntactic unit such as a statement or expression. Brackets are paired delimiters, e.g., parentheses or **begin** . . . **end** pairs. Delimiters may be used merely to enhance readability or to simplify syntactic analysis, but more often they serve the important purpose of removing ambiguities by explicitly defining the boundaries of a particular syntactic construct.

Free- and Fixed-Field Formats

A syntax is *free-field* if program statements may be written anywhere on an input line without regard for positioning on the line or for breaks between lines. A *fixed-field* syntax utilizes the positioning on an input line to convey information. Strict fixed-field syntax, where each element of a statement must appear within a given part of an input line, is most often seen in assembly languages. More commonly a partial fixed-field format is used; for example, in FORTRAN the first five characters of each line are reserved for a statement label. The first character of an input line is sometimes given special significance; for example, SNOBOL4 statement labels, comments, and continuation lines are distinguished by a character in the first position of a line.

Expressions

Expressions are the basic syntactic building block from which statements (and sometimes programs) are built. The various syntactic forms for expressions have been discussed at length in Sec. 6-2. We noted particularly the infix, prefix, and postfix forms and variants. Some languages, such as LISP and APL, adopt a single syntax for constructing expressions which is used uniformly. More commonly a mixture of forms is allowed, e.g., infix for arithmetic primitives, prefix for certain function calls. Translation of these mixed forms is more difficult, but the expressions are usually correspondingly more readable.

Besides the obvious syntactic differences in expression forms, there is a difference among languages in the importance given to expressions. In LISP and APL, for example, the expression is the central syntactic structure; statements, if they are used at all, take the form of single expressions. Thus in APL a program is simply a sequence of expressions. In languages such as FORTRAN and COBOL, on the other hand, expressions are much less important; instead statements are the primary syntactic form, and expressions are used within statements only occasionally when a value must be computed.

Statements

Statements are the most prominent syntactic component in most languages, and their syntax has a critical effect on the overall regularity, readability, and writeability of the language. Some languages adopt a single basic statement format, while others use a different syntax for each different statement type. The former approach emphasizes regularity, while the latter emphasizes readability. SNOBOL4 has only one basic statement syntax, the pattern-matching-replacement statement, from which other statement types may be derived by omitting elements of the basic statement. Most languages lean toward the other extreme of providing different syntactic structures for each statement type. COBOL is most notable in this regard—each COBOL statement has a unique structure involving special key words, noise words, alternative constructions, optional elements, and so on. The advantage of using a variety of syntactic structures, of course, is that each may be made to express in a natural way the operations involved.

A more important difference in statement structures is that between *structured* or *nested* statements and *simple* statements. A simple statement is one which contains no other embedded statements. APL and SNOBOL4 allow only simple statements. A structured statement is one which may contain embedded statements. The advantages of structured statements are discussed at length in Sec. 6-3.

Overall Program-Subprogram Structure

The overall syntactic organization of main program and subprogram definitions is as varied as the other aspects of language syntax. The languages of Part II illustrate a number of the most common structures.

Separate subprogram definitions. FORTRAN and APL illustrate an overall organization in which each subprogram definition is treated as a separate syntactic unit. In FORTRAN each subprogram is compiled separately and the compiled programs linked at load time. In APL, programs are separately translated and are linked only when one calls another during execution. The effect of this organization is particularly apparent in FORTRAN, where each subprogram is required to contain full declarations for all data elements, even for those which are in COMMON blocks and shared with other subprograms. These declarations are required because of the assumption of separate compilation.

Nested subprogram definitions. Pascal illustrates a nested program structure in which subprogram definitions appear as declarations within the main program and may themselves contain other subprogram definitions nested within their definitions to any depth. This overall program organization is related to the Pascal emphasis on structured statements but in fact serves a different purpose. Structured statements are introduced primarily to provide a natural notation for the common hierarchical divisions in algorithm structure, but nested subprogram definitions serve instead to provide a nonlocal referencing environment for subprograms which is defined at compile time and which thus allows static type checking and compilation of efficient executable code for subprograms containing nonlocal references. Without the nesting of subprogram definitions it is necessary either to provide declarations for nonlocal variables within each subprogram definition (as is done in FORTRAN) or to defer all type checking for nonlocal references until run time. The nesting also serves the less important function of allowing subprogram names to have less than global scope.

Data descriptions separated from executable statements. An altogether different organization is found in COBOL. In most languages each subprogram definition consists of declarations for local (and sometimes nonlocal) data and a set of executable statements. In a COBOL program the data declarations and the executable statements for all subprograms are divided into two separate program *divisions*, the *data division* and the *procedure division*. A third, the *environment division*, consists of declarations concerning the external operating environment. The procedure division of a program is organized into subunits corresponding to subprogram bodies, but all data are global to all subprograms, and there is nothing corresponding to the usual local data of a subprogram. The advantage of the centralized data division containing all data declarations is that it enforces the logical independence of the data formats and the algorithms in the procedure division—minor changes in data structure can be made by modification of the data division without modifying the procedure division. It is also convenient to have the data descriptions collected in one place rather than scattered throughout the subprograms.

Unseparated subprogram definitions. A fourth overall program organization (or lack of organization) is illustrated by the SNOBOL4 language. No syntactic distinction is made in SNOBOL4 between main program statements and subprogram statements. A program, regardless of the number of subprograms it contains, is syntactically just a list of statements. The points where subprograms begin and end are not differentiated. In fact any statement may be part of the main program and also part of any number of subprograms at the same time, in the sense that it may be executed at one point during execution of the main program and later executed again as part of execution of a subprogram. This rather chaotic program organization is valuable only in allowing run-time translation and execution of new statements and subprograms with relatively simple mechanisms. Most SNOBOL4 programmers introduce an artificial distinction between subprogram bodies by insertion of comments or other syntactic delimiters.

9-3   STAGES IN TRANSLATION

The process of translation of a program from its original syntax into executable form is central in every programming language implementation. The translation may be quite simple, as in the case of APL or LISP programs, but more often the process is complex and requires the major share of effort in a language implementation. Most languages could be implemented with only trivial translation if one were willing to write a software interpreter (software-simulated virtual computer) and if one were willing to accept slow execution speeds. In most cases, however, efficient execution is such a desirable goal that major efforts are made to translate programs into efficiently executable structures, especially hardware-interpretable machine code. The translation process becomes progressively more complex as the executable program form becomes further removed in structure from the original program. At the extreme an optimizing compiler for a complex language like PL/I may radically alter program structures to obtain more efficient execution. Such compilers are among the most complex programs in existence.

Logically we may divide translation into two major parts: the *analysis* of the input *source program* and the *synthesis* of the executable *object program*. Within each of these parts there are further divisions, as we shall see below. In most translators these logical stages are not clearly separate but instead are mixed so that analysis and synthesis alternate, often on a statement-by-statement basis. Figure 9-2 illustrates the structure of a typical compiler.

Analysis of the Source Program

To a translator, the source program appears initially as one long undifferentiated character string composed of thousands or tens of thousands of characters. Of course a programmer seing such a program almost instinctively structures it into subprograms, statements, declarations, and so forth. To the translator none of this is apparent. An analysis of the structure of the program must be laboriously built up character-by-character during translation.

Lexical analysis. The most basic phase of any translation is that in which the input program is subdivided into its elementary constituents: identifers, delimiters, operator symbols, numbers, key words, noise words, blanks, comments, etc. This phase is termed *lexical analysis*, and the basic program units which result from lexical analysis are termed *lexical items* (or *tokens*). Typically the lexical analyzer (or *scanner*) is the *input routine* for the translator, reading successive lines of input program, breaking them down into individual lexical items, and feeding these lexical items to the later stages of the translator to be used in the higher levels of analysis. The lexical analyzer must identify the type of each lexical item (number, identifier, delimiter, operator, etc.) and attach a type tag. In addition conversion to an internal representation is often made for items such as numbers (converted to internal binary fixed- or floating-point form) and

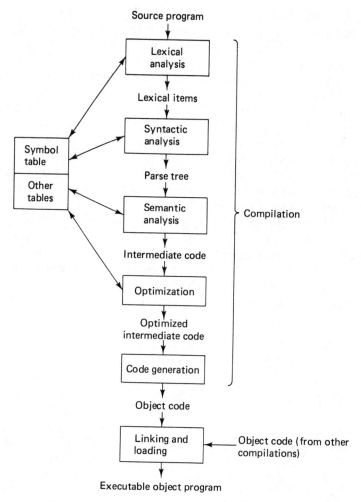

Fig. 9-2 Structure of a compiler

identifiers (stored in a symbol table and the address of the symbol table entry used in place of the character string).

While lexical analysis is simple in concept, this phase of translation often requires a larger share of translation time than any other. This fact is in part due simply to the necessity to scan and analyze the source program character by character, but it is also true that in practice it sometimes is difficult to determine where the boundaries between lexical items lie without rather complex context-dependent algorithms. For example, the two FORTRAN statements

$$\text{DO } 10 \text{ I} = 1,5$$

and

$$DO\ 10\ I = 1.5$$

have entirely different lexical structures—the first is a DO statement and the second is an assignment—but this fact cannot be discovered without fairly extensive analysis.

Syntactic analysis (parsing). The second stage in translation is *syntactic analysis* or *parsing.* Here the larger program structures are identified—statements, declarations, expressions, etc.—using the lexical items produced by the lexical analyzer. Syntactic analysis usually alternates with semantic analysis. First the syntactic analyzer identifies a sequence of lexical items forming a syntactic unit such as an expression, statement, subprogram call, or declaration. A semantic analyzer is then called to process this unit. Commonly the syntactic and semantic analyzers communicate using a stack. The syntactic analyzer enters in the stack the various elements of the syntactic unit found, and these are retrieved and processed by the semantic analyzer. A great deal of research has centered on discovery of efficient syntactic-analysis techniques, particularly techniques based on the use of formal grammars (see the next section).

Semantic analysis. Semantic analysis is perhaps the central phase of translation. Here the syntactic structures recognized by the syntactic analyzer are processed and the structure of the executable object code begins to take shape. Semantic analysis is thus the bridge between the analysis and synthesis parts of translation. A number of other important subsidiary functions also occur in this stage, including symbol-table maintenance, most error detection, the expansion of macros, and the execution of compile-time statements. The semantic analyzer may actually produce the executable object code in simple translations, but more commonly the output from this stage is some internal form of the final executable program, which is then manipulated by the optimization stage of the translator before executable code is actually generated.

The semantic analyzer is ordinarily split into a set of smaller semantic analyzers, each of which handles one particular type of program construct. For example, array declarations might be handled by one analyzer, arithmetic expressions by another, and **goto** statements by another. The appropriate semantic analyzer is called by the syntactic analyzer whenever it has recognized a syntactic unit to be processed.

The semantic analyzers interact among themselves through information stored in various data structures, particularly in the central symbol table. For example, a semantic analyzer which processes type declarations for simple variables may often do little more than enter the declared types into the symbol table. A later semantic analyzer which processes arithmetic expressions may then use the declared types to generate the appropriate type-specific arithmetic operations for the object code. The exact functions of the semantic analyzers vary greatly, depending on the language and the logical organization of the translator. Some of the most common functions may be described, however.

1. *Symbol-table maintenance.* A *symbol table* is one of the central data structures in every translator. The symbol table typically contains an entry for each different identifier encountered in the source program. The lexical analyzer makes the initial entries as it scans the input program, but the semantic analyzers have primary responsibility after that. In general the symbol-table entry contains more than just the identifier itself; it contains additional data concerning the attributes of that identifier: its type (simple variable, array name, subprogram name, formal parameter, etc.), type of values (integer, real, etc.), referencing environment, and whatever other information is available from the input program through declarations and usage. The semantic analyzers enter this information into the symbol table as they process declarations, subprogram headers, and program statements. Other semantic analyzers and perhaps the optimizer in the synthesis part of the translator use this information to construct efficient executable code.

The symbol table in translators for compiled languages is usually discarded at the end of translation. However, it may be retained during execution, e.g., in languages that allow new identifiers to be created at run time. APL, SNOBOL4, and LISP implementations all utilize a symbol table initially created during translation as a central run-time system-defined data structure.

2. *Insertion of implicit information.* Often in the source program, information is implicit which must be made explicit in the lower-level object program. Most of this implicit information goes under the general heading of *default conventions*—interpretations to be provided when the programmer gives no explicit specification. For example, a PL/I variable that is used but not declared is automatically provided a lengthy list of properties by default—it is of type FIXED BINARY if its name begins with I-N, it is AUTOMATIC, has scope equal to the block within which it is declared, and so on. All these default specifications can be overridden by explicit programmer declarations. The task of the semantic analyzers includes the insertion (into the symbol table or the object code) of these default specifications.

3. *Error detection.* The syntactic and semantic analyzers must be prepared to handle incorrect as well as correct programs. At any point the lexical analyzer may send to the syntactic analyzer a lexical item which does not fit in the surrounding context—a statement delimiter in the middle of an expression, a declaration in the middle of a sequence of statements, or perhaps an operator symbol where an identifier is expected. The error may

be more subtle—a real variable where an integer variable is required, a subscripted variable reference with three subscripts when the array was declared to have only two dimensions, or a statement label in a **goto** statement naming a statement within an iteration statement where such jumps are disallowed. At each step in translation a multitude of such errors might occur. The semantic analyzer must not only recognize such errors when they occur and produce an appropriate error message but must also, in all but the most drastic cases, determine the appropriate way to continue with syntactic analysis of the remainder of the program. Provisions for error detection and handling in the syntactic and semantic analysis phases may require greater effort than the basic analysis itself.

4. *Macro processing and compile-time operations.* Not all languages include macro features or provision for compile-time operations. Where these are present, however, processing is usually handled during semantic analysis.

A *macro*, in its simplest form, is a piece of program text which has been separately defined and which is to be inserted into the program during translation whenever an appropriate *macro call* is encountered in the source program. Thus a macro is much like a subprogram, except that rather than being separately translated and called at run time its body is simply substituted for each call during program translation. Macros may be just simple strings to be substituted, e.g., substitution of 3.1416 for PI whenever the latter is referenced. More commonly they look much like subprograms, with parameters which must be processed before the substitution for the macro call is made.

Where macros are allowed the semantic analyzers must identify the macro calls within the source program and set up the appropriate substitution of the macro body for the call. Often this task involves interrupting the lexical and syntactic analyzers and setting them to work analyzing the string representing the macro body before proceeding with the remainder of the source string. Alternatively the macro body may have already been partially translated so that the semantic analyzer can process it directly, inserting the appropriate object code and making the appropriate table entries before continuing with analysis of the source program.

A *compile-time operation* is an operation to be performed during translation to control the translation of the source program. PL/I provides a number of such operations. The PL/I compile-time assignment provides a simple macro capability by allowing an arbitrary string to be substituted for each occurrence of an identifier. More complex compile-time operations allow parts of a program to be translated only when certain conditions are satisfied or allow groups of statements to be repeatedly translated, as though a loop were executed by the translator, reprocessing the group of statements with each iteration. Again it is the semantic analyzers which must identify and execute these compile-time operations before translation proceeds.

Synthesis of the Object Program

The final stages of translation are concerned with the construction of the executable program from the outputs produced by the semantic analyzer. This phase involves code generation necessarily and may also include optimization of the generated program. If subprograms are translated separately, or if library subprograms are used, a final linking and loading stage is needed to produce the complete program ready for execution.

Optimization.   The semantic analyzer ordinarily produces as output the executable translated program represented in some *intermediate code*, an internal representation such as a Polish string of operators and operands or a table of operator-operand sequences. From this internal representation the code generators may generate the properly formatted output object code. Before code generation, however, there is usually some optimization of the program in the internal representation. Typically the semantic analyzers generate the internal program form piecemeal as each segment of input program is analyzed. This task is done most easily if the semantic analyzers do not have to worry too much about the surrounding code which has been generated immediately before. In doing this piecemeal output, however, extremely poor code may be produced; e.g., a register may be stored at the end of one generated segment and immediately reloaded from the same location at the beginning of the next segment. Often it is desirable to allow the generation of poor code sequences by the semantic analyzers and then during optimization replace these sequences by better ones which avoid obvious inefficiencies.

Many compilers go far beyond this sort of simple optimization and analyze the program for other improvements which can be made, e.g., computing common subexpressions only once, removing constant operations from loops, optimizing the use of registers, and optimizing the calculation of array-accessing formulas. Much research has been done on program optimization, and many sophisticated techniques are known (see the references at the end of this chapter).

Code generation.   After the translated program in the internal representation has been optimized, it must be formed into the assembly language statements, machine code, or other object program form which is to be the output of the translation. This process involves formatting the output properly from the information contained in the internal program representation. The output code may be directly executable, or there may be other translation steps to follow, e.g., assembly or linking and loading.

Linking and loading. In the optional final stage of translation the pieces of code resulting from separate translations of subprograms are coalesced into the final executable program. The output of the preceding translation phases typically consists of executable programs in almost final form, except where the programs reference external data or other subprograms. These incomplete places in the code are specified in attached *loader tables* produced by the translator. The *linking loader* (or *link editor*) loads the various segments of translated code into memory and then uses the attached loader tables to link them together properly by filling in data and subprogram addresses in the code as needed. The result is the final executable program ready to be run.

9-4 FORMAL DEFINITION OF SYNTAX

In the formal study of programming languages the topic of syntax and syntactic analysis has received the most attention. Initially the goal of this work was that of providing precise definitions of programming language syntax for the users and implementors of the language. It quickly became apparent, however, that these syntactic definitions could also be used directly as a basis for syntactic analysis in translators. Later work has developed and analyzed a variety of techniques for syntactic analysis based on formal syntactic definitions.

A formal definition of the syntax of a programming language is usually called a *grammar*, in analogy with the common terminology for natural languages. A grammar consists of a set of definitions (termed *rules* or *productions*) which specify the sequences of characters (or lexical items) that form allowable programs in the language being defined. A *formal grammar* is just a grammar specified using a strictly defined notation. The best-known type of formal grammar is the *BNF grammar* (or *context-free grammar*), which has found widespread application both in programming language definition and in natural language research. A variant of the BNF form of some importance is that used in the definition of COBOL, which for lack of a better name we shall term a *CBL* (COBOL-like) *grammar*.

BNF Grammars

The *BNF* (Backus-Naur form) *grammar* was developed for the syntactic definition of ALGOL by John Backus [1960]. At about the same time a similar grammar form, the *context-free grammar*, was developed by linguist Noam Chomsky [1959] for the definition of natural language syntax. The BNF and context-free grammar forms are equivalent in power; the differences are essentially only notational. For this reason the terms *BNF grammar* and *context-free grammar* are usually interchangeable in discussion of syntax.

A BNF grammar is composed of a finite set of BNF grammar rules, which together define a *language*, in our case a programming language. Before we look at the form of these grammar rules, the term *language* here deserves some further explanation. Because syntax is concerned only with form rather than meaning, a (programming) *language*, considered syntactically, consists of a set of *syntactically correct programs*, each of which is simply a character string. A syntactically correct program need not make any sense semantically; that is, if it were executed, it would not need to compute anything useful, or anything at all for that matter—it may just loop immediately. In general a formal grammar for a programming language allows many such syntactically correct but semantically meaningless programs. Remember that the grammar defines only a set of *character strings* but assigns no meaning to those strings. We carry this lack of concern with meaning one step further and admit the definition: A *language is any set of* (finite-length) *character strings* (with characters chosen from some fixed finite alphabet of symbols). Under this definition FORTRAN is a language (composed of all the character strings representing syntactically valid FORTRAN programs), but the set of all FORTRAN assignment statements is also a language, or the set of all LISP atoms, or even the set composed of sequences of a's and b's where all the a's precede all the b's (i.e., [ab, aab, abb, . . .]). A language may consist of only a finite set of strings— for example, the language composed of all Pascal delimiters: **begin**, **end**, **if**, **then**, and so on. The only restriction on a language is that each string in it must be of finite length and must contain characters chosen from some fixed finite alphabet of symbols. The language itself may contain an infinite number of strings, of course.

A BNF grammar defines a language in a straightforward manner. In the simplest case a grammar rule may simply list the elements of a finite language. For example,

$$\langle digit \rangle ::= 0 \mid 1 \mid 2 \mid 3 \mid 4 \mid 5 \mid 6 \mid 7 \mid 8 \mid 9$$

This BNF grammar rule defines a language composed of the ten single-character strings [0, 1, 2, 3, 4, 5, 6, 7, 8, 9] by listing a set of alternatives. The above grammar rule is read "A *digit* is either a '0' or a '1' or a '2' or a . . . ." The term *digit* is called a *syntactic category*; it basically serves as a name for the language defined by the grammar rule. The symbol ::= means "is defined as" or just "is" and the vertical bar | is read "or" and separates alternatives in the definition.

Once we have defined a basic set of syntactic categories (really sublanguages), we may use these in constructing more complex languages. For example, the rule

⟨*conditional statement*⟩ ::=
    if ⟨*Boolean expression*⟩ **then** ⟨*statement*⟩ **else** ⟨*statement*⟩|
    if ⟨*Boolean expression*⟩ **then** ⟨*statement*⟩

defines the language composed of ⟨*conditional statement*⟩s, using the syntactic categories ⟨*Boolean expression*⟩ and ⟨*statement*⟩, which must be defined in turn using other grammar rules. Note that the above rule shows two alternative forms of conditional statement (separated by the| symbol). Each alternative is constructed from the concatenation of several elements, which may be literal strings (e.g., **if** or **else**) or syntactic categories. When a syntactic category is designated, it means that any string in the sublanguage defined by that category may be used at that point. For example, assuming that the syntactic category ⟨*Boolean expression*⟩ consists of a set of strings representing valid Boolean expressions, the above rule allows any one of these strings to be inserted between the **if** and **then** of a conditional statement.

Another useful form of grammar rule uses the syntactic category being defined recursively in the definition. This is the technique used in BNF rules to specify repetition. For example, the rule

⟨*unsigned integer*⟩ ::= ⟨*digit*⟩ | ⟨*unsigned integer*⟩ ⟨*digit*⟩

defines an unsigned integer as a sequence of ⟨*digit*⟩s by using the syntactic category ⟨*unsigned integer*⟩ recursively. The first alternative in the rule allows a single ⟨*digit*⟩ to appear as an ⟨*unsigned integer*⟩. The second alternative allows a ⟨*digit*⟩ to be added to the end of any string which has already been classified as an ⟨*unsigned integer*⟩, with the result still being classified as an ⟨*unsigned integer*⟩. Thus two ⟨*digit*⟩s in a sequence still form an ⟨*unsigned integer*⟩, and since this is true for two ⟨*digit*⟩s, it is also true for three ⟨*digit*⟩s in sequence, and so on.

A complete BNF grammar is just a set of such grammar rules, which together define a hierarchy of sublanguages leading to the top-level syntactic category, which for a programming language is usually the category ⟨*program*⟩. Figure 9-3 illustrates a more complex grammar defining the syntax of a class of simple assignment statements using the basic syntactic categories ⟨*identifier*⟩ and ⟨*number*⟩.

⟨*assignment statement*⟩ ::= ⟨*variable*⟩ := ⟨*arithmetic expression*⟩
⟨*arithmetic expression*⟩ ::= ⟨*term*⟩ | ⟨*arithmetic expression*⟩ + ⟨term⟩
                    | ⟨*arithmetic expression*⟩ − ⟨*term*⟩
⟨*term*⟩ ::= ⟨*factor*⟩ | ⟨*term*⟩ × ⟨factor⟩ | ⟨*term*⟩ / ⟨*factor*⟩
⟨*factor*⟩ ::= ⟨*primary*⟩ | ⟨*factor*⟩ ↑ ⟨*primary*⟩
⟨*primary*⟩ ::= ⟨*variable*⟩ | ⟨*number*⟩ | (⟨*arithmetic expression*⟩)
⟨*variable*⟩ ::= ⟨*identifier*⟩ | ⟨*identifier*⟩ [⟨*subscript list*⟩]
⟨*subscript list*⟩ ::= ⟨*arithmetic expression*⟩
            | ⟨*subscript list*⟩, ⟨*arithmetic expression*⟩

Fig. 9-3 BNF grammar for simple assignment statements

Functions of a BNF Grammar

The use of a formal grammar to define the syntax of a programming language is important to both the language user and the language implementor. The user may consult it to answer subtle questions about program form, punctuation, and structure. The implementor may use it to determine all the possible cases of input program structures which are allowed and thus with which his translator may have to deal. And both programmer and implementor have a common agreed upon definition which may be used to resolve disputes about allowed syntactic constructs. A formal syntactic definition also helps to eliminate minor syntactic differences between implementations of a language.

The basic function of any grammar is that of distinguishing between syntactically correct and syntactically incorrect strings. The BNF grammar form does this through the set of BNF rules, which define the set of all syntactically correct strings. To determine if a given string in fact represents a syntactically valid program in the language defined by a BNF grammar, we must use the grammar rules to construct a syntactic analysis or *parse* of the string. If the string can be successfuly parsed, then it is in the language. If no way can be found of parsing the string with the given grammar rules, then the string is not in the language. Figure 9-4 illustrates the *parse tree* which results from a syntactic analysis of an assignment statement using the BNF grammar of Fig. 9-3.

While the basic function of a grammar is that of distinguishing correct and incorrect strings, BNF grammars serve a secondary function which is almost of equal practical importance. A BNF grammar assigns a *structure* to each string in the language defined by the grammar, as seen in Fig. 9-4. Note that the structure assigned is necessarily a tree because of the restrictions on BNF grammar rules. Each leaf of this parse tree is a single character or lexical item in the input string. Each intermediate branch point in the tree is tagged with a syntactic category which designates the class to which the subtree below it belongs. The root node of the tree is tagged with the syntactic category designating the whole language, in this case the category ⟨assignment statement⟩.

The parse tree assigned to each syntactically correct string in a language is important because it can be used to provide a sort of intuitive semantic structure for much of a program. Thus, for example, the BNF grammar for Pascal specifies a structure for a program as a sequence of declarations and statements, with nested blocks. The statements, in turn, are structured using expressions of various kinds, and the expressions are composed from simple and subscripted variables, primitive operators, functions calls, and so on. At the lowest level even identifiers and numbers are broken down into their constituent parts. By studying the grammar a programmer may gain a direct insight into the various structures which

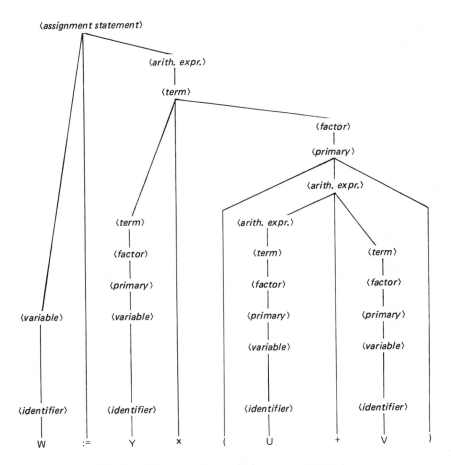

Fig. 9-4 Parse tree for an assignment statement

combine to form correct programs. It is important to note that no grammar must *necessarily* assign the structure one would expect to a given program element. The same language may be defined by many different grammars, as may be easily seen by playing with the grammar of Fig. 9-3 a bit. Figure 9-5, for example, gives a grammar defining the same language as the grammar of Fig. 9-3, but note that the structures assigned by this new grammar are quite at odds with the structures one would intuitively assign.

The BNF grammar, in spite of its exceedingly simple structure, can be used to do a surprisingly good job of defining the syntax of most programming languages. For example, the ALGOL BNF grammar (Naur [1963]), supplemented by only a few additional syntactic restrictions stated in English, describes the set of valid ALGOL programs very closely. The areas of syntax which cannot be defined by a BNF grammar are those which involve contextual dependence. For example, the ALGOL restrictions

⟨assignment statement⟩ ::= ⟨variable⟩ := ⟨arithmetic expression⟩
⟨arithmetic expression⟩::= ⟨term⟩ | ⟨arithmetic expression⟩ ↑ ⟨term⟩
                          | ⟨arithmetic expression⟩ × ⟨term⟩
                          | ⟨arithmetic expression⟩ + ⟨term⟩
⟨term⟩ ::= ⟨primary⟩ | ⟨term⟩ − ⟨primary⟩ | ⟨term⟩ / ⟨primary⟩
⟨primary⟩ ::= ⟨variable⟩ | ⟨number⟩ | (⟨arithmetic expression⟩)
⟨variable⟩ ::= ⟨identifier⟩ | ⟨identifier⟩ [⟨subscript list⟩
⟨subscript list⟩ ::= ⟨arithmetic expression⟩]
                    | ⟨arithmetic expression⟩,⟨subscript list⟩

Fig. 9-5 BNF grammar defining the same language as the grammar of Fig. 9-3.

"the same identifier may not be declared twice in the same block," "every identifier must be declared in some block enclosing the point of its use," and "an array declared to have two dimensions cannot be referenced with three subscripts" are each unspecifiable using only a BNF grammar. It is restrictions of this sort that must be defined by an addendum to the formal BNF grammar.

CBL (COBOL-like) Grammars: A Useful Notational Variant of BNF

Despite the power, elegance, and simplicity of BNF grammars, they are not an ideal notation for communicating the rules of programming language syntax to the practicing programmer. The primary reason is the simplicity of the BNF rule, which forces a rather unnatural representation for the common syntactic constructs of optional elements, alternative elements, and repeated elements within a grammar rule. For example, to express the simple syntactic idea "a *signed integer* is a sequence of digits preceded by an optional plus or minus" we must write in BNF a fairly complex set of recursive rules such as

⟨signed integer⟩::= + ⟨integer⟩ | − ⟨integer⟩ | ⟨integer⟩
⟨integer⟩::= ⟨digit⟩ | ⟨integer⟩ ⟨digit⟩

These notational shortcomings of BNF are largely unimportant to the theoretical development of the properties of the grammar, but many who have used BNF for syntactic description of actual languages have been moved to extend the notation in various ways to provide a more natural way of writing rules like that noted above. The most widely used of these alternative notations is that used in the definition of COBOL, which seems to have been developed independently and at about the same time as BNF. This notation has been used somewhat informally and has received little of the intensive analysis applied to BNF grammars.

It is convenient to consider the CBL rules as simply an extension of BNF which adds the following new notation:

1. Within a grammar rule, an optional element may be indicated by enclosing the element in square brackets, [. . .].

2. Alternative elements may be indicated by listing the alternatives vertically enclosed in braces, {. . .} (replacing the vertical bar of BNF).

3. Optional alternatives may be indicated by listing the alternatives vertically enclosed in square brackets, [. . .].

4. Repeated elements may be indicated by listing one element (enclosed in brackets or braces if necessary) followed by the usual ellipsis symbol, ...

5. Required key words are underlined, and optional noise words are not.

Examples:

1. $\langle signed\ integer \rangle ::= \begin{bmatrix} + \\ - \end{bmatrix} \langle digit \rangle \ \ldots$

2. $\langle identifier \rangle ::= \langle letter \rangle \begin{bmatrix} \langle letter \rangle \\ \langle digit \rangle \end{bmatrix} \ \ldots$

3. $\langle \underline{ALGOL}\ conditional\ statement \rangle ::= \underline{if} \langle Boolean\ expression \rangle\ \textbf{then}$
   $\langle unconditional\ statement \rangle\ [\textbf{else} \langle statement \rangle]$

4. $\langle COBOL\ ADD\ statement \rangle ::= \underline{ADD} \begin{Bmatrix} \langle identifier \rangle \\ \langle number \rangle \end{Bmatrix}$

   $\begin{bmatrix} ,\ \langle identifier \rangle \\ ,\ \langle number \rangle \end{bmatrix} \ \cdots\ \underline{TO} \langle identifier \rangle\ [\underline{ROUNDED}]$

   $[,\ \langle identifier \rangle\ [\underline{ROUNDED}]] \cdots$
   $[;\ ON\ \underline{SIZE}\ \underline{ERROR} \langle statement \rangle]$

The naturalness and conciseness of this CBL grammar form compared to BNF is easily seen by viewing the difference in the definition of ⟨*signed integer*⟩ in the two forms or by writing a full BNF definition of the ⟨COBOL ADD *statement*⟩ (see Problem 6). Note, however, that the BNF and CBL grammar forms are equivalent in power—any language that can be defined by a grammar in one form can also be defined by a grammar in the other.

9-5   REFERENCES AND SUGGESTIONS FOR FURTHER READING

The literature on the syntax and translation of programming languages is extensive. Backhouse [1980] and Aho and Ullman [1972], among others, survey the mathematical theory of formal syntax and parsing techniques.

Aho and Ullman [1977], Lewis, et al. [1976], Barrett and Couch [1979], and Hunter [1981] are representative of texts that treat the design and implementation of compilers. Bauer and Eickel [1976] provide a collection of papers on current practice.

Practical considerations in the design of the syntax of languages have also received attention. Sammet [1969] surveys much of the relevant material. The *Ada Rationale* (Ichbiah et al. [1979]) is another useful source.

9-6   PROBLEMS

1. Consider the following BNF grammar rules:

$$\langle pop \rangle \ ::= [\ \langle bop \rangle , \langle pop \rangle] | \ \langle bop \rangle$$
$$\langle bop \rangle \ ::= \langle boop \rangle \ | \ (\langle pop \rangle)$$
$$\langle boop \rangle ::= a \ | \ b \ | \ c$$

For each of the strings listed below, indicate all the syntactic categories of which it is a member, if any:

(a) c
(b) (a)
(c) $[b]$
(d) $([a,b])$
(e) $[(a),b]$
(f) $[(a),[b,a]]$

2. Write a BNF grammar for the language composed of all binary numbers which contain at least three consecutive 1's (the language including the strings 000011111110100 or 1111110 but not 0011000101011).

3. The syntax of the *monkey* language is quite simple, yet only monkeys can speak it without making mistakes. The alphabet of the language is { $a,b,d,$ ∧ }, where ∧ stands for a space. The grammar is

$$\langle stop \rangle \qquad ::= b \ | \ d$$
$$\langle plosive \rangle \ ::= \langle stop \rangle \ a$$
$$\langle syllable \rangle \ ::= \langle plosive \rangle | \langle plosive \rangle \langle stop \rangle \ | \ a \ \langle plosive \rangle \ | \ a \ \langle stop \rangle$$
$$\langle word \rangle \qquad ::= \langle syllable \rangle | \ \langle syllable \rangle \langle word \rangle \langle syllable \rangle$$
$$\langle sentence \rangle ::= \langle word \rangle | \ \langle sentence \rangle \ \wedge \ \langle word \rangle$$

Which of the following speakers is the secret agent in monkey disguise?

Ape: *ba* ∧ *ababadada* ∧ *bad* ∧ *dabbada*
Chimp: *abdabaadab* ∧ *ada*
Baboon: *dad* ∧ *ad* ∧ *abaadad* ∧ *badadbaad*

4. Write a CBL grammar for the language defined by the BNF grammar of Fig. 9-3.

5. Rewrite the grammar of Fig. 9-3 to show the proper structure for expressions assuming the APL rules for operator precedence and associativity: All operators

including assignment are of equal precedence and associativity is from right to left. For example, the assignment statement $W := Y \times W + U \times V$ should be assigned the structure

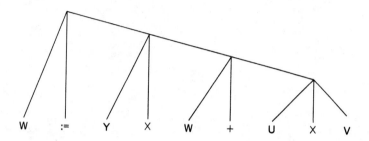

6. Write a BNF grammar for the COBOL ADD statement, defined using the CBL grammar in Sec. 9-4.

7. Construct parse trees for the following assignment statements using the BNF grammar of Fig. 9-3:

(a) $A[2] := B + 1$
(b) $A[I,J] := A[J,I]$
(c) $X := U - V \uparrow W + X / Y$
(d) $P := U / (V / (W / X))$

CHAPTER 10

Operating
and Programming
Environments

In the preceding chapters we have considered in detail the internal structure of programs and virtual computers during translation and execution. To get a complete view it is also helpful to consider the external environment in which programs are translated and executed. The external environment of a program during its execution is termed its *operating environment*. Batch-processing environments, interactive environments, and embedded-system environments are three different types of operating environments whose differing requirements have an important influence on language (and program) design.

The environment in which a program is designed, coded, tested, and debugged is usually different from the operating environment in which the program ultimately is used. This environment is termed the *programming environment*, because it is the environment of program creation. The requirements of programming environments also influence language design. Both APL and Ada are good examples of these influences (see Chapters 16 and 19).

10-1 BATCH-PROCESSING ENVIRONMENTS

The simplest operating environment consists only of external files of data, as discussed in Sec. 4-11. In this environment a program takes a certain set of data files as input, processes the data, and produces a set of output data files. For example, a program to process a payroll may process two input files containing master payroll records and weekly pay-period times and produce two output files containing updated master records and paychecks. This operating environment is termed a *batch-processing environment* because the input data are collected in "batches" on files and are processed in batches by the program (as opposed to an interactive environment, where single data items may be processed individually as received from a user at a terminal).

Effects on Language Design

Of the languages described in Part II, FORTRAN, COBOL, PL/I, Pascal, and SNOBOL4 are basically designed for a batch-processing environment. These languages may be used in an interactive or embedded-system environment, but their design is oriented toward batch processing. The influence of the environment is seen in four major areas: input-output features, error- and exception-handling features, timing facilities, and main program structure.

In a language designed for batch processing, sequential files are usually the basis for most of the input-output structure of the language. Pascal and SNOBOL4 provide only sequential files. FORTRAN, COBOL, and PL/I also provide direct-access files. Although a sequential file may be used for interactive input-output to a terminal, the special needs of interactive I/O are not addressed in these languages. The input-output structure also typically does not address the requirement for access to special I/O devices found in embedded systems.

In a batch-processing environment, an error that terminates execution of the program is acceptable but costly, because often the entire run must be repeated after the error is corrected. In this environment, too, no external help from the user in immediately handling or correcting the error is possible. Thus the error- and exception-handling facilities of the language emphasize error/exception handling within the program, so that the program may recover from most errors and continue processing without terminating.

The third distinguishing characteristic of a batch-processing environment is the lack of timing constraints on a program. In general the language provides no facilities for monitoring or directly affecting the speed at which the entire program or any part of it is executed. The presumption is that ordinarily the program is executed in an environment in which data may be input, processed, and output at any rate that is suitable for effective use of the overall computer system. For example, the operating system may allow the program to execute for a while, then swap it out to secondary storage for an indefinite period, and later bring it back into central memory to continue. The precise time required to complete execution of the program is not of great concern (within some broad bounds). The language itself ordinarily provides no means to monitor the timing of the program. Moreover, implementation of language features often reflects the lack of timing constraints. For example, input and output to files is usually buffered (as described in Sec. 4-11), so that a READ or WRITE operation transfers data to or from a buffer rather than directly to or from a file. Heap storage management may be implemented with a garbage collector, as described in Chapter 8, which causes program execution to halt for an indefinite period while garbage is collected and returned to the free-space list.

A final distinguishing characteristic of a language for a batch-processing environment is seen in the main program structure. In such languages, the main program looks much like an ordinary subprogram. That is, it consists of a sequence of declarations defining local variables, followed by a sequence of executable statements. Often the external files processed by the program appear as a "parameter list" in the program heading. Execution of the overall program consists simply of execution of the statements in the main program in sequence, after which the program terminates and execution is complete.

10-2 INTERACTIVE ENVIRONMENTS

In an interactive environment, a program during its execution interacts directly with a user at a terminal, by alternately sending output to the terminal and receiving input from the terminal. Examples include programs that implement word-processing systems, data-base management systems, and computer-assisted instruction systems. The terminal may be a simple one with a typewriterlike keyboard and a printer display or a complex graphics screen with a keyboard and light pen for input.

Effects on Language Design

The characteristics of interactive input-output are sufficiently different from ordinary file input-output that most languages designed for a batch-processing environment experience some difficulty in adapting to an interactive environment. These differences are discussed in Sec. 4-11. Buffering of data and timing constraints are the two major problem areas.

Error handling in an interactive environment is ordinarily treated somewhat differently. If a bad piece of input data is received from a terminal, the program may ordinarily flash an error message on the terminal screen and ask for a correction from the user. Language features for handling the error within the program (e.g., by ignoring it and attempting to continue) are of lesser importance. However, termination of the program in response to an error is usually not acceptable (unlike batch processing).

Interactive programs must often utilize some notion of timing constraints, although these are not usually severe. For example, in a program for administering a test to a student, the failure to respond within a fixed time interval may be taken as a wrong answer. An interactive program that operates so slowly that it cannot respond to an input command in a reasonable period is often considered unusable as well. However, the timing of the program's response to an input from the terminal is most often controlled by the operating system rather than from within the program itself (e.g., the operating system may have swapped the program out to secondary storage, so that a delay is caused by the time required to swap it back in to process the user's input).

Finally, in an interactive environment, the main program seen in a batch-processing environment is often nonexistent. Instead, the program consists of a set of subprograms, and the user enters the "main program" as a sequence of commands at the terminal. Thus the interaction with the user takes the form of a request for a command, followed by execution of that command, followed by a request for another command, and so on. Both LISP and APL exhibit this type of main program structure. Each command that the user enters invokes one (or more) of the subprograms in memory. Often each command automatically causes some results to be displayed at the terminal. Each subprogram, in turn, may also interact with the terminal.

10-3   EMBEDDED-SYSTEM ENVIRONMENTS

A computer system that is used to control part of a larger system such as an industrial plant, an aircraft, a machine tool, or an automobile is termed an *embedded computer system*. The computer system has become an integral part of the larger system, and the failure of the computer system usually means failure of the larger system as well. Often embedded computer systems are used in potentially life-critical applications, e.g., nuclear power plant or chemical plant monitoring, missile or aircraft control, and monitoring of critically ill hospital patients. These applications require high reliability. In addition, the computer is often connected directly to special-purpose input-output devices such as pressure or position sensors, motors and actuators of various kinds to control the system, and various warning devices. Of the languages in Part II, only Ada is expressly designed to meet some of the special requirements of embedded-system environments.

Effects on Language Design

Programs written for embedded systems often operate without an underlying operating system and without the usual environment of files and I/O devices. Instead the program must interact directly with nonstandard I/O devices through special procedures that take account of the peculiarities of each device. For this reason, languages for embedded systems often place much less emphasis on files and file-oriented input-output operations. Access to special devices is often provided through language features that provide access to particular hardware registers, memory locations, interrupt handlers, or subprograms written in assembly or other low-level languages.

Error handling in embedded systems is of particular importance. Ordinarily each program must be prepared to handle all errors internally, taking appropriate actions to recover and continue. Termination, except in the case of a catastrophic system failure, is often not an acceptable alternative, and usually there is no user in the environment to provide interactive error correction. The error handling must be able to account for failure of system components, in addition to the usual sorts of errors caused by bad data values. In Ada this concern for internal error handling is seen in the extensive features for exception handling.

Embedded systems almost always operate in *real time*; that is, the operation of the larger system within which the computer system is embedded requires that the computer system be able to respond to inputs and to produce outputs within tightly constrained time intervals. For example, a computer controlling the flight of an aircraft must respond rapidly to changes in its altitude or speed. Real-time operation of these programs requires language features for monitoring time intervals, responding to delays of more than a certain length of time (which may indicate failure of a component of the system), and starting up and terminating actions at certain designated points in time.

Finally, an embedded computer system is often a *distributed system*, composed of more than one computer (actual or virtual). The program running on such a distributed system is usually composed of a set of tasks that operate concurrently, each controlling or monitoring one part of the system. The main program, if there is one, exists only to initiate execution of the tasks. Once initiated, these tasks usually run concurrently and indefinitely, since they need to terminate only when the entire system fails or is shut down for some reason. Thus the set of concurrent tasks forms the top level of such an embedded program.

10-4   PROGRAMMING ENVIRONMENTS

The *programming environment*, in which programs are created and tested, tends to have less influence on language design than the operating environment in which programs are expected to be executed. However, it is widely recognized that the production of programs that operate reliably and efficiently is made much simpler by a good programming environment and by a language that allows the use of good programming tools and practices in this environment.

A programming environment consists primarily of a set of support tools and a command language for invoking them. Each support tool is another program that may be used by the programmer as an aid during one or more of the stages of creation of a program. Typical tools in a programming environment include editors, debuggers, verifiers, test data generators, and pretty printers.

The programs that are most affected by the presence of a good programming environment are large *production programs*—programs that are used repeatedly over a long period of time by many users other than the original designers. These large programs are usually constructed by groups of programmers who individually design and code different parts of the program. When the separate pieces are complete and tested, they must be integrated into a complete program for final testing. After the program is in production use, it must be repeatedly modified to repair latent errors and to add new features. The class of production programs includes all the major programs used in applications such as payroll and accounting, most embedded systems, data-base management systems, computer system software such as compilers and operating systems, and so on. A *single-user program* is a program created and used only by a single programmer, e.g., in learning a new language, in reformatting data, or for personal computing hobbies. Although a good programming environment is an aid in construction of any type of program, the tools of interest are primarily aimed at creation of production programs.

Effects on Language Design

Programming environments have affected language design primarily in two major areas: features aiding separate compilation and assembly of a program from components, and features aiding program testing and debugging. In a general way, of course, any programming language design is itself an attempt to provide a better programming environment than that provided by the bare computer.

Separate compilation. In the construction of any large program it is ordinarily desirable to have different programmers or programming groups design, code, and test parts of the program before a final assembly of all the components into a complete program. This requires the language to be structured so that individual subprograms or other parts can be separately compiled and executed, without the other parts, and then later merged without change into the final program.

Separate compilation is made difficult by the fact that in compiling one subprogram, the compiler may need information about other subprograms or shared data objects, such as:

a. The *specification* of the number, order, and type of the parameters expected by any subprogram called. This information allows the compiler to check whether a call of the external subprogram is valid. The language in which the other subprogram is coded may also need to be known, so that the compiler may set up the appropriate "calling sequence" of instructions to transfer data and control information to the external subprogram during execution in the form expected by that subprogram.

b. The *declaration of data type* for any variable referenced that is in an explicit common environment or that is imported from an external subprogram. The declaration is needed to allow the compiler to determine the storage representation of the external variable so that the reference may be compiled using the appropriate accessing formula for the variable (e.g., the correct offset within the common environment block).

c. The *definition of a data type* that is defined externally but is used to declare any local variable within the subprogram. This data-type definition is needed to allow the compiler to allocate storage and compute accessing formulas for local data.

To provide this information about separately compiled subprograms, shared data objects, and type definitions either (1) the language may require that the relevant information be *redeclared* within the subprogram (in PL/I and FORTRAN), (2) it may prescribe a particular *order of compilation* that requires that compilation of the subprogram be preceded by compilation of at least the specification of the called subprograms and shared data (in Ada and to some extent in Pascal), or (3) it may require the presence of a library containing the relevant definitions and specifications during compilation, so that the compiler may retrieve them as needed (in Ada).

The term *independent compilation* is usually used for option (1). Each subprogram may be independently compiled without any external information; the subprogram is entirely self-contained. Independent compilation has the disadvantage that ordinarily there is no way to check the consistency of the information about external subprograms and data that is redeclared in the subprogram. If the declarations within the subprogram do not match the actual structure of the external data or subprogram, then in the final assembly stage a subtle error appears (that will not have been detected during testing of the independently compiled program parts).

Options (2) and (3) require a means for specifications of subprograms, type definitions, and common environments to be given or placed in a library prior to the compilation of a subprogram. Usually it is desirable to allow the *body* (local variables and statements) of a subprogram to be omitted, with only the *specification* given. The body may be compiled separately later. In Ada, for example, every subprogram, task, or package is split into two parts, a specification and a body, which may be separately compiled or placed in a library as required in order to allow compilation of other subprograms. A subprogram call made to a subprogram that has not yet been compiled is termed a *stub*. A subprogram containing stubs may be executed, and when a stub is reached, the call causes a system diagnostic message to be printed (or other action taken) rather than an actual call on the subprogram. Thus a separately compiled subprogram may be executed for testing purposes even though code for some of the routines it calls is not yet available.

Another aspect of separate compilation that affects language design is in the use of *shared names*. If several groups are writing portions of a large program, it is often difficult to insure that the names used by each group for subprograms, common environments, and shared type definitions are distinct. A common problem is to find, during assembly of the final complete program, that several subprograms or other program units have the same names. Often this means a tedious and time-consuming revision of already tested code. For example, in FORTRAN each subprogram and COMMON block ordinarily must have a distinct name. When separate groups are coding in FORTRAN, *naming conventions* must be adopted at the outset so that each group has a distinct set of names they may use for subprograms and COMMON blocks (e.g., "all names used by your group must begin with QQ").

In Ada a more powerful set of features is provided. Any shared name X is usually part of a larger program unit P with a unique name. At the outermost level, all global names are part of the predefined environment STANDARD. If a subprogram is coded to directly reference X, and it later is discovered that there is a second shared variable X visible at the same point, from some other program unit, then the reference to X may be changed to P.X to designate that the X desired is that in program unit P. In Ada subprogram names (and some other names) may also be *overloaded*, so that several subprograms may have the same name. As long as the compiler can resolve the overloading based on the number, order, and types of parameters each time the overloaded name is used, no change is needed in the calling program. Language features of this sort make it possible to resolve any name conflicts through simple local changes in a single subprogram rather than requiring global changes in many parts of the program.

Testing and debugging. Most languages contain some features to aid program testing and debugging. A few typical examples are:

a. *Execution trace features.* SNOBOL4 (and many other languages) provides features that allow particular statements and variables to be tagged for "tracing" during execution. Whenever a tagged statement is executed or a tagged variable is assigned a new value, execution of the program is interrupted and a designated trace subprogram is called (which typically prints appropriate debugging information).

    b. *Breakpoints.* In an interactive programming environment, languages often provide a feature where the programmer can specify points in the program as *breakpoints.* When a breakpoint is reached during execution, execution of the program is interrupted and control is given to the programmer at a terminal. The programmer may inspect and modify values of variables and then restart the program from the point of interruption.

    c. *Assertions.* An *assertion* is a conditional expression inserted as a separate statement in a program, e.g.,

$$\text{ASSERT } (X>0 \textbf{ and } A = 1) \textbf{ or } (X= 0 \textbf{ and } A>B+10)$$

The assertion states a set of relationships that must hold between the values of the variables at that point in the program. When the assertion is "enabled," the compiler inserts code into the compiled program to test the conditions stated. During execution, if the conditions fail to hold, then execution is interrupted and an exception handler is invoked to print a message or take other action. After the program is debugged, the assertions may be "disabled" so that the compiler generates no code for their checking. They then become useful comments that aid in documenting the program.

10-5   REFERENCES AND SUGGESTIONS FOR FURTHER READING

Each language described in Part II shows influences from the programming and operating environments expected. APL, LISP, and Ada are the most strongly influenced by these considerations. A major part of the Ada design effort, after the design of the language itself was complete, was directed toward the design of a comprehensive programming environment that would contain a variety of support tools for Ada programming. The *Stoneman* requirements specification (Buxton [1980]) describes the major components expected in such an Ada programming environment. Work in the general area of *software engineering* is often concerned with the design of tools for programming environments. Howden [1982], Zelkowitz, Shaw, and Gannon [1979], and Zelkowitz [1978] provide good starting points. The *IEEE Transactions on Software Engineering* and *Software—Practice and Experience* are two journals that often carry relevant articles in this area.

    Operating environments for programs that must operate in *real-time* or on distributed computing systems introduce many special considerations not mentioned in Sec. 10-3. Wirth [1977a] discusses many of these. His MODULA (Wirth [1977b]) and MODULA2 (Wirth [1980]) show two language designs intended for use in programming such systems.

CHAPTER 11

Theoretical Models

In most areas of complex human activity, we see the progression:

$$\text{practice} \rightarrow \text{theory} \rightarrow \text{better practice}$$

in which theoretical models are constructed to explain and analyze current practice, leading to new methods and deeper insights, which lead in turn to new and better practice, which then provides the basis for new theories, and so on in a continuing cycle of deepening understanding. This progression appears as strongly in music or psychology as it does in physics or engineering. Theoretical models have played an important role in computing from the beginning of electronic computers, which of necessity are based on rather deep theoretical understandings about electronics and mathematics.

The design and implementation of programming languages illustrates a complex intermingling of theory and practice. Much early language design and implementation was based on practical concerns: what can we do to make this primitive piece of computer hardware usable for constructing the large programs needed for practical problems such as designing aircraft, analyzing radar data, or monitoring nuclear reactions? Many early language designs grew out of practical needs, with little input from theory. The flaws, failures and successes of this practice led to some early formal models of programming language syntax and semantics, which led in turn to better languages. Even though better, these languages still had numerous flaws in both design and implementation. Better theoretical models led to yet further refinements in design. The goal of this chapter is to briefly survey some of the major theoretical models that have been important for programming languages and to note their impact on practice.

A theoretical model may be *conceptual* (or qualitative), describing practice in terms of an underlying set of basic concepts, without an attempt to provide a formal mathematical description of the concepts. In this sense, the preceding chapters have constructed a theoretical model of the basic concepts underlying programming language design and implementation. Alternatively, a theoretical model may be *formal* (or quantitative), describing practice in terms of a precise mathematical model that can be studied, analyzed, and manipulated using the tools of mathematics. The theoretical models of this chapter are formal models. Many different formal models have been proposed for describing various individual aspects of languages and their implementations. Many of these are noted in the references at the ends of each of the preceding chapters. The discussion here concentrates on formal models intended to describe the entire syntax or semantics of a language, rather than just a single language feature. Because each formal model is constructed with a different terminology and notation, these models cannot be presented fully here. Instead we begin with a practical problem, describe with an informal sketch some of the formal models used in attacking the problem, and then look at the impact on practice of this theoretical work.

11-1 PROBLEMS IN SYNTAX AND TRANSLATION

The area of programming language design and implementation to receive the earliest deep analysis through theoretical models was that of syntax and translation.

Problem 1: Definition of Syntax

The practical problem. When a new programming language is designed, a precise, concise, and complete definition of its syntax is useful to both programmer and implementor. The programmer needs to know exactly what it is legal to write in the language, the format of each statement, its punctuation, optional phrases, and so on. The implementor needs to know the entire set of legal programs that the translator must accept. Description of exactly the set of syntactically valid programs in a language is thus an important practical problem. Working directly at the practical level, the problem appears difficult to solve. Not only are there many diverse syntactic components in a programming language, ranging from small elements such as numbers and identifiers to larger elements such as expressions, declarations, and statements to complete subprograms and programs, but there are also many complex interconnecting constraints that must be met to make a program syntactically valid. For example, it is usually invalid to declare the same identifier twice in the same local environment, or to write a **goto** statement, **goto** L, without also labeling some statement L. Attempting to put together a complete, concise, and readable definition of a language's syntax is thus difficult.

Some theoretical models and results. To solve the practical problem, it has been useful to build various theoretical models that treat the problem more abstractly. The theoretician asks the question: What is it that we are trying to describe? The abstract answer is: a *language*, which is just *a set of finite sequences of characters from some arbitrary alphabet*. The alphabet is just the set of characters that can be used in programs, and each finite sequence of these characters represents one complete valid program. Given the alphabet, any finite sequence of characters might be written by the programmer and given to the translator, but only some of those sequences represent valid programs; the others represent programs that contain syntax errors of various kinds.

The theoretician now looks for ways of defining sets of finite sequences of characters, rather than for defining programming languages. This same problem then is seen to arise in other areas; for example, the linguist has a similar problem in trying to characterize the syntax of natural languages, and the logician has the same problem in trying to define the set of mathematical formulae that meet different criteria. Not surprisingly, some formal models have been developed in these other areas to solve the problem that might be useful here as well.

The theoretical models that have proven most useful are termed *formal grammars*. The BNF grammar described in Chapter 9 is an example of a formal grammar. It consists of a set of *productions* or grammar rules that recursively define a set of valid character sequences. The BNF grammar model was developed by Backus and Naur for the description of the syntax of ALGOL 60, but at about the same time, the linguist Chomsky developed a hierarchy of four types of formal grammar, one of which, the context-free grammar, happened to be almost identical with the BNF grammar. The Chomsky hierarchy included one grammar form that was less powerful than the BNF form, and two that were more powerful. The less powerful form, now termed a *regular grammar*, was simpler than BNF but could not describe as complex a set of constraints. For example, a regular grammar might be used to define a language consisting of expressions containing parentheses, but the language could not be restricted to contain only expressions with properly paired parentheses. A BNF grammar could define the constraint that parentheses must be properly paired. However, there were constraints that could not be expressed using a BNF grammar, but that could be expressed using the more powerful grammars in the Chomsky hierarchy, the *context-sensitive* and *unrestricted* grammars. Where a BNF grammar cannot express the constraint that the label named in a **goto** statement must match the label on a statement somewhere in the program, these more powerful grammars can.

The Chomsky hierarchy of grammar form is an example of a common phenomenon in theoretical work: many different theoretical models of a practical situation may be constructed, each abstracting the practical problem in different ways. Some of these theoretical models turn out to be less useful than others and are studied for a while and then forgotten. Others turn out to capture some important element of the practical problem and enter into general use. Following Chomsky's pioneering work, many dozens of types of formal grammars were developed, each exploring a different way of defining the sorts of constraints needed for actual programming languages. The context-sensitive and unrestricted grammars in Chomsky's hierarchy turned out to be the wrong models for programming languages. While more powerful than BNF, they were also more complex to understand, analyze, and use in practice. Many of the later grammar forms were developed in an attempt to overcome the limitations of these models.

BNF grammars have a number of nice properties. They are rather easy to use in practical situations and are powerful enough to express most (but not all) of the syntactic constraints that are required for programming languages (linguists found them less useful for natural languages). They are also easy to analyze mathematically to discover facts about the languages they define that are not obvious directly. For example, one important practical question is whether a given BNF grammar for a programming language is *ambiguous*; that is, does the grammar define a unique parse for each valid program, or are multiple parses possible? Ordinarily each parse corresponds to a different meaning given to the program, so multiple parses lead to multiple meanings. The question arises: can you find a general procedure for determining whether a BNF grammar is ambiguous? The result from theoretical studies is surprising: don't bother to try to find such a procedure—there is none! In formal terms, the question of determining the ambiguity of a BNF grammar is said to be *undecidable*; there can be no general procedure for answering the question for any BNF grammar. The result is disappointing, because faced with a complex BNF grammar containing hundreds of productions, it would be nice to have a program that could check whether it is ambiguous. We might write a program that could give a yes or no answer most of the time, but the undecidability of the question tells us that no program could *always* give an answer—for some grammars, it would have to fail to produce an answer, no matter how long we let it run.

Study of alternative formal grammar models has led to many important results. Some of these relate formal grammars to implementations of parsers, the next problem taken up below. Others relate different models of formal grammars to each other, showing that many variants of BNF are equivalent in power, such as the CBL form described in Chapter 9, and also showing that there are many less powerful forms and many more powerful forms. Although some questions about BNF grammars are undecidable, many are decidable; for more powerful grammars, many of these same questions become undecidable.

Effect on practice. The description of the syntax of a new programming language is now routinely made using a formal grammar. Most commonly some variant of BNF grammar is used for the definition, but occasionally a more powerful form of grammar is used (e.g., the definition of ALGOL 68 uses a grammar form called a *two-level grammar* that can describe many of the contextual constraints on the language that cannot be described using only a BNF grammar). However, experience with the use of more powerful grammar forms has generally been disappointing, owing to their increased complexity. BNF grammars seem to hit about the right level of readability and descriptive power in practical use. Theoretical studies have clarified the limits of BNF grammars, so it is well understood that some classes of syntactic constraints cannot be described with them, and these must be described in some other way, often by attaching informal notes to the productions of a BNF grammar. The users of a language now routinely use a formal grammar to answer questions about syntax. Implementors of a language also routinely use a formal grammar to generate a parser for the language, as described below.

Problem 2: Efficient Parsing Algorithms

The practical problem. The implementation of a parser (syntactic analyzer) in the translator for a language is a common implementation problem. The parser is at the center of much of the translator structure, and its efficiency, reliability, and ease of modification are important for a successful translator. The parser must accept as input a sequence of characters, which it breaks down into lexical items, expressions, declarations, statements, and so on. A BNF grammar for the language is useful, because it defines precisely which input sequences are valid programs and also describes an appropriate structure for each valid program. However, the grammar describes the structure of a program in a "top-down" fashion, starting with a whole program, breaking that into subprograms and main program, each of these into statements and declarations, and so forth. The parser must begin with the individual characters and build up the structure from the bottom, working from left to right as the characters are input. Worse, the characters may not even form a valid program. The design and implementation of an efficient and correct parsing algorithm is potentially a difficult and time-consuming problem.

Some theoretical models and results.   Not too surprisingly, the theoretical studies of formal grammers provide a basis for the solution of this problem as well. First, it was understood from the time of Chomsky's work that each type of formal grammar is closely related to a type of automaton. An *automaton* is a simple abstract machine that is usually defined to be capable of reading an input tape containing a sequence of characters and producing an output tape containing another sequence of characters. An automaton thus represents a definition of an algorithm; the input tape represents the input data and the output tape represents the result data. The automaton associated with a formal grammar is a *recognizer* that reads its input tape and decides whether the character string on that tape is a valid string according to the grammar. If so, it writes *yes* on its output tape; otherwise it writes *no* (or indicates a yes-no answer in some other way).

The automaton associated with a BNF grammar is called a *pushdown automaton*, because it uses a third tape for auxiliary storage that serves as a pushdown stack. In theory, a pushdown automaton might serve as a model for how to implement a parser for the language defined by a BNF grammar, because the automaton reads the input program from left to right and "parses" it to decide if it is a valid program. Unfortunately, a problem arises: because a BNF grammar may be ambiguous and have some other troublesome properties, the automaton must be *nondeterministic*, that is, it must "guess" at the proper thing to do at various times during the parse. If some sequence of guesses leads to a complete parse of the input string, then the string is valid according to the grammar. But a sequence of guesses might lead to a dead end, either because the guesses were wrong or because the input string is not valid, and there is no way to tell which. What is needed is a more restricted automaton that never has to guess; such an automaton is called a *deterministic* automaton.

Theoretical studies into the relationship between formal grammars and automata models showed that, although for regular grammars there was always a corresponding deterministic automaton, for BNF grammars there was none unless the grammar was unambiguous and met some other restrictions as well. A major advance came with the discovery by Knuth of a class of grammars called *LR grammars*. These are a restricted class of BNF grammars for which simple automata exist that can parse an input string without guessing, i.e., that are deterministic. Study of the class of LR grammars and their associated automata led ultimately to various classes of LR grammars for which there exist extremely efficient parsing algorithms, defined as special types of automata. The theoretical studies also showed algorithms for taking a BNF grammar, determining if it meets the restrictions for an LR grammar (or a restricted LR grammar), and then generating the associated definition of an automaton to recognize the language defined by the grammar.

Effect on practice. The theoretical studies of grammars and automata provided the basis for the construction of a practical *parser generator*, a program that takes a BNF grammar as its input and produces as its output an efficient parser for the language defined by the grammar. Many different parser generators have been constructed, based on different models of formal grammars and automata. It is now a routine procedure to use a parser generator to automatically generate a good parser for a language from its BNF grammar. For the language implementor, a difficult problem has been reduced to a simple procedure.

Similar research efforts directed toward the other parts of a compiler, the lexical-analysis, semantic-analysis, optimization, and code-generation phases, have led to the development of methods for treating these phases that are also based on formal models. As a result of these theoretical studies, methods exist for automating most of the work of creating a compiler for a new language or machine.

11-2   PROBLEMS IN SEMANTICS

In this section we consider three problem areas that are concerned with the meaning of a program—that is, with the function that a program computes. The problems of syntax and translation in the preceding section are more concerned with the form of a program than with its function in any general sense. Of course, translation of a program must preserve the function computed by it, so semantics is necessarily a part of those issues as well, but in a less central way.

Problem 1: Definition of Semantics

The practical problem. A manual for a programming language must define the meaning of each construct in the language, both alone and in conjunction with other language constructs. The problem is quite similar to the problem of definition of syntax. A language provides a variety of different constructs, and both the language user and the implementor require a precise definition of the semantics of each construct. The programmer needs the definition so as to be able to write correct programs and to be able to predict the effect of execution of any program statement. The implementor needs the definition so as to be able to construct a correct implementation of the language.

In most language manuals, the definition of semantics is given in ordinary prose. Typically a production (or productions) from a BNF or other formal grammar is given, to define the syntax of a construct, and then a few paragraphs of prose and some examples are given to define the semantics. Unfortunately the prose is often ambiguous in its meaning, so that different readers come away with a different interpretation of the semantics of a language construct. A programmer may misunderstand what his program will do when executed, and an implementor may implement a construct differently from other implementors of the same language. As with syntax, some method is needed for giving a readable, precise, and concise definition of the semantics of an entire language.

Some theoretical models and results. The problem of semantic definition has been the object of theoretical study for as long as the problem of syntactic definition, but a satisfactory solution has been much more difficult to find. Many different methods for the formal definition of semantics have been developed. There are three general classes of such methods:

1. *Operational methods.* An operational definition of a programming language is a definition organized around a formal model of how programs in the language are executed on a virtual computer. It corresponds to an abstraction from our understanding of how languages are implemented. Typically the definition of the virtual computer is described as an automaton, but an automaton that is far more complex than the simple automata models used in the study of syntax and parsing. The automaton has an internal state that corresponds to the internal state of a program when it is executing; that is the state contains all the values of the variables, the executable program itself, and various system-defined housekeeping data structures. A set of formally defined operations are used to specify how the internal state of the automaton may change, corresponding to the execution of one instruction in the program. A second part of the definition specifies how a program text is translated into an initial state for the automaton. From this initial state, the rules defining the automaton specify how the automaton moves from state to state until (hopefully) a final state is reached. Such an operational definition of a programming language may represent a fairly direct abstraction of how the language might actually be implemented, or it may represent a more abstract model that might be the basis for a software interpreter for the language, but not for an actual production implementation. The *Vienna Definition Language* is an example of the operational approach.

2. *Functional or denotational methods.* A second class of semantic definition methods attempt to directly construct a definition of the function that each program in the language computes. This definition is built up

hierarchically through definition of the function computed by each individual program construct. As discussed in Chapters 3-5, each primitive and programmer-defined operation in a program represents a mathematical function. The sequence-control structures of the language may be used to compose these functions into larger sequences, represented in the program text by expressions and statements. Statement sequences and conditional branching are readily represented as functions constructed out of the functions represented by their individual components. The function represented by a loop is usually defined recursively, as a recursive function constructed from the components of the loop body. Ultimately, a complete functional model of the entire program can be derived. The method of *denotational semantics* of Scott and Strachey and the method of *functional semantics* of Mills are examples of this approach to semantic definition.

3. *Axiomatic methods.* A third class of methods for semantic definition define the semantics of each syntactic construct in the language directly by giving an axiom or rule of inference that may be used to deduce the effect of execution of that construct. To understand the meaning of an entire program, one uses the axioms and rules of inference somewhat as in ordinary proofs in mathematics. Beginning with the initial assumption that the values of the input variables meet certain constraints, the axioms and rules of inference may be used to deduce the constraints met by the values of other variables after execution of each program statement, until ultimately the results of the program are proven to meet the desired constraints on their values in relation to the input values (that is, that the output values represent the appropriate function computed from the input values). The method of *axiomatic semantics* developed by Hoare is an example of this method.

The various alternative semantic definition methods within each of these classes have provided the basis for extensive formal study of programming language semantic issues. The work on program correctness proofs, described below, has been closely associated with the development of axiomatic semantics. Denotational semantics has provided the basis for a deeper understanding of the sense in which a program computes a function. Operational semantic definitions have led to discovery of subtle issues in language implementations that are often not apparent to language implementors.

Effect on practice. Formal semantic definitions are becoming an accepted part of definition of a new language. For example, one of the requirements imposed during the definition of Ada was that a formal semantic definition be constructed for Ada. The operational formal semantic definition of PL/I was used as the basis for the standard PL/I definition, although the formal notation was not retained in the standard. The effect of axiomatic semantics on proofs of program correctness is discussed below. However, the effect of formal semantic definition studies on the practice of language definition has not been as strong as the effect of study of formal grammars on definition of syntax. No single semantic definition method has been found useful for both user and implementor of a language. The operational methods may provide a good formal model of implementation that an implementor can use, but these definitions are usually too detailed to be of much value to the user. Functional and denotational methods do not provide much guidance to the implementor and have usually proven too complex to be of direct value to users. Axiomatic methods are more directly understandable by a language user, but they cannot generally be used to define a language completely without becoming extremely complex, and they provide no guidance to the implementor.

The practical impact of semantic definition has been felt most strongly in the use of such definitions during the design of a language to detect and clarify subtle points that might otherwise lead to ambiguities in the definition. The final definition of a new language, however, is still ordinarily presented using prose. The denotational semantic definition of Ada played a significant role during the definition of that language; the final Ada manual, however, presents the language in English prose (with a BNF grammar defining the syntax formally).

Problem 2: Proving a Program Correct

The practical problem. Testing a program cannot insure that the program is without errors, except in very simple cases. A program is tested with some test-data sets and the results are compared with the input data. If the results are consistently correct for a substantial number of test cases, then the program is usually pronounced "debugged." However, in truth only those test-data sets actually tried are known to work correctly. The program may still be in error for other input-data sets. To test all the possible input-data sets for a program is ordinarily impossible. Thus the tester must be satisfied with a less-than-complete guarantee of a correct program. If some method could be found that would guarantee correctness of a program without relying on testing, then programs could consistently be made more reliable.

Some theoretical models and results. The theoretician observes that a program computes a function. The programmer must know what function the program should compute. Suppose a separate specification of the function were made, as part of the initial design of the program. And suppose that from the program, it were possible to determine the function that the program actually computed. If the program could in fact be shown to compute exactly the specified function, then it would have been proven to be correct, without testing. The axiomatic and denotational methods for semantic definition provide a formal basis for deducing the function computed by a program. Mathematics, and in particular the area of formal logic, provides various notations for specifying functions. The *predicate calculus* is a notation from formal logic that is particularly useful for specifying complex functions precisely. Several approaches to proving the correctness of programs rely on the basic idea that the function desired is specified using the predicate calculus, and the program is then analyzed to determine if the function it computes is in fact that specified by the predicate-calculus formula. The method of axiomatic semantics is particularly convenient for this purpose, because the use of axioms and rules of inference to derive the function computed by a program is quite similar to the methods used in formal logic to deduce the proof of a mathematical theorem. These studies of formal methods for proving the correctness of programs have led to some deep insights into the structures in programming languages that inhibit such proofs and that make such proofs easy. The same studies have illuminated some of the reasons that certain programming language constructs are hard for programmers to understand and work with correctly, for these often are the same structures that cause difficulty for formal methods of proof.

Another part of these theoretical studies has been the development of systems for *automating* the proof of correctness of a program. The proof methods developed in these studies tend to be tedious to apply to real programs. The proofs involve many formal steps and much detail. An error in the proof may make it appear that a program is correct when in fact it is not. For these reasons, it is desirable to automate the proof procedure, so that from the functional specification of the program and the program itself, an automatic program-proving system can derive the complete proof with little or no human intervention.

Effect on practice. Methods for program proving are now widely understood to be useful primarily during the design of a program, so that, in a sense, the program is proven as it is written. The use of program proofs for programs that have been written in ordinary ways, without being structured so as to be easy to prove correct, has generally been found to be difficult or impossible. The methods for program proof, although useful, are not powerful enough to deal with extremely complex program structures such as those found in older programs that have been modified repeatedly in production use. Program proof methods are commonly taught to practicing programmers, as well as being part of many introductory programming courses.

Another important impact of this theoretical work has been in its effect on the design of languages. Language features that inhibit proof of the correctness of programs are now generally considered undesirable if an adequate substitute is available that is more amenable to correctness proof.

For example, work on correctness proofs has been instrumental in showing the undesirability of *aliasing* in language design, as discussed in Sec. 7-1. The systems for automated correctness proofs that have been developed from theoretical studies are not generally powerful and efficient enough for proof of large programs, but they have proven useful in proof of small to medium-scale programs for applications where extremely high reliability is required. However, owing to the possibility of a correctness proof having a flaw (e.g., an automated correctness-proof system is itself a program that may contain errors), the practical combination of testing *and* proof of correctness is ordinarily used, rather than just correctness proof alone.

Problem 3: The Simplest Universal Language

The practical problem.   Our final problem is somewhat more general than the preceding. When programming in a language, say language A, it is usually apparent that an equivalent program might be written in language B. For example, if you write a payroll computation program in COBOL, the same program might equivalently be written in PL/I or FORTRAN, and perhaps with more difficulty in APL or LISP. Is there a program that can be written in one language for which there is really no equivalent program possible in one of the other languages? For example, is there a program that can be written in SNOBOL4 or Pascal that has no equivalent in FORTRAN? A *universal programming language* is a language that is general enough to allow any computation to be expressed. Our problem might be expressed by asking: *Are all the standard programming languages universal?* If not, then what sorts of programs can one express that another cannot; if so, then why do we need all these different languages? If all are universal, then perhaps we should find the simplest universal programming language and dispense with the others altogether.

Some theoretical models and results.   To abstract from this practical problem, note first that the question may be phrased in terms of the function computed by a program. To say that a program P written in language A is equivalent to a program Q written in language B must mean that the two programs compute the same function. That is, each program takes the same sets of possible input data and produces the same results in each case. A universal programming language is one in which any *computable function* can be expressed as a program. A function is computable if it can be expressed as a program in some programming language. This statement of the problem sounds a bit circular because we are up against a fundamental difficulty: how to define the concept of a computable function. To say a function is computable means, intuitively, that there is some procedure that can be followed to compute it, step-by-step, in such a way that the procedure always terminates. But to define the class of all computable functions, we must give a programming language or virtual computer that is universal—i.e., in which any computable function can be expressed. But we do not know how to tell whether a language is universal; that is the problem.

Surprisingly, this problem had already arisen in theoretical studies even before the invention of computers. Mathematicians in the 1930s had studied the problem of defining the class of computable functions. Several had invented simple abstract machines or automata that might serve to define the class of computable functions. The most widely known of these is the *Turing machine*, named for its inventor, the mathematician Alan Turing [1936].

A Turing machine has only a single data structure, a variable-length linear array called the *tape*. Each component of the tape contains just a single character. There is also a single pointer variable, called the *read head*, that points to some component of the tape at all times. The Turing machine is controlled by a program that involves only a few simple operations:

a. The character at the tape position designated by the read head can be read or written (replaced by another character). The program can branch depending on the value read. It can also use unconditional **goto**'s to construct loops.

b. The read-head pointer can be modified to point to the tape component one to the left or one to the right of its current position. If this shift of the read head moves its pointer off the end of the tape, then a new component is inserted at that end, with an initial value of # (the null character).

The operation of a Turing machine begins with its tape containing the input data and its read head positioned at the leftmost character in the input data. The Turing machine performs a sequence of the simple operations above, in the process modifying the contents of its tape (and possibly extending it as well). If it finally halts, the tape contains the results computed.

A Turing machine is an extremely simple abstract machine. Note that it cannot even do arithmetic. If you wish it to add two numbers, it must be programmed using only the operations above. And no other variables or data structures are allowed; only the single tape for storage (but note that the storage capacity of the tape itself is unlimited).

Can a Turing machine do *anything* useful? Several example programs might be given to convince you that it can at least be programmed to do some simple things like addition and subtraction. However, the argument that we really wish to make is a lot stronger: a Turing machine can do *everything* useful (in the realm of computations)! That is, we would like to show that every computation can be expressed as a program for a Turing machine, and thus the language used for programming a Turing machine is a universal language, in spite of the fact that it allows only one vector and no arithmetic,

352   Theoretical Models / Ch. 11

no subroutines, and none of the other structures that we associate with ordinary programming languages.

The formal statement of this idea is known as *Church's thesis* (after the mathematician A. Church): *any computable function can be computed by a Turing machine*. Church's thesis is not a theorem that can be proven. It is a hypothesis that might be disproven if a computation could be defined in some other programming language and be shown to have no equivalent as a computation for a Turing machine. However, Church's thesis has been considered for many years by many mathematicians. Many different real and abstract computers and languages have been invented, and it has been proven repeatedly that each alternative method proposed for producing a universal machine or language is in fact no more powerful than a Turing machine. That is, each function that can be computed using the new language or machine can be represented as a program for a Turing machine. Thus, although Church's thesis may sound absurd to anyone familiar with programming in a "real" programming language, we have to regard it as correct.

The central fact that the Turing machine illustrates is this: *It takes almost no machinery to achieve universality, other than some sort of unlimited storage capacity*. Even an extremely simple set of data structures and operations is sufficient to allow any computable function to be expressed. Many other simple universal machines and languages have been the object of theoretical studies. Another that is interesting is the *two-counter machine*, an abstract machine (or language) that has only *two* integer variables, together with operations that add one, subtract one, and test for zero on the values of these variables. Can you imagine trying to write a large and complex payroll program in a language that only allows you to use two integer variables? But it can be done (theoretically), provided only that the implementation allows the values of the variables to be arbitrarily large integers.

The study of Turing machines and other simple universal machines and languages has led to some other surprising results. Among these are a number of results showing that certain problems are *undecidable*; that is, there is no general algorithm for their solution, even in the context of these simple machines. The most widely known of these is the *halting problem*. Suppose you ask the question: Is there a general algorithm for determining whether any given Turing machine will ever halt when given any particular character string as its input data? This is the halting problem, and Turing's original theoretical studies in 1936 showed that the halting problem was undecidable: there could exist no general algorithm to solve the problem for all Turing machines and all input data sets.

Effect on practice.   The study of these simple universal languages and machines leads to the conclusion that any programming language that might reasonably be used in practice is undoubtedly a universal language, if bounds on execution time and storage are ignored. Thus the programmer who steadfastly refuses to use any language other than, e.g., FORTRAN, because he "can do anything he wants in FORTRAN," is in fact correct. It may be difficult, but it certainly can be done. The differences among programming languages are not *quantitative* differences in what can be done, but only *qualitative* differences in how elegantly, easily, and effectively things can be done.

Finally, becuse of the undecidability of questions associated with simple abstract machines, such as the halting problem for Turing machines, it is known that the similar problems for real languages also have no solutions. For example, it is quite hopeless to look for a general algorithm for deciding whether any Pascal program contains an infinite loop that will cause the program to fail to halt for some input data set. The problem for Pascal is just the halting problem in a slightly different context.

11-3 CONCLUSION

Practicing programmers often fail to appreciate the value of theoretical models and studies in the advancement of programming languages and programming techniques. The abstraction necessary as the first step in constructing a theoretical model of a practical problem sometimes appears to simplify to the point that the core of the practical problem is lost. In fact, this can and often does happen; by choosing the wrong abstraction, the theoretician may study a theoretical model and produce results that cannot be translated back into a solution to the original practical problem. However, as this chapter has tried to indicate, when the right abstraction is found, theoretical studies may produce results of the deepest practical impact.

11-4 REFERENCES AND SUGGESTIONS FOR FURTHER READING

Formal models of syntax, parsing, and translation are widely used in analysis and implementation of compilers and translators (see the references at the end of Chapter 9). Harrison [1978] and Hopcroft and Ullman [1979] provide overviews of some of the many different models of formal grammars and automata. Theoretical models supporting studies of various aspects of programming languages and their implementation are found in Wulf et al. [1981], the four volumes edited by Yeh [1977], Gries (ed.) [1978], Wasserman [1980], and another collection by Yeh [1976], among others.

Formal semantic definitions and program verification are a central concern of Dijkstra [1976], DeBakker [1980], Manna [1974], Neuhold (ed.) [1978], and Anderson [1979]. Two languages designed with particular attention to issues associated with the verification of program correctness are GYPSY (Ambler et al. [1977]) and EUCLID (Lampson et al. [1977]).

Marcotty et al. [1976] survey the issues in formal semantic definition and describe several methods. Gordon [1979] provides a good introduction to denotational semantics; Dunlop and Basili [1982] describe Mills functional semantics and contrast it with denotational semantics. Lucas and Walk [1969] describe the operational method called the *Vienna Definition Language* that was used for a formal semantic definition of PL/I. A denotational semantic definition of most of Ada is given in (Ada [1980]); an axiomatic definition of most of Pascal is given by Hoare and Wirth [1973]. Donahue [1976] and Hoare and Lauer [1974] contrast these varying approaches and recommend a combination of equivalent definitions, each used for different purposes.

This chapter has been able to touch on only a few of the many fascinating theoretical models and results in the study of universal languages and abstract automata such as the Turing machine. One of the best introductions to this area is given by Minsky [1967].

PART 2

LANGUAGES

CHAPTER 12

FORTRAN 77

FORTRAN is a language widely used for scientific and engineering computation. This chapter provides an overview of the major features and concepts found in FORTRAN 77, which is the most recent standard version of the language. Like the subsequent chapters describing other languages, this chapter does not attempt to give a complete description of FORTRAN 77. Instead it provides an overview that emphasizes the aspects of the language that are most important or that tend to set it apart from other languages. A comprehensive definition of the language may be found in (FORTRAN [1978]).

FORTRAN was the first high-level programming language to become widely used. The earliest versions were designed and implemented in the mid-1950s. At that point in time, the utility of any high-level language was open to question by programmers schooled in assembly language programming. Their most serious complaint concerned the efficiency of execution of code compiled from high-level language programs. As a result, the design of the earliest versions of FORTRAN was oriented heavily toward providing execution efficiency, and this concern has remained a major force guiding each subsequent revision of the design. The early history of FORTRAN development is described by Backus [1981] and Sammet [1969]. The first standard definition of the language was adopted in 1966 (FORTRAN [1966]). A major revision was made in this standard in the

1970s, leading to the current standard, which is generally known as *FORTRAN 77* to distinguish it from the earlier standard version.

12-1   BRIEF OVERVIEW OF THE LANGUAGE

The design of FORTRAN centers around the primary goal of execution efficiency. The language structures are generally simple, and much of the design is rather inelegant, but the goal of execution efficiency is achieved— FORTRAN can be implemented on most conventional computers so that program execution is more efficient than for any of the other languages described here.

A FORTRAN program consists of a main program and a set of subprograms, each of which is compiled separately from all the others, with the translated programs linked into final executable form during loading. Each subprogram is compiled into a statically allocated code segment and activation record. No run-time storage management is provided; all storage is allocated statically before program execution begins.

Only a restricted set of data types is provided in FORTRAN: four types of numeric data (integer, real, complex and double-precision real), Boolean data (called *logical*), arrays, character strings, and files. An extensive set of arithmetic operations and mathematical functions is provided, reflecting the orientation of the language toward engineering and scientific computation. Relational and Boolean operations and simple selection from arrays using subscripting are provided. Both sequential and direct-access files are supported, and a flexible set of input-output facilities and format specification features are available.

The greatest weakness of FORTRAN lies in its restricted data structuring facilities, which are essentially restricted to arrays and character strings of fixed declared length. No facilities are provided for type definitions or data abstraction. Subprograms (procedures and functions) provide the only abstraction mechanism.

Sequence-control structures include expressions with the usual infix and prefix operations and function calls. Statement sequence control relies heavily on statement labels and GOTO statements. An IF...THEN...ELSE conditional is provided and a single form of iteration statement. Subprogram sequence control involves nonrecursive call and return; alternatively, control may be returned to a labeled statement in a calling program through use of a label passed as a parameter.

Only two levels of referencing environment are provided, global and local. The global environment may be partitioned into separate common environments (called *COMMON blocks*) that are shared among sets of subprograms, but only data objects may be shared in this way. Subprogram names are global to the entire program. Parameters are uniformly trans-mitted by reference (or value-result).

The language is intended for a batch-processing operating and pro-gramming environment. No special features are included to support the construction of large programs beyond the provision for independent compilation of subprograms.

12-2 AN ANNOTATED EXAMPLE: SUMMATION OF A VECTOR

A simple FORTRAN program for summation of a vector of real numbers is given in Fig. 12-1. The program consists of a main program and a function subprogram. The subprogram, SUM, accepts a vector V and its length N as arguments and produces as its result the sum of the elements of the vector. The main program, MAIN, is a simple test program that reads in an integer K, followed by a sequence of K real numbers that are stored in a vector A. It then calls SUM to sum the vector. The result is printed and the program loops to read in a new set of test data until a zero value is read for K. This program is the FORTRAN analogue of the similar example programs given for PL/I, Pascal, and Ada in subsequent chapters. The annotations below refer to the line numbers to the left of the program listing, which are not a part of the program itself. Each statement actually begins with a *statement label* field (the first five characters of each line), which may contain an integer statement label, such as the labels 100 and 200 in Fig. 12-1.

```
Line

  1            PROGRAM MAIN
  2            PARAMETER (MAXSIZ=99)
  3            REAL A(MAXSIZ)
  4     100    READ *, K
  5            IF (K.LE.0 .OR. K.GT.MAXSIZ) STOP
  6            READ *, (A(I),I=1,K)
  7            PRINT *, (A(I),I=1,K)
  8            PRINT *, 'SUM =', SUM(A,K)
  9            GO TO 100
 10            END
 11            FUNCTION SUM(V,N)
 12            REAL V(N)
 13            SUM = 0.0
 14            DO 200 I = 1,N
 15     200    SUM = SUM + V(I)
 16            RETURN
 17            END
```

Fig. 12-1   Example of a FORTRAN 77 program

Line 1. The main program definition begins here and extends through line 10. Although both the main program, MAIN, and the subprogram SUM appear together, they are compiled completely independently by the FORTRAN compiler; that is, no information about MAIN is used during the compilation of SUM, and vice versa.

Line 2. A programmer-defined constant, MAXSIZ, is declared as having the value 99. The PARAMETER declaration is the FORTRAN equivalent of the constant definitions of Pascal and Ada.

Line 3. A vector A of real numbers is declared. The subscript range is from 1 (the default lower bound) to 99 (the value of MAXSIZ). Storage for A and all other FORTRAN data objects is ordinarily allocated statically during program execution.

Line 4. A single integer value is read from the standard input file, converted to the hardware integer representation, and stored as the value of variable K. Variable K is declared implicitly by its use in this statement. Its type is determined by a *naming convention* which specifies *integer* type because its name begins with a letter in the range I-N. The "*" indicates that *list-directed* input is being used, in which the FORTRAN *read* procedure scans the input file to find the next integer value. Alternatively, the programmer could explicitly define the format of the data on the input file.

Line 5. The main program terminates here if the value of K is not in the range 1-99. The STOP statement may be used to terminate execution of a program at any point.

Line 6. A sequence of K real-number values are read from the standard input file, converted to an internal floating-point number representation, and stored as the values of the elements of vector A. Again list-directed input is used so that the numbers on the input file are written separated by spaces, and no special programmer-defined format is needed. The variable I used in the statement serves only as a local integer counter within this statement and is not visible outside.

Line 7. The input data values are printed out immediately on the standard output file using a system-defined output format.

Line 8. On a separate line, the heading "SUM =" is printed, followed on the same line by the result returned by the function SUM. The arguments to SUM are the vector A and its length K.

Line 9. Control is transferred to line 4 to repeat the sequence until K has a value outside the range 1-99.

Line 10. Physical end of the main program.

Lines 11-17. Definition of the function SUM. These lines could be compiled separately, with the resulting object program linked to that for the main program during final loading prior to execution.

Line 11. The specification for function SUM is partially given. The formal parameters, V and N, are listed. The type of value returned by SUM is determined by the naming convention mentioned above to be *real* because the function name begins with S. By the same convention, N is of type *integer*.

Line 12. Formal-parameter vector V is explicitly declared as having elements of *real* type and a subscript range from 1 (the default lower bound) to N. Both V and N are transmitted by reference to SUM, so the length of the actual-parameter vector A transmitted from the main program is not affected by this declaration, but only the first N components of V are accessible within SUM regardless of its actual length.

Line 13. The value to be returned by the function is set initially to zero. The "=" indicates assignment in FORTRAN.

Line 14. A loop starts that is repeated, with the value of variable I moving through the range 1 to N in steps of 1. I is declared implicitly by use and is of type *integer* according to the naming convention. The loop body consists of the single statement labeled 200 in the next line.

Line 15 The elements of vector V are summed, using the function name as a local variable to collect the partial sums. The final value assigned to SUM before termination of the loop becomes the result returned from the function.

Line 16. Control returns to the caller of the function.

Line 17. Physical end of the function definition.

12-3   DATA TYPES

FORTRAN provides four numeric data types: integer, real, double-precision real, and complex. A Boolean (called *logical*) type is also included. Arrays, character strings, and files are the only structured data types.

Variables and Constants

The type of a variable must be declared. An explicit declaration such as

```
REAL A, B, SUM
DOUBLE PRECISION Q, R
LOGICAL T
```

may be given. If no explicit declaration appears, a *naming convention* based on the first character of the variable name determines the type. The default naming convention specifies that names beginning with I-N are *integer* variables; all others are *real* variables. However, the programmer may change the naming convention used in any subprogram by beginning the subprogram definition with an IMPLICIT statement. For example, the statement

IMPLICIT INTEGER (A-Z)

at the start of a subprogram causes the type *integer* to be assumed for all variables not explicitly declared.

The implicit declaration of variables simplifies the writing of a FORTRAN program. However, it has the troublesome effect that when a variable name is misspelled in writing a statement, the compiler assumes the variable is a new variable, gives it the implicit type, and proceeds without an error message, thus masking a common programming error.

Programmer-defined constants may be included by use of a PARAMETER statement at the beginning of a subprogram, e.g.,

PARAMETER (KMAX=100, MIDPT=50)

The implicit type determined by the naming convention applies to defined constants as well.

Type Checking

Static type checking is used in FORTRAN, but the checking is incomplete. Many language features, including arguments in subprogram calls and the use of COMMON blocks, cannot be statically checked, in part because subprograms are compiled independently. Constructs that cannot be statically checked are ordinarily left unchecked at run time in FORTRAN implementations.

Numeric Data Types

The numeric types *integer*, *real*, and *double-precision real* usually are represented directly using hardware number representations. Type *complex* is represented as a pair of real numbers, stored in a two-word block.

An extensive set of primitive operations for arithmetic and for conversion between the four numeric types is provided. The basic arithmetic operations (+, −, *, /) and exponentiation (**) are supplemented by a large set of predefined *intrinsic functions* that include trigonometric and logarithmic operations, square root, maximum and minimum, as well as explicit type-conversion functions for the various numeric types. The usual relational operations on numeric values are also provided, represented as .EQ. for *equal*, .LT. for *less than*, and so on.

Booleans

The Boolean type is called LOGICAL, with the constants .TRUE. and .FALSE.. The operations .NOT., .AND. and .OR. represent the basic Boolean operations; .EQV. and .NEQV. represent Boolean equivalence and its negation, respectively.

Arrays

The subscript ranges for arrays must be explicitly declared, either in a DIMENSION statement (which allows the component type to be determined by the implicit naming convention) or by declaring the array and its component type using one of the declarations mentioned above, e.g.,

$$\text{REAL M(20), N(-5:5)}$$

If the lower subscript bound is omitted, it is assumed to be 1. An array may have up to seven dimensions. Arrays to be shared between subprograms may also be declared directly in COMMON statements (see Sec. 12-6). Subscripts are used to select array components, using the same syntax as for function calls, e.g., M(3) or N(I+2).

Unlike most language definitions, the definition of FORTRAN defines the major features of the storage representation for arrays. Arrays are stored in *column-major order*, as described in Sec. 4-5; e.g., a matrix is stored sequentially by columns rather than by rows. Each array component occupies one *storage unit* (whose size is implementation dependent) if the component type is REAL, INTEGER, or LOGICAL and two storage units if DOUBLE PRECISION or COMPLEX. No descriptor is stored with an array; if needed, it must be stored separately.

The sequential storage representation is critical in the definition of the COMMON and EQUIVALENCE declarations. COMMON is discussed in Sec. 12-6 because its primary purpose is that of setting up shared data between subprograms. The EQUIVALENCE declaration allows more than one simple or subscripted variable to refer to the same storage location.

Example. EQUIVALENCE (X,Y). This declaration specifies that the simple variable names X and Y are to be associated with the same storage location. The value stored at that location may later be retrieved or modified through either of the identifiers X or Y.

Example. EQUIVALENCE (A(1,1),K(1)). This also assumes the declaration

DIMENSION A(10,20),K(21)

The EQUIVALENCE declaration defines the first element of matrix A and the first element of vector K to share the same storage unit. Because of the sequential storage representation assumed for both arrays, however, much more is actually declared implicitly: The entire 21 elements of vector K share storage with the first 21 elements of the sequential representation of matrix A, as shown in Fig. 12-2.

One intent of the EQUIVALENCE statement is to allow the *reuse* of storage reserved for variables and arrays. Because all storage is allocated statically during translation in FORTRAN, an array which is used only in part of the program cannot be destroyed and the storage recovered and used to create another array. The EQUIVALENCE declaration allows the programmer to shoulder the burden of reuse of storage if he wishes. The EQUIVALENCE declaration above, for example, might be used if the programmer were planning to use matrix A only during the first part of his program and vector K only during the last part. He could then set up the storage allocated for A to be used also for K.

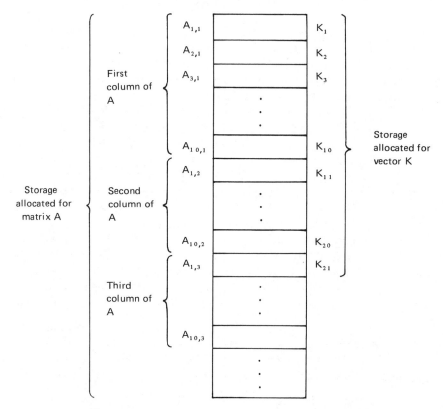

Fig. 12-2 Effect of an EQUIVALENCE statement

The EQUIVALENCE declaration, although useful in a language with only static storage management, is a poor substitute for true dynamic storage management. Essentially the burden of storage allocation and reuse is placed on the programmer, and no safeguards are provided. Note, for example, that arrays A and K are of types real and integer, respectively, in the above. It is possible to store a real number in A(1,1) and later retrieve it through K(1), thinking it an integer. As no run-time descriptors are present in most FORTRAN implementations this most subtle error cannot be detected—the programmer is left to track it down.

Character Strings

Fixed-length character-string variables may be declared; e.g.,

CHARACTER S*10, T*25

defines S and T to contain character strings of length 10 and 25, respectively. The IMPLICIT declaration may also be used to provide a default length and CHARACTER type for variables not explicitly declared. Arrays of character strings and functions that return character strings as their values may also be defined. The concatenation operation (syntax //) allows two character strings to be joined. The relational operations (.EQ., .GT., etc.) are also defined for character strings, using the lexicographic ordering.

The character positions in the value of a character-string variable are numbered from 1 to the declared bound. A substring of a character string may be selected, using the syntax

⟨*char variable name*⟩(⟨*first char posn*⟩:⟨*last char posn*⟩)

Either the first or last character position indicators may be omitted, and the defaults of ⟨*first char posn*⟩=1 and ⟨*last char posn*⟩=*declared bound* are used. Omitting both gives the entire character string.

Assignment and Initialization

Assignment (syntax =) is the basic operation for modifying elements of arrays and values of simple variables. Static type checking is performed, with type conversion between certain numeric data types set up implicitly when the type of the value to be assigned differs from the type declared for the variable or array element which is to be modified.

A number of forms of assignment statement are provided. An *arithmetic assignment statement* is used to assign a numeric value to a simple variable or array element. For example,

$$X = Y + Z \quad \text{or} \quad A(1,2) = U - V * W$$

A *logical assignment statement* is used to assign a logical (Boolean) value to a logical variable or array element, using a logical expression to define the value. For example,

$$L = X.LT.Y.AND.Z.GT.0.0$$

Assignment to a variable of type CHARACTER causes the assigned string to be adjusted to the declared length of the receiving variable, either by truncation (if too long) or extension with spaces (if too short). A *statement number assignment statement* is described in Sec. 12-5.

The language contains rather elaborate facilities for assignment of initial values to variables and arrays. Since storage for these data structures normally is allocated during translation, the initial value assignments are also done during translation, and no run-time cost is incurred. A *data initialization statement* is used for this purpose. The data initialization statement is composed of a list of simple and subscripted variables together with a corresponding list of initial values to be assigned. For example,

$$DATA X/1.0/,Y/3.1416/,K/20$$

defines the initial values of the variables X, Y, and K to be 1.0, 3.1416, and 20, respectively. X, Y, and K must be local variables. Initial values may be assigned to global variables and arrays (defined in COMMON blocks; see Sec. 12-6), but such assignments must be made using the data initialization statement within a special *block data subprogram* which consists only of the special header BLOCK DATA, followed by COMMON declarations and data initialization statements for the COMMON variables and arrays. The result of translation of such a block data subprogram is a set of loader tables which are used by the loader at the end of translation to initialize the appropriate storage locations before execution begins.

Files and Input-Output Operations

Both sequential and direct-access files are supported and an extensive set of input-output operations is provided. There are nine special statements used for input-output operations. READ, WRITE, and PRINT specify the actual transfer of data. OPEN, CLOSE, and INQUIRE allow the status, access method, and other properties of a file to be set or queried. BACKSPACE, REWIND, and ENDFILE provide positioning of the file-position pointer.

A textfile (sequence of characters) in FORTRAN is termed a *formatted* file; other files are *unformatted*. READ, WRITE, and PRINT statements convert data values from internal storage representations to character form during transfer to formatted files. Data transfer to an unformatted file leaves the data in its internal representation. A READ, WRITE, and PRINT to a formatted file may be *list-directed*, which means that no explicit format specification is given; an implicit, system-specified format is used instead, as in the example of Fig. 12-1. Alternatively an explicit format may be provided by the programmer. Ordinarily a FORMAT statement is used:

⟨*stmt number*⟩ FORMAT (⟨*sequence of format specifications*⟩)

and the ⟨*stmt number*⟩ is designated in the READ, WRITE, or PRINT statement. For example, to read input data that consists of a sequence of integers formatted eight per line in five-character fields, the READ and FORMAT statements might be

$$\text{READ } 200, \text{ N, (M(K), K=1,7)}$$
$$200 \quad \text{FORMAT (8I5)}$$

The READ statement specifies that the first integer is read into variable N, and the next seven into the components 1-7 of vector M. The FORMAT statement specifies "I" (integer) format, five digits per integer, repeated eight times across the line beginning in the first character position. A large number of possible format specifications are provided for the various kinds of numeric and character data, as well as specification of spacing, tabs, line breaks, and the like.

To specify an exception handler for an end-of-file condition or an error during an input-output operation, a statement number is provided in the READ or WRITE statement designating a statement in the subprogram executing the READ or WRITE to which control should transfer if the exception is raised. For example

READ (UNIT=2, FMT=200, END=50, ERR=90) N, (M(K), K=1,7)

is the extended form of the READ above which specifies a transfer to statement number 50 on an end-of-file condition and statement number 90 on an error. The UNIT=2 designation specifies that the file is to be found on the input device numbered "2".

The format conversions provided by the input-output operations may also be invoked to convert a character string stored in a variable or array into internal binary storage representations in another variable or array of numeric or logical type (or vice versa). The same READ, WRITE, and FORMAT statements are used, but the "UNIT" specification is now a variable name; e.g.,

READ (UNIT=A,...*as above*...) ...

specifies that the data is to be "read" from character-string variable A, just as though A were an external file, converted to internal integer representation, and stored in M and N as before. Input using such *internal files* is often useful where the exact form of the input data is not known in advance. The data may be read in character form, inspected, and then converted as required.

The format specifications used to control input and output are treated as character strings. During translation they are stored in character-string form and interpreted dynamically by the READ, WRITE, and PRINT procedures as needed during execution. A format specification (character string) may be dynamically created or read in during program execution and subsequently used to control input-output conversions. The result is a flexible and powerful input-output system.

12-4   SUBPROGRAMS

Subprograms form the only abstraction mechanism in FORTRAN. There are no provisions for definition of new data types or data abstractions.

Three types of subprograms are provided. *Function* subprograms allow the return of a single value of numeric, logical, or character-string type. An example of a function is given in Fig. 12-1. A *subroutine* returns results through changes in its parameters or through nonlocal variables in COMMON blocks. The heading provides only the names of formal parameters, e.g.,

SUBROUTINE SUB1(A, B, C)

and the types and other attributes of the parameters are declared separately within the subroutine. The subroutine call statement has the form

CALL ⟨*name*⟩(⟨*actual parameter list*⟩)

Execution of a subprogram ordinarily begins with its first statement. However, an ENTRY declaration may be used to provide another point where the subprogram may begin execution when called using a different name. For example, in the subroutine SUB1, whose heading is given above, an ENTRY declaration

ENTRY SUB2(X, Y)

may be placed at another point in the body, between two statements. A call, CALL SUB2(. . .) then invokes execution of SUB1 at the point of the ENTRY declaration (with possibly a different number and type of parameters). The effect is as though SUB1 and SUB2 were two separate subprograms which share parts of their bodies.

Statement functions.   A function whose value may be computed in a single arithmetic or logical expression may be defined as a *statement function*, local to a particular subprogram. A statement-function definition appears as a single declaration at the beginning of a main program or subprogram definition, following all the other declarations but before executable statements begin. The definition consists only of the function name, a formal parameter list, and the expression by which the value may be computed, e.g.,

$$FN(X,Y) = SIN(X)**2 - COS(Y)**2$$

The implicit typing rules for variable names apply to determine the type of both the formal parameters and the type of the result returned by the function (or types may be declared explicitly in the declarations of the program).

Statement functions may be called as ordinary functions within expressions in the body of the program in which they are defined. They serve mainly as a shorthand in writing expressions that occur repeatedly in assignments. Because the statement-function definition is local to the subprogram in which it is used, each function call is ordinarily replaced by the body of the function during translation, and no execution call and return overhead is necessary—the code is in-line within the executable program.

12-5 SEQUENCE CONTROL

The sequence-control facilities of FORTRAN are straightforward.

Expressions

An expression may be used to compute a single number, logical value, or character string. Associativity of primitive operations is from left to right for all operations except ** (exponentiation), which associates from right to left. Parentheses may be used to control the order of evaluation in the usual way. The primitive operations have the precedence order (from highest to lowest):

$$**$$
$$* /$$
$$+ -$$
$$//$$
$$.EQ. \quad .NE. \quad .LT. \quad .GT. \quad .LE. \quad .GE.$$
$$.NOT.$$
$$.AND.$$
$$.OR.$$
$$.EQV. \quad .NEQV.$$

Functions may not have side effects that affect the result of expression evaluation. The FORTRAN definition explicitly allows any FORTRAN implementation to rearrange the order of evaluation of an expression for optimization in any manner, provided, of course, that the tree structure of the expression defined by the precedence rules and parentheses is not violated. Unfortunately, there is no way that the prohibition on side effects which affect evaluation can be enforced.

Statement Sequence Control

The executable statements are always executed in their physical program sequence unless the sequence is modified by an explicit control statement.

Statement labels. Most explicit sequence control is based on statement labels and GOTOs. Statement labels are restricted to positive integers and thus have little mnemonic value. Each statement begins with a fixed-length *statement-number field* of five characters, which is either left blank or contains the integer statement number.

GOTO statements. Three types of explicit GOTO statements are provided. To effect a direct transfer of control to another statement, the *unconditional* GOTO is used, e.g., GOTO 21. The *assigned* GOTO allows transfer to different statements depending on the value of a *label variable.* The statement has the form GOTO K, where K is a simple integer variable. The value of K must be specified by a special *statement-number assignment statement* of the form

ASSIGN 21 TO K

where 21 is a statement label in the same subprogram. The statement number must be given explicitly in the ASSIGN statement and cannot be computed. These restrictions allow the assigned GOTO to be compiled into a simple run-time unconditional jump, with the ASSIGN statement simply filling in the address of the code for the designated statement.

A third form of GOTO allows multiway branching based on the value of an integer variable. This statement, termed a *computed* GOTO, has the form

$$\text{GOTO } (n_1, n_2, n_3, \ldots, n_p), \text{I}$$

The sequence of statement numbers n_1, n_2, $\ldots$, n_p essentially serves as a vector of statement numbers and I as a subscript. If the value of I is in the range $1 \cdots p$, control is transferred to the statement numbered n_i; otherwise the statement has no effect. Again this structure allows efficient execution because no run-time computation of statement numbers is involved; a *jump-table* implementation may be used (see Sec. 6-3).

Conditional statements. Three conditional branching statements are provided in addition to the computed and assigned GOTOs described above. An *arithmetic* IF statement provides a three-way branch depending on whether the value of an arithmetic expression is negative, zero, or positive:

$$IF(expr)n_{neg}, n_{zero}, n_{pos}$$

where the n's are statement numbers to which control is to be transferred.

A *logical* IF statement allows only execution of a single statement if the value of a logical expression is true, using the syntax

$$IF(expr) \; statement$$

The *statement* may not be a DO statement or another logical IF, thus disallowing any sort of nested statement structure.

A *block* IF statement allows an *if...then...else...endif* alternation of statements without the use of statement labels. The form is

IF ⟨*test expression*⟩ THEN
        — sequence of statements on separate lines
ELSE IF ⟨*test expression* ⟩ THEN
        — sequence of statements on separate lines

        ⋮

ELSE
        — sequence of statements on separate lines
END IF

where the ELSE IF or ELSE parts may be omitted. Note that because of the statement-per-line syntax of FORTRAN, each of the IF, ELSE IF, ELSE, and END IF delimiters must appear as a separate line in the program.

Iteration statements. The FORTRAN iteration statement has only a single form. The header has the structure

$$DO \; stmt\text{-}num \; int\text{-}var = init\text{-}val, term\text{-}val, increment\text{-}val$$

where *int-var* is a simple integer variable to be used as a counter during repeated executions of the body of the loop. *Init-val* is an expression specifying the initial value of the counter, *term-val* likewise specifies the final value for the counter which terminates the loop, and *increment-val* specifies the amount to be added to the value of *int-var* each time through the loop. If omitted, the increment is 1.

The body of the loop extends from the DO statement itself to the statement which is labeled with the *stmt-num* specified in the DO statement. Neither the value of *int-var* nor the values of variables used to specify *init-val, term-val,* or *increment-val* may be modified during execution of the loop. This restriction allows all the loop parameters to be calculated once on first entry to the loop and never recomputed.

Previous versions of FORTRAN tested the termination condition on a DO loop only *after* the first execution of the loop body, with the result that a DO loop body was always executed at least once, even if the initial value of the loop variable was less than the final value specified on first entry to the

372 FORTRAN 77 / Ch. 12

loop. However, FORTRAN 77 provides for the test to be made *before* the body is executed for the first time, so that in the above case, the loop body is never executed at all.

Subprogram Sequence Control

Only the basic call and return structure, without recursion, is provided. The entire execution of a program may be terminated at any point by a STOP statement.

12-6   DATA CONTROL

Referencing in FORTRAN is either local or global; no provision for intermediate levels of nonlocal referencing is made. All identifiers must be declared (explicitly or implicitly) in the program. These structures allow determination of each subprogram's referencing environment during translation and efficient handling of environments during execution with essentially no overhead.

Local Referencing Environments

The local environment of a subprogram consists of the variables and arrays declared at the start of that subprogram. As FORTRAN is ordinarily implemented, the local environment is retained between calls, because the activation record is allocated storage statically as part of the code segment (see Sec. 12-9 below). However, the language definition does not require the retention of local environments unless the programmer explicitly includes the statement "SAVE" within the subprogram. SAVE indicates that the complete local environment is to be retained between calls. Alternatively only specified variables may be saved, e.g., SAVE A,X indicates that only variables A and X must be retained.

Common Environments

If simple variables or arrays are to be shared between subprograms, they must be explicitly declared part of the global referencing environment. This global environment is not set up in terms of single variables and arrays but rather in terms of *sets of variables and arrays*, which are termed COMMON *blocks*. A COMMON block is a named block of storage and may contain the values of any number of simple variables and arrays. For example,

COMMON/BLK/X,Y,K(25)

appearing in a subprogram declares a COMMON block named BLK which contains the variables X and Y and the vector K. Assuming that X and Y have type real and K has type integer, the block BLK occupies 27 storage units in sequence in memory. Suppose that two subprograms SUB1 and SUB2 both contain the above COMMON declaration. Then the block BLK is accessible to both of them, and the identifiers X, Y, and K have the same association (and values) in each. Any other subprogram may gain access to this same COMMON block by inclusion of the same COMMON declaration in the subprogram definition.

The effect of the COMMON declaration is effectively to allow the global referencing environment to be partitioned into *blocks*, so that every subprogram need not have access to all the global environment. The COMMON declaration allows efficient run-time processing, because any reference to a global variable in a subprogram may be immediately compiled into a base-address-plus-offset computation at run time, where the base address is the address of the beginning of the COMMON block.

The COMMON statement is most often used in an identical form in each subprogram accessing a given COMMON block. However, the structure allows other possibilities as well. Observe that it is only the *name* of a COMMON block that is actually a global identifier; the variable and array names in the COMMON statement list are *local* to the subprogram in which the statement appears; i.e., it is only the block of storage containing the values of the identifiers which is actually being shared, not the identifiers themselves. It is thus possible to have different identifiers and to organize the COMMON block differently in each subprogram which uses it. For example, if subprogram SUB1 contained the COMMON statement given above, SUB2 might contain

$$\text{COMMON/BLK/U,V,I(5),M(4,5)}$$

This COMMON block also occupies 27 storage units, and the type assigned to each element of the block is the same in each case. The second COMMON statement assigns a completely different set of identifiers and array structures to the 27 storage units, but such an assignment is valid as long as the overall length and type structure of the block is preserved.

Subprogram Parameters and Results

Parameter transmission is uniformly by reference. Actual parameters may be simple variables, literals, subscripted variables, array names, subprogram names, or arithmetic or logical expressions. The details of transmission by reference for these types of parameters are given in Sec. 7-8.

Results of function subprograms are transmitted by assignment within the subprogram to the name of the subprogram. The name of the subprogram acts as a local variable within the subprogram, and the last assignment made before return to the calling program is the value returned. Functions may return only single numbers, character strings, or logical values as results.

12-7   OPERATING AND PROGRAMMING ENVIRONMENT

FORTRAN is designed for a batch-processing operating and programming environment. The operating environment consists only of sequential and direct-access files, as discussed in Sec. 12-3. Most implementations make provision for calls to subprograms coded in other languages (e.g., assembly languages), to allow access to the operating environment at a low level.

The language provides few features to support a programming environment beyond the provisions for independent compilation of subprograms. However, the simple global referencing environment consisting only of COMMON block names and subprogram names makes it straightforward to combine groups of subprograms written by different programmers into larger programs. The major weakness here is the lack of error checking (e.g., type checking) when program groups are combined. Parameter list and COMMON block inconsistencies must ordinarily be found by the programmer during testing.

12-8   SYNTAX AND TRANSLATION

FORTRAN subprograms are designed to be separately compiled, with the compiled programs linked together by the loader before execution. As a result each subprogram definition contains full declarations for all global as well as local identifiers—variables and arrays in COMMON blocks, parameters, called subprograms and functions, etc. This structure allows translation of each subprogram into efficient executable code, with most error checking performed during translation.

Syntax

Program syntax is semifixed field. A program is a sequence of *lines*, each of 72 characters. The first five characters of a line are reserved for the statement number, if any. Character positions 7-72 contain the statement itself, written in free format with spaces inserted as desired. If a statement is continued to a second line, character position 6 is used to designate a *continuation line*. Each program has a fairly fixed structural format consisting of an initial header followed by declarations, statement function definitions (if any), executable program statements, and a terminating END statement, in that order. Each statement and declaration begins with a key word identifying its type—DO, IF, etc.—except assignment statements and statement function definitions. FORTRAN uses only a standard basic character set, with no unusual special characters.

Individual lines of a FORTRAN program are usually easily understandable. The overall structure of programs, however, tends to be rather opaque because of the heavy use of statement labels and GOTOs in the sequence control mechanisms. Thus it is often difficult to see the overall flow of control in a FORTRAN program. Also the use of mnemonic identifiers is hampered by a restriction to six character identifiers.

Translation

Translation of most FORTRAN statements is straightforward and may proceed on a simple line-by-line basis. Each FORTRAN subprogram is translated separately. The language structures are designed so that the storage requirements of a subprogram may be determined by the translator. The translator is thus able to set up the entire run-time structure for a subprogram as a contiguous block of memory, divided into areas of compiled code, system data, and programmer-defined data structures. Only the linkages to COMMON blocks, system run-time routines, and called subprograms cannot be filled in during initial compilation. However, these linkages may be filled in by the loader when the various separately compiled programs are assembled in memory prior to execution.

Formal Syntax

Although formal definitions of FORTRAN syntax exist, they have been of relatively little importance in the FORTRAN development. In fact, the definition of standard FORTRAN does not utilize a formal grammar for syntax specification. Complete syntactic definition of FORTRAN is made complex by the semifixed field format and by the numerous minor restrictions on various constructs.

12-9 STRUCTURE OF A FORTRAN VIRTUAL COMPUTER

Simulation of a FORTRAN virtual computer on a conventional computer poses few problems. Because storage allocations are static, the entire run-time memory organization may be set before execution begins. Figure 12-3 illustrates a typical run-time memory layout. The memory area is divided

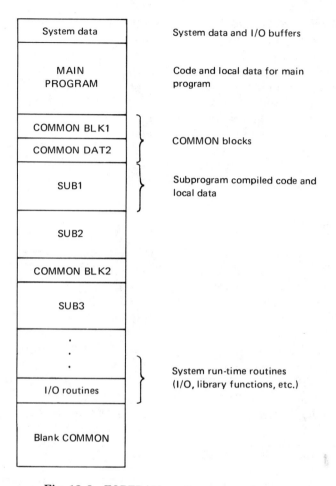

Fig. 12-3 FORTRAN run-time memory layout

into blocks of varying size. Each block contains one subprogram (including code segment and activation record), one COMMON block, or a run-time system routine. The special *blank* COMMON block is used for the COMMON block with a null name. In the usual implementation the loader initially is stored in this block at the beginning of loading. The loader brings in each of the separately compiled subprogram and COMMON blocks, stores them in memory starting at the other end of the available area, and links them together appropriately as required by the compiler-produced loader tables. The space occupied by the loader is allocated for blank COMMON. Although this organization is hidden from the programmer, it gives the special blank COMMON block the property that it cannot be initialized using the DATA statement (because such initialization would entail the loader loading initial values on top of itself).

12-10 REFERENCES AND SUGGESTIONS FOR FURTHER READING

Numerous texts describe the essentials of FORTRAN 77 programming and also the earlier versions of the language, which are still widely used. The standard definition is found in (FORTRAN [1978]). Most implementations extend the standard in various ways. A set of proposed extensions for *real-time processing* is found in (FORTRAN [1981]).

Sammet [1969] provides an extensive collection of references on various aspects of the language as well as an excellent history of its development. Backus [1981] provides a more personal view of FORTRAN's early history. Backus was the leader of the original design group which produced the first published description of the language in 1957 (Backus et al. [1957]).

12-11 PROBLEMS

1. The SAVE statement in FORTRAN allows some or all of the local variables of a subprogram to be retained between calls. The implementation using static storage allocation described in Sec. 12-9 retains *all* local variables regardless of the use of SAVE (the SAVE statement did not appear in older versions of FORTRAN). However, because SAVE must be used in FORTRAN 77, alternative implementations are possible. Describe a different implementation that allows local variables not SAVE'd to be deleted between calls (so that storage is not reserved for them when they are not in use).

2. In FORTRAN (and many other languages, including PL/I and Ada), the same syntax is used for references to array components and for calls to function subprograms and statement functions. For example, in the statement

$$X = Y + F(I,J)$$

F(I,J) might be a reference to a component of an array F or a call on a function F. However in FORTRAN, the compiler has no information when compiling the above statement about the function subprograms that are available. Thus if F is not declared as an array or statement function, the compiler must assume it is a function subprogram, leaving it up to the link editor to determine whether a function subprogram F exists. Explain the problems that arise for the programmer in the case of the two common programming errors: (a) missing declaration for array F and (b) array reference with a misspelled array name, e.g., F instead of FN.

CHAPTER 13

COBOL

COBOL (COmmon Business Oriented Language) has been widely used since the early 1960s for business applications of computers. Like most other widely used languages, COBOL has evolved through a sequence of design revisions, beginning with the first version in 1960 and leading to the latest revision in 1974 (COBOL [1974]). Sammet [1969] gives an excellent history of the development of COBOL through 1968.

COBOL is perhaps the most widely implemented of the languages described in this book, but few of its design concepts have had a significant influence on later languages, with the exception of PL/I. Both of these facts may be partially attributed to its orientation toward business data processing, a major area of computer application, but one in which the problems are of a somewhat unique character: relatively simple algorithms coupled with high-volume input-output (e.g, computing the payroll for a large organization). Most of the other languages described in this book emphasize features supporting complex computations with relatively small amounts of input-output and thus do not benefit greatly from the COBOL design.

Because input-output is a prime concern in business applications programs, the COBOL design emphasizes features for specification of the properties and structure of input-output files. Another important and obvious language characteristic is the English-like syntax of the language statements (aimed at making programs readable enough to be largely self-documenting).

The widespread implementation and use of COBOL has led to efforts to standardize the language definition. The first COBOL standard definition was published in 1968; the latest revised and updated standard appeared in 1974. The standard is organized in a modular fashion which allows the language to be implemented on a wide range of hardware. The definition consists of a *nucleus* and a set of ten *modules*, each of which has one to three *levels*. A minimal COBOL implementation consists of implementation of the features making up the lowest level of the nucleus and of each of the modules (table handling and sequential input-output are the only modules with a nonnull lowest level). Increasingly more powerful and complex COBOL implementations which include more powerful data and control structures and more complex interactions with external files may be constructed by adding higher levels of the nucleus or of some of the modules. On a small computer with limited I/O equipment the minimal COBOL may be reasonable, but for larger computers larger COBOL subsets are appropriate. In this manner the standard COBOL definition attempts to maintain flexibility in implementation without loss of standardization. COBOL programs which run on one COBOL implementation should run with only minor modification on any other COBOL implementation which includes the subset of the original implementation.

13-1 BRIEF OVERVIEW OF THE LANGUAGE

Perhaps the most striking aspect of a COBOL program is its organization into four *divisions*. This organization is largely a result of two design goals: that of separating *machine-dependent* from *machine-independent* program elements and that of separating data descriptions from algorithm descriptions, so that each might be modifiable without affecting the other. The result is a tripartite program organization: The PROCEDURE division contains the algorithms, the DATA division contains data descriptions, and the ENVIRONMENT division contains machine-dependent program specifications such as the connections between the program and external data files. A fourth IDENTIFICATION division begins each program and serves to name the program and its author and to provide other commentary as program documentation.

The COBOL design is based on an essentially static run-time structure. No run-time storage management is required, and many aspects of the language are designed to allow relatively efficient run-time structures to be used (although this goal is less important than that of hardware independence and program transportability).

Data representations in COBOL have a definite business-applications flavor but are rather flexible. The basic data structure is the *record*. Records are also the basis for external data file structures, which play an extremely important role in COBOL. Records may be mixed with ordinary arrays, so that arrays may be components of records and vice versa. Such structures must be fully declared in a program and no run-time variability of structure size is allowed. Individual record elements, array elements, or simple variables must be declared as to type, but an almost unbounded set of possible type declarations may be constructed through PICTURE specifications. Numbers and character strings are the basic elementary data types. The language also provides rather extensive facilities for specifying the properties of external data files.

Built-in primitive operations include simple arithmetic, logical and relational primitives, and some simple character-string scanning and substitution operations. Assignment, which includes automatic type conversion of the assigned value to the type of the receiving variable, is particularly important because of the large variety of possible type specifications allowed. As might be expected, a powerful set of input-output primitives are provided for accessing and manipulating various kinds of external files. These include input-output for sequential, indexed-sequential, and random-access files; a SORT primitive; and a *report generator* for automatic generation of complex output formats.

Sequence control in COBOL includes a statement label—**goto** structure, a rather restricted **if** . . . **then** . . . **else** construct, and a PERFORM statement which serves both as a simple subprogram call statement and as an iteration statement. An exception-handing facility is provided for use on various types of input-output errors. Expressions play a minor role in the language, and no programmer-defined functions are allowed. True subprograms (with parameters and local variables) are infrequently seen; they need not even be implemented in less than full COBOL. The PERFORM statement provides a call-return structure without change in referencing environment. Many (perhaps most) COBOL programs are written as a single routine using a common global referencing environment defined by the DATA DIVISION of the program.

The language is notable for its English-like syntax, which makes most programs relatively easy to read. The language provides numerous optional *noise words* which may be used to improve readability. The syntax makes COBOL programs easy but relatively tedious to write because even the simplest program becomes fairly lengthy (as is seen in the next section). Translation of COBOL into efficient executable code is a complex compilation problem, because of the number of different data representations which may be defined and the large number of options in the way in which many statements may be written. Most of the early COBOL compilers were extremely slow, but more recently improvements in compilation techniques have led to relatively fast COBOL compilers, producing fairly efficient executable code.

13-2 AN ANNOTATED EXAMPLE: SUMMING A LIST OF PRICES

The simple COBOL program illustrated in Fig. 13-1 processes an input file composed of a sequence of *item-name—price* pairs. Each input pair is listed in the output and a final count of the number of input pairs and the total of the item prices is output at the end. The following annotations refer to the line numbers to the left of the listing, which are not a part of the listing.

Lines 1-3. These lines form the IDENTIFICATION DIVISION of the program. They serve only as commentary.

Lines 4-11. These lines form the ENVIRONMENT DIVISION of the program. Line 4 is the required initial statement.

Lines 5-7. The CONFIGURATION SECTION of the ENVIRON-MENT DIVISION. The SOURCE-COMPUTER paragraph identifies the computer on which the program is to be compiled. The OBJECT-COMPUTER paragraph specifies the computer on which the compiled program is to be executed. These designations may serve only as comments, but alternatively the compiler or run-time system may check them and abort compilation or execution if the actual configuration is not the same as that specified.

Lines 8-11. These lines form the INPUT-OUTPUT SECTION, consisting of a single FILE-CONTROL "paragraph," whose purpose is to relate the file names used within the program to actual external files. In this case the file called INP-DATA within the program will actually be the standard system input file INPUT. Similarly, the file called RESULT-FILE within the program will actually be the standard system output file OUTPUT. The names INPUT and OUTPUT are peculiar to the particular COBOL implementation being used.

Lines 12-31. These lines form the DATA DIVISION. Line 12 is the required header. The remaining lines define all the variables and data structures used in the program.

Lines 13-20. These lines form the FILE SECTION of the DATA DIVISION. Each external file used for input or output by the program must be defined, its characteristics specified, and the format (or formats) of a typical data record specified. For this program standard files are used and thus relatively little need be specified. Line 13 is the required header.

Line 14. This line begins the file description (FD) for the file named INP-DATA. Since the file is a standard input file, only the required LABEL

Line

```
1        IDENTIFICATION DIVISION.
2        PROGRAM—ID. SUM—OF—PRICES.
3        AUTHOR. T—PRATT.
4        ENVIRONMENT DIVISION.
5        CONFIGURATION SECTION.
6        SOURCE—COMPUTER. CDC—CYBER.
7        OBJECT—COMPUTER. CDC—CYBER.
8        INPUT—OUTPUT SECTION.
9        FILE—CONTROL.
10           SELECT INP—DATA ASSIGN TO INPUT.
11           SELECT RESULT—FILE ASSIGN TO OUTPUT.
12       DATA DIVISION.
13       FILE SECTION.
14       FD INP—DATA LABEL RECORD IS OMITTED.
15       01   ITEM—PRICE.
16           02   ITEM PICTURE X(30).
17           02   PRICE PICTURE 9999V99.
18           02   FILLER PICTURE X(44).
19       FD RESULT—FILE LABEL RECORD IS OMITTED.
20       01   RESULT—LINE PICTURE X(132).
21       WORKING—STORAGE SECTION.
22       77 TOT PICTURE 9999999V99, VALUE 0, USAGE IS COMPUTATIONAL.
23       77 COUNT PICTURE 9999, VALUE 0, USAGE IS COMPUTATIONAL.
24       01   SUM—LINE.
25           02   FILLER VALUE '  SUM = ' PICTURE X(12).
26           02   SUM—OUT   PICTURE   $$,$$$,$$9.99.
27           02   FILLER VALUE ' NO. OF ITEMS = ' PICTURE X (21).
28           02   COUNT—OUT  PICTURE ZZZ9.
29       01   ITEM—LINE.
30           02   ITEM—OUT   PICTURE X(30).
31           02   PRICE—OUT   PICTURE ZZZ9.99.
32       PROCEDURE DIVISION.
33       START.
34           OPEN INPUT INP—DATA AND OUTPUT RESULT—FILE.
35       READ—DATA.
36           READ INP—DATA AT END GO TO PRINT—LINE.
37           ADD PRICE TO TOT.
38           ADD 1 TO COUNT.
39           MOVE PRICE TO PRICE—OUT.
40           MOVE ITEM TO ITEM—OUT.
41           WRITE RESULT—LINE FROM ITEM—LINE.
42           GO TO READ—DATA.
43       PRINT—LINE.
44           MOVE TOT TO SUM—OUT.
45           MOVE COUNT TO COUNT—OUT.
46           WRITE RESULT—LINE FROM SUM—LINE.
47           CLOSE INP—DATA AND RESULT—FILE.
48           STOP RUN.
```

Fig. 13-1 Example COBOL program

RECORD IS clause is given, specifying that the file has no label at its beginning. The information provided here, together with that obtained from the FILE-CONTROL paragraph (line 10) enables the compiler to set up code for the proper accessing of the file at run time.

Lines 15-18. Description of a typical record in the external file INP-DATA. This declaration sets up a record data structure in central memory having the specified form. Each time a new logical record is read from the external file (as a character string) the input characters are stored in this data structure and then accessed through the identifiers specified in this declaration.

Line 15. The record data structure is named ITEM-PRICE. The 01 preceding the name is a *level number* used to define the hierarchical grouping of elements within the record. The level 01 indicates that a new structure definition is being initiated.

Lines 16-18. The record ITEM-PRICE contains three components. However, because only the first two components, ITEM and PRICE, contain significant data here, the third component, which appears only to fill out the record definition to 80 characters (the length of a record derived from punched card input data), is named with the null name FILLER. This record data structure must be large enough to accommodate the entire record input from the external file at each READ statement, so the FILLER element is required here.

Line 16. The type of the component named ITEM is declared using a PICTURE clause. The PICTURE specification X(30) designates a simple character-string data type of 30 character positions.

Line 17. The component PRICE is declared, using the PICTURE specification 9999V99, to be a number in character-string form consisting of six digits (the six 9's) with the decimal point assumed between the fourth and fifth digits. Because the ITEM element is declared to occupy the first 30 characters of an input record, the PRICE element occupies the thirty-first through thirty-sixth positions. The thirty-seventh through eightieth positions (44 characters) are declared as a *filler* in the next line.

Lines 19-20. The declaration for the output file named RESULT-FILE. Because output lines of varying formats are to be output, it is convenient to define the record structure in central memory for this file to consist of a single long character string of 132 character positions, representing the length of a print line on an external printer. The actual output lines will be built up in other data structures and moved into the RESULT-LINE structure only immediately before output.

Lines 21-31. These lines make up the WORKING-STORAGE SECTION of the DATA DIVISION. Simple variables and records used only as local data structures in the program and not associated with an external file for input and output are declared here.

Line 22. A simple variable (indicated by level number 77) named TOT is declared. The value of TOT will be a positive real number less than 10 million with at most two digits to the right of the decimal. Initially TOT has the value zero. The USAGE IS COMPUTATIONAL clause specifies that TOT is primarily used in arithmetic calculations and should be stored in binary floating-point form (or other form appropriate for direct use in hardware arithmetic operations). Without the USAGE clause TOT would be stored in character-string form as a string of nine digits, and it would then have to be converted to an appropriate hardware representation before each arithmetic operation, at a substantial cost in execution speed.

Line 23. Simple variable COUNT is declared as an integer less than 10,000.

Lines 24-28. These lines define a record data structure of four elements which is used to build up the character-string representing the final output line printed by the program. Line 24 declares the structure name as SUM-LINE.

Line 25. The first element of the record is a character string with a fixed value consisting of six blanks followed by SUM =. Because there will never by any need to access this element individually, it is given the null name FILLER.

Line 26. The element SUM-OUT will contain the number representing the total of the individual item prices input. Because this number is to be part of the output line, the PICTURE clause specifies an appropriate output format for the number. The specification $$,$$$,$$9.99 declares that the value of SUM-OUT will be a number less than 10 million with two digits to the right of the decimal point (all but the leftmost $ counts as a 9). The decimal point will be explicitly inserted between the seventh and eighth digits, any leading zeros beyond the units position will be suppressed and replaced by blanks, commas will be inserted in the usual positions as needed, and a single $ will be printed immediately to the left of the leading digit of the number.

Lines 27-28. The remaining two elements of SUM-LINE are declared: the constant string NO. OF ITEMS, and the four-digit integer COUNT-OUT, whose value will have leading zeros replaced by blanks.

Lines 29-31. The declaration for the record ITEM-LINE, which serves as the record in which another format of output line is constructed. This line is simply the *echo print* of the input line, formatted slightly differently.

Lines 32-48. These lines form the PROCEDURE DIVISION of the program containing the executable program statements. Line 32 is the required header. The division is broken into "paragraphs" by statement labels such as START and READ-DATA, which may be used as objects of GOTO control transfers.

Line 34. The external files names INP-DATA and RESULT-FILE are set up for processing. INP-DATA is to be used for input, and RESULT-FILE for output.

Line 36. The next record of file INP-DATA is read in (as a character string) and stored in the internal record data structure ITEM-PRICE associated with the file. If an end-of-file indicator is read, showing that the file has been completely processed, then control is transferred to the statement labeled PRINT-LINE.

Lines 37-38. The values of variables TOT and PRICE are incremented. Both TOT and COUNT are stored in the hardware number representation, but PRICE is in character-string form and must be converted to hardware form before the addition.

Line 39. The newly input value of PRICE is assigned as the value of PRICE-OUT. Because the PICTURE declarations for the two elements differ, the assigned value is converted to the appropriate format for a value of PRICE-OUT.

Line 40. The character-string value of ITEM is assigned to ITEM-OUT. Because the PICTUREs of the two elements are the same, no conversion is needed.

Line 41. The entire contents of record ITEM-LINE (a string of 37 characters) is copied into the record RESULT-LINE and filled out with blanks to make 132 characters. The resulting character string is output to file RESULT-FILE as the next record.

Line 42. Control is transferred back to the statement labeled READ-DATA to read the next input record (line 35).

Lines 44-45. Control is transferred here when the input file has been completely processed. The final output line is now formatted and output. Line 44 assigns the total of the item prices which has been collected in simple variable TOT to the element SUM-OUT of record SUM-LINE. Because the PICTURE declarations differ, the number is converted from internal binary format (or other hardware representation) to character-string form. Line 45 specifies a similar assignment of the value of COUNT.

Line 46. The contents of record SUM-LINE are copied to record RESULT-LINE, filled out to 132 characters with blanks, and output to file RESULT-FILE.

Lines 47-48. The two external files are "closed" to further processing, and the program ends.

13-3   DATA TYPES

All data declarations in a COBOL program are collected into the separate DATA DIVISION. This division is split into a number of *sections*, the most important of which are the WORKING-STORAGE SECTION and the FILE SECTION. The former includes declarations for each simple variable and local data structure used by the program. The latter contains similar declarations for data records transmitted between central memory and external files. In both these sections the same basic data declaration formats are used. Less commonly used sections contain formats for the optional report generator and declarations for formal parameters (in programs to be called as subprograms).

The central principle of data representation in COBOL is that all data are stored in character-string form at run time, with the exception of those numeric data items explicitly declared with a USAGE IS COMPUTA-TIONAL clause. This character-string data representation serves two important purposes. First, because COBOL is oriented toward applications with high-volume input-output, it allows data to be stored in central memory in a form which may be directly transmitted to an external file without conversion. Numbers, in particular, are not automatically converted to a hardware binary representation on input but instead are converted only when needed as operands in an arithmetic operation. Second, the character-string representation allows data descriptions to be almost entirely independent of particular hardware characteristics such as word length or number representation. As a result COBOL programs are relatively easy to transport.

The character-string machine-independent data declarations exact a price in execution speed, because (1) data items may be split across word boundaries and thus be difficult to access and (2) numbers must be converted to the hardware representation before arithmetic operations and then the result converted back to character-string form before being stored. As a compromise the language provides the optional SYNCHRONIZED declaration which forces a data item to begin or end at a word boundary (or other natural memory division) and the USAGE IS COMPUTATIONAL declaration which allows a hardware number representation to be used for a particular data item. Use of these optional declarations makes the length of data structures or individual items implementation-dependent but may have a dramatic effect on execution speed.

Elementary Data Items and Simple Variables

Every variable used in a COBOL program must be explicitly declared in the DATA DIVISION. COBOL allows individual type declarations to be built up in a large variety of ways. A simple variable occupies a fixed number of character positions at run time, and the declaration of the variable defines the number of character positions as well as the format of the data item.

The PICTURE *Clause.* The primary type declaration for a simple variable (or an element of a larger structure) is specified through a PICTURE *clause* attached to the declaration of the variable in the DATA DIVISION. The simplest form of PICTURE clause specifies only the number of character positions occupied by the data value, as in

77 VAR PICTURE XXXXXXXX.

or equivalently

77 VAR PICTURE X(8).

In these declarations, VAR is the variable name, 77 indicates a simple variable, and XXXXXXXX or X(8) specifies that the value of VAR is a string of eight characters.

A number being input as a simple sequence of digits but which represents an amount in dollars and cents might be described by the PICTURE

AMT PICTURE 9999V99

indicating a data value composed of six digits, with the decimal point positioned between the fourth and fifth digits.

For output a much more elaborate format might be desirable, e.g., if the amount is to appear on a bill or check to be mailed. An appropriate PICTURE might then be

AMT-OUT PICTURE $$$$9.99

The value of AMT-OUT is an *edited number*, a character string of eight characters composed of zero to three blanks, followed by a $, followed by one to four decimal digits, followed by a ., followed by two decimal digits. The number of blanks before the $ is determined by the number of leading zeros in the actual value. Leading zeros are suppressed and the $ "floats" to the right.

These examples illustrate only a few of the possibilities for PICTURE construction. In general, a data item may occupy any fixed number of character positions; each of these character positions may be tagged as containing a digit, a letter, or an arbitrary character; *editing* characters may be added to specify insertion of blanks, zeros, DB, CR, or one of the characters ".,$ / + −"; leading zeros may be suppressed or replaced by *; and so on.

Other clauses for elementary data items. The declaration of a variable or element of a data structure may contain other clauses in addition to the PICTURE declaration. The VALUE clause may be used to define an initial value for the variable; the JUSTIFIED clause determines left or right justification of a character-string value when the value is shorter than the receiving variable. The SYNCHRONIZED and USAGE IS COMPUTA-TIONAL clauses have already been mentioned.

Arithmetic, Relational, and Boolean Operations

Addition, subtraction, multiplication and division operations may be written as separate statements, e.g.,

> ADD X, Y GIVING Z.
> DIVIDE P BY Q GIVING R REMAINDER S.

or alternatively (in most cases) in more conventional form using a COM-PUTE statement:

> COMPUTE Z = X + Y.

COMPUTE assignment statements may also include exponentiation (**). The programmer may specify whether the result assigned is to be truncated or rounded and also may specify an action to be taken in case the result is too large to fit in the receiving location, e.g.,

> MULTIPLY K BY L GIVING M ROUNDED;
> ON SIZE ERROR GO TO MULT-ERR.

Relational and Boolean operations may be used in Boolean expressions in IF, PERFORM, and SEARCH statements. The usual arithmetic relations are provided, and these may be applied to nonnumeric data using the collating sequence defined by the implementation to determine the ordering. The Boolean operators AND, OR, and NOT are primitive. In addition, primitives are provided for testing if the value of a particular data item is strictly numeric or alphabetic.

Records

The basic data structure in COBOL is the *record*. The records used by a program must be completely declared in the DATA DIVISION of the program. Because full declarations are provided, static type checking and relatively efficient run-time storage and accessing of elements of records are possible. Records are declared using an outline format of nested levels, each with a *level number*, as described in Sec. 4-6. Elementary items are declared using the same PICTURE and other clauses described for simple variables. Each elementary item or group of items in the record receives an identifier as a name, which may be used as a subscript in accessing those elements.

At run time a record is represented as a contiguous block of storage. If the record does not involve items declared as COMPUTATIONAL, then this storage area may be considered simply as a long character string, with the elementary item and group names serving as names for various substrings within the area.

Arrays and Mixed Arrays and Records

Records may contain arrays (called *tables*) of one to three dimensions as components. For example, to set up a vector of ten elements, each of which is a five-digit integer, the declaration might be

```
01   ARR.
    02   A OCCURS 10 TIMES PICTURE 99999.
```

ARR is the name of the entire vector; the individual elements may be referenced as A(1), A(2), . . . , A(10).

The OCCURS clause is used to declare a vector, each element of which may be an elementary data item or another record or array. If an element contains an OCCURS clause as well, then the result is a two-dimensional array. Up to three levels of such nesting are allowed. For example,

```
01   THREE-DIM-ARRAY.
    02   PLANE OCCURS 20 TIMES.
        03   ROW OCCURS 30 TIMES.
            04   ELEM OCCURS 10 TIMES PICTURE 9999.
```

defines THREE-DIM-ARRAY as a three-dimensional $20 \times 30 \times 10$ homogeneous array of four-digit integers. Individual elements are accessed by subscripting in the usual way, e.g., ELEM(7,21,3). In addition, individual rows and planes may be accessed as units, e.g., PLANE(12) or ROW(4,5).

More interesting than simple arrays are mixed structures containing both records and arrays. For example, the record declared as

```
01   POPULATION-DATA.
    02   TOTAL-US-POP PICTURE 9(10).
    02   STATE OCCURS 50 TIMES.
        03   STATE-NAME PICTURE X(30).
        03   STATE-POP PICTURE 9(9).
        03   CAPITAL-NAME PICTURE X(30).
        03   CAPITAL-POP PICTURE 9(8).
```

contains an elementary item, TOTAL-US-POP, and a vector, STATE, of 50 items, each of which is a record of four elements.

Most of the complexity of referencing and accessing in such mixed arrays may be dealt with at compile time because of the presence of full declarations with fixed bounds for all arrays. At run time a simple sequential representation suffices.

The REDEFINES *Clause.* The REDEFINES clause allows more than one structure to be described for the same record storage area or part of a storage area. For example, the declaration

        01   ARR.
        02   A OCCURS 10 TIMES PICTURE 99999.

reserves a block of 50 character positions, structured into a vector of 10 five-digit integers. If this declaration were immediately followed by the declaration

        01   NEW-ARR REDEFINES ARR.
        02 B PICTURE 99999.
        02 C OCCURS 5 TIMES.
            03   D PICTURE XXXX.
            03   E PICTURE 99999.

then the same 50-character block would also be used for the record NEW-ARR, as shown in Fig. 13-2. The REDEFINES clause allows an arbitrary number of different structures to be imposed on a single storage area, thus allowing a single character string to be taken apart or built up in a variety of ways. A second use is to provide a form of *variant record* (see Sec. 4-6) in which no explicit tag field is used.

Accessing, Assignment, and Type Conversion

Implicit type conversions caused by an attempt to store a data value in a variable with a different type declaration are an important part of COBOL. Much formatting of data for output is done through such implicit type conversions. The primitive used in making such data transfers (with their associated implicit conversions) is the simple assignment operator MOVE. The statement

                    MOVE A TO B.

assigns a copy of the current value of A as the new value of B. Figure 13-1 contains numerous examples of the use of MOVE. Other COBOL statements involve assignments as well, e.g., the arithmetic statements ADD, SUBTRACT, MULTIPLY, DIVIDE, and COMPUTE.

Accessing of elements of data structures is controlled by subscripting.

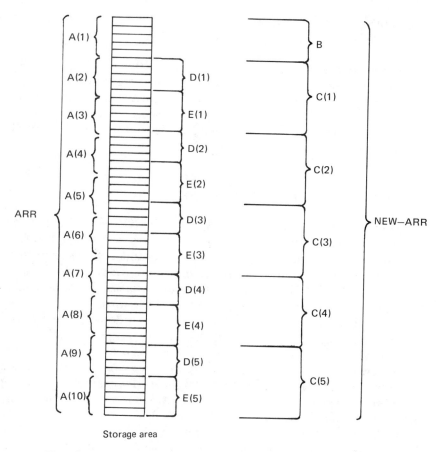

Storage area

Fig. 13-2 A storage area with multiple definitions showing the names by which various substrings may be referenced

In records each element or group of elements is provided with an identifier as subscript. Elements of arrays within records (defined using the OCCURS clause) are accessed through integer subscripts. The same identifiers may be used to designate elements within different structures. For example, there may be an element named CITY in three different records named EMPLOYEE-RECORD, NEW-EMPLOYEE, and EMPLOYER. Because such an element name by itself is ambiguous, each use of the name must be *qualified* by adding the name of some higher-level grouping (such as a record name) which will uniquely identify the desired elements, as in CITY OF NEW-EMPLOYEE or CITY OF EMPLOYER. In general, any reference is acceptable as long as it is unambiguous.

The use of the same identifier to name elements in more than one structure is made particularly useful by the CORRESPONDING *option—* the ability in COBOL to access in one step all the elements with identical names in two different structures. For example, the statement

MOVE CORRESPONDING A TO B.

will cause the value of each element of A which has a like named element in B to be assigned as the new value of that corresponding element (with the necessary implicit type conversions). The corresponding elements need not occupy identical positions within the records A and B. This accessing of corresponding elements is also possible in the ADD and SUBTRACT statements.

External Files and File Declarations

The FILE SECTION of the DATA DIVISION contains a declaration for each external file accessed by the program. The declaration specifies various gross characteristics of the file and defines each format that a record on the file might assume. Additional declarations in the ENVIRON-MENT DIVISION specify the particular external files to be used and certain implementation-dependent properties of the files.

Files may be sequential, indexed, or random. These different types of organization are discussed in Sec. 4-11. The programmer specifies the organization of the file and whether records are to be accessed sequentially or at random. In addition, declarations may specify the presence or absence of labels on the files, the contents of labels if present, the indexing key if the file is indexed, the number of buffer areas to be used during input-output (which affects the speed of input-output operations), and a variable to be used as a *status indicator* during input-output operations, so that the programmer may monitor the result of each operation.

Besides these declarations of the gross external characteristics of the file and related data areas to be used in file processing, the program specifies the internal structure of the file. In general, the file is composed of a sequence of physical records or *blocks*, each containing in turn a sequence of logical records, each of which is a simple character string. As part of the file declaration the programmer specifies the number of logical records that comprise a block and the length of a logical record. The BLOCK CON-TAINS is used for the former purpose. The length of a record is defined by the record declarations which comprise the major part of the file description.

After the initial line describing the gross characteristics of the file, a sequence of record declarations follows, each in exactly the same form as the record declarations found in the WORKING-STORAGE SECTION for local record data structures. The sequence of record declarations here, however, has a different significance: Each declaration describes a different format for a record which might appear on the external file. A single central storage area, called the *record area*, is allocated for the file. Its length is equal to the length of the longest record defined by any of the record declarations. Each of the record declarations essentially redefines the structure of this single record area, but no explicit REDEFINES clause is necessary.

Input-Output and Sorting

Input is straightforward. A READ operation reads the next (or other specified) record from the external file (using an internal buffer for temporary storage). This record is a character string which is stored in the record area for the file without modification. If only a single record declaration for the file was given, as in the example of Sec. 13-2, then the record just input has a known format specified by the record declaration, and the programmer can proceed to access the various substrings of the record using the identifiers and type declarations defined by the record declaration. However, more generally, the file declaration may contain more than one record declaration, indicating that the external file may contain records in various formats. In this case after the record is input to the record area, the programmer must first determine its format before he can select the proper set of identifiers (specified by some one record declaration) to use in accessing the substrings of the record. This format identification is commonly done by using a *format tag* field which each format has in common, with a unique tag number designating the format of the individual record (see Problem 3).

The WRITE operation is equally straightforward: A character string is copied from the record area of the file to the buffer area and ultimately to the external file. Output lines, however, are usually formatted in a record in WORKING-STORAGE and moved to the file record area only immediately before output, because this allows fixed headings and other constant data to be entered into the WORKING-STORAGE records at compile time and never modified, as illustrated in the example program of Fig. 13-1.

The operations ACCEPT and DISPLAY are used for input and output, respectively, to low-speed devices such as computer consoles or small terminals. On random-access files REWRITE allows substitution for an existing record and DELETE allows deletion of a record.

Most data files processed by COBOL programs must be sorted before they can be processed. For example, a file of weekly payroll inputs must be sorted (perhaps by social security number) before it can be processed if the weekly inputs are to be matched to entries in a (presorted) master payroll file. Because the sorting opertion is so common, most COBOL implementations include a SORT primitive which allows a file to be sorted using a given *key* element as the basis for the ordering.

Other Operations in COBOL

A variety of other primitives is provided. A SEARCH statement allows an efficient search of a homogeneous array data structure. Some simple character-string-processing primitives are provided which allow a string to be scanned for special characters and replacements made. The optional report-writer module, when available, provides a set of primitives for formatting and outputting printed matter by setting up page formats directly into the same paragraphs or sections in the normal-sequence of WRITE primitive.

13-4 SUBPROGRAMS

COBOL has few features to support abstraction and encapsulation of programmer-defined operations (subprograms); it has none to support type definitions or data abstraction. The basic COBOL subprogram is simply a paragraph (labeled sequence of statements) in the PROCEDURE division which may be executed via a PERFORM statement. Subprograms with parameters and a separate referencing environment are an optional feature. These subprogram facilities are described in the sections that follow.

13-5 SEQUENCE CONTROL

COBOL sequence-control structures are heavily oriented toward statement sequence control. Expressions play only a minor role in the language, and subprograms are restricted to simple calls and returns without recursion. In addition, exception-handling facilities are provided in certain special cases.

Expressions

The minimal COBOL language uses no expressions at all. In full COBOL they occur in only three places. In the COMPUTE assignment statement an arithmetic expression using the basic arithmetic operations and parentheses may be used to specify the value to be assigned. In an IF conditional statement and the SEARCH statement the condition may be specified by an expression involving arithmetic, relational, and Boolean operators in the usual manner. No provision is made for function calls within expressions, and thus expression evaluation is straightforward.

Statement Sequence Control

The executable portion of a COBOL program, the PROCEDURE DIVISION, begins with an optional set of exception handlers together with the associated exception names. Following these *declaratives* the program statements are grouped into *sentences*, the sentences into *paragraphs*, and the paragraphs (optionally) into *sections*. Each paragraph and section begins with a label which may be used as the object of a GOTO or PERFORM control transfer. Execution follows the physical statement sequence without regard to sentence, paragraph, or section boundaries unless a GOTO, PERFORM, or IF statement is used to explicitly transfer control. Particularly notable is the fact that there are no explicit subprogram boundaries within the PROCEDURE DIVISION. Paragraphs or sections may be used as simple subprograms, but control is also allowed to flow directly into the same paragraphs or sections in the normal sequence of execution.

Labels and GOTOs. A simple GOTO may transfer control to any paragraph or section label. A multiway branch using a vector of labels and a computed subscript (similar to the FORTRAN *computed* GOTO) is also provided using the syntax

GO TO L1,L2,...,L*n* DEPENDING ON ⟨*identifier*⟩.

A third option allows a simple GOTO to be written as the only statement in a separate paragraph. The label specified may then be modified at run time by execution of an ALTER statement, e.g.,

ALTER L1 to PROCEED TO L25.

where L1 is the label of the paragraph containing the GOTO to be modified. These facilities are essentially the same as those provided by FORTRAN.

Conditional (IF) *statements.* An *if-then-else* statement is provided, using the syntax

IF ⟨*condition*⟩ ⟨*statement sequence*⟩ ELSE ⟨*statement sequence*⟩.

The ⟨*condition*⟩ specified may be a relational or Boolean expression.

PERFORM *statements.* The COBOL PERFORM statement serves both as an iteration statement and as a simple parameterless subprogram call. In its simplest form,

PERFORM L1. or PERFORM L1 THRU L*n*.

it causes execution of the designated paragraph (or section) or sequence of paragraphs (or sections) as a simple parameterless subprogram. Control is transferred to the paragraph labeled L1; the statements in that paragraph, or in following paragraphs through paragraph Ln, are executed; and control returns to the point of call (the PERFORM statement). No parameters or local variables are involved; only control transfers occur. The other forms of PERFORM are straightforward extensions of this basic concept. The statement

PERFORM L1 THRU Ln k TIMES.

serves to call the *subprogram* repeatedly k times. The statement

PERFORM L1 THRU Ln UNTIL ⟨*condition*⟩.

iterates execution of the subprogram until the condition evaluates to true. The fourth version of the statement,

PERFORM L1 THRU Ln
VARYING I1 FROM J1 BY K1 UNTIL ⟨*condition$_1$*⟩
AFTER I2 FROM J2 BY K2 UNTIL ⟨*condition$_2$*⟩
AFTER I3 FROM J3 BY K3 UNTIL ⟨*condition$_3$*⟩.

allows iterative execution of the subprogram with from one to three loop indices moving through integer ranges. In the above statement, index I3 cycles completely for each step in the value of I2, and so on.

Special condition checking. In addition to the basic statement sequence-control structures mentioned above, many COBOL statements provide for execution of one or more statements when a special condition arises during execution of the base statement. For example, each arithmetic statement may contain a suffix designating actions to be taken in case of a *size error*, an error caused by the result of the arithmetic operation being too large to fit in the designated result variable location. Thus the statement

ADD A TO B, ON SIZE ERROR PERFORM ERROR1.

would cause execution of subprogram ERROR1 should the sum of the values of A and B exceed the space allocated for B. Other special condition checks include end-of-file checking on READ statements and end-of-page checking on WRITE statements.

Subprogram Sequence Control

True subprograms play a minor role in COBOL programming. In fact, early versions of COBOL (1960-1965) included no subprogram facilities beyond the primitive structure associated with the PERFORM statement, described above. True subprograms with parameters and local referencing environments first appeared as an optional language feature in the 1968 version of the language. They are not required in any COBOL implementation. When implemented, subprograms are restricted to simple nonrecursive calls and returns.

The only other sequence-control structure of interest provides a limited exception-handling capability for monitoring input-output errors or end-of-file conditions (e.g., parity errors). The programmer may specify at the beginning of the PROCEDURE DIVISION an exception handler (set of paragraphs or sections) to be executed should such an I/O error occur on a given file.

13-6 DATA CONTROL

The data-control mechanisms in COBOL are the most primitive of any language described in this book. This fact is basically a reflection of the lack of emphasis on subprograms in the language. The DATA DIVISION of a program sets up a single global referencing environment which is used throughout the PROCEDURE DIVISION for referencing. Although paragraphs or sections in the PROCEDURE DIVISION may be called like subprograms using PERFORM, these "subprograms" must use only the common global referencing environment and may have no parameters or local identifiers. The only identifiers not appearing in the DATA DIVISION are the labels for paragraphs and sections in the PROCEDURE DIVISION and again these cannot be made local but are implicitly global (e.g., GO TO L1 appearing anywhere in the PROCEDURE DIVISION transfers control to the same label L1).

In versions of COBOL since 1968 the optional true subprogram facility allows subprograms (written as complete COBOL programs) to be separately compiled and to have parameters and their own local referencing environments (defined by the DATA DIVISION of each subprogram). These local environments are retained between calls, as in FORTRAN. Parameters to such subprograms are transmitted by reference, and actual parameters are restricted to single identifiers naming simple variables or records. Full declarations for the corresponding formal parameters must be provided in a special LINKAGE SECTION of the DATA DIVISION of the subprogram. The only nonlocal identifiers in COBOL are the names of separately compiled subprograms, the external file names mentioned in the ENVIRONMENT DIVISION, and a few other minor implementation-dependent identifiers. The simple data-control structures used in COBOL allow all referencing to be set up at compile time. Direct access to the appropriate data locations is then possible at run time without any referencing overhead.

13-7   OPERATING AND PROGRAMMING ENVIRONMENT

A batch-processing operating environment containing large data files is assumed in the COBOL design. Major parts of the language are concerned with the description of the characteristics of these files. COBOL is probably strongest in this area of file description, compared to the other languages described here. Sequential files, direct-access files, and indexed sequential files are supported, and a variety of features for accessing these files are provided. The *report-writer* features provide a simple means to format and output pages of results to be printed. Sorting and merging of data on external files is supported by a *sort-merge* feature.

The language also includes a number of features that are intended to support a programming environment in which large COBOL programs must be developed and maintained by groups of programmers over extended periods. Most prominent is the separation into the ENVIRONMENT division of the aspects of the program that are presumed to be machine dependent, e.g., the relation of internal file descriptions to actual external files. This separation attempts to make it simpler to transport a COBOL program to another computer or to modify a program when the underlying operating system or hardware changes. The language also contains a *debug module* to support program testing and a *library module* to support the assembly of a COBOL program from components stored in a program library. This library feature provides a COPY statement that may be used to copy source program text from a library into a program being constructed. In a typical COBOL programming environment, many programs process the same set of files, and thus the file descriptions must be repeated in the ENVIRONMENT and DATA divisions of many programs. The COPY statement is used to retrieve these repeated parts of program text from a common library and insert them into a source program before compilation. Similarly, COPY may be used to retrieve the source form of commonly used "subprograms" (paragraphs) for insertion into the PROCEDURE division of a program.

13-8   SYNTAX AND TRANSLATION

The major features of the COBOL syntax have been mentioned in the preceding sections. Programs are broken into four divisions, each composed of sections, which in turn are broken into paragraphs (in the ENVIRON-MENT and PROCEDURE divisions). The statement formats are English-like, and many optional noise words are allowed to improve readability. The goal of this syntactic organization is a language in which programs are readable without extra documentation. However, the language design only partially accomplishes this goal. The natural English-like syntax makes individual statements or groups of statements quite readable, but the weakness of the COBOL subprogram capabilities and limited use of expressions and structured statements tend to obscure the overall organization of a program. The control structures natural to an algorithm often cannot be directly reflected in the program.

Because of the relatively simple and natural syntax, COBOL programs are not particularly difficult to write, but programming in COBOL is tedious because of the large amount of code which must be produced (even for simple programs) in the form of division, section, and paragraph headers, and because of the full declarations required for each data item used. Also, every key word or noise word used in a COBOL statement is a reserved identifier which cannot be used by the programmer. The list of reserved words fills an entire printed page (about 300 words). Conflicts between programmer-chosen identifiers and reserved words are common COBOL programming errors.

Translation

The COBOL syntax is not designed for simplicity of translation. The language syntax itself, with the numerous statement types, optional elements within statement types, and variety of syntactic constructs, is difficult to parse efficiently. Run-time efficiency is highly desirable in compiled COBOL programs, because such programs are often compiled into executable form and then used repeatedly from their compiled form (e.g., a payroll computation program may be run every pay period for years). The language is designed to allow reasonably efficient executable code to be produced, but the task of actually producing the optimized code is made difficult by the sheer bulk of a large COBOL program. Usually a *multipass* compiler is used, which consists of a number of processing stages brought into memory one at a time in sequence to compile the input program. The initial stages perform syntactic analysis and construct tables for later stages which generate and optimize the resulting code.

The COBOL Formal Grammar

The CBL grammar form discussed in Sec. 9-4 has been used successfully since the initial COBOL design to describe the syntax of the language. This grammar form allows a succinct and readable representation of the rather complex syntactic options of the many COBOL statement and declaration types.

13-9   STRUCTURE OF A COBOL VIRTUAL COMPUTER

The overall memory organization imposed by a COBOL program during execution is static. Thus there is no run-time storage management. Programs are compiled into machine code and executed by the hardware interpreter. Input-output operations require fairly extensive run-time software support on most computers. The most obvious area of incompatability between the COBOL virtual computer and conventional hardware, however, is in data representations. For the most part COBOL data are stored in the form of character strings, and each substring representing a data element has a complex type declaration. Accessing data elements and converting among the different data types requires fairly extensive run-time software support. Some of the more special COBOL primitives are also software-simulated, in particular the SORT operation and the SEARCH command for searching arrays.

13-10   REFERENCES AND SUGGESTIONS FOR FURTHER READING

Many texts are available that provide an introduction to COBOL and its applications. The complete standard definition is found in COBOL [1974]. Sammet [1981, 1969] gives an excellent history of the early development of the language. Jackson [1977] provides a delightful comparison of the COBOL design to more current views of language design.

13-11   PROBLEMS

1. Explain why use of the SYNCHRONIZED clause in a data structure declaration can make the size of the structure implementation-dependent.

2. For the storage area of Fig. 13-2, write a record declaration that REDEFINES record ARR to allow each individual character in the storage area to be accessed by an integer subscript.

3. Suppose that a COBOL program for processing public school student records contains the following input file declaration:

```
        FD INP-FILE LABEL RECORD IS OMITTED . . .
        01   ELEM-STUDENT.
            02   GRADE PICTURE 99.
            02   NAME . . .
                :
                :
```

```
01   JR-HIGH-STUDENT.
     02   GRADE PICTURE 99.
     02   SCHOOL . . .
               :
               :

01   SR-HIGH-STUDENT.
     02   GRADE PICTURE 99.
     02   NAME . . .
               :
               :
```

The statement READ INP-FILE causes the next record to be read from the file and stored in the record area for the file. The record may have any one of the three formats designated in the file description. Write a COBOL conditional statement that will transfer control to paragraph PARA1 if the record read is that of an ELEM-STUDENT (GRADE = 1-6), to PARA2 if the record is that of a JR-HIGH-STUDENT (GRADE = 7-9), and to PARA3 if the record is that of a SR-HIGH-STUDENT (GRADE = 10-12).

CHAPTER 14

PL/I

PL/I is a large, multipurpose language designed during the early 1960s by a committee organized by the IBM Corporation. The initial goal of the committee was to design a successor to FORTRAN which would include more extensive data-structuring facilities and a more sophisticated operating environment and which would thus be applicable to a broader range of problem areas. The committee decided that FORTRAN compatibility could not be maintained if these goals were to be met and proceeded with the design of the new language that became PL/I. PL/I is applicable to a rather wide range of problem areas—scientific applications, business applications, and to some extent systems programming, as well as applications which overlap these areas.

The design of PL/I draws heavily on the earlier languages FORTRAN, ALGOL, and COBOL. PL/I contains fairly direct analogues of the FORTRAN parameter-transmission mechanisms, separately compiled subprograms, formatted input-output, and COMMON blocks; of the ALGOL block structure and structured statements; and of the COBOL records, record-oriented input-output, and PICTURE type declarations. However, in each case the design of PL/I extends these earlier constructs and supplies many new concepts, particularly in the areas of control structures and storage management.

The most significant aspects of the PL/I design stem from the attempt of the designers to balance two sets of conflicting goals: generality and flexibility without loss of execution efficiency, and ease of use for unsophisticated programmers without loss of detailed control for experienced programmers. In both cases the solution involves placing a considerable extra burden on the PL/I compiler. Generality and flexibility are obtained through the inclusion in the language of a large variety of different data structures, primitives, and control structures. To allow the compiler to produce relatively efficient executable code, however, extensive declaration of the properties of the structures used by a program is required. The variety of structures and the detailed declarations required also advanced the goal of programmer control—an experienced programmer may control the run-time structures and execution costs by careful choice of program structures and declarations. In addition, the language provides explicit storage management primitives and storage classes that allow the experienced programmer to provide detailed control of storage.

The resulting language is large and complex. To make it also usable by the less experienced programmer the design adopts the philosophy of extensive *default declarations*—declarations provided by the compiler whenever the programmer fails to specify all the attributes of a data or program element. The inexperienced programmer may thus write straight-forward programs without concern for many language details, and the compiler is expected to provide the necessary additional information. (Unfortunately, the default-declaration concept, in practice, is sometimes more confusing than helpful to the programmer, because the default declaration provided may not be that which is expected.)

The design of PL/I represents one extreme in design philosophy. Basically, the design attempts to meet the needs of a broad range of applications by including a wide variety of often overlapping features within a fixed framework. Relatively few features are provided for programmer-defined abstractions; instead most of the features needed by a programmer are included directly in the language. The merits of this approach versus the smaller but more easily extensible base language have been widely debated but with no definite resolution.

PL/I exists in a number of different versions on different computers. Although the language was designed in the early 1960s, a standard definition was not adopted until 1976 (PL/I [1976]). The standard definition, on which this chapter is largely based, does not contain a definition of the features supporting concurrent tasks and the *compile-time* features described in Sec. 14-8, even though many PL/I implementations contain such features. The subset of PL/I known as PL/C (see Conway and Gries [1975]) has seen extensive use in the teaching of programming.

14-1   BRIEF OVERVIEW OF THE LANGUAGE

A PL/I program consists of a set of separately compiled routines, each of which has a nested block structure similar to that of a Pascal program. Each block or subprogram definition contains a set of declarations and a set of executable statements, which may be freely intermixed. Generally, each statement or declaration type has a basic form and numerous options which the programmer may either use or omit and accept the compiler-provided default option. The resulting syntax is rather complex, and programs are not particularly easy to read or write.

PL/I contains a wide variety of elementary data types, including an extensive set of possible type specifications for numeric data. Character and bit strings, pointers, and labels may also be used. Arrays and records are the basic data structure types, and full declarations must be provided. The same structures provide the basis for a primitive *programmer-defined data type* facility with provision for creation and destruction of new structures at arbitrary points during program execution. The language also includes a complex set of features supporting use of external files for input-output.

A large range of primitive operations are built into the language. The major emphasis falls on arithmetic and other numeric operations and on input-output. Extensive automatic type conversions are provided, including conversions between different hardware number representations and COBOL-like conversions between formatted character-string data items. Many operations may be applied to entire arrays as operands, although the facilities for array operations are not as powerful as those of APL. In addition, array *cross sections* may be treated as subarrays. Some basic string-processing operations are also provided.

PL/I expressions and statement sequence-control features are powerful but standard in form. Subprogram sequence control includes exception handling as well as ordinary subprogram calls with recursion.

Subprogram facilities are emphasized in PL/I. Subprograms may be either separately compiled, in which case a FORTRAN-like explicitly declared global referencing environment may be used, or definitions may be nested within other subprogram definitions, in which case the static block structure determines the nonlocal referencing environment. Parameters are transmitted by reference (or by value-result in some implementations). Declarations for formal parameters are required in subprograms, but the programmer may either specify automatic conversions of actual parameters to match the corresponding formal parameter types or, alternatively, specify different entry points for a subprogram depending on the types of the actual parameters transmitted.

Compilation of PL/I programs is difficult because of the complexity of the language and the need to compile efficiently executable code. Substantial run-time software support is necessary for storage management and simulation of the large number of primitives used. Run-time storage management requires, in general, a static area, a stack, and a heap (which may be split into many small heaps by the programmer). Only the simple explicit allocation and freeing method of heap management is used, however; the programmer is responsible for avoiding the generation of garbage or dangling references.

14-2   AN ANNOTATED EXAMPLE: SUMMATION OF A VECTOR

Figure 14-1 shows a PL/I program analogous to the FORTRAN and Pascal example programs of Chapters 12 and 15, respectively. The program consists of a main program and a subprogram. The subprogram SUM is a function which sums the elements of an argument vector V of real numbers. The main program tests SUM by creating a sequence of vectors, reading in values for the vector elements, calling SUM, and then printing the value computed by SUM for each test vector. The annotations below refer to the line numbers to the left of the listing, which are not a part of the program.

Line 1. Beginning of the main program. The main program takes the form of a *procedure* (subprogram) named TEST. The OPTIONS (MAIN) attribute specifies that this procedure is the main program.

Line 2. First executable statement in the main program. The statement is labeled START. Integer variable K is declared implicitly. A value for the variable K is to be read in from the standard input file. The GET indicates input; the LIST indicates that the input value will appear on the external file as an ordinary decimal number separated from other data items by blanks or commas. LIST-directed input is the simplest of four basic input format options.

```
Line

  1          TEST: PROCEDURE OPTIONS (MAIN);
  2              START:  GET LIST (K);
  3                  IF K > 0 THEN BEGIN;
  4                      DECLARE A(K) FLOAT;
  5                      GET LIST (A);
  6                      PUT LIST ('INPUT IS',A,'SUM IS',SUM(A));
  7                      GO TO START;
  8                  END;
  9              SUM: PROCEDURE (V) RETURNS (FLOAT);
 10                  DECLARE V(*) FLOAT,
 11                      TEMP FLOAT INITIAL (0);
 12                  DO I = 1 TO DIM(V,1);
 13                      TEMP = TEMP + V(I); END;
 14                  RETURN(TEMP);
 15                  END SUM;
 16          END TEST;
```

Fig. 14-1   Example PL/I program

Line 3. A one-branch conditional statement begins here and extends to line 8. If the test $K > 0$ is not satisfied, then control transfers to the first executable statement following line 8, which in this case is the terminating END for the main program in line 16.

Line 4. Lines 4-8 form a BEGIN-block which is executed if the test on line 3 is satisfied. The block begins with a declaration of a vector A of K elements, where the value of K is the value just read in. FLOAT gives the type of each element of A: real numbers represented in an appropriate hardware floating-point format. A new vector A is created each time control enters this block during program execution, and the vector is destroyed on block exit.

Line 5. K values for the newly created vector A are read in from the standard input file. Again LIST-directed input is used so that the values may be entered on the file separated by blanks or commas without any special formatting.

Line 6. The input values stored in A are printed, together with the sum of the values returned by function subprogram SUM, with appropriate headings. PUT indicates output to the standard output file. LIST-directed output is used, which requires no programmer-supplied format specification. Output values are printed in a simple sequence separated by blanks.

Line 7. Control is transferred back to line 2 to begin another test loop.

Line 8. End of the BEGIN-block begun on line 3 as well as the conditional statement begun on the same line.

Lines 9-15. Definition of the function subprogram SUM. This declaration could have been placed anywhere within the body of the main program. The PL/I compiler is expected to process all declarations appearing anywhere within a program unit (subprogram) as though they had occurred at the beginning of the program unit.

Line 9. Beginning of the procedure named SUM, which has one formal parameter, V, and returns a result of type FLOAT.

Line 10. PL/I requires declarations for all formal parameters. V is declared to be a vector of decimal floating-point numbers (represented in the appropriate hardware representation). The * in the subscript list for V designates that the subscript range is to be that of the actual parameter vector transmitted to SUM.

Line 11. A local variable TEMP is declared with zero as its initial value. A new variable TEMP, initialized to zero, is created on each entry to SUM and destroyed on exit.

Line 12. A DO iteration statement begins here and ends with the END on the next line. The function call DIM(V,1) calls a built-in primitive function which returns the size (subscript range) of the first dimension of vector V; thus it is possible to find out the dimension of a vector or array dynamically during execution. The variable I is initialized to 1 and incremented by 1 each time through the loop until the size of V is reached. Note that variable I need not be explicitly declared; its use without a declaration causes the compiler to assume that it is a fixed-point variable.

Line 13. Body of the iteration statement begun on line 12. The successive elements of V are summed using the temporary variable TEMP.

Line 14. Control is transferred back to the calling program. Since SUM is a function subprogram, an expression designating the function value to be returned is given, which in this case consists of the value of variable TEMP.

Line 15. End of the body of subprogram SUM.

Line 16. End of the main program.

14-3   DATA TYPES

PL/I contains an extensive selection of data types and primitives for accessing and modifying data elements. In general, full declarations of data types (with the exception of array subscript ranges and string lengths) are provided at compile time for each identifier, either explicitly or by default. The declarations are structured in terms of *attributes*—each declaration specifies a set of values for the various attributes which a variable or data structure may have. The compiler uses these attribute declarations to determine an appropriate run-time representation for each data item and the manner in which it is accessed and modified.

Numbers

Numbers in PL/I are classified on the basis of four attributes: (1) *mode*, which may be real or complex; (2) *scale*, which may be fixed-point or floating-point; (3) *base*, which may be decimal or binary; and (4) *precision*, which is specified in terms of the number of digits. For example, the declaration

DECLARE X FIXED BINARY(31,0)

declares identifier X to represent a simple variable whose value will be an integer (fixed-point number) with 31 bits of precision (no bits past the decimal point). Complex numbers are represented as pairs of real numbers. Although there are four basic types of real numbers (decimal and binary fixed-point and decimal and binary floating-point) and a large number of possible specifications of precision, in fact, each number type is represented by the closest hardware number representation at run time—no run-time software simulation of real-number representations is ordinarily used.

Numeric data may also be stored in character-string form. Again the programmer controls the choice of representation by the form of his declaration—to specify character representation of numbers a PICTURE declaration similar to that in COBOL is used.

Arithmetic Operations

The basic arithmetic operations are represented by the infix operators $+, -, *,$ $/,$ and $**$ (exponentiation) and prefix $-$ (negation). In addition, a full set of built-in functions for square root, absolute value, max, min, trigonometric operations, and the like are provided. In general, each arithmetic primitive may be used with operands of any type or mixture of types which can be converted to a form appropriate for the operation. Great emphasis is placed on providing fully automatic conversion between data types. Owing to the large number of different arithmetic type specifications, the details of these automatic conversions are extremely complex. In general, static type checking is possible, numbers are represented in the appropriate hardware representation at run time, and hardware arithmetic operations are used directly. The full type declarations which are required allow the necessary type conversions to be determined at compile time, but the run-time software necessary to actually perform the conversions may be substantial.

Character and Bit Strings

Variables and data structure elements may be of type *character string* or *bit string*, but the declaration must specify either a fixed string length or a maximum string length. The hardware bit or character representation is utilized, and because of the required declared bounds, a fixed-size block of storage may be allocated for each string variable at run time. Character-string variables may alternatively be declared using a COBOL-like PICTURE declaration.

Relational Operations

Eight primitive relational operations are provided in infix form: $=, >, <, >=,$ $<=, \neg =, \neg <,$ and $\neg >.$ Each may be applied to numbers, bit strings, or character strings (using the implementation-defined collating sequence for character ordering). Again, automatic conversion between data types is provided whenever possible.

Boolean and String Operations

There is no Boolean data type as such in PL/I; a bit string of length 1 is used instead. The basic Boolean operators, **and** (&), **or** (|), and **not** (¬) are provided as operators on bit strings. In addition, a concatenation operation (||) on both character and bit strings is provided. Other basic string-manipulation primitives are provided as built-in functions, e.g., LENGTH, which returns the length of an argument string; INDEX, which searches a string for a given substring and returns its position; and SUBSTR, which retrieves a specified substring of a given string.

Assignment

The assignment operation (syntax =) provides automatic type conversion of the assigned value to the type of the receiving element. Assignments may list multiple receiving locations on the left-hand side, each with a different required type conversion. For example,

$$K(2),X,Z = 2*Q;$$

assigns the value of $2*Q$ to each of K(2), X, and Z, converting the assigned value as needed.

Certain built-in functions, termed *pseudovariables*, may also be used on the left of an assignment. For example, the SUBSTR built-in function is ordinarily used to retrieve a substring of designated length from a designated position within another string. However, SUBSTR may be used on the left of an assignment as a pseudovariable, in which case the value of the right-hand expression (which must be a string) is stored in the designated position within the receiving string. For example, the assignment

$$SUBSTR(STR1,2,5) = SUBSTR(STR2,17,5);$$

stores a copy of the five-character string beginning at the seventeenth character position in STR2 in the five character positions beginning at position 2 in STR1.

Arrays and Structures

Arrays and records (called *structures*) are the basic data structure types of PL/I. Full declarations of dimensions and element types are required, except that the subscript ranges in arrays may be provided at run time. The techniques for declaration, run-time storage, and accessing of elements of such arrays and structures are standard and are discussed in Secs. 4-5 and 4-6. Structures may include arrays as elements, and arrays may include structures as elements.

An array *cross section* may be accessed as a unit by using a subscripted variable with an asterisk in one or more of the subscript positions. For example, a 10 × 20 array A of five-digit integers might be declared:

DECLARE A (10,20) FIXED (5);

The third row of A is accessed by A (3,*), the fifth column by A(*,5), and the entire array by A or A(*,*). A cross section is also an array and may be treated as such in general, even though its elements may not be stored in a contiguous block of storage. Many of the PL/I primitives will accept arrays (including cross sections) as well as single data items as operands.

Two or more arrays or structures may be declared to utilize the same storage area by specifying the second to be DEFINED in terms of the first. For arrays the technique is similar to the FORTRAN EQUIVALENCE construct; for structures the technique resembles the COBOL REDEFINES construct.

Array and Structure Operations

The primitive infix and prefix operators may be applied to array operands to produce array results, under the restriction that the arrays be identical in number of dimensions and subscript ranges. The types of array elements may differ provided that appropriate conversions can be made. For example, if A and B are two arrays of identical dimension and subscript range, then A+B results in an array of the same size, each of whose elements is the sum of the corresponding elements of A and B.

Infix and prefix operators may also be applied to structures provided that both structures have the same organization (but not necessarily the same element names) and that appropriate conversion of data types and corresponding elements is possible.

The result of an array or structure expression must ordinarily be immediately assigned to another array or structure of identical shape. Assignments are made between values in the generated structure and corresponding elements in the receiving structure according to the usual rules for assignment. The array or structure assignment basically serves as a shorthand for a sequence of element-by-element assignments.

Storage Classes and Programmer-Defined Data Types

One of the attributes included in the declaration of a simple variable, array, or structure is its *storage class*: STATIC, AUTOMATIC, CONTROLLED, or BASED. The STATIC and AUTOMATIC classes are those ordinarily used.

In these two cases the storage class attribute simply defines the lifetime of the declared structure: STATIC structures are retained throughout program execution (as in FORTRAN), and AUTOMATIC structures are created on entry to the block or procedure in which the declaration occurs and are deleted on exit (as in Pascal).

When the CONTROLLED or BASED storage class attribute is specified, however, the significance of the declaration for the associated structure is modified. The declaration now becomes a *template* defining a *typical structure* in a class of structures which may be considered as a new *programmer-defined data dype*. A new structure of the defined type may be created by use of an ALLOCATE statement and subsequently destroyed by a FREE statement.

The difference between the CONTROLLED and BASED attributes lies in the accessing arrangements. When ALLOCATE is used to create a new structure of a type declared as BASED, a pointer to the new structure is stored at the time of creation in a pointer variable (designated either in the ALLOCATE statement or in the original declaration). Subsequent attempts to access the structure must use this pointer as an access path. Many ALLOCATE statements may be executed in sequence, and the pointers returned may be used to link together the created structures to form arbitrary graph structures. Subsequent FREE statements must specify a pointer to the particular structure which is to be destroyed.

When a structure type is declared as CONTROLLED, on the other hand, only a single structure of the declared type may be accessed at any time during program execution. The CONTROLLED declaration basically serves to set up a stack (initially empty) of structures of the declared type. Each ALLOCATE statement creates a new structure of the specified type and pushes it down on the top of the associated stack; a FREE statement pops the top element off of the stack and destroys it. Between an ALLOCATE and FREE statement only the top structure on the stack is accessible.

There is no restriction on the type of the data structure declared as BASED or CONTROLLED. Thus it is possible to declare a complex data structure type and then create and manipulate a stack of such structures (by a CONTROLLED attribute) or a set of such structures accessed through pointers (by a BASED attribute). Run-time accessing is fairly efficient because the compiler has a template for a typical structure and may compile a base-address-plus-offset type of accessing formula into the executable code for each reference to an element of such a structure, leaving the base address to be determined at run time.

The storage class attributes are obviously closely related to the underlying storage management structures used: The STATIC attribute implies static storage for the associated data structure, AUTOMATIC implies a stack storage mechanism based on activation records for the associated block or procedure, and BASED and CONTROLLED imply a heap structure because the use of ALLOCATE and FREE require storage allocation and recovery at arbitrary points during execution.

Pointers

The data type POINTER is one of the elementary data types in PL/I. A simple variable or element of an array or structure may be declared to be of type POINTER and at run time may then contain a pointer to a data structure of a type declared as BASED (pointer data may also be generated for non-BASED data structures, but this is less common). The pointers to BASED structures generated by the ALLOCATE statement must be stored in POINTER variables. Each reference to a BASED variable must specify a pointer variable which contains the pointer which is to serve as the *base address* for the accessing calculation.

PL/I pointers, in general, are handled without any run-time descriptors or data type checking (see Problem 2). This structure provides efficient execution but places the burden of insuring correct pointer use on the programmer. In particular, dangling references and garbage may easily be generated through incorrect pointer use, and no system protection is provided. For example, if A is declared

DECLARE A (10) FLOAT BASED (P);

then the statement

ALLOCATE A;

creates a vector of ten elements and stores a pointer to it in P. A subsequent ALLOCATE A creates another vector of ten elements and assigns the pointer to P, destroying the pointer to the original vector. The original vector has become garbage unless the programmer has explicitly copied the original pointer in P to some other POINTER variable. If the original ALLOCATE A statement were followed instead by

Q = P;
FREE A;

then the pointer to the vector stored in P would be destroyed along with the vector itself, but pointer variable Q would be left with a dangling reference, a pointer to the destroyed structure.

Areas and Offsets

BASED and CONTROLLED data are allocated storage in a central heap. Because both types of data utilize absolute pointers for access, it is not, in general, possible to output such data to an external file for later input, because the data would be returned to different memory locations, thus invalidating all the pointers involved. PL/I also provides for the use of relative pointers (called *offsets*) and *areas* that serve as small heap storage blocks, as described in Sec. 4-9. In general, any BASED or CONTROLLED data may be created using ALLOCATE in any desired area. The offset produced may be treated as pointer data. However, when it is desirable to output the data stored in an area, the entire area as a simple sequential block of memory may be output. Subsequently, the stored area may be read back into new memory locations, and the offset pointers retain their original relationships.

Input-Output Files

PL/I provides facilities for declaration of the properties of external files and of the accessing methods to be used. In basic organization, an external file is treated either as a *stream*—a single sequence of bits or characters—or as a sequence of *records*, each of which is individually accessible. Input and output operations on a STREAM file always involve conversions of the data from the external form into appropriate internal memory representations, as in the FORTRAN formatted input-output operations. A RECORD file allows direct input and output of records without conversion, as in the COBOL input-output operations. RECORD files may be structured as sequential, random-access, or indexed sequential; STREAM files are necessarily sequential.

Input-Output Operations

For RECORD files a READ statement reads the next record from the external file to an internal storage area without conversion of individual data items. A WRITE statement transmits a copy of a storage area to the external file without conversion. REWRITE and DELETE statements allow replacement or deletion of individual records in an external file. RECORD files are generally used when a large volume of input and output is required, especially when the output files produced are to be used only as input for some later processing, e.g., in updating a master file in a business application.

STREAM files are commonly used when the input-output volume is smaller and when the output is to be printed. Data received from a STREAM file are immediately converted to the appropriate type for the receiving variable or data structure; on output the inverse conversion is made. The basic STREAM input operation is the GET statement; the basic output operation is the PUT statement. However, three different *modes* of STREAM input-output are provided, which give different levels of convenience and programmer control of the conversions provided. The EDIT-*directed* mode utilizes a programmer-supplied format which specifies the exact conversions desired for each input or output data item. EDIT-directed input-output is essentially the same as the FORTRAN input-output structure discussed in Chapter 12.

The other two modes of STREAM file input-output provide greater convenience for the programmer by utilizing simple *free-field* formats. In DATA-*directed* transmission each data item on the external file consists of an identifier and a value. On input, the identifier specifies the variable to which the value is to be assigned. On output the name of the variable whose value is being output is output along with the value. A more generally useful alternative is LIST-*directed* input-output in which the programmer specifies a list of variable names in the GET or PUT statement whose values are to be transmitted. The input or output file contains only values in this case. For input the values must be on the external file in sequence separated by blanks or commas with no special formatting. On output, values are written using a system-defined format.

Statement Labels

A variable or data structure element may be declared to be type LABEL. However, labels cannot be computed, and as a result the compiler may convert labels to an appropriate internal run-time representation and no run-time labels table need be maintained. This topic is discussed further in Sec. 14-5.

14-4 SUBPROGRAMS AND PROGRAMMER-DEFINED DATA TYPES

The design of PL/I predates the development of the notions of data abstraction discussed in Chapter 5. A primitive concept of type definition is part of the language. Subprograms form the primary abstraction mechanism.

Subprograms

A subprogram is defined using the syntax

⟨*name*⟩: PROCEDURE (⟨*formal-parameter list*⟩)

RETURNS (⟨*result-type*⟩);

      — type declarations for formal parameters;

      — declarations of local variables and subprograms;

      — executable statements

END ⟨*name*⟩;

where the RETURNS (⟨*result-type*⟩) in the heading is included only if the subprogram is a function. If the subprogram is to be called recursively, the keyword RECURSIVE must follow the formal-parameter list. The language allows the declarations of parameters, variables, and nested subprograms to be written in any order, and even to be interspersed with the executable statements. The compiler collects the declarations and treats them as if they had been written at the beginning of the subprogram definition.

The implementation of subprograms follows the general methods described in Chapters 5 and 6. Each subprogram is compiled into a code segment and an activation record. However, if the subprogram is not declared RECURSIVE, then a single copy of the activation record may be allocated storage statically along with the code segment. If RECURSIVE is declared, then the activation record must be created dynamically on a central stack when the subprogram is called during execution. The full declarations that are required allow the compiler to determine the structure of the activation record and to compute offsets for references to variables.

Programmer-Defined Data Types

A primitive type-definition facility is provided in conjunction with the use of BASED and CONTROLLED variables whose storage allocation is explicitly controlled by the programmer using ALLOCATE and FREE statements. The declaration of a BASED or CONTROLLED variable has the same form as an ordinary variable declaration, but it actually serves as a type definition. The declaration is used as a template when a structure of the type is created using ALLOCATE, as described in the preceding section. Type checking for accesses to elements of CONTROLLED variables is provided, but no checking is done for accesses to BASED variables using pointers. The abstraction possible using these mechanisms is extremely limited.

14-5 SEQUENCE CONTROL

The PL/I sequence-control structures within expressions and between statements are relatively straightforward. The most novel features of the language are found in the facilities for exception handling.

Expressions

Only the basic arithmetic, relational, and Boolean operations, plus concatenation of strings, are represented by infix or Polish prefix operators.
Other primitives are invoked using the syntax for a programmer-defined
function call. The prefix and infix operators have the hierarchy (from
highest precedence to lowest)

$**$ (exponentiation), prefix $+$ and $-$, $\neg$ (Boolean *not*)
$*$ (multiplication), $/$ (division)
$+$ (addition), $-$ (subtraction)
$||$ (concatenation)
$=, >=, <=, >, <, \neg =, \neg <, \neg >$
$\&$ (Boolean *and*)
$|$ (Boolean *or*)

Operators of equal precedence associate from left to right. Parentheses may
be used for explicit control within expressions in the usual way.

Statement Sequence Control

Within a single subprogram, execution follows the physical executable
statement sequence except where explicit control transfers are specified by
the programmer.

Conditional statements. A Pascal-like IF . . . THEN . . . ELSE . . . ;
conditional statement is used, with the ELSE . . . part optional. Conditional
statements may be nested by using another IF as the statement following
THEN or ELSE; the ambiguity introduced by nesting conditionals with
optional ELSE clauses (see Sec. 9-1) is resolved by always matching an
ELSE with the closest preceding unmatched THEN.

Iteration statements. The iteration statement has the form

DO ⟨*test*⟩; ⟨*statement sequence*⟩ END;

where the ⟨*test*⟩ may take one of the two forms:

WHILE ⟨*Boolean expression*⟩

or

⟨*variable*⟩ = ⟨*initial value*⟩ TO ⟨*final value*⟩ BY ⟨*increment*⟩

or may include both forms, e.g., DO I=1 TO K WHILE (X<Y); . . . END;. In
addition, the test may be entirely omitted, in which case the DO; . . . END;
syntax serves only to create a single *compound statement* out of the
statements in the ⟨*statement sequence*⟩. The order of evaluation of the

expressions in the DO statement head is clearly specified: The ⟨*initial value*⟩, ⟨*final value*⟩, and ⟨*increment*⟩ expressions are evaluated only once before the iteration begins, and the test for termination is always made before the initial execution of the ⟨*statement sequence*⟩ as well as after each iteration.

GOTOs and labels. PL/I includes a GOTO-label structure of intermediate run-time complexity: labels may not be computed during execution, but label parameters, label variables, and label arrays are allowed. A GOTO statement may transfer control to a local label in the usual way but may also transfer control to a nonlocal label or to the label value of a variable or array element of type LABEL. In each of the latter cases the label must be treated at run time as an *environment pointer-code pointer* pair, and the proper referencing environment must be reinstated whenever a transfer to the label is made, as discussed in Sec. 7-8.

Subprogram Sequence Control

The ordinary CALL-RETURN subprogram control structure is basic. Recursive calls are allowed only when a subprogram has been explicitly declared RECURSIVE in its definition.

Exceptions and exception handlers. An extensive system is provided for checking and handling exceptions that may arise during program execution. The exception conditions for which run-time checking may be enabled fall into three main categories:

1. *Computational conditions*, e.g., test for overflow or underflow on arithmetic operations, division by zero, an illegal character in a string being converted to a number or bit string, or truncation of significant leading digits of a number during an assignment.

2. *Input-output conditions*, e.g., test for end-of-file on input, end-of-page on output, or data transmission hardware errors.

3. *Program testing conditions*, e.g., test for a subscript outside of the declared range, assignment of a new value to a variable, or transfer of control to a label.

In general, checking is automatically enabled for computational and input-output conditions and disabled for program testing conditions. However, the programmer may control explicitly the enabling and disabling of all but input-output conditions through explicit *prefixes* attached to statements, blocks, or subprograms within his program. Each condition is assigned a key word, e.g., OVERFLOW, SUBSCRIPTRANGE, and ZERO-

DIVIDE. By writing the appropriate key word in parentheses preceding a statement, block, or subprogram, checking for the corresponding condition is enabled throughout execution of that program segment. A condition is disabled by writing NOOVERFLOW, NOZERODIVIDE, etc., as a prefix. For example, the programmer may wish to have subscript ranges checked in a given block during program testing but not within an enclosed sublock. This may be accomplished by writing

(SUBSCRIPTRANGE): BEGIN

⋮

(NOSUBSCRIPTRANGE): BEGIN

⋮

END;

⋮

END;

For each exception condition there is an implementation-defined system exception-handler which is executed automatically when the associated exception is raised during program execution. The system action may be to print out an appropriate message and then either continue execution or, more commonly, terminate the program. The programmer, however, may explicitly specify his own handler in place of the system handler through use of the ON statement:

ON ⟨*condition keyword*⟩ ⟨*statement or block*⟩;

The ⟨*statement or block*⟩ is treated as a simple parameterless subprogram. ON statements may be inserted anywhere within a program. When executed, the ON statement does nothing more than to substitute the programmer-defined statement or block in place of the system handler (or previously specified program-defined handler) as the code to be executed should the specified exception occur. The effect of an ON statement is local to the block within which it is executed.

14-6   DATA CONTROL

PL/I provides a variety of techniques for data control.

Referencing Environments

On entry to a BEGIN block or procedure a local referencing environment is established, which includes explicitly declared local variable and data structure names, formal parameters (in procedures), statement labels, and simple variables declared implicitly by use. For simple variables and data structures the programmer controls whether associations are created on entry and deleted on exit or whether they are retained between calls by attaching the AUTOMATIC or STATIC storage attribute to the declaration. AUTOMATIC is assumed by default, so that, in general, local environments are recreated on each entry, using a run-time stack.

Nonlocal referencing is ordinarily based on the static block structure of the program. However, the programmer has an alternative: by attaching the EXTERNAL attribute to the declaration of an identifier, that identifier and its association may be entered into a global referencing environment. Any number of subprograms may have declarations for the same EXTERNAL identifier (and the declarations must then be identical). At run time all references to this identifier in any of the subprograms retrieve the same global association. The major use of the EXTERNAL attribute is in sharing data between separately compiled subprograms, in which case it serves essentially the same function as the COMMON statement in FORTRAN. For identifiers declared EXTERNAL the global referencing environment may be created at load time before program execution begins.

Parameter Transmission

Subprogram parameters are ordinarily transmitted by reference (or value-result in some implementations). Actual parameters may be any of the types discussed in Sec. 7-8, including statement labels and subprograms. Full declarations (with the exception of array subscript ranges and string lengths) must be specified in each subprogram for each formal parameter.

Because PL/I subprograms may be separately compiled, it is not always possible for the compiler to check whether actual and formal parameters in subprogram calls are declared identically. In general, no run-time descriptors and type checking are provided, and thus the programmer is responsible for insuring correct correspondence between actual and formal parameters. As a rule the actual parameter provided at the point of call must be of an appropriate type to match the formal parameter. However, the programmer may specify an actual parameter of a different type and have it converted to the appropriate type at the time of call during execution, provided that he tells the compiler what conversion will be required so that the appropriate conversion can be compiled into the executable code without run-time type checking being necessary. Such an automatic conversion is specified by giving a separate declaration in the *calling program* of the parameter types of the *called program*. For example, if subprogram SUB is declared to have a single real number as argument, then in another subprogram in which SUB is called, the added declaration

DECLARE SUB ENTRY (FLOAT);

allows SUB to be called with an actual parameter of any type which can be converted to FLOAT form. The compiler will match the declared parameter type with the actual parameter type and compile appropriate code for the run-time type conversion. A similar structure provides for declaration of the type of value returned by a function subprogram. Function values are restricted to elementary data items.

Generic Subprograms

Often it is desirable to be able to call a single subprogram with various types of actual parameters. The parameter type declaration discussed above provides a means to get all actual parameters converted to the appropriate type automatically before transmission to the subprogram. An alternative is to define the subprogram as a *generic subprogram*.

A generic subprogram is actually a set of subprograms defined in the ordinary way, each with a different set of declarations for its formal parameters. For example, suppose that we have the declarations

```
SUB1: PROCEDURE (X,Y);          SUB2: PROCEDURE (W,Z);
         DECLARE X FIXED,                  DECLARE W FLOAT,
                 Y FLOAT;                           Z FLOAT;
              ⋮                                  ⋮
         END SUB1;                         END SUB2;
```

and we wish to use SUB1 and SUB2 as the two alternatives for a generic subprogram named SUB—a call to SUB with a FIXED first argument is to be treated as a call to SUB1, and with a FLOAT first argument as a call to SUB2. Then in the calling program where we wish to use the generic subprogram SUB the declaration

```
DECLARE SUB GENERIC
        (SUB1(FIXED,FLOAT),SUB2(FLOAT,FLOAT));
```

is added. Within this routine the statement

```
                    CALL SUB(U,V);
```

will be compiled into a call to either SUB1 or SUB2 depending on the declared type of U. Thus the effect of the GENERIC declaration is to *overload* the name SUB; the compiler resolves the overloading by comparing the type of the first actual parameter in the call of SUB with the types declared for the various definitions of SUB in the GENERIC declaration.

14-7 OPERATING AND PROGRAMMING ENVIRONMENT

PL/I is designed for a batch-processing operating and programming environment. The major components of the operating environment are the external data files used for input-output. The exception-handling features allow program control of many of the errors that may occur in interacting with these files and input-output devices. The programming environment features include provision for separate compilation of program units and for construction of a global common referencing environment. No major features supporting more extensive operating or programming environments are included.

14-8 SYNTAX AND TRANSLATION

The syntax of PL/I is designed to restrict the programmer as little as possible without leading to ambiguity. As a result, statements and declarations usually may be written in a number of equivalent forms, with the burden falling on the compiler to collect the appropriate information necessary to compile efficient executable code. The complex syntax of the language together with the desire for efficient executable code make compilation difficult.

Syntax

PL/I programs are written in a free format (with line boundaries ignored) without reserved words. Each statement or declaration ordinarily takes the form of a key word followed by some required information, followed by a choice of *attributes*, each of which consists of an additional key word possibly followed by further specifications in parentheses. For example, a full declaration for a simple integer variable might take the form

DECLARE X FIXED DECIMAL REAL (7) STATIC EXTERNAL;

In this declaration only the key word DECLARE and the identifier X are required. The remaining attributes—FIXED, DECIMAL, REAL, STATIC, EXTERNAL, and precision 7—are entirely optional and may occur in any order. If any are omitted, default attributes are assumed by the compiler.

 Where two or more identifiers share the same attributes, *factoring* of attributes is allowed. For example, the declaration

$$\text{DECLARE (X,Y,Z) FIXED DECIMAL (7);}$$

declares a common set of attributes for each of the identifiers X, Y, and Z. As an additional convenience certain key words may be abbreviated, as in the equivalent

$$\text{DCL (X,Y,Z) FIXED DEC (7);}$$

Most PL/I control statements are structured, so that other statement sequences may be nested within them. In addition, a Pascal-like block structure dominates the overall program organization.

In general, PL/I attempts to balance readability and writeability—statement forms use meaningful key words, but abbreviations and default options may be used to reduce the amount which must be coded.

The Compile-Time Facilities

Most PL/I implementations provide a number of special features which allow modification of a program *during compilation*, in a special prepass before ordinary compilation begins. These *compile-time facilities*, as they are termed, allow the programmer to specify the replacement of certain identifiers with arbitrary strings, the inclusion of program text taken from an external library, the repeated translation of a program segment, or deletion of part of the program text from compilation.

A statement to be *executed at compile time* is designated by an initial % character on the statement. Only a few statement types may be used at compile time, e.g., assignment, GOTO, IF, DO, and END. Special compile-time variables and functions may be declared using DECLARE and PROCEDURE declarations, but only integer and character data types are allowed. Text from an external file is entered into the program text by a %INCLUDE statement. %ACTIVATE and %DEACTIVATE statements allow the compile-time associations for declared identifiers to be activated and deactivated at arbitrary points.

The compile-time facilities may be used by the programmer to speed up execution of his program by moving certain computations to compile time which ordinarily would be performed at run time. For example, suppose that the program contains a simple loop:

```
DO I = 1 TO 5;
A(I) = 2 * B(I);
END;
```

The sequence of statements

$$A(1) = 2 * B(1);$$
$$A(2) = 2 * B(2);$$
$$A(3) = 2 * B(3);$$
$$A(4) = 2 * B(4);$$
$$A(5) = 2 * B(5);$$

is equivalent and faster to execute but tedious to write (and the compiled code probably takes more storage). If the programmer writes instead

%DECLARE I FIXED;
%DO I = 1 TO 5;
A(I) = 2 * B(I);
%END;
%DEACTIVATE I;

the result is that the statements written are actually replaced by the simple five-statement sequence above before the main stage of compilation begins. This replacement occurs as follows. The %DECLARE statement sets up I as a compile-time integer variable. The %DO statement acts as an ordinary DO statement in the manner in which I is initialized and incremented through the values 1, 2, 3, 4, 5. The body of the *compile-time* DO is treated differently, however. Instead of being executed, it is treated as a character string to be scanned. On the initial pass through the loop each occurrence of identifier I in the statement is replaced by the current value of compile-time variable I (converted to a character string). Thus the result on the first iteration is the string $A(1) = 2 * B(1)$. Each subsequent iteration through the loop produces another copy of the body with the appropriate substitution for I made. After five iterations the resulting program text is the simple sequence above. The %DEACTIVATE I statement allows I to be used in subsequent program statements without a substitution occurring.

The result of the initial pass during compilation in which compile-time statements are executed is simply another PL/I program in which the original compile-time statements have been deleted and the designated substitutions in other parts of the program made. These features can be a useful aid to the programmer in avoiding tedious coding without introducing any additional execution cost. However, there is also a danger, as the example above illustrates: use of the compile-time facilities may cause a large increase in the size of the compiled program for only a small decrease in execution time.

14-9 STRUCTURE OF A PL/I VIRTUAL COMPUTER

PL/I programs are compiled into executable machine code, but a substantial amount of run-time software support is required for simulation of many PL/I features, e.g., input-output, exception handling, and data type conversions. In general, hardware data representations are used and run-time data descriptors are not required, except in the case of variable-size arrays, variable-length character strings, and array cross sections. Most of the primitive operations, outside of the basic arithmetic, relational, and Boolean operations, require software simulation. The large number of data types and primitive operations provided in the language make the number of necessary run-time support routines correspondingly large.

PL/I run-time storage management is rather complex. A static area is required to store the compiled code for the executable program, the run-time support routines, STATIC data structures and variables, and various pieces of system-defined data. A central stack is used for subprogram and block activation records. Each activation record in general contains a static chain pointer, return point, storage areas for AUTOMATIC variables and data structures, and various other pieces of system data. Ordinarily the central stack is used for most run-time storage allocation.

A heap is necessary only when a program uses BASED or CONTROLLED variables or data structures, which can be created and destroyed anytime during program execution within the block or subprogram in which they are declared. Management of storage in the heap is simple. Storage is allocated and freed only upon explicit use of ALLOCATE and FREE statements, and no attempt is made to avoid the generation of garbage and dangling references. Free storage in the heap is allocated in variable-size blocks.

14-10 REFERENCES AND SUGGESTIONS FOR FURTHER READING

The standard definition of PL/I is found in (PL/I [1976]); the definition of the standard subset of the language is given in (PL/I [1981]). A more readable semantic description of the language is provided in an excellent article by Beech [1970]. Nicholls [1975], Elson [1973], and Harrison [1973] also treat various aspects of PL/I in depth. Proposed extensions to the language for real-time applications are presented by Barnes [1979].

The history of the PL/I development is treated at length by Sammet [1969]. The article by Radin [1981] provides a more personal view of the early history of the language.

One of the first formal semantic definitions for a major language was developed by the IBM Vienna Laboratory for a definition of PL/I. Lucas and Walk [1969] give an overview of the methods used. The standard PL/I definition referenced above uses a less formal method based closely on the Vienna techniques; Marcotty and Sayward [1977] describe these methods.

Two implementations of the language are described briefly by Conway and Wilcox [1973] and Freiburghouse [1969].

14-11 PROBLEMS

1. Determine whether subprogram parameters are transmitted by *reference* or by *value-result* in your local PL/I implementation by experimenting with some test programs. [*Hint*: A main program and a subprogram are needed. Viewed from the main program both transmission techniques should appear indistinguishable, but in the subprogram there are some subtle differences which appear when parameter transmission is coupled with nonlocal referencing.]

2. Consider the program segment

```
DECLARE 1 NODE BASED (P),
          2 CAR POINTER,
          2 CDR POINTER;
DECLARE (Q,Z) POINTER;
ALLOCATE NODE SET (Q);
              .
              .
              .
```

(1) $Q \to CDR = Z;$

```
              .
              .
              .
```

In line (1) an assignment is made to the CDR field of the structure of type NODE pointed to by Q. Unfortunately Q may not point to a structure of type NODE at the time of the assignment. For example, if another BASED structure type, TAB, has also been declared, line (1) might be preceded by a statement ALLOCATE TAB SET(Q) and then the assignment to the CDR field of Q would be nonsense. In PL/I implementations the programmer usually has no protection against such errors. *Problem*: Design two *safe* PL/I systems that will not allow an access or an assignment to a field of a BASED structure through an incorrect pointer:

(a) *System 1*. This system utilizes *dynamic* (run-time) *type checking* to protect against such errors. Specify the run-time mechanisms and data necessary to make use of BASED variables safe.

(b) *System 2*. This system utilizes *static* (compile-time) *type checking* but requires some slight restriction and modification of the language. Specify how the language needs to be modified to make this possible.

Do not concern yourself with problems of BASED and POINTER variables transmitted as parameters but only with local structures and variables. (*Hint*: Hoare [1968] provides some useful suggestions.)

CHAPTER 15

Pascal

The original design of Pascal was aimed at creation of a simple language suitable for teaching purposes and for construction of system software such as compilers. The original definition and implementation appeared in 1971. A revised definition and implementation appeared in 1973. Subsequently the language is found in Pascal [1983] and provides the basis for this struction in a variety of application areas. The standard definition of the language is found in (Pascal [1983]) and provides the basis for this chapter.

The earlier language ALGOL 60 (Naur [1963]) played an important role in the Pascal design, not only in providing some particulars such as the general syntactic form and block-structured layout, but also, more importantly, in emphasizing simplicity and elegance in design. The design of ALGOL 60 influenced many other language designs during the 1960s and also played a central role as the object for many theoretical studies in language syntax and semantics. Pascal has played a somewhat similar role during the 1970s. It has formed the object and basis for many theoretical studies and has heavily influenced the design of later languages such as Ada (Chapter 16), Euclid (Lampson et al. [1977]), Gypsy (Ambler et al. [1977]), CLU (Liskov et al. [1977]), and Concurrent Pascal (Brinch Hansen [1975]).

15-1 BRIEF OVERVIEW OF THE LANGUAGE

Pascal is a block-structured language. A Pascal program is always formed from a single main program block, which contains within it definitions of the subprograms used. These definitions may be nested to as many levels as required. Each block (main program or subprogram) has a characteristic structure: a header giving the specification of parameters and results, followed by constant definitions, type definitions, local variable declarations, other (nested) subprogram definitions, and the statements that make up the executable part, in that order.

The most innovative part of the design lies in the treatment of data types. A large selection of different data types is provided: integers, reals, characters, enumerations, Booleans, arrays, records, sequential files, and a limited form of sets. In addition a pointer type and an operation to create new data objects of any type allow the programmer to construct new linked data objects during program execution. More important perhaps is the fact that Pascal allows the separate definition of a data type to be given by the programmer. Individual variables of the type may then be declared by giving only the name of the new type, without repeating the definition. These type definitions provide the beginnings of a true abstract data type facility, as discussed in Chapter 5, although they do not provide grouping and encapsulation of the type definition with a set of subprograms for operating on data objects of the new type.

Subprograms take the form of functions (if they return a single value) or procedures (if they act by modifying their parameters or global variables). Type specifications must be provided for all parameters, and complete static type checking is possible for correspondence of actual and formal parameter types in each subprogram call.

Sequence-control structures in Pascal are straightforward. Statement labels and **goto** statements are seldom used. Instead statement-level sequence control is based on structured control statements: compound statements, conditional and **case** statements, and three forms of iteration statement. Subprograms are invoked with the usual call-return structure, with recursion.

Since Pascal is a block-structured language, most of its data-control structure for variable references uses the standard static scope rules and nested program format characteristic of block structure. Parameters may be transmitted either by value or by reference. Subprograms may be passed as parameters, but statement labels may not.

Pascal may be implemented efficiently on conventional computer hardware. The design includes only language features for which there exist well-understood and efficient implementations. During translation, static type checking for almost all operations is possible, so that little dynamic checking is required but full security of execution is still provided. Translation is ordinarily into executable machine code, although some Pascal implementations instead translate into a virtual machine code, which is interpreted and executed by a software interpreter.

During execution of a Pascal program a central stack is used for subprogram activation records, with a heap storage area for data objects created directly for use with pointer variables, and a static area for subprogram code segments and run-time support routines. Few run-time support routines are required beyond the standard procedures for input-output to sequential files and procedures for storage management.

15-2 AN ANNOTATED EXAMPLE: SUMMATION OF A VECTOR

The Pascal program of Fig. 15-1 represents a main program and a function subprogram. The subprogram, SUM, computes the sum of the components of an argument vector of real numbers. The main program serves as a driver for the subprogram, creating a vector, reading numbers into the vector, calling SUM to compute the sum, printing the result, and looping to input a new set of numbers and repeat the cycle. The program is the Pascal equivalent of the FORTRAN example of Sec. 12-2. The following explanation of the details of the program structure is keyed to the line numbers on the left of Fig. 15-1, which are not part of the Pascal program itself.

Line 1. Beginning of the main program, MAIN, which extends to line 31. The main program forms the outermost block, within which all other subprogram definitions are nested in typical block-structured program style. Two external files, INFILE and OUTFILE, are declared as formal parameters to the main program.

Line 2. Beginning of the constant-definitions section of the main program. The layout of the program (line divisions and indentation) is unrestricted; this example shows a typical Pascal style.

Line 3. A constant SIZE is defined. A subsequent use of the identifier SIZE in the program is equivalent to use of the literal 99 at that point.

Line 4. Beginning of the type-definitions section of the main program. Both this section and the constant-definitions section are optional in any program or subprogram.

Line

```
1     program MAIN(INFILE,OUTFILE);
2     const
3         SIZE = 99;
4     type
5         VECT = array [1 . . SIZE] of real;
6     var
7         INFILE,OUTFILE: text;
8         A: VECT;
9         J,K: integer;
10    function SUM(V: VECT; N: integer): real;
11        var
12            TEMP: real;
13            I: integer;
14        begin {SUM}
15            TEMP := 0;
16            for I := 1 to N do TEMP := TEMP + V[I];
17            SUM := TEMP
18        end; {SUM}
19    begin {MAIN}
20        read(INFILE, K);
21        while (K > 0) and (K < = SIZE) do
22            begin
23                for J := 1 to K do
24                    begin
25                        read(INFILE, A[J]);
26                        write(OUTFILE, A[J])
27                    end
28                writeln(OUTFILE, 'SUM = ',SUM(A,K));
29                read((INFILE,K)
30            end
31    end. {MAIN}
```

Fig. 15-1   Example Pascal program

Line 5. A new type VECT is defined. Each data object of type VECT is a one-dimensional array of 99 components, each a real number.

Line 6. Beginning of the variable-declarations section for the main program.

Line 7. The two input files are declared to be textfiles, where TEXT is a predefined type:

$$TEXT = \textbf{file of } CHAR;$$

A textfile is thus a sequential file in which each component is a single character.

Line 8. Variable A is declared to be of type VECT, so A is an array of 99 real numbers. Alternatively, the type VECT could have been replaced by the definition of VECT in line 5 to give

A: **array** [1..SIZE] **of** real;

However, then A could not be passed as a parameter to function SUM in line 28, because SUM expects its first parameter to be a VECT. Even were A not passed as a parameter, the use of an explicit type definition makes the program easier to modify later.

Line 9. J and K are declared to be simple integer variables.

Lines 10-18. Definition of the function subprogram SUM. This definition forms a second block nested within the outer main program block.

Line 10. The function subprogram heading declares the name of the function, SUM, the names and types of the two formal parameters, V and N, and the type of the result (*real*). Since no explicit designation of method of transmission is given, the actual parameters corresponding to V and N are transmitted by value. This means that the actual parameter vector is copied into the local vector V on entry. Alternatively, the name V could be preceded by **var** in the formal-parameter list, indicating transmission by reference. A new level of referencing environment begins here. The name SUM is part of the main program local environment, but the formal parameters V and N are part of the local environment of SUM.

Line 11. Beginning of the variable-declarations section of subprogram SUM. Note that the constant- and type-definition sections have been omitted, since no new types or constants are defined.

Lines 12-13. Local variables TEMP and I are declared as part of the local environment of SUM.

Line 14. Beginning of the executable-statements part of subprogram SUM.

Line 15. Pascal uses ":=" to indicate the assignment operation. The variable TEMP is set initially to zero.

Line 16. A loop that sums the first N components of the vector V, using TEMP to collect the partial results. The loop body is always a single statement, either a simple statement as in this case or a compound statement. Note that the loop index variable must be explicitly declared as a local variable.

Line 17. The sum collected in TEMP is assigned to the function name SUM to indicate that this value is to be returned as the value of the function when execution is complete (unless modified by some subsequent assignment to SUM).

Line 18. End of the definition of subprogram SUM. When execution of the body of SUM reaches this point, a return to the caller occurs.

Line 19. Beginning of the body (executable statements) of the main program. At run time, execution of the overall program begins at this point.

Line 20. An integer is read from external file INFILE into local variable K. The predefined READ procedure provides automatic conversion from the character format on the file to internal binary data representations. This statement shows the form of a Pascal procedure call.

Lines 21-30. The main loop of the program, repeated until a value of K is read that is not in the range 1 to 99. Note that a new value for K is read at the end of each iteration in line 29. Line 21 is the loop header; lines 22-30 are a single compound statement that forms the body of the loop.

Lines 23-27. An inner loop that reads K values from INFILE into the components of vector A. After each value is read, it is output also to file OUTFILE. The predefined WRITE procedure provides automatic conversion and line formatting so that the values output are in character form and appropriately spaced on one or more lines for possible printing.

Line 28. The predefined WRITELN procedure is the same as the WRITE procedure, but it also terminates the current line of output by writing an "end-of-line" character. The first value output is the string "SUM ="; the second is the number returned as the result of the call to function SUM with vector A and integer K as arguments.

Line 29. A new value for K is read.

Line 30. The **while** loop ends. A new iteration begins with the termination test in line 21.

Line 31. End of the main program. Execution of the program terminates.

15-3   DATA TYPES

The major area in which Pascal represents an advance over earlier languages such as ALGOL 60 lies in its treatment of data types. A broad range of built-in data types is provided, and type definitions may be used to construct definitions of new programmer-defined types. The primitive types are described in this section.

Specification and Implementation

The specifications for the various Pascal primitive data types are generally straightforward, with a few simple restrictions intended to allow efficient implementation. Little software simulation is ordinarily required for the operations on primitive types, beyond the usual routines for input-output to files.

Declarations and Type Checking

Every variable name (and most other identifiers) used in a Pascal program must be declared explicitly at the beginning of a program or subprogram. These declarations allow the complete local and nonlocal referencing environments for each subprogram to be determined during compilation, along with the type of each variable used. Complete static type checking is performed for both local and nonlocal variable references for each operation used in a program. The declarations also allow the storage required for each variable to be determined during compilation.

A declaration of a variable takes the form

$$\langle variable\text{-}name\rangle : \langle type\rangle;$$

where the type may be one of the primitive types discussed below or a programmer-defined type defined in the same subprogram or an outer block. Type definitions are described in the next section.

Constant Definitions

Any program or subprogram may begin with a set of *constant definitions* that allow identifiers to be used in place of literal constant values in a program. The general form of a constant definition is

$$\langle identifier\rangle = \langle literal\text{-}constant\rangle$$

Note that an expression is not allowed on the right side of a constant definition, so one constant cannot be defined in terms of the value of another defined constant. Figure 15-1 shows such a definition of a constant SIZE at the beginning of the main program. References in the program to a defined constant are resolved entirely during compilation, so that it is just as though the program were originally written with the literal value in place of the constant identifier.

Assignment and Initialization

The assignment operation (:=) is defined for all Pascal data types except files, provided that both left- and right-hand side arguments are of the same type. In particular, assignment of a whole data structure such as an array, record, or set to another structure of the same type is defined (provided the data structure has no *file* components) and results in all the component values in the receiving structure being replaced by their corresponding values in the structure named on the right of the assignment. The implementation of the assignment operation is simply an operation of copying the values in one block of storage into another block, since all elementary and structured data objects in Pascal are represented as sequential blocks of storage at run time (with the exception of files and data objects constructed by the programmer using pointers).

An inconvenience in Pascal is the lack of a facility for specifying initial values for variables. Instead an explicit assignment of initial value is required after entry to the subprogram where the variable is declared. All variables are uninitialized (have arbitrary values) when first created.

Integers

Data objects of type integer, ordinarily represented using the hardware integer number representation, are provided. Arithmetic and relational operations are defined using the usual infix notation for the binary operations: +, −, *, **div** (division), **mod** (remainder), =, <> (inequality), <, >, <= (less than or equal), and >= (greater than or equal). The largest integer value is the value of the predefined constant MAXINT (set by the implementor to reflect the largest conveniently representable integer value). The arithmetic operations are generally implemented using the corresponding hardware primitive operations.

Reals

The predefined type *real* usually corresponds to a hardware floating-point representation (if available). A simple set of operations is supported, again using the usual infix notation: +, −, *, =, <>, <, >, <=, >=, and / (division). No exponentiation is provided, but some basic arithmetic functions are built in, e.g., SIN (sine), COS (cosine), and ABS (absolute value).

Enumerations

An enumeration type may be defined using the syntax

$$\langle \textit{type-name} \rangle = (\langle \textit{literal}_1 \rangle, \langle \textit{literal}_2 \rangle, \dots, \langle \textit{literal}_k \rangle)$$

where the literals are programmer-chosen identifiers. The literals represent a sequence of values, ordered as listed, so that $\textit{literal}_1 < \textit{literal}_2$, and so on.

The relational operations (=, <, etc.) are defined on enumeration types, as well as the successor and predecessor operations, SUCC and PRED, which give the next and previous literals in an enumeration sequence for a given argument from that sequence. For example, given the declaration

$$CLASS = (FRESH,SOPH,JUNIOR,SENIOR)$$

then PRED(SOPH) = FRESH, SUCC(SOPH) = JUNIOR, and SUCC(SENIOR) is undefined.

Enumeration values are implemented as small integers at run time, as described in Sec. 3-9. The first literal is represented by zero, the second by one, and so forth. The operation ORD returns as its value the integer representing an enumeration value at run time; e.g., if X := SENIOR, then ORD(X) = 3.

Booleans

A predefined Boolean data type is specified as the enumeration

$$BOOLEAN = (FALSE,TRUE)$$

The Boolean operations AND, OR, and NOT are primitive, as well as the relational (and other) operations available for any enumeration type. The Boolean values are implemented as the values 0 and 1, as for other enumerations.

Characters

A predefined type CHAR is defined as an implementation-defined enumeration, listing the available characters in the character set in the order of their collating sequence (see Sec. 3-11). Besides the relational operations SUCC, PRED, and ORD available for any enumeration type, the operation CHR takes an integer argument in the range 0 up to the number of characters (minus one) in the character set and returns the corresponding character value. Thus CHR is the inverse of ORD for character data; i.e., if CH is a variable of CHAR type, then CHR(ORD(CH)) = CH.

Subranges

A subrange of the sequence of values defined by the type **integer** or by an enumeration type may be specified using the syntax ⟨ *first value* ⟩..⟨ *last value* ⟩, e.g., 2..10 or SOPH..SENIOR. An enumeration or a subrange of an enumeration may be used to specify an array subscript range. For example, the declaration

$$Q: \text{ \textbf{array} [CLASS] \textbf{of} STUDENTREC};$$

gives an array of four components selected by Q[FRESH], Q[SOPH], etc.

Arrays

The basic array data structure in Pascal has only a single dimension with an arbitrary subscript range, which may be defined as an integer subrange or an enumeration. Significantly, the subscript range must be fixed at compile time; it cannot involve computed values. Thus the size of an array is always known during compilation. Array components may be of any type, either primitive or programmer-defined. Thus an array of records, an array of files, and an array of sets are all possible structures. An array is declared as

array [⟨*subscript-range*⟩] **of** ⟨*component-type*⟩

A multidimensional array is constructed out of single-dimensional arrays by constructing a one-dimensional array whose components are each a one-dimensional array (i.e., a vector of vectors). For example, to define a 3×6 matrix of real numbers, the declaration might be

array [1..3] **of array** [1..6] **of** real

For convenience, the declaration of a multidimensional array may be shortened by listing all the subscript ranges together, e.g.,

array [1..3,1..6] **of** real

The latter form also allows use of a simpler subscripting syntax for selecting array components, e.g., A[3,4] instead of A[3][4].

The implementation of arrays typically follows the standard sequential representation and uses the accessing formulas described in Sec. 4-5. Since all array subscript ranges are known during compilation, the most efficient form of each accessing formula may be used.

An array may be designated **packed**, e.g.,

packed array [1..6] **of** char

and the implementation is then allowed to use a space-efficient run-time representation instead of the standard array representation. The packed representation is particularly important for character strings (see below) and for bit strings, which may be represented as packed arrays of Boolean components. Generally, selection of a component from a packed array is more expensive at run time because the standard accessing formula cannot be used. Also components of packed arrays may not be transmitted by reference as arguments to subprograms. Two predefined procedures, PACK and UNPACK, allow the components of an unpacked array to be copied to a packed array, and vice versa, using a single procedure call instead of an explicit loop.

Character Strings

A character string is represented in Pascal as a packed array (vector), each of whose components is a single character. Since the subscript range of an array is fixed during compilation, this representation of strings corresponds to the "fixed declared length" representation discussed in Sec. 4-7. The only operations provided for character-string data are the relational operations (=, <, etc.) which apply to strings of the same length. The result is determined by the ordering of characters defined in the enumeration of the CHAR type (discussed above). Assignment to a character-string variable is allowed, but only of another string of the same length. Character strings may be output to textfiles, but they must be read in a character at a time to an ordinary variable or array with components of type CHAR, and subsequently packed into strings using PACK.

Because of the limited facility for creating and manipulating character strings in Pascal, the usual method is to store character data as strings, in packed arrays, but to unpack them before any manipulation. In unpacked form, single characters and sequences of characters may be manipulated by appropriate loops and array subscripting. After processing, the new string may be repacked using the PACK procedure.

Records

The basic Pascal record data type is described fairly completely in Sec. 4-6, with examples of both syntax and implementation. The components of a Pascal record are termed *fields*, and the component names are the *field names*. Each field name and the data type of the associated field must be declared explicitly. The general syntax is

> **record**
> ⟨field-name⟩: ⟨type⟩;
> ⟨field-name⟩, . . . ,⟨field-name⟩: ⟨type⟩;
> ⟨variant-part⟩
> **end;**

where a sequence of one or more fields with the same type may be declared by listing the field names followed by the type.

A record may have a variant part, as shown above, using the syntax

> **case** ⟨tag-field-name⟩: ⟨tag-type⟩ **of**
> ⟨literal-constant⟩: (⟨field-list⟩);
> :
> :
> ⟨literal-constant⟩, . . . , ⟨literal-constant⟩: (⟨field-list⟩)

where each field-list is just a list of field-names and types, possibly ending in another variant, as in the general record syntax above. An example of a Pascal record with a variant part is given in Sec. 4-6. Note that a variant part must always appear as the last part of a record in Pascal. This allows a record to be implemented as described in Sec. 4-6, and the offset of every component may be determined during compilation.

The tag field may be omitted from a variant record, by giving only the tag type and omitting the tag-field name in the syntax above. If omitted, no checking is possible at run time to determine which variant is present when a selection is made of a field in a variant. Thus without the tag field, use of variant records may lead to subtle run-time errors. If the tag field is present explicitly at run time (by declaring the variant with a tag-field name), then run-time checking to determine the validity of selections of fields in a variant is possible in principle, although not all implementations of the language may provide such checking. The variant record structure is regarded as one of the least secure features of Pascal.

A record may be declared as **packed** by beginning the declaration with **packed record**. The implementation may then use a run-time representation for records that minimizes the space required for each field. Only the operations of component selection and assignment are provided for records.

Sets

Pascal provides a limited form of set data type. A set is composed of a set of components, each from some base type, which is restricted to be an enumeration or integer subrange containing less than some maximum number of values. The maximum is determined by the implementor and ordinarily corresponds to the number of bits in one or several words of storage in the underlying hardware computer. The set may then be implemented as a sequence of Boolean values (single bits), where each bit corresponds to one possible element in the base set. If a bit is TRUE, then the element is in the set value, and if FALSE then the element is not in the set value, as described in Sec. 4-10.

The syntax for declaration of a set type is:

$$\langle type\text{-}name \rangle = \textbf{set of } \langle base\ type \rangle$$

where the base type is as described above. A variable of a set type may then have as its values any subset of the values of the base type, including the empty set (written [   ]). A literal constant representing a set value may be written:

$$[\langle value \rangle, \ldots, \langle value \rangle]$$

where each ⟨value⟩ is either a single value or a subrange of values from the base set.

For example, suppose the base type is taken as the enumeration type CLASS defined in the discussion above, and variable S is declared as:

S : set of CLASS;

In the implementation of this set, a sequence of four bits is required because the base set CLASS has four values. Thus the value of S may be represented as a sequence of four bits: 0000 is the empty set, 0010 is the set [JUNIOR], 1100 is the set [FRESH,SOPH], 1111 is the set [FRESH..SENIOR], and so on.

The operations provided for sets are union (syntax "+"), intersection ("*"), and difference ("−"). The relational operations =, <>, <=, and >= are also defined for set types, where the latter two operations denote a test for the inclusion of one set in another; e.g., A <= B means: "Is A a subset of B?" To test whether a particular value is in a set, the operation **in** is used. For example, "SOPH **in** S" means: "Is the value SOPH in the set represented by the current value of S?" Given the implementation of sets using sequences of bits, as described above, these operations are efficiently implementable using the hardware operations on bit sequences (see Problem 5).

Pointers and Programmer-Constructed Data Objects

A data object may contain a pointer to another data object in Pascal. The type of the first data object is then declared to be ↑⟨second-type⟩, where ⟨second-type⟩ is the type of the data object pointed to. A variable may be declared to be of pointer type using the syntax

⟨variable-name⟩: ↑⟨type⟩

and the value of the variable may then be either the null pointer, denoted *nil*, or an actual pointer to a data object of the declared type. By using pointer data objects, arbitrarily linked data objects may be constructed in Pascal.

No operations are defined on pointer values except assignment (which copies the pointer value), the relational operations = and <> (not-equal) which compare pointer values, and the operation NEW. When a program begins execution, no pointer values are defined. During execution a pointer value may be created and assigned as the value of a pointer variable (or pointer component of a data structure) only through execution of the built-in procedure NEW. If P is a pointer variable, declared by "P: ↑T", then execution of "NEW(P)" causes a block of storage to be allocated (in the heap storage area) for a data object of type T, and a pointer to that new data object to be assigned as the value of P. Once a pointer value has been created using

NEW, additional assignments may be used to get copies of the pointer value; e.g., Q := P creates a pointer in Q pointing to the same data object as P. An operation for freeing storage allocated by NEW is provided as a predefined procedure DISPOSE (see Sec. 15-9 and Problem 1).

Files and Input-Output Operations

Sequential files are the only type of file structure provided in Pascal. The syntax for declaring a file is:

file of ⟨*component-type*⟩

where ⟨*component-type*⟩ may be any type except a file or pointer type. Thus the components of a file may be arrays, records, or other structured data objects, in addition to data objects of elementary types.

The first line of a program has the syntax:

program ⟨*prog-name*⟩ (⟨*file-list*⟩)

where ⟨*file-list*⟩ is a list of file names that are presumed to be provided from some external environment to the program. These files must be declared in the local declarations for the main program. Other "local files" may be declared within the main program or a subprogram just as for variables of any other type. These local files may be used as "scratch files" which are written during one part of the program and later are read by another part of the program. Local files disappear upon exit from the program or sub-program in which they are declared, just as any other locally declared data objects in Pascal.

When a file is declared, the file name also is used as the name of a "buffer variable," referenced as ⟨*file-name*⟩↑. This buffer variable is not declared explicitly but may be referenced and assigned in the program. For example, if F is declared as:

F: **file of** integer

then within the program declaring F, the assignment F↑ := 2 or X := F↑ is valid. The buffer variable is the data object representing the local temporary storage for a single component of the file. Two predefined procedures GET and PUT are used to move data from the file to the buffer variable (GET) or from the buffer variable to the file (PUT).

When a new component is to be written to a file, two steps are necessary: (1) the value for the new component must be assigned to the buffer variable for the file, and (2) the procedure PUT must be called to transfer the data from the buffer variable to the file, inserting a new component at the end of the file with the specified value and advancing the file position indicator past the new component. For example, the two statements "F↑ := 2; PUT(F)" must be executed to write the value 2 on file F. A similar sequence is required to read the value of the current component from the file into a local variable; e.g., "X := F↑; GET(F)" copies the current component (in the buffer variable F↑) into variable X and then advances the file to the next component, bringing its value into the buffer variable F↑.

Because most file processing involves many repetitions of these two-step sequences, predefined procedures READ and WRITE are provided that combine the sequences into a single procedure call. For example, READ(F,X) is equivalent to X := F↑; GET(F).

Textfiles. A textfile is a file of single-character components, declared using the predefined type TEXT. A textfile is presumed to be organized into "lines," which are sequences of characters ending with a special "end-of-line" character. Textfiles may be processed using the ordinary file operations, GET, PUT, READ, and WRITE. However, the READ and WRITE procedures are extended to allow a variable of other than character type to be used as an argument; e.g., READ(F,N) is allowed, where N is an integer variable rather than being of type CHAR. When given an argument of numeric rather than character type, READ and WRITE provide automatic conversion between the character representation on the file and the internal binary representation needed for the value of the variable. READ scans the input file until a complete number of the required type is found; WRITE provides automatic formatting of the output data on the output file. READLN and WRITELN procedures provide the same actions as READ and WRITE, but they also advance the file to a new line before they terminate.

In general, the Pascal facilities for file processing are rather simple and limited. Many Pascal implementations extend this basic set of features to include more sophisticated facilities.

15-4   SUBPROGRAMS AND TYPE DEFINITIONS

Two abstraction mechanisms are provided in Pascal: the programmer may define new operations using procedure and function subprograms, and new data types may be defined using type definitions. However, there is no mechanism for constructing true abstract data types, because a set of type definitions and the operations on those types cannot be conveniently encapsulated.

Subprograms

A Pascal subprogram may be either a *function*, if it returns a single value of elementary data type, or a *procedure*, if it returns results only by changing the values of its arguments or of nonlocal variables. The specification for a procedure or function is contained in the heading that begins the definition:

function ⟨ *fn-name* ⟩ (⟨ *formal-parameter-list* ⟩) : ⟨ *result-type* ⟩;

or

procedure ⟨ *proc-name* ⟩ (⟨ *formal-parameter-list* ⟩);

The formal-parameter list contains, for each parameter, its name, data type, and mode of transmission (by value or by reference).

The body of a subprogram has the form:

label
  — list of statement labels used
const
  — list of constant definitions
type
  — list of type definitions
var
  — list of variable declarations
  — list of (nested) procedure and function definitions
begin
  — sequence of executable statements
end;

where any of the sections may be omitted except the executable statement sequence.

A main program has a body of the same form, but it begins with the heading

program ⟨ *main-program-name* ⟩ (⟨ *list of file-names* ⟩);

Figure 15-1 illustrates this program structure, except for the statement label list part (see the discussion of GOTO's in Sec. 15-5).

Implementation of a Pascal subprogram follows rather closely the discussion in Chapters 5 and 6 for subprogram structures with recursion. Each subprogram definition is compiled into a code segment and an activation record template. During compilation the lists of labels, constant definitions, and type definitions are used to set up the appropriate activation record and code segment, but they do not directly appear in the run-time structure.

Type Definitions

A new named type may be defined by using a *type definition* at the beginning of a program or subprogram. The form is

$$\langle \textit{type-name} \rangle = \langle \textit{type-definition} \rangle$$

where the type definition gives the structure of the data objects in the new type, using existing primitive or defined types. An example is seen in the definition of the type VECT in Fig. 15-1.

Type definitions in Pascal are used only during compilation. The compiler enters the information from type definitions into its symbol table and then uses the information to perform static type checking of variable references and to lay out the structure of subprogram activation records. Type definitions do not exist during program execution.

Two variables are considered to have the same type in some cases if the variables are declared using the same type name; in other cases they have the same type if the declared types have the same structure. Thus Pascal uses a mixture of *name* and *structural* equivalence for determining if two variables have the same type. Name equivalence is used in most cases for determining if formal and actual parameters in subprogram calls have the same type; structural equivalence is used in most other situations. Because these rules were not clearly set out in the original Pascal definition, different implementations of the language have used slightly different rules for type equivalence.

15-5   SEQUENCE CONTROL

The sequence-control structures in Pascal are straightforward. The statement-level sequence-control structures, in particular, have served as a model for many later languages.

Expressions

The basic arithmetic, Boolean, relational, and set operations mentioned in the preceding sections may be combined with variable references, constants, data structure component selectors, and function subprogram calls to form expressions in the usual ways. Infix notation is used for binary operations. Parentheses may be used to group parts of an expression to control the sequence in which the operations are executed. In the absence of parentheses, the following precedence of operations is used to determine the execution sequence (from highest to lowest precedence):

$$\textbf{not}$$
$$* \quad / \quad \textbf{div} \quad \textbf{mod} \quad \textbf{and}$$
$$+ \quad - \quad \textbf{or}$$
$$= \quad <> \quad < \quad <= \quad > \quad >=$$

Left-to-right associativity is used if two or more operations at the same precedence level appear in sequence.

One somewhat controversial aspect of Pascal has been the position of the Boolean operations **and** and **or** in this precedence table (see Problem 6). The use of only four precedence levels for operations has the advantage of simplicity, but the lack of a separate precedence level for the **and** and **or** operations causes some surprising results. For example, to test if X is in the range MAX to MIN, one might write

$$\text{if MIN} <= \text{X and X} <= \text{MAX then} \ldots$$

which in Pascal means something unexpected, because it is grouped as

$$\text{if (MIN} <= \text{(X and X))} <= \text{MAX then} \ldots$$

Within a Pascal expression, no coercions of types are performed except to convert an *integer* operand to type *real* where required by the context. The philosophy in the Pascal design is that the programmer should be made explicitly aware of any other type conversions that need to be performed, by invoking explicit type-conversion functions.

Statement Sequence Control

The sequence in which Pascal statements are executed is controlled primarily by the use of structured control statements: conditional and **case** statements, compound statements, and iteration statements. **Goto** statements and statement labels are provided, but their use is discouraged.

Compound statements.   The Pascal compound statement is bracketed by **begin** and **end**:

$$\textbf{begin}$$
$$\langle \textit{statement} \rangle;$$
$$\vdots$$
$$\langle \textit{statement} \rangle$$
$$\textbf{end}$$

The entire statement sequence, including the **begin** and **end**, becomes a single statement that may be nested within other statements.

Conditional statements.   The simple one- and two-branch conditional statements have the forms

$$\textbf{if} \ \langle \textit{Boolean-expression} \rangle \ \textbf{then} \ \langle \textit{statement} \rangle$$

and

$$\textbf{if} \ \langle \textit{Boolean-expression} \rangle \ \textbf{then} \ \langle \textit{statement}_1 \rangle \ \textbf{else} \ \langle \textit{statement}_2 \rangle$$

When the two forms are combined, e.g., as in

$$\text{if } A=0 \text{ then if } B<C \text{ then } S_1 \text{ else } S_2$$

the ambiguity discussed in Sec. 9-1 regarding the execution sequence is resolved by always pairing an **else**-*part with the nearest preceding unmatched* **then**. Thus the statement above is parsed as though it were grouped

$$\text{if } A=0 \text{ then (if } B < C \text{ then } S_1 \text{ else } S_2)$$

rather than

$$\text{if } A=0 \text{ then (if } B < C \text{ then } S_1) \text{ else } S_2$$

CASE *statements.* The **case** statement takes the form

```
case ⟨expression⟩ of
    ⟨constant⟩: ⟨statement⟩;
         .
         .
         .
    ⟨constant⟩, . . . , ⟨constant⟩: ⟨statement⟩
end
```

where the constants represent possible values of the expression. For example, if variable DEVSTATUS is declared as an enumeration

$$\text{DEVSTATUS} = (\text{READY,INUSE,NOTREADY})$$

then a **case** statement might take the form

```
case DEVSTATUS of
    READY,INUSE:⟨statement₁⟩;
    NOTREADY:⟨statement₂⟩
end
```

When a **case** statement is executed, the expression in the head of the statement is evaluated, and the value is used to determine which of the following statements is executed next. If the value does not match one of the constants labeling any of the following statements, then it is considered a run-time error. This form of case statement may be implemented using the jump-table structure described in Sec. 6-3.

Iteration statements. Three forms of iteration statement are provided in Pascal. The two basic forms, the **while** and **repeat** statements provide for the loop termination test to be made before each iteration (**while**) or after each iteration (**repeat**). The syntax is

$$\textbf{while} \langle \textit{Boolean-expression} \rangle \textbf{ do } \langle \textit{statement} \rangle$$

and

repeat ⟨ *statement-sequence* ⟩ **until** ⟨ *Boolean-expression* ⟩

In either case, the body of the loop may be a sequence of statements, but an explicit **begin . . . end** compound statement must be used to bracket the sequence for the **while** statement.

The third form of iteration statement is a **for** loop, which provides iteration while incrementing or decrementing a counter. The syntax is

for ⟨ *simple-variable* ⟩ := ⟨ *initial-value* ⟩ **to** ⟨ *final-value* ⟩ **do**
⟨ *statement* ⟩

or

for ⟨ *simple-variable* ⟩ := ⟨ *initial-value* ⟩ **downto** ⟨ *final-value* ⟩ **do**
⟨ *statement* ⟩

where the **to** form indicates an increment of one in the value of the simple variable after each iteration and **downto** indicates an increment of minus one. No other increments are allowed in Pascal. The initial value and final value are specified by arbitrary expressions that are evaluated at the time of initial entry to the loop. Assignments to the controlled variable within the loop are prohibited.

GOTO *statements and statement labels.* A Pascal statement may be labeled with an integer label, and control may then be transferred to it using a **goto** statement. Each statement label that is used in a subprogram must be "declared" in the statement-label list at the beginning of that subprogram. Statement labels used in one subprogram are visible in subprograms whose definitions are nested within that subprogram, according to the usual static scope rules. Thus a **goto** statement in a subprogram may transfer control to a statement in an enclosing subprogram. The statement-label list at the beginning of a subprogram allows the Pascal compiler to determine, in a single pass through the source program, whether the statement named in a **goto** statement is local or nonlocal to the subprogram containing the **goto**. When a **goto** to a nonlocal label is executed, execution of the current subprogram is terminated, as well as execution of each subprogram back down the dynamic chain of subprogram calls, until the subprogram is reached that contains the labeled statement.

Because of the availability of other structured control statements in Pascal, it is seldom necessary to use **goto** statements other than for exception handling. Thus many Pascal programs contain no **goto** statements at all.

Subprogram Sequence Control

Pascal provides only the standard call-return structure for control of subprogram execution, with recursive subprogram calls allowed. Function calls are written in prefix form within expressions; procedure calls are written as separate statements. The syntax is

⟨*subprogram-name* ⟩(⟨*actual-parameter-list* ⟩)

The details of parameter transmission are taken up in the next section. Execution of a subprogram terminates after the last statement in the subprogram body is executed. No explicit **return** statement is provided. Alternatively, a **goto** statement to a nonlocal label may be used to terminate execution of a subprogram, as mentioned above.

Since recursive subprogram calls are allowed in Pascal, there may be multiple simultaneous activations of the same subprogram during execution. Implementation of this control structure typically uses a central stack of activation records, with an activation record created on the stack on subprogram entry and deleted from the stack on exit, as described in Sec. 6-5.

15-6   DATA CONTROL

Pascal is a block-structured language in which static scope rules are used to determine the meaning of nonlocal references to names. Parameters are passed by value or reference.

Names and Referencing Environments

A global system-defined referencing environment is predefined to contain definitions of procedures such as GET, PUT, READ, and WRITE; functions such as SIN and SQRT; constants such as MAXINT; and types such as INTEGER, REAL, and BOOLEAN. All other names are part of a local referencing environment for some subprogram or the main program. Every name used in a Pascal statement must be explicitly declared unless it is part of the predefined global environment.

A Pascal program has the nested structure characteristic of block-structured languages. A program consists of an outer block defining the main program and blocks representing subprogram definitions nested within the main program block or within each other.

Local Environments

All local variables are created on entry to a subprogram and are deleted on exit. The implementation structure is described in Sec. 7-4.

WITH *statements.*   Pascal provides a **with** statement that sets up a special local referencing environment just for execution of a single group of statements. The **with** statement has the syntax

$$\textbf{with} \; \langle \textit{record-variable} \rangle \; \textbf{do} \; \langle \textit{statement} \rangle$$

where the statment ordinarily is a compound statement. Within a **with** statement, the fields of the named record variable may be referenced without prefixing the field name with the record name. For example, if R is a variable defined as a record with fields named A, B, and C, then the statement

$$\textbf{with} \; R \; \textbf{do} \; A := X + B$$

causes field R.A to be assigned the sum of the value of variable X and the field R.B; i.e., the above **with** statement is equivalent to the single statement

$$R.A := X + R.B$$

Within this **with** statement, an ordinary variable named A, B, or C would be hidden and could not be referenced.

In small programs, the **with** statement is seldom used. Its main utility occurs in large programs which use record data structures with many fields, which are often again records. References to fields of such records often require long sequences of field selectors, e.g., EMPLOYEE.ADDRESS. STREET.NUMBER. To simplify writing such a program, a group of statements that process, for example, the address part of the employee record may then be put inside a **with** statement that begins

$$\textbf{with} \; \text{EMPLOYEE.ADDRESS} \; \textbf{do} \ldots$$

and references within these statements may then be written using only the shortened field name, e.g., STREET.NUMBER. **With** statements are processed by the compiler and have no effect on the run-time structure (except to allow some special optimizations of record field references to be used).

Nonlocal Environments

Data may be shared between subprograms through nonlocal references to variables. The mechanisms are those typical of languages using static scope and block structure, as described in Secs. 7-3 and 7-7.

Parameters and Parameter Transmission

Parameter transmission both by value and by reference are provided in Pascal. The concepts are as discussed in Sec. 7-8. Each subprogram heading lists the names and data types of each formal parameter. The choice of transmission by value or reference for each parameter is indicated by prefixing each reference-parameter name by the keyword **var** in the formal-parameter list. For example, in the procedure heading

procedure SUB (X: integer; **var** Y: real)

the first parameter, X, is transmitted by value (since **var** does not appear) and the second, Y, is transmitted by reference.

A function subprogram may return a single value of elementary data type. Figure 15-1 shows the syntax for specifying the type of a function value. Function subprograms may also have reference parameters, so they may return results through modification of their parameters in addition to returning an explicit function value.

The implementation of Pascal parameter transmission follows the structure described in Sec. 7-8. Reference parameters are implemented by transmitting a pointer to the actual parameter, while value parameters are implemented by copying the actual-parameter value into the formal parameter, which is treated as a local variable.

Subprogram Names as Parameters

Procedures and functions may be passed as parameters to other subprograms. The basic mechanisms are as described in Sec. 7-8. In the original version of Pascal, the formal parameter consisted of the specification "**procedure** ⟨*proc-name*⟩" or "**function** ⟨*fn-name*⟩" with the corresponding actual parameter consisting of simply the actual subprogram name to be used. This structure makes it impossible to perform static type checking of the actual parameters in the call of the subprogram transmitted as a parameter (see Sec. 7-8).

The standard version of Pascal remedies this design problem by requiring that the formal-parameter specification for a subprogram name being transmitted as a parameter include the complete procedure or function heading, including the number, order, and type of parameters required by the subprogram. The compiler may then check that any call of the subprogram using the formal-parameter name is correct.

15-7   OPERATING AND PROGRAMMING ENVIRONMENT

Pascal is designed for a straightforward batch-processing operating environment containing only sequential files. No provision is made for more complex file structures or for direct access to user terminals or external devices. However, the simple, regular, and generally elegant structure of the language makes the addition of new predefined procedures and data types for special purposes rather easy.

The Pascal design also contains no special provisions for separate compilation of subprograms or for any other special characteristics of a programming environment. Programs are assumed to be assembled into complete units that include all subprograms, type definitions, and other components, before compilation begins. Thus merging of separately written program components is done at the source language level, before compilation, rather than through linking of separately compiled components before execution. The rationale for this aspect of the design is that a Pascal compiler may be made efficient enough that recompilation of an entire program is no more expensive than relinking of a set of separately compiled program components, and the compiler provides much more extensive checking and error detection.

15-8   SYNTAX AND TRANSLATION

The examples of the preceding sections illustrate the general style of Pascal syntax. The division of programs into lines and the indentation of each line is entirely the programmer's choice. Reserved words are used to delimit the parts of most statements and declarations. Nesting of syntactic elements is found in all parts of the language; statements, declarations, and subprogram definitions may all be nested. The extensive use of nested syntactic elements makes it possible to construct complex programs using only a few different types of syntactic constructs. The resulting simplicity and regularity of the syntactic structure makes most aspects of parsing of Pascal programs straightforward.

Formal Syntax

Most definitions of Pascal include a BNF grammar that gives a formal definition of its syntax. However, a second form of syntactic definition has also seen wide use with Pascal, the *syntax chart*. A syntax chart can be used to describe exactly the same set of constructs as a BNF grammar. The syntax chart looks somewhat like a flow chart, defining a single class of syntactic constructs. For example, Fig. 15-2 shows syntax charts defining the Pascal constructs *program* and *block* (subprogram body). In a syntax chart, each possible path through the chart, beginning at the upper left corner and proceeding through the chart to an exit point, defines a sequence of elements that represent a valid syntactic construct in the language. The circles and ovals contain elements that must be written exactly as given; the rectangles contain the names of constructs defined by other syntax charts. The syntax chart for *program* in Fig. 15-2 is equivalent to the BNF grammar productions

program

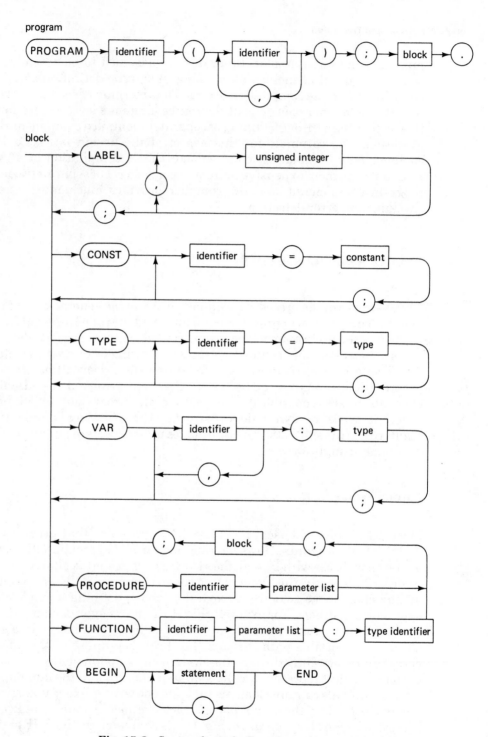

Fig. 15-2   Syntax charts for Pascal programs and blocks

$\langle\,program\,\rangle ::=$
$\qquad$ PROGRAM $\langle identifier\rangle$ $(\langle identifier\text{-}list\rangle)$; $\langle block\rangle$.
$\langle\,identifier\text{-}list\,\rangle ::=$
$\qquad \langle\,identifier\,\rangle \mid \langle\,identifier\text{-}list\,\rangle,\langle\,identifier\,\rangle$

Note that a single syntax chart may combine many BNF productions and thus be easier to read than the corresponding BNF grammar.

Translation

Pascal source programs are ordinarily compiled into machine code that is directly executable by the hardware interpreter on larger computers. On small computers, many implementations instead compile into an intermediate code (usually termed *P-code*) that is then executed by a software interpreter. The P-code compilation has the advantage that the executable object code requires less storage space, but execution using a software interpreter is considerably slower than direct execution by the hardware interpreter. Another advantage of the P-code implementation is that the compiler is more easily transported to another computer, because less of the implementation structure is dependent on the underlying hardware organization.

A Pascal compiler may be structured so that it is extremely efficient, and so that it also produces efficient object code for execution. Parsing in a Pascal compiler is often based directly on the structure of the syntax charts (or BNF grammar) defining the Pascal syntax (see Wirth [1971b] for a description of such an implementation). The compiler can provide full static type checking for almost all language constructs. It may also determine the size and organization of subprogram activation records so that creation of an activation record during execution involves only allocation of a block of storage of known size on the central stack. The offsets within the activation record of each data object referenced may be computed during compilation as well, so that run-time data referencing is extremely efficient.

One aspect of the overall language design that contributes substantially to efficient compilation is that each identifier in a program is required to be *defined* before it may be *referenced*. For example, a statement may contain a reference to a variable X, but the declaration for variable X must appear in the current subprogram or an outer containing subprogram before the reference to X. Similarly, the declaration for X may contain a reference to a defined type T, but the definition for T must appear in the type-definitions section of a subprogram before it is referenced in the declaration for X, and so on. Even statement labels must be declared before they can be referenced in a **goto** statement, even though the actual statement with that label appears later in the statement sequence.

There is one instance in which, inherently, it is difficult to define an identifier before it is referenced for the first time: the case of two mutually recursive subprograms. For example, if A and B are subprograms and A calls B and B calls A, then if the definition of A appears before the definition of B, then the call to B in A necessarily appears before B's definition. Reversing the order of the definitions of A and B only makes the call to A (in B) appear before the definition of A. This problem is solved in Pascal by requiring that a **forward** *declaration* be given for whichever of the subprograms is defined last. The **forward** declaration has the form of the heading for the subprogram definition, including the full parameter list, followed by the word **forward** in place of the subprogram body. For example,

procedure A (⟨*formal-parameter-list*⟩); **forward;**

Following this forward declaration for A, subprogram B could be defined, and then later the full definition for the body of A is given (but the formal-parameter list is not repeated). The **forward** declaration gives the compiler enough information to correctly compile the call on A found in B, even though the complete definition of A has not yet appeared.

The reason for the Pascal emphasis on definition before use of an identifier lies in the intent that a Pascal compiler be a *one-pass compiler*. A one-pass compiler makes a single sweep through the source program, reading and processing it one subprogram definition at a time, generating the executable object program as it goes. In order to process the program in one pass, the compiler must have enough information at each point about the meaning of each identifier so that the correct object code can be generated. A one-pass compiler is usually substantially faster than a multipass compiler that must repeatedly traverse the entire source program or some internal representation of it before generating object code, because the multipass compiler must usually store the intermediate program representation on a file between passes.

15-9 STRUCTURE OF A PASCAL VIRTUAL COMPUTER

Implementation of Pascal requires a static storage area for procedure code segments and various items of system-defined data. A central stack is required for allocation of subprogram activation records at the time each subprogram is called. A heap storage area is also required for storage of data objects constructed dynamically by the NEW operation. The general layout of the Pascal storage areas during program execution is shown in Fig. 8-2.

Note that the stack and the heap areas are set up in a single large statically allocated block of storage. The stack grows from one end toward the middle in response to subprogram calls. The heap grows from the other end toward the middle in response to invocations of NEW. The stack shrinks as storage for activation records is recovered automatically on subprogram exit. However, if the stack and heap ever meet, then execution of the program must be aborted on the next request for either stack or heap allocation, because in general it is impossible with this implementation scheme to add storage to either area. Of course, alternative implementation methods might be used to allow one or both areas to expand further.

Management of storage recovery in the heap area is a troublesome issue in Pascal implementation. Freeing of storage is programmer controlled, using a predefined procedure DISPOSE. The procedure DISPOSE is called with a pointer to a programmer-constructed data object as its argument. DISPOSE sets the pointer value to NIL, so as to destroy the access path to the data object, and it may free the storage for reuse. However, the usual potential for generation of dangling references or garbage is present, as discussed in Sec. 8-3. Although a garbage-collection or reference-count method might be implemented to manage storage in the Pascal heap, these mechanisms are not generally used because of their extra cost in storage and execution efficiency. Most Pascal implementations instead use a simpler implementation of DISPOSE (see Problem 1) that potentially may generate garbage and/or dangling references.

The run-time structure of Pascal ordinarily requires little software simulation if the compiler produces object code that is directly executable by the hardware interpreter. Most of the language constructs may be represented by hardware instructions or simple instruction sequences (with the exception of the predefined procedures for input-output). No run-time checking is required except in the case of assignments to subrange type variables, subscript range checking, and a few other cases. In only a few circumstances does Pascal allow constructs to be used that are neither checked during compilation nor execution and that potentially may lead to run-time errors, e.g., variant records without a tag field. In general, execution of a Pascal program is both very efficient and very secure in comparison with other languages.

15-10 REFERENCES AND SUGGESTIONS FOR FURTHER READING

Pascal was designed by Niklaus Wirth in the late 1960s. The first published report appeared in 1971 (Wirth [1971a]). Unlike most languages, an implementation of the language was constructed during the design stage, and the language was used to write its own compiler (Wirth [1971b]). Thus from the beginning Pascal compilers have been written in Pascal. Based on experience with the original design, some features of the language were extensively modified, and a revised report on the language appeared in 1973 (see Jensen and Wirth [1978]). The standard definition is found in (Pascal [1983]). A formal semantic definition of much of the language also was prepared (Hoare and Wirth [1973]). Two texts by Wirth describe applications of the language (Wirth [1973, 1976]). The basic reference manual is by Jensen and Wirth [1978]. Barron [1981] gives a collection of articles on the language and its implementation; see also Pemberton and Daniels [1982].

The language fairly quickly became the basis for other language designs because of its many innovations, particularly in the area of data types and type definitions. References to many of these languages are given at the beginning of this chapter. Wirth himself designed two languages, MODULA (Wirth [1977b]) and MODULA2 (Wirth [1980]), that used many of the Pascal concepts in the framework of a language for construction of operating systems and other low-level system software.

Feuer and Gehani [1982] give a comparison of Pascal and the C language. Numerous critiques of the Pascal design have also appeared; Wasserman [1980] contains a collection of these. Moffat [1981] gives a comprehensive bibliography of the Pascal literature.

15-11 PROBLEMS

1. Implementations of Pascal have handled the DISPOSE operation in various ways. Some of the strategies have been:

   (a) Have DISPOSE(P), when executed, do nothing except assign NIL as the value of pointer variable P. Implement heap storage management using a single pointer to the current top (first free location) in the heap. Advance the pointer to allocate storage when NEW is called. Never retreat the pointer.
   (b) Implement heap storage management as in part (a), using a single pointer that is advanced by NEW, but have DISPOSE both assign NIL to its pointer parameter P and also move the heap top pointer back to the position below the data object to which P points, so that storage for P is recovered and returned to the heap. [Hint: Consider the sequence NEW(P); NEW(Q); DISPOSE(P);]
   (c) Implement the heap using a free-space list for variable size blocks of storage, as described in Sec. 8-8. Use a first-fit or best-fit allocation strategy for storage requested by NEW. Implement DISPOSE so that it sets its pointer parameter P to NIL and returns the block of storage to which P points to the free-space list.

   Discuss the problems of garbage, dangling references, and fragmentation that result with each of these possible implementations of NEW and DISPOSE.

2. The ORD function is defined as taking a single argument, which must be a value

from some enumeration. ORD returns the integer representing the position of that value in the enumeration sequence (0 if the value is first in the sequence, 1 if it is the second, etc.). However, since a value from an enumeration is represented at run time by the integer representing the position of the value in the sequence anyway, ORD really has nothing to do. For example, given the enumeration type

CLASS = (FRESH,SOPH,JUNIOR,SENIOR)

and a variable X of type CLASS, the assignment X := SENIOR actually assigns the value 3 to X, and subsequently ORD(X) evaluates to 3. Thus ORD gets 3 as its argument and returns 3 as its result, so it does nothing useful (and a Pascal implementation may eliminate any call on ORD from the executable object code altogether). However, ORD does have a purpose, but its effect appears during compilation.

(a) Explain the purpose of ORD. Why does Pascal provide this function when it has no run-time effect at all?

(b) For the variable X defined above, explain the actions taken during *execution* for the two program fragments:

if X = SENIOR **then** . . .

and

if ORD(X) = 3 **then** . . .

(c) For the two program fragments in part (b), explain the actions taken during *compilation* in type checking the two fragments above and the third fragment

if X = 3 **then** . . .

3. A component of a data structure declared as **packed**, e.g., a component of a packed array or record, cannot be transmitted as a reference parameter to a subprogram in Pascal (although transmission by value is acceptable). For example, if procedure P is specified as

procedure P(**var** X: integer); . . .

and array A is declared

A: **packed array** [1 . . 5] **of** integer

then the procedure call P(A[2]) is not allowed, but if array B is identical to A except that B is not packed, then P(B[2]) is allowed. Explain the implementation problem that causes this restriction in the language.

4. Give a set of BNF productions that define the syntactic construct BLOCK, whose definition is given by a syntax chart in Fig. 15-2.

5. Given the representation of Pascal sets using bit strings, as described in Sec. 15-3, and assuming that the maximum number of elements in a set must be less than the word length of the underlying hardware computer, give algorithms for implementing the operations of set union, intersection, difference, and the

membership test (**in**), using the hardware primitives of *logical and*, *logical or*, and *logical complement* on entire words.

6. Define a new precedence table for the basic Pascal operations that occur in expressions, to replace the table given in Sec. 15-5. The new table should provide the most "natural" meaning for an expression that is written without parentheses, such as "MIN $<=$ X **and** X $<=$ MAX". Explain the advantages and disadvantages of your definition as compared to the original Pascal definition.

CHAPTER 16

Ada

The development of the Ada language followed a pattern unique in the history of major programming languages. In the early 1970s the U.S. Department of Defense undertook to develop a standard programming language for embedded-system applications, in which one or more computers are part of a larger system such as an aircraft, ship, or a communications system. Before the design of the language began, a detailed set of specifications were produced that outlined the various capabilities required. These specifications were progressively refined through a series of preliminary documents known as "Strawman," "Woodenman," "Tinman," "Ironman," and finally "Steelman." Each of the preliminary specifications was critiqued by a large group of programming language experts. The "Tinman" specification was used in 1976-77 to determine if an existing language would satisfy all the given requirements, but no suitable language was found. The final specification then became the basis for an international design competition.

Seventeen proposals were received from various groups, and four groups were chosen to construct preliminary designs. Each of the four groups proposed to base their design on Pascal (PL/I or ALGOL 68 were the other possible base languages). After an extensive critique of the four designs by languages and applications experts, two designs were chosen to proceed to the "finals." After some revision of these designs, an extensive critique was again held, leading to the final selection in 1979 of a design that subsequently was named "Ada" (after Ada Lovelace, an early pioneer in computing). Whitaker [1978] gives a more extended history of the early development of Ada.

The Pascal design was the starting point for the design of Ada, but the resulting language is different in many major aspects from Pascal. Most prominently, Ada is a much larger and more complex language than Pascal, and it includes several major sets of features that have no analogue in Pascal—in particular, tasks and concurrent execution, real-time control of tasks, exception handling, and abstract data types. The language has undergone some minor revisions since its original definition. The description of this chapter is based on (Ada [1982]). Because the language has not yet seen extended use, some further changes are likely as more experience is gained.

16-1   BRIEF OVERVIEW OF THE LANGUAGE

Ada is intended to support the construction of large programs by teams of programmers. Rather than being constructed as a single main program and a hierarchy of subprograms, as in Pascal and most other languages, an Ada program is ordinarily designed as a collection of larger "software components" called *packages*. A package may represent an abstract data type or a set of data objects shared between subprograms, but more generally a package contains an integrated set of type definitions, data objects, and subprograms for manipulating these data objects. For example, a package for computer graphics, for input-output to textfiles, for manipulation of large arrays, or for processing a data base might be part of a large Ada program. Such packages would be available to the Ada programmer through a program library, and the programmer's primary task is taken to be construction of a program through combination of existing packages rather than through generation of an entirely new program from scratch. Much of the special nature of Ada and Ada programming comes from this emphasis on program construction using packages.

At the top level, an Ada program consists of a single procedure that serves as a main program. This main program declares variables, giving the type of each, and gives statements to be executed, including calls on other subprograms. However, these data types and subprograms are often part of separately defined packages, which are simply "imported" from a program library as needed. The Ada program may involve a set of separate tasks that are to execute concurrently. If so, then these tasks often are directly initiated by the main program and form the top level of the program structure. Again, however, these tasks ordinarily use data types and subprograms defined in separately defined packages.

Ada provides a broad range of built-in data types, including integers, reals, enumerations, Booleans, arrays, records, character strings, and pointers. The powerful type-definition facilities allow other types such as files to be defined in a package, rather than being built into the language as primitive types. The usual operations on data objects of these types are provided.

Abstraction and encapsulation of programmer-defined data types and operations are provided through the package features and through subprograms. The encapsulation mechanisms are particularly important in allowing the internal structure of data objects and subprograms to be made "invisible" to the user, so that true abstraction of both data and operations is enforced.

Sequence-control structures within an Ada subprogram utilize expressions and statement-level control structures similar to those in Pascal. Conditional and case statements, several types of loops, and a restricted form of **goto** statement are provided. An extensive set of features are available for exception handling. Subprogram-level sequence-control includes the ordinary subprogram call and return, with recursion. In addition, exceptions may cause subprograms to be terminated. The most notable aspect of the sequence-control features of Ada, however, is the provision of tasks that may be executed concurrently and controlled using a time clock and other scheduling mechanisms. These concurrent tasks may be used to respond to and control external devices where the interactions must occur under set time constraints.

The data-control structures of Ada utilize the static block-structure organization for nonlocal references within small groups of subprograms, as in Pascal. However, the language also provides means for nonlocal references to type names, subprogram names, and other identifiers in an explicit common environment defined by a package, where often the same identifier may be used in many different packages. Each formal parameter in a subprogram is tagged as **in**, **out**, or **in out**. The compiler then chooses the appropriate parameter-transmission method (by constant value, by value, by value-result, or by reference).

Ada has a rather complex syntactic structure. Full declarations are given for each variable, and complete static type checking is provided except in a few cases that require run-time checking. These aspects make the construction of an Ada compiler difficult.

The Ada virtual computer utilizes a central stack for each separate task. Each stack is used to create and delete subprogram activation records during execution of that task. Since tasks may run concurrently, they may execute subprograms independently of each other. A heap storage area is also required for programmer-constructed data objects. Because the separate tasks in an Ada program may potentially be executed by separate computers, the storage areas utilized by each task may be distributed among the memories of the various computers. The distributed nature of data storage and task execution produces special problems in Ada implementation that are not present in the other languages discussed here. Many of these implementation problems are still the subject for research.

16-2   AN ANNOTATED EXAMPLE: A PACKAGE FOR VECTOR PROCESSING

Because Ada programming is heavily oriented toward the use of packages, the example of Fig. 16-1 shows a package called VECT_PACKAGE for "vector processing," together with a program that uses the package. The package defines a data type REAL_VECT, together with several operations on vectors (in a full package, other operations would be included). The program using the package declares a data object to be a REAL_VECT and then applies one of the operations from the package to manipulate its REAL_VECT. The annotations below refer to the line numbers at the left of Fig. 16-1, which are not a part of the Ada program.

Lines 1-6. The *specification part* of the package includes the type definition for REAL_VECT together with the specifications for three subprograms to manipulate REAL_VECTs. The specifications part contains all the information about the package that is *visible* to a user of the package.

Line 2. The type definition for REAL_VECT is given. The subscript range is specified as an integer subrange, but the exact bounds are left unspecified (using the "<>" as the range designation). FLOAT is the Ada designation for the predefined real-number type.

Lines 3-5. The specifications for subprograms SUM, VECT_PRODUCT, and MAX are given. Besides the name and type of each formal parameter, the transmission method is designated by **in** (transmission by constant value) or **out** (transmission by result). A third alternative is **in out** (transmission by reference or value-result). These specifications provide enough information to the compiler so that it can effectively compile a call on one of these subprograms from within a program using the package. The SUM function is the Ada analogue of the SUM function in the Pascal, PL/I and FORTRAN examples of previous chapters.

Lines 7-18. This is the body of the package VECT_PACKAGE, containing the complete definitions of the subprograms whose specifications appear in lines 3-5. Only the definition of function SUM is given for this example. The package body encapsulates these subprogram definitions so that they are not visible to the package user. The package body may be compiled separately from the package specification.

Line

```
 1    package VECT_PACKAGE is
 2        type REAL_VECT is array (INTEGER range <>) of FLOAT;
 3        function SUM(V: in REAL_VECT) return FLOAT;
 4        procedure VECT_PRODUCT(V1,V2: in REAL_VECT; RES: out REAL_VECT);
 5        function MAX(V: in REAL_VECT) return FLOAT;
 6    end;
 7    package body VECT_PACKAGE is
 8        function SUM(V: in REAL_VECT) return FLOAT is
 9            TEMP: FLOAT := 0.0;
10        begin
11            for I in V'FIRST . . V'LAST loop
12                TEMP := TEMP + V(I);
13            end loop;
14            return TEMP;
15        end;
16            —definitions of VECT_PRODUCT and MAX subprograms would
17            —appear here
18    end;

19    with VECT_PACKAGE, TEXT_IO;
20    procedure MAIN is
21        use VECT_PACKAGE, TEXT_IO;
22        package INT_IO is new INTEGER_IO(INTEGER);
23        package REAL_IO is new FLOAT_IO(FLOAT);
24        use INT_IO, REAL_IO;
25        K: INTEGER range 0..99;
26    begin
27        loop
28            GET(K);
29            exit when K<1;
30            declare
31                A: REAL_VECT(1 . . K);
32            begin
33                for J in 1 . . K loop
34                    GET(A(J));
35                    PUT(A(J));
36                end loop;
37                PUT("SUM = ");
38                PUT(SUM(A));
39            end;
40        end loop;
41    end;
```

Fig. 16-1 Example Ada package and program

Line 8. The specification for the SUM function is repeated in the package body.

Line 9. A local variable TEMP is declared and given the initial value 0. TEMP is created and initialized on each entry to the SUM function.

Lines 10-15. This is the body of subprogram SUM. The **for** loop sums the values in the argument REAL_VECT, V, using TEMP as the running partial sum. I is declared implicitly and exists only for the duration of the loop. The final value of TEMP is returned as the value of the function.

Line 11. The expressions V'FIRST and V'LAST reference the *attributes* FIRST (the lower bound on the subscript range) and LAST (the upper bound on the subscript range) of the array V. These values are part of the run-time descriptor for the data object V, so they need not be passed to SUM as separate parameters.

Lines 19-41. This is an Ada program that uses the package VECT PACKAGE, as well as the standard predefined input-output package TEXT_IO. This program may be compiled separately from the VECT PACKAGE package, provided that the specification part for the package is compiled first.

Line 19. This line indicates to the compiler that the specifications for the packages VECT_PACKAGE and TEXT_IO are required in order to compile this program. After this line, any identifier (type name, subprogram name, etc.) defined in the specification part of either package may be referenced by prefixing it with the package name; e.g., VECT_PACKAGE. SUM(. . .) may be used to call the SUM function. The compiler uses the package specification to check the validity of the reference.

Line 20. The main program is simply a procedure in Ada. The choice of the name MAIN is arbitrary.

Lines 21-24. These lines are primarily concerned with gaining access to the input-output routines needed by the main program.

Line 21. The USE statement makes the identifiers defined in the packages VECT_PACKAGE and TEXT_IO available in the main program *without* prefixing them with the package name. Thus all these identifiers are part of the local referencing environment of the main program after this point.

Lines 22-23. To get access to the input-output routines for integers and floating-point reals which provide conversions between the internal number representations and the character representations of numbers, the two *generic packages* INTEGER_IO and FLOAT_IO must be *instantiated* to create two new packages INT_IO and REAL_IO that contain the required routines. INTEGER_IO and FLOAT_IO are package templates (generic packages) defined within package TEXT_IO. Thus the specification part of package TEXT_IO contains definitions of these generic package names. The **use** statement in the preceding line has made these names visible here.

Line 24. The identifiers (primarily the names of input-output routines) defined in the new packages INT_IO and REAL_IO are made part of the local environment of the main program.

Line 25. A local variable K is defined to have the integer subrange 0 through 99 as its type.

Lines 26-41. This is the body of the main program. An integer value is input as the value of K, a REAL_VECT of that number of components is created, and the REAL_VECT is filled with real-number values, which are input one at a time and output immediately. The values are summed, using a call on the SUM function, and the sum is output. This process is repeated until a zero value is read for K.

Lines 27-40. This outer loop is executed repeatedly until the EXIT test in line 29 is satisfied.

Line 28. The GET procedure is called with an argument of type INTEGER (subrange). GET for an INTEGER argument is defined in package INT_IO, so this statement is compiled as a call on the procedure INT_IO.GET. GET reads an integer value from the standard input file, converts it to internal integer representation, and stores it as the new value of K. Before the value is stored, it is checked to insure it is within the declared range 0..99.

Line 29. If the condition K<1 is satisfied, control is transferred out of the enclosing loop to line 41.

Lines 30-39. This is a *block* that represents a local referencing environment within the MAIN procedure. Local variables may be declared and used in a sequence of statements within the block.

Line 31. A local variable A of type REAL_VECT is declared. A new vector A will be created on each entry to this block (i.e., on each iteration of the enclosing outer loop). Since type REAL_VECT is defined without any particular subscript range in the package VECT_PACKAGE, each declaration of a variable of REAL_VECT type must supply the particular subscript range to be used. The range here is specified with upper bound equal to the current value of K, so the vector A is created to be just the appropriate size to contain the data items to be input.

Lines 32-39. Body of the block. A **for** loop is used to read the data values into vector A; then SUM is used to sum the values. J exists only for the duration of the loop.

Lines 34-35. The GET and PUT procedures are used to read a single value from the standard input file and write a single value to the standard output file. Since the argument to GET is of type FLOAT, the compiler determines that the GET procedure to be called is that in package REAL_IO (rather than the GET in INTEGER_IO or TEXT_IO). This multiple use of the same identifier to name several procedures is termed *overloading* in Ada. The name PUT is similarly overloaded; the compiler determines that procedure REAL_IO.PUT is the one desired here.

Line 37. This call on PUT, with a character-string argument, is

compiled into a call on the PUT in package TEXT_IO, i.e., procedure
TEXT_IO.PUT.

Line 38. A call on procedure REAL_IO.PUT, because the SUM function returns a result of type FLOAT.

Line 39. End of the block in which A is declared; the vector A
disappears, to be recreated on the next block entry.

Lines 40-41. End of the outer loop and the main program.

16-3   DATA TYPES

The basic types described in this section extend only slightly the data types
available in Pascal. However, the Ada facilities for programmer definition
of new types are considerably more powerful than those provided by Pascal,
and the package facility allows encapsulation of type definitions and
subprograms to obtain true data abstractions. These features are described
in the next section.

The notion of "built-in" type is somewhat different in Ada from that
common in other languages. Types such as INTEGER, REAL (called
FLOAT in Ada), CHARACTER, BOOLEAN, and STRING (character
string) are *predefined* types, defined in a package STANDARD that is
automatically available to each Ada program. Thus these "built-in" types
are actually defined using a more primitive set of type constructors
available in the language. Examples of these constructors are enumerations, arrays, and records. For example, both BOOLEAN and CHARACTER
are defined as enumerations and STRING is defined as a vector of
CHARACTERs. Because the type-definition mechanism is used throughout the language, for both primitive and programmer-defined types, many
of the examples in this section include type definitions.

Constants and Variables

Ada allows any data object to be defined as either a constant or a variable. If
a declaration begins with the keyword **constant**, then the data object is a
constant. An initial value must be given (an initial value for every
component of a data structure), and this value cannot be changed during
execution. If the keyword **constant** is omitted, the same declaration defines
a variable data object. An initial value may be given, and the value may be
modified through assignment. For example, a constant MAX_SIZE and a
variable CURRENT_SIZE may be declared by

```
MAX_SIZE : constant INTEGER := 500;
CURRENT_SIZE: INTEGER := 0;
```

This integrated treatment of constants and variables is considerably more elegant than the separate and restricted sort of constant definition allowed in Pascal and FORTRAN 77. In these other languages, variables are often used as constants (i.e., a variable is often assigned an initial value that is never modified), but no language structure is provided for stating this fact. Thus the language implementation cannot provide checking against inadvertent modification of "constant" values. The Ada structure allows the implementation to insure that declared constants are never modified. Note that Ada constants may be arrays and records as well as elementary data objects, e.g.,

WEEKDAYS: **constant array** $(1..5)$ **of** STRING$(1..3)$:=
("MON","TUE","WED","THU","FRI")

Declarations and Type Checking

The type of each data object in an Ada program must be fully declared. The Ada compiler provides strong static type checking, so that almost all type errors are detected during compilation. Run-time type checking is required in only a few circumstances. The few constructs that provide unchecked operations that may lead to undetected type errors are set aside in special features that must be intentionally invoked by the programmer.

The Ada design pays careful attention to type errors that might occur at the interface between subprograms, packages, and tasks, e.g., where a subprogram is using a type defined in a separate package. The design allows each interaction between separate program components to be checked for type errors during compilation, so that when separate components of a large program are brought together from different programming groups, the possibility of undetected errors at the interface between modules is minimized.

Attributes

An unusual feature is the provision in Ada of more than 40 predefined *attributes*. Each attribute designates an important binding or property of a data object, data type, subprogram, or of the underlying hardware computer. The attribute name, prefixed by ', is used with the name of the data or program object or data type to retrieve the value of the attribute. For example, one of the attributes of any vector data type, VECT, is the lower bound on its subscript range, denoted VECT'FIRST. The upper bound is VECT'LAST. By using these attributes, a program may be written so that it is independent of the particular type definition of VECT; thus if the definition of VECT is modified, the program statements using VECT'FIRST and VECT'LAST may remain the same. Predefined attributes exist for most of the basic data types discussed below; other attributes are taken up in subsequent sections as appropriate.

Numeric Data Types

Integers, floating-point reals, and fixed-point reals are the basic numeric data types.

Integers. The predefined type INTEGER is defined in the STANDARD package as

type INTEGER **is** *implementation-defined*;

This definition allows the implementor to use the underlying integer representation provided by the hardware. If the hardware also supports representations and operations on integers of more than one length, other types such as SHORT_INTEGER or LONG_INTEGER may also be provided by the implementation. The programmer may directly use one of these predefined types or may define a new type giving only the range of integer values desired. For example

type DAY_TYPE **is range** 1..366;
DAY: DAY_TYPE;

declares DAY as an integer variable, using one of the predefined integer types chosen by the compiler, but with the value of DAY constrained to the declared range. System-defined constants SYSTEM.MIN_INT and SYSTEM.MAX_INT allow a program to determine the range of integer values allowed in a particular Ada implementation (where a program is to be transported between several implementations). The usual arithmetic and relational operations are provided, using infix representation for binary operations.

Floating-point real numbers. There is a predefined type FLOAT in the package STANDARD, and an implementation may include other shorter or longer forms such as types SHORT_FLOAT or LONG_FLOAT. Each floating-point type ordinarily corresponds to an underlying hardware supported representation and set of arithmetic primitives. As with integers, the programmer may declare a variable using one of the predefined types or may define a new type by specifying the number of digits of accuracy desired and (optionally) a range of values. For example

type RESULT **is digits** 10 **range** −1.0E12 . . 1.0E12

declares a floating-point type requiring 10 digits of accuracy and a possible range of values that includes -10^{12} through 10^{12}.

One unique aspect of Ada is the large number of predefined attributes of the floating-point types that are accessible. For example, for any floating-point type T, the attributes T'DIGITS gives the number of (decimal) digits declared for T, T'MANTISSA gives the number of bits in the mantissa for the declared number of decimal digits, T'EMAX is the largest exponent value for the declared range, and so on. These attributes allow a program to be written so that it checks machine characteristics that might affect the validity of floating-point computations when the program is transported to different hardware.

The usual arithmetic operations, including exponentiation, are provided. Other operations are ordinarily provided through appropriate library packages.

Fixed-point real numbers. Provision is made in the language for access to a hardware-provided fixed-point real-number representation if one exists. To define a fixed-point type, the program declares the required maximum difference between two consecutive values of the type, called the *delta value*. For example, to specify a range of decimal fixed-point numbers with two digits after the decimal point, a delta value of .01 would be declared:

type SMALL_AMOUNT **is delta** 0.01 **range** −100.0..100.0

The usual arithmetic operations are provided for fixed-point numbers. If the hardware does not directly provide an appropriate fixed-point number representation, the floating-point representation may be used by an implementation, provided the specified accuracy constraints are satisfied (i.e., numbers must provide at least the accuracy specified by the delta value).

Enumerations

Enumerations may be defined in Ada using a Pascal-like style of definition and implementation as described in Sec. 3-9. For example, the definition

type CLASS **is** (FRESH,SOPH,JUNIOR,SENIOR);

defines an enumeration type, which may then be used in variable declarations. Unlike Pascal, an enumeration cannot be defined directly in a variable declaration but must be defined in a separate type definition. The run-time representation of enumeration values uses the "position number" for each literal value, starting with 0 for the first value listed, 1 for the second value, and so on. The basic relational comparisons (equal, less than, etc.) are provided for enumeration values, as well as the successor and predecessor functions and assignment.

The same literal name may be used in several enumerations (unlike Pascal, where all enumeration literals must be distinct). Such a literal name is said to be *overloaded*. For example, given the definition of CLASS above, the definition

type BREAD_STATUS is (STALE,FRESH);

overloads the literal name FRESH. In some contexts the compiler may be able to resolve the overloading directly, e.g., in the assignment B := FRESH where B is of type CLASS. To specify explicitly which meaning of FRESH is intended at a point in the program where both the types CLASS and BREAD_STATUS are visible, the programmer may qualify the literal name with the name of the base type, e.g., CLASS(FRESH) or BREAD_STATUS (FRESH). This mechanism is particularly important in allowing a program to use several packages which may have many enumerations with over-loaded literal names.

Character and Boolean Types

Two predefined enumeration types are provided in the package STAN-DARD. The type CHARACTER is an enumeration of the full ASCII character set. The type BOOLEAN is predefined as the enumeration (FALSE,TRUE). Besides the usual operations on enumerations, the special Boolean operations AND, OR, XOR (exclusive OR), AND THEN, and OR ELSE are provided. The latter two are discussed in Sec. 16-5.

Vectors and Arrays

An array data object may be declared with any number of dimensions, with arbitrary subscript ranges, and with any type of component. The basic storage representations and accessing formulas for selecting components are as described in Sec. 4-5. For example, the declaration

TABLE: array (1..10,1..20) of FLOAT;

creates a 10×20 matrix of real numbers. Subscripting is used to select components, e.g., TABLE(2,3).

Type definitions may be used to declare classes of array data objects. Ada differs from Pascal in allowing an array type definition to be given without a particular subscript range for one or more dimensions. When a variable is declared as being of that type, the particular dimensions to be used for that data object are then given. For example, the array type definition might be:

type MATRIX is
       array (INTEGER **range** $\diamond$, INTEGER **range** $\diamond$) **of** FLOAT;

where the $\diamondsuit$ indicates a subscript range to be filled in when a variable of type MATRIX is declared. A later variable declaration would then provide the particular subscript range for the MATRIX data object, e.g.,

TABLE: MATRIX(1..10,1..20);

The subscript range used need not be an integer range; it may be a range from any enumeration type. Also the subscript bounds may be defined by expressions that involve computed results, e.g.,

NEW_LIST: **array** (1..N) **of** LIST_ITEM;

where N is a variable with a computed value. Each time the subprogram containing this declaration is entered, a different length of vector NEW_LIST is created, depending on the value of N at the time of entry.

Two other features are of interest. First, subscripting may be used to select a *slice* out of a vector instead of a single component, where a slice is defined as a contiguous subvector of the original vector. For example, the reference NEW_LIST(2..4) results in selection of the three-component slice composed of the second through fourth components of NEW_LIST. Slices are particularly valuable in breaking up character strings (which are represented as vectors of characters) into subparts.

The second feature of note allows array components to be assigned initial values in the declaration that creates the array. For example,

POWERS_OF_TWO: **array** (1..6) **of** INTEGER := (2,4,8,16,32,64);

Character Strings

Character strings are treated as a predefined vector type using two other predefined types, POSITIVE (the positive integers) and CHARACTER (enumerating the characters in the ASCII character set):

type STRING **is array** (POSITIVE **range** $\diamondsuit$) **of** CHARACTER;

A particular string data object may then be declared by giving the maximum length (as a subscript range) for the string, e.g.,

NAME: STRING(1..30);

Character strings have the usual operations that are provided for vectors, including subscripting and slices to access individual characters and substrings. The concatenation operation (&) is provided, and the relational operations are also extended to strings (using the lexicographic ordering of strings that is determined by the ordering of the individual characters in the enumeration type CHARACTER).

Records

Record data objects in Ada are similar to Pascal records. A record may have any number of components of arbitrary type. If the record has several variants, the variant components must come at the end. Unlike Pascal, however, a record with variants must always have a tag field, called the *discriminant*, that explicitly indicates at run time which variant currently exists. Thus selection of the component that does not currently exist in the variant part of a record may be detected at run time and an exception raised.

A simple record, without variants, is declared using the syntax

> **record**
> ⟨*component-name*⟩ : ⟨*component-type*⟩;
> ⋮
> ⟨*component-name*⟩ : ⟨*component-type*⟩;
> **end record;**

In Ada, unlike Pascal, a record data object must be defined by first using a *type definition* to define the structure of the record and then giving a variable declaration using the type name. Similarly, if a component of a record is itself a record, then that record structure must be defined as a separate type definition; the second record definition cannot be nested inside the definition of the larger record.

A *default initial value* may be given for any component of a record, for example,

> **type** BIRTHDAY **is**
> **record**
> MONTH: STRING(1..3) := "JAN";
> DAY: INTEGER **range** 1..31 := 17;
> YEAR: INTEGER **range** 1950..2050 := 1969;
> **end record;**

Every data object of type BIRTHDAY has the initial values given in the type definition, unless an initial value assignment is given in the declaration itself, in which case the stated initial values are used. Thus, if variable MY_DAY is declared

> MY_DAY : BIRTHDAY;

then MY_DAY has the default initial values for its components. However, if YOUR_DAY is declared

> YOUR_DAY : BIRTHDAY := ("MAR",13,1968);

or alternatively

YOUR_DAY : BIRTHDAY := (MONTH => "MAR", DAY => 13,
                              YEAR => 1968);

then the given initial values are used in place of the default values. Assignment of a complete set of values to a record variable is also possible using either of the forms above, e.g.,

MY_DAY := ("DEC",30,1964);

or

MY_DAY := (YEAR => 1964, MONTH => "DEC", DAY => 30);

Note that an *aggregate* composed of a complete set of values for the components of a record may be constructed either by listing the values of the components in the order of their appearance in the declaration or by giving each component name individually (and in any order) following by the value for that component. Selection of a component of a record uses the "." operation, as in Pascal, e.g., MY_DAY.YEAR or YOUR_DAY.MONTH.

Two methods in Ada allow a single record type definition to be used to define records of similar but not identical structure. The simplest method allows a record declaration to have parameters, called *discriminants*, that determine the subscript ranges of array components, so that each data object declared of the type may have array components of different sizes. For example, to define a record type that contains information about each month, including a vector of reals having one entry for each day of the month (which might be used to save daily sales totals), the following definition might be used:

```
type MONTH (LENGTH : INTEGER range 1..31) is
    record
            NAME : STRING(1..3);
            DAYS : array (1..LENGTH) of FLOAT;
    end record;
```

Then individual records of type MONTH may be declared, e.g.,

JAN : MONTH(31);
FEB : MONTH(28);

to get a DAYS vector of the correct length in each record.

The second method for using a single record type definition to define similar but not identical record data objects is to use a variant record structure, similar to that in Pascal. The tag field, used to indicate which variant is present, is always listed as a discriminant in the record type definition (in the same form as given above). The syntax for the variant part itself is then

```
case ⟨ discriminant-name ⟩ is
    when ⟨ discriminant-value ⟩ => ⟨ component-list ⟩;
    when ⟨ discriminant-value ⟩ => ⟨ component-list ⟩;
        ⋮
    when others => ⟨ component-list ⟩;
```

where the component list may be the reserved word NULL, indicating no components for that variant, or it may be a sequence of component names and types, as for an ordinary record definition. The tag field (discriminant) is automatically included as a component of the record at run time, so run-time checking of the validity of the references to variant records is possible. In many cases, however, variant record types are used only to allow different data objects to be created from the same type definition, and no run-time change in the variant occurs. Where such cases can be detected during compilation, no run-time checking of the validity of references to components of a variant is required. For example, an employee record might appear as

```
type WAGE_TYPE is (HOURLY,SALARIED);
type EMPLOYEE-REC (PAY_TYPE : WAGE_TYPE) is
    record
        NAME: STRING(1..30);
        AGE: INTEGER range 15..100;
        case PAY_TYPE is
            when HOURLY =>
                HOURS: FLOAT;
                HOURLY_RATE: FLOAT;
            when SALARIED =>
                MONTHLY_RATE: FLOAT;
    end record;
```

and then particular data objects might be declared, e.g.,

```
PRESIDENT: EMPLOYEE_REC(SALARIED);
CHAUFFEUR: EMPLOYEE_REC(HOURLY);
```

where the variant chosen never changes during execution (for example, the wage type of PRESIDENT never changes to HOURLY).

If the variant of a record data object is to change at run time, an assignment to the entire record variable must be made; the discriminant value cannot be changed in any other way. Such an assignment overwrites the block of storage representing the record with a complete set of new values, including a new discriminant value.

The implementation of Ada records, including variants, follows the usual structure outlined in Sec. 4-6. Each record is represented as a sequential block of storage. Storage is allocated for the largest variant, if there are several of different sizes, unless it can be determined during compilation that the variant will not change during execution.

Pointers and Programmer-Constructed Data Objects

A pointer type, called an **access** type, is provided in Ada, together with a primitive function **new** that creates a new data object (allocating storage in a heap area) and returns a pointer to it, which may then be assigned to a variable of an access type. A variable cannot be directly declared to be of an access type, instead a type definition must be used, e.g.,

> **type** ⟨ *access-type-name* ⟩ **is access** ⟨*type-name*⟩;

and then variables may be declared to be of the defined access type. A variable of access type is thus constrained to point to data objects of only a single type. All variables of access types have the null pointer value, NULL, as their initial value by default, unless an explicit pointer value is assigned in the declaration.

The **new** function is called an *allocator*. It may be used to create a data object of any primitive or defined type, including a task data object created from a task type (Sec. 6-9). The **new** allocator allows the specification of discriminant values for records and subscript ranges for arrays if these options are used in the definition of the type. For example, using the definition of the EMPLOYEE_REC record type above, two pointer variables T1 and T2 might be declared:

> **type** EMPLOYEE_PTR **is access** EMPLOYEE_REC;
> T1 : EMPLOYEE_PTR;
> T2 : EMPLOYEE_PTR := **new** EMPLOYEE_REC(HOURLY);

Variable T1 has an initial null pointer value; T2 is initialized to point to an EMPLOYEE_REC record with the HOURLY variant structure. Either variable may be assigned a different pointer value through assignment; e.g., T1 := T2 assigns T1 a pointer to the same data object as T2. The assignment

> T1 := **new** EMPLOYEE_REC(SALARIED);

creates a new EMPLOYEE_REC record and assigns T1 a pointer to it.

Selection using pointer variables uses the same syntax as for selection in the base data type. For example, T1.AGE selects the AGE component of the record to which T1 currently points. T1.**all** selects the entire data object to which T1 points. Implementation of pointer variables and the **new** operation in Ada follows the general structure described in Sec. 4-9.

TABLE 16-1   Predefined Input-Output (I-O) Packages in Ada

Package Name	Package Function
SEQUENTIAL_IO	Sequential file types and I-O operations.
DIRECT_IO	Direct-access file types and I-O operations.
TEXT_IO	Textfile type and character I-O operations, incl.
INTEGER_IO	I-O and format conversions for INTEGER types.
FLOAT_IO	I-O and format conversions for FLOAT types.
FIXED_IO	I-O and format conversions for FIXED types.
ENUMERATION_IO	I-O and format conversions for ENUMERATION types.
IO_EXCEPTIONS	Exception names common to all I-O packages.
LOW_LEVEL_IO	Types and I-O operations for direct access to special external devices.

Files and Input-Output

Files and input-output operations in Ada are defined as abstract data types, using several predefined packages (see Table 16-1). Besides these packages, an implementation would ordinarily supply additional input-output packages built using the basic data types and operations defined in the predefined packages, e.g., a package for graphic output to a terminal.

This use of packages to define the structure of files and input-output operations illustrates the importance of the package facility to the overall language design. The Ada programmer sees files as data types whose internal structure is largely hidden by being encapsulated within these predefined packages. The procedures and functions provided by the packages provide the only means to access and manipulate files. No special syntax for input-output statements or file declarations is necessary in the language.

Because the type of component in a file differs among files (e.g., a file of characters, a file of integers, a file of vectors), each predefined package that defines a type of file is actually a *generic* package (see Secs. 5-5 and 16-4) with a parameter that is the type of component desired in the file. To get a package for input-output to files with a particular type of component, the generic file package must be *instantiated* to get a particular package that contains file type definitions and operations for files with that particular type of component. For example, to get a package for input-output to a sequential file of FLOAT numbers, the procedure doing the I-O operations would begin with an instantiation of the package SEQUENTIAL_IO using FLOAT as a parameter:

package REAL_FILE_IO **is new** SEQUENTIAL_IO(FLOAT);

```
use REAL_FILE_IO;
procedure DO_IO(. . .) is
        — declare sequential files with components of type FLOAT
    begin
        — OPEN a file of FLOAT components
        — READ and WRITE to the file
        — CLOSE the file
    end;
```

The predefined packages listed in Table 16-1 provide an extensive set of file types and input-output operations. The packages support both sequential and direct-access file organizations, with the usual operations for input-output, testing file status, and so on. Textfiles have a more complex structure than in Pascal. An Ada textfile is organized as a sequence of *pages*, each of which is a sequence of *lines*, each of which in turn is a sequence of *characters*. Lines, pages, and the file itself are each ended with special terminators. The current position within a textfile is indicated by three special counts, the *current page number*, the *current line number*, and the *current column number*. These structures within a textfile make it possible to format entire pages at a time (rather than just single lines) for output. The basic TEXT_IO package provides operations for character and character-string input-output. To get operations for conversion of numeric data to character form, the packages INTEGER_IO, FLOAT_IO, and FIXED_IO that are part of the basic TEXT_IO package must be used. These packages provide options for format control during input-output operations. If input-output of data of an enumeration type is required, the generic package ENUMERATION_IO must be instantiated, using the enumeration type name as a parameter. The run-time representation of enumeration values as small integers (the position numbers) may then be converted during output to the actual literals used in the enumeration type definition. Similarly, enumeration literals may be read from a file and converted to their position number before storage.

16-4 SUBPROGRAMS, TYPE DEFINITIONS, AND PACKAGES

The Ada facilities for definition and encapsulation of new data types and operations are the most sophisticated of any language described here. The subprograms and type definitions in general follow the Pascal pattern. Packages provide a general method for programmer definition of new abstract data types.

Subprograms

Procedures, functions, and tasks are the three varieties of Ada subprogram. Note that there is no main program as such; instead a procedure is designated as the main program (through some means not defined in the language).

Procedures and functions. A procedure or function definition has the form of a specification

procedure ⟨ *proc-name* ⟩ (⟨*formal-parameter list*⟩) **is**

or

function ⟨ *fn-name* ⟩ (⟨*formal-parameter list*⟩) **return** ⟨ *result-type* ⟩ **is**

followed by a body in the form

            — sequence of declarations
    begin
            — sequence of statements
    exception
            — exception handlers
    end;

In the formal-parameter list, each parameter name is given, together with its type and the method of transmission to be used: **in** for transmission by constant value, **out** for transmission by result, and **in out** for transmission by reference or value-result (depending on the implementation). A function subprogram is only allowed to have **in** parameters because, in principle, a function should return no results through modification of its parameters (but side effects are still possible, e.g., through modification of nonlocal variables). Parameter transmission is discussed further in Sec. 16-6.

A procedure or function definition may also be used to *overload* (assign an additional meaning to) an operator symbol or a subprogram name that is already in use. For example, suppose that the programmer has defined a new type COMPLEX and wants to provide a definition for the "+" symbol when applied to COMPLEX data objects. The function definition might be

function "+"(A,B: **in** COMPLEX) **return** COMPLEX **is** . . .

Within the scope of such an overloading for the "+" symbol, an expression involving +, such as X+Y, may indicate any one of the current definitions for "+", including those predefined in the language, such as integer addition, and those defined by the programmer, such as COMPLEX addition. The compiler determines which meaning of "+" is intended by checking the types of the operands, X and Y. If X and Y are integer variables, then an integer addition instruction is used in the object code; if X and Y are type COMPLEX, then a call on the function defined above is inserted into the object code. In general, the Ada compiler resolves any reference to an overloaded operator symbol or subprogram name during compilation, by checking the types of the arguments in the call and matching them against the types specified for the formal parameters of the various primitive and defined subprograms with that name. If this matching process does not lead to a unique subprogram (or primitive operation), the the call of the overloaded name is considered an error.

Procedures and functions are implemented using the basic methods described in Chapter 5. Each procedure or function definition is compiled into a code segment and an activation record template. Since recursive subprogram calls are allowed, activation records must be created on a central stack at the time of call during execution. The code segment is allocated storage statically and is shared by all activations.

Tasks. A task is a subprogram that may be executed concurrently with other tasks. A fairly extended description of the Ada facilities for task definition, initiation, and synchronization is given in Sec. 6-9, so only a brief overview is given here.

A task definition has the general form

```
task 〈 task-name 〉 is
          — entry declarations
     end;
task body 〈 task-name 〉 is
          — sequence of declarations
     begin
          — sequence of statements
     exception
          — exception handlers
     end;
```

Note that the task definition has two separate parts. The first part, the *specification*, gives the entry declarations for the task. The second part, the *body*, has the same general structure as a procedure or function body. The specification of the task provides all the information necessary for another subprogram or task to communicate with the task, and thus it serves the same general purpose as the specification part (formal-parameter list, etc.) of a procedure or function. The task body is encapsulated, so that any contained declarations or statements are invisible to users of the task, and in Ada this task body may even be compiled separately (see Sec. 16-7). Instead of a separate definition for each task needed in a program, a *task type* may be defined. Using a task type, multiple tasks may be created from a single definition. Section 6-9 discusses this aspect of task definition further.

Type Definitions

Type definitions play a central role in the structure of most Ada programs. Numerous examples are found in the previous sections. The general syntax is

type ⟨ *type-name* ⟩ **is** ⟨ *type-definition* ⟩

If the type is defined as a record, a list of discriminants may appear after the type name. Two aspects of type definitions have not been seen in the above examples, *subtypes* and *derived types*.

Subtypes. Any defined type gives a name to a class of data objects having certain attributes. A *subtype* of that *base type* consists of a subset of those data objects that meet a particular *constraint*. A constraint for the base type INTEGER would be a restriction to a subrange of the integers; a constraint for an array base type defined with unspecified INTEGER subscript range ("<>") would be a particular subscript range. A constraint for a base type defined as a record with a discriminant would be a particular value for the discriminant (which might determine a particular variant of the record).

A subtype is defined using the syntax:

subtype ⟨ *subtype-name* ⟩ **is** ⟨ *base-type-name* ⟩⟨ *constraint* ⟩;

For example:

subtype GRAPH_SCALE **is** INTEGER **range** −20..20;
subtype EXECUTIVE **is** EMPLOYEE_REC(SALARIED);

A subtype does not define a new type; it simply defines a subset of the data objects defined by the base type. In particular, the same operations that can be used on data objects of the base type can be used on objects of the subtype, and data objects of different subtypes of the same base type may be mixed as operands in an expression. The utility of subtypes in Ada comes from the fact that the subtype allows a tighter constraint on the allowable set of data objects without losing access to any of the operations provided for the base type. When operations create new data objects of the subtype, the Ada implementation checks whether the constraint defined for the subtype is met (at compile time if possible, otherwise at run time). Thus the programmer can be sure that data objects meet the subtype constraint.

Derived types. A derived type is similar to a subtype, but a derived type is a *new type*, different from the base type. The syntax for a derived type definition is:

type ⟨ *derived-type-name* ⟩ **is new** ⟨ *base-type-name* ⟩

where the base type might be defined with a constraint (and thus actually be a subtype). For example:

type METERS **is new** INTEGER;
type LITERS **is new** INTEGER;

A derived type is allowed to use all the operations defined on the base type (or subtype), but because the derived type is a distinct type from the base type, operations cannot be applied to mixtures of operands of the base type and the derived type. For example, given the above definitions, "+" is defined for base type INTEGER, and thus it is also defined for derived types METERS and LITERS. However, if X, Y, and Z are variables of types INTEGER, METERS, and LITERS, respectively, then no pair of these variables may be added together; e.g., X+Z is illegal. Thus by use of a derived type, the programmer is protected against the inadvertent addition of two variables that represent distinct kinds of data, even though the base representation of the data may be identical (all represented as integers in this example).

Type equivalence. Ada generally treats two variables as being of the same type only if they are declared using the identical type name. Thus *name equivalence* of types is the rule in this language. The concept of derived types allows the programmer to use the name equivalence rule to obtain protection through type-checking of variables in the case where classes of variables need to be totally separated. The concept of subtype allows the programmer to obtain range checking and similar constraints of the values of a variable, without keeping that variable separate from other variables of the base type.

Implementation of the Ada type-definition features is primarily handled during compilation. However, many aspects also have an impact on the run-time structure because they require some run-time checking of constraints.

Packages

Packages are the major innovation supporting abstraction in Ada. A package definition has two parts, a *specification* (containing a *visible part* and a *private part*) and a *body*. The specification provides the information necessary for the correct use of the package; the body provides the encapsulated local variables and subprogram definitions, as well as the bodies of subprograms callable from outside the package. In some cases a package does not need to have a body. The general form of a package definition is

package ⟨*package-name*⟩ **is**
    — declarations of visible types, variables,
    —   constants, and subprograms

```
private
        —   complete definitions of private types
        —       and private constants
end;
package body ⟨package-name⟩ is
        —   definitions of local variables, types, and
        —       subprograms, and complete bodies for subprograms
        —       declared in the specification part above
begin
        —   statements to initialize the package when it is
        —       first instantiated
exception
        —   exception handlers
end;
```

Package specifications. The visible part of the package specification (everything preceding the keyword **private**) defines what the outside user of the package can make use of in a program. If type definitions are given in the visible part, the user can declare variables of those types; if variables and constants are defined, he can reference those data objects, and so on.

Private types. In many cases where the package defines an abstract data type, we want the user to be able to declare variables of the abstract type, but we do not want the detailed type definition to be visible to him. In this case, the type definition in the visible part is

type ⟨type-name⟩ is private;

and the complete type definition is given in the private part of the specification. For example, if the type is EMPLOYEE_REC, defined as a record with several components such as NAME and AGE, then the complete type definition could be given in the visible part, and the user could then declare variables of type EMPLOYEE_REC and also access the components NAME and AGE. If later we wish to modify the package so as to delete the component AGE from EMPLOYEE_REC's, then every user of the package might have to be modified also, since the AGE component was visible. To hide the component names from the users, while still making the type name visible, the *private* declaration is used:

type EMPLOYEE_REC is private;

and then in the private part:

```
private
        type EMPLOYEE_REC is
            record
                —   full declarations of components
            end record;
```

The reason why the private type definition must be part of the package *specification* rather than the package *body* is due to implementation requirements. Note that subprogram definitions are also split into a visible part (in the specification) and a hidden part, but the hidden part (the subprogram body) is given in the package body rather than in the private part of the package specification. For type definitions, however, the Ada compiler must know the complete type definition for any visible type when a program that uses the package is being compiled; for subprogram calls, the compiler need only know the specification of argument and result types for the subprogram.

For example, suppose a subprogram SUB declares a variable NEWHIRE of type EMPLOYEE_REC, using the package in which that type is defined as a private type. When SUB is compiled, storage for variable NEWHIRE must be allocated in the activation record (template) for SUB. Without the complete type definition for EMPLOYEE_REC, the compiler cannot determine how much storage NEWHIRE requires, so the complete type definition must be part of the specification part of the package, since that is the only part that the compiler sees when compiling SUB. At the same time, since the type definition is specified as **private** in the package, the compiler can insure that SUB does not reference component AGE of NEWHIRE. SUB may only manipulate the components of NEWHIRE by calling subprograms provided in the package that defined type EMPLOYEE_REC, because only these subprograms have access to the private components.

Usually it is desirable to have the primitive operations of assignment and the tests for equality and inequality available automatically even for a private type, e.g., so that A := B is defined for A and B of private types. In Ada these are the only operations provided directly for a private type without explicit programmer definition. However, in many cases even these operations should not be predefined for a private type. If the programmer declares the type as **limited private** then no operations at all are predefined for the type.

The encapsulation mechanism provided by private types is an important part of the data abstraction mechanisms in Ada. It makes possible the efficient compilation of programs that use packages, while still enforcing the information hiding that is necessary to insure that an abstract type may be changed at any time without modifying programs outside the package that use the type.

Packages may be used for several purposes. Definition of abstract data types is one of their primary functions. An example of this use of packages is seen in the program of Fig. 16-1, which contains a package defining an abstract type REAL_VECT.

A second major purpose for packages is to define a common environment of shared variables, constants, and related type definitions. The effect is similar to the FORTRAN COMMON block. In this case, the visible part of the package contains the declarations of the shared variables and constants (plus any type definitions needed for those declarations). No package body is needed because no subprograms are defined.

Generic packages. A generic package is a package specification that has "parameters" giving the types of particular package elements, the sizes of particular arrays in the package, and so forth. For example, a generic package that defines the abstract type STACK might have a parameter giving the type of component stored in the stack. An example of such a generic package is given in Sec. 5-5. In the example program of Fig. 16-1, the packages INTEGER_IO and FLOAT_IO used by the main program are generic packages. Before one of these packages could be used, the template represented by the generic package had to be *instantiated* to create a particular package using a particular set of values for the parameters to the generic package. Lines 22 and 23 of Fig. 16-1 illustrate how this instantiation is done in Ada. The general form is

> **package** ⟨*actual package name*⟩ **is**
> **new** ⟨*generic package name*⟩ (⟨*parameters*⟩);

Instantiation of a package is an operation done by the compiler. At compile time, each reference to a "formal-parameter name" within the package is replaced by the "actual parameter" in the statement that instantiates the package. The resulting package can then be compiled in the same way as an ordinary package. The generic package and its instantiation have no effect on the run-time structure; only the resulting package (after the instantiation) actually is compiled into run-time data objects and executable code. However, since instantiation of generic packages is a rather frequent operation in Ada, especially where library packages are involved, most Ada compilers optimize this operation in various ways, often by a partial precompilation of the generic package itself, leaving only those aspects directly dependent on the parameters to be compiled anew at each instantiation.

16-5 SEQUENCE CONTROL

Sequence-control structures in Ada are extensive at the expression, statement, and subprogram level. The facilities for control of concurrent tasks and exception handling are particularly notable.

Expressions

Expressions in Ada allow primitive and defined functions to be combined into sequences in the usual way. Infix notation is used for the usual binary arithmetic, relational, and Boolean operations. Prefix notation is used for unary operations (+, −, and NOT), and function calls use the ordinary mathematical prefix representation "**fn-name**(*argument list*)". Parentheses may be used to group operations, and in the absence of parentheses the following precedence order is followed (highest-precedence operations listed first):

$$** \quad \text{(exponentiation)}$$
$$* \quad / \quad \textbf{mod} \quad \textbf{rem}$$
$$+ \quad - \quad \textbf{abs} \quad \textbf{not} \quad \text{(unary + and −)}$$
$$+ \quad - \quad \& \quad \text{(binary + and −)}$$
$$= \quad /= \quad < \quad <= \quad > \quad >= \quad \textbf{in} \quad \textbf{not in}$$
$$\textbf{and} \quad \textbf{or} \quad \textbf{xor} \quad \textbf{and then} \quad \textbf{or else}$$

Operations with the same precedence are associated from left to right. These rules give Ada expressions the same general character as expressions in Pascal, FORTRAN, and PL/I, with minor differences in the precedence order for operations. Note that Ada contains the *short-circuit* Boolean operations **and then** and **or else**, which evaluate only their first operand if that value is enough to determine the value of the expression (see the discussion in Sec. 6-2). The operations **in** and **not in** are used to test if a value is within a particular range or satisfies a particular constraint.

Statement Sequence Control

The statement sequence-control structures are the usual conditional statements (**if** and **case**) and iteration statements (loops). Three forms of loop statement are provided, and an **exit** statement allows direct exit from a loop. A limited form of **goto** statement is also provided. All the major control statements terminate with the keyword **end** followed by the initial keyword of the statement, e.g., **end if**, **end loop**, so that separate **begin**...**end** pairs are seldom needed to bracket component statements in Ada.

IF *statements.*   The **if** statement has the general form

if ⟨*Boolean-expression₁*⟩ **then**
     — statement-sequence₁
elsif ⟨*Boolean-expression₂*⟩ **then**
     — statement-sequence₂
elsif ⟨*Boolean-expression₃*⟩ **then**
     ⋮
else
     — statement-sequence$_k$
end if;

where any of the **elsif** or **else** parts may be omitted.

CASE *statements.* The general form of the **case** statement is

        case ⟨*expression*⟩ **is**
            when ⟨*choice*⟩ | ... | ⟨*choice*⟩ => ⟨*statement-sequence*$_1$⟩;
            when ⟨*choice*⟩ | ... | ⟨*choice*⟩ => ⟨*statement-sequence*$_2$⟩;
                .
                .
                .
            when others => ⟨*statement-sequence*$_k$⟩
        end case;

Each ⟨*choice*⟩ indicates either one or a range of possible values for the expression at the head of the statement; i.e., it is a literal value or a subrange of integer values (or values from some other enumeration), e.g.,

        case GRADE_LEVEL **is**
            when FRESH => ⟨*statements*⟩;
            when SOPH | JUNIOR => ⟨*statements*⟩;
            when SENIOR => ⟨*statements*⟩;
        end case;

One particularly important requirement in Ada is that the set of choices include all the possible values for the expression, or that the final case be **when others** to explicitly indicate an action for all the remaining values. Thus no run-time error is possible because of computation of a value for the **case** expression for which no action is specified. If no action is required for some of the choices, the statement part may be the keyword **null**.

Iteration statements. The basic iteration statement has the form

        loop
                — sequence of statements
        end loop;

Since no loop header is given to indicate a termination condition, this form of loop iterates endlessly until terminated by an explicit **exit, goto,** or **return** statement or an exception. The **exit** statement has the form

        exit when ⟨*Boolean-expression*⟩;

or simply **exit**. When an **exit** statement is executed, it transfers control to the end of the innermost enclosing loop (if the condition indicated by the Boolean expression is satisfied). Alternatively, loops may be labeled and the **exit** statement may give the label of the enclosing loop to be exited, e.g.,

        exit OUTER_LOOP **when** A(I,J) = 0;

Instead of an **exit** statement, a *header clause* may be used at the beginning of a loop to make it into the usual **while** or **for** loop, as in Pascal.

The **while** clause has the form

$$\text{\textbf{while}} \langle \textit{Boolean-expression} \rangle$$

and the **for** clause is

$$\text{\textbf{for}} \langle \textit{variable-name} \rangle \text{ \textbf{in}} \langle \textit{discrete-range} \rangle$$

or

$$\text{\textbf{for}} \quad \textit{variable-name} \quad \text{\textbf{in reverse}} \quad \textit{discrete-range}$$

where ⟨*discrete-range*⟩ may be a subrange of an enumeration or integer type, e.g., 1..10 or FRESH..JUNIOR. The keyword **reverse** indicates that the iteration begins with the final value of the range assigned to the given variable and works down to the initial value. Examples of **for** loops are given in Fig. 16-1.

An important feature of the **for** loop is that the ⟨*variable-name*⟩ given in the **for** clause is *not* declared as an ordinary local variable, as in Pascal. Instead it is declared *implicitly* by its occurence in the **for** clause, and it may be referenced only within the loop. Once the loop is exited, this variable disappears and can no longer be referenced. This structure allows a number of important loop optimizations to be performed by the Ada compiler.

GOTO statements. **Goto** statements are provided in Ada, but their use is tightly restricted. In general, a **goto** may transfer control only to another statement within the same subprogram and at the same or an outer level of statement nesting.

Subprogram Sequence Control

The usual subprogram call-return structure, with recursion, is used in Ada. The syntax for a subprogram call is

$$\langle \textit{subprogram-name} \rangle (\langle \textit{actual-parameter-list} \rangle)$$

and the parentheses must appear even if the subprogram has no parameters. The normal exit from the procedure or task is via execution of the statement **return**; **return** ⟨*expression*⟩ is used for exit from a function, where the value of the expression becomes the value returned by the function.

Exceptions and exception handlers. At the end of each program unit (subprogram, block, task, or package) a set of exception handlers may be specified. These handlers may be used to process exceptions raised within the program unit, or propagated to the unit from some called subprogram that does not handle the exception. Each exception has a name. There are a few predefined exceptions, such as CONSTRAINT_ERROR (raised when a subscript is out of its declared range, when a subrange constraint is violated in an assignment, etc). All other exceptions are declared using the form

⟨*exception-name*⟩: **exception**

An exception handler begins with the names of the exceptions that it handles, followed by a sequence of statements that take the action appropriate for handling the exception. The general syntax for the exception handlers section of a program unit is

> **exception**
> **when** ⟨*exception-name*⟩ | . . . | ⟨*exception-name*⟩
> => ⟨*statement-sequence*⟩;
>
> ⋮
>
> **when others** => ⟨*statement-sequence*⟩;

where each sequence of statements may handle one or more named exceptions. The **others** handler need not be specified, but if it is, it handles all exceptions not named in previous handlers.

An exception is raised either implicitly, by a primitive operation, or explicitly, by execution of a statement

raise ⟨*exception-name*⟩

When an exception is raised, control is transferred to the handler in the currently executing program unit, if that unit has a handler for it. If no handler is present, then the exception is propagated down the dynamic chain of subprogram calls to the most recently called subprogram that does have a handler for it, or ultimately to a system-defined handler if no program-defined handler is present. Exceptions are not propagated from a task.

Once an exception has been processed by a handler, the subprogram (or other program unit) terminates execution normally and transfers control back to its caller. Thus the exception handler in Ada is viewed as *completing* the execution of the subprogram body that was interrupted when the exception was raised. There is no provision for resumption of execution of the program unit in which the exception occurred. An exception handler may itself partially process the exception, and then propagate the same exception to a handler back down the dynamic chain by executing the statement **raise** with no exception name.

Tasks and concurrent execution. The Ada facilities for definition of concurrent tasks and for their subsequent initiation and synchronization during execution are an important part of the language. Section 6-9 gives an extended discussion of these features, especially the *rendezvous* and the various statements that support this synchronization mechanism, the

select statement (a form of *guarded command*), the **accept** statement, and the **entry** call.

16-6 DATA CONTROL

Data-control structures, particularly the rules for visibility of names at different points in a program, are a central concern in Ada. A program is usually assembled as a collection of packages and subprograms, each of which defines a set of identifiers as type names, variable names, subprogram and task names, exception names, enumeration literals, and so on. Since these packages are often obtained from a library or are written by separate programming groups, names may be duplicated between packages. The rules for resolving these ambiguities are important in Ada.

Local Referencing Environments

The local referencing environment of a subprogram is created when the subprogram is called and is deleted when it returns control to its caller. For a task, the local environment is created when the task is initiated and deleted when it terminates. A separate activation record is created on entry to a subprogram or task, and local variables are referenced using their offsets from the base address of this block. The implementation structure follows the general pattern described in Sec. 7-4.

All local names are explicitly declared in the program, so the compiler may build the usual symbol table of local names and then use the type definitions and other declared information to lay out the structure of the local activation record for each subprogram and to compute the required offsets for references. In some cases, however, this computation of offsets must be done during execution.

Blocks

The term *block* has a particular technical meaning in Ada. Any single statement may be a *block*, which is a compound statement that also includes its own local referencing environment, including new declarations of variables and exception handlers. The general form of a block is

> **declare**
>   — sequence of declarations
> **begin**
>   — sequence of statements

exception
      — exception handlers
end;

The block allows the programmer to limit the scope of particular identifiers to a single sequence of statements within a larger subprogram. It also allows special exception handlers to be used for a sequence of statements that differ from those used in the larger subprogram. A third use for a block is to allow a subprogram to read in or compute the sizes of the arrays that it needs, and then enter a block in which those arrays are declared using expressions for the subscript ranges that involve the computed values. The arrays may then be made just the proper size for the data to be stored, rather than a static size equal to the maximum amount of data expected. The example program in Fig. 16-1 shows this use of blocks.

    A block is most easily implementable by treating it as an unnamed, parameterless procedure that is called at the place where it appears in the program. The compiler may combine the code segment with that of the surrounding subprogram, but the use of a separate activation record for the block allows the change in referencing environment on entry to the block to be implemented in a straightforward manner.

Static Block Structure

Nonlocal references are treated according to the usual static scope rules for programs that have the static block structure form, as discussed in Sec. 7-7. Package definitions, as well as procedures, functions, tasks, and blocks, may be nested, and a nonlocal reference is resolved by searching the local environments of enclosing program units at compile time in the usual way. At run time, the nonlocal referencing is usually implemented using a static chain or display to link subprogram activation records.

Common Referencing Environments

An alternative to the use of static nesting of program units, and the sharing of data through nonlocal references, is provided by the package structure. Any package may be considered as defining an explicit *common referencing environment* containing type definitions, constant definitions, subprograms, and so forth. To gain access to the common environment defined by a package, the package name itself must be visible to the subprogram. The simplest way to do this is to precede the subprogram definition by a **with** statement that names the packages to be used, e.g.,

with VECT_PACKAGE, TEXT_IO

in the example of Fig. 16-1. The **with** statement makes the package names visible, and identifiers defined within the specification part of a visible package may be referenced as ⟨*package-name*⟩.⟨*identifier*⟩, e.g., VECT_PACKAGE.SUM or TEXT_IO.GET. The prefixing insures that each identifier reference is unambiguous, even though the same identifier may be defined in several packages.

The **use** statement allows the identifiers in a package to be referenced without the package name as prefix. The **use** statement has the form

use ⟨*package-name*⟩, . . . , ⟨*package-name*⟩

and has the effect of adding the visible identifiers in the named packages to the local referencing environment of the subprogram, so that they may be referenced as though they were defined locally within the subprogram. If the same identifier is defined in several packages, then it becomes *overloaded* in the local environment, and the compiler must be able to resolve the overloading each time such an identifier is referenced, to produce an unambiguous reference. Figure 16-1 illustrates this overloading in the case of the procedure names GET and PUT that were defined in several input-output packages.

A predefined common environment, the package STANDARD, is implicitly visible in every program unit, as though the program unit were preceded by

with STANDARD; **use** STANDARD;

The STANDARD package contains definitions of the predefined types (BOOLEAN, INTEGER, FLOAT, CHARACTER, etc.), the basic arithmetic, relational, and Boolean operations, the predefined exceptions (NUMERIC_ERROR, CONSTRAINT_ERROR, etc.), and various other predefined identifiers.

Parameters and Parameter Transmission

Three modes of parameter transmission are provided, **in** (transmission by constant value), **out** (transmission by result), and **in out** (transmission by reference or value-result). Each formal parameter is tagged with its transmission mode in the formal-parameter list of a subprogram. Function subprograms are allowed to have only **in** parameters and to return a single elementary data item as a result. There is no provision in Ada for subprograms to be passed as parameters to other subprograms.

There are three methods provided for pairing formal and actual parameters in a subprogram call:

a. *Positional correspondence.* The usual list of actual-parameter expressions may be given in a subprogram call. These expressions are evaluated, and the resulting actual parameters are paired with the formal-parameter names in the sequence given in the list (first actual with first formal, etc.).

b. *Named correspondence.* Each actual-parameter expression may be preceded by "⟨*formal-parameter name*⟩ =>" to indicate explicitly the particular formal parameter with which the actual parameter is to be paired. The actual-parameter expressions may then be given in any order. The compiler translates this form into the appropriate positional correspondence.

c. *Default value.* An actual-parameter expression may be omitted altogether if the corresponding formal parameter is an **in** parameter and a *default value* is given for the formal parameter in the subprogram specification. The default value is then used as the actual parameter. A default value is specified as

⟨ *formal-parameter name* ⟩: **in** ⟨*type*⟩ := ⟨*default value*⟩;

in the specification part of a subprogram.

Shared Data and Tasks

Two tasks ordinarily share data through actual parameters given in an **entry** call. The corresponding **accept** statement provides the formal-parameter list, just as for an ordinary procedure. The entry declaration in the task specification repeats the formal-parameter list so that the compiler can check that an entry call on the task has the correct number and types of actual parameters (see Sec. 7-9).

Alternatively, two tasks may share data through references to the same nonlocal variable, using the static block structure. For example, the definitions of tasks A and B may both be nested within the procedure definition C. If C declares a local variable X, then both A and B may reference X and assign new values to X. If references to X are made only within an **accept** statement during a rendezvous of tasks A and B, then mutual exclusion is assured, since only the task executing the **accept** statement has access to X during the rendezvous. However, Ada also allows access to X by A and B without a rendezvous by using a special predefined procedure SHARED_VARIABLE_SYNCHRONIZE to enforce mutual exclusion. Other references to a shared nonlocal variable are allowed, but the effects of assignment by one task to the shared variable may not immediately be visible in the other task because an implementation may keep a hidden local copy of the variable and actually update the real shared variable only when a rendezvous occurs.

16-7 OPERATING AND PROGRAMMING ENVIRONMENT

Considerations of both the operating environment in which programs are executed and the programming environment in which programs are written are important in the Ada design.

Operating Environment

Predefined packages provide access to the usual sequential and direct-access files, which form one level of operating environment. However, Ada is designed for an embedded-system operating environment, as discussed in Sec. 10-3. In the embedded-system environment, the program is a crucial component of a larger system such as an aircraft or satellite. The program must often run on a small computer with limited resources. It must interact directly with special-purpose input-output devices such as sensors for measuring air speed or temperature and actuators for moving control surfaces or closing valves. Failure of the program often means failure of the entire system, with possibly costly consequences. In this environment, many programs do not use ordinary file structures, since these generally require support from an underlying operating system, which may not be present.

The major effects of the special requirements of embedded systems are seen in the careful attention to features for exception handling and in the inclusion of a number of features that allow an Ada program to be tightly coupled to the particular requirements of the hardware and external devices that form its run-time environment. Some of the most important of these features are mentioned here.

Pragmas. A **pragma** is a statement used to convey information to the compiler. The general form is

pragma ⟨*pragma-name*⟩ (⟨*parameter list*⟩)

where the major pragma-names are predefined in the language, and an implementation may define others. Some pragmas simply control compiler functions, such as the generation of a program listing (**pragma** LIST). However, the majority are intended to allow some control over the run-time structure of a particular subprogram. For example, **pragma** INLINE(⟨*subprogram name list*⟩) specifies to the compiler that calls on the listed subprograms are to be replaced by in-line code sequences whenever possible; **pragma** OPTIMIZE(TIME **or** SPACE) specifies that the subprogram within which it occurs should be compiled so as to minimize its execution TIME or storage SPACE requirements.

Address specifications. The particular location in memory at which a data object, subprogram, or task is to be located at run time may be specified, using the statement

for ⟨*object-name*⟩ **use at** ⟨*memory-address*⟩

where the memory address is given by the value of an expression.

Interrupts. It is often important in embedded systems for a program to be able to process interrupts generated by the hardware or external devices. Such an interrupt may be associated with an entry name for a task using

for ⟨*entry-name*⟩ **use at** ⟨*interrupt address*⟩

When an interrupt occurs, it acts as a highest-priority entry call on the task with the given entry. Thus the task responsible for processing the interrupt may respond immediately if it is waiting at an appropriate **accept** statement for the entry.

Other features allow specification of particular storage representations, the insertion of machine code segments within subprograms, and specification of special interfaces to subprograms written in other languages.

Programming Environment

The language has many features intended to support a programming environment. The package structure is one major feature that supports the construction of libraries of "software components" that can be assembled into programs.

The separate compilation features are particularly tuned to the production of programs by groups of programmers. In general, any package, task, or subprogram may be compiled in two phases. First the specification may be compiled, so that subsequently any other program unit that uses the package, task, or subprogram may be compiled with full checking that any calls or references to the first unit are correct. At some later time, the body of the package, task, or subprogram may be compiled, so that subsequently any other program unit using the first unit may be executed. This separate compilation of specification and body allows one programming group to provide specifications to another group, so that the second group may write and compile their programs before the first group has completed coding the bodies of their program units.

The language also has provisions for use of libraries of program units. The general rules for **with** and **use** statements and for the resolution of references to overloaded names are intended to make it easy to incorporate a library package, task, or subprogram into another program, even though identifiers defined in the library unit may conflict with local names or names in other packages.

16-8   SYNTAX AND TRANSLATION

Ada is a complex language to compile, owing to the large number and variety of features in the language, and the need to provide an efficient run-time organization. The syntax is generally straightforward. The general style of the syntax is seen in the examples in this chapter. Nested syntactic constructs are used throughout the language, in the usual style of block-structured languages.

The language manual provides a complete BNF grammar for the language, and most implementations utilize a parser generator to generate a parser directly from some form of this grammar. The later phases of translation, particularly the static type-checking required throughout every aspect of an Ada program, have been the basis for a number of research studies, as they raise new issues not found in older languages.

16-9   STRUCTURE OF AN ADA VIRTUAL COMPUTER

The most novel aspect of the Ada virtual computer is that it may be considered to be a *distributed computer*, in which each separate task defined by a program is executed by a separate processor. The actual implementation need not have more than one hardware processor, shared by all the tasks, with each given a "time slice" in which to execute. In such an implementation, priorities are used to control the scheduling of time slices for tasks, so that the most crucial tasks are executed first. However, conceptually, the virtual computer has as many processors as there are tasks defined in the program (or at least as many as there are tasks executing concurrently at any time). The manner in which a particular task is initiated (begins execution) on a processor is an implementation decision.

Once a task is executing, it requires its own central stack area to store the activation records of subprograms that it calls. Thus execution begins with a single stack for the main procedure that begins execution. As tasks are initiated, each requires a new stack area (possibly in a separate processor memory in a truly distributed system). The original stack thus has split into several new stacks, which may split again if more tasks are initiated. This storage management structure is usually known as a *cactus stack*, since it resembles the splitting of the arms of a saguaro cactus. The connection of the stack of the newly initiated task to the stack of the program unit within which it is statically nested must be maintained at run time because of the possibility that the task may make nonlocal references to shared data back in the stack of the original program unit. Thus a link such as a static chain pointer must be maintained to allow such nonlocal references to be satisfied correctly at run time.

Each task must in general have its own heap storage area, with provision for storage management within the heap. A static area is also required for the storage of code segments and run-time support routines for a task. The language requires relatively little run-time support, however, because programs must often execute on a hardware system with little or no operating system software. Thus the assumption of underlying operating system support for files, input-output, and other complex run-time activities cannot be made (note that files and I-O operations are part of a library package which need not be used by a program).

The run-time organization within a single task is similar to that for other block-structured languages. The central stack is used for the allocation of activation records on subprogram entry and their recovery on exit. Storage representations for data objects and subprograms follow the general patterns outlined in Part 1 for Pascal-type languages. Because data objects in an activation record may in general have initial values, the prologue code of a subprogram usually includes a section that assigns the appropriate initial values to data objects in the activation record at the beginning of subprogram execution.

Heap storage allocation is handled in a way that provides the programmer some control over the details. The **new** operation is used to create a data object of a given type and obtain a pointer to it. A block of storage may be set aside for allocation of storage for all data objects of a particular access (pointer) type, using the statement

for ⟨*access-type-name*⟩ **use** ⟨*expression*⟩

where the expression gives the size of the block of storage to be reserved. Any subsequent use of **new** for that access type allocates storage within the reserved block. When the block is full, the exception STORAGE_ERROR is raised by **new**.

The programmer may choose to prohibit recovery of storage within a heap block by the pragma CONTROLLED(⟨*access-type-name*⟩). Alternatively, explicit freeing of storage may be performed using a predefined procedure UNCHECKED_DEALLOCATION. Explicit freeing may cause dangling references and thus is unsafe ("unchecked"). In either case, the block of storage for a particular access type may be recovered by an underlying storage management system when the program unit defining the access type is exited during execution. If the program does not declare a special block for use by NEW with a particular access type, then a general heap storage area is used for data objects of that access type. The storage management methods used within this heap are not a part of the language definition.

16-10 REFERENCES AND SUGGESTIONS FOR FURTHER READING

The basic definition of the standard language is found in (Ada [1982]). A preliminary version of the language design appeared in *SIGPLAN Notices* (Ichbiah et al. [1979]). Although this version is no longer of importance, the accompanying *Rationale* for the design provides many useful insights into the reasons behind the design choices that went into the final language. Another useful document for the study of language design is the *Steelman* report (Ada [1978]) that sets out the final form of the requirements that the Ada design had to meet. Wasserman [1980] includes this report and some related articles. A formal semantic definition of the language (exclusive of the task features) may be found in (Ada [1980]).

Numerous texts describing the language have appeared. The June 1981 issue of *IEEE Computer* includes a series of more general articles on Ada and the Ada development. Because Ada is a new language, many aspects of its implementation and application are still under study. The two conference proceedings found in the November 1980 and October 1982 issues of *SIGPLAN Notices* are excellent sources for study of some of these research issues.

The promise of widespread use of Ada has spurred a number of projects to develop special computer hardware organizations tailored especially to meet the requirements of the Ada run-time virtual computer. The goal of many of these projects is to represent most of the Ada run-time structure directly in terms of hardware-supported data objects and operations.

The development of special programming environments for Ada is also a major area for research. Subsequent to the Ada design, a set of requirements for an Ada programming environment have been developed, again through a sequence of requirements specifications that have received widespread public scrutiny. The *Stoneman* report (Buxton [1980]) is currently the most recent in this sequence.

16-11 PROBLEMS

1. In Fig. 16-1, the outer loop in the main program is an example of the loop form called the *loop and a half*. Rewrite this loop using a **while** loop. Comment on the readability and writeability of the two versions.

2. Because Ada allows actual parameters to be paired with formal parameters by using the *names* of the formal parameters in the call statement, the formal-parameter names become *visible* in the caller. Ordinarily formal-parameter

names are local to the called subprogram and are not visible in the caller. Explain the effect on ease of modification of a subprogram caused by the visibility of its formal-parameter names.

3. Contrast the Ada **for** loop and the Pascal **for** loop in respect to the treatment of the loop-control variable. Give one advantage and one disadvantage of the Ada approach.

CHAPTER 17

LISP

The LISP language was first designed and implemented by John McCarthy and a group at the Massachusetts Institute of Technology around 1960. The language has become widely used for computer science research, most prominently in the area of artificial intelligence (robotics, natural language processing, theorem proving, intelligent systems, etc.). The basic definition of LISP is found in McCarthy et al. [1965]. However, almost every implementation extends and modifies the basic definition in various ways. There is no generally accepted standard LISP language, although several proposals have been made. This chapter is based primarily on the original LISP definition, but it includes extensions that are typical of more modern LISP systems such as INTERLISP (Teitelman [1974]), Franz LISP (Foderaro [1980]), and the Standard LISP proposal of Marti et al. [1979].

LISP is different from most other languages in a number of aspects. Most striking is the equivalence of form between programs and data in the language which allows data structures to be executed as programs and programs to be modified as data. Another striking feature is the heavy reliance on recursion as a control structure, rather than the iteration (looping) which is common in most programming languages. A third key feature is the use of linked lists as the basic data structure together with operations for general list modification. List processing is the basis of most LISP algorithms, although numbers and characters may also be manipulated to a limited extent. The important storage management technique of *garbage collection* was also first introduced in LISP.

17-1   BRIEF OVERVIEW OF THE LANGUAGE

LISP is the only example in this book of a *functional programming language*, a language in which expressions composed of function calls, rather than statements, are the basic unit from which programs are constructed. LISP programs run in an interactive environment (ordinarily), and as a result, a main program does not exist in the usual form. Instead, the user at a terminal enters the "main program" as a sequence of expressions to be evaluated. The LISP system evaluates each expression as it is entered, printing the result automatically at the terminal. Ordinarily some of the expressions entered are function definitions. Other expressions contain calls on these defined functions with particular arguments. There is no block structure or other complex syntactic organization. The only interactions between different functions occur through calls during execution.

LISP functions are defined entirely as expressions. Each operator is a function which returns a value, and subprograms are written as single (often very complex) expressions. Various special constructs have been added to the language to make this pure expression syntax appear somewhat like the ordinary *sequence of statements* syntax, but the expression form remains basic.

Data in LISP are rather restricted. *Literal atoms* (symbols) and *numeric atoms* (numbers) are the basic elementary types. Linked lists and property lists (represented as a special case of linked lists) form the basic data structures. All descriptor processing is done during execution, and no declarations of any sort are necessary.

LISP provides a wide variety of primitives for the creation, destruction, and modification of lists (including property lists). Basic primitives for arithmetic are provided. Run-time program translation and execution are also provided as primitives, and programs may be created and executed dynamically.

LISP control structures are relatively simple. The expressions used to construct programs are written in strict Cambridge Polish form and may include conditional branching. The PROG feature provides a simple structure for writing expressions in a sequence with provision for labels and gotos. Generator primitives (called *functionals*) are also provided for generating elements of lists in sequence. Recursive function calls are heavily emphasized in most LISP programming.

LISP referencing is primarily based on the *most-recent-association* rule for nonlocal referencing, often implemented using a simple linked list of current associations, the *A-list*, which is searched for the current association each time an identifier is referenced. A number of twists are provided, however, to allow this simple but slow technique to be replaced by faster methods. The most important allows any identifier to be given a global association, which takes priority over any other association for the identifier.

Function parameters are transmitted either all by value or all by name depending on the classification of the function, with transmission by value being the usual case.

LISP is most easily implemented with a software interpreter and software simulation for all primitives. Most implementations also provide a compiler which can be used to compile selected function definitions into machine code. These compiled functions are then executable by the hardware interpreter (but still require software simulation for many operations). LISP is rather poorly suited for compilation because most bindings are not made until execution. A complex storage management structure based on a garbage-collected heap is used as the primary storage for data and programs.

17-2   AN ANNOTATED EXAMPLE: BUILDING A LIST OF ATOMS

Figure 17-1 shows an example of a LISP interactive terminal session. The user begins by defining a function LISTATOMS. LISTATOMS takes a list structure as its argument. It finds all the "atoms" in the list structure and constructs a new linear list containing the atoms. For example, if the argument to LISTATOMS is the list structure shown in Fig. 17-2, then the result of the call to the function is the list shown in Fig. 17-3. After the user defines the function, he tests it three times with different arguments. The LISP system automatically prints the value returned from each function call; these values are indicated in italics in Fig. 17-1.

LISTATOMS operates by scanning the elements of the input list in

```
Line

  1    (DEF LISTATOMS (LAMBDA (X)
  2        (COND
  3            ((NULL X) NIL)
  4            ((ATOM (CAR X)) (CONS (CAR X) (LISTATOMS (CDR X))))
  5            (T (APPEND (LISTATOMS (CAR X)) (LISTATOMS (CDR X))))))))
  6    (LISTATOMS)
  7    (LISTATOMS '(JOE (TOM SALLY) FRANK MARY))
  8    (JOE TOM SALLY FRANK MARY)
  9    (LISTATOMS '())
 10    NIL
 11    (LISTATOMS '((A B) (((C)) D) A))
 12    (A B C D A)
```

Fig. 17-1 Example LISP terminal session

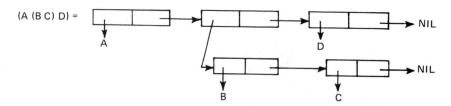

(A (B C) D) =

A

D

NIL

B

C

NIL

Fig. 17-2 Argument list structure for LISTATOMS

sequence. Each element is either an atom or a sublist. If an atom, the atom is added to the output list being constructed. If a sublist, then LISTATOMS is called recursively to create a list of the atoms on the sublist, and this list is then concatenated onto the list being constructed as the function value. The annotations below refer to the line numbers to the left of the program listing, which are not a part of the listing itself.

Line 1. The user begins the session by defining the function LIST-ATOMS, whose definition begins on this line and extends through line 5. The line begins with the name of the primitive function DEF that is used to define a user function to the LISP system. DEF requires two arguments, the name of the function being defined (LISTATOMS in this case), and a single expression forming the definition of the function body. The function body has the form (LAMBDA *(formal-parameter list) (expression))*. In this case X is the single formal parameter. Lines 2-5 contain the expression that forms the "executable part" of the function body.

Line 2. The expression that makes up the executable part of the function body in this case consists of a single *conditional expression*. A conditional expression, represented as a call on the special function COND, is the LISP equivalent of the usual **if . . . then . . . elseif then . . . elseif . . . endif** conditional statement, except that it returns a value. Since the COND expression makes up the entire body of the function definition, the value returned by COND becomes also the value returned by the function LISTATOMS.

Line 3. The first **if . . . then . . .** part of the COND conditional begins with the test (NULL X). NULL is a function that tests if its argument list is the empty list, represented in LISP as () or NIL. The second expression on the line is the value to be returned if the test is satisfied, in this case the value

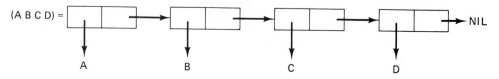

(A B C D) =

A

B

C

D

NIL

Fig. 17-3 Result list returned as value of LISTATOMS

NIL. Thus this line might be read: "If the value of X is the empty list, then return NIL as the value of the COND (which in turn is returned as the value of the call to LISTATOMS)." Stated more clearly, "If the argument list is empty, then it contains no atoms, so return an empty list as the result."

Line 4. The second **else if** . . . **then** . . . part of the COND conditional begins with the test (ATOM (CAR X)). CAR is a primitive which returns as its value the first component of its argument list. Since the test (NULL X) of the previous line was not satisfied, we know X must have at least one component at this point. The component retrieved by (CAR X) must be either a pointer to an atom or a pointer to another list. The primitive function ATOM tests whether its argument is a pointer to an atom. Thus the entire expression (ATOM (CAR X)) evaluates to T (true) if the first component of list X is an atom. If the test is satisfied, then the remainder of the line specifies the result to be returned as the value of the COND expression. The result in this case is the value of the expression (CONS (CAR X) (LIST-ATOMS (CDR X))). The CONS function is used to concatenate the atom represented by the value of its first argument (CAR X) onto the front of the list returned as the value of its second argument (LISTATOMS (CDR X)). This second argument uses the primitive CDR to get the remainder of the list X, with the first component deleted, and then calls LISTATOMS recursively to construct a list of the atoms on the remainder of list X. To summarize, this line might be read: "If the first component of X is an atom, then the result to be returned as the value of the COND is the list composed of this atom followed by the atoms in the remainder of the list X."

Line 5. The final **else if** . . . **then** . . . **endif** part of the COND conditional begins with the trivial test T (true), which of course is always satisfied if execution reaches this point. The result to be returned as the value of the COND is the value returned by execution of the expression following. Because of the tests on the two preceding lines, we know execution can reach this point only if the first component of the list X is a pointer to a sublist. The APPEND function is the general list concatenation function that makes one long list from the two shorter lists given to it as arguments. The first argument for APPEND is the value of the expression (LISTATOMS (CAR X)), which returns a list of the atoms in the sublist retrieved by (CAR X). The second argument to APPEND is the expression (LISTATOMS(CDRX)) seen in the preceding line, which returns a list of the atoms in the remainder of the list X. APPEND concatenates these two lists and returns as its value the final list containing all the atoms in both lists.

Line 6. The LISP system immediately evaluates the call to the DEF function as soon as its arguments have been completely entered. The result is automatically printed. DEF returns a list containing the name of the function defined, in this case (LISTATOMS).

Line 7. The programmer now tests the newly defined function by calling it with the argument list (JOE (TOM SALLY) FRANK MARY). The single quote mark before the argument list indicates that this argument to LISTATOMS is *quoted*, that is, the argument list is actually written literally; (JOE (TOM SALLY) FRANK MARY) is not an expression to be evaluated to get the actual argument. The quote mark is a shorthand representing a call on the function QUOTE, explained in the next section.

Line 8. The result returned from the call of LISTATOMS is printed automatically.

Lines 9-10. LISTATOMS is tested again with the empty list () as its argument. The result returned is also the empty list, printed by the LISP system as NIL.

Lines 11-12. LISTATOMS is tested again with a more complex list structure that contains several sublists, including a list having only a single component, where the component is a list with only a single component, ((C)). The argument also contains a repeated atom, A, which appears twice in the result because LISTATOMS does not remove duplicates.

17-3   DATA TYPES

The primary types of data objects in LISP are lists and atoms. Function definitions and property lists are special types of lists of particular importance. Arrays, numbers, and strings usually are also provided, but these types play a lesser role.

Two features are common to all LISP data objects:

a. Each data object carries a run-time descriptor giving its type and other attributes.

b. If a data object has components (i.e., is a structured data object) then the components are almost never represented directly as part of the data object; instead a pointer to the component data object is used.

Atoms

A LISP atom is the basic elementary type of data object. An atom is sometimes called a *literal atom* to distinguish it from a number (or *numeric atom*), which is also classified as an atom by most LISP functions. Syntactically an atom is just an identifier—a string of letters and digits beginning with a letter. Within LISP function definitions, atoms serve the usual purposes of identifiers; they are used as variable names, function names, formal-parameter names, and so on. In LISP list structures, they also serve as basic symbolic data items, as in the example of Fig. 17-1, where the atoms were extracted from a complex list structure and inserted in a separate list.

A LISP atom is not simply an identifier, however, at runtime. An atom is a complex data object represented by a location in memory which contains the type descriptor for the atom together with a pointer to a *property list*. The property list contains the various properties associated with the atom, one of which is always its *print name*, which is the character

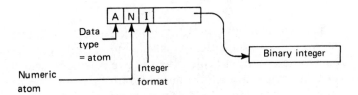

Fig. 17-4 Literal atoms and numeric atoms

string representing the atom for input and output. Other properties represent various bindings for the atom, which may include the function named by the atom and other properties assigned by the program during execution. The detailed structure of a property list is taken up below. Figure 17-4 illustrates the structure of a LISP atom.

Whenever an atom appears as a component of another data object such as a list, it is represented by a pointer to the memory location serving as the run-time representation of the atom. Thus every reference to the atom ABC during execution of a LISP program appears as a pointer to the same location in memory, as shown in Fig. 17-4.

Every atom also ordinarily appears as a component in a central, system-defined table called the *object list* (ob-list). The ob-list is usually organized as a hash-coded table that allows efficient lookup of a print name (character string) and retrieval of a pointer to the atom with that print name. For example, when a list is input that contains the character string "ABC", representing the atom ABC, the READ operation searches the ob-list for the entry "ABC", which also contains a pointer to the storage location for the atom ABC. This pointer is inserted into the list being constructed at the appropriate point.

Operations on Atoms

A few primitives are defined on literal atoms, but most manipulations involve either modifying the property lists associated with atoms or modifying lists that contain pointers to atoms, without modifying the atoms themselves. The operations on atoms typically include the function ATOM, which distinguishes between a pointer to a list word and a pointer to an atom (by checking the descriptor of the word); NUMBERP, which tests whether an atom is a literal atom or a number; EQ, which tests if two literal atoms are the same (by simply testing if its two arguments point to the same location); GENSYM, which generates a new atom (and does not put it on the ob-list); INTERN, which puts an atom on the ob-list; and REMOB, which removes an atom from the ob-list.

Numbers

Numbers (numeric atoms) in integer or floating-point format may be used. The hardware representation is used, but a run-time descriptor is also required, so each number typically uses two words. However, this representation coordinates well with that used for literal atoms; a number is an atom with a special type designator and a pointer to the bit string representing the number instead of a pointer to a property list, as shown in Fig. 17-4.

Arithmetic, Relational, and Boolean Operations

LISP contains the basic arithmetic primitives: PLUS, DIFFERENCE, TIMES, and DIVIDE, and a few others. The syntax is the same as for other LISP operations; thus $A + B * C$ is written (PLUS A (TIMES B C)). All arithmetic operations are generic operations, accepting arguments of either real or integer data type and making type conversions as necessary.

The relational operations for comparing numbers are also provided as functions: ZEROP tests for a zero value, GREATERP and LESSP represent the usual greater-than and less-than comparisons. The results of these operations are either the atom NIL, representing *false*, or T, representing *true* (any non-NIL value ordinarily represents *true* in LISP).

There is no Boolean data type in LISP. The Boolean operations AND, OR, and NOT are provided as functions. The AND operation takes an arbitrary list of unevaluated arguments; it evaluates each in turn and returns a NIL result if any of its arguments evaluates to NIL. The OR operation works in a similar manner. Every LISP implementation extends this basic list of arithmetic, relational, and Boolean operations, often including dozens of functions for various useful operations on numeric data.

Lists

LISP lists are simple singly linked structures, as shown in Fig. 17-5. Each list element contains a pointer to a data item and a pointer to the following list element. The last list element points to the special atom NIL as its successor. The two pointers in a list element are termed the CAR pointer and the CDR pointer. The CDR pointer points to the successor of the list element. The CAR pointer points to the data item. (The terms CAR and CDR originated from the hardware organization of the first computer on which

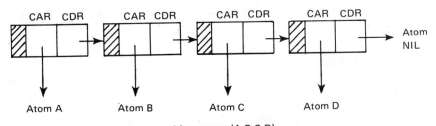

List syntax: (A B C D)

(hashed area contains system-defined data)

Fig. 17-5 Simple list representation

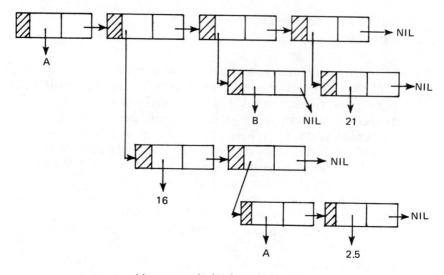

List syntax: (A (16 (A 2.5))(B)(21))

Fig. 17-6 List with sublists

LISP was implemented but became such a basic part of the LISP jargon that their use has continued.)

A list element may contain (have as its CAR pointer) a pointer to a data object of any type including a literal or numeric atom, or a pointer to another list. Each case is distinguished by a data type flag stored in the location pointed to. Since a list element may contain a pointer to another list, it is possible to build up list structures of arbitrary complexity. Ordinarily these are tree structures, but it is possible to have shared sublists, to build circular structures, and the like. Figure 17-6 illustrates a typical list with sublists.

Syntactically a list is represented by writing its elements in sequence with the whole enclosed in parentheses. Atoms are written using their print names, and numbers are written in the usual number syntax. Lists which share sublists or which are circular cannot be written down, but every other list may be so represented. Figures 17-5 and 17-6 illustrate the syntax for lists.

List Manipulation

The central primitives are those for list manipulation.

CAR *and* CDR. The primitives CAR and CDR retrieve the CAR pointer and CDR pointer of a given list element, respectively. Effectively, given a list L as operand, (CAR L) returns a pointer to the first list element, and (CDR L) returns a pointer to the list with the first element deleted.

CONS. The CONS primitive takes two pointers as operands, allocates a new list element memory word, stores the two pointers in the CAR and CDR fields of the word, and returns a pointer to the new word. Where the second operand is a list the effect is to add the first element to the head of this list and return a pointer to the extended list.

CAR, CDR, and CONS are the basic operations for selecting list components and constructing lists. By using CONS any list may be constructed element by element. For example, (CONS A (CONS B (CONS C NIL))) constructs a list of the three elements referenced by A, B, and C. Similarly, if L = (A B C) is a list, then (CAR L) is A, (CAR (CDR L)) is B, and (CAR (CDR (CDR L))) is C. By using CAR, CDR, and CONS appropriately any list may be broken down into its constituent elements, and new lists may be constructed from these or other elements.

LIST *and* QUOTE. The primitive LIST may be used to replace a long sequence of CONS operations. LIST takes any number of arguments and constructs a list of its arguments, returning a pointer to the resulting list. QUOTE allows any list or atom to be written as a literal in a program. For example, if L = (B C) is a list, then (CONS (QUOTE A) L) produces the list (A B C). The function name QUOTE (and the parentheses surrounding QUOTE and its argument) may be replaced by a single quote symbol, ', in most LISP systems, as shown in Fig. 17-1. For example (CONS 'A '(B C)) is equivalent to (CONS (QUOTE A) (QUOTE (B C))).

REPLACA *and* REPLACD. The REPLACA primitive is used to replace the CAR pointer field in a list word with a new pointer; REPLACD is used to change the CDR pointer. These two primitives must be used with care in LISP because they actually modify the contents of a list word as well as returning a value, and thus they have *side effects*. Because of the complex way that lists are linked in LISP, these side effects may affect other lists besides the list being modified.

Other list-manipulation primitives. NULL tests if a list is empty (equals the atom NIL), APPEND may be used to concatenate two lists, and EQUAL compares two lists for equality of corresponding elements (applying itself recursively to corresponding pairs of elements). Every LISP implementation extends this basic set to include a variety of other list-manipulation primitives as well.

Property Lists

Each literal atom has an associated property list, accessible through a pointer stored in the memory location representing the atom. A property list is simply an ordinary LISP list, differing only in that its elements are logically paired into an alternating *property name/property value* sequence. Every atom's property list contains at least the property PNAME whose associated value is a pointer to a list containing the print name of the atom in character string form. If an atom is a function name, its property list contains the property name giving the function type and a pointer to the list representing the function definition. Other properties may be added by the programmer as desired, and certain primitives also add properties. In much LISP programming the property lists of atoms are the central structures where much of the data are stored.

Operations on Property Lists

Basic functions are provided for insertion, deletion, and accessing of properties on property lists. PUT is used to add a property name/property value pair to a property list; GET returns the current value associated with a given property name; and REMPROP deletes a name/value pair from a property list. For example, to add the name/value pair AGE, 40 to the property list of atom MARY, one writes

(PUT 'MARY 'AGE 40)

Later in the program the AGE property of MARY may be retrieved through the function call

(GET 'MARY 'AGE)

Deletion of the AGE property of MARY is accomplished by the call

(REMPROP 'MARY 'AGE)

The primitives that define functions also may modify property lists for special property names such as EXPR and FEXPR (see below).

Assignment

Direct assignment does not play as central a role in LISP programming as it does in other languages. Many LISP programs are written entirely without assignment operations, using recursion and parameter transmission to get somewhat the same effect indirectly. However, assignment is used within PROG segments, where the LISP program takes on the ordinary sequence-of-statements form. The basic assignment operator is SETQ. The expression (SETQ X VAL) assigns the value of VAL as the new value of variable X; the result of the expression is the value of VAL (thus SETQ is a function, but its value is usually ignored). The variable name (X above) must be explicitly given in a call to SETQ. The primitive SET is identical to SETQ except that the variable (which is just an atom) to which assignment is made may be computed. For example, (SET (CAR L) VAL) is equivalent to (SETQ X VAL) if atom X happens to be the first element of list L. RPLACA and RPLACD allow assignment to the CAR and CDR fields, respectively, of any list element. For example, (RPLACA L VAL) assigns the value of VAL as the new first element of list L, replacing the current first element.

Vectors and Arrays

Most LISP implementations provide some type of vector or array data object. However there is little uniformity in treatment between different implementations, reflecting the relative lack of importance of vectors and arrays in most LISP programming. A typical implementation provides a function MKVECT(⟨*bound*⟩) that creates a vector data object with subscript range 0 to a given ⟨*bound*⟩. Each component of the vector may contain a pointer to any LISP data object; initially all pointers are set to NIL. A function GETV(⟨*vector*⟩,⟨*subscript*⟩) returns the pointer stored in the indicated component of the argument vector; thus GETV is the LISP version of subscripting to retrieve the value of a vector component. PUTV is used to assign a new value to a vector component.

Character Strings

A character-string type of data object is provided in many LISP systems, together with a limited set of operations for string manipulation. Again the details vary widely among different LISP implementations.

Files and Input-Output

Most LISP output is automatic. For each function call in the main program the system automatically prints out the function name, its arguments, and the value returned by the function. A TRACE primitive allows any other function (programmer- or system-defined) to be tagged for similar treatment. When such a tagged function is entered during execution its name and parameters are printed out, and when it is exited its value is printed. Because there is little need in many LISP applications for specially formatted output, these simple automatic output features often suffice.

Input data may be included directly in the form of actual parameters in the main program function calls, as seen in Fig. 17-1. Thus many LISP programs run entirely without any explicit input-output commands.

Simple primitives are also provided for reading and writing sequential external files. READ reads in the next list, list structure, or atom from an input file; PRINT prints a list; and PRINTPROP prints a property list. Another set of functions allows the input file to be read character by character and an output line to be built up element by element under programmer control.

Function Definitions as Data Objects

Programmer-defined functions are written in the form of lists for input, as seen in Fig. 17-1. The LISP input routines make no distinction between function definitions and data lists but simply translate all lists into the internal linked-list representation. Each atom encountered is looked up in the ob-list and the pointer to the atom retrieved if it already exists or a new atom created if not. All the LISP primitive operations are named by atoms which are system-defined at the beginning of execution but which otherwise are like any other atoms. Figure 17-7 shows a simple LISP function definition and its corresponding internal linked list form. As noted in the introduction, this common internal representation for programs and data structures allows LISP programs to be created dynamically by other programs during execution and later executed. Thus a *data list* may turn into a *program list*, and conversely, as required.

17-4 SUBPROGRAMS

LISP provides no abstraction mechanisms beyond function subprograms. There are no provisions for programmer-defined types or data abstractions. Most LISP implementations distinguish three classes of functions: *interpreted functions, compiled functions*, and *macros*.

Interpreted functions. An interpreted function is one whose definition is represented in list structure form at run-time, as shown in Fig. 17-7. The software interpreter, represented by the primitives EVAL and APPLY, is used to execute the function definition when the function is called. Two modes of parameter transmission are possible in each function, either evaluating all actual parameters before transmission or evaluating none of them (see Sec. 17-6). The function is classified as an EXPR function if its arguments are always evaluated, and a FEXPR function if its arguments are never evaluated. Most programmer-defined functions are EXPR's.

When an interpreted function is called with a particular actual-parameter list, the LISP system sends the function name and its argument list to APPLY. APPLY evaluates the arguments (if required) and adds them to the current referencing environment, as described in Sec. 17-6. APPLY then calls EVAL to actually evaluate the expression that forms the body of the function. EVAL traverses the list structure representing the body of the function. It evaluates atoms representing variables by looking up their current value in the referencing environment, and it evaluates internal function calls by calling APPLY (recursively) with the function name and argument list. Thus EVAL and APPLY interact with each other to traverse

Program list: (LAMBDA (X)(COND ((NULL X) X)

(T (CAR (CDR X)))))

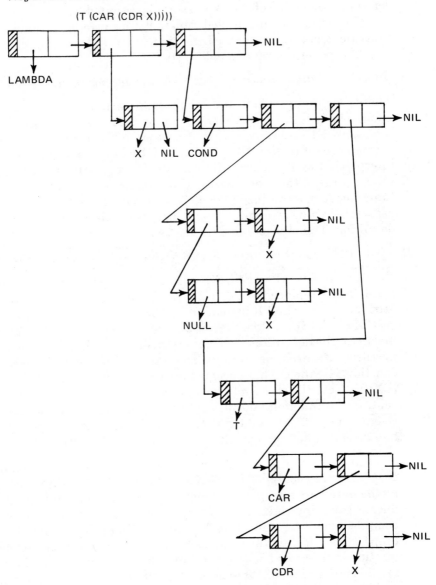

Fig. 17-7 Executable form (list structure) of a LISP program

the list structure representing the function definition and ultimately determine the value of the expression represented by the list structure.

To define an interpreted function, the primitive function DEF (or equivalent, depending on the LISP system) is used, as in the example of Fig. 17-1. The general form of a call to DEF is

(DEF *function-name* (LAMBDA (*formal-parameter list*) (*body*)))

where the function name and each formal-parameter name are just atoms, and the body is any expression involving primitive or programmer-defined functions. DEF may be called at any point during program execution to define a new function. The action of DEF is quite simple. Definitions of interpreted functions are ordinarily stored as an attribute-value pair on the property list of the atom representing the function name. For an ordinary function, such as defined above, the attribute name EXPR is used, and the associated value is a pointer to the list structure representing the function definition. Thus the call to DEF above is equivalent to the call

(PUT '*function-name* 'EXPR '(LAMBDA (*parameters*) (*body*)))

If the function is to be a FEXPR (unevaluated argument transmission), then LAMBDA is replaced by NLAMBDA in the call to DEF, and DEF uses the attribute name FEXPR instead of EXPR on the property list entry.

Many LISP systems reserve a special location in the atom (header block) for the definition of the function named with that atom, to avoid the necessity to search the property list for the function definition each time the function is called. This special location designates the type of function (EXPR, FEXPR, etc.) and contains a pointer to the list structure representing the function definition. In these implementations, special primitives GETD, PUTD, and REMD are usually provided to directly get, insert, and delete a function definition from the special location.

Compiled functions. The second general class of functions are those that have been compiled into a block of machine code that can be executed by the hardware interpreter. Compiled and interpreted function definitions may be freely intermixed in a LISP system. The run-time representation of a compiled function definition has an attribute-value pair stored on the property list of the atom representing the function name (or in a special location in the atom head), just as for an interpreted function. However, the attribute name is CEXPR (compiled EXPR) or CFEXPR (compiled FEXPR) and the associated value is a pointer to a special block of storage containing the compiled code. EVAL and APPLY, when given a compiled function to execute, invoke the hardware interpreter to execute the compiled code after they have transmitted the arguments as appropriate for a compiled function. The compiled function body may contain calls on interpreted functions, in which case EVAL and APPLY are invoked recursively by calls from the hardware interpreter. Thus the software and hardware interpreters in a LISP implementation cooperate to execute the entire LISP program.

Primitive functions such as CAR, CDR, and CONS are usually represented as a special class of compiled functions (using the attribute names SUBR and FSUBR). Special forms of compiled code are used to make these functions especially efficient, since they never invoke other interpreted or compiled functions. Thus they form the bottom level in the calling hierarchy.

Various methods are used to compile a function definition in different versions of LISP. A special COMPILE primitive may be provided, or, more commonly, a special system-defined variable may be used, e.g., *COMP. *COMP is set by the programmer to be NIL or non-NIL. When DEF is called, if *COMP is NIL then DEF defines the function as an interpreted function. IF *COMP is non-NIL then DEF compiles the function being defined.

Macros. The third general class of LISP function is the *macro*. Again the DEF primitive is used to define such a function, but MACRO must replace LAMBDA in the function definition. A macro is just an ordinary LISP function (it may be interpreted or compiled), but its execution has a special twist. A macro always has only a single argument, which consists of the complete expression that invoked the macro, including the macro name and the unevaluated actual-parameter list. Rather than evaluating this expression, the macro function constructs a second equivalent expression as its result, and this result expression is then evaluated instead of the original expression by the LISP system. The process of substitution of the result expression for the original macro call expression is termed *macro expansion*. Thus when the LISP interpreter encounters a macro call, a two-step evaluation sequence is invoked: first the macro function is called, and then the result from that call is itself evaluated to get the final result.

For example, a common use of macros is to provide a more readable syntax for common LISP operations. An **if** . . . **then** . . . **else** . . . syntax for the usual COND conditional might use the syntax (IF (*test-expr*) THEN (*expr₁*) ELSE (*expr₂*)). Note that this is still a LISP list (of six components), so it may be included as part of an ordinary LISP function definition. However, the atom IF is not the name of a LISP primitive function, so it must be defined by the programmer as a function. The programmer defines IF as a macro function:

$$(DEF\ IF\ (MACRO\ (X)\ (body)))$$

When the LISP interpreter APPLY encounters an IF call during execution, it sends the entire expression (IF (*test*) THEN (*expr₁*) ELSE (*expr₂*)) to the IF macro as its argument X. The body of the IF macro is defined so that it takes apart the input list and constructs the list (COND ((*test*) (*expr₁*)) (T (*expr₂*))) which it returns as its result. This list represents a valid COND conditional expression. APPLY then sends this expression to EVAL to be evaluated in place of the original IF expression. For the programmer, it appears that the original IF expression has been directly executed; the macro expansion and subsequent evaluation of the COND expression are invisible.

17-5 SEQUENCE CONTROL

A LISP main program is composed of a simple sequence of function calls, each consisting of a function name followed by a list of actual parameters. These *top-level* function calls are executed in sequence by the LISP system, using EVAL or APPLY.

Each function subprogram definition is composed of a single expression. Thus in LISP the expression structure is the key element in sequence control. The special PROG expression allows use of a syntax which roughly resembles an ordinary sequence of statements.

Expressions

LISP expressions are written in strict Cambridge Polish notation (function name followed by sequence of actual parameters) with full parenthesization. Expressions may be built most simply by use of nested function calls, e.g., (CONS (CAR L) (CAR (CDR L))). In such expressions the usual sequence of evaluation applies: First the arguments are evaluated, and then the function is applied to the result. However, certain special functions are applied without evaluating their arguments (see below). Actual parameters are evaluated from left to right, and otherwise the nesting of parentheses completely determines evaluation order.

The COND primitive used in previous sections allows branching within expressions. Like all LISP primitives COND is written as a function with a list of parameters, but COND invokes a special evaluation rule which gives the effect of a branching control structure. The form is

$$(\text{COND } (test_1 \ result\text{-}expr_1)$$
$$(test_2 \ result\text{-}expr_2)$$
$$\vdots$$
$$(test_k \ result\text{-}expr_k))$$

Each *test* is an expression which must evaluate to true (non-NIL) or false (NIL). The test expressions are evaluated in sequence, and when one evaluates to true the corresponding result-expression is evaluated and the value returned as the value of the COND expression.

Statements and the PROG Feature

Any LISP program may be written using only simple expressions, conditionals, and recursive function calls. However, for many algorithms which ordinarily would be coded using a loop, such noniterative coding requires heavy reliance on recursion to give the effect of looping. The PROG *feature* allows a loop to be coded directly. The necessity to keep within the usual expression syntax makes the syntax for PROGs somewhat odd. A PROG takes the form

$$\text{(PROG (\textit{list of-local-variables})}$$
$$(\textit{expr}_1)$$
$$(\textit{expr}_2)$$
$$\vdots$$
$$(\textit{expr}_n))$$

An atom may be put between any pair of expressions in a PROG to serve as a label for the following expression. A goto is provided in the form (GO *label*), which transfers control to the expression following the designated *label*.

The expressions in a PROG are evaluated in sequence, skipping over atoms representing labels, with the GO transferring control in the usual way. A PROG may be exited either by completing evaluation of the last expression (in which case the PROG as a whole has the value NIL) or by a call to the primitive RETURN. The argument to RETURN is the value to be returned as the value of the PROG.

To illustrate the use of PROG, the following is a PROG version (not entirely equivalent) of the function LISTATOMS of Fig. 17-1.

```
(DEF LISTATOMS (LAMBDA (X)
    (PROG (RES)
    LOOP (COND
        ((NULL X) (RETURN RES))
        ((ATOM (CAR X)) (SETQ RES (CONS (CAR X) RES)))
        (T (SETQ RES (APPEND (LISTATOMS (CAR X)) RES))))
    (SETQ X (CDR X))
    (GO LOOP))))
```

Note that an explicit loop is coded within the PROG, using the atom LOOP as a statement label and the function GO to transfer control. Function SETQ is used to code explicit assignments to local variable RES in order to construct the result list to be returned as the value of the PROG (using function RETURN). This version returns a list containing the atoms in *reverse order* of their occurrence in the argument list. Note how much less readable this version is as compared to the elegant recursive version of Fig. 17-1.

Two special functions, PROG2 and PROGN, provide a means of executing a simple sequence of expressions (with no looping) in place of a single expression. The function call (PROG2 ⟨*expression₁*⟩ ⟨*expression₂*⟩) causes both expressions to be evaluated in sequence, with the value of ⟨*expression₂*⟩ returned as the value of PROG2. The value of ⟨*expression₁*⟩ is lost. PROGN takes an arbitrary number of expressions as arguments, evaluates them in sequence, and returns the value of the last as its value.

Subprogram Sequence Control

Function subprogram calls, with recursion, are the primary means of subprogram sequence control in LISP. A limited facility for exception handling is provided by two functions, ERROR and ERRORSET. ERROR is used to raise an exception within a function, specifying an error number and an error message. When ERROR is called, the LISP system takes control and begins to unwind the dynamic chain of function calls that led to the call on ERROR. Each function activation in the dynamic chain is terminated until an activation of the function ERRORSET is reached. ERRORSET represents the exception handler for the exception raised by ERROR. ERRORSET prints the message specified in the original call to ERROR and returns the error number as its value. Any further handling of the exception is left to the function that originally invoked ERRORSET. Most LISP systems extend this basic exception-handling capability to include more sophisticated facilities.

Generators for List Elements

A simple set of list *generators* is provided; these generators are called *functionals* in LISP terminology. The functional MAPCAR is typical. The function call (MAPCAR *list fn-name*) applies the function *fn-name* to each element of the list *list* in sequence. The value of MAPCAR is the list composed of the values produced by *fn-name* during this processing. MAPCAR may be used to replace the use of an explicit loop or recursion for the sequential processing of a list. Most LISP implementations provide a variety of other generators (functionals) for processing lists in various ways. In addition the programmer may easily write his own.

17-6 DATA CONTROL

In most language implementations the referencing environment is maintained as a system-defined data structure hidden from the programmer. LISP is unusual in making the referencing environment an explicit data structure which is both visible and accessible to the programmer. The exact representation of referencing environments varies widely among LISP implementations. Compiler-based implementations tend to use rather complex representations which allow efficient referencing. However, the simplest and most general technique is that using an explicit association list, the A-list. We shall describe this technique here.

A-Lists and Referencing Environments

An A-list (association list) represents a referencing environment. The A-list is an ordinary LISP list, each of whose elements is a pointer to a word representing an identifier (atom) and its current association. These association pairs are list words whose CAR points to the atom and whose CDR points to the value (list, atom, or other data object) associated with the atom. Figure 17-8 illustrates this A-list structure.

Referencing in LISP is strictly according to the most recent association rule, which is implemented by a simple search of the A-list from beginning (most recent associations) to end (oldest associations) until an appropriate association is found. Thus to find the current value of X, for example, the A-list is searched until an entry is found whose CAR is the atom X. The CDR of that entry is then the current value of X.

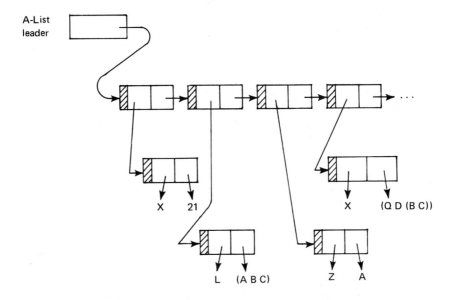

(Atoms, numbers, and lists serving as identifiers and values are themselves linked lists, although this structure is not diagrammed)

Fig. 17-8 An A-list for a referencing environment containing associations for L, Z, and two occurrences of X

The A-list is modified during program execution in three basic ways. When a function call occurs to a programmer-defined function, the LISP interpreter (the function APPLY) pairs the atoms representing formal parameters with their corresponding actual-parameter values and adds the resulting pairs to the beginning of the A-list. A similar thing happens when a PROG is entered. The atoms listed as local variable names for the PROG are each paired with the value NIL and added to the beginning of the A-list. When a function or PROG execution is completed, the associations added on entry are deleted. The programmer may directly modify the most recent association for an atom on the A-list by using SETQ (or SET). The effect of (SETQ X VAL) is to replace the current value of X on the A-list by the value of VAL. X may occur on the A-list more than once, but SETQ affects only the most recent entry.

Global Common Environment

The A-list represents the dynamically changing local and nonlocal referencing environment for a function during its execution. A global common environment is also provided in most LISP implementations. The details of implementation vary widely, but the general method is to allow any atom to be associated with a value which is used when the atom is referenced as a variable name, instead of an association on the A-list. This global value, rather than being paired with a pointer to the atom on the A-list, is stored directly in the atom itself, either on the property list of the atom (using the attribute name VALUE or APVAL) or in a special location reserved in the atom head to contain a pointer to the global value.

When an atom is referenced that has a global value, this value is retrieved directly, and no search of the A-list is performed. Thus such an atom cannot be used as a formal-parameter name or a PROG local variable, because any bindings on the A-list are hidden as long as the atom is in use as a global variable name. Assignment of a value to a global variable may require use of a special assignment function, or a special function may be used to tag atoms as global variable names, with SET and SETQ being used for assignment as usual.

Parameters and Parameter Transmission

The actual parameters in a function call are always expressions, represented as list structures. LISP provides two main methods of parameter transmission:

1. *Transmission by value.* The most common method is to evaluate the expressions in the actual-parameter list, and transmit the resulting values.

A pointer to each value is paired with a pointer to the corresponding formal-parameter name (atom) and the pair is inserted at the top of the A-list. The programmer specifies this method of transmission by using LAMBDA before the formal-parameter list in the function definition. The function type is then tagged as EXPR (interpreted functions) or CEXPR (compiled functions).

2. *Transmission by name.* A less common method is to transmit the expressions in the actual-parameter list *unevaluated,* and let the called function evaluate them as needed using EVAL. In this method the entire actual-parameter list is simply passed as a single parameter and paired on the A-list with the single formal-parameter name of the called function. This method is used primarily in two situations: (1) where a function accepts a variable number of arguments on different calls, and (2) where the evaluation of one or more of the arguments may be undesirable (e.g., the COND and DEF primitives require their arguments transmitted uneval- uated). Transmission by name is standard for macro functions. For other functions, the programmer may specify transmission by name by using NLAMBDA in place of LAMBDA in the function definition. The function definition is then tagged as FEXPR (interpreted functions) or CFEXPR (compiled functions).

When a function call is made, the interpreter function APPLY checks the type of the function; if EXPR or CEXPR, then it evaluates the actual parameter list before calling the function; if MACRO, FEXPR, or CFEXPR, then it transmits the unevaluated list.

Results of Functions

LISP functions may create and return arbitrary data objects as their values, in contrast to most other languages. Since these data objects are represented by pointers when transmitted as results, the transmission is straight- forward. Because an executable expression is represented as a list structure at run time, a function may create a new expression or complete function definition and return that as its value. Thus it is possible to write a LISP program that creates or modifies other LISP programs (see Problem 5).

Functions as Parameters

Special provision is made for transmitting the referencing environment along with a function name (when the function is transmitted as an actual parameter to a subprogram) by using the primitive FUNCTION. The referencing environment at the point of transmission is represented by a pointer to the current top of the A-list. For example, to call a function SUB with another function NUB as actual parameter, the expression (SUB (FUNCTION NUB) *other-params*) is used. The atom NUB is then transmitted together with a pointer to the beginning of the current A-list, and whenever NUB is executed through a reference in SUB to the corresponding formal parameter, the transmitted A-list pointer is taken as the beginning of the A-list to be used as referencing environment during execution of NUB. This general problem of passing the correct referencing environment along with a function name when it is transmitted as a parameter is termed the *funarg problem* in LISP (funarg = functional argument).

17-7 OPERATING AND PROGRAMMING ENVIRONMENT

LISP was originally designed for a batch-processing environment, but it has evolved through use into a language that is primarily used interactively. The simple top-level command interpreter (ordinarily the EVAL function) provides a natural basis for an interactive environment both for LISP program development and for execution of LISP programs. The top-level interpreter simply accepts a function call as input and executes the call.

LISP supports only rather simple sequential file structures. In addition to sequential files and an interactive terminal, a LISP program ordinarily has access to external libraries of function definitions, from which additional functions may be retrieved and executed. Thus the set of functions available for use by a LISP program during execution may change dynamically as the course of execution proceeds.

Most LISP implementations provide an extensive programming environment to support program development. Since LISP function definitions are entirely independent until calling linkages are made during execution, a group of programmers may develop separate sets of function definitions and simply add them to a library as appropriate. Compiled and interpreted functions may be freely intermixed, so that debugged and tested functions may be compiled (for execution efficiency) while others remain uncompiled (for debugging ease).

A typical LISP programming environment includes special functions for tracing program execution and setting "breakpoints" at which execution will halt. Most of the LISP run-time system is usually visible to the programmer through special functions that provide information about the status of various system-defined data structures (such as the A-list, the pushdown list, the object list, and the free-space list). Thus the programmer can obtain a rather complete picture of the execution state at any time. Other features available usually include a special *function editor* that can be used to retrieve and modify the definition of a function. A sophisticated package of error-recovery and other debugging aids is also usually a part of the programming environment. Because LISP has seen its primary use in computer science research, many innovative ideas about programming environments have been tried out in LISP systems.

17-8   SYNTAX AND TRANSLATION

Syntax

The key points of LISP syntax have already been mentioned in the preceding sections: the main program form as a sequence of function calls and the function definitions as list structures using fully parenthesized Cambridge Polish notation. Both programs and data share the same syntax. Even the primitive operations are named with the same atoms used for data.

The regularity and simplicity of the LISP syntax is both a virtue and a vice. The basic rules of LISP syntax may be learned in a few minutes by the beginner, and then writing programs is mainly a matter (syntactically) of getting the right arguments listed for each function call. The problem with this simple syntax lies in the parentheses. Every expression is fully parenthesized, and since each function body is a gigantic expression, the parentheses in a function definition often pile up ten or fifteen levels deep. The result may be extremely difficult to read and debug, and a parenthesis out of place is perhaps the most common LISP error. Most LISP systems include an automatic parentheses counter which, when used, outputs integers beneath parentheses in the program listing to indicate parenthesis pairings.

A second common feature used to ease the parenthesis-matching problem in LISP is the use of brackets, [and], as *superparentheses*. A right bracket is treated as equivalent to as many right parentheses as are needed to close all the pairs back to a preceding left bracket, or to close every unclosed pair if no preceding left bracket occurs. Thus where a function definition may end in five to ten right parentheses, for example, a single "]" may be used instead.

Translation

The LISP translator is simply the READ function. READ scans a character string from the input file or terminal, looking for a complete identifier or list structure. If a single identifier is found, it is looked up in the ob-list to obtain a pointer to the corresponding atom (or to create a new atom if none is found with that print name). If a list structure is found, beginning with "(", then each item in the list is scanned until a matching ")" is found. Each list item is translated into internal form and a pointer is inserted into the list as a CAR pointer at the appropriate point. Numbers are translated into their binary equivalents, with a descriptor in a separate word. If a sublist is found, beginning with another "(", then READ is called recursively to build the internal representation of the sublist. A pointer to the sublist is then inserted as the CAR pointer of the next component of the main list. Note that this translation process does not depend on whether the list is a function definition or a data list; all lists are treated the same way.

17-9 STRUCTURE OF A LISP VIRTUAL COMPUTER

The run-time memory organization in a typical LISP implementation is briefly described in Sec. 8-5. Figure 8-3 illustrates the pattern of memory usage. The major memory area is the heap, which contains both data list structures and list structures representing function definitions. Property lists are stored in the heap, and some of the system-defined lists, such as the A-list, also use part of this storage. The heap is managed in fixed-size one-word units, utilizing a free-space list and garbage collector. One part of the heap block is restricted to *full-word* data items—numbers and character strings—and requires a special garbage-collection scheme.

Other memory areas include a statically allocated area for system programs, including the interpreter, compiler (if used), primitive operations, and storage management routines. A third area, called the *pushdown list*, is allocated for a stack of activation records. Each activation record contains a return point and temporary storage areas for use by a function during its execution. The referencing environment for a function is maintained on the separate A-list. Execution of a function by the LISP interpreter, APPLY and EVAL, is described in the preceding sections.

The most significant feature of the LISP run-time structure is the amount of simulation necessary. Almost no hardware features can be used directly on a conventional computer; instead everything must be software-simulated. Each primitive is represented by a software routine, PROG and recursion—the central control structures—are simulated, and even arithmetic must be simulated to the extent of doing run-time type checking (and possibly type conversion) for each arithmetic operation. The LISP virtual computer structure is almost completely at odds with conventional computer design.

17-10 SPECIAL TOPICS

In many ways LISP is the most unconventional language described in this book. Some of these aspects have been mentioned in the preceding sections: the *functional programming* nature of the language, linked lists as the central data structure, recursion as the central control structure, the A-list representation of referencing environments, and the equivalence in run-time representations of programs and data. Garbage collection, at the time of the first LISP implementations, was a decidedly unconventional storage management technique, although it has been widely copied since then.

Two important topics about LISP have not yet been mentioned.

Pure LISP

Pure LISP is the simple subset of LISP composed of (1) the basic primitives CAR, CDR, CONS, EQ, and ATOM; (2) the control structures using COND, recursion, and functional composition; (3) list structures containing only atoms and sublists, without numbers or property lists; and (4) some means for function definition. With this subset most of the usual LISP list processing may be done. In fact, pure LISP is a *universal language*, in the sense described in Chapter 11.

Pure LISP has been the basis for many theoretical studies of programs. It is particularly amenable to study because programs written in this subset have an exceedingly simple, regular, recursive structure, which simplifies formal analysis.

The LISP Definition

The LISP manual (McCarthy et al. [1965]) is one of the few programming language manuals that provides a fairly clear description of the run-time structures on which the language implementation is built. The center of this description is a complete definition of the *interpreter* which executes LISP programs, given in the form of LISP programs for the two primitives EVAL and APPLY. The interpreter mechanisms are so straightforward that the entire definition takes less than two pages. (The fact that the definitions take the form of LISP programs is of interest but not central—EVAL and APPLY are of course represented by machine language primitives in an actual implementation.)

There is more to the LISP definition of run-time structures than just the EVAL and APPLY definitions. The A-list as a mechanism for representation of referencing environments; the use of property lists to associate function names with their definitions; the descriptions of run-time representations for lists, atoms, property lists, and numbers; and the description of the garbage collection mechanisms all contribute to provide a picture of the run-time structure which is easy to understand.

This clarity of definition has been important for both the LISP programmer and the LISP implementor, because it provides a common point of reference. Programmers use the definition to answer subtle questions of language semantics, and implementors use it as an implementation guide showing how particular constructs are supposed to work (although each implementation may modify the implementation details considerably from those described). This LISP definition is perhaps the most widely known *virtual computer* definition of a language.

17-11 REFERENCES AND SUGGESTIONS FOR FURTHER READING

The basic LISP definition is still the original MIT LISP manual by McCarthy et al. [1965]. Meehan [1979], Teitelman [1974], and Foderaro [1979] describe current LISP systems. Friedman [1974], Siklossy [1976], and Weissman [1967], among others, provide more elementary introductions. Sandewall [1978] describes experience with the interactive use of LISP. McCarthy [1981] gives an interesting account of the early history of the language. Winston [1977] and Minsky [1968] describe applications of LISP in artificial intelligence research. The influence of LISP on subsequent language design for work in this research area is described by Bobrow and Raphael [1974].

An excellent discussion of LISP and its implementation issues is given by Allen [1978]; see also Winston and Horn [1981]. Harrison [1973] and Bobrow and Murphy [1967] discuss implementation issues, especially storage management. Some of the articles in Berkeley and Bobrow [1964] also treat implementation questions. The subtleties of the *funarg problem* are the subject of a paper by Moses [1970]. Two computers oriented toward direct execution of LISP and similar languages are described by Sansonnet et al. [1982] and Sussman et al. [1981].

Functional programming languages such as LISP are of interest also because they suggest an alternative style of programming that might be generally effective. Henderson [1980] and Backus [1978] are good starting points for study of these ideas.

17-12 PROBLEMS

1. Trace the execution of the purely recursive version of LISTATOMS given in Fig. 17-1 when applied to the argument list (((A B) (((C)) D) E)); i.e., give the argument and result of each recursive activation of LISTATOMS. The PROG version of Sec. 17-5 produces a result list which is the reverse of the list produced by the LISTATOMS of Fig. 17-1. Can you rewrite the PROG version of LISTATOMS so it produces a result identical to that of the original LISTATOMS?

2. In the property-list examples of Sec. 17-3, explain why the atoms AGE and MARY must be quoted in each call to PUT, GET, and REMPROP. In Fig. 17-1, explain why the argument given in the call of LISTATOMS in line 4 is not quoted, while that in line 7 is quoted.

3. In the syntactic representation of a list in the usual *list notation* (as a sequence of elements in parentheses), the terminating CDR pointer to NIL is implicit; e.g.,

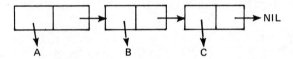

is written (A B C). Occasionally it is desirable to allow the last element of a list to have a CDR pointer to an atom other than NIL. In this case an alternative notation, the *dot notation*, may be used. In dot notation each list element is written as a pair of subelements representing the CAR and CDR of the element. The subelements are enclosed in parentheses and separated by a dot. For example,

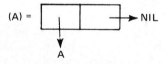

is written (A . NIL), (A B) is written (A .(B . NIL)), and, ((A B) C) is written ((A .(B . NIL)). (C . NIL)) Now the element

which cannot be written in list notation can be written (A . B) in dot notation. Write in dot notation

(a) (A (B C)).
(b) (((A)) B (C D)).
(c) The program list of Fig. 17-7.
(d) The A-list of Fig. 17-8. Note that this list cannot be written in list notation.

4. Property lists of atoms which contain properties other than the print name (PNAME) of the atom can never be garbage-collected, even if they are entirely inaccessible from any active list structure at the time of garbage collection. Explain why.

5. *The self-reproducing function.* The equivalence of program and data representations in LISP makes it possible to write many subtle programs easily that would be much more difficult in other languages. Some of these have the status of *classical* LISP *problems*, of which the *self-reproducing function problem* is typical: *Write a* LISP *function* SRF *whose value is its own definition.* SRF has no inputs. If SRF is defined as (SRF (LAMBDA () (. . . *body* . . .))), then the result of the call (SRF) is the list structure (SRF (LAMBDA () . . . *body* . . .)). SRF must construct its result list piecemeal—it cannot access the property list of atom SRF to obtain its definition list.

6. Write the macro definition for the IF macro described in Sec. 17-4. You will need only the primitives CAR, CDR, QUOTE ('), and LIST or CONS.

7. *Shallow binding.* The A-list representation for LISP referencing environments is sometimes called *deep binding*, because the association for a variable X may be deep within the A-list and require an extended search every time X is referenced. An alternative is to provide each variable name (atom) with its own small A-list, giving only the associations (bindings) for that variable. This *shallow binding* method puts a pointer to a list of bindings for an atom directly in the head location of the atom. No A-list is used. When a variable (atom) such as X is referenced, the head location of the atom X is accessed, and the first binding on its bindings list is retrieved. Thus referencing is much more efficient than a search of an A-list. However, the setting up of the bindings of actual and formal parameters on entry to a function, and their removal on exit from the function, is simpler with the A-list deep binding method, because all the bindings are inserted as a group at the head of the A-list when the function is called and may be removed as a group when the function activation is complete. Explain what must be done on function entry and exit when the shallow binding method is used instead of deep binding.

8. While ordinarily a LISP programmer may consider each list as a separate data object, often this is not strictly true. During the manipulation of lists, the tails of lists that are apparently separate are often in fact joined. For example, suppose that X and Y are variable names on the A-list, and the value associated with X is the list (A B C). If the assignment (SETQ Y (CONS 'R (CDR X))) is executed, then Y gets the list (R B C) as its value. Subsequent manipulation of list Y does not appear to affect X, but in truth, lists X and Y have a common tail composed of the sublist (B C). Explain why the assignment to Y produces a list that has a common tail with X.

     In Sec. 17-3 it is mentioned that the assignment operations REPLACA and REPLACD, which change the CAR and CDR pointers, respectively, of a given list word, must be used with care because of the possibility of *side effects* from such assignments. It is because of the joining of many lists in common tails that these side effects are particularly troublesome. Explain the side effects that occur if the value of list Y above is now modified by execution of (REPLACA (CDR Y) 'Z), which assigns a pointer to the atom Z to the CAR field of the list word retrieved by (CDR Y), thus giving Y the value (R Z C) without changing the list words pointing to R and C.

CHAPTER 18

SNOBOL4

SNOBOL4 is the last and most widely implemented of a series of character-string-processing languages developed at Bell Telephone Laboratories during the 1960s. Its major application is to problems in which substantial amounts of character-string data must be processed in complex ways, e.g., in processing natural-language text. However, the language includes many features of general applicability to other types of data, and thus it has become widely used in a variety of other areas. An excellent text, written by the language designers (Griswold et al. [1971]), describes the language. The original SNOBOL4 implementation design (on which this chapter is partially based) is described by Griswold [1972].

SNOBOL4 is different from the other languages described in this book in a number of important aspects. Most obvious is the emphasis on character-string data and the associated pattern-matching operation. In addition, the language is one of the first to include facilities for adding new programmer-defined data types. SNOBOL4 shares with LISP the ability to translate and execute at run time programs which have been either constructed or read in as data. It is also similar to LISP in its overall emphasis on generality and flexibility at the expense of execution efficiency—SNOBOL4 implementation requires extensive software simulation on most computers.

18-1   BRIEF OVERVIEW OF THE LANGUAGE

The most novel aspect of SNOBOL4, compared to other languages such as Pascal or PL/I, is the extremely *late binding* of almost every part of a program. During execution, new variables may be defined, new subprograms created, the types of variables may change, the sequence-control structure of a subprogram may change, and so on. Even the meaning of the basic operations such as "+" and "*" may vary dynamically. This late-binding aspect of the design provides a language that is extremely flexible, at the cost of making possible during program execution many errors that in most other languages would be caught by the compiler.

SNOBOL4 provides an extensive selection of data types, of which character strings are the most important. The central primitive operation is pattern matching on character-string data. A large collection of primitives are provided for the creation of patterns to be used in pattern matching. Patterns are themselves treated as a separate data type. Using pattern matching, a character string may be decomposed into substrings, and the substrings reassembled into new strings in very general ways.

The type of a variable is not declared in the program. Instead each variable name may refer to different data objects (of potentially different types) at various points during program execution. Thus the type of a variable may vary at run time. A variable is implemented by associating the variable name with a pointer to the data object that it currently designates in the *central strings table*, described below. Multidimensional arrays and property lists (called *tables*) are also provided, with the data type of each component allowed to vary dynamically at run time. Data structure creation operations are extremely flexible. At any point during program execution a new simple variable, array, or other data object may be created. Structures are not destroyed explicitly, but become garbage as all pointers to them are lost. New data types may be defined during program execution as well, and the SNOBOL4 run-time system automatically generates the appropriate functions for creating data objects of the new type and for selecting components of such data objects. Input-output operations are restricted to transmission of character strings to and from sequential files.

Sequence control in SNOBOL4 is rather simple. Expressions defining strings, numbers, and patterns are used extensively. Statements may be labeled, and each statement contains a *success-failure goto* field through which the successor to a statement may be explicitly specified. Each statement may succeed or fail for a variety of reasons—most commonly dependent on the success or failure of a pattern-matching operation. A simple call-return mechanism with recursion allows transfer of control to subprograms. Referencing is based on the most-recent-association rule, using a central referencing environment table.

The most common SNOBOL4 implementation (the *macro implementation* described by Griswold [1972]) is based on complete software simulation of the SNOBOL4 virtual computer. Programs are translated only into an internal Polish prefix executable *code string*, which is then decoded and executed by a software interpreter. The run-time memory organization centers around a central table of character strings, which contains a unique entry for each string currently existing at each point during execution, including variable names, statement labels, and other identifiers, as well as strings used as values of variables and array elements. As character strings are created during execution, they are entered into this table if they do not already exist. The table values are stored in a heap storage area along with arrays, patterns, executable code strings for program statements, and programmer-defined data structures. The heap is managed using garbage collection and full compaction, as described in Sec. 8-8.

A compiler-based implementation of the language is an attractive alternative because of the cost of the software simulation, and a number of such implementations have been constructed, e.g., the SPITBOL implementation (Dewar and McCann [1977]). However, the extensive run-time variability allowed by the language makes compilation difficult. This chapter is based on the simpler software-interpreted implementation, but where a compiler-based implementation is available, substantial savings in program execution speeds may be possible (usually with some slight restrictions on the language).

18-2 AN ANNOTATED EXAMPLE: REVERSING A STRING OF ELEMENTS

Figure 18-1 illustrates a simple SNOBOL4 subprogram and main program. The subprogram REVERSE reverses the elements of a given argument character string. The string consists of some arbitrary sequence of elements (words, numbers, etc.) separated by spaces. REVERSE picks off the elements of the string one by one and concatenates them in turn onto the front of a new string, which is built up and returned as the value of the function. The main program reads in a sequence of test strings and tests REVERSE on each in turn. The annotations below are keyed to the line numbers on the left of the figure, which are not a part of the program.

Line 1. The main program begins with a call to the DEFINE function to set up a subprogram definition. DEFINE simply enters the appropriate

Line Number		SNOBOL4 Program	
1		DEFINE ('REVERSE (X)Y','REV')	:(MAIN)
2	REV	X POS(0) SPAN(' ') =	
3	LOOP	X BREAK(' ') . Y SPAN(' ') =	:F(LAST)
4		REVERSE = Y ' ' REVERSE	:(LOOP)
5	LAST	IDENT(X,' ')	:S(RETURN)
6		REVERSE = X ' ' REVERSE	:(RETURN)
7	MAIN	A = INPUT	:F(END)
8		OUTPUT = 'INPUT IS:' A	
9		OUTPUT = 'INPUT REVERSED:' REVERSE(A)	:(MAIN)
10	END		

Fig. 18-1   Example SNOBOL4 program

information in a run-time table of defined subprogram names. The arguments to DEFINE are (1) the subprogram name REVERSE, (2) the formal-parameter name X, (3) the local-variable name Y, and (4) the label REV of the statement which begins the body of the subprogram. After the call to DEFINE is completed, control is transferred to the statement labeled MAIN. This **goto** is required because otherwise control would transfer to the next statement in sequence, which happens to be the first statement in the body of REVERSE. As an alternative the body of REVERSE might have been put after the main program, immediately before the END, thus avoiding the necessity of transferring control around the subprogram body.

Line 2. Because this statement is labeled REV, it is the first statement of the body of REVERSE. When REVERSE is called, the formal parameter X is set to the value of the actual parameter, local variable Y and the variable REVERSE (used for the function value to be returned) are initialized to have null string values, and control transfers to this statement. This is a pattern-matching statement which is used to delete leading blanks from the argument string X. The pattern is defined by POS(0) SPAN(' '), which may be read: "Starting at the beginning of the subject string (position zero), match a sequence of blank characters of maximum length." The subject string X is named before the pattern. The following = designates that the string matched in X (if any) is to be replaced by the string which follows the =. Since nothing follows the =, the null string is to be used; i.e., the matched substring is to be deleted from X.

Line 3. This statement, labeled LOOP, is the main pattern-matching statement of REVERSE. This statement picks off the first element remaining in string X, assigns it to the local variable Y, and deletes the element and any following blank characters from X. Again X is the subject string in the pattern matching. The pattern is BREAK(' '). Y SPAN(' '). The first part of the pattern, BREAK(' '), matches the first part of string X up to the leftmost blank character. The following .Y indicates that the substring matched by BREAK is to be assigned as the value of Y. The final portion of the pattern, SPAN(' '), again matches a sequence of blanks, as in line 2. The following = indicates that the entire matched substring is to be deleted from X. The **goto** field of the statement, following the :, specifies a transfer of control to statement LAST if the pattern matching *fails*; control otherwise continues to the next statement in sequence. Pattern matching in this case fails when string X has been reduced to at most a single element followed by no trailing blanks or, alternatively (if the original string had trailing blanks), to the null string.

Line 4. Control reaches this statement if the preceding pattern matching did in fact pick off an element from X and assign it to local variable Y. In this statement the value of Y is concatenated (together with an intervening blank character) onto the beginning of the string being built up for output as the value of REVERSE, and the resulting string is assigned as the new value of REVERSE. The subprogram name REVERSE is used here as a local variable. Concatenation of strings is specified by a blank character. Thus the expression on the right of the assignment operator = specifies two concatenations: concatenation of the value of Y and the literal string " " (a single blank) and concatenation of the result and the value of local variable REVERSE. Control is transferred from this statement back to the preceding statement LOOP, where another element is retrieved from X and the process repeated.

Line 5. When the string X has been exhausted, except for possibly one terminating element, control is transferred here. This statement tests whether X has been reduced to the null string by an identity test between X and the null string (represented by a pair of single quotes ' '). If the test *succeeds*, control is returned to the calling program; otherwise, control passes to the next statement in sequence. The final value of the variable REVERSE becomes the function value returned.

Line 6. Final statement of the body of REVERSE. At this point X contains one final element, which is simply concatenated onto the beginning of the result string and control returned to the calling program.

Line 7. Second line of the main program. Control is transferred here directly from line 1. This statement reads the next input string from the standard input file and assigns the string read to variable A. The input occurs automatically whenever the special variable INPUT is referenced. The value of the reference to INPUT is always the next input string. If the input file is empty because all the input data have been read, then the reference to INPUT fails. In this case control is transferred to the statement labeled END.

Line 8. The newly input string is output immediately to the standard output file, but first the literal string INPUT IS: is concatenated onto the beginning. Output is specified by an assignment to the special variable OUTPUT. Whenever the value of OUTPUT is changed the new value is automatically output.

Line 9. REVERSE is tested on the input string A. The result of REVERSE is output, preceded by the string INPUT REVERSED:. Control is transferred back to the statement labeled MAIN for another input-test loop.

Line 10. End of the main program.

18-3   DATA TYPES

An extensive and flexible set of data types is found in SNOBOL4. Several aspects of the general treatment of variables and data types are particularly noteworthy:

   a. All data objects include a run-time descriptor.

   b. No declarations for variables are given, and the type of data object associated with a variable name may change during program execution.

   c. All type checking is dynamic (performed immediately before execution of each operation at run time).

Character Strings

Character strings are the central data type in this language. A character-string data object may contain a string of arbitrary length. A character string is represented by a block of storage containing a run-time descriptor (indicating data type = "string" and giving the length of the string) and the character values. A variable whose value is a character string is represented by a pointer to the block of storage representing the string.

In the usual SNOBOL4 implementation, all character-string data objects are stored in a *central strings table*. This run-time table contains a *unique* entry for each string that has been computed or input by the program during its execution. Whenever a new string is created during program execution, the central table is searched to determine if the string has already been entered in the table. If so, then the existing table entry is used. Thus, for example, if the string 'XYZ' is the value of both variables A and B at some point during program execution, then both A and B will be represented by a pointer to the same block of storage in the central strings table.

In a rather subtle but important variation on the usual distinction between a variable name and the value of the variable, in SNOBOL4 each variable name is itself considered as a character string, which is entered into the central strings table. Thus if the identifiers A and B appear in a SNOBOL4 program as variable names, then they are entered into the central strings table as the strings 'A' and 'B' during translation. Thus at the beginning of program execution, each identifier that has appeared in the source program is present in the central strings table. As the program executes, new strings are created and entered into the central table. At any point during execution, any string in the central table may be used as a variable name, a statement label, a subprogram name, or other identifier. Thus in SNOBOL4, identifiers used as variable names become data objects that may be manipulated as character strings. This simple scheme allows new variables to be created at will during program execution and is the source of much of the flexibility of the language. The major disadvantage of the central strings table lies in the cost of the table search each time a new string is created. Since many SNOBOL4 statements create new strings, the table search occurs frequently during execution. The various uses of the central strings table to implement different language features are discussed further in the following sections. The initial concern here is simply with strings as data objects.

Simple String-Manipulation Operations

Concatenation of two character strings is the most basic string-manipulation primitive. A blank symbol appearing between two string-valued expressions indicates concatenation. For example, in

'LAUGHING' 'LIONS'

the blank between the two strings LAUGHING and LIONS indicates concatenation; the result is the string LAUGHINGLIONS.

Other primitive functions may be used to find the length of a string (SIZE), to substitute characters within a string (REPLACE), and to duplicate a given string an arbitrary number of times (DUPL). In general, however, more complex string manipulations are performed using the pattern-matching operation.

Pattern Matching

The basic specification of the pattern-matching operation is

pattern-match: character string × pattern → substring × success/fail.

The argument character string is called the *subject string*. The pattern is a data object that controls the search through the subject string for a desired substring. If found, the result is the matched substring together with a Boolean value indicating success; if not found, the result is a null (empty) string and a value indicating failure.

Patterns and pattern matching are such a specialized and central part of SNOBOL4 that they form almost a sublanguage of the entire language. A pattern serves essentially as a *program* for the pattern-matching operation, which scans the subject string and at the same time interprets the pattern, using it to guide the search through the subject string.

The pattern-matching operation is specified in a SNOBOL4 program through use of the special *pattern-matching* or *pattern-matching and replacement* statement. The former has the syntax

⟨*subject string*⟩ ⟨*pattern*⟩

where ⟨*subject string*⟩ is a string-valued expression whose value is the string that is to be searched for a substring matching the pattern that is the value of the expression ⟨*pattern*⟩. The pattern-matching and replacement statement has the form

⟨*subject string*⟩ ⟨*pattern*⟩ = ⟨*replacement string*⟩

where ⟨*subject string*⟩ and ⟨*pattern*⟩ are as above, and ⟨*replacement string*⟩ is a string-valued expression whose value is to replace the matched substring of the subject string if pattern matching succeeds.

A pattern-matching operation, if it succeeds, always results in the identification of some contiguous substring of the subject string. The pattern-matching and replacement statement allows another string to be designated to replace the matched substring within the subject string (thus permanently altering the subject string). In the simple pattern-matching statement, the subject string is left unaltered, with the pattern matching serving only as a test for the presence of an appropriate substring. In either case the *success* or *failure* output of the pattern matching may be used to control a program branch. Besides these explicit results, a pattern-matching operation may also produce side effects through assignments of substrings to variables during matching. Often these side effects are as important as the explicit results of the matching. Although the matching operation itself always searches for a contiguous substring, these side effects during matching allow all or part of the subject string to be broken down into any number of substrings and reconstructed from the same or other pieces during the course of a single pattern match.

The pattern-matching operation for a given subject string STR and pattern PAT is most easily understood in terms of three pointers:

1. The left end pointer, LEFT, which points to the character in STR which represents the left end of the substring being matched at any point during matching.

2. The right end pointer, CURSOR, which marks the rightmost matched character within STR at any point during matching.

3. The NEEDLE, a pointer to the element of PAT which is currently the pattern element being matched.

Pattern matching proceeds left to right through the subject string STR. LEFT and CURSOR initially point to the leftmost character in STR, and NEEDLE points to the first alternative in PAT. NEEDLE is advanced through the pattern structure, which basically has the form of a tree of alternatives. Simultaneously, CURSOR moves right through the subject string. The various alternatives specified by PAT are tried exhaustively until either a complete match is found (if NEEDLE traverses PAT to a terminal point) or no match is found (if all alternatives are exhausted). If a complete match is found, then the pattern-matching operation succeeds and the final positions of LEFT and CURSOR delimit the substring of STR which has been matched. If the statement causing the pattern match was a pattern-matching and replacement statement, then this substring is replaced by the designated replacement string; otherwise the subject string is left unmodified.

The action taken on failure of pattern matching when the pointer LEFT is positioned at the left end of STR depends on the pattern-matching *mode*. In *anchored mode* LEFT must remain positioned at the left end of STR, and thus the entire pattern-matching operation fails if no match is found with LEFT in its initial position. In *unanchored mode*, however, pattern matching continues after initial failure: LEFT is advanced one character position to the right in STR, and again CURSOR and NEEDLE are used to exhaustively test for an appropriate substring beginning at the new position of LEFT. In unanchored mode, pattern matching ultimately fails only when LEFT has advanced to the right end of STR without an appropriate substring being matched.

The exhaustive search required for this pattern-matching operation is obviously extremely time-consuming if STR is very long or PAT is very complex. In general, it is only the success or failure of pattern matching which is of concern to the SNOBOL4 programmer, and thus it is desirable insofar as possible to avoid searching "blind alleys." SNOBOL4 implementations typically utilize a number of heuristic rules to avoid useless searching. Occasionally a special situation arises where the full exhaustive search is desirable, an option which the programmer may choose when needed. Other than the anchored/unanchored mode designation and the heuristics/no heuristics choice, the remainder of the pattern-matching operation is controlled through the manner in which the programmer constructs the pattern PAT used in the matching operation.

Patterns and Pattern Creation

A pattern is a data structure. Patterns are created by the evaluation of pattern-valued expressions. Once created, the elements of a pattern cannot be accessed or modified; the only use of a pattern is as an argument for a pattern-matching operation. In the simplest case the pattern-valued expression defining a pattern is inserted directly into the pattern-matching statement in which the pattern is to be used. For example,

STR 'AND' | 'OR'

is a pattern-matching statement containing the pattern-valued expression 'AND' | 'OR' which defines a pattern that matches either the string AND or the string OR. Alternatively, the pattern may be created using a separate assignment statement:

PAT = 'AND' | 'OR'

and the created pattern later used in the pattern-matching statement

STR PAT

The advantage of the latter alternative is that the pattern data structure need be created only once even though it may be later used repeatedly in pattern matching. In the former case the identical pattern structure is created and then immediately discarded each time the pattern-matching statement is executed, causing a considerable waste of storage and execution time.

Patterns are a separate data type in SNOBOL4. This means that patterns are legitimate values for variables and components of arrays and tables. A pattern is represented during execution in a specialized form that is suitable for efficient interpretation by the pattern matcher. Commonly this form is as a linked set of storage areas forming a tree data structure, which reflects the natural structure of a pattern as a set of alternatives and concatenated subpatterns.

A pattern is constructed from various primitive pattern elements, which we shall now consider individually. Each primitive element may be viewed as defining a valid way in which the CURSOR may be advanced from its current position during pattern matching.

Strings as patterns. The simplest pattern element is a single character string, e.g., AND or 2. A pattern consisting only of such a string may be used to search the subject string for that substring. For example, the pattern-matching statement

STR 'AND'

causes the subject string which is the value of STR to be searched for the leftmost occurrence of AND. The details of this search clarify the use of more complex pattern structures (for this example we ignore the obvious heuristics that would ordinarily be used to speed the search). In the search, LEFT and CURSOR initially point to the first character of STR. The pattern 'AND' allows CURSOR to be advanced from its current position only if the next three characters in the string are A, N, and D in that sequence. Assuming that the value of STR is the string GREEN EGGS AND HAM, the attempt to advance CURSOR from its initial position at the left end of the string will fail. Because there are no other alternatives in the pattern, both LEFT and CURSOR are advanced to point to the second character position in the subject string. Again, CURSOR cannot be advanced, and both LEFT and CURSOR move to the third character position in the subject string. Eventually both LEFT and CURSOR are positioned at the first A in GREEN EGGS AND HAM, and CURSOR may then be advanced to the blank character following the D. Since there are no other following pattern elements, the matching operation is complete and matching succeeds, with the final positions of LEFT and CURSOR designating the matched substring.

Pattern-valued functions. Pattern-valued functions are built-in primitives which produce pattern data structures as values. SNOBOL4 contains a large set of such primitives, the most important of which are:

LEN. The function LEN, given a positive integer k as argument, produces a pattern structure which matches any string of k characters. Thus, for example, LEN(5) in a pattern expression specifies that CURSOR is to be advanced five character positions from its current position in the subject string.

ANY. The argument to ANY is a single character string composed of a set of distinct characters. The value of ANY is a pattern structure which matches any occurrence of one of those characters. Thus, for example, ANY('012') in a pattern expression specifies that CURSOR may be advanced one character position provided that the character passed over is one of 0, 1, or 2.

SPAN. SPAN is like ANY except that CURSOR is advanced as far to the right as possible until a character is found that is *not* a character in the argument string. For example, SPAN('012') matches any string composed entirely of zeros, ones, and twos that is followed by the end of subject string or by a symbol other than 0, 1, or 2.

NOTANY. NOTANY is like ANY except that CURSOR is advanced one character position only if the character involved is *not* a character in the argument string.

BREAK. BREAK is like SPAN except that CURSOR is advanced as far as possible until a character is found which *is* in the argument string.

REM. The value of REM is a pattern which matches the entire remainder of the subject string; i.e., REM specifies that CURSOR is to be advanced to the right end of the subject string.

TAB *and* RTAB. Given a positive integer k as argument, TAB produces a pattern which allows CURSOR to be advanced to the kth character position in the subject string, provided its current position is to the left of the kth position. RTAB is the same except that CURSOR advances to the kth position from the right end of the subject string.

ARB. The value of ARB is a pattern that matches any string of zero or more characters beginning at the current CURSOR position.

BAL. The value of BAL is a pattern that matches any string of zero or more characters beginning at the current position of CURSOR which contains no unpaired parentheses.

POS *and* RPOS. Given an integer k as argument, POS produces a pattern which matches only if CURSOR is positioned at the kth character of the subject string, and otherwise has no effect. RPOS is similar but uses the kth character position from the right end of the subject string.

Concatenation and alternation. Complex pattern data structures may be built up from explicit strings and pattern-valued functions using the operations of concatenation and alternation. If P and Q are two patterns, then the concatenation of P and Q, written P Q, is a new pattern that matches any string which begins with a string matched by P and whose remainder is matched by Q. The alternation of P and Q, written P | Q, is a pattern which matches any string matched by P or by Q. In such composite pattern structures the order of matching often becomes critical. The rule for matching in an alternation P | Q is as follows: Try all the alternatives for P first at the current CURSOR position, and then try the alternatives for Q. For the concatenation P Q the sequence is as follows: Match one alternative for P at the current CURSOR position, advance CURSOR to the end of the matched substring, and then try to match the pattern Q beginning at the new CURSOR position. If no match for Q is found, back up CURSOR to its original position and try to find another substring which matches P. If one is found, advance CURSOR and try Q again; if none is found, then the match of the concatenated pattern fails.

Assignment during pattern matching. A successful pattern-matching operation identifies a substring of the subject string which is matched by the entire pattern structure used. Often it is desirable to also identify sub-substrings of this substring which were matched by subelements of the overall pattern. For example, the pattern

$$\text{SPAN(' ') BREAK(' ') SPAN(' ')}$$

matches the leftmost substring of the subject string which begins and ends with blanks and which has at least one nonblank character. Ordinarily it would be desirable to obtain the nonnull part of the substring matched, the component matched by BREAK(' '). A copy of such a substring may be obtained by specifying a *conditional value assignment* (operator .) in the pattern. For example,

$$\text{SPAN(' ') BREAK(' ') . WD SPAN(' ')}$$

specifies that after a successful match of the pattern a copy of the substring matched by the BREAK(' ') part of the pattern is to be assigned to the variable WD. Using conditional value assignment a copy of any part of a matched string may be obtained. A less frequently used alternative is *immediate value assignment* (operator $), which allows assignment during a pattern match even though the matching operation ultimately fails. The most common use for immediate value assignment is during program testing—an immediate value assignment to variable OUTPUT may be used to print a trace of the steps during pattern matching.

Parameters in patterns (unevaluated expressions).   Ordinarily the structure of a pattern is fixed at the time of evaluation of the pattern-valued expression which creates the pattern. In particular, every variable in the pattern expression is evaluated and its current value copied into the pattern structure being created. Sometimes it is desirable to leave certain variables or expressions as parameters in the pattern and evaluate them only at the time during pattern matching when their values are actually required. The * operator before a variable name (or any subexpression) in a pattern indicates that the variable is to be left unevaluated until the time of *use* of the pattern in pattern matching. For example, the assignment

$$\text{PAT = LEN(*N)}$$

creates a pattern structure with parameter N, whose value may vary each time the pattern PAT is used. Unevaluated expressions in patterns also allow recursive patterns to be used. For example, the pattern

$$\text{P = *P 'A'| 'B'}$$

matches any sequence composed of a B followed by zero of more A's.

Numbers

Real and integer numbers are provided. Each carries a run-time type descriptor in addition to the bit-string hardware representation of the number itself.

Arithmetic, Relational, and Boolean Operations

The basic arithmetic operations (including exponentiation) on integers and reals are provided, as well as the usual relational primitives (represented by the functions EQ, NE, LT, GT, LE, GE). Run-time type checking and type conversion are necessary. Character strings may be compared for equality using the primitive IDENT; e.g., IDENT(X,Y) succeeds if the values of X and Y are identical strings.

No Boolean operations are included directly except *not* (syntax ¬). Boolean values are treated in a novel way. There are no explicit Boolean values in SNOBOL4. Instead an operator such as EQ (= on numbers) either succeeds or fails, and this result may be tested in the goto field of the statement. When an operator fails, the entire statement immediately fails. When an operator succeeds, execution of the statement continues without interruption. One result of this approach is that relational and other tests may be inserted in the middle of expressions. When the expression is evaluated, if the test succeeds, nothing is changed, but if the test fails, then evaluation is immediately terminated and the entire statement containing the expression fails. For example, the assignment

$$N = NE(N,0) \; N - 1 \qquad :S(LOOP)F(NEXT)$$

causes the value of N to be decremented by 1 and control transferred to the statement labeled LOOP, provided that the initial value of N is not already zero. If zero, the value of N is not modified and control is transferred to statement NEXT.

Simple Variables and Assignment

A simple variable in SNOBOL4 is simply a character string entered into the central strings table. Each entry in this table consists of both a pointer to a character string (which may be considered as the *name* of the variable) and a pointer to a value, which may be another character string in the same table (and it, of course, may also have an associated value), or it may be a number, an array, a pattern, or any other type of data object. The assignment operation applied to a simple variable operates by first finding the variable name (string) in the central strings table and then changing the associated value pointer to point to the new data object assigned. For example, if the following sequence of assignments is executed:

$$Y = \text{'GREEN'}$$

$$X = Y$$

then three entries, for each of 'X', 'Y', and 'GREEN', are made in the central strings table. Execution of the first assignment causes the value pointer for

Y to be set to point to the table entry for 'GREEN'. The second assignment causes the value pointer for X to be set to be a copy of the value pointer for Y, so that both X and Y end up pointing to the table entry for 'GREEN'. If instead the assignment X = 'Y' were executed, then the value pointer for X would point to the table entry for Y, whose value pointer in turn would point to the entry for 'GREEN'.

Arrays

SNOBOL4 arrays are created dynamically by a primitive operation (function) ARRAY, which may be called at any point during program execution. Types of elements may vary during the lifetime of the array, but the array may not change in length once created. The fixed size allows an array representation as a sequential block of storage with attached descriptor. Each entry in this block contains a pointer to the value of an array element, except in the case of numeric values which are usually stored directly. Names are not directly associated with array data objects; instead an array is represented by a pointer to the block of storage containing the descriptor and values. If an array pointer is assigned as the value of some string (in the central strings table), then that string serves temporarily as the name of the array. Array elements may be accessed individually by subscripting this temporary name. For example, the statement

$$X = ARRAY(10)$$

creates an array of ten elements (through the call on the ARRAY primitive). The pointer to this array returned by the ARRAY function is immediately assigned as the value of the variable X, stored in the central strings table. A later reference to X⟨3⟩ accesses the third element of this array in the usual way. However, the assignment

$$Y = X$$

causes a copy of the same pointer to be assigned as the value of Y. Now the array has two temporary names, and both X⟨3⟩ and Y⟨3⟩ access the same element of the array. The array may become lost altogether (i.e., may be made garbage) if subsequent assignments change both the values of X and Y.

Arrays may have arbitrary numbers of dimensions and subscript ranges. The values of array elements may be numbers or strings, but they also may be of other data types: patterns, tables, or other arrays. Thus it is possible to construct arrays of arrays, where each element of one array contains as its value a pointer to another array.

Tables

A SNOBOL4 *table* is a heterogeneous linear array of variable size accessed through subscripts which are arbitrary strings rather than integers. Thus a table is a type of *property list*. Each table entry consists of a *subscript*, which is a pointer to a string in the central strings table, and a *value*, which is either a number or a pointer to a string, array, or other data item. A table is created by use of a primitive function, TABLE, with arguments specifying an initial size and an increment size for the table. For example, the statement

$$T = TABLE(50,30)$$

causes creation of a block of storage for a table of 50 subscript-value pairs plus descriptor. The function TABLE returns a pointer to this block, which is then assigned to the variable T. T serves as the temporary name for the table. Reference to table elements and creation of new table elements is done by subscripting the variable T. For example, T⟨'AGE'⟩ = 25 causes a table search for the subscript AGE. If found, its associated value is changed to 25. If AGE is not found, then a new entry of the pair AGE-25 is made. Entries in a table may not be deleted. When 50 entries have been made in the table a new block of storage for 30 (the second parameter in the initial call of TABLE) pairs is allocated and linked to the original block via a pointer. Ultimately then the table appears in storage as a linked list of blocks of storage, each of the same length except the first.

Files and Input-Output

The SNOBOL4 input-output system is based on the direct transmission of character strings between central memory and external sequential files. Using the pattern-matching operation and the other string-manipulation primitives, input strings may be broken down into components and output strings formatted easily. As a result the input-output operations need transmit only character strings.

Input and output operations utilize an interrupt scheme. Certain variables are tagged as *input variables* and others as *output variables*. Each tagged variable is associated with a particular external file. Whenever the value of an input variable is referenced during execution, execution is interrupted and a new record (character string) is read in from the associated external file. This character string becomes the new value of the input variable, and execution proceeds. If the file is empty (i.e., if all the data have been read), then the reference to the variable fails, causing the statement being executed to fail. Similarly, when a new value (which must be a string or number) is assigned to an output variable, execution is interrupted and the new character string value is copied to the external file. The variables INPUT and OUTPUT are predefined as input and output variables, respectively, but other input and output variables may be designated by the programmer at any point during execution. Use of INPUT and OUTPUT is illustrated in the example of Sec. 18-2.

Keywords

Access to various items of system-defined data is provided by a set of keywords. A *keyword* is actually just a simple variable whose name begins with the symbol &. Keyword variables may be *protected*, in which case their values may be accessed but not modified, or *unprotected*, in which case their values may be both accessed and modified. Protected keywords usually contain system-defined data items which may occasionally be of value to the programmer. For example, the number of statements which have been executed is accessible as the value of the keyword &STCOUNT, the number of the statement currently being executed is the value of &STNO, the number of the last statement executed is accessed through &LASTNO, the current depth of subprogram calls is found through &FNCLEVEL, and so on. Unprotected keywords serve as *flags*, which may be set by the programmer to modify execution parameters. For example, tracing output is produced if the value of &TRACE is nonzero, and execution terminates if the number of statements executed exceeds the value of &STLIMIT.

The two most important keywords are &ANCHOR and &FULLSCAN, which control the actions of the pattern-matching operation. Both have only two possible values. &ANCHOR, if nonzero, indicates that pattern matching is to occur in *anchored* mode (where the matched substring must begin at the left of the subject string); &FULLSCAN, if nonzero, indicates that the pattern matcher is to perform a full exhaustive search of all possible alternatives, rather than using various heuristics to avoid blind alleys and speed up the search.

Labels and Subprogram Names

The presence of all identifiers in the central strings table during program execution allows a simple direct use of statement labels and subprogram names as data items. The central table is augmented by two auxiliary tables. The *labels table* contains pairs consisting of a pointer to a string used as a statement label and a pointer to the corresponding code position in the executable program structure. The *subprograms table* consists of similar pairs of *pointer to string/pointer to subprogram definition* (an entry in yet another auxiliary table). The presence of these run-time tables allows any string to be read in or computed and then subsequently used as a statement label in a **goto** or as a subprogram name in a subprogram call. The string is simply looked up in the appropriate table at the time of **goto** or call, and an appropriate transfer of control is made. If the string has not been used as a statement label or subprogram name, then a run-time error message results and execution terminates.

Programs as Data

Program execution in the usual SNOBOL4 implementation is done by a software interpreter. Programs are represented at run time in a special internal form which is a variant of a Polish prefix representation. We shall term this program representation a *code string*. A program to be executed is immediately translated into a code string before execution begins. During execution, additional program segments may be translated and later executed as though they had been part of the original program. This translation is initiated by a call on a primitive function CODE. The argument to CODE is a character string representing a valid SNOBOL4 program segment (with statements separated by semicolons), and the result returned is a pointer to the new code string representing the translated program. Code strings are a separate data type, and as with other data types in SNOBOL4, code strings may be saved as the value of variables, array elements, and so on. A code string may be executed beginning at its first statement, or any **goto** may lead into a labeled statement in a code string.

18-4   SUBPROGRAMS AND PROGRAMMER-DEFINED DATA TYPES

SNOBOL4 provides features for the programmer to define operations (subprograms) and data types. However, these features provide only limited abstraction and encapsulation. In particular, true abstract data types cannot be defined, because the language provides no mechanism for grouping and encapsulation of type definitions and operations.

Subprograms

SNOBOL4 subprograms have a number of novel aspects. Subprogram definition is strictly a run-time operation. During translation a main program and a set of subprograms are simply a long list of statements, with no syntactic distinction among the elements of the different routines.

Execution begins with no subprograms defined other than system-defined primitives. Before a subprogram may be called it must first be defined by means of a call to the DEFINE primitive:

DEFINE('⟨subprog-name⟩(⟨formal-params⟩)⟨local-vars⟩',
       '⟨label of first statement in body⟩')

The DEFINE primitive enters into a run-time table of *defined subprograms* the subprogram name, the number and names of its formal parameters, the number and names of its local variables, and the label of the first statment in its body. The label of the first statement may be omitted, in which case the subprogram name is also taken to be the label of the first statement. Subprogram definition and calling structure is taken up in more detail in Sec. 18-6.

The statements forming the body of a subprogram have no necessary syntactic relation with the DEFINE call which defines the subprogram. They may be placed anywhere, but the programmer is responsible to see that control does not inadvertently flow into a subprogram body during execution of the main program or another subprogram. The statements in a subprogram body need not even exist when the subprogram is defined— they may be read in or constructed as strings and then later translated into executable form by the primitive CODE before the subprogram is called.

A subprogram may be defined at any point during program execution prior to the first call on it. A later DEFINE may redefine a previously DEFINE'd subprogram name (because only run-time table entries need to be modified). The names of system primitives such as LEN and SIZE as well as infix or prefix operator symbols may also be redefined to name programmer-defined subprograms, but the special system function OPSYN must be used instead of DEFINE. For example, the statement

OPSYN('+','ADD',2)

causes any subsequent use of + as a binary operator to be executed as a call of the subprogram ADD; thus the statement Z = X + Y is made equivalent to Z = ADD(X,Y).

Programmer-Defined Data Types

SNOBOL4 provides some simple but flexible features which allow a programmer to define and use data structures of new types. Basically a data type definition specifies a class of record data objects, fixed-length linear arrays whose elements are referenced by character string subscripts. The definition of the data type itself defines only the name of the type, the length of each array of that type, and the subscripts of the elements of each array of that type. Data type definition is done with a call to the primitive function DATA. For example,

$$\text{DATA('EMP-REC(NAME,AGE,ADDRESS)')}$$

defines a data type called EMP-REC. Each data structure of this type, when created, will consist of a linear array of three elements, accessible by the subscripts NAME, AGE, and ADDRESS, respectively. The primitive DATA acts to create and enter into run-time tables a descriptor for the data type EMP-REC, which specifies the length of an element and the subscripts. In addition, a *pseudosubprogram* is entered into the run-time subprograms table under each of the names EMP-REC, NAME, AGE, and ADDRESS. The EMP-REC subprogram represents a *creation primitive* for arrays of type EMP-REC. Whenever it is called, it allocates space for a new array of type EMP-REC and initializes the values of the array elements. For example, the statement

$$\text{X = EMP-REC('KING',29,'1708 HALIFAX')}$$

creates a three-element array of type EMP-REC and initializes the values of the array elements to the string KING, the number 29, and the string 1708 HALIFAX, respectively. The value returned by the function EMP-REC is a pointer to this new array, which is assigned as the value of X. A later reference to an element of this new array is made using one of the functions NAME, AGE, or ADDRESS. For example, the statements

$$\text{Y = AGE(X)}$$

$$\text{AGE(X) = 30}$$

have the effect of retrieving the value of the second array element and assigning it the new value 30, respectively.

Using these basic facilities for the creation and use of programmer-defined data types, the programmer may construct arbitrary linked structures by letting the value of an element in one structure be a pointer to another structure. Thus linked lists, trees, and general directed graphs may be created and processed.

18-5   SEQUENCE CONTROL

SNOBOL4 sequence-control mechanisms are rather simple. The most complex control structures arise in the control of pattern matching; these are described in Sec. 18-3.

Expressions

SNOBOL4 expressions produce values which are either strings, numbers, or patterns. Expressions are constructed from a mixture of infix binary operators, Polish prefix operators, and ordinary mathematical prefix operators. The usual precedence order and associativity rules for arithmetic operations are extended to include the operations of concatenation, alternation, and conditional and immediate value assignment. Parentheses may be used for explicit control as needed.

Statement Sequence Control

Only one construct for controlling statement execution sequence is provided. Each statement execution may succeed or fail. For example, a statement involving pattern matching may fail because the pattern was not found, a statement referencing INPUT may fail if the input file is empty, or a statement involving a call to a programmer-defined subprogram may fail because the subprogram returns via FRETURN (see below). Each statement may contain an optional **goto** *field* which specifies either an unconditional transfer of control to a designated successor statement, a transfer only if the statement execution succeeds, a transfer if execution fails, or transfers on both conditions. Omission of part of the **goto** field specifies an implicit transfer of control to the next physical statement in sequence. Statements may be labeled by identifiers.

This basic **goto**—*statement label* structure is made more flexible by allowing any label to be computed. The **goto** field of a statement may specify an arbitrary string-valued expression to be used to compute the string representing the statement label to which control is to be transferred. Implementation requires maintenance of a run-time table of statement labels and their associated code positions. The computed string is looked up in the table when the **goto** is reached during execution, and a transfer to the associated code position is made.

Subprogram Sequence Control

The usual subprogram call is provided, with recursion. The control flow through a subprogram is rather novel, however. When a subprogram is called, control is transferred to the first statement of the subprogram (this statement's label is given in the DEFINE statement defining the subprogram). From there control may pass to any other statement in the whole program, including statements in the main program or other subprograms. Return from a subprogram occurs only when a **goto** to one of the labels RETURN, NRETURN, or FRETURN is specified, and such a **goto** causes a return only from the last subprogram entered (as designated by the activation record on the top of the run-time stack). RETURN and NRETURN cause an ordinary return; FRETURN causes the statement to which return is made to fail.

A set of tracing features provides an alternative subprogram calling structure based on exceptions. Statement execution may be interrupted on one of six exception conditions: change in value of a designated variable; transfer of control to a designated label; call, return, or call and return from a designated subprogram; or change in the value of certain key words. For each type of exception the programmer may specify a subprogram to be executed whenever the exception is raised or a default system-defined action may be used. This exception structure is most useful for tracing during program debugging but may also be used to advantage in other situations; for example, pattern matching may be interrupted for execution of a programmer-defined subprogram by setting an exception to occur upon conditional or immediate value assignment to a variable within a pattern.

18-6 DATA CONTROL

The current referencing environment of a SNOBOL4 program is closely tied to the *central strings table* used for character-string storage. Because each string which is currently in use is treated also as the name of a simple variable, every string in the central strings table may have an association and may be referenced. Of course the program text itself contains only certain variable identifiers which were known when the program was written. However, any string created during program execution may be referenced as a variable using the *indirect reference operator*, $. The operator $ applied to any string retrieves the value associated with that string in the central strings table. For example, if the variable X has as its value the string ABC, then the value of the variable ABC may be obtained by the expression $X. If the value of ABC is the string QRS, then $$X retrieves the value of QRS, etc.

The assumption that every string is automatically a usable variable, and thus is part of the current referencing environment, allows the central strings table to serve also as a central referencing environment table. Each table entry is augmented by a *value pointer* which points to the data item that serves as the value of the associated string. When a new string is created it is entered into the table with a null value (the *null string*). Subsequent references may assign it a nonnull value, or retrieve its value. Ultimately strings which are in the table but are not accessible from any other point, and which have a null value, may be garbage-collected and the storage reused. New strings are always entered in the central table as global variables, and thus their existence is not affected by subsequent subprogram entries or exits.

Local variables are designated when a subprogram is defined through a call of the primitive function DEFINE. For example, execution of the statement

DEFINE('SUB(X,Y),U,V')

defines a subprogram named SUB by entering the name SUB into a run-time table of subprogram names. Part of this same entry is a list of formal parameter names and local variables. In the example X and Y serve as formal parameter names and U and V serve as local variable names. The name of the subprogram, SUB, also serves as a local variable whose value is returned as the value of the subprogram. When subprogram SUB is called during program execution, the central strings table is modified to reflect the appropriate referencing environment for execution of SUB. First the existing values of the strings SUB, X, Y, U, and V in the central table must be saved. These are saved (along with the return point and other system-defined data) as an activation record on a *hidden* stack. Then new values for each of the strings are entered into the central table. SUB, U, and V receive null values. X and Y are initialized to the values passed as the values of the corresponding actual parameters in the call. Once this updating of the central table is complete, control is passed to the first statement of the subprogram (the statement labeled SUB in this case) just as in an ordinary **goto**. The subsequent execution of a **goto** to one of the special labels RETURN, NRETURN, or FRETURN signals the end of execution of the subprogram body. The top activation record on the hidden stack is accessed to provide a return point and to indicate the appropriate string-value pairs in the central table whose values must be restored. After the values are restored control is returned to the point of call, with the last value of the subprogram name SUB becoming the value of the subprogram (function) call.

The effect of using the central strings table as the referencing environment is basically to make nonlocal referencing follow the most recent association rule. On subprogram entry the current associations for all local identifiers are deactivated and on exit they are restored, but all other identifiers retain their existing (and thus most recent) associations.

Parameter Transmission and Value Return

Parameters to programmer-defined subprograms are transmitted uniformly by value. The actual parameter is evaluated to obtain a pointer to a data item, which may be a string, number, pattern, array, and so on. The pointer is transmitted to the subprogram and becomes the initial value of the corresponding formal parameter (stored in the central strings table). Neither subprogram names nor statement labels may be transmitted directly as parameters; instead the *string* representing the name or label is trans-mitted. Within the subprogram the string may be used as the object of a **goto** or subprogram call by referencing the associated formal parameter (using $ or the primitive APPLY as appropriate). This technique ignores the problems of referencing-environment transmission usually associated with subprogram name and label parameters—the only referencing-environment modifications made automatically are those prescribed by the DEFINE statement for a subprogram.

Although parameter transmission is strictly by value in SNOBOL4, some of the effects of transmission by reference and by name may be obtained without difficulty. For example, to transmit variable Q to SUB by reference, the string 'Q' is transmitted. If the corresponding formal parameter within SUB is X, then $X references Q as a variable within SUB. The value of Q may be modified or accessed through such indirect references. Similarly, an expression such as A*B*C may be transmitted *unevaluated* by transmitting the string 'A*B*C' as an actual parameter. The primitive function EVAL may then be used to evaluate the string as an expression. Both these techniques, however, suffer from the defect that the referencing environment is not updated before evaluation of either $X or A*B*C, and thus the local referencing environment may interfere with evaluation (see Problem 3).

A subprogram may return any data item as its value, including strings, patterns, arrays, tables, and numbers. The last value assigned to the subprogram name within the subprogram is returned as the value of the subprogram call. If the result is to be used immediately as the object of an assignment, then the return must be by a goto the special label NRETURN; otherwise the label RETURN is used. In both these cases the call of the subprogram is said to succeed, and evaluation of the expression containing the subprogram call is resumed, using the value returned. An alternative is that of returning through a goto the label FRETURN. Such a return causes the subprogram call to fail. In this case no value is returned, and instead the execution of the calling statement is terminated immediately and the failure branch of the calling statement is taken.

18-7 OPERATING AND PROGRAMMING ENVIRONMENT

SNOBOL4 is designed for a batch-processing environment. Input-output of character strings to external sequential data files is the major means provided for access to the environment. In addition, access to an external library of precompiled programs (written originally in FORTRAN or assembly language) is provided at run time through a LOAD primitive. For example, the statement LOAD('SUB(REAL,INTEGER)REAL') causes run-time loading of a subprogram SUB and entry of the subprogram name and the types of its parameters and result into the run-time subprogram names table.

The main features of the languages that might be considered primarily intended to affect the programming environment are the features for program tracing. These tracing features allow the programmer to follow the course of execution of a program during testing. Tracing is particularly valuable in checking the correctness of complex pattern-matching operations. However, the general lack of structure in SNOBOL4 programs also makes tracing necessary to track down subtle errors in the flow of control through a program.

18-8   SYNTAX AND TRANSLATION

The most striking aspect of the syntax of SNOBOL4 is the complete *lack* of any syntactic distinction among the bodies of subprograms and the main program. A program consists basically of a list of statements. There is no way to determine syntactically whether a particular statement is part of the main program or of any particular subprogram. In fact, a single statement may be part of both the main program and any number of subprograms simultaneously.

This rather chaotic program structure allows new program segments and subprograms, translated into executable form at run time, to be easily integrated with existing program elements. In many cases, however, the structure leads to errors because omission of an explicit **goto** on a statement may cause control to flow into or out of a subprogram body inadvertently.

Statements.   Individual statements have a common syntactic base—the pattern-matching and replacement statement. The basic syntax is

⟨ *label* ⟩ ⟨ *subject string* ⟩ ⟨ *pattern* ⟩ = ⟨ *replacement string* ⟩ :⟨ *goto* ⟩

The ⟨*label*⟩ is a single identifier beginning in the first character position. The ⟨*subject string*⟩ and ⟨*replacement string*⟩ are defined by string-valued expressions. The ⟨*pattern*⟩ is defined by a pattern-valued expression. The ⟨*goto*⟩ may specify an unconditional branch or alternatives for success and failure of the statement. Labels and **gotos** are optional in any statement.

Assignment statements follow the above syntax with the ⟨*pattern*⟩ field omitted. Simple pattern matching without replacement is specified by omission of the = ⟨*replacement string*⟩. A subprogram call may be specified by omission of both ⟨*pattern*⟩ and ⟨*replacement string*⟩ fields. For an unconditional **goto** alone, all except the ⟨*goto*⟩ field may be omitted. SNOBOL4 provides no structured statements of any form.

Translation.   In the usual implementation of SNOBOL4, programs are translated into an executable form which is decoded and executed by a software interpreter. The syntactic structure of SNOBOL4 programs makes translation relatively trivial. Because there are no subprogram boundaries, declarations, or structured statements, each statement in a program may be translated without regard for the context in which it appears. Thus translation may proceed essentially line by line. The late binding time of most elements of SNOBOL4 statements also simplifies translation, because so little of the interpretation of a statement is fixed at translation time. For example, in translating the expression X + Y, none of the properties of the variables X and Y are known to the translator, and the symbol + may not even represent addition when the expression is evaluated during execution (because the meaning of + may be changed by the primitive OPSYN). The translator is thus reduced to making simple syntactic checks and translating each statement into a block of executable code, which is largely just a direct encoding of the original statement in a somewhat more convenient form for execution. In the usual SNOBOL4 implementation these code blocks take the form of a sequence of prefix instructions, each composed of an operator symbol and list of operands. The operands may themselves be prefix form instructions to be evaluated, so the overall form is similar to a tree structure of operator-operand combinations.

18-9 STRUCTURE OF A SNOBOL4 VIRTUAL COMPUTER

The run-time structure of a SNOBOL4 implementation is made complex by the large amount of run-time variability that the language allows. Considerable software simulation is required, regardless of whether a software interpreter with a simple translator or the hardware interpreter with a compiler is used as the basis for the implementation. The software-interpreter-based system is the simplest and thus is the one which has been used in this chapter.

Storage Management

A tripartite memory organization is required: a static area for storage of system routines (including the translator) and various fixed-size tables, a stack for storage of subprogram activation records, and a heap for storage of translated user programs, user data structures, variable-size system tables, and other system data. The heap is allocated in variable-size blocks, and garbage collection and full compaction occur when free space is exhausted.

The static area and stack require little comment. Subprogram activation records in the stack contain the deactivated values for formal parameters, local variables, and the subprogram name identifiers, because the central referencing environment table method is used to maintain the current referencing environment. Thus the stack serves as a hidden stack and plays no direct role in referencing.

The heap is the central storage area. SNOBOL4 allows a programmer to create strings, arrays, tables, and programmer-defined data structures at arbitrary points during program execution, and as a result all programmer-defined data (each with full run-time descriptor) are allocated space in the heap. In addition, the translator may be called at any point during execution to translate a character string representing a set of SNOBOL4 statements into executable form. Such run-time-translated programs also require storage allocation in the heap. These aspects of the language have been discussed in previous sections.

Run-Time System Data

Almost every aspect of program and data structure in SNOBOL4 is subject to change at unpredictable points during program execution. As a result a large amount of run-time data must be maintained by the run-time system and continuously accessed and modified as execution proceeds. Most of these data are the sort which in other languages would be generated and used by the translator in creating the executable program form and then discarded before execution. It is most convenient to characterize this run-time system data in terms of a set of tables, although different implementations may store these system data in different ways. The run-time tables which must be maintained during execution of a SNOBOL4 program include:

1. *Central strings table* (*referencing environment*). The central run-time table in which character strings and their associated values are stored has been discussed in the preceding sections. Each entry in the central table consists of a character string and a pointer to its current value. Ordinarily, because the table must be accessed frequently, it is structured as a hash-coded table of fixed size in which each entry is a bucket consisting of a linked list of all the entries with the same hash index. Strings and their values are stored in the heap, but the basic fixed-size hash table (with pointers to the buckets in the heap) is stored in the static area.

2. *Statement labels table*. The label designated in the **goto** field of a statement may be an arbitrary computed string. This structure requires a run-time table of statement labels and pointers to their associated code positions in the executable code. Because strings are always entered into the central strings table, this labels table need only contain a pointer to the entry for the string and a pointer to the code position for each label. The possibility of translating new program statements containing labels into executable form during program execution means that the labels table may grow unpredictably during program execution and thus must be allocated storage in the heap.

3. *Subprogram and operator names.* A new subprogram name is defined whenever the DEFINE function is called during program execution. In addition, the OPSYN primitive allows any operator symbol (e.g., +) to be associated with a programmer-defined subprogram. This run-time variability requires a run-time table of associations between subprogram names and subprogram definitions and between operator symbols and operator definitions which may be modified by DEFINE and OPSYN and accessed whenever an operator is invoked or a subprogram called.

4. *Input, output, and trace associations.* The input, output and trace features of SNOBOL4 are activated by interrupts which occur whenever tagged identifiers are referenced in certain contexts. For example, an output interrupt occurs whenever an assignment to a tagged *output variable* is made, a label trace interrupt occurs whenever control is transferred to a tagged label, and so on. Such tagged identifiers may be created at any point during program execution through execution of one of the primitives functions TRACE, INPUT, or OUTPUT. A run-time table is required to specify the associations which are current for each tagged variable, which may include association with an input file, with an output file, or with tracing when used as a label, subprogram name, or when its value is modified. In addition to the run-time table (or tables) of associations, each reference to an identifier requires run-time checking for an appropriate interrupt tag because the interrupt system is unlikely to be supported by hardware and thus must be software-simulated.

5. *Data types and fields.* Programmer-defined data types may be created at arbitrary points during execution. Each component (field) of such a data element receives an identifier as its name, and the same field name may be used in many different data types. A run-time table must be maintained specifying for each *data type-field name* pair, the position of that field within a data element of that data type.

It should be clear from this discussion that the maintenance of the run-time system data in a SNOBOL4 implementation is a substantial part of the run-time virtual computer structure. The storage and execution time required for this system data handling represents a substantial part of the cost of program execution.

18-10 REFERENCES AND SUGGESTIONS FOR FURTHER READING

The basic definition of the SNOBOL4 language is found in the text by Griswold et al. [1971]. The early history of the design and implementation of the language is described by Griswold [1981]. A "primer" by Griswold and Griswold [1973] provides a more elementary introduction to the language.

Chapter 8 of the text by Organick et al. [1978] emphasizes data representations and data-control structures in the language, using partial
implementation models. Books by Gimpel [1976] and Griswold [1975]
provide many examples of applications of the language.

The standard implementation of the language is described at length in
Griswold [1972]; this book contains excellent discussions of many of the
issues that arise during SNOBOL4 implementation. A very different
approach is found in the SPITBOL compiler implementation described by
Dewar and McCann [1977]. An extensive critique of the pattern-matching
features of the language is made by Griswold and Hansen [1980].

18-11 PROBLEMS

1. Consider the program segment

$$X = \text{'GREEN EGGS AND HAM'}$$
$$Y = X$$
$$X \text{ 'AND'} = \text{'PLUS'}$$

The final value of X is the string GREEN EGGS PLUS HAM.
(a) What is the final value of Y?
(b) Explain the run-time changes that occur in the central strings table (including
the values of X and Y) as a result of execution of each of these statements.

2. Explain why strings in the central table to which no path exists may be garbage-
collected only if they have a *null value*.

3. The indirect referencing operator $ makes it possible to get some of the effects of
parameter transmission by reference (or by name), even though SNOBOL4
parameters are always transmitted by value. A simple example is the subprogram
ADD1, which when called with a simple integer-valued variable as argument will
add 1 to the value of the variable. In FORTRAN the program would be

```
        SUBROUTINE ADD1(I)
        I = I + 1
        RETURN
        END
```

In SNOBOL4 ADD1 would be written as

```
        DEFINE('ADD1(I)')            :(NEXT)
ADD1    $I = $I + 1                  :(RETURN)
```

The calling sequence in FORTRAN

```
        K = 2
        CALL ADD1(K)
```

(which results in K's being given the value 3), is written in SNOBOL4 as

$$K = 2$$
$$ADD1('K')$$

Unfortunately, while this sequence results in K's being given the value 3, the sequence

$$I = 2$$
$$ADD1('I')$$

results in a run-time error diagnostic because an argument given to + is not a number.

(a) Explain why ADD1('K') works, while ADD1('I') fails.

(b) Suppose that your SNOBOL4 subprogram SUB is defined to have formal parameters P1, P2, . . . , Pm, local variables L1, L2, . . . Ln, and the first actual parameter is expected to be a string representing a variable name (as in ADD1) which will be referenced indirectly as $P1 in SUB (i.e., you wish to use P1 as a *by reference* parameter). To make SUB available as a useful SNOBOL4 subprogram, what restrictions must be placed on the string (identifier) transmitted as the first actual parameter to SUB to insure that SUB will work correctly?

4. In the SNOBOL4 implementation described in this chapter, strings are entered in the central strings table at the time of their *creation*. An alternative would be to enter strings into the central table only when they are used as identifiers (i.e., when they are given an association as a subprogram name or label or when they are given a value). Strings with no association would be saved in temporary storage only until they became garbage and could be destroyed. Discuss the advantages and disadvantages of this alternative representation.

CHAPTER 19

APL

The original APL programming language was defined in a book by Kenneth Iverson, *A Programming Language*, published in 1962. The acronym APL is derived from the title of the book. Iverson's original intent was not to develop a conventional programming language that might be implemented on a computer as much as to develop a *notation* adequate to express concisely many important algorithms in mathematics. As a result the original APL utilized a myriad of special notational conventions and symbols, including subscripts, superscripts, and a two-dimensional program syntax with arrows designating flow of control that made the notation difficult if not impossible to directly implement on a computer. The original APL proved to be a useful conceptual tool for the precise statement of algorithms, which might then be translated by hand into conventional programming languages. Applications of this original APL included a concise and complete formal description of the IBM 360 computer hardware (Falkoff et al. [1964]).

A modified version of the original APL, termed APL\360, was implemented in the late 1960s by Iverson, Falkoff, and a group at IBM. Since then many other APL implementations have appeared, all based largely on the APL\360 design. A proposed standard APL definition is in preparation. It is this implemented version of APL that is described in this chapter. APL has two distinguishing characteristics that set it apart from the other languages described in this part:

1. *Interactive language.* APL is the only language of those described here that is expressly designed to be *interactive*. By interactive we mean a language designed to be used by a programmer sitting at a computer terminal who is building, testing, modifying, and using programs dynamically. APL includes a number of special features designed expressly for an interactive environment, including immediate execution of expressions entered at the terminal and facilities for subprogram creation, editing, and storage.

2. *Direct processing of entire data structures.* In APL the primitive operations accept whole arrays as arguments and produce whole arrays as results. Thus in APL the basic unit of data tends to be an entire array, rather than a single array element as in languages such as FORTRAN and Pascal. This emphasis on array processing gives programming in APL a unique "style" quite different from other languages.

APL has attracted a devoted group of users and evoked much controversy in its lifetime. Iverson's original notation is remarkable in its conciseness, power, and elegance, and most of this has been carried over into the implemented APL, even to the extent of insisting on a character set for APL which provides a greatly expanded set of special characters. The power and conciseness of the language make it well suited to the interactive environment, because a line of only a few characters typed in at a terminal can accomplish a surprising amount of computation. Often, such a *one-liner* is sufficient to define the body of an entire subprogram. The interactive features added to the original APL notation have also been nicely designed to enhance the convenience of using the language. The resulting APL language is particularly attractive to the programmer who wishes to get on the computer at a terminal, do some computing, obtain the desired results, and get off in a minimum amount of time—e.g., when using a personal computer. The language is much less suitable for construction of large programs which will be used repeatedly for production computing. In addition, because arrays are the only data structures in the language, it is difficult to apply to problem areas where flexible data structuring is a prime consideration, such as work in business data processing or artificial intelligence.

19-1   BRIEF OVERVIEW OF THE LANGUAGE

APL is based on simple homogeneous array data structures with components of type number or character. Typing is strictly dynamic and of no direct concern to the programmer (except that certain operators apply only to arrays of numbers). A large class of primitive operators are built in, including many which create, destroy, and modify arrays. Every APL primitive is defined as a function which returns a value. From these primitives extremely powerful expressions may be constructed. APL control structures are quite simple. Within expressions there is no hierarchy of operations, and right-to-left associativity is used in place of the more usual left-to-right technique. Between statements all that is provided is a simple **goto**, which allows a computed statement number, and recursive subprogram calls. Additionally, various kinds of interrupts may be set to interrupt program execution and return control to the programmer at his terminal, allowing him to enter new data, modify old data values, or modify the program before restarting the interrupted program at a designated statement.

Subprograms are restricted to at most two arguments, transmitted by value, and a single result. However, the ability to accept array arguments and return array results in any subprogram makes these restrictions relatively minor. Subprograms have the form of a simple sequence of statements, each of which has a system-generated *line number* and which may, in addition, have a programmer-supplied label. **Goto** statements may designate their object either by a line number or statement label. A subprogram may have a designated set of local identifiers. The local environment is created on subprogram entry and deleted on exit. Nonlocal referencing obeys the most-recent-association rule.

There is no concept of main program in APL. Subprogram execution is initiated either by a call from another subprogram or by the programmer at his terminal through entry and execution of an expression containing a function call. In the latter case control returns to the programmer at the terminal after subprogram execution is complete. In a sense the programmer creates and executes the main program line by line during a session at the terminal.

APL has perhaps the most extensively specified operating environment of any language described in this book. This environment, of course, includes the programmer at his terminal. Control may be passed back and forth between an executing program and the programmer as necessary. For external storage, programs and data are grouped into *workspaces*; these may be saved from session to session by the programmer. Each workspace may contain various program and data structures, including partially written programs and programs that have been partially executed and then interrupted. *System commands* are provided to allow workspaces to be brought into central memory from external storage and stored back again after being updated. In addition, subprogram definitions and data structures may be transferred individually by name between a stored workspace and the currently active one. Two APL programs executing concurrently may communicate through a special *shared variable* facility.

A typical APL implementation is based on purely software-interpreted program execution. Programs are stored essentially as entered, with only slight translation done. Two static storage areas are allocated, one for system routines and one for the workspace currently in use by the programmer. The system routines are ordinarily shared between several users, each with his own workspace area. The workspace area contains some static storage for system data and three dynamic storage areas: a stack for subprogram activation records (local referencing environments and return points), a heap for array storage and storage of the bodies of defined subprograms, and a table of global identifier associations. Garbage collection and full compaction are used when necessary.

19-2   AN ANNOTATED EXAMPLE TERMINAL SESSION: A PROGRAM TO COMPUTE THE FIRST N PRIMES

Figure 19-1 contains the listing of a partial APL terminal session in which the programmer enters, tests, corrects, and saves a function subprogram that computes a vector containing the first N prime numbers, for a given input parameter N. The programmer is assumed to already have gained access to the APL system and to have completed any earlier work. The annotations below refer to the line numbers to the left of the example listing, which are not a part of the program.

Line 1. The programmer clears his workspace of previous work. All subprogram and data structure definitions entered previously and not explicitly saved in the workspace library are destroyed.

Line 2. The programmer enters *definition mode* by typing the ∇ and follows with a subprogram header. The subprogram is defined in lines 3-9 following. The header declares the subprogram name, PRIMES, the name of its formal parameter, N, and two local variables, RES and T. The final value of RES is to be returned as the value of the function.

Line 3. Initial values are assigned to RES and T. The ← indicates assignment, and the "," indicates concatenation. The expression is evaluated from *right to left* as follows: (1) T is assigned the value 3, and 3 becomes the value of the expression T ← 3 (thus assignment is a function returning the value assigned as its value); (2) the value 3 is concatenated with the value 2 to form a vector of two elements; and (3) the two-element vector is assigned as the value of the variable RES. Note that the statement created a two-element vector during its execution. The right-to-left evaluation of expressions is standard throughout APL.

Line 4. This statement indicates a transfer of control because it begins with →. Control is returned to the calling program if the length of the vector

Line

1		)CLEAR
2		∇ RES ← PRIMES N; T
3	[1]	RES ← 2, T ← 3
4	[2]	→0 X ι N < ρ RES
5	[3]	T ← T + 2
6	[4]	→3 X ι v/0 = RES ⏐ T
7	[5]	RES ← RES, T
8	[6]	→2
9		∇
10		PRIMES 4
11		2 3 5 7 11
12		∇ PRIMES [2 □ 8]
13	[2]	→0 X ι N < ρ RES
14		/1
15	[2]	→0 X ι N ρ RES
16		=
17	[2]	→0 X ι N = ρ RES
18		[□] ∇
19		∇ RES ← PRIMES N;T
20	[1]	RES ← 2, T ← 3
21	[2]	→0 X ι N = ρ RES
22	[3]	T ← T + 2
23	[4]	→3 X ι v/0 = RES ⏐ T
24	[5]	RES ← RES,T
25	[6]	→2
26		∇
27		PRIMES 4
28		2 3 5 7
29		X ← PRIMES 10
30		X
31		2 3 5 7 11 13 17 19 23 29
32		)CONTINUE

Fig. 19-1 An APL terminal session

that is the value of RES is greater than the value of N input. If not, then control passes to the next statement. In other words, the routine terminates here if $N + 1$ primes have been computed (an error which is corrected below). In detail the statement is evaluated from right to left as follows: (1) The operator ρ returns the length of a vector argument, so ρ RES gives the length of the vector named by RES; (2) the operator $<$ compares the value of N and the length of RES, returning 1 for true and 0 for false; (3) the operator ι, for an integer argument k, produces a vector of the first k integers, or the *null vector* if k is zero, which in this case (argument either 1 or 0) gives either the vector containing only 1 or the null vector as result; (4) the operator $\times$ represents multiplication, in this case multiplication of zero times the result of step (3), giving either the null vector or the vector containing only a single zero; and finally (5) the branch operator $\rightarrow$ does nothing if its operand is the null vector and otherwise it transfers control to the statement whose number is the value of the first element of its vector argument, which in this case would be a branch to the statement numbered zero; no statement has the number zero, and such a branch is by definition a subprogram return. This structure seems inordinately complicated at first, but the trick of reading the expression $\rightarrow 0 \times \iota$ as "branch to 0 if the following expression is true, and otherwise continue to the next statement" simplifies things somewhat.

Line 5. The value of T is increased to the next odd integer.

Line 6. Another *test and* **goto**, this time to the statement numbered 3 (line 5) if the expression $\vee/0 = \text{RES} \mid T$ returns true. This expression is evaluated from right to left as follows: (1) T contains the next number to be tested for primeness, while RES contains a vector of the primes found to this point; the operator $\mid$ returns the remainder (residue) of division of its two arguments; thus the expression RES $\mid$ T produces a vector of the remainders obtained by dividing each element of the vector RES into the value of T; (2) each element of the vector resulting from step (1) is compared to zero, giving a vector of Boolean values (1's and 0's) depending on whether the remainder in the original vector was zero or nonzero, respectively; and finally (3) the operator $\vee$ is applied *between* each two adjacent elements of the Boolean vector resulting from step (2), giving a result of 1 (true) if the vector produced in step (2) contains any 1's and a result of 0 (false) if the vector is all zeros. Since the vector contains a 1 in some position only if the corresponding prime in RES exactly divides the test integer T, a vector of all zeros indicates that the test number is a prime.

Line 7. If the value of T is a prime, the value is concatenated (operator ,) onto the vector RES, giving a new vector, and the new vector is assigned as the new value of RES.

Line 8. Direct **goto** to statement number 2 (line 4).

Line 9. End of subprogram definition. The definition is automatically stored in the programmer's active workspace as the association for the identifier PRIMES. The terminal is returned to *immediate execution* mode, where any APL expression entered is immediately executed.

Line 10. First test of the new subprogram PRIMES. PRIMES is called with the argument 4. It should return as its value a vector of the first four primes. The result of the function call is printed automatically unless it is assigned as the value of a variable.

Line 11. Program bug detected. PRIMES returned the first five primes.

Lines 12-17. The subprogram definition is edited to correct the error, which is due to the $<$ comparison in statement [2].

Line 12. The programmer reenters definition mode (with ∇) and specifies listing of statement [2] of subprogram PRIMES, set for editing to begin on character 8 of the line.

Lines 13-14. Statement [2] is displayed and the terminal carriage is positioned on the next line beneath the eighth character. The programmer then spaces over or back to the exact position to be modified and enters /1, with the slash beneath the character to be deleted and the 1 indicating that the deleted character is to be replaced by one new character.

Lines 15-16. Statement [2] is redisplayed with the character deleted and the carriage positioned beneath the empty space. The programmer types the character to be inserted.

Line 17. The corrected statement is displayed again.

Line 18. The programmer requests display of the entire corrected function before leaving *definition mode.*

Lines 19-26. The function definition is listed.

Lines 27-28. The function is tested again and this time returns correct results.

Line 29. A vector of the first ten primes is computed and assigned as the value of the variable X. Since X has not been referenced previously, it is created automatically before the assignment is made.

Lines 30-31. The programmer requests and gets a printout of the value of X.

Line 32. The programmer ends the terminal session. The active workspace, containing the definition of subprogram PRIMES and the vector X of the first ten primes, is saved in the programmer's workspace library under the name CONTINUE. When the programmer signs on for his next terminal session, this workspace will be automatically loaded as his initial active workspace.

19-3 DATA TYPES

APL is quite restricted in its data-structuring facilities. Numbers and single characters are the elementary data types. Data structures are restricted to homogeneous multidimensional arrays containing elements of one of these two types. The arrays may have an arbitrary number of dimensions. The lower bound on subscript ranges is implicitly 1 but may be set at 0 by a special system command. Arrays are stored sequentially with a full run-time descriptor. Characters are stored in their hardware representation. Numbers are stored in fixed- or floating-point formats and are automatically converted as the need arises during execution; the programmer has no control over the internal storage representation of numbers.

No declarations for data are used in APL. Identifiers are not declared explicitly unless they are formal parameters or local identifiers in a subprogram, in which case the declaration serves only to indicate a scope of definition. An identifier may name a simple variable, an array, or a subprogram at different points during a terminal session. Full run-time descriptors are carried for all data items.

Syntax. The usual syntactic representation is provided for numbers and characters. Vectors of numbers may be written directly as a sequence of numbers separated by spaces. Character vectors are written as a character string. Arrays of higher dimension may be created from vectors using built-in operators.

The APL primitive operation set is the most powerful and elegant of any language described here. Primitives are provided for a wide variety of simple and complex manipulations on arrays. In general, each primitive operation takes arrays as operands and produces an array as a result. The primitives themselves are powerful, but equally important they may be combined into expressions in very complex ways, allowing a single expression to compute results which would require a lengthy program in other languages. It is this powerful expression capability that leads to the APL phenomenon of *one-liners*—an entire complex computation written as a one-line program composed of a single expression.

A complete description of the entire set of APL primitives is unnecessary. Detailed definitions of the various operators may be found in the reference manuals, e.g., Pakin [1972]. We shall classify the various operators into categories to give an idea of the diversity and power of the operations.

Arithmetic operations. The usual arithmetic operations—addition, subtraction, multiplication, division, negation, and exponentiation—are provided, but many others also appear as primitives: absolute value, reciprocal, logarithm, square root, sine, cosine and other trignometric functions, maximum, minimum, factorial, and random-number generation. These operations may be applied to single numbers (or pairs of numbers) in the usual way, but more importantly they may be applied to any array of numbers (or pairs of arrays of the same shape and size). When applied to arrays, the operations are applied to each element (or each pair of elements), and the result is a new array of the same size. For example, if A and B are arrays of the same shape and size, then the expression A + B produces a new array by adding corresponding elements of A and B. Similarly, A ⌈ B produces a new array whose components are the maximum of corresponding pairs of components in A and B.

Relational and logical operations. In APL the Boolean values are represented by the numbers 1 (true) and 0 (false). Thus the relational and logical operations are special cases of arithmetic operations. This representation is useful because it allows arithmetic, relational, and logical operations to be interspersed without type conflicts. The logical and relational operations may be applied to arrays in the same manner as the arithmetic operations. The primitive relational operations are the usual *equal, not-equal, less-than, greater-than, less-than-or-equal*, and *greater-than-or-equal*. Logical operations include *not, and, or, nand,* and *nor.*

Selection and assignment. In keeping with the basic APL design philosophy that every primitive should be generalized as far as possible, the basic operations of selection and assignment appear in a much more general form than usually seen. Any variable may have an array as value (or a single number or character). The entire array is retrieved just by referencing the variable in the usual way. Individual array elements may also be selected by subscripting; e.g., A[2;3] designates the element in the second row and the third column of the array which is the value of A. Subscripting is extended to allow arbitrary subarrays of an array to be accessed. For example, A[;3] accesses the third column of the matrix value of A; similarly, A[2;] gives the second row. But also A[1 2;] gives a matrix composed of the first two rows of A; A[1 2; 2 4] gives a 2 by 2 matrix composed $A_{1,2}, A_{2,2}, A_{1,4},$ and $A_{2,4}$.

Assignment (symbol ←) is performed differently depending on whether the variable on the left is subscripted or not. If a simple variable appears, then the value being assigned replaces the current value of the variable in the usual way, except that the value assigned may be an array. For example, if A and B are arrays of the same shape and size, then

$$C \leftarrow A + B$$

assigns the sum array as the new value of C, destroying the old value of C, which may also have been an array. It is not appropriate in APL to think of A, B, or C as the names of particular arrays, in the way one would in FORTRAN or Pascal. Because assignment may associate any of these identifiers with a new array at any time, it is best to think of A, B, and C as simple variables whose *values* happen to be arrays.

Assignment to a subscripted variable works differently. Subscripting indicates that the array which is the current value of the variable is to be retained (rather than destroyed) and only the values of selected elements of the array are to be modified. Thus A[2;3] ← 7 assigns 7 as the new value of A[2;3] as expected. The assignment, however, is not restricted to a single element of A. For example,

$$A[2;] \leftarrow 7$$

assigns 7 as the new value of each element in the second row of A. The assignment

$$A[1\ 2;\ 2\ 4] \leftarrow 7$$

sets the elements $A_{1,2}$, $A_{1,4}$, $A_{2,2}$, and $A_{2,4}$ each to 7. Assignment is extended further to allow any array to be assigned to a subarray of another array of the same shape and size. For example, if B is a 2×2 matrix, then the assignment $A[1\ 2;2\ 4] \leftarrow$ B changes the value of each specified element of A to the value of the corresonding element of B.

Array modification. A variety of other operators that modify arrays in various ways, without changing values of array elements, is provided. A basic operator, ρ, allows access to the descriptor of an array, returning a vector of upper bounds on each subscript of the array. For example, if A is a 3×4 matrix, then ρA returns the two-element vector (3 4) as its value. A double application of ρ produces the number of dimensions of an array, e.g., $\rho\rho$A = 2. Thus a program may always determine dynamically the size and shape of any array.

An array of any number of dimensions may be turned into a vector using the operator ",". The array elements are taken in row-major order. An array of any number of dimensions may be formed from a vector or another array using the operator ρ as a binary operation. For example, if A is the vector (2 3 4 5 6 7), then the expression 2 3 ρ A produces the 2×3 matrix

$$\begin{array}{ccc} 2 & 3 & 4 \\ 5 & 6 & 7 \end{array}$$

as its value.

Two vectors or arrays may be concatenated to form a new array. A vector may be modified by deletion of leading or trailing elements. A matrix transpose primitive and a rotation operator which rotates the elements of a vector (or rows or columns of a matrix) end-around are also provided. Expansion and compression operators allow arbitrary insertions and deletions of elements within an array. Moreover, each of these primitives applies to arrays of higher dimension as well, with a choice of which dimension is to be used (where such extension is appropriate).

Much of the power of APL lies in this set of primitives for structural modification of arrays. In general, given a set of arrays, these primitives allow the arrays to be taken apart, restructured, and the pieces recombined in almost any desired manner. In the process, of course, the array element values may also be modified using the arithmetic, logical, and relational operations.

Generators. Several built-in *generator* operations play a central role in much APL programming. Each accepts one or two other primitives and one or two arrays as arguments and applies the primitives to the elements of the arrays in a fixed sequence. The most basic of these is the *reduction* operation (symbol /), which accepts a vector (or an array) and one of the basic binary arithmetic, relational, or logical primitives as arguments. The primitive is applied to the last two elements of the vector, then to the result of that operation and the third from the last vector element, and so on. The effect is as though the elements of the vector were written out in sequence with the primitive between each adjacent pair and then the resulting expression executed from right to left in the usual APL manner. For example, if A has as its value the vector (2 3 4 5 6 7), then +/A evaluates to the sum of the elements of A, −/A gives the value (2−(3−(4−(5−(6−7))))) or 2−3+4−5+6−7. The *scan* operation (symbol \) applies the reduction operation to each partial vector, starting at the left of a given vector, and produces a vector of results. For example, +\A evaluates the sequence of expressions

$$+/(2) \qquad +/(2\ 3) \qquad +/(2\ 3\ 4) +/(2\ 3\ 4\ 5) \ldots$$

giving the result vector

$$2 \quad 5 \quad 9 \quad 14 \quad 20 \quad 27$$

Both reduction and scan may be applied to arrays of higher dimension by designating the dimension along which the reduction is to be made. For example, if B is a matrix, then +/[1]B produces a vector of the sums of the columns of B, and +/[2] B produces a vector of the row sums.

The other two generator primitives are inner product (symbol .) and outer product (symbol °.). The *inner-product* primitive takes two binary primitive operations and two arrays (of conformable shapes) as arguments. The second primitive is applied to corresponding pairs of elements of the two arrays, and then the first primitive is applied to reduce the result. More specifically, the expression A+.× B, where A and B are vectors of the same length, is equivalent to the expression +/(A × B); i.e., corresponding elements of A and B are multiplied to produce a new vector of the same length, and then this new vector is summed to produce a single number. If A and B are matrices, then A+.× B is ordinary matrix multiplication. Other uses for the inner-product primitive abound; for example, two vectors may be tested for component-by-component equality by the expression A+.≠B, which evaluates to zero only if A and B are identical.

The final generator primitive, *outer product*, takes two arrays and a binary primitive as arguments and applies the primitive to each pair of elements of the two arrays, generating a new array with number of dimensions equal to the sum of the number of dimensions of the two original arrays. Thus the outer product of two vectors results in creation of a matrix, the outer product of a vector and a matrix gives an array of three dimensions, and so on.

A number of other more specialized array-manipulation primitives are provided, including matrix division, matrix inverse, and sorting primitives. Creation and destruction of arrays is an implicit aspect of almost every APL primitive. Unlike other languages, it has no special creation and destruction operations.

Input-output. APL input-output operations are restricted to simple input and output of numbers, character strings, and arrays to the programmer's terminal. No access to external data files is ordinarily provided (although some APL implementations include such features). The input symbol is □. The occurrence of □ as a variable in an expression being evaluated causes evaluation to be interrupted and a request for input sent to the programmer's terminal. After he has entered a number, vector of numbers, or character string, evaluation of the expression is resumed. Output is handled similarly: The appearance of □ as the object of an assignment within an expression specifies that the value is to be printed at the programmer's terminal. In addition, automatic output of the value of an expression occurs when the expression has been input by the programmer for immediate evaluation.

Translating and executing data as program. The *execute* (or *unquote*) operation (symbol ⍎) takes a vector or matrix of characters as its argument. The vector (or each row of the matrix) is treated as an expression to be translated and executed as though it had been entered directly by the programmer at the terminal. Thus the execute operation allows an array of characters that ordinarily would be considered as data to be turned into part of an APL program. For example, if vector C is assigned the value "+\A" (i.e., C is a vector of three characters), then at some later point, evaluation of ⍎C has the effect of evaluating the expression +\A, producing the vector of results shown above.

The execute operation has a variety of uses. One that is particularly important is that it allows an APL program to accept user input that does not utilize APL syntax, transform it as a character string into a valid APL expression, and then execute it. For example, the user might input the string "SUM VECTOR A", which the APL program could transform into the expression "+/A" and execute using *execute*.

19-4 SUBPROGRAMS

Function subprograms defining operations are the only abstraction mechanism provided by APL. The details of function definition are straightforward and are treated in Sec. 19-6 below. An example of function definition and invocation is seen in Fig. 19-1.

19-5   SEQUENCE CONTROL

APL is rather weak in sequence-control mechanisms, particularly in statement sequence control. However, much of the sequence-control structure ordinarily needed for array processing in languages like FORTRAN and Pascal is made unnecessary by the powerful APL primitives, and thus this weakness is not as significant as it might appear. Note, for example, that the summation of the elements of a vector, which would require a set of statements including a loop in FORTRAN or Pascal, may be written in APL as

$$SUM \leftarrow +/V$$

No statement sequence control is required.

Expressions

APL operations appear only in two forms, regardless of whether they are primitives or programmer-defined subprograms:

1. Binary (called *dyadic*) operations are written in infix notation, e.g., A−B or A?B.

2. Unary (called *monadic*) operations are written in prefix notation (without parentheses), e.g., −C or ?C.

The only exception to this rule is the *subscripting operation*, which is represented by enclosing the subscript in a pair of brackets, e.g., D[2].

The simple syntax for expressions allows an equally simple evaluation rule, the *right-to-left* rule: An APL expression is always evaluated from right to left, with the operands of an operation evaluated before the operation is applied. Parentheses may be used in the usual way to control the order of evaluation. For example,

$$A−B−C−D \quad \text{is evaluated as} \quad A−(B−(C−D)).$$
$$A\times B+C\times D \quad \text{is evaluated as} \quad A\times(B+(C\times D)).$$

Note that the right-to-left rule applies to programmer-defined function subprograms as well as built-in primitives. Since no special syntax is provided for function subprogram calls, they also appear as infix operations; for example, A FUN B represents the function call FUN(A,B). The expression A−B FUN C÷D is evaluated as A−(B FUN (C÷D)) or in the more common function notation as a A−FUN(B,C÷D).

The right-to-left rule leaves open the question of the order of evaluation of the two operands of a binary operation; e.g., in (A−B) + (C−D) both (A−B) and $(C-D)$ must be evaluated before the $+$ operation is applied, but the order of evaluation of $(A-B)$ and $(C-D)$ is not defined. The order makes no difference except where side effects occur, but then it may be crucial. APL function subprograms may have side effects; moreover, because assignment is defined as a function, direct side effects through assignments embedded in expressions may occur. For example, the result of the expression

$$A-(B\leftarrow C)-B$$

is dependent on the order of evaluation of the assignment to B and the reference to B, and this order is not defined by the right-to-left rule. Similarly, if FUN has the side effect of changing the value of B, then the result of $(A\ FUN\ C)-B$ is undefined. The result of evaluation in such cases is implementation-dependent.

Implementation of expression evaluation is made complex by a number of language features. Intermediate results of evaluation may be arbitrarily large arrays, for which temporary storage must be allocated. In addition, any expression may include the $\square$ operation specifying a request for input from the programmer's terminal. This requires an interruption of evaluation, during which the active workspace is ordinarily copied to external storage by the APL system, to be brought back into central memory when the programmer has entered his data. Evaluation of a function call in an expression may be interrupted by an error, during which the programmer is given control. The programmer may attempt to modify the statement containing the partially evaluated expression by editing the original function definition. Careful monitoring of such editing attempts is necessary to insure that execution can still be continued.

Statement Sequence Control

Each statement in a function definition receives a line number automatically upon input. In addition, statements may be labeled by preceding the statement by ⟨*label*⟩:. Statements are executed in sequence in the usual way. The **goto** operator (symbol $\rightarrow$) may be used to modify this sequence. A **goto** statement must begin with $\rightarrow$ followed by an arbitrary expression. The value of the expression must be either an integer or a statement label. The $\rightarrow$ operator transfers control to the statement with this line number or label in the usual way.

This simple computed **goto** command is made more flexible by a number of conventions. First, notice that since a single APL expression may perform a complex computation which includes testing conditions of various sorts and varying the computation accordingly, the basic **goto** command can be used either as a simple **goto**, as in $\rightarrow 3$, which transfers control unconditionally to statement 3, or as a two-way or multiway branch by using more complex expressions. This basic structure is extended by the following conventions:

1. If the expression evaluates to a vector, the first element of the vector is taken as the integer line number for the **goto**.

2. If the expression evaluates to the special null vector (the vector of no elements), then no transfer occurs, and control passes to the next statement in sequence.

The same **goto** may also be used as a subprogram return or halt (see below).

Subprogram Sequence Control

Subprogram execution is controlled by the ordinary call and return structure, with recursive calls allowed. Return from a subprogram is done by a **goto** to a nonexistent statement number, usually statement number zero, e.g., →0. Return from an entire subprogram calling chain back to the top level, where the programmer is again free to enter commands directly, may be accomplished by a statement consisting only of the **goto** arrow without an operand, →.

Besides the subprogram call and return it is also possible to interrupt subprogram execution, leaving the subprogram in a *suspended state*. Execution is interrupted automatically if an error occurs during execution. The interrupted subprogram is placed in a suspended state, and control returns to the programmer at his terminal. Programs may be left in the suspended state indefinitely while other subprograms are executed. In fact, any number of subprograms may be in the suspended state simultaneously. Interruption of the subprogram execution also may be specified to occur when particular lines of the subprogram are reached during execution. This is done by setting up a *stop vector*—a vector of line numbers at which execution is to be suspended. For example, if subprogram SUB is to be interrupted prior to execution of lines 6 and 17, the statement

$$S\Delta SUB \leftarrow 6\ 17$$

entered at the terminal will tag the appropriate statements in SUB for interruption when SUB is executed.

When subprogram execution is interrupted and the subprogram is put into the suspended state, control returns to the programmer at the terminal, who may now proceed to modify the suspended subprogram, write new subprograms, and the like. The only real restriction on his activity is that he must be careful not to modify in certain ways subprograms which are partially executed, for the obvious reason that then return of control might be made impossible.

The interrupt features of APL are useful in allowing very flexible program testing schemes. For example, a partially written subprogram may be tested by setting interrupts for statements leading into missing program segments. Or execution may be interrupted just prior to a call on a subprogram which has not yet been written.

19-6   DATA CONTROL

The first line of a subprogram definition is used to declare the identifiers local to that subprogram, including formal parameters and a result parameter used as a local variable to designate the result returned (if the subprogram is a function). For example, a subprogram definition might begin

$$\nabla \ \ R \leftarrow A \ SUB \ B; \ L;M;N$$

This statement identifies the subprogram name as SUB, the formal parameters as A and B, the result parameter as R, and the local variables as L, M, and N. Parameter transmission is always by value, so that A and B are treated identically with L, M, and N during execution, the only difference being that A and B are assigned initial values (the values of the actual parameters) while the initial values of L, M, and N are undefined. The result parameter R also acts as a local variable, except that on termination of execution the value of R is transferred back to the calling program as the value of SUB. Subprograms are restricted to at most two parameters. The result parameter may be omitted if the subprogram returns no value and is not to be used as a function. The formal parameters, result parameter, and local variables make up the local referencing environment of a subprogram.

Global identifiers may be defined in two ways. Subprogram names automatically become global identifiers when a subprogram is defined. Global variables may be defined implicitly by an assignment to an identifier which has not previously been used (or declared as local). Such assignments may be entered directly by the programmer for immediate execution or may occur in subprograms being executed. This structure allows identifiers to be added to the global referencing environment at any time. Identifiers may be deleted from the global environment by the ERASE command. For example,

$$)ERASE \ SUB \ X \ Y$$

deletes the identifiers SUB, X, and Y from the global environment (and frees the space taken up by their values, whether arrays or function definitions).

Nonlocal referencing in subprograms is controlled by the most recent association rule, but with a twist. Recall that using the most recent association rule, if the subprogram being executed references identifier X and X is not a local variable, then the association used for X is found by simply searching back down the calling chain to a subprogram having an association for X. This is the basic nonlocal referencing technique in APL. Should there *fail* to be an association for X in the calling chain, however, the search continues back through the subprograms and their calling chains that are in *suspended execution* because of an interrupt. This search is made in the reverse order of suspension, so that the most recently suspended subprogram and its calling chain is searched first, then the next previously suspended subprogram, and so on. If no association for X is found in this search (which covers all the local identifiers which have any current association), then the global association for X is used. If X has no global association, then a referencing error is signaled.

APL provides facilities for programmer access to the current referencing environment and subprogram calling chains at any point during execution. The list of subprograms which are in the calling chain of the subprogram currently being executed and of subprograms whose execution has been suspended by an interrupt (and their calling chains) is termed the *state indicator list* and may be printed by executing the command)SI. For example, the state indicator list during execution of the third statement of a subprogram SUB might be

SUB[3]*
Q[5]
P[17]
SUB1[3]*
R[5]

The asterisks indicate subprograms interrupted during execution and placed in the suspended state. In this example, SUB was called from the fifth line of subprogram Q, which was called in turn from the seventeenth line of subprogram P, which was called directly by the programmer in an expression entered for immediate execution. Prior to entry of that expression, subprogram SUB1 had been interrupted at line 3 and placed in the suspended state. SUB1 had been called from the fifth line of subprogram R, which was directly invoked by the programmer.

To obtain a complete list of all local identifiers for each subprogram in the state indicator list the command)SINL is executed. The listing then also includes on each line a list of the local identifiers declared in the subprogram header. The programmer thus at any time may interrupt execution of a subprogram and ask for a listing of its referencing environment.

19-7 OPERATING AND PROGRAMMING ENVIRONMENT

One of the most elegant aspects of the APL design is its combination of interactive operating and programming environment. The key components of the APL environment are (1) the *programmer* at his terminal; (2) the *active workspace*, which serves as temporary storage for programs and data during a terminal session; and (3) the *workspace library*, which serves as permanent storage for workspaces between sessions. Workspaces and libraries are manipulated through four subsystems of the APL virtual computer: an *active workspace manager*, which manipulates the active workspace; a *library manager*, which provides access to private and public libraries of workspaces; an *editor*, which manipulates individual subprogram definitions within the active workspace; and an *interpreter*, which executes APL programs. The programmer directs these subsystems through various *system commands*, which he enters at his terminal for immediate execution.

A terminal session begins when the APL programmer signs on to an APL terminal. Immediately an active workspace is set up for him, and he is put in contact with his private workspace library through the library manager. The initial active workspace is empty unless the programmer has left a workspace named CONTINUE in his library from a previous session, in which case a copy of this workspace becomes the initial active workspace.

Workspace and Library Structure and Manipulation

The workspace is organized around a table of identifiers, called the *symbol table*. Each identifier in the symbol table is usually the name of a subprogram, a simple variable, or an array, and in these cases the table entry contains a pointer to the subprogram or data structure, which is stored in another part of the workspace. Some identifiers in the symbol table may be identifiers without a current definition, representing, for example, subprograms which have been referenced but not yet defined.

Initially the symbol table of a workspace is empty. The programmer may add entries to the symbol table in a number of ways. Subprogram names are added when the programmer enters the special character ∇ at his terminal, followed by a subprogram definition and a terminating ∇ . The body of the subprogram is then stored in the workspace, and the subprogram name is entered into the symbol table with a pointer to the stored body. Similarly, assignment of an array to an identifer causes the array to be stored in the workspace and the identifer to be entered into the symbol table with an associated pointer to the array.

Once having set up these various symbol table entries, the programmer may now access the symbol table to obtain listings of the various identifiers, using the system commands:

)FNS   gives a list of subprogram names
)VARS   gives a list of variable names

Any individual subprogram definition or variable value may be listed also. Symbol table entries may be deleted using the command)ERASE *list-of-names*, or the entire symbol table (and thus the entire workspace) may be cleared by the command)CLEAR.

The *workspace library* serves as permanent storage for the workspaces which the programmer constructs. Whenever the programmer wishes to permanently save the contents of the current active workspace, he first provides a name for the workspace, using the command)WSID *name*, and then enters a copy into his workspace library using the command)SAVE. A saved workspace may later be retrieved by the command)LOAD *name*, which replaces the current active workspace with a copy of the named workspace from the library. A listing of the names of all library workspaces may be obtained with the command)LIB; deletion of library workspaces is accomplished through)DROP *name*. Selected subprogram definitions or data structures may be copied from a library workspace to the currently active workspace using the command)COPY *wksp-name list-of-names*. These facilities combine to make access to workspace libraries simple. Besides the programmer's *private library* of workspaces, other *public libraries* and the private libraries of other programmers may be accessed through special library numbers.

Entering and Editing Subprogram Definitions

Another component of the operating and programming environment in APL is an *editor*, which the programmer may use to enter or modify subprogram definitions. Note that system commands which communicate with the active workspace or library managers always begin with a). To gain contact with the editor, the programmer enters a line beginning with the symbol ∇. His communication is then with the editor until another ∇ is entered. An example of initial subprogram entry and editing is given in Sec. 19-2.

Shared Variables

An extension found in many APL systems allows two APL programs running concurrently to communicate through *shared variables*. A single

APL user at a terminal cannot execute two programs concurrently, so the use of shared variables is to communicate with another APL program being executed by another user or to communicate with system programs providing special services that are outside of standard APL (such as access to external files). The conceptual view provided to the APL user is that there are other processors executing programs concurrently in the operating environment of the APL program. The APL virtual computer controls the operation of all these concurrent processors, and it also coordinates access to the public libraries to which the various users have access. Ordinarily each user has his own processor that executes his programs and which is entirely separate from the processors of other users. However, by use of shared variables, one processor may communicate with another processor.

The central data structure involved is a global table of shared variables to which all users have access. In order to set up the sharing of a variable between two processors, both must cooperate. One offers to share a variable by entering the name of the variable in the global table (via a call on the primitive operation SVOFFER), together with a tag identifying the other processor with which it is willing to share. The other processor executes a similar call on SVOFFER naming the same variable and giving the ID tag of the first processor. The named variable immediately becomes a communication link between the two processors. In general it serves as a two-way link, with one processor assigning a value to the variable and the other referencing the value, and vice versa. Access is synchronized by the central APL virtual computer, so that if one processor attempts to reference the variable a second time before the other has assigned a new value, the referencing processor is forced to wait until the new value is assigned. Simultaneous access is prevented by a mutual-exclusion mechanism enforced by the central virtual computer. As an example, a special processor for reading external files might be provided, with a shared variable serving as the communication link during reading of the file. The **read** processor reads the next file component and stores it in the shared variable; the user program references the shared variable to get the next component. Storing a new value and referencing the new value must alternate, with neither processor allowed to get ahead of the other.

Either one of the processors participating in the sharing of a variable may decide to *retract* the offer to share, using the primitive SVRETRACT. Also a processor may query the central table of shared variables to determine which processors have variables that are currently available for sharing. In making an entry in the table, a processor may offer to share a variable with any other processor (i.e., without giving an explicit processor ID). Any other processor may then query the table to find the ID of the offering processor and then execute a call on SVOFFER naming that processor in order to set up the communication link.

Shared variables establish communication links dynamically between processors. When a program terminates, all its shared-variable links are automatically retracted if the variables are local to the program. Shared-variable links through global variables in the current workspace are lost when the terminal session terminates or when a new workspace is loaded to replace the current one.

19-8   SYNTAX AND TRANSLATION

The syntactic structure of APL is the simplest of any language discussed here, with the possible exception of LISP. Each subprogram definition is entirely separate from the others. The only interaction between subprograms comes when one calls another during execution. Each subprogram definition is composed of a simple sequence of lines, each with an attached line number. Each line is composed of a single expression. Each expression is a combination of numbers, character strings, variables, and prefix and infix operators. The entire syntactic structure is so simple and regular that it can be mastered easily even by beginning programmers.

The most problematic feature of the APL syntax is the use of a large set of special characters to represent operators. The APL character set includes the following special characters, many of which must be produced by backspacing the terminal typewriter and overstriking:

$$< > = \neq \leq \geq \lor \land \sim \land \!\!\!\!\!/ \; \lor \!\!\!\!\!/ \; + - \times \div * ? \; \epsilon$$
$$\uparrow \; \iota \; \phi \; \circledast \; \lceil \; \nabla \!\!\!\!\!\sim \; ! \perp \mid \; / \; . \; \circ \; \circ \; \boxplus \rho \downarrow \; \llcorner \; \Delta$$
$$[\;] \; (\;) \; \top \; \bullet \; , \; \backslash \; \square \; \square \; ' \; \leftarrow \rightarrow \; A \; \nabla \; \Delta \; ; \; :$$
$$\lozenge \; \Phi \; \Phi \; \theta \; \cap \; \cup \; \supset \; \subset \; \alpha \; \omega \; \not\!+ \; \not\!+$$

The special characters for operators have an obvious advantage: programs are shorter because fewer characters need be used. However, they have what is probably a more serious disadvantage: programs are so compact that they are difficult to read. This extreme conciseness is a particular problem because of the power of the individual operations, which allow rather large computations to often be compressed into a single expression. For example, an expression such as the following (from a program by Greiner [1972] in the APL newsletter *Quote-Quad*)

$$\rightarrow \times \rho, M[\times \rho M;] \leftarrow D \times M[\times \rho M \leftarrow 1 \; 1 \downarrow M\text{-}M[;1]^{\circ}. \times M[1;1] \div D \leftarrow 1 \rho M;]$$

may take many minutes, or even hours, to decode. Programming languages specialist Daniel McCracken [1970] notes that it once took him *four hours* to decode a *four-line* APL program.

Related to the overly concise expression syntax is the almost total lack of redundancy in APL expressions. Each operator symbol usually represents not just one powerful operation but two, one when used as a prefix operator with one operand and a different one when used as an infix operator with two operands. For example, $X \div Y$ represents division, but $\div Y$ alone represents the reciprocal. When an expression is input, the omission of an operand like the X in the first expression above results in another expression which looks very similar to the correct one. Unfortunately the incorrect expression is probably still executable, but it computes something quite different from the intended result. Such errors are difficult to track down in a complex expression.

Translation

The usual APL implementation executes APL programs with a software interpreter. Only a trivial translation of each program line into an internal form is made when a program line is input. These translated lines are then stored as the executable program form to be interpreted by the software interpreter. During the translation to internal form, numbers are converted into their hardware representation (with descriptor attached), identifiers are converted into pointers to symbol table entries, and operator symbols are left as character codes. This trivial translation makes reconversion of the program to its original input form easy. Since this reconversion must be done frequently, e.g., for listings, editing, and error messages, simple reconversion is of value. Also since APL programs tend to be relatively short, the cost of line-by-line software interpretation, while high, is not so expensive as might otherwise be the case.

19-9 STRUCTURE OF AN APL VIRTUAL COMPUTER

A typical APL implementation is structured around two memory areas: an active workspace area and an APL system area. The *system area* contains the programs which simulate the APL virtual computer; these cannot be modified by the programmer. The system area is usually shared by all the APL programmers who are using APL at any one time—each may use the various routines in the system area. The system area also contains the monitor which supervises interactions with the various APL terminals, including access to shared variables. Each APL programmer who is at a terminal also has an *active workspace* area which contains his private programs, data, and system-defined status indicators and data items.

The active workspace may be viewed as organized into four major parts, as shown in Fig. 19-2. The contents of these parts are

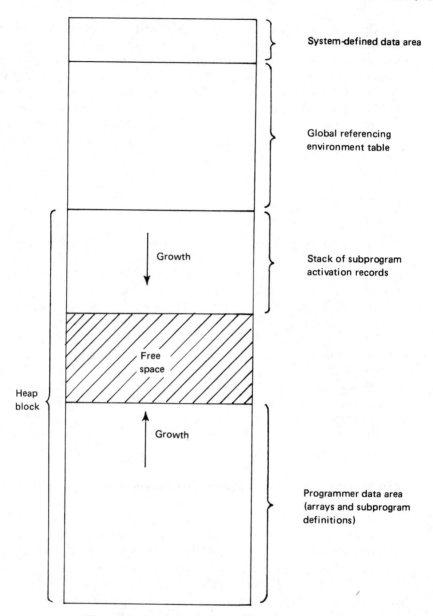

Fig. 19-2 Organization of an APL active workspace

1. *Programmer data area.* This heap storage area contains definitions of programmer-defined subprograms and programmer-created data structures (arrays). Space is used beginning at the bottom of the heap block and is allocated toward the middle as needed. No free-space list is maintained as storage is freed; instead, a garbage collection and compaction is initiated when all available storage has been exhausted.

2. *Global referencing-environment table.* This area is of fixed size (typically 256 table entries) and contains one entry for each identifier which the programmer uses at his terminal which is not a local variable in a subprogram. Entries are made as the programmer introduces new identifiers in expressions entered at his terminal.

3. *Subprogram activation record stack.* A stack of subprogram activation records is maintained during subprogram execution. Subprograms may be recursive, so the stack is allowed to grow as necessary. The stack is allocated sequentially and maintained at the opposite end of the heap block from the programmer data area. The stack and programmer data area grow toward each other, with garbage collection and compaction of the programmer data area taking place when the two areas meet.

4. *System-defined data area.* A small statically allocated area is reserved for special system data items. Some, such as the length of a print line and the number of significant digits printed for numbers, may be modified by the programmer; others represent hidden system data that is not directly accessible by the programmer.

The APL virtual computer is almost entirely software-simulated. The key simulation routines, which reside in the system area, are (1) the *expression interpreter*, which decodes and executes single APL expressions when entered directly by the programmer, or when called by (2) the *subprogram interpreter*, which executes APL subprograms, setting up activation records, calling the expression interpreter to execute each line of the subprogram as appropriate, and deleting activation records; (3) the *primitive operations*, each of which is simulated by a routine in the system area; and (4) the *storage manager*, which manages allocation, recovery, and compaction in the heap storage area and also allocation and recovery in the symbol table and stack.

Data representations for arrays, numbers, and characters are based on hardware representations. Arrays, in particular, are stored sequentially in a block of memory. However, all APL data must carry a run-time descriptor because no data properties are fixed by declarations. Thus numbers and characters must be tagged as to data type, and arrays must be accompanied by descriptors giving number of dimensions, type, subscript bounds, and so on.

19-10 REFERENCES AND SUGGESTIONS
FOR FURTHER READING

The original definition of APL is found in Iverson [1962]. A proposed
standard version of the language is (APL [1982]). Pakin [1972] describes the
implemented version of APL on the IBM 360. Breed and Lathwell [1968]
provide an overview of this implementation. Harrison [1973] discusses APL
and a related language SETL. Falkoff and Iverson [1981] describe the early
history of APL and its implementation. Iverson [1979] suggests how the
operators in APL might be extended. In general, APL language extension
and implementation activities center around the ACM Special Interest
Group on APL (SIGAPL), which publishes a regular newsletter.

19-11 PROBLEMS

1. Right-to-left associativity (with all operators of equal precedence) is the usual
   evaluation rule when Polish prefix notation is used in expressions, but it is quite
   surprising to find it coupled with *infix* operators in APL. Give two advantages
   and two disadvantages of the use of this expression evaluation rule in APL.

2. Give a BNF grammar for APL statements, using the basic syntactic categories
   ⟨*infix operator*⟩, ⟨*prefix operator*⟩, and ⟨*number*⟩. There are only two classes of
   APL statements, a ⟨GOTO *statement*⟩ and a ⟨*simple statement*⟩ (actually just an
   ⟨*expression*⟩).

References

JOURNALS

The most important journals in the area of programming language design and implementation are the following, although many other journals occasionally carry articles of interest.

> *ACM Computing Surveys*
> *ACM Transactions on Programming Languages and Systems*
> *Acta Informatica*
> *Communications of the ACM*
> *Computer Languages*
> *IEEE Transactions on Software Engineering*
> *SIGPLAN Notices* (Newsletter of the ACM Special Interest Group on Programming Languages)
> *Software Engineering Notes* (Newsletter of the ACM Special Interest Group on Software Engineering)
> *Software—Practice and Experience*

BOOKS AND ARTICLES

ADA [1978] *Requirements for High Order Computer Programming Languages—"STEELMAN"*, U.S. Dept. of Defense, Adv. Res. Projects Agency. Reprinted in WASSERMAN [1980].

——— [1980] *Formal Definition of the Ada Programming Language*, Honeywell, Inc. (preliminary).

——— [1982] *Reference Manual for the Ada Programming Language (Draft Proposed ANSI Standard)*, U.S. Dept. of Defense.

AHO, A., J. HOPCROFT and J. ULLMAN [1983] *Data Structures and Algorithms*, Addison-Wesley, Reading, MA.

———, and J. ULLMAN [1972] *The Theory of Parsing, Translation and Compiling*, Prentice-Hall, Englewood Cliffs, NJ.

——— and ——— [1977] *Principles of Compiler Design*, Addison-Wesley, Reading, MA.

ALLEN, J. [1978] *The Anatomy of LISP*, McGraw-Hill, New York.

AMBLER, A. et al. [1977] "GYPSY: A Language for Specification and Implementation of Verifiable Programs," *SIGPLAN Notices*, 12, 3, 1-10. Reprinted in WASSERMAN (ed.) [1980].

ANDERSON, R. [1979] *Proving Programs Correct*, Wiley, New York.

APL [1982] *Second Working Draft Standard for Programming Language APL*, ISO TC97/SC5 WG APL N2, International Standards Organization.

BACKHOUSE, R. [1980] *Syntax of Programming Languages*, Prentice-Hall, Englewood Cliffs, NJ.

BACKUS, J. [1960] "The Syntax and Semantics of the Proposed International Algebraic Language of the Zurich ACM-GAMM Conference," *Information Processing*, UNESCO, Paris, 125-132.

——— [1978] "Can Programming be Liberated from the von Neumann Style? A Functional Style and its Algebra of Programs," *Comm. ACM*, 21, 8, 613-641.

——— [1981] "The History of FORTRAN I, II, and III." In WEXELBLAT (ed.) [1981], 25-44.

——— et al. [1957] "The FORTRAN Automatic Coding System," *Proc. Western Jt. Comp. Conf.*, AIEE (now IEEE), Los Angeles, 188-198.

BAER, J. [1980] *Computer System Architecture*, Computer Science Press.

BARNES, R. [1979] "A Working Definition of the Proposed Extensions for PL/I Real-time Applications," *SIGPLAN Notices*, 14, 10, 77-99.

BARRETT, W. and COUCH, J. [1979] *Compiler Construction: Theory and Practice*, SRA, Chicago.

BARRON, D. [1968] *Recursive Techniques in Programming*, American Elsevier, New York.

——— [1972] *Assemblers and Loaders* 2d ed., North-Holland, New York.

——— [1977] *An Introduction to the Study of Programming Languages*, Cambridge Univ. Press.

—————— (ed.) [1981] *Pascal: The Language and Its Implementation*, Wiley, New York.

BAUER, F., and J. EICKEL (eds.) [1976] *Compiler Construction, An Advanced Course*, 2d ed., Springer-Verlag, New York.

BEECH, D. [1970] "A Structural View of PL/I," *Computing Surveys*, 2, 1, 33-64.

BERKELEY, E., and D. BOBROW (eds.) [1964] *The Programming Language LISP: Its Operation and Applications*, M.I.T. Press, Cambridge, Mass.

BOBROW, D., and D. MURPHY [1967] "Structure of a LISP System Using Two-level Storage," *Comm. ACM*, 10, 3, 155-159.

——————, and B. RAPHAEL [1974] "New Programming Languages for Artificial Intelligence," *ACM Computing Surveys*, 6, 3, 153-174.

——————, and B. WEGBREIT [1973] "A Model and Stack Implementation of Multiple Environments," *Comm. ACM*, 16, 10, 591-602.

BOHM, C., and G. JACOPINI [1966] "Flow Diagrams, Turing Machines and Languages with Only Two Formation Rules," *Comm. ACM*, 9, 5, 366-371.

BREED, L., and R. LATHWELL [1968] "The implementation of APL/360." In KLERER and REINFELDS (eds.), *Interactive Systems for Experimental Applied Mathematics*, Academic Press, New York.

BRINCH HANSEN, P. [1973] "Concurrent Programming Concepts," *ACM Computing Surveys*, 5, 4, 223-245.

—————— [1975] "The Programming Language Concurrent Pascal," *IEEE Trans. on Soft. Engr.*, 1, 2, 199-207. Reprinted in WASSERMAN (ed.) [1980].

—————— [1977] *The Architecture of Concurrent Programs*, Prentice-Hall, Englewood Cliffs, NJ.

BURGE, W. [1975] *Recursive Programming Techniques*, Addison-Wesley, Reading, MA.

BUXTON, J. [1980] "Stoneman: Requirements for Ada Programming Support Environments," U.S. Dept. of Defense, Advanced Research Projects Agency.

CHOMSKY, N. [1959] "On Certain Formal Properties of Grammars," *Information and Control*, 2, 137-167.

COBOL [1974] *American National Standard Programming Language COBOL*, X3.23, Amer. Natl. Standards Inst., New York.

COHEN, J. [1981] "Garbage Collection of Linked Data Structures," *ACM Computing Surveys*, 13, 3, 341-368.

CONWAY, R., and D. GRIES [1975] *An Introduction to Programming*, 2d ed., Winthrop, Cambridge, MA.

——————, and T. WILCOX [1973] "Design and Implementation of a Diagnostic Compiler for PL/I," *Comm. ACM*, 16, 3, 169-179.

DAHL, O. [1968] "Discrete Event Simulation Languages." In GENUYS [1968], 349-395.

————, and C. A. R. HOARE [1972] "Hierarchical Program Structures." In DAHL et al. [1972], 175-220.

————, E. DIJKSTRA, and C. A. R. HOARE [1972] *Structured Programming*, Academic Press, New York.

DeBAKKER, J. [1980] *Mathematical Theory of Program Correctness*, Prentice-Hall, Englewood Cliffs, NJ.

DEWAR, R., and A. McCANN [1977] "MACRO SPITBOL—A SNOBOL4 Compiler," *Software—Practice and Experience*, 7, 1, 95-114.

DIJKSTRA, E. [1975] "Guarded Commands, Nondeterminacy and Formal Derivation of Programs," *Comm. ACM*, 18, 8, 453-457. Reprinted in WASSERMAN [1980].

———— [1976] *A Discipline of Programming*, Prentice-Hall, Englewood Cliffs, NJ.

———— [1972a] "Notes on Structured Programming." In DAHL et al. [1972], 1-82.

———— [1972b] "The Humble Programmer," *Comm. ACM*, 15, 10, 859-866.

DONAHUE, J. [1976] *Complementary Definitions of Programming Language Semantics*, Lect. Notes in C.S., No. 42, Springer-Verlag, New York.

DUNLOP, D., and V. BASILI [1982] "A Comparative Analysis of Functional Correctness," *ACM Computing Surveys*, 14, 2, 229-244.

ELSON, M. [1973] *Concepts of Programming Languages*, SRA, Chicago.

FALKOFF, A., and K. IVERSON [1981] "The Evolution of APL." In WEXELBLAT (ed.) [1981], 661-673.

————, K. IVERSON, and E. SUSSENGUTH [1964] "A Formal Description of SYSTEM/360," *IBM Syst. J.*, 3, 3, 198-263.

FATEMAN, R. [1982] "High-level Language Implications of the Proposed IEEE Floating-point Standard," *ACM Trans. on Prog. Langs. and Systems*, 4, 2, 239-257.

FEUER, A., and N. GEHANI [1982] "A Comparison of the Programming Languages C and Pascal," *ACM Computing Surveys*, 14, 1, 73-92.

FEUSTAL, E. [1973] "On the Advantages of Tagged Architecture," *IEEE Trans. Comps.*, C-22, 7, 644-656.

FODERARO, J. [1980] "The Franz LISP Manual," *UNIX Programmers Manual*, Univ. of Calif., Berkeley, CA.

FORTRAN [1966] *American National Standard Programming Language FORTRAN*, X3.9-1966, Amer. Natl. Standards Institute, New York.

———— [1978] *American National Standard Programming Language FORTRAN*, X3.9, Amer. Natl. Standards Inst., New York.

———— [1981] "Draft Standard, Industrial Real-time FORTRAN," *SIGPLAN Notices*, 16, 7, 45-60.

FREIBURGHOUSE, R. [1969] "The Multics PL/I Compiler," *Proc. AFIPS Fall Jt. Comp. Conf.*, 35, 187-199.

FRIEDMAN, D. [1974] *The Little Lisper*, SRA, Chicago.

GENUYS, F. (ed.) [1968] *Programming Languages*, Academic Press, New York.

GHEZZI, C., and M. JAZAYERI [1982] *Programming Language Structures*, Wiley, New York.

GIMPEL, J. [1976] *Algorithms in SNOBOL4*, Wiley, New York.

GOODENOUGH, J. [1975] "Exception Handling: Issues and a Proposed Notation," *Comm. ACM*, 18, 12, 683-696.

GORDON, M. [1979] *The Denotational Description of Programming Languages, An Introduction*, Springer-Verlag, New York.

GREINER, W. [1972] "Algorithm 81: Determinant," *Quote-Quad*, III, 4, in *SIGPLAN Notices*, 7, 4, 33.

GRIES, D. (ed.) [1978] *Programming Methodology*, Springer-Verlag, New York.

GRISWOLD, R. [1981] "A History of the SNOBOL Programming Languages." In WEXELBLAT (ed.) [1981], 601-644.

―――― [1975] *String and List Processing in SNOBOL4: Techniques and Applications*, Prentice-Hall, Englewood Cliffs, NJ.

―――― [1972] *The Macro Implementation of SNOBOL4*, W. H. Freeman, San Francisco.

――――, and M. GRISWOLD [1973] *A SNOBOL4 Primer*, Prentice-Hall, Englewood Cliffs, NJ.

――――, and D. HANSEN [1980] "An Alternative to the Use of Patterns in String Processing," *ACM Trans. on Prog. Langs. & Systems*, 2, 2, 153-172.

――――, J. POAGE, and I. POLONSKY [1971], *The SNOBOL4 Programming Language*, 2nd ed., Prentice-Hall, Englewood Cliffs, NJ

HARRISON, MALCOLM [1973] *Data Structures and Programming*, Scott Foresman, Glenview, IL.

HARRISON, MICHAEL [1978] *Introduction to Formal Language Theory*, Addison-Wesley, Reading, MA.

HENDERSON, P. [1980] *Functional Programming: Application and Implementation*, Prentice-Hall, Englewood Cliffs, NJ.

HOARE, C. A. R. [1968] "Record Handling." In GENUYS (ed.) [1968], 291-348.

―――― [1972] "Notes on Data Structuring." In DAHL et al. [1972], 83-174.

―――― [1981] "The Emperor's Old Clothes," *Comm. ACM*, 24, 2, 75-83.

――――, and P. LAUER [1974] "Consistent and Complementary Formal Theories of the Semantics of Programming Languages," *Acta Informatica*, 3, 135-153.

—— and N. WIRTH [1973] "An Axiomatic Definition of the Programming Language Pascal," *Acta Informatica*, 2, 335-355. Reprinted in WASSERMAN (ed.) [1980].

HOLT, R., et al. [1978] *Structured Concurrent Programming with Operating System Applications*, Addison-Wesley, Reading, MA.

HOPCROFT, J., and J. ULLMAN [1979] *Introduction to Automata Theory, Languages, and Computation*, Addison-Wesley, Reading, MA.

HOROWITZ, E., and S. SAHNI [1976] *Fundamentals of Data Structures*, Computer Science Press, Woodland Hills, CA.

HOWDEN, W. [1982] "Contemporary Software Development Environments," *Comm. ACM*, 25, 5, 318-329.

HUNTER, R. [1981] *The Design and Construction of Compilers*, Wiley, New York.

HUSSON, S. [1970] *Microprogramming Principles and Practices*, Prentice-Hall, Englewood Cliffs, NJ.

ICHBIAH, J., et al. [1979] "Rationale for the Design of the Ada Programming Language," *SIGPLAN Notices*, 14, 6, Part B.

IVERSON, K. [1962] *A Programming Language*, Wiley, New York.

—— [1979] "Operators," *ACM Trans. on Prog. Langs. & Systems*, 1, 2, 161-176.

JACKSON, M. [1977] "Cobol." In PERROTT, R. (ed.) *Software Engineering*, Academic Press, New York.

JENSEN, K., and N. WIRTH [1978] *Pascal: User Manual and Report*, 2d ed., Springer-Verlag, New York.

JONES, N., and S. MUCHNICK [1978] *TEMPO: A Unified Treatment of Binding Times and Parameter Passing Concepts in Programming Languages*, Lect. Notes in C.S., Springer-Verlag, New York.

KNUTH, D. [1967] "The Remaining Trouble Spots in ALGOL 60," *Comm. ACM*, 10, 10, 611-617.

—— [1973a] *The Art of Computer Programming*, Vol. 1: *Fundamental Algorithms*, 2d ed., Addison-Wesley, Reading, MA.

—— [1981] *The Art of Computer Programming*, Vol. 2: *Seminumerical Algorithms*, 2d ed., Addison-Wesley, Reading, MA.

—— [1973b] *The Art of Computer Programming*, Vol. 3: *Sorting and Searching*, Addison-Wesley, Reading, MA.

—— [1974] "Structured Programming with GOTO Statements," *ACM Computing Surveys*, 6, 4, 261-301. Reprinted in WASSERMAN (ed.) [1980].

KUCK, D. [1978] *The Structure of Computers and Computations*, Wiley, New York.

LAMPSON, B., et al. [1977] "Report on the Programming Language EUCLID," *SIGPLAN Notices*, 12, 2.

———— and REDELL, D. [1980] "Experience with Processes and Monitors in MESA," *Comm. ACM*, 23, 2, 105-117.

LEAVENWORTH, B. (ed.) [1972] *Control Structures in Programming Languages* (special issue), *SIGPLAN Notices*, 7, 11.

LEDGARD, H., and M. MARCOTTY [1981] *The Programming Language Landscape*, SRA, Chicago.

LEWIS, P., D. ROSENKRANTZ, and R. STEARNS [1976] *Compiler Design Theory*, Addison-Wesley, Reading, MA.

LISKOV, B., et al. [1977] "Abstraction Mechanisms in CLU," *Comm. ACM*, 20, 8, 564-576. Reprinted in WASSERMAN (ed.) [1980].

LUCAS, P., and K. WALK [1969] "On the Formal Description of PL/I," *Ann. Rev. Auto. Prog.*, 6, 3, 105-182.

MANNA, Z. [1974] *Introduction to the Mathematical Theory of Computation*, McGraw-Hill, New York.

MARCOTTY, M., H. LEDGARD, and G. BOCHMANN [1976] "A Sampler of Formal Definitions," *ACM Computing Surveys*, 8, 2, 191-275.

————, and F. SAYWARD [1977] "The Definition Mechanism for Standard PL/I," *IEEE Trans. Soft. Engr.*, SE-3, 6, 416-430.

MARLIN, C. [1980] *Coroutines*, Lect. Notes in C.S., No. 95, Springer-Verlag, New York.

MARTI, J., et al. [1979] "Standard LISP Report," *SIGPLAN Notices*, 14, 10, 48-68.

MCCARTHY, J. [1981] "History of LISP." In WEXELBLAT (ed.) [1981], 173-184.

———— [1965] *LISP 1.5 Programmer's Manual*, 2d ed., M.I.T. Press, Cambridge, Mass.

MCCRACKEN, D. [1970] "Whither APL," *Datamation*, Sept. 15, 53-57.

MEEHAN, J. [1979] *The New UCI LISP Manual*, Lawrence Erlbaum Assoc., Hillsdale, NJ.

METROPOLIS, N. [1980] *A History of Computing in the Twentieth Century*, Academic Press, New York.

METZNER, J., and B. BARNES [1977] *Decision Table Languages and Systems*, Academic Press, New York.

MINSKY, M. [1967] *Computation: Finite and Infinite Machines*, Prentice-Hall, Englewood Cliffs, NJ.

———— (ed.) [1968] *Semantic Information Processing*, M.I.T. Press, Cambridge, MA.

MOFFAT, D. [1981] "1981 Pascal Bibliography" *SIGPLAN Notices*, 16, 11, 7-21.

MOSES, J. [1970] "The Function of FUNCTION in LISP," *SIGSAM Bull.*, July, 13-27.

MYERS, G. [1981] *Advances in Computer Architecture*, 2d ed., Wiley, New York.

NAUR, P. (ed.) [1963] "Revised Report on the Algorithmic Language ALGOL 60," *Comm. ACM*, 6, 1, 1-17.

NEUHOLD, E. (ed.) [1978] *Formal Description of Programming Concepts*, North-Holland, New York.

NEWELL, A., et al. [1964] *Information Processing Language V Manual*, Prentice-Hall, Englewood Cliffs, NJ.

NICHOLLS, J. [1975] *The Structure and Design of Programming Languages*, Addison-Wesley, Reading, MA.

ORGANICK, E., A. FORSYTHE, and R. PLUMMER [1978] *Programming Language Structures*, Academic Press, New York.

PAKIN, S. [1972] *APL-360 Reference Manual*, 2d ed., SRA, Chicago.

PARNAS, D. [1972] "On the Criteria to be Used in Decomposing Systems into Modules," *Comm. ACM*, 15, 12, 1053-1058.

PASCAL [1983] *American National Standard Pascal Computer Programming Language*, IEEE Computer Society, Los Alamitos, CA.

PEMBERTON, S., and M. DANIELS [1982] *Pascal Implementation*, Wiley, New York.

PFALTZ, J. [1977] *Computer Data Structures*, McGraw-Hill, New York.

PL/I [1976] *American National Standard Programming Language PL/I*, X3.53. American Natl. Standards Inst., New York.

———— [1981] *American National Standard Programming Language PL/I General Purpose Subset*, X3.74, Amer. Natl. Standards Inst., New York.

PRENNER, C., et al. [1972] "An Implementation of Backtracking for Programming Languages." In LEAVENWORTH (ed.) [1972].

PRESSER, L. [1975] "Multiprogramming Coordination," *ACM Computing Surveys*, 7, 1, 21-44.

————, and J. WHITE [1972] "Linkers and Loaders," *Computing Surveys*, 4, 3, 149-168.

RADIN, G. [1981] "The Early History and Characteristics of PL/I." In WEXELBLAT (ed.) [1981], 551-574.

SAMMET, J. [1981] "The Early History of COBOL." In WEXELBLAT (ed.) [1981], 199-242.

———— [1969] *Programming Languages: History and Fundamentals*, Prentice-Hall, Englewood Cliffs, NJ.

———— [1972] "Programming Languages: History and Future," *Comm. ACM*, 15, 7, 601-610.

SANDEWALL, E. [1978] "Programming in an Interactive Environment: The LISP Experience," *ACM Computing Surveys*, 10, 1, 35-72.

SANSONNET, J., et al. [1982] "Direct Execution of LISP on a List-directed Architecture," *SIGPLAN Notices*, 17, 4, 132-139.

SHAW, M., et al. [1977] "Abstraction and Verification in ALPHARD: Defining and Specifying Iteration and Generators," *Comm. ACM*, 20, 8, 553-564. Reprinted in WASSERMAN (ed.) [1980].

SIEWIOREK, D., C. BELL, and A. NEWELL (eds.) [1982] *Computer Structures: Principles and Examples*, McGraw-Hill, New York.

SIKLOSSY, L. [1976] *Let's Talk LISP*, Prentice-Hall, Englewood Cliffs, NJ.

STANDISH, T. [1980] *Data Structure Techniques*, Addison-Wesley, Reading, MA.

SUSSMAN, G., et al. [1981] "SCHEME 79—LISP on a Chip," *IEEE Computer*, July 1981.

TANENBAUM, A. [1976] *Structured Computer Organization*, Prentice-Hall, Englewood Cliffs, NJ.

TEITELMAN, W. [1974] *INTERLISP Reference Manual*, Xerox Palo Alto Res. Cntr., Palo Alto, CA.

TENNENT, R. [1981] *Principles of Programming Languages*, Prentice-Hall, Englewood Cliffs, NJ.

TOU, J., and P. WEGNER (eds.) [1971] *Proc. Symp. on Data Structures & Prog. Langs.*, *SIGPLAN Notices*, 6, 2.

TURING, A. [1936] "On Computable Numbers, with an Application to the Entscheidungs-Problem," *Proc. London Math. Soc.*, 42, 230-265.

WASSERMAN, A. (ed.) [1980] *Programming Language Design (Tutorial)*, IEEE Computer Society Press, New York.

WEISSMAN, C. [1967] *LISP 1.5 Primer*, Dickenson Publishing Company, Inc., Encino, Calif.

WEIZENBAUM, J. [1963] "Symmetric List Processor," *Comm. ACM*, 6, 9, 524-544.

WELSH, J., W. SNEERINGER, and C. A. R. HOARE [1977] "Ambiguities and Insecurities in Pascal," *Software—Practice and Experience*, 7, 6, 685-696. Reprinted in WASSERMAN (ed.) [1980].

WEXELBLAT, R. (ed.) [1981] *History of Programming Languages*, Academic Press, New York.

WHITAKER, W. [1978] "The U.S. Dept. of Defense Common High Order Language Effort," *SIGPLAN Notices*, 13, 2, 19-29.

WINSTON, P. [1977] *Artificial Intelligence*, Addison-Wesley, Reading, MA.

————, and B. HORN [1981] *LISP*, Addison-Wesley, Reading, MA.

WIRTH, N. [1971a] "The Programming Language Pascal," *Acta Informatica*, 1, 1, 35-63.

———— [1971b] "The Design of a Pascal Compiler," *Software—Practice and Experience*, 1, 4, 309-333.

———— [1973] *Systematic Programming: An Introduction*, Prentice-Hall, Englewood Cliffs, NJ.

————[1976] *Algorithms + Data Structures = Programs*, Prentice-Hall, Englewood Cliffs, NJ.

————[1977a] "Toward a Discipline of Real-time Programming," *Comm. ACM*, 20, 8, 577-583.

———— [1977b] "MODULA: A Language for Modular Multiprogramming," *Software—Practice and Experience*, 7, 1, 3-35.

———— [1980] "MODULA-2," Rept. 36, Institut für Informatik, ETH, Zurich.

WULF, W., M. SHAW, P. HILFINGER, and L. FLON [1981] *Fundamental Structures of Computer Science*, Addison-Wesley, Reading, MA.

YEH, R. (ed.) [1976] *Applied Computation Theory*, Prentice-Hall, Englewood Cliffs, NJ.

———— (ed.) [1977-78] *Current Trends in Programming Methodology*, Vols. I-IV, Prentice-Hall, Englewood Cliffs, NJ.

YOURDON, E. (ed.) [1979] *Classics in Software Engineering*, Yourdon, Inc., New York.

ZELKOWITZ, M. [1978] "Perspectives on Software Engineering," *ACM Computing Surveys*, 10, 2, 197-216.

————, A. SHAW, and J. GANNON [1979] *Principles of Software Engineering and Design*, Prentice-Hall, Englewood Cliffs, NJ.

Index

Bucket list, 111
Buffer:
  for a file, 114-16
  in message passing, 275
  storage for, 282
Buffer variable for a file, 113-14, 116
Built-in function, 56
Burge, W., 209
Busy waiting, 200
Buxton, J., 338, 495

C (programming language), 454
Cactus stack, 493
Call-return operation and storage
  management, 282-83
Call-return sequence control, 175-85
Call statement, 175-77
Cambridge Polish notation, 153-54
Case statement, 169-71
CBL grammar, 321, 326-27
Central referencing environment
  table, 240-42
Central stack:
  and dynamic scope, 239-42
  and local data, 231-33
  with static chain, 246
  and storage management, 285-89
  and subprogram activations,
    184-87
Central strings table in SNOBOL4,
  122
CEP (See Current environment
  pointer)
Character data type, 69-70
Characteristic function, 109
Character set, 69, 309
Character string data type, 98-102
Chomsky, N., 321, 341-42
Chomsky hierarchy of grammars,
  341-42
Church, A., 352
Church's thesis, 352
CIP (See Current instruction
  pointer)
Clock in real-time processing, 205
Close operation on a file, 114
CLU, 147, 208, 210, 426
COBOL, 378-401
  array data type, 389-92
  assignment, 390-92
  data control, 397
  data representations, 386
  data types, 386-94
  debug module, 398
  edited data item, 387
  elementary data types, 387-88
  example program, 381-86
  exceptions, 396-97
  expressions, 394
  files, 392-93
  formal grammar, 399
  input-output, 393
  library module, 398
  modules, 379
  nucleus, 379
  numeric data types, 387-88
  operating environment, 398
  overview, 379-80
  PICTURE clause, 387
  programming environment, 398

COBOL (cont.):
  record data type, 388-92
  report writer, 380, 394, 398
  sequence control, 394-97
  sorting, 393
  standards, 379
  statement sequence control,
    395-96
  subprograms, 394
  subprogram sequence control,
    396-97
  syntax, 398-99
  translation, 399
  type conversion, 390-92
  variant records, 390
  virtual computer, 400
COBOL-like grammar, 326-27
Code, storage for, 133-35
Code generation, 320
Code segment, 133-35 .
  and retained local data, 230-33
  storage for, 281
  for a subprogram, 178-85
Coercion, 56-57
Cohen, J., 300
Collating sequence, 69
Collision, in hash table, 110-11
Column-major order, 87
Comment, 311
Common block (See Common
  environment)
Common environment, 234-38
Compaction of storage, 284, 300
Compilation:
  independent, 336
  order of, 336
  separate, 335-37
  stages in, 314-21 (See also
    Translation)
  theory of, 343-45
Compiled language, 24-25
Compiler, 21
  one-pass, 452
Compile time, 31
Compile-time operation, 319-20
Complex number data type, 66
Component:
  of a data object, 40
  of a data structure, 73
  existence of, 82
  type of, 82
Compool, 234
Composite name, 217
Composition:
  and compound statements, 168
  of functions, 151
  of statements, 162
Compound statement, 168
Computable function, 350-52
Computer:
  actual, 14, 25
  alternatives for construction, 25
  definition, 14
  firmware, 20
  hardware, 14, 19-20
  hardware realization, 19
  hierarchies of, 28-30
  high-level language, 19-20, 22
  host, 20
  microprogrammed, 20
  software-simulated, 14, 22-25

Computer (cont.):
  structure and operation, 14-19
  virtual, 14, 25-30
Computer state, 18-19
Concatenation, 99
  of strings, 121
Conceptual model, 340
Concurrent Pascal, 426
Concurrent subprogram, 196-206
Conditional **goto** statement, 163
Conditional in an expression, 159
Conditional statement, 168-171
Consistency of static and dynamic
  scope rules, 223, 243-45
Constant, 41-42
  programmer-defined, 42
  storage for, 133-34, 281
Constant value, parameter
  transmission by, 255
Context-free grammar (See
  Grammar, BNF)
Context-sensitive grammar, 342
Contour model, 275
Controlled variable in a loop (See
  Index variable in loop)
Control statement, 167-75
Control structure (See Sequence
  control; Data control)
Conversion (See Type conversion)
Conway, R., 403, 425
Copy rule for subprograms, 176-77
Coroutine, 177, 191-94
  recursive, 213
  and scheduled subprograms, 195
Correctness proof, 348-50
Correspondence of actual and
  formal parameters, 253
Cost of use of a language, 12
Counter in a loop, 172-73
Creation operation and storage
  management, 283
Critical region, 273
Cross section of an array, 120
Current environment pointer,
  179-85
  definition, 179
  and local data referencing, 231-32
Current instruction pointer, 178-85
  definition, 178-79

Dahl, O., 13, 209
Dangling reference, 80-81
  in heap storage, 292-97, 299-300
Data:
  in a computer, 15-16
  shared (See Shared data)
Data abstraction (See Abstract
  data type)
Data control, 215-79
  in a computer, 15, 18
  definition, 215
Data descriptor in hardware, 123
Data object, 42
  definition, 39
  elementary, 40, 44
  lifetime of, 40
  programmer-constructed (See
    Pointer data type)
  programmer-defined, 39
  structured, 40

Simulation:
  using microprograms, 20
  using software, 22–25
Simultaneous execution of subprograms (*See* Subprogram, concurrent)
Single execution sequence, 177
Single-user program, 335
SLIP, 207, 301–2
SNOBOL4, 528–57
  alternation, 539
  anchored mode, 536, 544
  arrays, 542
  assignment, 541–42
    during pattern matching, 539–40
  assignment example, 59
  Boolean operations, 541
  central strings table, 122, 533–34, 549–50, 554
  character strings, 533–34
  code string, 545
  compiler, 530
  concatenation:
    of patterns, 539
    of strings, 534
  data control, 549–51
  data types, 533–45
  data types table, 555
  example program, 530–33
  exceptions, 549
  expressions, 547–48
  files, 543–44
  goto statements, 548
  hidden stack, 550
  indirect reference operation, 549
  input-output, 543–44
  keywords, 544
  labels table, 544, 554
  late binding, 529
  macro implementation, 530
  numbers, 540–41
  operating environment, 551
  overview, 529–30
  parameters in patterns, 540
  parameter transmission, 550–51
  pattern creation, 537–40
  pattern matching, 534–36
  patterns, 537–40
    with parameters, 540
  pattern-valued functions, 538–39
  program as data object, 545
  programming environment, 552
  property list, 543
  result of a subprogram, 551
  run-time system data, 554–55
  sequence control, 547–49
  simple variables, 541
  statement labels, 544
  statement sequence control, 548
  storage management, 553–55
  subprogram name as a data object, 544–45
  subprograms, 545–46
    table of, 544–45, 555
  subprogram sequence control, 548–49
  syntax, 552

SNOBOL4 (cont.):
  system data at run-time, 554–55
  table data type, 121–22, 543
  tracing, 555
  translation, 552–53
  type definitions, 546–47
  unevaluated expressions, 540
  unevaluated parameters, 551
  virtual computer, 553–55
Software engineering, 338
Software interpretation (*See* Software simulation)
Software simulation, 22–25
  of a computer, 14, 22–25
  of a data type, 44
  of an operation, 49
Source language, 21
Source program, 315–20
Space as syntactic element, 311
Spaghetti logic, 166
Spaghetti stack, 300
Specification:
  of a data type, 43–48
  of a subprogram, 129–30
SPITBOL, 530, 556
Stack, 102
  as an abstract data type, 145–46
  hidden, 241
  spaghetti, 300
  storage management using, 285–89
  and subprogram activations, 184–87
Stack pointer, 285–86
Standardization, 7, 13
Standish, T., 118, 300
Statement:
  basic, 162
  call, 175–77
  case, 169–71
  compound, 168
  conditional, 168–71
  control, 167–75
  exit, 173–75
  goto (*See* **Goto** statement)
  guarded command, 171, 201–5
  if, 168–69
  iteration, 171–75
  multi-purpose, 166
  raise, 175, 188–89
  resume, 191–94
  return, 175
  as syntactic element, 312–13
Statement label, 163–67, 174–75
  approaches to use, 164–65
  as a data object, 164–65
  as a parameter, 271–72
Statement sequence control, 162–75
  basic forms, 162–63
State of a computer, 18–19
  final, 19
  initial, 19
State transition of a computer, 19
Static allocation of storage, 285
Static block structure, 225–27
Static chain, 246–50
Static chain pointer, 247

Static nesting of subprogram definitions, 244–45
Static organization of a computer, 18
Static scope, 223–27
  importance, 223–25
  and shared data, 241, 243–50
Static scope rule, 223–27
Static storage management, 285
Static type checking, 53–56
  and subprogram parameters, 265–66
Stepwise refinement, 127
Stoneman, 338
Storage location of a data object, 40
Storage management, 280–302
  for activation records, 286–87
  in a computer, 15, 18
  and dangling references, 292–97, 299–300
  and data structures, 79–81
  dynamic, 285–300
  elements requiring, 281–82
  of fixed-size blocks, 290–97
  fragmentation, 300
  and garbage, 292–97, 299–300
  heap, 290–300
  methods:
    best-fit allocation, 299
    first-fit allocation, 299
    garbage collection, 295–97, 299–300
    reference counts, 294–95
    stack-based, 285–89
    static, 285
  and operating systems, 300–301
  operations requiring, 282–83
  and paging, 301
  phases, 284
    compaction, 284, 300
    initial allocation, 284
    recovery, 284
    reuse, 284
  for pointer data, 106–8
  programmer-controlled, 283–84, 292–94
  and segments, 301
  system-controlled, 283–84
  of variable-size blocks, 297–300
  for variant records, 96
Storage representation:
  of a data type, 43, 48–49
  and declarations, 51–52
  and type checking, 53
Structural equivalence of types, 140–41
Structure assigned by a grammar, 324
Structure data type (*See* Record, data type)
Structured control statement, 167–75
  problems of, 174–75
Structured programming, 10, 13, 127
  definition, 166

602